CONSTITUTION

# CONSTITUTIONAL TEXTS

*Materials on Government and the Constitution*

EDITED BY
RODNEY BRAZIER

CLARENDON PRESS · OXFORD
1990

*Oxford University Press, Walton Street, Oxford* OX2 6DP
*Oxford New York Toronto*
*Delhi Bombay Calcutta Madras Karachi*
*Petaling Jaya Singapore Hong Kong Tokyo*
*Nairobi Dar es Salaam Cape Town*
*Melbourne Auckland*
*and associated companies in*
*Berlin Ibadan*

*Oxford is a trade mark of Oxford University Press*

*Published in the United States*
*by Oxford University Press, New York*



*British Library Cataloguing in Publication Data*
*Constitutional texts: materials on government and the constitution.*
*1. Great Britain. Government*
*I. Brazier, Rodney*
*354.41*
*ISBN 0–19–876246–1*
*ISBN 0–19–876245–3 pbk*

*Library of Congress Cataloging in Publication Data*
*Constitutional texts: materials on government and the Constitution / edited by Rodney Brazier.*
*1. Great Britain—Constitutional law. I. Brazier, Rodney.*
*KD3930.C66 1990 342.41'023—dc20 [344.10223] 90–6752*
*ISBN 0–19–876246–1*
*ISBN 0–19–876245–3 (pbk.)*

*Typeset by Hope Services (Abingdon) Ltd.*
*Printed in Great Britain by*
*Biddles Ltd.*
*Guildford & King's Lynn*

# PREFACE

In writing my book *Constitutional Practice* (Oxford University Press, 1988) I had to seek out a large number of materials on the constitution. Some of these were not particularly easy to find; others were scattered throughout many different parts of various libraries, or were to be found within large series of published works; yet others could only be found in one place in this country (usually the Public Record Office). Even though we do not have a written constitution as every other developed state would understand it, most of the British constitution *is* in writing. The obvious difficulty which faces the student of the British constitution is to locate the basic source materials. I hope that a fair spread of these sources appears in sufficient depth in the following pages.

The subjects covered in this book are the same as in *Constitutional Practice*, although there is an additional chapter on the Opposition. This book is, therefore, a collection of materials about British central government and the constitution. Anyone writing about the British constitution is faced with a choice of what to include; inevitably some of the writer's idiosyncracies, based on what he thinks is important or interesting, will find their way in. As well as allocating room for reports of departmental and parliamentary committees, Cabinet papers, the Standing Orders of both Houses of Parliament, and statutes, much space is given over to excerpts from autobiographies and biographies, diaries and letters, written by or about politicians who have practised the tenets of the constitution. The views of historians, political scientists, and other academic writers are also reproduced. Their contributions to the meaning and requirements of constitutional rules can be just as important as the more traditional sources. A very large number of sources are quoted. The citations should indicate further reading for those who wish to investigate particular topics more fully.

R.B.

*University of Manchester*
*January 1990*

# ACKNOWLEDGEMENTS

THE author and publisher thank the following for permission to reproduce copyright material: Aurum Press Ltd. (Lord Whitelaw, *The Whitelaw Memoirs*); Basil Blackwell (Peter Hennessy, *Cabinet*); Butterworth & Co. Ltd. (Erskine May, *Parliamentary Practice*); Cambridge University Press (Vernon Bogdanor, *Multi-Party Politics and the Constitution*; Sir Ivor Jennings, *Cabinet Government*); Jonathan Cape Ltd. (Bernard Donoughue, *Prime Minister: The Conduct of Policy under Harold Wilson and James Callaghan*; Patrick Gordon Walker, *The Cabinet*; David Marquand, *Ramsay MacDonald*; D. R. Thorpe, *Selwyn Lloyd*); Cassell PLC (Winston S. Churchill, *The Second World War*, volume 5); Century Hutchinson Ltd. and Curtis Brown Ltd. (Tony Benn, *Out of the Wilderness: Diaries 1963–1967*); Collins (Walter Bagehot, *The English Constitution*; James Callaghan, *Time and Chance*; Lord Carrington, *Reflect on Things Past*; J. A. G. Griffith, *The Politics of the Judiciary*; Lord Home, *The Way the Wind Blows*; Roy Jenkins, *Asquith*); Controller of Her Majesty's Stationery Office (*Hansard*, parliamentary papers, and government publications); Hamish Hamilton Ltd. (Lord Butler, *The Art of the Possible*; James Prior, *The Balance of Power*; Francis Pym, *The Politics of Consent*); Hamish Hamilton and Jonathan Cape Ltd. (Richard Crossman, *Diaries of a Cabinet Minister*, volumes 1 and 3); William Heinemann Ltd. (Martin Gilbert, *Never Despair: Winston S. Churchill 1945–1965*, copyright C. and T. Publications 1988); Hodder and Stoughton Ltd. (Sir John Colville, *The Fringes of Power: Downing Street Diaries 1939–1955*; Anthony Seldon, *Churchill's Indian Summer: The Conservative Government 1951–1955*); Lord Hailsham of St. Marylebone, 'Will Cabinet Government Survive?', (The Granada Guildhall Lecture 1987); Incorporated Council of Law Reporting of England and Wales (extracts from the Law Reports); Michael Joseph Ltd. (Phillip Whitehead, *The Writing on the Wall*, copyright Brook Productions Ltd. 1985); The Labour Party (extracts from the Party's *Constitution, Standing Orders*, and Parliamentary Labour

Party *Standing Orders*); Longman Group (George Hutchinson, *Edward Heath*; E. C. S. Wade and A. W. Bradley, *Constitutional and Administrative Law*); Macmillan (David Butler, *Governing Without a Majority*; Alistair Horne, *Macmillan 1957–1986*; Harold Macmillan, *At the End of the Day, Pointing the Way, Riding the Storm*; Kenneth Rose, *King George V*; Sir John Wheeler-Bennett, *King George VI: His Life and Reign*; Hugo Young, *One of Us*); Oxford University Press (Geoffrey Marshall, *Constitutional Conventions*, copyright Geoffrey Marshall 1984); Routledge and Kegan Paul (S. A. Walkland and M. Ryle (eds.), *The Commons Today*); The Social and Liberal Democratic Party (extracts from the Party's *Constitution*); Sweet and Maxwell Ltd. (David Bonner, *Emergency Powers in Peacetime*; R. W. Blackburn, 'Prorogation and Adjournment Before a Dissolution of Parliament' [1987] *Public Law* 533, 'The Queen and Ministerial Responsibility' [1985] *Public Law* 361; A. W. Bradley, 'Judges and the Media—The Kilmuir Rules' [1986] *Public Law* 383; Margaret Brazier, 'Judicial Immunity and the Independence of the Judiciary' [1976] *Public Law* 397; D. L. Ellis, 'Collective Ministerial Responsibility and Collective Solidarity' [1980] *Public Law* 367; P. M. McDermott, 'Queensland Revisited' [1988] *Public Law* 31; John Mackintosh, *The British Cabinet*; Philippa Hughes and Stephanie Palmer, 'Voting Bishops' [1983] *Public Law* 393; Lord Hunt of Tamworth, 'Access to a Previous Government's Papers' [1982] *Public Law* 514; P. F. Smith and S. H. Bailey, *The Modern English Legal System*); Unwin Hyman Ltd. (Geoffrey Marshall and Graeme C. Moodie, *Some Problems of the Constitution*, copyright Unwin Hyman Ltd. 1971); Weidenfeld and Nicolson Ltd. (Robert Rhodes James, *Anthony Eden*; Kenneth Harris, *Attlee*; Keith Middlemas and John Barnes, *Baldwin*; Lord Rawlinson, *A Price Too High*; Norman Tebbit, *Upwardly Mobile*; Colin Turpin, *British Government and the Constitution: Texts, Cases and Materials*; Lord Wilson of Rievaulx, *Final Term: The Labour Government 1974–1976*, *The Governance of Britain*, *The Labour Government 1964–1970: A Personal Record*).

# CONTENTS

# TABLE OF STATUTES

1. *Acts*

# TABLE OF OFFICIAL PAPERS

# [1]

# CHOOSING A PRIME MINISTER

## Leader of the Party

## 1. QUALIFICATIONS OF A PRIME MINISTER

*The Prime Minister must be an M.P. (or be about to take his seat as an M.P. after a general election), and so cannot be a peer (unless he can disclaim his peerage: see below, p. 504. He must usually be the elected Leader of his party. The Leadership election rules of the three main political parties follow.*

## 2. PARTY LEADERSHIP ELECTION RULES

### (1) THE CONSERVATIVE PARTY

*Procedure for the Selection of the Leader of the Conservative Party*

Timing of elections and general responsibilities

1. If the position of Leader of the Party is vacant, an election shall be held as early as possible.

2. Otherwise there shall be an election in the House of Commons beginning within twenty-eight days of the opening of each new session of Parliament, except that in the case of a new Parliament the election shall be held not earlier than three months nor later than six months from the date of assembly of that Parliament. The actual date will be determined by the Leader of the Party in consultation with the chairman of the 1922 Committee.

3. The chairman of the 1922 Committee will be responsible for the conduct of all ballots and will settle all matters in relation thereto.

Nominations and lists of candidates

4. Candidates will be proposed and seconded in writing by Members of the House of Commons in receipt of the Conservative whip.

The chairman of the 1922 Committee and scrutineers designated by him will be available to receive nominations. Each candidate will indicate on the nomination paper that he is prepared to accept nomination, and no candidate will accept more than one nomination. The names of the proposer and seconder will not be published and will remain confidential to the scrutineers. Nominations will close by noon on a Thursday five days before the date of the first ballot.

5. If only one valid nomination is received, the chairman of the 1922 Committee shall declare this person elected. If more than one valid nomination is received, the chairman of the 1922 Committee and his scrutineers will publish a list of the valid nominations and immediately transmit a copy to the two vice-chairmen of the 1922 Committee, the Chief Whip in the House of Commons, the chairman of the National Union, the chairman of the Executive of the National Union, the president of the Scottish Conservative and Unionist Association, the chairman and deputy chairman of the Party, the chairman of the Party in Scotland, the Leader of the Party in the House of Lords and the Chief Whip in the House of Lords.

Procedure for consultation with members of the party outside the House of Commons

6. During the period between the close of nominations and the date of the first ballot, it shall be the responsibility of the constituency associations, represented by Conservative Members of Parliament, to inform the Member of their views regarding the candidates.

7. Similarly, the Leader of the Party in the House of Lords and the Chief Whip in the House of Lords will make such arrangements as appropriate to obtain the views of peers in receipt of the Conservative whip.

8. In order that all sections of the Party shall be consulted, area chairmen of the National Union will obtain the opinions of constituency associations, through their chairmen, and report their findings to the chairman of the National Union and the chairman of the Executive of the National Union. In Scotland the area chairmen will similarly consult and report to the president of the Scottish Conservative and Unionist Association. They will also report to Conservative Members of Parliament within the area of their responsibility the views of constituencies not represented by a Conservative Member of Parliament.

9. The Leader of the Party in the House of Lords, the Chief Whip in the House of Lords, the chairman of the National Union and the chairman of the Executive of the National Union, together with the president of the Scottish Conservative and Unionist Association, will on the Monday attend a meeting of the Executive of the 1922 Committee for the purpose of conveying to them the collective views of the peers in receipt of the Conservative whip, the National Union and the Scottish Conservative and Unionist Association respectively.

First ballot

10. The first ballot will be held on the Tuesday immediately following. For this ballot the scrutineers will prepare a ballot paper listing the names of the candidates and give a copy for the purpose of balloting to each Member of the House of Commons in receipt of the Conservative whip.

11. For the first ballot each voter will indicate one choice from the candidates listed.

12. Where any Member is unavoidably absent from the House on that day, through sickness or by being abroad, the scrutineers will make arrangements to receive their votes.

13. The ballot will be secret and neither the names of those who have voted for a particular candidate nor the names of those who have abstained from voting shall be disclosed by the scrutineers.

14. If, as a result of this ballot, one candidate *both* (i) receives an overall majority of the votes of those entitled to vote *and* (ii) receives fifteen per cent more of the votes of those entitled to vote than any other candidate, he will be elected.

15. The scrutineers will announce the number of votes received by each candidate, and if no candidate satisfies these conditions a second ballot will be held.

Second ballot

16. The second ballot will be held on the following Tuesday. Nominations made for the first ballot will be void. New nominations will be submitted by the Thursday, under the same procedure and with the same arrangements for consultation as described in paragraphs 4–9 for the first ballot, both for the original candidates if required and for any other candidates.

17. The voting procedure for the second ballot will be the same as for the first save that paragraph 14 shall not apply. If, as a result of this second ballot, one candidate receives an overall majority of the votes of those entitled to vote, that candidate will be elected.

Third ballot

18. If no candidate receives an overall majority, the three candidates receiving the highest number of votes at the second ballot will be placed on a ballot paper for a third and final ballot on the Thursday following.

19. For the final ballot each voter must indicate two preferences amongst the three candidates by placing the figure 1 opposite the name of his preferred candidate and the figure 2 opposite the name of his second choice.

20. The scrutineers will proceed to add the number of first preference votes received by each candidate, eliminate the candidate with the lowest number of first preference votes and redistribute the votes of those giving him as their first preference amongst the two remaining candidates in accordance with their second preference. The result of this final count will be an overall majority of votes cast for one candidate, and he will be elected.

Party meeting

21 The candidate thus elected by the Party in the House of Commons will be presented for confirmation as Party leader to a Party meeting constituted as follows: Members of the House of Commons in receipt of the Conservative whip; Members of the House of Lords in receipt of the Conservative whip; Adopted Parliamentary candidates; Members of the Executive Committee of the National Union not already included in the above categories.

(*a*) *The first Conservative election (1965)*

Peter Emery, a former Parliamentary Private Secretary to Heath, was secretary of the 1922 Committee. It fell to him and his chairman, Sir William Anstruther-Gray, to receive the nominations in the contest which Sir Alec's decision [to resign as Conservative Leader] immediately set in train. At first, nobody could be sure how many there might be. Besides Heath, Maudling and Macleod, who seemed certain runners, Hogg, Soames and Peter Thorneycroft were also expected, at one moment or another, to let their names go forward.

Then Macleod, to the astonishment of some of his most ardent supporters, decided not to enter the lists. He calculated that he could not beat either Heath or Maudling, and he preferred to avoid the contest. Hogg also remained on the sidelines, as did Soames and Thorneycroft. In the event the only other contender was Enoch Powell—and he was a late starter.

Nominations had to be in by 11.30 a.m. on Monday 26 July [1965] for the first ballot to open twenty-four hours later. Over the weekend the Chief Whip, William Whitelaw, detected a strong feeling in the Parliamentary Party that there should be only two nominations, not more. The Heath and Maudling camps were already at work; but then Enoch Powell let it be known that he too would be running.

A friend of mine in the Commons has described the Heath and Maudling campaigns to me. 'Ted's camp left nothing to chance,' he recalls. 'Everybody was canvassed—everybody. Nothing was left undone. It was a beautifully organised campaign run by Peter Walker from H.Q. in Gayfere Street. They treated it like a war, and they were determined to win. Reggie's campaign was charming, easy-going, rather haphazard, very nice—like the man himself. But his side got a lot of things wrong. They were not fully organised. They took too much for granted, and they made mistakes of a kind that they ought not to have made.' Enoch Powell, who needed nobody to tell him that he couldn't win (he knew that perfectly well), was not the object of anything that could properly be called a campaign: he was a loner with just a few devoted friends behind him.

William Whitelaw and his Whips did not take sides in any outward way. Each of them exercised his right to vote as an individual, but as Whips they were all expected to avoid any open expression of preference. Hour by hour, they were of course sizing things up: nobody was better placed to judge the feeling in the House. Lord St Aldwyn, the Opposition Chief Whip in the Lords, was also taking soundings among Conservative peers—he consulted sixty-five of them. Within the National Union, Sir Clyde Hewlett, as chairman of the Executive Committee, spoke to the area chairmen and other officers. While neither the National Union nor the peers could have a direct say in the choice of leader it was nevertheless thought desirable, if only for reasons of tact, to know their views. Though the Lords expressed a slight preference for Heath, the upshot of all these inquiries was that most people, in the House of Commons and out of it, intimated that they would be equally happy with either Heath or Maudling. This suggested a very close contest and was gratifying to both camps—to such activists for Maudling as Robert Carr, Lord Lambton and Richard Stanley, and equally to Peter Walker, Robin Chichester-Clark and Anthony Kershaw, who were foremost in promoting Heath.

The result of the ballot stood up pretty well to the Whips' calculations. The figures, announced about two o'clock in the afternoon on Tuesday 27 July, were: Heath 150 votes, Maudling 133, and Powell 15. But the ballot was inconclusive because Heath had failed to secure the necessary 15 per cent lead—he had not received 15 per cent more of the votes cast than any other candidate. According to the rules there would have to be a second ballot. Then an hour later, having heard the outcome in the City, where—rather characteristically—he was lunching, Maudling decided to withdraw. Powell did the same. Thus the evening newspapers were able to report Heath's victory that day; and it was confirmed at 11.30 next morning when the second ballot closed and there was only one nomination—for Heath. Sir William Anstruther-Gray formally declared him the victor and his election was duly rubber-stamped at the ceremonial party meeting six days later. A total of 298 votes had been cast. There were then 304 Conservative M.P.s. William Whitelaw believes, however, that there were no abstainers: the six who did not vote were either too far away to present themselves at Westminster, or they were ill.

[George Hutchinson, *Edward Heath* (London, 1970), 141–4.]

*The voting in the first-ever Conservative ballot was:*

| | |
|---|---|
| Edward Heath | 150 |
| Reginald Maudling | 133 |
| Enoch Powell | 15 |

*Maudling and Powell immediately withdrew.*

(*b*) *The second Conservative election (1975)*

Our defeat [at the October 1974 general election] was nothing like as heavy as most of us had feared. But within twenty-four hours I told Ted that his only chance of carrying on as Leader was if he submitted himself to an early election through the 1922 Committee.

He replied that he didn't intend to submit himself to a leadership election because he was determined to fight the right wing, I told him that if he refused to go he would probably end up giving them exactly what they wanted. Maybe I delivered my opinion more bluntly than I should have, but I had always been candid with Ted.

I felt that there was no chance that he could sustain his position. An early decision to submit himself to re-election was probably his only chance of holding on, though I doubted if he could in any circumstances. My impression was that Ted by then was only hearing the advice he wished to hear, including some from sources to which previously he had paid scant attention.

I was surprised by the number of people who were saying that they disliked him, and by the degree of bitterness and the spiteful determination that he had to go. The executive of the 1922 Committee met at the home of its chairman, Edward du Cann, on October 14, and decided to press for a leadership election. The executive had been dubbed the 'Milk Street Mafia', after a more public meeting at Edward's City office at Keyser Ullman, in Milk Street.

Again Ted demurred, but the Parliamentary Party's unease over the procedure for new leadership elections caused him to set up a review committee under Alec Home. The conclusions of Alec's review committee, however, were not at all helpful to Ted. There should be a provision for annual leadership elections in the Parliamentary Party. If there was a second ballot, new candidates could stand at that stage.

The most likely of Ted's challengers was Keith Joseph, the most senior 'dissident' who had been in Ted's Cabinet. No one had then realised that, however decent the man, his political antennae were too insensitive. But they very soon did, for within a few days, on October 19, Keith made a speech in Edgbaston which demonstrated almost unbelievable ineptitude for someone in the running for the Leadership. He referred to social classes 4 and 5 as being the least able to bring up children without resort to the state, and appeared to suggest that they should be encouraged through birth control to have fewer.

In fairness to Keith, he realised very quickly that he lacked the requisite qualities and threw in the towel. This posed the dissidents with quite a problem. They did not really want Edward du Cann—he was recognised as having been disloyal to Ted Heath, and his

City activities, with Lonrho and Keyser Ullman, were not universally accepted. He soon announced his decision not to run.

At this stage most people would have given up the struggle and for a time settled for Ted, who by now had enlisted new blood into his team, including the trusty old campaigner, John Peyton, and Peter Walker, who was re-engaged as Ted's campaign manager. But we reckoned without the persistence and almost obsessive scheming of Airey Neave.

Airey was a man of great courage—he had escaped from Colditz—and bitter determination. He was an implacable enemy of Ted's, from the 1950s when Ted had been Chief Whip, and they had a great row. Someone who had been determined enough to escape from Colditz was unlikely to be put off by losing a couple of potential candidates, so the next in line was pushed forward. This was Margaret Thatcher.

Up to that time, I do not believe that she had thought of herself as a candidate for the Leadership. My conversations with her gave me no inkling to that effect, and, although she was ambitious, I do not think she felt that her time had come. However, Airey ran a brilliant campaign—I was in a good position to judge because at that time Margaret had the little box of an office immediately opposite mine in the Shadow Cabinet corridor at the Commons, and this became Airey's headquarters. There was a constant flow of MPs to see them, and I began to realise that these were drawn from a wide cross-section of the Party.

Although Margaret knew I would not support her, I was on reasonable terms with her—so much so that during the battle for the Leadership I attended her constituency annual dinner and dance as guest of honour.

Airey Neave's exercise was carried out by a combination of promises and flattery, and was brilliantly masterminded. Margaret's stature in the Party had been enhanced by her performances at the dispatch box as Robert Carr's deputy opposing Labour's Finance Bill. Her courage in opposing Ted went down well in the Party and in much of the press. Other potential candidates, who were remaining loyal to Ted but who it was known would come in on the second ballot if Ted were defeated, were quietly being accused of cowardice by the Neave camp. The fact that a vote for Margaret was the only way to secure a second ballot was also turned to advantage.

There was only one really bitter outbreak of in-fighting, prompted by a story which Peter Walker had raked up from somewhere that gave an account of Margaret hoarding food during the miners' strike. The intention had been to brand her as a 'hoarder' as well as the 'milk snatcher', but most of us thought this seemed an eminently sensible thing for her to have done.

On the day of the first ballot, February 4, 1975, I was on a political tour of the East Midlands. I had allowed plenty of time to return to the Commons to vote, but the train was one and a half hours late. I arrived at the House in time to be greeted by the sight of Alan Clark, the maverick right wing MP for Plymouth Sutton, rushing out of Westminster Hall shouting at the top of his voice, 'She's won, she's won.'

Margaret received 130 votes to Ted's 119 and Hugh Fraser's 16. Thank goodness my vote would not have made any difference. It was one of the most miserable days in my life.

The next day I received a visit from Humphrey Atkins, by then our Chief Whip, telling me in enthusiastic and forceful terms that I should stand for the leadership. This surprised me, as I had not thought of him as someone who would favour me, and in any case I presumed that he would support Willie Whitelaw.

My main supporters were my former PPSs, Michael Jopling and Barney Hayhoe, the former retiring to bed with 'flu for the rest of the week between the two ballots.

I received a number of approaches to withdraw. Ian Percival, the lawyer on the right of the party, suggested that Margaret as Leader and myself as Deputy would be a winning team and the votes could be delivered. I cannot believe he came without Airey Neave's permission, but it did not look a very comfortable arrangement, and I declined.

On the second ballot on February 11, Margaret won 146 votes, Willie Whitelaw 79, myself and Geoffrey Howe each won 19 votes, and John Peyton 11. It was clear that Geoffrey Howe and myself would be the also-rans, but I was a little surprised that I ran so badly. I discovered when I later spoke with Geoffrey that he too had been persuaded to stand by Humphrey Atkins.

Margaret had won convincingly. The party was greatly relieved to get the whole business over and done with.

I have no doubt that Willie lost his chance of being leader and perhaps Prime Minister as a result of his loyalty to Ted during this period. If he had been free to enter the leadership stakes immediately after our October election defeat, he would almost certainly have been elected. No one can fault the absolute loyalty that Willie gave to Ted and then Margaret. He has had a very distinguished career and by dint of old-fashioned virtues and a marvellously warm personality has held the Party together on many occasions.

There was no way that the Party was going to be generous to Ted Heath after three General Election defeats out of four. The right wing hated Ted and the scenes of rejoicing when he was beaten in the leadership contest by Margaret Thatcher left me feeling very sad.

[James Prior, *A Balance of Power* (London, 1986), 98–101.]

*First ballot*:

| | |
|---|---|
| Margaret Thatcher | 130 |
| Edward Heath | 119 |
| Hugh Fraser | 16 |

*Second ballot*:

| | |
|---|---|
| Margaret Thatcher | 146 |
| William Whitelaw | 79 |
| James Prior | 19 |
| Geoffrey Howe | 19 |
| John Peyton | 11 |

## (2) THE LABOUR PARTY

### *Constitution, clause VI*

(1) There shall be a leader and a deputy leader of the Labour Party who shall be *ex-officio* leader and deputy leader of the Parliamentary Labour Party.

(2) The leader and deputy leader of the party shall be elected or re-elected from amongst the Commons members of the Parliamentary Labour Party at the party conference . . . and with the provision as may be set out in the standing orders for the time being in force.

### *Standing Orders, No. 5*

(2)(a) The leader and deputy leader of the party shall be elected separately at a party conference.

(b) Affiliated organisations, Constituency Labour Parties and Commons Members of Parliament may nominate for each of the offices of leader and deputy leader, one Commons Member of the

Parliamentary Labour Party attending conference (unless excused attendance as provided in sub-section (c) below) as a delegate or *ex-officio* delegate.

(c) Nominees who do not attend the party conference shall be deemed to have withdrawn their nominations unless they send to the secretary on or before the date on which the conference opens an explanation in writing of their absence, satisfactory to the party Conference Arrangements Committee.

(d) Before sending in nominations on the prescribed form, the consent in writing of the nominees must be obtained and each nomination must be supported by twenty per cent of Commons Members of the Parliamentary Labour Party. Unless the written consent is attached to the nomination paper and twenty per cent of Commons Members have indicated their support, the nomination shall be null and void. Valid nominations shall be printed in the agenda together with the names of the nominating organisations and Commons members supporting the nomination.

(3)(a) Voting in the election of the leader and deputy leader of the party shall take place consecutively in three sections as follows:

(i) Section 1 shall consist of those Commons Members of the Parliamentary Labour Party who are at present at Party Conference and each such Commons Member shall be entitled to one vote in each ballot held under this section in the election. Commons Members unable to attend conference through sickness or because they are abroad on parliamentary business may send instruction to the secretary of the party or to a parliamentary colleague on how their vote shall be cast provided that they send to the secretary on or before the date on which conference opens an explanation in writing of their absence.

(ii) Section 2 shall consist of those delegates from affiliated Constituency Labour Parties present at Party Conference and each Constituency Labour Party shall be entitled to vote in each ballot under this section. . .

(iii) Section 3 shall consist of those delegates from affiliated trade unions, socialist societies, co-operative societies and other organisations present at party conference and each delegation shall be entitled to vote in each ballot under this section . . .

(b) The votes for each nominee in a section shall be calculated as a percentage of the total votes cast in that section and then shall be apportioned in the following manner,

| | |
|---|---|
| Section 1 Parliamentary Labour Party | 30% |
| Section 2 Constituency Labour Parties | 30% |
| Section 3 Affiliated organisations | 40% |

(c) The votes apportioned as provided in paragraph (b) above shall be totalled and the candidate receiving more than half of the votes shall be declared elected and if no candidate reaches this total on the first ballot further ballots should be held on an elimination basis.

(d) (i) Subject to sub-paragraph (iii) below, when the Parliamentary Labour Party is in opposition in the House of Commons the election of the party leader and deputy leader shall take place at each annual party conference.

(ii) When the party is in government and the party leader is prime minister, the election shall take place only if requested by a majority of the party conference on a card vote.

(iii) Subject to paragraph (4) below, in any other circumstances an election shall be held when a vacancy occurs.

(e) The votes cast for each nominee by each affiliated organisation, Constituency Labour Party and Commons Members of the Parliamentary Labour Party shall be recorded and made available as soon as possible.

(4) When the party leader, for whatever reason, becomes permanently unavailable, the deputy party leader shall automatically become leader until a new party leader is elected at a party conference.

*(a) Election for Deputy Leader (1981)*

*The electoral college was first used in 1981 to elect the Deputy Leader. The results of the second ballot were:*

| | |
|---|---|
| Denis Healey | 50.43% |
| Tony Benn | 49.57% |

*(b) Election for Leader 1983*

*The first-ever use of the electoral college to elect a Leader took place on the resignation of Michael Foot. The results were:*

| | |
|---|---|
| Neil Kinnock | 71.27% |
| Roy Hattersley | 19.29% |
| Eric Heffer | 6.30% |
| Peter Shore | 3.14% |

*(c) Election for Deputy Leader 1983*

*On the same occasion, the Deputy Leadership votes were:*

| | |
|---|---|
| Roy Hattersley | 67.27% |
| Michael Meacher | 22.27% |
| Denzil Davies | 3.53% |
| Gwyneth Dunwoody | 1.32% |

*(d) Election for Leader 1987*

*The figures in this ballot were:*

| | |
|---|---|
| Neil Kinnock | 88.63% |
| Tony Benn | 11.37% |

*(e) Election for Deputy Leader*

*On the same occasion, the Deputy Leadership votes were:*

| | |
|---|---|
| Roy Hattersley | 66.82% |
| John Prescott | 23.69% |
| Eric Heffer | 9.48% |

## (3) THE SOCIAL AND LIBERAL DEMOCRATIC PARTY

*Constitution, articles 8 and 10*

8.5. The Federal Executive shall have power, after appropriate consultations and subject to ratification by the Federal Conference, to make and from time to time vary Party rules as to membership, elections and such other matters as it may consider necessary or desirable to give effect to or supplement the provisions of this

Constitution. Any election rules must provide for elections to be by STV and secret ballot.

10.1 The Leader of the Party shall be elected by the members of the Party in accordance with election rules made pursuant to Article 8.5.

10.2 An election for the Leader shall be called upon:

(a) the Leader asking for an election;
(b) the death or incapacity of the Leader;
(c) the Leader ceasing to be a Member of the House of Commons (other than a temporary cessation by reason of a dissolution);
(d) the receipt by the President of the resignation of the Leader or of a declaration of intent to resign upon the election of a new Leader;
(e) a vote of no confidence in the Leader being passed by a majority of all Members of the Parliamentary Party in the House of Commons;
(f) the receipt by the President of a requisition submitted by at least 75 Local Parties following the decision of a quorate general meeting; or
(g) the second anniversary of the preceding general election being reached without an election being called under any of paragraphs (a) through (f), provided that:
    (i) in exceptional circumstances, the Federal Executive may postpone such an election for no more than one year by a two-thirds majority of those present and voting; and
    (ii) this paragraph (g) shall not apply if the Leader is a member of the Government.

10.3 Upon election, the Leader shall hold office until death, incapacity or resignation or the completion of an election called under this Article.

10.4 Upon the calling of an election, the Federal Executive shall publish a timetable for nominations, withdrawals, despatch, and receipt of ballot papers and the holding of ballots and shall appoint a disinterested person or body to receive and count the ballot papers.

10.5 Nominations must be of a Member of the Parliamentary Party in the House of Commons, who must be proposed and seconded by other such Members and supported by 200 members in aggregate in not less than 20 Local Parties (including, for this purpose, the Specified Associated organisations representing youth and students as provided by Article 13.8) following the decision of a quorate general meeting and must indicate acceptance of nomination.

*In the ballot for the Leadership of the new, merged party, the votes were as follows:*

| | |
|---|---|
| Paddy Ashdown | 41,401 |
| Alan Beith | 16,202 |

## 3. CONSTITUTIONAL CONSEQUENCE OF PARTY LEADERSHIP ELECTION RULES

*Now that each party has formal election procedures through which to choose its Leader, the Queen in normal circumstances will not have to make a personal choice between rival candidates for Prime Minister, a choice which she had to make in 1957 and in 1963 before the Conservative Party adopted election rules.*

### (1) 1957

On the morning of 9 January 1957 I was working at the Treasury when a message was delivered summoning me to Number 10 at 3 o'clock. I remember asking my private secretary to enquire what would be the main subjects of our discussion. The state of the sterling exchanges, the progress of the negotiations for financial aid, the estimates of the likely flow of oil—these were all matters on which I knew the Prime Minister would want the latest information. But from the nature of the reply which came from his private office, it was clear that he wanted a personal talk.

Eden was in the little drawing-room, the smallest of the three saloons which occupy the front of the famous house. All these face north and seldom see the sun; but in this room there is a window to the west, looking over the garden, and the afternoon and evening sun give it, even through the gloom of a London winter, a touch of warmth and glow. He told me with simple gravity, as a matter decided and not to be discussed, that he had decided to resign his office. The Queen had already been informed; this had been the purpose of his visit to Sandringham the previous day, which had generally been regarded as part of the normal routine, and not as marking any special occasion. He had already spoken with Salisbury and Butler. There was no way out. The doctors had told him the truth about his health and, though he was not doomed as a man, it must be the end of his political life.

I was deeply shocked, for I had not been at all prepared for this sudden and tragic end to the adventure on which we had set out so gaily some twenty months before. I had certainly learned from my talk with Sir Horace Evans of the nature and seriousness of Eden's malady; but the great doctor had seemed hopeful in November that a few weeks' rest, followed by the normal holiday at Christmas, would be sufficient. Indeed, when Eden returned from Jamaica in the middle of December, he had seemed almost, if not fully, restored. He himself had no suspicion of the advice the doctors were to have to give in January. Nevertheless, the doctors were inexorable, and there was nothing to be done but accept the verdict. Throughout our short and painful conversation he was as charming, as elegant and as dignified as ever. I could hardly believe that this was to be the end of the public life of a man so comparatively young, and with so much still to give . . .

I walked sadly back through the connecting passage to Number 11, and waited almost stunned with the news. The Cabinet had been summoned for 5 o'clock, but nothing had leaked out. When, therefore, Ministers were told the truth for which they were wholly unprepared, they were dazed. On his return in mid-December all his colleagues had felt encouraged by the Prime Minister's buoyancy; he had conducted the last debates with all his old skill and command of the House. Attributing his illness to the mental stresses and strains of the last few months, they were ignorant of the true medical causes. It was a painful, and unforgettable scene.

Eden spoke shortly, and with great dignity. The doctors' decision was irrevocable. He must resign. Salisbury spoke—with great emotion, almost in tears—of his lifelong friendship. Butler spoke next—very appropriately. I said a few words. Then it was all over. It was a dramatic end to an extraordinary and, in many ways, unique career. What seemed so dreadful was that he waited so long for the Premiership, and held it for so short a time . . .

I was one of the first to leave, making my way back to Number 11 unobserved. I heard afterwards that Butler left also, and that Lord

Salisbury, as senior Cabinet Minister, invited the remaining Ministers to give their opinion about who should succeed to the vacant and, in the circumstances, not very alluring post. The Ministers were asked to see Lord Salisbury (the Lord President) and Lord Kilmuir (the Lord Chancellor) one by one in the Lord President's room in the Privy Council offices, which could be reached without leaving the building. There were two light reliefs. Practically each one began by saying, 'This is like coming to the Headmaster's study.' To each Bobbety [Salisbury] said, 'Well, which is it, Wab or Hawold?' As well as seeing the remainder of the ex-Cabinet, we interviewed the Chief Whip and Oliver Poole, the Chairman of the Party. John Morrison, the Chairman of the 1922 Committee, rang me up from Islay the next morning. An overwhelming majority of Cabinet Ministers was in favour of Macmillan as Eden's successor, and back-bench opinion, as reported to us, strongly endorsed this view.

There was no attempt by either Salisbury or Kilmuir to use what one might call a prefect's influence on the opinion of those they interviewed. They merely asked a question and received an answer. Since both were senior members of the Government and neither, from the nature of things, was a potential candidate for the Premiership, they acted with strict propriety in a difficult situation.

These two senior Ministers had agreed on this course before the Cabinet met. They were rightly anxious to preserve the Queen's Prerogative, and not to allow the election of a Prime Minister as the result of a Party meeting. This point had some importance because, in Gaitskell's absence in America, there was an attempt by Griffiths, the Deputy Leader, to object to the course which had been adopted. He even accused the Conservatives of having placed the Crown in a very difficult and embarrassing position. When Parliament returned, the Opposition would take the matter up and proceed to a vote of censure. However, Gaitskell was much too sensible to fall for this nonsense. No more was heard of any such protest. Nevertheless, in view of the controversy which was later to follow when illness brought my own tenure of office to an end, it is perhaps worth rehearsing the true story.

While this novel but not ineffective procedure was at work, Eden had gone to the Palace. In the evening, a bulletin signed by Sir Horace Evans and three other doctors was published in the following terms:

> The Prime Minister's health gives cause for anxiety. In spite of the improvement which followed his rest before Christmas there has been a recurrence of abdominal symptoms. This gives us much concern because of the serious operations in 1953 and some subsequent attacks of fever. In our opinion his health will no longer enable him to sustain the heavy burdens inseparable from the office of Prime Minister.

At the same time the Queen's acceptance of her Prime Minister's resignation was announced . . . The next morning I thought it wiser not to go to the Treasury.

I heard that Lord Salisbury and Sir Winston Churchill had been sent for by the Queen. But since no one had told me about what had taken place the night before, I had no idea of what advice they would give. It is since clear that Lord Salisbury did not give his own views. He merely informed the Queen of the general view among the leading members of the Party . . . Since the Socialists afterwards tried to make out that this was a personal and private effort by the head of the Cecils, it is important to record that Lord Salisbury merely acted as a means of conveying to the Queen the general view inside the Party. I gathered from Anthony (whom I saw later on Thursday) that he had neither been asked for his advice nor had volunteered it.

I passed the morning in the downstairs sitting-room, to which I had restored the picture of Mr Gladstone, and I read *Pride and Prejudice*—very soothing. At noon Sir Michael Adeane rang up and asked me to be at the Palace at 2 o'clock. So it was settled.

We had then a small dining-room at the top of Number 11, which my wife and I used when we were alone. I sent a message to ask if we could have some luncheon at one o'clock, sharp. I had not told her about my summons to the Palace, but when I appeared in a tail coat, this unusual costume, combined with the insistence on punctuality, led her to make an accurate deduction.

The Queen received me with the greatest kindness and consideration. Although in various posts, especially as Foreign Secretary, I had seen her not infrequently, yet this was the beginning of a quite different relationship. The Prime Minister is above all the Queen's First Minister. His supreme loyalty is to her. I could not disguise from her the gravity of the situation. Indeed, I remember warning her, half in joke, half in earnest, that I could not answer for the new

Government lasting more than six weeks. She smilingly reminded me of this at an audience six years later.

[Harold Macmillan, *Riding the Storm* (London, 1971), 180–5.]

Anthony returned from his enforced rest on 14th December. He at once declared his intention to carry on as Prime Minister. Suddenly, on 8th January, he telephoned me to say that he was going to Sandringham to tender his resignation to the Queen. Cabinet Ministers were 'corralled' to give an immediate judgement between Harold Macmillan and me as successor. Selwyn Lloyd objected to this procedure being carried out by two peers, Kilmuir and Salisbury. A majority of the Cabinet decided for Harold. The Queen sent for Churchill and Salisbury. I had no doubt what Salisbury's advice would be. I had served Churchill for ten years and for four as his Chancellor, but he told me later 'I went for the older man.' It was clear from the representations that had been made to the Chief Whip's office that there were many on the back-benches who would oppose my succession; there was no similar anti-Macmillan faction. Ted Heath was sent to inform me of the result. As I wrote at the time, I was not surprised. I had been overwhelmed with duties as head of the government, and had made no dispositions for the emergency which occurred. Horace Evans had told me that Anthony Eden would get better, and I had relied on him going on. That night Anthony's wife sent me the following balm from Chequers:

Dear Rab,
Just a line to say what a beastly profession I think politics are—and how greatly I admire your dignity and good humour.
Yours ever,
Clarissa.

In the precarious situation that now confronted the government and the party, it was my duty to give the new Prime Minister loyal and sincere co-operation. I thought I could best do this at the Foreign Office, since in the aftermath of Suez so many dangerous tangles remained to be unravelled and so many ruptured friendships to be mended. However, as he pungently states in his memoirs, Macmillan 'felt one head on a charger should be enough', and was accordingly anxious not to dislodge the faithful Selwyn Lloyd. His memory plays him false in averring that I 'chose the post of Home

Secretary'. But he was clearly relieved when I agreed to accept it at his hands. Dining a few nights later at the Beefsteak, I was reminded by a bright spark that Home Secretaries scarcely ever become Prime Ministers. But since the exceptions include Melbourne and Churchill, this 'rule' need depress no incumbent; nor was I ever Home Secretary *tout court*. Other jobs and dignities, including the leadership of the House, the chairmanship of the party, the conduct of Central African affairs, the oversight of European negotiations, the first Secretaryship of State, and even the Deputy Premiership, were to be added unto me for varying periods in the years that followed; and each time Macmillan went abroad—notably during his Eastern tour in 1958 and his African trip in 1960—I was automatically invited to act as head of the government. But to do him justice, the Prime Minister never gave me any impression that he wanted me to succeed him . . .

[Lord Butler, *The Art of the Possible* (London, 1971), 195–6.]

## (2) 1963

When we assembled for Cabinet on 8 October we found that the Prime Minister had suffered a severe attack of his prostate gland trouble during the night and had to see his doctor again. It was apparent that his attendance at the coming Party Conference must be assumed to be very unlikely, and that the question of replacing him as leader could arise.

In Cabinet in his absence we had a short discussion. The Lord Chancellor (Viscount Dilhorne) said that, as he was not himself a candidate for the leadership, if anyone wished to have any private talk he would be available. I said that the same applied to me. Enoch Powell later cited this indication of my position as a kind of pledge from which, when events turned out as they did, I should have had the whole Cabinet's leave formally to withdraw. It was, however, nothing so dramatic or pompous—merely a statement revealing that at that time the question of my succession to Macmillan had simply not crossed my mind.

When the others went off to Blackpool I stayed behind to attend to Foreign Office business, as my speech to the Conference was not to be until later in the week.

On 9 October I went to see Macmillan in the nursing home and he talked about the future leadership. He asked me whether I had thought of taking it on, and if not why not. I replied that I had not done so—that I was happy in the Foreign Office, and in the House of Lords which I had never contemplated leaving, and that it was in these fields that my strong preferences lay. He seemed to accept that, and said that he had concluded after much thought that Lord Hailsham might be the best choice. I had watched Quintin under pressure during the Suez crisis where he had shown admirable calm at the Admiralty in testing circumstances; and while I had some misgivings about his famous 'judgement' I felt that he could take on the leadership and the job of Prime Minister, and make a success of it. I left it with Macmillan that he would continue his talks with him and others. He asked me to take a message to the Blackpool Conference conveying to the delegates that he felt that he could not lead the Party at the General Election, and inviting those whose business it was to do so, to take soundings about the future leadership.

I did not enjoy the journey to Blackpool with these grim tidings; and when I came to the platform to deliver his message to the audience of 4,000 the hall was hushed with anticipation that something ill was in the wind.

As President of the National Union for the year I read the message which contained Macmillan's decision. 'I will not be able to carry the physical burden of leading the Party at the next General Election. I hope that it will soon be possible for the customary consultations to be carried out within the Party about the leadership.' All of us felt a long way from the happy days when 'we never had it so good'.

I walked back from the Meeting with Quintin who knew by then that he was Macmillan's selection, and I told him that the idea had my support. Had I known that he intended to throw his claim to the leadership into the ring within a matter of hours, I would have tried to dissuade him from it then and there, for people never like being bounced, and least of all at a time of emotional stress. As it was, others advised him against precipitating the issue, and I had a late word with him shortly before his evening meeting with the Conservative Political Centre; but by then it was too late for he considered himself to be committed to his friends. In his speech he declared himself a runner. The immediate instinct of his audience was to acclaim, but there followed a swift reaction against his candidature, and the tactical advantage which he had seemingly tried to gain by such instant action fell right away. This had been predictable; and the opposition increased rapidly in the succeeding days. It was sad. He had many of the qualities of an inspiring leader; for he combined a keen intellect with an ability to speak from the heart; and over and above that the power to make up his mind and to decide.

It was after this débâcle that a number of Conservatives came and told me that I ought to consider coming forward as a leader of the Party and a potential Prime Minister. I was the last thing which I had anticipated, and the last thing which I sought. At first my reply was that which I had given to Macmillan. I was happy in my Office; it was exacting but I could carry it easily in the House of Lords; and I had no wish to re-submit myself to the rough and tumble of electioneering and the House of Commons . . .

One thing was clear in the confusion—that I could not even let myself think about the matter unless my physical health was up to it. Overstrain had brought on tuberculosis in 1939 and I had been having a lot of trouble with my eyes. I told Lord Dilhorne that I would ask my doctor whether in his opinion I could last the course if the task were laid upon me. After a thorough examination he said that I was well enough to hold it down. That escape route was closed.

I then had to consider all the political and governmental aspects of the matter. There was one rather serious minus in the count-down. I was not trained in economics, and economic matters were sure to figure largely in the run-up to the election and in the years to come. Unluckily, in 1962, in an interview with Kenneth Harris of the *Observer*, I had publicly admitted this deficiency. He had asked me whether I felt that I could ever be Prime Minister, and I had answered light-heartedly, 'No, because I do my sums with match-sticks'. It did not worry me unduly because all that was needed would be to choose a good Chancellor of the Exchequer; but Harold Wilson was not likely to miss a trick like that.

On the plus side was the fact that the Foreign Office and the years spent in Cabinet were a good apprenticeship, while in addition I had never been afraid of taking decisions. That, above all else, is what a Prime Minister is for.

Naturally I talked over every aspect of it with Elizabeth and the family; and in the end I concluded that if—and only if—convincing evidence was brought to me that a substantial majority in both Houses wished me to take on the job I would do so. The procedure for ascertaining the opinion of members of the Commons and of Peers and of prominent people in the Party Organization was then conducted by persons who were later to be christened 'the Magic Circle'. They were in the main Conservative Whips in both Houses, for if they did not know the form then nobody else would. When the result of the canvass was conveyed to me I had no doubt whatever that it had been thorough and honest and that I could command the necessary support in Parliament. There was therefore no longer any reason for or point in hesitation; and I said that if I were the choice that I would respond to the best of my ability . . .

On 18 October I was sent for by Her Majesty and invited to form a Government. I expressed my gratitude, but explained to the Queen that I must ask leave to go away and see if I could form an administration. I was by no means sure, after the drama of the recent weeks, what the attitude of some of my colleagues would be. I had to enlist Butler, Maudling and Hailsham at the very least, to have the foundation on which to build a Cabinet and Government which would command support in the country and respect overseas.

Butler had for long been heir-apparent, and had given devoted and distinguished service to the Conservatives. Maudling was the best equipped on economics, and Hailsham was the possessor of a keen brain and was a colourful and popular figure. None of them could have been happy at that time. With kindness and loyalty and sacrifice they gave me their support, as did all but two of my colleagues in Macmillan's Cabinet. They were Ian Macleod and Enoch Powell, who were not natural bedfellows, but who for the moment had got into a huddle. The reason which they gave to me was that they did not believe that a man with my social background could win a General Election for the Conservative Party at that time in the twentieth century. I said that I thought they were wrong; but that if that was their reason for declining to serve I could only accept it and be sorry. I had a feeling that at the back of their minds was the calculation that, although we might lose in 1964, the next opportunity would not be long and that then we would win under another leader. But in politics one cannot do such clever mathematical sums and hope that events will conform. When a General Election comes it is necessary to fight flat out to win.

[Lord Home, *The Way the Wind Blows* (London, 1976), 180–5.]

As Randolph Churchill so eloquently described in *The Fight for the Tory Leadership*, Macmillan had seen Hailsham on the Monday before the Conference and indicated that in the event of retirement he would support his candidature. Accordingly the 'cohorts'—including the family, especially Maurice Macmillan and Julian Amery—warmly urged the case for Hailsham at the Imperial Hotel. Randolph himself returned from America with hundreds of badges marked Q for Quintin. He came up to my room and obligingly handed me some for my wife, myself and friends. These I consigned to the waste-paper basket.

Meanwhile Home with great determination had been to the hospital in London and obtained Macmillan's written resignation, which was read to the Conference on Thursday afternoon: 'I hope that it will soon be possible for the customary processes of consultation to be carried on within the party about its future leadership.' Alec Home obtained this and himself read it out. The fact that the P.M. asked for the processes of selection of his successor to be undertaken in the middle of a party conference was bound to create consternation, confusion and intrigue, and indeed it did. I cannot imagine an atmosphere less suited to such a declaration with scores of journalists, television interviewers, *et hoc genus omne*. It turned Blackpool into a sort of electoral Convention *à l'Américaine*. After that there was no peace.

The effect of Macmillan's encouragement was that Quintin Hailsham announced to the C.P.C. meeting on the Thursday night his determination to renounce his title. When I entered the Winter Gardens he was emerging surrounded by an hysterical crowd, having been greeted by a demonstration described to me by a hostile witness as 'reminiscent of a Nuremberg Rally'. He had been up to my room that afternoon and asked my advice. I had recommended him to say he was considering his position and no more. He said he thought it very good advice but would not take it. Alec Home gave him similar advice. Home's biographer implies that if Hailsham had taken it and not publicly shown his judgement faulty, Home would have supported Hailsham as Macmillan's designated heir.

We had frequent opportunities for meeting the Homes, who had the next-door set of rooms. He told us on more than one occasion that he could not himself contemplate coming down from the House of Lords and denuding it of himself as well as its leader. He appeared to Mollie and me to stick to that view during the Conference until the Saturday when he told us he was consulting his doctor. The Lord Chancellor, travelling down with us in the train, took Mollie a bet of £5 to 5*s*. that he would not stand. At that time the Lord Chancellor seemed fairly sure that, with the slump in Quintin's stock, my position was good. He was, however, extremely discreet and did not tell us any results of the Cabinet soundings in detail.

It became clear to me at Blackpool that there was considerable support for Alec, partly because he made a good speech on foreign policy, partly because he took the chair at my meeting in his capacity as President of the National Union, and partly because of lobbying by back-benchers who saw him as the best compromise candidate. His wife, Elizabeth, has told Mollie that they did not really get the view that it was coming their way until the next week; but, in fact, it was. My speech to the party conference on the Saturday had a good reception, but those who favour 'democracy by decibels' noted a victory for Home on points . . .

I returned to London and the Prime Minister made clear what I had always known, that, had he not been stricken down, he would have made a speech on the Saturday at Blackpool saying that he was going on. This would have avoided all discussion of the succession. Rather to my surprise popular support, especially in the *Daily Express* of the 16th, showed me to be in the lead—Butler 39½, Hailsham 21½, Maudling 11, Home 9½. I also had many more letters than usual and much assurance from Michael Fraser at the Research Department that the national polls really indicated a very considerable measure of support in the country. The situation was not however quite the same in the Parliamentary party. There was an element of criticism there of which I was informed by the Chief Whip and the Lord Chancellor, just as there was an element of criticism of Hailsham, and it seemed quite possible that the Whips would prefer a compromise candidate. On the other hand I was assured by the Lord Chancellor and by the Prime Minister that the Cabinet would be perfectly happy to work either under me or Alec Home.

I think that Harold himself always had a feeling, despite the nine years between us, that my succession would not make enough difference between his regime and the next, and he mentioned this argument to me on the 17th. I pointed to the fact that I was younger than when he took over. I also pointed out the difficulty of bringing a peer down from the Upper House—not only the short-term difficulty of the delay but also the psychological impact on the country. I therefore did my best to keep the doors open. Despite the unpleasantness of the situation personal relations were maintained. I saw Alec Home, Reggie Maudling and Quintin Hailsham. In my talk with Alec he himself expressed grave doubts whether he wished to take it on. He said his wife was encouraging him, but that he realized the difficulties of coming back to the Commons and of the years after the election if we were in office or even more if we were in opposition. He said he would be perfectly happy to back me. I got the impression that he was personally not keen to stand himself but could be persuaded. He said he hoped that if he had to do it he could count on me. My talk with Reggie was very short. He simply said that he did not know how the M.P.s would react in his favour but that he counted on me to work with him. My talk with Quintin had more content since he said that if another peer came down from the Upper House he would withdraw from public life whether he was in the Upper or Lower House. He would then go back to the Bar and try to make a living there. I reminded him of my advice that he should not have renounced the Upper House so speedily. He agreed that this advice had been good but said that things had now gone too far. I besought him if the decision went against him to return to the Upper House and do his bit there. He said he would be perfectly ready to serve with me.

There then followed the inquiry by the Whips in the Commons about whom M.P.s wanted as Leader. I have never seen the result of this operation. I simply heard from numerous of my friends that they were rung up by quite junior Whips who stressed that Alec was standing, having decided to renounce his peerage. The Whips had a difficult job and were as usual a good body of men, but the accounts sent in to me showed me that each man in conducting this inquiry adopted a different emphasis according to his own character. At any rate we were informed that the Chief Whip had carried a document to the sick Prime Minister showing the majority preference.

By the Thursday afternoon the newspapers had smelt that things were going Home's way. A meeting took place that night at Enoch Powell's house at which Toby Aldington, Iain Macleod, Reggie Maudling and Freddie Erroll were present. They were later joined by the Chief Whip. This was a meeting of revolt against the choice of

Home. They telephoned me at the St. Ermin's Hotel, where Mollie and I were staying while our house in Smith Square was under repair, to pledge their support. Quintin himself rang saying 'This simply won't do' and Mollie answered him. She was superb throughout, counselling me to stay out, and this made my eventual decision all the more poignant. Other members of the Cabinet who were friendly to me were Henry Brooke, Edward Boyle and John Boyd-Carpenter. I was also spoken to by the Chief Whip who reiterated that the majority of the party were for Alec. One presumes and hopes that the Chief Whip informed the Prime Minister, as he was requested to do, that seven or eight members of the Cabinet were opposed to the choice of Home. What is certain is that Macmillan decided to ignore this powerful objection and acted (as he had done in 1962) with utter determination and dispatch, making a definite recommendation of Home.

[Butler, *Art of the Possible,* 242–3, 246–8.]

Before 1965 the Crown's role in choosing a Prime Minister was greater than it has now become. If a Labour Prime Minister had died or retired whilst in office the Parliamentary Party election procedure would have produced a new leader. But the death or retirement of a Conservative Prime Minister made it necessary for a choice to be made by the Queen in accordance with the convention that the office should be filled by an incumbent most likely to command the support of a Commons majority. That principle dictated the choice as the Prime Minister's successor of a leading figure in the party, but it did not indicate precisely who the appointee should be when the Conservative party was in office and there were competing claimants for the succession. Between 1945 and 1965 that situation arose on two occasions (in 1957 and in 1963), on the retirement of the Conservative Prime Ministers Eden and Macmillan. The practice was that the Queen with the aid of her Private Secretary would take soundings from a variety of sources including Privy Councillors, senior politicians and party whips. It was agreed that the retiring Prime Minister did not have any right to nominate or give binding advice as to his successor, though he might be consulted along with others.

The choice by the Queen of Lord Home in 1963 was of some importance since the circumstances in which it took place illustrated the difficulties of the process and led fairly quickly to the adoption by the Conservative Party of a leadership election process that was designed (like the Labour Party's leadership election) to make the choice of a Prime Ministerial successor a constitutional formality.

The events surrounding the appointment of Lord Home (as he then was) have been the subject of rival accounts. A criticism made by those in both parties who were opposed to the appointment was that on Mr Harold Macmillan's prompting the Queen had allowed herself to be urged prematurely into a decision without having at her disposal all the available evidence about feeling in the Conservative Party. In effect the process of consultation and decision was cut off at a point where the situation was changing rapidly and when the leading contenders for office had in fact agreed to express their willingness to serve under Mr R. A. Butler. It was alleged that efforts to convey this information to the Queen's advisers on the morning when she saw Macmillan were unsuccessful. It is still unclear from the account given in Macmillan's memoirs what facts were made known to the Queen when the Prime Minister read to her from his hospital bed a memorandum of advice containing the suggestion that she should invite Lord Home to attempt to form an administration. What is said is that mention was made of the 'so-called revolt of certain ministers'. When asked about this revolt the Prime Minister replied that he 'thought speed was important and hoped she would send for Lord Home immediately—as soon as she got back to the Palace'. Randolph Churchill reported a similar sentiment as being expressed by Macmillan to Home: '. . . We can't change our view now. All the troops are on the starting line. Everything is arranged.'

This perhaps supports the criticism that the Queen's advisers should not have allowed her to be urged into an immediate invitation to Lord Home and that she should have taken at least a little time fully to apprise herself of the changing political situation and of the views of the Conservative leadership, as it was then emerging. If she was aware of the situation as it was on the morning of 18 October 1963 she was possibly mistaken in her action. If she was not aware of it she was deceived. Mr Harold Macmillan was admittedly fortified by an informal poll of Conservative members and notables, but it may be argued that he should not have been the sole fountain-head of advice, if it is indeed a constitutional principle that a retiring

Prime Minister has no special title or status to advise on the choice of his successor. In fact, at the time when Macmillan's advice was sought he had ceased to be Prime Minister and it is the more odd that the Queen on this occasion should have, in Macmillan's words, said that 'she did not need and did not intend to seek any other advice but mine'.

Other criticisms were of less validity. Macmillan related that the Queen believed, or at least agreed, that 'Lord Home was really the best and strongest character'. On the publication of Macmillan's memoirs Mr Humphrey Berkeley wrote to *The Times* to complain about this as being a 'gross constitutional impropriety'. The impropriety was not, it is to be assumed, the expression of this arguably valid assessment of the political talents of Messrs Maudling, Butler, and Hogg, but the fact that it should have been revealed to the general public. The complaint, if valid, would suggest the existence of a constitutional practice or convention, which has certainly not been observed with complete fidelity in the past. Lord Attlee's memoirs, for example, as well as Sir John Wheeler-Bennett's biography of George VI described a number of views held by the King without the authors being accused of constitutional impropriety. In 1963 Queen Elizabeth, like her father, was exercising one of Bagehot's three monarchical Prerogatives—the right to encourage, the right to be consulted, and the right to warn. No doubt she encouraged Mr Macmillan at a time when he needed some encouragement; and there seemed little danger to the Constitution in this fact being revealed in1973 to those readers of Sir Harold's memoirs who had stayed the course through the *Winds of Change*, the *Blast of War*, and the *Tides of Fortune* to the *End of the Day*.

Conservative dissatisfaction with the episode of 1963 led almost immediately to the adoption of a procedure for election of the party leader by a ballot of members taking the Conservative whip. Recent changes in the party system, however, suggest that there may still be situations in which it may be necessary for the Prerogative of appointment to be excercised in accordance with the independent judgment of the Queen and her advisers.

[Geoffrey Marshall, *Constitutional Conventions* (Oxford, 1984), 29–32.]

## Summary of Changes of Prime Minister since 1900

| Reason for change | Outgoing P.M. | New P.M. and date |
|---|---|---|
| Defeat of government at general election | Baldwin | MacDonald (1924) |
| | MacDonald | Baldwin (1924) |
| | Baldwin | MacDonald (1929) |
| | Churchill | Attlee (1945) |
| | Attlee | Churchill (1951) |
| | Douglas-Home | Wilson (1964) |
| | Wilson | Heath (1970) |
| | Heath | Wilson (1974) |
| | Callaghan | Thatcher (1979) |
| Resignation of P.M. (illness or old age) | Salisbury | Balfour (1902) |
| | Campbell-Bannerman | Asquith (1908) |
| | Bonar Law | Baldwin (1923) |
| | MacDonald | Baldwin (1935) |
| | Churchill | Eden (1955) |
| | Eden | Macmillan (1957) |
| | Macmillan | Douglas-Home (1963) |
| Voluntary retirement | Baldwin | Chamberlain (1937) |
| | Wilson | Callaghan (1976) |
| To form or break up a coalition | Asquith | Asquith (1915) |
| | Asquith | Lloyd George (1916) |
| | Lloyd George | Bonar Law (1922) |
| | MacDonald | MacDonald (1931) |
| | Chamberlain | Churchill (1940) |
| | Churchill | Churchill (1945) |
| Change of party government without general election | | Campbell-Bannerman (1905) |

## Possible Causes of Change of Prime Minister

### 1. GENERAL ELECTION

#### (1) SUCCESS OF THE GOVERNMENT

*No constitutional action is necessary when the government is returned with an absolute Commons' majority, as happened in 1906, 1918, 1922, 1931, 1935, 1950, 1955, 1959, 1966, October 1974, 1983 and 1987.*

So it was all over, with a new House of Commons containing [after the 1959 general election] 365 Conservative, 258 Labour and 6 Liberal members. Since on the morning of Polling Day *The Times* had forecast a majority of twenty-two I felt more than satisfied—but it was impossible not to feel, with all the excitement and gratification, a sense of humility and even awe. At a Press Conference at the Central Office I tried to express this. 'We must try,' I said, 'to emphasise the fundamental unity of our people and not exaggerate the differences which divide us, important as they may be.' Nevertheless, it was a staggering result. No Party has been victorious three times running increasing its majority each time.

One more duty I was able to perform the next day. I had advised Her Majesty the Queen not to break her holiday and leave Balmoral because of the General Election. Accordingly I was glad to be able to write to her formally on 10 October:

Madam,

Mr Macmillan with his humble duty to The Queen.

I was glad that in the course of the night of 8/9 October it became clear that it would not be necessary to trouble Your Majesty to return to London. I must admit that this situation caused me some anxiety at an earlier stage, but no point was made about this in the Press either before or after the Election. The new Americanised habit of one of the Leaders 'conceding' the Election in the early hours of the morning was an advantage from this point of view.

I propose to think over the situation of the Government generally during the week-end and I have not yet made any definite decisions as to possible changes of Ministers. I do not anticipate that these will be on a very substantial scale and I do not see any reason why it should be necessary to ask Your Majesty to return to London prematurely. Ministers can go from London to Balmoral as well as Sovereigns from Balmoral to London, and the former has to my mind a far better and longer tradition behind it. At any rate, perhaps I may be allowed to communicate with Your Majesty on this point, or ask my Private Secretary to discuss it with Sir Michael Adeane.

With regard to the general result of the Election, naturally my colleagues and I, and those who think with us, are more than satisfied. But we realise the heavy work that lies ahead, both at home and abroad. The people at home have become accustomed to a very high and stable economic situation. The slightest change in the barometer, although it might be due to factors quite outside our control, would correspondingly depress them. Abroad, although hopeful, they are a little more realistic.

The most encouraging feature of the Election however, from Your Majesty's point of view, is the strong impression that I have formed that Your Majesty's subjects do not wish to allow themselves to be divided into warring classes or tribes filled with hereditary animosity against each other. There was a very significant breakdown of this structure of society which, in spite of its many material advantages, was one of the chief spiritual disadvantages of the first industrial revolution. It will be curious if the second industrial revolution, through the wide spread of its amenities of life to almost every home in the country, succeeds in destroying this unfortunate product of the first. At any rate, anything that makes Your Majesty's subjects more conscious of their unity and of their duty to each other seems to me to be a real gain.

With my humble duty,
I remain,
Your Majesty's faithful
and devoted servant.

To this the Queen returned a gracious reply which while maintaining the full impartiality of the Crown encouraged me to continue to do my best to serve her as her First Minister.

[Harold Macmillan, *Pointing the Way* (London, 1972), 14–15]

## (2) SUCCESS OF THE OPPOSITION

*The Opposition was returned with an absolute Commons' majority in 1924, 1945, 1951, 1964, 1970 and 1979.*

The procedures followed in the very different circumstances that arise from the electoral defeat of the party in power are inevitably simpler, provided that the result creates a viable situation for the majority party. The Queen, without of course receiving any advice from the outgoing prime minister, sends for the leader of the successful party. In this generation there has not been any doubt about his identity.

[Harold Wilson, *The Governance of Britain* (London, 1976), 24.]

### (3) SUCCESS FOR NO SINGLE PARTY

*This is discussed below:* *see p. 64*

## 2. RESIGNATION THROUGH ILLNESS OR OLD AGE; DEATH

A solution is suggested which combines the requirements of always having someone, with next to no power vacuum, at the helm, together with what today may be taken as being the common preference in the political parties for the Leader (and hence Prime Minister) to be elected. Save for the case where a Prime Minister is to resign as the result of advanced years, and therefore where speed is not essential and an ordinary party election could take place, the following course of action is proposed to find a new Prime Minister for a continuing government. First, the outgoing Prime Minister would inform the Queen and his parliamentary party of his illness and desire to resign. Secondly, the Queen would ask the Prime Minister's deputy (if there were one), or the number two in the order of precedence in the Cabinet list (if there were no formal deputy), to take charge of the government, while retaining his portfolio, but *without* appointing him Prime Minister. He would look after the government on as much of a care and maintenance basis as circumstances permitted, deciding only urgent matters and then only with Cabinet consent if this were possible. Thirdly, the government party would proceed to an election as expeditiously as might be and, when a successful candidate was elected, the Prime Minister (if able, or the deputy or number two if not) would recommend him as successor, resign, and the new Leader would kiss hands on appointment as Prime Minister. In such a way the democratic ideal would be preserved; at no time would the government be rudderless, and the Queen would remain isolated from party politics.

It might be objected that for a politician to act as a 'caretaker' might in itself enhance his chances in the subsequent Leadership election, simply by his being seen to fulfil the duties of the office of Prime Minister. But it is equally possible that he could spoil any chances he might have had by making some political slip. And even if the 'caretaker' solution is still disliked, would not a strong argument in its favour be that the automatic selection of the 'caretaker' by virtue of his position preordained either by the stricken Prime Minister or (in the case of a Labour government) by his position as Deputy Leader of the Labour Party mean that that selection would keep the Queen above the party infighting, and overall would ensure that the royal prerogative of choice of a new Prime Minister in this context would have no part to play?

As a matter of strict law, party elections can neither preclude nor pre-empt the prerogative of choice. If a Prime Minister indicated that he wished to resign because he was ill, the Queen would indeed be acting in accordance with constitutional law if she were then and there to accept his resignation and appoint a successor after taking whatever soundings seemed appropriate. But that law has upon it a rich gloss of practice, realism, and political sophistication which, I suggest, would preclude a repeat of events such as those which occurred in 1963. This gloss was added when all the parties came to accept the desirability of Leadership elections—that is, after 1965.

[Rodney Brazier, *Constitutional Practice* (Oxford, 1988), 11–13]

Accepted procedural rules appear to be that the person selected must have the support of a majority in the House of Commons (if need be, after a new general election), and that the Monarch must 'secure the strongest Government in the minimum time' while still observing the need for public impartiality. Most frequently, under the two-party system, all these requirements are met easily by sending for the Leader of the Opposition or of the majority party, as the case may be, upon the fall of government—as happened, for example, in 1945 and 1951. Here the facts are such as to allow of no other choice. There was until recently one situation in which the Monarch might be called upon to exercise a degree of discretion but even this has now in practice been removed as the result of party political developments that took place between 1957 and 1965 . . .

This situation arose when a Prime Minister died in office or resigned for personal reasons, that is to say, when a vacancy occurred which was not accompanied by any change in the position of the parties. Even then, there might sometimes be no room for choice, as when Sir Anthony Eden succeeded Sir Winston Churchill. But when Sir Anthony retired in his turn in 1957, the Queen was not presented with any one obvious successor. Under such circumstances it was normally assumed that, although the Monarch would probably seek advice in order to discover what persons would be acceptable to the party in power, yet for the final choice she alone was morally and constitutionally responsible. It was clear, however, that an unwise or ill-advised Monarch might conceivably act in a manner which could be construed as partial, in that it appeared to reflect a royal preference for one particular group within the party. It is true, and important, that a party in a majority is able to reject any selection of which it does not approve—if it is prepared to undergo the internal conflict this would probably entail. A royal 'mistake' is not final; but it could still harm the Monarch's own reputation. To prevent this there must exist rules capable of serving as effective guides to action. In 1957, on Sir Anthony Eden's resignation, the Queen apparently sought and acted upon the advice of Sir Winston Churchill and Lord Salisbury, both elder statesmen of the Conservative Party who had themselves no personal ambitions at stake, and who appeared to have the confidence of their own party. At the same time the Labour Party took the opportunity of outlining the procedure it wished to be adopted in the selection of a Labour Prime Minister under comparable conditions. It declared that the Monarch should make no selection until a new Leader had been elected by the Parliamentary Labour Party in the same way as a Leader is chosen when the Party is in opposition. The Labour Party, thus, had given notice that it would not be prepared to accept a Leader chosen for it by the Monarch. The Conservatives, on the other hand, appeared still to accept traditional methods of selection. It is to be doubted, however, whether they would have done so had the Monarch exercised a wide personal discretion without seeking the advice of Conservative elders. Both parties, nevertheless, seemed concerned to limit or even abolish the Monarch's culpability in this situation, and to insist upon a new procedural rule of what might be called 'party responsibility'. Such a 'rule' should not conflict with authority and precedent which require, essentially, only that the person selected be acceptable to the party in question. What it does is extend the requirements to include methods of selection which should virtually guarantee that the 'proper' choice is made for each party. To acknowledge this rule should thus have the double advantage of eliminating any appearance of royal partiality in selecting a Prime Minister on these occasions, and of ensuring that the parties obtain the leaders they want by the methods they want.

[Geoffrey Marshall and G. C. Moodie, *Some Problems of the Constitution* (London, 5th edn., 1971), 47–8.]

This afternoon to the Commons and talked to Frank Barlow, the Secretary of the PLP, who told me in detail the arrangements that had been made in the event of Harold Wilson dying. The news will be conveyed to a meeting of Ministers at Number 10, which will include the heads of all Departments, i.e. Ministers of Cabinet rank, as well as Cabinet Ministers themselves. Though there is no Deputy Prime Minister, George Brown is Deputy Leader of the Parliamentary Labour Party and will therefore have Harold's Party responsibilities.

Bowden as Leader of the House would be responsible for informing the House. As soon as Ministers know, letters or telegrams will be sent to every Commons Member of the Parliamentary Labour Party and a meeting will be summoned within twenty-four hours if the House is sitting or within forty-eight hours during a recess. No Lords will be present. At this meeting, nominations will be received and ballot papers will be duplicated on the spot. Four tellers will be appointed and the Party will proceed immediately to a vote.

It will be the usual exhaustive ballot procedure and if the first vote does not give an overall majority to one of the candidates there will be an adjournment for fifteen or twenty minutes in the same room to give candidates the opportunity to withdraw. There will then be another ballot and so on, until a new Leader of the Parliamentary Labour Party is appointed. The press will not be admitted until that is decided. The announcement will be made in a statement by Frank Barlow, as Secretary to the Parliamentary Labour Party, and will be conveyed to Sir Michael Adeane at Buckingham Palace. The Queen has been told that she is not to summon anybody to form a Government until she has heard who the new Leader is. Adeane understands this and the man elected Leader will be summoned. These arrangements have been agreed with the Liaison Committee of the Parliamentary Labour Party under Manny Shinwell's chairmanship and approved by Harold.

[Tony Benn, *Out of the Wilderness: Diaries 1963–1967* (London, 1987), 263.]

## 3. VOLUNTARY RETIREMENT

### (1) BALDWIN 1937

Retirement is one of the few moments which a politician can choose with deliberation and Baldwin had been preparing for it for months, if not for years. There could be no doubt, after 1935, that Neville Chamberlain would succeed him. Only the Abdication had prevented Baldwin from going at the end of 1936. Some of those very close, including Dugdale, urged him to withdraw as soon as that episode was over. But he refused. His conduct of the crisis could be seen as a great achievement, yet something so negative and distasteful was not what he would have wished for his last service. Instead, he would see the new King firmly into the saddle and retire after the Coronation.

For five months, therefore, after Edward VIII signed the Instrument of Abdication, Baldwin remained Prime Minister, steadily handing over control to Chamberlain, but keeping a watching brief in matters of defence. The domestic events of the spring of 1937 were not without importance but he took small part in them, and a cursory reading of the Cabinet minutes might suggest that he had already retired in mind. His position was not unlike that of MacDonald two years before: but he was able to exert his influence with most of his former strength when he thought it right to do so.

Wrapped in the adulation which expressed the country's relief at being saved from a constitutional crisis, Baldwin went down to Astley in December. 'We had a wonderful day yesterday,' he wrote to Tom Jones, on Boxing Day. 'The sunlight was as the opening of the gates of heaven itself and the glow it threw on the western hills transfigured the whole landscape for half an hour. The strange unearthly light lasted nearly all day . . . I am feeling quietly content and very thankful.'

Early in January, the Baldwins stayed at Sandringham for a weekend with the new King—'a family gathering, with the Bishop of Jarrow as preacher and the only other visitor.' On the Sunday, a crowd of eight thousand cheered the Royal Family on their way to church and Baldwin was given a most cordial reception. He found the King's strength and confidence increasing and he had no doubts about his fitness to rule; but the King was still anxious for time in which to adjust himself to his new station and duties. When Baldwin returned to London, Tom Jones showed him an article in the *Political Quarterly*, suggesting that the new Monarch should mix with a wider range of people. 'Oddly enough,' Baldwin replied, 'I was talking over this very matter with the King. I asked him if he would be willing to meet some members of the House, if Lucy and I fixed up some small dinner parties after my resignation. I am going round about Whitsun, perhaps May 20th . . .'

Neville Chamberlain returned that day from France, where he had taken ten days' rest, and the last session of Baldwin's leadership began. The key dates were soon fixed: the Coronation for 12 May and Baldwin's resignation for the 27th. Since these cut across both the Finance Bill and the Imperial Conference, Chamberlain had to make his dispositions in advance.

[Keith Middlemas and John Barnes, *Baldwin* (London, 1969), 1018–19.]

## (2) WILSON 1976

In the relatively simple hand-over of what is in fact, though not constitutionally, a continuing government, the test, given the normal circumstances of a party majority, is whether A or B can in fact command a majority in the House of Commons. Where the party's procedure for selecting a leader is laid down and is seen to have worked, e.g. the eliminating ballot procedure used by the Parliamentary Labour Party in March–April 1976, the selection is fairly clear, though it still has to be made. The Parliamentary Party was not in fact electing a prime minister; it was electing a new party leader.

When the process is complete, the outgoing prime minister goes straight to the Palace and formally tenders his resignation; the most he needs to do is inform the monarch, who will have been given the figures already, that the ballot has produced a given result, probably adding that in his view the newly elected leader can command a majority in Parliament. (The procedure might be somewhat different in a situation where the Government was in a minority, for example had I resigned between March and October 1974.) Contrary to widespread belief, there is no duty on the prime minister, still less any inherent right, to recommend the man to be sent for. It is the sovereign who decides whom to send for and invite to form a government.

[Wilson, *Government*, 21–2.]

Harold's secret was well guarded and the Cabinet gathered at No. 10 on the following Tuesday without the slightest inkling of the dramatic news they were to hear. Whilst Ministers were assembling, Harold called Ted Short, the Deputy Leader, Denis Healey and me to his study and there broke the news to the three of us. I do not know whether the other two also had prior knowledge, but no one gave any indication to this effect as we all filed silently to the Cabinet Room.

The Prime Minister opened the meeting. Ministers had hardly settled themselves in their seats before the bombshell burst. It was several seconds before they recovered their breath. The purport of his remarks is already familiar. This was no sudden decision on his part, as he had never intended to stay longer than two years after the 1974 election. The task of the Prime Minister was unremitting, for he was on duty every minute of the day and night and must know all that was going on in the Government. That demanded constant attention, and yet the Prime Minister must also be able to stand back from the pressure of events and think about the future. He recalled that he had led the Party for thirteen years, nearly eight of them as Prime Minister. We were living in a period of change and he wanted to avoid the danger of rejecting courses of action merely because they had been considered and turned down on some earlier occasion during his leadership. He had stayed long enough to see the first stage of the counter-inflation policy accepted and the clash and confrontation of two years earlier replaced by a new partnership.

His next sentence unobtrusively removed an argument that might have been used against me in the leadership contest. He said the fact that he was leaving at the age of sixty should have no bearing on the choice of his successor. I was grateful for not only was I four years older than he but I would also be the oldest of the potential candidates.

It was a great regret to me that our partnership was to come to an end. Except for our differences over Barbara Castle's proposals for trade union reform, he and I had worked closely together since 1964, and during my early days as Chancellor of the Exchequer when sterling was under great strain he was a considerable strength and comfort.

When we were in difficulties his sagacity and sangfroid were beyond doubt, as was his kindliness to his colleagues. There had been a period when he allowed Barbara Castle, Dick Crossman and George Wigg, all of whom suffered from the belief that politics was a conspiracy, to influence him too much, but in later years he had broken free from them and I suddenly realised how much I had got used to him being there to shoulder the final responsibility, to feeling able to turn to him naturally for a second opinion and for well-informed advice. Now in a short time he would be gone, and the era that had begun in the 1960s with the triumvirate of Harold Wilson, George Brown and myself would be at an end. Only I would be left. Three weeks later, on the day I became Prime Minister, my first impulse was to sit down in the study which had been Harold's and write him a letter of appreciation and grateful thanks.

Strangely enough, at no time did I have real doubts that I would be elected, and this determined my public attitude during the three successive ballots that were necessary. Merlyn Rees, Gregor Mackenzie and John Cunningham, all of whom were friends who had served me as Parliamentary Private Secretaries, rallied at once and with Tom McNally, my Political Adviser, formed a small inner team to conduct the contest on my behalf.

I told them I would prefer to give no interviews to press or television. In my view our fellow Members, who lived with us cheek by jowl, were fully aware of my strengths and weaknesses and were unlikely to be impressed by pictures of me on their TV screens dressed in a striped apron and pretending to wash up in the kitchen, as had happened during the Tory leadership election. Coincidentally, I had a very busy schedule as Foreign Secretary at that time. During the ensuing three weeks the French Foreign Minister, M. Sauvagnargues, was due to visit me in London for talks, as was the Turkish Foreign Minister. There was to be a European Council

Meeting in Luxembourg which required the attendance of both the Prime Minister and myself, and in an important improvement in Anglo-Soviet relations, Andrei Gromyko, the Soviet Foreign Minister, had accepted my invitation to pay an official visit to London—his first for some years—for discussions on East-West relations and bilateral affairs.

All of these meetings required careful preparation and I was relieved when my election team agreed with my general tactics, although they added that I must make myself available for private talks with any colleague who asked to see me. We further agreed that we would make no promises and twist no arms, and having decided on this general strategy, my friends urged me to leave the campaign to them. We expected Michael Foot, Roy Jenkins and Tony Wedgwood Benn to stand, but when Denis Healey and Tony Crosland also announced they were candidates, my team calculated that I would lose a number of votes to them, for the three of us were close in our thinking and attitudes. As far as I am aware, there was good feeling between the candidates during the election, and I was somewhat surprised to read in Susan Crosland's splendid biography of her husband that Roy Hattersley had told him I was angry that he was standing, and that he must give me his support before the first ballot or I would have no interest in him. If this happened, it was a piece of private enterprise and done without the agreement of my election team or myself.

[James Callaghan, *Time and Chance* (London, 1987), 390–2.]

## 4. EMERGENCY COALITION

### (1) SITTING PRIME MINISTER TO CONTINUE

It is doubtful whether any Government could have surmounted the world slump in trade and the financial crisis of 1931; but MacDonald's was memorably inept. The Prime Minister allocated no fewer than three of his Cabinet colleagues to stem unemployment, which throughout 1930 rose from 1.5 to 2.75 million. Thomas and Lansbury, however, lacked both imagination and thrust; and Mosley, who did produce a Keynesian scheme of public works, resigned after the Cabinet had rejected it as impracticable.

The misery which unemployment inflicts on human lives cannot be measured; but its impact on the Exchequer was all too calculable. The mounting cost to the nation of State benefits pointed, if not to bankruptcy, at least to a dangerously unbalanced budget. Conclaves of economists argued this way and that. But it was not until March 1931 that the Government appointed an independent committee to recommend how national expenditure could best be reduced. Its chairman was Sir George (later Lord) May, who had spent nearly half a century in the Prudential Assurance Company, broken only by a wartime interlude administering soldiers' canteens. After four and a half months of deliberation, the committee presented its report. It offered neither tea nor sympathy. To meet an estimated budget deficit for 1932 of £120 million, a majority of the committee recommended cuts in Government expenditure of £97 million: £67 million to be saved from a reduction in unemployment benefits and the remaining £30 million to be found out of taxation. Brooding on this severe prospect, MacDonald and his colleagues departed for their summer holidays.

They were soon summoned back to London. The May Committee's indictment of an unbalanced budget had further undermined confidence in Britain's financial stability and accelerated a run on the pound. On 12 August, a Cabinet Committee met to act on May's recommendations. It consisted of MacDonald, Snowden, Thomas, Henderson and William Graham, President of the Board of Trade. The Chancellor revealed to his shocked colleagues that May had underestimated the budget deficit for 1932; it would not be £120 million but £170 million. This unexpected blow left the Big Five (as the Cabinet Committee came to be called) with scarcely any room for manœuvre. Only by raising loans in New York and Paris could the Bank of England prop up the pound; but foreign bankers were unwilling to risk their money unless the British Government balanced its budget. There would thus have to be drastic cuts in public expenditure, particularly in the soaring cost of unemployment benefits.

By 19 August, the Big Five had reluctantly agreed to economies of £79 million, of which nearly £50 million was to be met by cuts in unemployment benefits; the remainder of the budget would be balanced by additional taxation. In proposing such unpalatable measures, albeit with reluctance, the Big Five were showing both realism and courage. For among the rank and file of the Labour movement, no issue was more emotive than the relief of unemployment. 'It was a bitter day,' wrote MacDonald, 'and grievous is our just complaint against Providence.'

On Wednesday, 19 August, from 11 in the morning until 10.30 at night, the Cabinet debated the report of the Big Five. There was a majority in favour of its recommendations, although many were unhappy about the scale of cuts in unemployment benefits. A minority rejected any reduction whatsoever in the dole, and instead pleaded for a tariff revenue. In spite of its indecision, the Cabinet did not reject the report, but hoped to reach an agreed solution during the next forty-eight hours.

Thursday, 20 August, brought a setback. The Conservative and Liberal leaders told the Prime Minister that they could not countenance new taxation of the order of £100 million, and that only further substantial cuts in expenditure, particularly in unemployment benefits, could restore public confidence. But even as the country's gold and currency reserves continued to drain away, worse was to come. The general council of the Trades Union Congress, led by Walter Citrine and Ernest Bevin, warned MacDonald that there must be no tampering with the social services, least of all with the dole. Thus was the Prime Minister ground between the millstones of rigid retrenchment and obstructive idealism.

The Big Five sat late that night, but failed to agree. 'We're done,' Thomas exclaimed in disgust as he left the Cabinet room. 'Bloody cowards!' For by then two of the Big Five had defected. Henderson and Graham, in deference to the TUC, would no longer support any but the most exiguous cuts in unemployment benefits. MacDonald was tempted to bring his frustrated administration to an end there and then. But by the following morning, Friday, 21 August, he had recovered some of his resilience and determined to make one last appeal to the divided Cabinet. It was in vain. Forty-eight hours earlier, the Cabinet had agreed in principle to the Big Five's recommended savings of £70 million, of which nearly £50 million was to come from cuts in unemployment benefits. These were now reduced to £56 million, of which only £22 million was to be cut from unemployment benefits. The revised figures were unlikely to satisfy the Opposition, much less the foreign bankers on whom Britain depended for her rescue from imminent bankruptcy. But the intransigent majority of Cabinet members would not be moved by threats. Rather than compromise on welfare payments, they were prepared to resign and leave social butchery to the Tories.

Throughout these painful exchanges, the King had remained at Sandringham; it was not for the sovereign to intervene between one faction of the Cabinet and another. But before leaving by train for his annual Scottish holiday on that Friday evening, he inquired whether the Prime Minister wished him to change his plans. MacDonald thought that it would further alarm the public if he cancelled his journey. That was an unwise decision; for already the leaders of the Opposition parties had told him that the Cabinet's latest financial proposals were 'wholly unsatisfactory', and had suggested that he should consult the King. Hardly had the King reached Balmoral on the Saturday morning when the Prime Minister sent a message that it might after all be necessary for him to return to London. 'I at once spoke to His Majesty,' Wigram later wrote, 'who quite rightly said that there was no use shilly-shallying on an occasion like this, and he would proceed south that night.' The King afterwards explained his sudden decision in a letter to the Archbishop of Canterbury: 'When I realized how serious the situation both political and financial had become, I felt that it was necessary for me to be in close touch with my Prime Minister and of course he couldn't come here.'

It proved to be one of the most important interventions of his reign. Within two hours of arriving back at Buckingham Palace on Sunday morning, the King received MacDonald. 'The Cabinet is divided,' he noted in his diary, 'and he fears he will have to resign.' The only gleam of hope the Prime Minister could offer was that the Cabinet had on the previous day agreed to ask the Bank of England whether an increase of cuts from £56 million to £76 million, including a ten per cent cut in unemployment benefits, would be enough to ensure an American loan. The Bank of England had at once consulted the New York banking house of J. P. Morgan, and an answer was expected that Sunday evening. But it was not an offer by the Cabinet, merely an inquiry. Even if New York agreed to a loan in return for promised cuts in expenditure of £76 million, the Cabinet remained free to reject such a solution.

MacDonald's lack of trust in that slippery manœuvre emerges from his conversation at the palace on Sunday morning. He wrote in his diary:

King most friendly and expressed thanks and confidence. I then reported situation and at end I told him that after tonight I might be of no further use and should resign with the whole Cabinet. He asked if I would advise him to send for Henderson. I said 'No', which he said relieved him. I advised him in the meantime to send for the leaders of the other two parties and have them report position from their points of view. He said he would and would advise them strongly to support me. I explained my hopeless parliamentary position if there were any number of resignations. He said that he believed I was the only person who could carry the country through . . . He again expressed thanks and sorrow.

The King, acting upon his Prime Minister's advice, next summoned the leaders of the Opposition parties to the palace. Lloyd George had in 1926 succeeded Asquith as leader of a reunited Liberal Party. Throughout the crisis of 1931, however, he was confined to bed after an operation. His place was taken by Sir Herbert Samuel, Postmaster General during the first years of the King's reign. He told the King that he would prefer MacDonald to remain in office in order to carry out the necessary programme of economies; but that if he failed to carry enough of his colleagues with him, then the best alternative would be for MacDonald to head a National Government containing members of all three parties. Later that afternoon, Baldwin gave similar advice on behalf of the Conservatives and agreed that if necessary he would serve under MacDonald.

Both in his contemporary record of those conversations and in a separate note a month later, Wigram wrote that it was Samuel's clarity of exposition which had convinced the King of the need for a National Government. That is also the view taken by Nicolson in his biography of the King. Certainly the Liberal leader, a spare-time philosopher, put the case with conviction. As he himself later recalled: 'The King listened attentively. He was quite a good listener sometimes.' But the Prime Minister's account of his own conversation at the palace earlier that morning reveals that the King had already determined to try for a National Government headed by MacDonald. What else could the King have meant when he told MacDonald that he was 'the only person who could carry the country through' and that he, the King, would strongly advise the leaders of the other parties to support him? Even as early in the ministerial crisis as that Sunday morning, the King needed no prompting on what his course should be.

That evening, while the Prime Minister waited at No. 10 for a telegram from the New York bankers in reply to the Cabinet's inquiry, the King had a single guest to dine. He was Mr (later Sir) Edward Peacock, one of the two directors of the Bank of England in day-to-day touch with the Prime Minister about the deterioration in Britain's gold and currency reserves. Left-wing partisans were later to refer to the establishment of the National Government on the following day as a 'bankers' ramp': and here, it seems, is evidence of just such a conspiracy. The truth is more prosaic. Peacock was indeed a director of the Bank of England; but he was also the partner in Baring's who two years earlier had succeeded the late Lord Revelstoke as adviser on the King's private finances. It was in that personal role that he had been summoned to dine at short notice. Peacock afterwards recalled that the political crisis had not been mentioned during dinner; instead, he and his sovereign, like two farmers at a cattle sale, had discussed fluctuations in the price of wheat and barley over the past ten years.

At about nine o'clock on Sunday evening, the reply of the New York bankers reached Downing Street. It offered only a short-term credit, and that hedged about with oppressive conditions. In plain language it meant that there could be no public loan unless the British Government was prepared to commit itself to severe retrenchment, including a cut of ten per cent in unemployment benefits. After the Prime Minister had appealed to his colleagues to weigh the proposed reduction in the dole against the sacrifices to be made by the country as a whole, each was invited to give his opinion. Eleven ministers supported the cuts; nine, including Henderson and Graham, Clynes and Lansbury, rejected them. No Government could continue on so wafer-thin a majority. MacDonald declared that he would at once see the King and advise him to hold a conference on the following morning attended by Baldwin, Samuel and himself. On his way out he said: 'I'm off to the Palace to throw in my hand.' Twenty-four hours later he was still Prime Minister—but of a National Government.

There can be no doubt that MacDonald truly intended to resign. For the past two days he had been saying so to all who would listen. He telephoned his son Malcolm with the message on both Saturday and Sunday. At Buckingham Palace on Sunday morning he declared that he had no other course, and afterwards wrote in his diary: 'I commit political suicide to save the crisis.' He repeated that there was no alternative when again received by the King late that night. And on returning to Downing Street for talks with the Opposition leaders, he spoke of his death warrant. Were he to join a Government of Conservatives and Liberals, he continued, he would be a ridiculous figure, unable to command support and bringing odium on them as well as on himself. Whatever else persuaded MacDonald to head a National Government, it was not premeditated ambition.

Yet that audience with the King on Sunday night did produce an improvement in spirits if not a change of mind. Peacock, who had not yet left the palace after dining with the King, noticed that the Prime Minister had gone into the King's room like a shattered man—'scared and unbalanced' was Wigram's phrase—and emerged with head erect and confidence restored. For the second time that day, his sovereign had assured him that he was the only man to lead the country through the crisis and had asked him to reconsider his resignation. The King added that he knew MacDonald could depend on Conservative and Liberal support, and he agreed to preside over a meeting of the three party leaders on the following day. Until then MacDonald must withhold his resignation.

Next morning at 10 o'clock, when MacDonald, Baldwin and Samuel assembled in the Indian Room of the palace, the Prime Minister repeated his by now familiar litany; indeed, he had the resignation of the entire Cabinet in his pocket. For the third time in twenty-four hours, the King replied that it was out of the question. He told MacDonald that by remaining at his post with such colleagues as were still faithful to him, his position and reputation would be much more enhanced than if he succumbed; the Prime Minister must come to some arrangement with Baldwin and Samuel to form a National Emergency Government which would restore British credit and the confidence of foreigners. And in his best quarterdeck manner, the King impressed on the three party leaders that before they left the palace there should be a communiqué to end speculation at home and abroad. Then he withdrew to his own rooms to let them get on with it.

Rather more than an hour later, the party leaders sent a message asking the King to return. They had drawn up a memorandum agreeing to a National Government led by MacDonald; it would dedicate itself to economies of £70 million, including a cut of ten per cent in the dole. Although supported by both the Conservatives and the Liberals, the new ministry would not be a Coalition but a 'co-operation of individuals', to last only as long as the emergency. It was to be followed by a general election which the three parties would fight on their individual platforms. The King was pleased by his stage management. Wigram's note on the meeting with the three statesmen concludes:

His Majesty congratulated them on the solution of this difficult problem, and pointed out that while France and other countries existed for weeks without a Government, in this country our constitution is so generous that leaders of Parties, after fighting one another for months in the House of Commons, were ready to meet together under the roof of the Sovereign and sink their own differences for a common good and arrange as they had done this morning for a National Government to meet one of the gravest crises that the British Empire had yet been asked to face.

With that comforting little homily, the King sent them on their way.

At 12 noon MacDonald returned to Downing Street, where the Cabinet awaited him. Still hopelessly divided, they expected to hear that he had tendered their collective resignations to the King. Had he not left them the night before, exclaiming: 'I am off to the Palace to throw in my hand'? Instead he announced that he was to lead a National Government. 'Consternation when I reported,' he wrote in his diary. That morning there had been a renewed run on the Bank, and he asked his colleagues to share with him the burdens both of office and self-sacrifice. Only three agreed to do so: Snowden, Thomas and Sankey. But that token Labour force was enough to justify the formation of a National Government in name as well as in purpose.

'Looking worn and weary', as Wigram described him, MacDonald went back to the palace at four o'clock that afternoon. At last he was allowed to resign as Prime Minister of the Labour Government, but only in order to kiss hands as Prime Minister of a National administration. When its members received their seals of office two days later, MacDonald's mournful countenance was accentuated by his frock coat and black tie. 'You look as if you were attending your own funeral', the King chaffed him. 'Put on a white tie and try to think it is your wedding.' The Prime Minister was not to be comforted. 'This is a lonely job,' he wrote.

Without the King's initiative there would have been no National Government. Three times in twenty-four hours MacDonald tried to resign and three times the King dissuaded him. Then he gave way and agreed to remain Prime Minister, an eminence for which he professed no enthusiasm. The motives of public men are rarely as base or as quixotic as their enemies would have us believe; and no portrait of MacDonald is complete which depicts him as the ambitious, fawning courtier of Labour mythology or the martyred patriot of his own invention. He did not become less willing to relinquish office during those forty-eight hours of crisis; but he did become less willing to relinquish office at the behest of Arthur Henderson. As one of the Big Five, Henderson had at first accepted the need for cutting the dole in order to save the credit of his country; then he changed his mind under pressure from the trade unions and carried half the Cabinet with him. 'They chose the easy path of irresponsibility and leave the burdens to others,' MacDonald wrote as his divided ministry broke up. And on the following day he told Margaret Bondfield: 'Until there is some new spirit in the Labour Movement, a Labour Government will run away from two things: (1) [At] the orders of the T.U.C. and (2) An awkward crisis.'

[Kenneth Rose, *King George V* (London, 1983), 371–7.]

## (2) A NEW PRIME MINISTER

Lloyd George did not receive Asquith's letter until the following morning—Tuesday, December 5th [1916]. He replied at length and almost at once. There was no question of his accepting the new situation. He intended to fight; and, to a much greater extent than Asquith had done, he wrote a manifesto and not a letter:

As all delay is fatal in war, I place my office without further parley at your disposal.

It is with great personal regret that I have come to this conclusion. In spite of mean and unworthy insinuations to the contrary—insinuations which I fear are always inevitable in the case of men who hold prominent but not primary positions in any administration—I have felt a strong personal attachment to you as my chief. As you yourself said, on Sunday, we have acted together for ten years and never had a quarrel, although we have had many a grave difference on questions of policy. You have treated me with great courtesy and kindness; for all that I thank you. Nothing would have induced me to part now except an overwhelming sense that the course of action which has been pursued has put the country—and not merely the country, but throughout the world, the principles for which you and I have always stood throughout our political lives—in the greatest peril that has ever overtaken them.

As I am fully conscious of the importance of preserving national unity, I propose to give your Government complete support in the vigorous prosecution of the War; but unity without action is nothing but futile carnage, and I cannot be responsible for that. Vigour and vision are the supreme need at this hour.

This letter of strong but not unexpected challenge reached Asquith soon after noon. So did one from Balfour, written from a sick-bed in Carlton Gardens. This announced, quietly but determinedly, that Balfour did not want Asquith's backing for the Admiralty:

I am well aware that you do not personally share Lloyd George's view in this connection. But I am quite clear that the new system should have a trial under the most favourable possible circumstances; and the mere fact that the new Chairman of the War Council *did* prefer, and, as far as I know *still* prefers, a different arrangement is, to my mind, quite conclusive, and leaves me in no doubt as to the manner in which I can best assist the Government which I desire to support.

It is doubtful whether Asquith fully assimilated the shift of allegiance which this letter quietly announced. He saw Balfour and Lloyd George in such different lights that, the issue of the Admiralty apart, the idea of an alliance between them hardly entered his head. In any event he had little time to give careful immediate consideration to the letter; he merely wrote a short reply pressing Balfour to reconsider his position. At 12.30 Crewe arrived at Downing Street. He had been to Buckingham Palace for a Privy Council, and he was able to inform Asquith that the King still hoped for a solution without a change of Prime Minister. Then, at one o'clock, all the Liberal ministers with the exception of the Secretary of State for War assembled. Lloyd George was resentful at the absence of a summons, but as he had chosen to work almost exclusively with Unionists during the preceding weeks, this resentment was hardly justified. The business of the meeting was to consider the situation created by Lloyd George's letter of resignation. Montagu apart, there was unanimous agreement that his challenge must be resisted, and that Asquith could best do this by resigning. The outcome, it was believed, would then turn on the attitude of the Unionist ministers. Montagu's alternative proposal was that the King should be asked to convene a conference of Asquith, Lloyd George, Bonar Law and Henderson. 'My suggestion was derided,' he recorded, 'and McKenna most helpfully asked me if I wanted four Prime Ministers, or, if not, which one I wanted.'

The attitude of the Unionist ministers was made clear during the afternoon. At 11 o'clock in the morning they had met—Curzon, Cecil, Long and Chamberlain—in the Secretary of State's room at the India Office. At three o'clock the 'three C's' were summoned to Downing Street. Asquith asked them two questions. Were they prepared to continue in a Government from which both Lloyd George and Bonar Law had resigned; and what would be their attitude towards Lloyd George if he attempted to form an administration? To the first question, in Austen Chamberlain's words,

> we replied that our only object was to secure a Government on such lines and with such a prospect of stability that it might reasonably be expected to be capable of carrying on the war; that in our opinion his Government, weakened by the resignations of Lloyd George and Bonar Law and by all that had gone on during the past weeks, offered no such prospect and we answered the question therefore with a perfectly definite negative.

'This was evidently a great blow to him,' Chamberlain added. 'Had we replied in the affirmative, he would clearly have been prepared to make the attempt . . .'

To the second question their reply was equally discouraging. In effect they said that if Lloyd George looked like succeeding, they would join him. Cecil urged Asquith to do the same, but, Chamberlain said, Asquith 'would not allow (him) to develop this idea, which he rejected with indignation and even with scorn.' The three Unionists then crossed Downing Street for a meeting with Bonar Law. From this meeting they sent back Curzon with a formal resolution, urging Asquith's immediate resignation, and saying that he must in any event accept and publish theirs. In the meantime Asquith had received Balfour's second letter, written at 4.0 p.m. Once again the style was casual but the intention was firm. Balfour would offer no opposition to Lloyd George.

In these circumstances immediate resignation was the only course open to Asquith. He announced this to the Liberal ministers who had once again congregated in 10, Downing Street. Perhaps one or two of them were so blinded by hatred of Lloyd George as to believe that the move would still show up his impotence. But this was not the general view. Montagu testified that they never seriously doubted Lloyd George's ability to form a Government. And it was certainly not Asquith's view. He decided to resign, not as a tactical manoeuvre, but because he did not have sufficient support to carry on.

He gave effect to his decision at seven o'clock that evening. He had been Prime Minister for eight years and 241 days.

'The Prime Minister came to see me,' the King recorded in his diary,

> and placed his resignation in my hands, which I accepted with great regret. He said that he had tried to arrange matters with Lloyd George about the War Committee all day, but was unable to. All his colleagues both Liberal and Unionist, urged him to resign as it was the only solution to the difficulty. I fear that it will cause great panic in the City and in America and do harm to the Allies. It is a great blow to me and will I fear buck up the Germans.

Back in Downing Street, Asquith dined with Crewe. The King in the meantime had asked for a constitutional memorandum, dealing with a new Prime Minister's right to a dissolution, from Haldane, and had summoned Bonar Law. His interview with Law went as badly as it is easily possible to imagine. They argued about a dissolution, about the course of the war, about the relations between politicians and the military. Having established this happy basis of almost universal disagreement, the King performed his constitutional duty by asking Law to form a Government.

The Unionist leader then went immediately to see Lloyd George, with whom he had conferred before his visit to the Palace. Afterwards he went to Downing Street where he called Asquith out from dinner and asked him if he would serve under him. Asquith demurred, and also responded discouragingly to a suggestion that they might all serve under Balfour. He did not believe that any such combinations would work, but he did not close his mind on continuing consultation.

Later that evening Bonar Law again saw Lloyd George, this time at Carson's house. The following morning (Wednesday, December 6th) they went together to see Balfour, still in his sick-room. It was probably this occasion which prompted Lloyd George to write of Balfour: 'I confess that I underrated the passionate attachment to his country which burnt under that calm, indifferent, and apparently frigid exterior'; upon which Balfour's latest biographer has somewhat severely commented: 'By "passionate attachment to his country," Lloyd George, presumably meant Balfour's backing for him as Prime Minister . . .' But this may be a little hard. Such a firm commitment was not sought at this stage.

A Buckingham Palace conference was to take place that afternoon. There is doubt as to where this idea originated. Beaverbrook said that it came from Henderson; Balfour said that it came from Bonar Law; Law's biographer said that it came from Balfour; and Crewe said that it came from Montagu and Derby. Whoever sowed the seed, the conference was due to meet within a few hours. Balfour's role was likely to be crucial. He had kept himself the most aloof from the crisis so far. The main concern of Bonar Law and Lloyd George was that he should give no support for an Asquith restoration. Law that morning, according to Montagu, 'had objected to any Conference to put Asquith back.' They went away reassured.

Balfour saw the King for half an hour before the others came. He gave his opinion that no one man could be effectively Prime Minister, leader of the House of Commons, and chairman of the War Committee. It was arranged that he should open the discussion with a statement of this and other views. Then the other participants—Asquith, Lloyd George, Bonar Law and Henderson arrived. Beaverbrook, presumably informed by Law, wrote that Asquith's mood differed from that of the other members of 'this grave assembly'. 'His manner in fact was fairly like that of a schoolboy who has got an unexpected half-holiday. He was jocular with everybody.'

This is to some extent contradicted by Lloyd George, who subsequently wrote: 'It is now a matter of history how we expressed our readiness to serve under Mr Balfour—all of us except Mr Asquith, who asked indignantly, "What is the proposal? That I who have held first place for eight years should be asked to take a secondary position." This broke up the conference.'

Whatever else this interchange may be, it is not a matter of history. There is no hint in the contemporary accounts of either Balfour or Stamfordham that such a conversation ever occurred; indeed it seems unlikely that the premiss of a Balfour premiership was ever before the conference. Lord Stamfordham's memorandum describes how Asquith was urged by all the other participants to serve under Bonar Law, and then continues:

> Mr Asquith maintained that the Prime Minister and nobody else could preside over the War Committee, otherwise decisions might be arrived at which he could not agree to, which would result in friction and delay . . . Mr Asquith continued by denouncing in serious terms the action of the Press. The Prime Minister's work was sufficiently heavy and responsible without

being subjected to daily vindictive, merciless attacks in the columns of the newspapers, and he urged that whatever government might come into office, measures should be taken to prevent the continuance of this Press tyranny. He had been accused of clinging to Office, but he appealed to all those present to say whether such a charge was justifiable. He could honestly say that on waking this morning he was thankful to feel he was a free man. Mr Asquith referred in touching terms to the unquestioning confidence the King had invariably placed in him, of which he had received His Majesty's assurance only two days ago. He deeply valued it, and only hoped that his successor might enjoy the same generous trust and support which His Majesty had graciously reposed in him.

This may not have been very constructive, but, except towards the newspaper proprietors, it did not sound particularly bitter. Furthermore, it is an account almost exactly borne out by Balfour. But what next? The King, after Asquith had spoken, pointed out that no decision had been reached. Balfour attempted to sum up:

(He) said that he considered it was impossible for Mr Asquith to form a Government after what Mr Bonar Law had said about his party. A Government without Mr Lloyd George was impossible. Apparently Mr Bonar Law was ready to form a Government if Mr Asquith would agree to accept a subordinate place, but, failing this, he would propose that Mr Lloyd George should form an Administration.

The result of the meeting was an agreement that Mr Asquith should consider the proposals made to him, and let Mr Bonar Law know as soon as possible whether he would join the Government under him. If the answer was in the negative, Mr Bonar Law would not form a Government, but Mr Lloyd George would endeavour to do so.

Again Balfour's account is in substantial agreement, although he adds the gloss that when, at one stage in his summing up he referred to his assumption that Asquith would not serve under either Law or Lloyd George, Asquith intervened to say that he had not gone quite so far as that; he must consult his friends before giving a final answer.

The conference broke up at 4.30. Asquith returned to Downing Street and immediately began this consultation. There was a full turn up of Liberal ministers, with the exception of Lloyd George. Henderson was also present. Decisions were taken in two stages. First it was agreed (the meeting in this respect giving the impression of being a little behind events) that Asquith should make no attempt to form a Government without Lloyd George and the Unionists. Then came the question of whether he would serve in a subordinate post. Crewe, Grey, McKenna, Runciman, Buckmaster and McKinnon Wood all urged him not to. Three others (Harcourt, Samuel and Tennant) apparently indicated silent agreement with this view. Montagu and Henderson were alone in dissenting, not only from the advice tendered but also from the implied assumption that if Asquith did not serve, none of the others present would either.

'Mr Asquith', Crewe recorded, 'entirely concurred with our statements . . .' He did so, the account continued, not out of 'personal dignity or *amour propre*'. What, then, were his reasons? First, he could hope to exercise no real influence in the new Government. Its tone would be set by those who were most distrustful of his leadership. It was doubtful whether he would even be a member of the War Committee. He saw no prospect of avoiding for long a head-on collision. It was better to stand out at the beginning than to go in with the expectation that he would soon have to provoke a further crisis by resignation.

Secondly, if on the other hand he were completely to subordinate himself to the new Government his influence in Parliament and the country would quickly be eroded. This was not a selfish consideration. Politicians exist to exercise influence. Unless they believe that they can do so beneficially they have no *raison d'être*. Asquith thought that the erosion of his would lead to the growth of an irresponsible opposition, undermining the near unanimity of support for the war effort. This may have been something of a rationalisation of his instinctive desires, but it was a perfectly defensible attitude. While not the most encouraging offer which a Prime Minister can receive, support from outside is a time-honoured formula and one which has frequently been used with much less excuse than Asquith had on this occasion. Furthermore he interpreted it in such a way that 'support' was not an empty word. He did not cause Lloyd George a tenth of the trouble that Lloyd George, outside, would have caused him.

There was a third consideration, not mentioned by Crewe, in Asquith's mind. He believed that so long as he remained in the Government the Press attacks would continue and that his supposedly malevolent influence would be blamed for every failure. This would further undermine his position both with his colleagues and with the public. It would be an extreme form of responsibility without power.

By six o'clock Asquith had conveyed his decision, in a letter, to Bonar Law. The importance of the communication was symbolised by Lord Curzon, who had come across to 10, Downing Street to hear the news, acting as messenger boy. At seven Law went to Buckingham Palace and declined the King's commission. At 7.30 the commission was passed on to Lloyd George. Within 24 hours he had succeeded in discharging it. 'Mr Lloyd George came . . . and informed me that he is able to form an administration and told me the proposed names of his colleagues,' the King wrote in his diary. 'He will have a strong Government. I then appointed him Prime Minister and First Lord of the Treasury.'

The new Government was principally but not exclusively a Unionist one. The War Cabinet was composed of Lloyd George, Curzon, Milner, Bonar Law and Henderson. Carson, although not after all included in this body, became First Lord of the Admiralty. Balfour, directed by the pistol's point, moved with speed but dignity from the Admiralty to the Foreign Office. No Liberal member of the late Cabinet (except for Lloyd George himself), not even Montagu, joined the new Government. None was formally invited, except for a late and not very attractive offer to Montagu, but Lloyd George would probably have been glad to have two or three of them had he believed that they would accept. A few lesser-known Liberals were brought in, and there were two Labour heads of departments, apart from Henderson.

[Roy Jenkins, *Asquith* (London, Fontana edn., 1967), 510–19.]

*If a new Prime Minister were needed for an emergency coalition and no obvious successor existed, the Sovereign would have to make the best choice possible. In deference to democracy, and if time permitted, perhaps the House of Commons as a whole might elect the new Prime Minister.*

## 5. LOSS OF THE PARTY LEADERSHIP

*If a Prime Minister were to be ousted from the Leadership of his party, he would have to resign as Prime Minister. A formal party vote might not be necessary to remove him: senior members of his party might make it clear to the Prime Minister that he no longer had the confidence of the parliamentary party (as, in a sense, happened with Churchill in 1955), or the lack of support might become clear as the result of a Commons vote (as in 1940, when Chamberlain obtained a drastically-reduced majority in a vote of confidence). A formal party Leadership vote could take place against the wishes of the Leader and Prime Minister in any of the main parties: the constitutional problems could be particularly acute in the Labour Party.*

Although at the time it was seen as no more than the correction of an anomaly, only at the Labour Party's annual conference in 1979 was the formal position of the Leader of the Parliamentary Labour Party brought into line with the *de facto* position by his being accorded the title of 'Leader of the Labour Party'. The changes in the method of electing the Leader, introduced at the special conference at Wembley in January 1981, and the 1980 requirements about reselection of candidates have, however, possibly laid a constitutional minefield.

Broadly, the rules require that an electoral college choose the Leader. A weighted voting system is used, giving seventy per cent of the votes to the Party outside Parliament—forty per cent to trade unions and other affiliated organizations, thirty per cent to the constituency Labour parties—leaving the previously autonomous Parliamentary Labour Party (PLP) with only thirty per cent. The system was first used in 1981 to elect the Deputy Leader. In 1983, on the retirement of Mr Foot, Mr Kinnock was elected Leader by the electoral college and Mr Hattersley was elected Deputy Leader. This system could present three separate constitutional problems. The first is centred on the attitude of the PLP. Now, the Leader of that parliamentary party with an overall majority is entitled to be asked to form a government. Under the old system, the Leader of the PLP would be seen to enjoy the confidence of that body because it had elected him through an exhaustive ballot. The obvious danger under the 1981 arrangements is that, given the overwhelming percentage of votes from outside the Commons, a new Leader might have little support in the PLP. Leaving aside for present purposes the polarizing of the different parts of the Party which would take place, the constitutional issue may be highlighted by examining a hypothetical House of Commons. Suppose that a Labour Prime Minister, A, with an overall majority gives notice of his intention to retire as soon as a new Leader is elected (following the Wilson precedent of 1976). The electoral college elects B, mainly through trade union and constituency votes. But it is obvious, through public statements, media polls, and so on, not only that B would have fared badly under the old PLP electoral system, but that another MP, C, would have won convincingly under it, because in this example the PLP is to the right (or to the left) of the Party outside the House of Commons. B enjoys the full-hearted support of only a small percentage of the PLP. Assuming, as it seems safe to do, that the opposition parties would not support B as Prime Minister in the Commons, his parliamentary majority just does not exist. What 'right' would B have to become Prime Minister? One plausible result might, of course, be that the PLP would make the best of it, tolerating B as their Leader because he was the choice of the Party. The consequences of rejecting him could be (*a*) a fatal split in the Labour Party as a whole; (*b*) an utterly confused state of party politics in the Commons; and—most serious of all in the immediate term for Labour—(*c*) the danger that the Queen might refuse to appoint B Prime Minister because of his obvious lack of a Commons majority. Constitutional development could be thrown back to before 1965, with the Queen exercising the prerogative of choice based on the best advice available to her. No one in the Labour Party would want that; the Party outside Parliament would be outraged; the Sovereign would be seen, however unavoidably, to be taking sides. And there would be no solution in appointing a Labour Prime Minister conditionally on a request for a dissolution, because were Labour to be returned to power the Leadership question would still be there. A compromise (which by definition would not satisfy everyone) can be suggested. It would avoid, on the one hand, the use of the prerogative of choice in appointing C as Prime Minister (not as Leader of the Party but as the Leader of the majority of the PLP) and, on the other, an automatic use of prerogative of appointment to install B (as Leader of the Party), knowing that he had no Commons majority. The PLP could conduct a poll of its members to test which man had the greater support. Presumably, in the hypothesis presented, C would win and he would become Prime Minister. Even as this is written, howls of anger from Labour ranks can be imagined, but every political party must remember that it cannot effect changes in British constitutional law or practice merely by changes in its internal rules if the consequence of those changes clashes with clear constitutional practice.

A second difficulty could arise from the Labour Party rule (again dating from 1981) that a Leader in office as Prime Minister can be challenged for the Leadership at a Party conference if an election is requested by a majority of the conference on a card vote. Now it could be argued that this likelihood is so remote as not to be worthy of consideration. After all, the Conservative Party has had provision for electing a new Leader while in office since 1975 and it has not been used in that circumstance. In 1975, Mr Heath, as Leader, accepted amended rules which had been drawn up under Lord Home's chairmanship and announced that the first ballot would be held on 4 February 1975 (the Party, of course, then being in opposition). Of relevance here is the rule that a ballot for the Conservative Leadership *must* take place if the post is vacant, or within twenty-eight days of the beginning of *every* session, or between three to six months after the opening of *every* new Parliament. (In the event, Mr Heath, who had lost three general elections, lost the 1975 ballot to Mrs Thatcher.) There is thus a Conservative *requirement* of an annual election—although, of course, if there is no challenger, no election will be necessary. The Conservative Party has no record of loyalty to failed Leaders or Prime Ministers. So is it safe to be sanguine about Labour's procedures, given the mood which deepened in the early 1980s and which strives for even greater accountability in the Labour Party, of which this rule is an example? I suggest that an attempt may well be made at some future Labour Party conference to dislodge a Labour Prime Minister. If it were successful, he would have to resign as Prime Minister. Whether his successor took over smoothly would depend on the issues discussed above in relation to the Leadership changing hands in a hypothetical House of Commons.

The last major problem potentially caused by changes in Labour rules in 1980 is that every Labour MP must undergo a reselection process. This must happen once in each Parliament, usually not later than thirty-six months after the last general election. It is very unlikely that a Labour Prime Minister would be deprived of his seat in this way, but it deserves to be noted that, however unwittingly, a piece of machinery has been created which could be used locally to deprive a Labour Prime Minister of his seat. *If* this were ever done, then unless some other constituency took him on board in time for the general election, or perhaps unless he stood and won in his constituency as some kind of independent Labour candidate with at least PLP support, then, on the declaration of the result in his constituency, he would lose any right to remain Prime Minister. Labour might be in the extraordinary position of winning a general election with its Leader outside Parliament.

[Brazier, *Constitutional Practice*, 18–21.]

(1) The desirability of contesting the constituency for parliament shall be considered by the Executive Committee of this party in consultation with the National Executive Committee or its officers prior to the procedure laid down in this clause being set in motion.

(2) The General Committee shall be asked to give authority to the Executive Committee of this party in co-operation with the National Executive Committee to secure nominations for the candidature.

(3) The normal procedure shall be as follows:

(*a*) A circular, in terms prescribed by the National Executive Committee, shall be sent to affiliated and party organisations entitled to appoint delegates to the General Committee inviting nominations. Such nominations to be made within a period of time and under conditions mentioned therein.

(*b*) Affiliated and party organisations entitled to appoint delegates to the General Committee and the Executive Committee of this party, may nominate an individual member of the Labour Party who is not disqualified under the constitution of the Labour Party, or under the decisions of party conference as a parliamentary candidate.

(*c*) No nomination shall be valid unless made on the form in terms prescribed by the National Executive Committee and bearing thereon the consent in writing of the member nominated. In the event of the name of a member nominated being on the official panel of available parliamentary candidates of an affiliated organisation the consent in writing of the Executive Committee thereof must also be obtained and sent in with the form of nomination.

(*d*) Prior to a meeting of the General Committee being

called to consider the nominations, the Executive Committee of this party shall consult with the National Executive Committee or its officer to determine the validity of the nominations received.

(*e*) The Executive Committee of this party may tender such advice as it deems necessary to the General Committee on the nominations found to be valid, and may suggest to the General Committee the manner in which they shall be dealt with provided that all valid nominations shall be placed before that body for its consideration at an ordinary meeting. The notice calling such meeting must indicate the business to be transacted. The General Committee shall then fix a date for a special meeting to decide which nomination, if any, shall be submitted to the National Executive Committee for endorsement as prospective parliamentary candidate.

(*f*) The last day for the appointment of delegates to attend this special meeting of the General Committee shall be decided in accordance with regulations sanctioned by the National Executive Committee.

(*g*) To be eligible to attend a meeting of the General Committee referred to in paragraphs (e) or (h), a person must have been a member of this Constituency Labour Party for at least twelve months prior to the date of the relevant meeting and have attended at least one previous meeting of the General Committee during the same period.

(*h*) The special meeting of the General Committee to select a prospective candidate shall be convened by circular in terms prescribed by the National Executive Committee. It shall be attended by a representative of the National Executive Committee, appointed for the purpose. When a vote is necessary to determine which nomination is to be sent to the National Executive Committee for endorsement, it shall be taken by an eliminating ballot on the basis of one delegate, one vote.

(*j*) The selection of a prospective parliamentary candidate shall not be regarded as completed until the name of the member selected has been placed before a meeting of the National Executive Committee, and his or her selection has been duly endorsed. Until such endorsement has been received this party shall not introduce its prospective candidate to the public.

(4) Where no valid nominations are received, or when an emergency arises, or when the Executive Committee of this party or the National Executive Committee are of opinion that the interests of the Labour Party demand the suspension of the procedure laid down in section (3) of this clause, normal procedure may be dispensed with by the National Executive Committee.

(5) If a parliamentary by-election occurs in the constituency the procedure laid down in section (3) of this clause shall be suspended and the National Executive Committee shall co-operate with the Executive Committee of this party in the nomination of a candidate. The National Executive Committee may, if it deems it necessary in the interests of the Labour Party, advise the Executive Committee of this party to select a nomination it may submit to it. The National Executive Committee may also give advice and guidance on any special issue to be raised or in the conduct of the campaign during the by-election.

(6) In accordance with the constitution of the Labour Party the General Committee of this party or the executive committee of a nationally affiliated organisation shall by resolution formally accept responsibility for the election expenses of the prospective candidate selected and a copy of such resolution shall be attached to the application of the constituency party to the National Executive Committee for endorsement.

(7)(*a*) If this party is represented in parliament by a member of the Parliamentary Labour Party, the procedure set out in section (3) of this clause (for the selection of a prospective parliamentary candidate) shall be set in motion not later than thirty-six months after the last time the said Member of Parliament was elected. Where a member of the Parliamentary Labour Party is representing this party in parliament for the first time the above (normal) proceedure shall be set in motion not earlier than eighteen months after his or her election as Member of Parliament.

(*b*) The Member of Parliament shall be eligible for nomination for selection as the prospective parliamentary candidate and, whether nominated or not, he or she shall be entitled to appear as if they had been nominated before the special meeting of the General Committee convened in accordance with section (3) of this clause and to be considered for selection as the prospective parliamentary candidate.

(*c*) If the said Member of Parliament is not selected as the prospective parliamentary candidate at the special meeting referred to in paragraph (b) above to be the prospective parliamentary candidate, he or she shall have the right to appeal to the National Executive Committee on the grounds, and only on the grounds, that the procedure laid down in these rules and the general provision of the constitution and rules have not been properly carried out.

(*d*) Where there is a formal announcement of a royal proclamation to dissolve parliament before the special meeting referred to in paragraph (b) above has been held the provisions of this section (other than this paragraph) shall be suspended and the said Member of Parliament shall be reselected as the prospective parliamentary candidate unless he or she intimated his or her intention to retire in which case the provisions of section (4) of this clause shall apply.

(8) Where the prospective parliamentary candidate has been selected and subsequently intimates his or her intention not to stand for parliament in the constituency as the Labour Party candidate at the next election, the procedure set out in section (3) of this clause shall (subject to section (4) of this clause) be forthwith set in motion again.

(9) When this party has selected the prospective parliamentary candidate, section (3) of this clause shall be applicable only when section (8) applies or, having received a written request from the General Committee of this party for permission to reconsider the selection of the prospective parliamentary candidate, the National Executive Committee has decided that in its opinion there are changed circumstances relating to the prospective parliamentary candidate since his or her selection, and has given authority to this party to convene a special meeting of the General Committee in accordance with regulations sanctioned by the National Executive Committee to consider a resolution that the prospective candidate selected previously shall not be the candidate at the next general

election. The prospective parliamentary candidate against whom such action is taken shall have the right of appeal to the National Executive Committee, which committee shall have the power to confirm, vary, or reverse the action taken by the General Committee.

(10) An election shall cancel any parliamentary candidature.

(11) Every parliamentary candidate must undertake to stand as 'the Labour Party candidate' independent of all other political parties and, if elected, join the Parliamentary Labour Party.

(12) This clause shall be read with clause X of the constitution of the Labour Party, and the provisions of the latter shall apply to this party.

[Rules for Constituency Labour Parties and Branches, cl. XIV.]

## 6. A HUNG PARLIAMENT

### (1) HUNG PARLIAMENTS THIS CENTURY AND THEIR CONSEQUENCES

*(a) January 1910*

| Party | Seats |
|---|---|
| Liberal | 275 |
| Conservative | 273 |
| Irish Nationalist | 82 |
| Labour | 40 |

*(b) December 1910*

| Party | Seats |
|---|---|
| Conservative | 272 |
| Liberal | 272 |
| Irish Nationalist | 84 |
| Labour | 42 |

*The Liberal government which had taken office in 1905 won the 1906 general election by a landslide, and remained in office after the two inconclusive general elections of 1910 with tacit support from the small parties.*

(*c*) *1923*

| Party | Seats |
|---|---|
| Conservative | 258 |
| Labour | 191 |
| Liberal | 159 |
| Others | 7 |

*Several outcomes were theoretically possible, but neither Labour (under MacDonald) nor the Conservatives (under Baldwin, who had played an important part in breaking up the Lloyd George coalition in 1922) would countenance a coaliton. The Liberals would not support the Conservatives, who had campaigned for protection. A minority Labour government, with tacit Liberal support, was the result.*

What had happened was that Birkenhead, Austen Chamberlain, Worthington Evans, Derby and Joynson Hicks had, together or separately (and, according to Bridgeman, backed by Beaverbrook and Rothermere) succeeded in persuading Balfour that Baldwin intended to resign; that he should, if asked by the King, advise him to choose not MacDonald nor Asquith, but another Conservative—Derby or Austen Chamberlain, because he held Baldwin personally to blame rather than his party; further, they had so worked on Stamfordham, that if Baldwin had gone to resign at once, the advice tendered to the King by his private secretary would have been the same. It is not certain how many of the leading members were privy to this scheme: Lloyd-Greame seems to have sat on the fence; Hoare, Wood, Cave, Salisbury and some of the other peers stood out for Baldwin, but this was not contained in the advice which convinced Stamfordham. Of course the plot depended on Balfour, and on the King following his private secretary's advice. In the circumstances the latter was unlikely: he had not done so in May on an infinitely more difficult decision. But the intention of the rebels was to bundle Baldwin out of the leadership before opinions had time to come to terms with the election results.

The plotters represented the hard core of the right wing. In other sections of the party there was no lack of advice, only of agreement. Neville Chamberlain wrote that the Cabinet was a nest of intrigue, which was, considering everything, an understatement. His voice was cast on the side of moderation—he 'was clear on all grounds that Labour should be given office'. He added, cynically, that if Labour came in 'it would be too weak to do much harm, but not too weak to get discredited'. On the fringe of the political scene, the *Daily Mail* campaigned vigorously for a coalition under a new leader and various important figures in the City of London let it be known that a Socialist Government would be a financial disaster. Walter Long favoured an Asquith government with Conservative support and Austen Chamberlain hoped, rather improbably, that the King would call on Asquith and MacDonald together.

Balfour (who was not wholly convinced by the plotters and who refused finally to do their bidding) sent a message to Baldwin to say that the constitutional course was to meet Parliament. His reversal astonished Derby, who realised that the plot was dead and wrote at once to Austen Chamberlain to explain that he intended to turn about and support Baldwin's decision to meet Parliament.

The message which Balfour sent was that, 'He is also of the opinion that it will be a serious danger if the Socialist Party is allowed to assume office at the present time and he thinks every means ought to be taken to avert the Parliamentary defeat which would bring them into office in your place.' 'This meant,' so Balfour advised, 'a working arrangement with Asquith, which he believed could be done without loss of dignity or authority.' Such an alliance was popular with many backbenchers: James Hope, lately Chairman of Ways and Means, suggested, 'a composite Government but not a coalition. Let some patriot of repute (Grey?) form a Government of whomsoever he pleases or can get. Let Liberals and Conservatives take office under him without prejudice to their party allegiance—but let the leaders stand out, keeping their party machinery intact, and promise support say for a year only. At all hazards we must avoid the creation of an amalgamated "bourgeois block" which leaves the Socialists as the sole alternative. This was Bonar's greatest fear . . .' Meanwhile, to forestall the wreck, the party secretariat prepared to wind up the secret Supply and Transport Committee before the Labour Party uncovered its strike-breaking organisation.

Most remarkable of all the suggestions put to Baldwin came from

Lord Haldane, who only a month later was to take office as Lord Chancellor in the Labour Government, and who advised him to continue in office; 'It may seem the odder in as much as I have supported the Labour Party and free trade through this general election. But you are placed in a great difficulty. The King's Government has to be carried on and I think that you are the only man who has a chance of doing this successfully. I think it especially because you are much esteemed, even by your political opponents, for your exceptional personal qualities.'

Baldwin's own opinion of the Labour Party had been shown by his conduct during fifteen years in the House of Commons. He believed that it was the official Opposition and had an undoubted right to take its place as the next in line. He was close to MacDonald and trusted him to respect the constitution. He was far too honourable to approach Asquith with a deal which could only mean the compromise of both their principles for a period of artificial power, not unlike the last years of the Coalition; and he saw that an anti-socialist alliance could only lead, in the end, to a major Labour victory. But to make certain that MacDonald would be chosen, he had to be sure of his own party and the Liberals. G. M. Young suggested that he wavered before coming to his courageous decision not to resign at once. On the contrary, he could do nothing else without playing into the hands of those plotting his downfall and a return to a form of Coalition. He judged Asquith's sense of probity correctly—meeting him in the Travellers' Club later, the Liberal leader said 'You have done quite right.' Asquith's confirmed his own rejection of an anti-socialist alliance on 18 December and maintained it, in spite of what he called 'virulent manifestations of political hysteria . . . I have been intreated during these weeks, cajoled, wheedled, almost caressed, tortured, threatened, brow-beaten and all but blackmailed to step in as the saviour of society.'

Once Baldwin's decision was made, the right-wing plot collapsed as suddenly as it had grown up and, as always after prolonged but successful mental strain, he felt free. Tom Jones found him more than merry, preparing his final speech for 21 January, when it was obvious that Labour would defeat the Government. 'I found him in great spirits. "I have not felt so well for a long time and I shall be tempted to be very vulgar in my speech."' Nervousness had left him entirely, when the crisis of decision was past. The Government were defeated that evening by 72 votes and MacDonald was summoned to the Palace next day.

[Middlemas and Barnes, *Baldwin,* 251–3.]

Polling was on December 6th. In Aberavon, MacDonald was returned in a straight fight with Byass by a majority of 3,512. Nationally, the Conservatives lost 115,000 votes as compared with 1922, while the Liberal and Labour Parties gained 180,000 and 120,000 votes respectively. Thanks to the quirks of the electoral system, however, the change in seats was much more striking. The Conservative Party now had 259 seats in the House of Commons, the Labour Party 191 and the Liberals 159. Neither the Labour nor the Liberal Party had won, but it was clear that the Conservatives had lost—and in an election called by them on an issue of their own choice. MacDonald returned to London on December 8th to find that the evening papers were prophesying that Baldwin would resign after the weekend and advise the King to send for him. 'Ah! were she here, to help me,' he noted. 'Why are they both dead—my mother and she?'

The evening-paper headlines turned out to be premature. A group of Conservative malcontents, headed by Lord Birkenhead, tried to use the prospect of a Labour Government as an excuse for removing Baldwin from the leadership of the Conservative Party. They failed; but Baldwin had to abandon his original intention of resigning straight away, and decided to stay in office until the new Parliament met. In the next few days there was much wild talk about the dangers of allowing Labour to take office, and many wild schemes were designed to avert them. The *English Review* thought that the 'sun of England seems menaced by final eclipse'. Winston Churchill, who had just been defeated as Liberal candidate for Leicester, West, declared that a Labour Government would be a 'national misfortune such as has usually befallen a great state only on the morrow of defeat in war'. *The Times* advocated a coalition between Liberals and Conservatives. Lord Balfour thought it was Asquith's duty to keep Baldwin in power, Lord Long that the Conservatives should offer their support to Asquith. In some quarters it was suggested that the best solution would be to set up a government of 'national trustees', headed by McKenna, who had deserted politics for banking and had not sat in Parliament since 1918.

Consternation in the more excitable sections of the older parties was mirrored by a revealing mixture of awe, incredulity and apprehension in the Labour movement. Over the weekend, when it still seemed possible that Baldwin would resign in the next few days, Sydney Arnold and Lees Smith advised MacDonald not to take office, on the grounds that a Labour Government would be bound to fail and that the party would then be 'overwhelmed'. The Clapham I.L.P., H. N. Brailsford reported, held a discussion on the pros and cons of taking office, in which 'every single speech was against'. Little by little, however, MacDonald and his closest colleagues became convinced that if they were given the opportunity to form a Government it would be folly to turn it down. On December 9th, as well as talking to Arnold and Lees Smith, MacDonald discussed the situation with J. A. Hobson and J. H. Thomas. Hobson, he noted later, advised him to 'risk it', and to appeal to the nation with a policy of 'European settlement, improved unemployed [*sic*] schemes, housing, co-ordinate pensions etc., Committees on Agriculture [and] National Debt'. 'Not sure', MacDonald wrote, 'if party wd. give confidence to do this moderate work, but think it would.' Thomas's view, he noted, was the 'same as is forming in my own mind'. On December 10th, the party leaders decided to jump the fence if it were presented to them . . .

In the next two days, the position was considered, in turn, by the Labour Party National Executive, by a joint meeting of the National Executive and the T.U.C. General Council, and by the executive of the Parliamentary Labour Party. At each of these meetings, MacDonald pointed out that if the Labour Party were to refuse office after defeating the Government with the aid of the Liberals, and if Asquith were then to form a Government instead, the Liberals would sit on the Government benches. The Opposition front bench, and most of the other Opposition benches as well, would be occupied by the Conservatives. The Labour Party would be relegated to the position of a group, and would probably sit below the gangway on the Liberal side of the House. When the Liberals were defeated, as they would be in due course, it would be they, and not the Labour Party, who would take the Opposition front bench. By refusing office, Labour would lose all the parliamentary advantages it had gained by becoming the official Opposition in 1922; its position in the country might be put back by a decade. These arguments proved conclusive. On December 12th the National

Executive resolved that 'should the necessity for forming a Labour Government arise, the Parliamentary Party should at once accept full responsibility for the Government of the country without compromising itself with any form of coalition.' 'One against taking office,' MacDonald noted, 'but he voted for to make unanimity.' On December 13th the joint meeting of the National Executive and General Council followed suit; and in the afternoon the Parliamentary Labour Party executive did the same. On December 18th, Asquith made it clear, in a speech to the Parliamentary Liberal Party, that the Liberals would not keep the Conservatives in office or join in any combination to keep Labour out. If a Labour Government were ever to be tried, he declared, 'it could hardly be tried under safer conditions.' Whoever might be in office, 'it is we, if we really understand our business who really control the situation.' To all intents and purposes, a Labour Government was now certain.

Early in January, MacDonald returned to London from Lossiemouth. Parliament met on January 8th, and that evening MacDonald addressed a great demonstration at the Albert Hall. With characteristic skill, he managed at one and the same time to tap the vein of emotional, utopian socialism which played such a large part in the Labour movement, and yet to make it clear that the Labour Party would take office in a severely pragmatic spirit. He wanted a Labour Government, he delcared,

> so that the life of the nation may be carried on. Nineteen-twenty-four is not the last in God's programme of creation. My friends, we will be dead and gone and forgotten and generation after generation will come, and there will still be the search for the Holy Grail by knights like Keir Hardie. The shield of love and the spear of justice will still be in the hands of good and upright men and women, and the ideal of a great future will still be in front of our people. I see no end, thank God, to these things . . . I see my own skyline, but I am convinced that when my children or children's children get there there will be another skyline, another horizon, another dawning, another glorious beckoning from heaven itself.

On January 15th came the King's speech, announcing a full legislative programme. On January 17th, Clynes moved an amendment to the address in the name of the Labour Party. On the 13th, MacDonald had noted in his diary that Cabinet-making looked 'as if it is to be the most horrible job of my life. Am beginning to suspect human nature.' By the 19th his depression had become more acute.

'C. making worse than I thought,' he wrote. 'All but two or three disappointed . . . One after another behave as though I insulted them in offering them anything but a Cabinet place. To-day a wild letter had come from the wife of one who refused subordinate office which will give me a sleepless night. I feel like an executioner, I knock so many ambitious heads into my basket.' Little by little, however, the process was completed. January 21st was the culminating day. As MacDonald described it later:

Consultation with Thomas, Henderson, Clynes, Snowden, Spoor. Produced my proposals for Ministers and under Secys, etc. List generally approved after explanations of why and wherefore. Wheatley finally fixed. Necessary to bring Clyde in. Will he play straight . . . Hurried dinner with Leach's party; Speech at 9.47. Govt. defeated and so I am to be P.M. The load will be heavy and I am so much alone.

On January 22nd, Baldwin left office. At midday, MacDonald went to the palace to be sworn of the Privy Council. The King complained about the singing of the 'Red Flag' and the 'Marseillaise' at the Labour Party meeting in the Albert Hall a few days before. MacDonald told him that if he had tried to stop it, there would have been a riot, and that it had required all his influence to prevent his followers from singing the 'Red Flag' in the House of Commons itself on the night the Baldwin Government fell. They had 'got into the way of singing this song', he explained, and it was 'by degrees that he hopes to break down this habit'. In the afternoon he returned to kiss hands as prime minister. Later he noted privately:

My dear Ishbel is splendid. The little maid is sedate as a judge and reminds me every day of her mother. 10.30 Party meeting. Watched the disappointed ones and charity came into my heart. H. raised his special grievance, but his complaint published in the *Sunday Express* has only added to the completeness of his downfall . . . Had to go to Buckingham Palace and meeting had to be adjourned—12. sworn member of the Privy Council, and afterwards had 55 minutes with the King. He explained as House met today, better not to swear me in as First Lord of the Treasury until it rose. He talked so steadily that I could hardly thank him. Most friendly. Referred to Lansbury's King Charles speech and Albert Hall songs. I pointed out that if there had been any counter demonstration effect would have been serious and very uncomfortable to both of us. He agreed. Fixed appointment after the adjount. of the House. 2.45 House met. One or two ineffective speeches. I took no part and declined to be drawn—4.30 Returned to King and 'kissed hands'. Another long talk. Referred to Russia. Hoped I would do nothing to compel him to shake hands with the murderers of his relatives. King plays the game straight, though I feel he is apprehensive. It wd. be a miracle were he not.

[David Marquand, *Ramsay MacDonald* (London, 1977), 296–305.]

In any case, a Conservative-Liberal alliance to exclude Labour from office depended on Asquith's support; and this he declined to countenance, in spite of what he described as 'appeals, threats, prayers from all parts, and from all sorts and conditions of men, women and lunatics, to step in and save the country from the horrors of Socialism and Confiscation'. Disliking the Tories more than he disliked Labour, he declared that on the defeat of Baldwin's Government in the new Parliament, the King should ask MacDonald to form an administration, which he and his fellow Liberals would keep in office as long as it avoided extremist policies. Asquith could also reflect with satisfaction that 'if a Labour Government is ever to be tried in this country, as it will be sooner or later, it could hardly be tried under safer conditions'.

After an initial hesitation in December that lasted no more than forty-eight hours, the King's sense of fair play had led him to the same conclusion. He told Davidson that 'a Socialist Government would have an opportunity of learning their administrative duties and responsibilities under favourable conditions and that it was essential that their rights under the Constitution should in no way be impaired'. Stamfordham, too, could look back with satisfaction on his conduct of negotiations with the party leaders. He wrote to a friend in mid-January:

Ever since the result of the General Election, I have taken for granted that, on Baldwin's defeat in the House of Commons, the King would send for Ramsay MacDonald; and I have deprecated any attempt to prevent his having the same facilities which would be accorded to any Minister entrusted by the Sovereign with the formation of a Government. I therefore entirely agree with what you say—as things are the sooner the Labour Party comes into power the better. Personally I am not alarmed and, unless they are upset by their own extremists, it would not surprise me were they to remain in office for some time, during which they may do considerable good.

So it came to pass. The King opened the new Parliament on 15 January 1924. Six days later, at the end of the customary debate on the Address, Labour and Liberals united to defeat the Conservatives by seventy-two votes. Baldwin at once resigned as Prime Minister and MacDonald was summoned to the palace. The King wrote in his diary for 22 January 1924:

> I held a Council, at which Mr Ramsay MacDonald was sworn in a member. I then asked him to form a Government, which he accepted to do. I had an hour's talk with him, he impressed me very much; he wishes to do the right thing. Today 23 years ago dear Grandmama died. I wonder what she would have thought of a Labour Government.

Members of the new Cabinet who celebrated over lunch the next day were burdened by no such solemnity. 'We were a jolly party,' wrote Beatrice Webb, wife of the President of the Board of Trade, 'all laughing at the joke of Labour in Office.'

MacDonald faced unusual difficulties in forming his Cabinet. Most newly-appointed Prime Ministers are embarrassed by a plethora of well-qualified supplicants; MacDonald could scarcely find enough party stalwarts with the ability or experience to fill even the major posts. For the second most important place in the Government, that of Foreign Secretary, he initially chose J. H. Thomas, a man of coarse speech and coarser wit who had demonstrated his administrative talents in directing a succession of railway strikes. But there was fierce hostility to the appointment within the Labour ranks; Thomas instead accepted the Colonial Office, where his instinctive patriotism and robust utterances were more appreciated.

In the absence of any more eligible candidate, MacDonald became his own Foreign Secretary. He was encouraged to assume this double burden by Arthur Ponsonby, the younger brother of Fritz, who after nine years in the Diplomatic Service had resigned to sit in the Commons as a Liberal; finding his colleagues inadequately radical, Ponsonby had then joined the Labour Party and in January 1924 was installed at the Prime Minister's elbow as Parliamentary Under-Secretary for Foreign Affairs. Philip Snowden, dour but competent, became Chancellor of the Exchequer; and the avuncular Arthur Henderson, who alone of his colleagues had sat in the Cabinets of Asquith and Lloyd George, Home Secretary. J. R. Clynes, the new Lord Privy Seal, wrote picturesquely of 'the strange turn in Fortune's wheel which had brought MacDonald the starveling clerk, Thomas the engine driver, Henderson the foundry labourer and Clynes the mill-hand, to this pinnacle beside the man whose forebears had been Kings for so many splendid generations. We were making history.'

[Rose, *King George V*, 324–7.]

In 1922 the Conservative/Liberal Coalition led by Lloyd George which had ruled Britain since 1918 was overthrown by a revolt of Conservative back-benchers who refused to accept the advice of their leaders that the Coalition should continue. A purely Conservative government was formed under the leadership of Bonar Law, and Parliament was dissolved in October 1922. Bonar Law's leadership of the Conservatives was, however, by no means secure, since the majority of leading Conservatives, including such figures as Austen Chamberlain, Lord Birkenhead (formerly F. E. Smith), Lord Balfour and Sir Robert Horne, remained loyal to the Coalition. They hoped and believed that Bonar Law would fail to secure an overall majority for the Conservative Party. It would then become apparent that the experiment of resuscitating an independent Conservative Party had failed, and a new coalition between Conservatives and Liberals would be the only way of meeting the socialist threat.

The Liberal Party was also divided, between the supporters of Lloyd George, who, like Austen Chamberlain and Birkenhead, hoped for a revival of the Coalition, and the independent Liberals under the leadership of Asquith who had opposed the Lloyd George Coalition from the Opposition benches since 1918. But it was the Labour Party which had become the official Opposition in 1918. It was the most united of the three parties, and, having adopted a socialist constitution in 1918, it was in no mood to form a coalition with either of the 'capitalist' parties. It sought a socialist majority in its own right, but most of its leaders believed that a long period of education and propaganda would be necessary before that majority could be secured.

In the event, the general election of 1922 gave the Conservatives an overall majority of 37, albeit on only 38.2% of the vote, a consequence of the fact that the Conservatives were competing with three other parties—Lloyd George Liberals, independent Liberals, and Labour. However, the Conservative Government of 1922 was destined to prove an ill-fated one, for in May 1923, only six months after assuming office, Bonar Law was found to be suffering from incurable cancer of the throat, and he immediately resigned. Most of the leading Conservatives who might have hoped to succeed him were disqualified as supporters of the Lloyd George Coalition, and the succession went to the relatively unknown Chancellor of the Exchequer, Stanley Baldwin. After six months as Premier, however, Baldwin told the Conservative Party Conference that unemployment was the gravest domestic issue which the country had to face, and that 'if we go pottering along as we are we shall have grave unemployment with us to the end of time'. The remedy, in his view, lay in a protective tariff keeping out those imports likely to damage British manufactured goods. Unfortunately, however, Baldwin was prevented from applying this remedy because of a pledge given by his predecessor Bonar Law that there should be no fundamental change in the fiscal arrangements of the country. 'I am not a man to play with a pledge', Baldwin told the Conference. 'I am not a clever man. I know nothing of political tactics, but I will say this: Having come to that conclusion myself, I felt the only honest and right thing as a leader of a democratic party was to tell them, at the first opportunity I had, what I thought, and submit it to their judgment.'

Baldwin therefore decided to seek the dissolution of a Parliament which was barely a year old. George V tried to dissuade him from this course and indeed went so far as to register a formal protest:

> I then pointed out to him that I strongly deprecated a dissolution at this moment as I had implicit confidence in him and in the Conservative Party now in power, and I considered that as most countries in Europe, if not in the world, were in a chaotic and indeed dangerous state, it would be a pity if this country were to be plunged into the turmoil of a General Election on a question of domestic policy which will arouse all the old traditional bitterness of the hard fought battles between Protection and Free Trade: also that it was quite possible that his majority might be reduced, or that he might not get a majority at all.
>
> I was therefore prepared to take the responsibility of advising him to change his mind, and I was also prepared for him to tell his friends that I had done so.

But Baldwin was not to be moved.

> He answered that he had gone too far now and that the Country expected a dissolution.

Parliament was dissolved on 13 November, and the election announced for 6 December.

Baldwin's declaration for Protection had the immediate effect of reuniting the two sections of the Liberal Party around the historic cause of Free Trade, and Asquith and Lloyd George came together at public meetings to exchange insincere pleasantries. The leading Coalitionists in the Conservative Party—Austen Chamberlain and Birkenhead—had, perforce, to come to terms with Baldwin, and sustained him as unwillingly as Lloyd George accepted Asquith's leadership.

Labour, the most united of the three parties, fought the election on the basis that socialism was the true answer to Protection. But it did not seriously expect to win. Indeed, according to Beatrice Webb, 'So far as I know, no member of the Labour Party, certainly not any Front Bench man, foresaw the possibility of a Labour Government arising out of the election', and most expected either a continuation of the Conservative government or a renewal of Conservative/Liberal coalition.

Memories of the Lloyd George Coalition, however, and the taint of corruption which adhered to it—Baldwin had regarded the Lloyd George Cabinet as a 'thieves' kitchen'—made most politicians unwilling to contemplate a renewal of the experiment. Moreover, there was in both the Conservative and Labour Parties at this time a widespread mistrust and fear of Lloyd George. Thomas Jones, Deputy Secretary to the Cabinet from 1916 to 1930, recorded that at Baldwin's Worcestershire home, there was an 'L. G. obsession . . . I came across a picture of Lloyd George as Chancellor of the Exchequer defaced. How they do hate him', while the second Labour government of 1929 'like their predecessors, are apparently haunted by the spectre of Ll.G. never absent from the Cabinet Room'. This hatred of Lloyd George on the part of both Baldwin and MacDonald made it very difficult for the Conservative or Labour Parties to contemplate either coalition with the Liberals, or even a tacit understanding with them to sustain a minority government; and the politics of the 1920s cannot therefore be understood without appreciating the widespread antagonism both to coalition and to Lloyd George personally.

The electorate, to the surprise of many, rebuffed Baldwin and denied him a mandate for Protection. The result was as follows:

| | |
|---|---|
| Conservatives | 258 seats |
| Labour | 191 seats |
| Liberals | 158 seats |
| Others | 7 seats |

Such a distribution of seats allowed, in the abstract, for a wide variety of possible governments. The Conservatives might seem to have a legitimate claim as the largest single party; but they had failed to obtain a mandate for Protection. Therefore, perhaps Labour as the largest anti-Protection party, should be allowed to govern. Yet Labour had not fought the election solely on a negative programme of hostility to Protection but on its socialist programme; and the electors had given even less of a mandate to socialism than to Protection.

Since the election had been fought on the issue of Protection, there was an argument for the two Free Trade parties—Labour and the Liberals—joining together in a coalition. But Labour saw the Liberals as being a 'capitalist' party, and therefore hardly better than the Conservatives; and there were, in addition, powerful social factors predisposing Labour to a dislike of the Liberals whom they regarded as haughty and patronising in manner.

Socialism, however, had been repudiated at the polls even more decisively than Protection, and there seemed to be a stronger case for an anti-socialist coalition composed of the Conservative and Liberal Parties than for a Free Trade one. The Liberals, although the smallest of the three parties, would seem to be the only party whose programme had not been rejected by the electors; and, as the only party which could co-operate with either of the other two, it would seem to have been put in a particularly strong position by the result of the election. Certainly Asquith saw the situation in much this light. But, as events were to show, the Liberals were quite unable to take advantage of their pivotal role, and their high hopes were to be rapidly dashed.

It was possible, therefore, to argue for any of a range of governments—Conservative/Liberal Coalition, Labour/Liberal Coalition, or minority Conservative, Labour or Liberal governments—depending upon which principle of government formation one believed to be the most important. The outcome, however, would be settled not by determining the relative validity of different principles of government formation, but by the complex process of political manoeuvering which began as soon as the election results were known.

The election was held on Thursday 6 December, and the result known the next day. Baldwin returned to London on the Friday, and told his friend Geoffrey Dawson, the editor of *The Times*, that he would resign immediately and would probably be succeeded by a Conservative/Liberal coalition, possibly led by Asquith, in which he, Baldwin, might well participate. On the 8th, Baldwin saw the King's Private Secretary, Lord Stamfordham, and told him that although he 'had come to no decision', his inclination was 'not to meet Parliament but to resign'. 'He had asked the country for a mandate for Tariff Reform, this had been refused, and the honourable thing would be for him to resign at once.' As regards his successor, 'it seemed to him that there were only two alternatives—a Liberal/Conservative Government or a Liberal/Labour Government'. Stamfordham reports Baldwin as saying:

> The latter seemed to him almost impossible, as the Labour policy was primarily based upon the two principles of a Levy on Capital and Nationalisation. Also, he did not believe that Labour would coalesce with a Government of which Mr Lloyd George was a member. But he thought that Mr Asquith might form a Coalition with the Conservatives, although there again Mr Lloyd George might be a difficulty.

Baldwin was encouraged in his inclination to resign immediately not only the Premiership but also the leadership of the Conservative party, by the Conservative Party Chairman, F. S. Jackson, and his immediate predecessor, Sir George Younger. Their advice was not wholly disinterested, however, since there seems to have been a move in the Conservative Party at this time to replace Baldwin as Party leader by Austen Chamberlain, and so prepare the ground for another Conservative/Liberal Coalition—a reversal, as Cowling puts it, of the verdict of the Carlton Club which had destroyed the Lloyd George Coalition. The Marquess of Lincolnshire, a former Liberal Minister (as Earl Carrington) and confidant of Asquith, wrote in his diary on 8 December with emphasis, '*The general opinion is that Baldwin has made such a mess of it that he must go at once*', and on 18 December, '*There is a Chamberlain-Birkenhead intrigue going on backed by the "Daily Mail"*.' Lord Birkenhead, who lunched with Lord Derby (the Secretary of State for War in Baldwin's Cabinet) on 10 December, told him that Baldwin would resign, that the King would then send for Lord Balfour, the only living Conservative ex-Prime Minister, to seek advice. Balfour would say that Austen Chamberlain should be sent for; and, according to Birkenhead, Balfour thought that this was 'the right course to pursue as it gave the King one other alternative before sending for Ramsay MacDonald'. There was some possibility that Asquith and the Liberals would support a reconstituted Conservative government, and in this way the nation could be saved from the perils of socialism. Certainly the general belief was that, having wantonly thrown away a Conservative majority, Baldwin could not remain as Party leader let alone Prime Minister; and Randolph Churchill, the biographer of Lord Derby, comments that 'It is interesting to notice in Derby's correspondence, and in that of other leading Tories of the time, how for the first two or three weeks after the Party's defeat in the Election there was an unchallenged assumption that Baldwin could not survive the catastrophe.'

However, no sooner was the intrigue launched than Baldwin killed it by the simple expedient of deciding to remain in office and meet Parliament. For, by Monday 10 December, on the same day that Birkenhead told Derby of the plot, Baldwin saw the King and told him that he had decided not to resign. His decision was clothed in the rhetoric of constitutionalism. His supporters, Baldwin said, thought that he should meet Parliament, 'and that former precedent did not apply in this instance, in which the question at issue was one concerning not two but three Parties, and that the House of Commons was the proper place for the choice of the Electorate to be made known'.

The King approved of this decision, and indeed Lord Stamfordham wrote a memorandum which revealed that the King had seen Balfour on 8 December and told him that, 'If Mr Baldwin wishes to resign, the King will refuse, on the grounds that he is still the head of the largest Party in the House of Commons and for every reason, constitutional and otherwise, it would be right and proper for the Government to meet Parliament and leave it to the representatives of the people to decide whether or not they will support the Government.'

Comments of this type have led some commentators to accept an exaggerated interpretation of the King's role. The King could hardly 'refuse' to accept Baldwin's resignation if Baldwin insisted on going. All that he could do would be to advise him strongly against resigning, and, as he had done when attempting to dissuade him from dissolving Parliament, back up his advice with a formal protest, allowing Baldwin to tell his colleagues that the King objected to the course he was taking. It is therefore quite wrong for Maurice Cowling, whose account of the crisis is by far the best, to write of 'The King's *decision to make Baldwin stay in office*.' (My italics.) The King was in no position to make such a decision and, in any case, Baldwin had already decided to meet Parliament when he met the King on 10 December, and so the King did not even have to persuade him to adopt what he believed to be the correct course.

After telling the King of his new-found resolve to meet Parliament, Baldwin added that he was 'absolutely opposed' to Coalition. He had, after all, played a prominent part in destroying the Lloyd George coalition fourteen months before, and had no wish to be involved in another one. The King responded by asking whether a working arrangement with the Liberals might be possible, and Baldwin said that he would find out. The Cabinet met on Tuesday 11 December and unanimously approved of Baldwin's decision that the government meet Parliament in five weeks' time on 15 January.

With this, the first phase of the crisis was over, and the intrigue against Baldwin collapsed. His continued leadership of the Conservatives, at least until the government met Parliament, was now assured. Had Baldwin resigned immediately after the election, on the other hand, the King might well have sought to ascertain whether another Conservative could have formed a government and secured Liberal support. Baldwin's decision, therefore, limited the options available to the Liberals. If they wished to prevent Labour forming a government, they would have to come to an arrangement with Baldwin, rather than any other Conservative; and since the Liberals had only just fought an election opposing Baldwin's policy of Protection, this would be a difficult course for them to take. On the other hand, if the Liberals voted against Baldwin, they would be putting Labour into power, something which many Liberal electors had not envisaged when they had voted Liberal to preserve Free Trade. In making up their minds what to do when faced with the expected no-confidence motion from Labour therefore, the Liberals were put in a most unenviable position.

Asquith, however, was in no doubt as to his course of action. On 18 December he addressed the Liberal MPs assembled at the National Liberal Club, making what one observer called 'the speech of his life'. He began by declaring that Liberal members 'were not sent here by your constituents to play the part of soldiers of fortune to settle squalid fights'. He declared that if either Protection or the capital levy were submitted to the Commons, they would be defeated by a majority of more than 200. Neither the Conservatives nor

Labour, therefore, had a chance of retaining or obtaining office unless they abandoned for the time being the principal position which they fought the election to obtain. 'Whoever may be the incumbents of office, it is we who really control the situation.'

Asquith then made it clear that he would do nothing to assist the Conservatives. 'The days of the present Government are numbered. They will go, and they will go with short shrift . . . Their record is an almost unbroken one of impotence and humiliation.' In the Debate on the Address when Parliament reassembled, Asquith made clear the reason why the Liberals would turn the government out.

> There may be many theories, I have no doubt there are, why we have been sent here by the electorate in such strange proportions. But there is one theory which will not hold water for a moment; and that is, that we were sent here to maintain the present Government in office. It was their election, not ours. It was they, not we, who threw down the challenge. It was they again, not we, who invited the judgment of the electorate. They have got it.

The Liberals, then, would support Labour's amendment declaring no confidence in the government. The consequence would be that the King would send for Ramsay MacDonald, the leader of the Opposition. Labour, however, was determined to govern on its own, without recourse to coalition. How, then, could the Liberals hope to gain advantage from the situation? At the National Liberal Club meeting, Asquith revealed his thinking. He made it clear that he thought a minority Labour government would have no right to a dissolution if it was rapidly defeated in the Commons. The King could legitimately refuse a request to dissolve for the third time in a little over a year. Asquith claimed:

> the Crown is not bound to take the advice of a particular Ministry to put its subjects to the tumult and turmoil of a series of general elections so long as it can find other Ministers who are prepared to give it a trial. The notion that a Ministry which cannot command a majority in the House of Commons . . . a Ministry in a minority of 31 per cent . . . in these circumstances is invested with the right to demand a dissolution is as subversive of constitutional usage, as it would, in my opinion, be pernicious to the general and paramount interests of the nation at large.

Either, therefore, Labour would govern with the support of the Liberals which would indeed make the Liberals the arbiters of government; or Labour would be defeated in the House, and seek a dissolution which would be denied to them. 'Father asks me to say', wrote Asquith's daughter Violet Bonham-Carter to Winston Churchill, 'that there are an immense number of Dominion precedents for refusing one [i.e. a dissolution] under such conditions.' Asquith would then be summoned to form a government which would be supported by the Conservatives.

Asquith gave Stamfordham his views on how he imagined the situation would develop. He saw the Labour Party's position as a difficult one, and began his conversation with Stamfordham by saying rather patronisingly that in MacDonald's position, he, Asquith, would decline office 'on the grounds that he and his Party were not yet fit to undertake the responsibility'. But if MacDonald did form a government, the Liberals would sit on the Opposition benches. Stamfordham reported:

> The next step that he foresaw would be that Mr Ramsay MacDonald comes to the King and asks for a Dissolution: indeed Mr Asquith believes that in accepting office Mr Ramsay MacDonald will very probably ask His Majesty to promise a Dissolution in the event of an early defeat of the Government in the House of Commons . . . Mr Asquith considers the King would be constitutionally justified in giving an absolute refusal . . . there can be no possible justification for a third Election within a year; and, if on the King's refusal to dissolve Parliament Mr Ramsay MacDonald resigned, and his Majesty sent for Mr Asquith, the latter would accept all responsibility for the King's action. No doubt he himself would have difficulties: but he thought that the Conservatives, without entering into any general undertaking, would support his Government, which would not embark upon any extravagant legislation; and in this way the King's Government might be carried on for another Session or even longer.

Asquith's approach caused some alarm to the Labour Party and to the King. Labour's suspicions were immediately aroused that Asquith's speech at the National Liberal Club was part of an 'Establishment' plot to deny Labour fair play, and that a Labour government defeated in the Commons would be denied the right which other governments had enjoyed, of an immediate dissolution. Asquith's remarks, therefore, gave rise to the expression of some anti-monarchical sentiment. The Rev. Campbell Stephen, a prominent figure on the Labour Left, declared that if Labour was refused a dissolution, the monarchy would be in danger. George Lansbury, speaking at Shoreditch Town Hall in January 1924, reminded the monarch that 'Some centuries ago a King stood against the common people and he lost his head.' MacDonald in a speech at Elgin in December voiced his 'suspicion that between now and January . . . there was going to be a serious attempt to wangle the Constitution so that the democracy of this country might not have fair play given to them'.

The King, understandably enough, did not thank Asquith for implying that he would deviate from the role of strict constitutionality by denying to Labour what he had given to the other parties. Hugh Dalton, whose father was Canon of Windsor, reports a conversation which he had with Stamfordham at Windsor Castle on 26 December. According to Stamfordham, 'The King frightened by Glasgow speeches, including especially one by Campbell Stephen, saying that if J. R. M [i.e. MacDonald] is refused a dissolution, that will be the end of the Monarchy. The King had rung up S [i.e. Stamfordham] about this from Sandringham. S blames Asquith for raising the constitutional aspects of the right to obtain a dissolution in his recent speech.'

Whatever the constitutional value of Asquith's approach in the abstract, his speech ignored political realities. If he were to defeat a Labour government as soon as it had taken office, the Liberals would be accused of frivolity in precipitating an unnecessary election, especially if Labour contented itself with moderate policies as it intended to do. No one could predict with certainty whether or not the King would grant a dissolution in such circumstances, but his inclination was to ensure that the Labour government be given every privilege that previous governments had enjoyed. The King was particularly anxious to dispel the view expressed by Campbell Stephen and Lansbury that he was hostile to Labour; and he told J. C. C. Davidson, a confidant of Baldwin, on 21 January after the Conservatives had been defeated in the Commons, that 'it was essential that their rights under the Constitution should in no way be impaired'. 'I must confess', Stamfordham wrote to St Loe Strachey, editor of the *Spectator*, ' . . . at the present moment I feel that His Majesty should do his utmost not to hamper in any way Ramsay MacDonald in, what we must all admit will be, a task of almost incalculable magnitude. And I expect that the King would be interpreting the general feeling of the people of the country that, true to British ideas, the Government, whoever they may be, should have a fair chance . . .'

Nor was there any reason to believe that the Conservatives would support an Asquith government when Asquith had been responsible for turning them out of office. Asquith 'rather took for granted', Stamfordham confided to the Archbishop of Canterbury, 'that the Conservatives would help keep him in office, although without any agreement'. The Conservatives, Winston Churchill predicted, with rather more prescience than Asquith, would not 'act as bottle holders to those who kicked us into the street three months ago and deliberately erected this Socialist monstrosity'.

In fact, the first Labour government which took office in January 1924, after Baldwin had been defeated on an amendment to the Address, lasted until October, when the new government in turn was defeated on a Liberal amendment to a Conservative motion which MacDonald chose to regard as a matter of confidence; and the Conservatives rather than the Liberals were to be the beneficiaries of MacDonald's fall.

[Vernon Bogdanor, *Multi-Party Politics and the Constitution* (Cambridge, 1983), 91–101.]

### (*d*) *1929*

| Party | Seats |
|---|---|
| Labour | 288 |
| Conservative | 260 |
| Liberal | 59 |
| Others | 8 |

*Several of the factors which had produced a minority Labour government in 1923–4 still existed, and MacDonald accordingly formed another minority government.*

The general election was now only a few months away. As in 1923, Labour had to fight on two fronts; as in 1923, the Liberals were, in many ways, a more dangerous enemy than the Conservatives. On November 6th, MacDonald noted that the by-election results showed only that the Government would be defeated, not that an independent Labour Government would succeed it. 'If the three party system is to remain,' he wrote gloomily, 'it is obvious that the question of coalitions in some shape or form has to be faced. Our immediate duty is to place every obstacle we can in the way of the survival of the three party system.' Despite occasional misgivings, however, he was optimistic enough to speculate about the form which the next Labour Government might take . . .

During the next few weeks, however, it became clear that the result of the election was not yet a foregone conclusion. The Conservatives were fairly quiescent, but the Liberals were buzzing ominously with activity. On January 31st, R. H. Tawney wrote to warn Arthur Henderson:

An acquaintance who is well-informed as to the intentions of the Liberals writes to me that they propose to make a big plan of public works the centre of their election programme. The idea is to create employment until the total unemployment is brought down to half a million.

If the Labour Election Programme is to be any use it *must have something concrete and definite* about unemployment. The pages on what subject in Labour and the Nation are . . . not up to the mark . . . [W]hat is required is a definite statement that (a) A Labour Government will initiate productive work on a larger scale, and will raise a loan for the purpose. (b) that it will maintain from national funds all men no absorbed in such work . . .

This matter ought to occupy a prominent place in the Election Manifesto. Do get the Leader to authorise a bold statement.

Tawney's letter was sent to MacDonald by Arthur Greenwood, accompanied by a covering note: 'Middleton passed this to me today. It happens to be in line with what is being done. But I thought you ought to see it.' Greenwood's assurances turned out to be wildly overconfident. At a dinner for Liberal candidates on March 1st, Lloyd George announced that the Liberal Party had prepared a series of public-works projects, which could be put in hand the moment a Liberal Government came to power, and which would reduce unemployment to 'normal proportions' in a year. The projects were set out in a pamphlet with the alluring title, *We Can Conquer Unemployment*: 350,000 men were to be employed on road-building, 60,000 on housing, 60,000 on telephone development and 62,000 on electrical development. The cost would be £250 million, and the money would be raised by loan. Since the increase in tax revenue and the fall in unemployment expenditure would compensate for the cost of servicing the loan, there would be no burden on the exchequer. In the next three months, Keynes and his protégé, Hubert Henderson, published a pamphlet in support; Lloyd George addressed a series of great meetings up and down the country; and the Government was provoked into issuing a special white paper, proving that the plan was unworkable. In Trevor Wilson's words, it was the 'Indian summer of the old Liberal Party'; and, as sometimes happens with Indian summers, it was at least as spectacular as anything that had happened during the real one . . .

At the Manchester Free Trade Hall on May 24th, MacDonald delivered a brisk attack on Lloyd George's record, and returned to the well-worn, but still telling, argument that the Liberals were trying to steal Labour's clothes. In a broadcast appeal to the electors on May 28th, he denounced the idea that unemployment could be cured by 'patchwork' and declared that Labour's solution was 'not a programme of relief works upon which the capital spent will be mainly lost to the country. It is a programme designed to add to the wealth and efficiency of the nation, to give a spur to industry and to open the way to markets.' A vote for the Liberals, he concluded, would be a vote for a minority Government, dependent on parliamentary compromises and without real responsibility for its actions. For the most part, however, he concentrated on other issues—the defects of the Government's 'safeguarding' policy, the need for a body to co-ordinate the economic activities of the state, the responsibility for the general strike and, above all, the danger of a drift to war. The last was probably his strongest card, and no one who heard this broadcast on May 28th could doubt that it was the one about which he cared the most. What, he asked, had happened to British foreign policy since 1924? . . .

Polling day was on May 30th. In Seaham, MacDonald was returned with a majority of 28,794. In the country as a whole, the Conservatives won 8,664,000 votes, the Labour Party 8,360,000 and the Liberals 5,300,000. But the bias of the system worked in Labour's favour, and in the House of Commons the Labour Party had 287 seats, the Conservatives 261 and the Liberals 59. Labour had gained over 130 seats, and for the first time in history it was the strongest party in the state. Egon Wertheimer had written not long before:

After the inglorious fall of his Government, accompanied as it was by a whole series of *faux pas*, Ramsay MacDonald's future, crowed the wiseacres of London, was not worth a single cent. Yet he sits more firmly in the saddle than ever. His leadership was never less disputed than at the present moment. For this his ability to compromise and reconcile is beyond doubt responsible in part. The true reason, however, is to be sought outside the immediately political. In the imagination and consciousness of thousands his position is beyond party politics . . . [I]n the slums of the manufacturing towns and in the hovels of the countryside he has become a legendary being—the personification of all that thousands of downtrodden men and women hope and dream and desire. Like Lenin . . . he is the focus of the mute hopes of a whole class.

Wertheimer's judgment would have been echoed by most of MacDonald's followers.

[Marquand, *Ramsay MacDonald*, 483–8.]

At No. 10 on the evening of 30 May, the gloom deepened as the results came in, worsening as the night dragged on. Central Office experts had to confess that their harshest forecast had been far exceeded. Baldwin found it hard to reconcile the results with his reception during the election campaign. By next morning the rout was obvious. Conservatives dropped to 261, Labour rose to 287 and the Liberals came home with a mere 59. Labour had swept Lancashire, Yorkshire, Cheshire, the West Midlands and London. The peculiarity of the electoral system was shown again, for the Conservatives had kept the majority of votes—8.66 million against the Labour 8.36; and there was something to be said for the view that a drift of mainly middle-class population southward, and the absence of an up-to-date register of the already enfranchised voters, had benefited Labour in the tally of actual seats. What hurt most was that the Liberals had, by fighting the Conservatives rather than Labour, let in many Socialists. Many of the best young men were lost—Macmillan, Duff Cooper, O'Connor, Bentinck and Charles Rhys, the Prime Minister's Private Secretary, all went down. 'So we are beaten,' wrote Lucy Baldwin, 'but, God willing, will flourish again.'

Baldwin was stricken more by this result than that of any other election in his life. His administration had been the most productive of the century, save only that of the Liberals in 1906. But gratitude, as his son was to comment later, is not a political category. Patrick Duff wrote, 'This reverse has come as a great shock. The Party Headquarters thought we were going to get about fifty over all other Parties, and they are wrong by about eighty. When one thinks of all the PM's work these last four and a half years and of all he is and stands for, and that this is the response it gets, it makes one lose faith a bit. But he and Mrs B. are wonderful. Never a word of bitterness or complaint. They both "treat those two imposters just the same" if ever anyone did. And this, after spending themselves to the last ounce, only within the last three weeks, and being greeted everywhere with roaring crowds and cheering streets and the appearance of universal applause and approbation. It must make it all the harder that this reception has availed so little in the result . . . still this isn't the end of everything. As the PM says, no one has ever done anything big and good if he has always had success and hasn't had some thumping clouts on the head on the way. And this may be just the recoil for a bigger jump, like 1923 was.'

In Central Office, Patrick Gower consoled himself, 'It has been a strenuous year but it has been worth it and it has been fun. I was hoping that our humble efforts would help bring S.B. back. I never before worked with such complete belief in and admiration for any man or any government and one's faith in democracy is apt to be shattered when one sees a man like S.B. defeated by falsehood and misrepresentation. But I am convinced that it is only temporary and we've damn well got to see it is.'

The immediate problem, like that of 1923, was whether to resign at once or wait and meet Parliament. Lengthy research went on to find suitable precedents but the overriding consideration was the position of Lloyd George and the Liberals. If Baldwin met Parliament, Lloyd George might keep the Conservatives in for a few weeks to humiliate them. On the other hand, the King was ill and there was the usual pressure for a Tory/Liberal combination to keep Labour out. Baldwin had intended to resign at once if Labour got a majority and this was still his instinct, but now he retired to Chequers where on 1 June came Davidson, Eyres Monsell, Austen Chamberlain and Hoare. He also consulted constitutional experts who assured him that it was in the Prime Minister's hands to do as he chose. Dawson wrote in his diary for 1 June, 'the Prime Minister was undecided and Mrs Baldwin urging him to go!'

Chamberlain wanted to meet Parliament, saying 'the loss of Steel-Maitland need not determine an essential question of policy.' Churchill agreed, but later changed his mind. On Sunday came Salisbury, whose advice was indecisive. Tom Jones and Duff argued for resignation, and Lady Astor helped to sway Dawson to the same line, which was duly reflected in *The Times* leader of Monday morning. But already on the Sunday Baldwin had seen Stamfordham: 'He had appealed,' he told the King's Private Secretary, 'to the people to trust him, as in 1924, and they had refused. He was beaten and he accepts it and thinks this sporting attitude will count in his favour next time. If he hangs on they will say, "Here is this man clinging to office, he won't take his defeat, he is trying to prevent the Labour Party from enjoying their victory." ' As always, when he had taken the decision, Baldwin's care fell away. He overbore Neville Chamberlain and the others who still wanted to ride for a fall on a bold safeguarding policy. On Tuesday he went to Windsor to resign.

[Middlemas and Barnes, *Baldwin*, 526–7.]

Had some bold prophet told the King that he was one day to preside over a change of Government wearing a Chinese dressing-gown, he would scarcely have believed his ears. But immediately after the general election of 1929, the reopening of a surgical wound obliged him to receive both Baldwin and MacDonald in his bedroom at Windsor. That was indeed a revolution. So too was the instant transfer of power from Conservative to Labour. After the general election of 1923, the King had asked the defeated Prime Minister, Baldwin, to defer his resignation until the new Parliament could meet. Disputable even in 1923, that narrow constitutional doctrine had become outmoded by 1929. Labour now commanded 287 seats, compared with 261 Conservative and 59 Liberal: an effective though not overall majority. There was nothing to recommend preserving the old Government until it had been formally defeated at Westminster. As Stamfordham wrote: 'We must recognise that Democracy is no longer a meaningless sort of shibboleth; with the enormous increase of voters by the women's franchise it is the actual voice, for better or worse, the political voice of the State.'

Baldwin agreed. If he were to hang on, he told Stamfordham, the nation would say: 'Here is this man clinging to office, he won't take his defeat, he is trying to prevent the Labour Party from enjoying their victory.' So he at once resigned, and the King sent for MacDonald.

[Rose, *King George V*, 367.]

In December 1923, the key decision had been that made by Baldwin not to resign immediately. In 1929, the Parliament elected in 1924, having nearly run its course, was dissolved, and the election, held on 30 May produced another hung Parliament. The result was as follows:

| | |
|---|---|
| Labour | 288 seats |
| Conservatives | 260 seats |
| Liberals | 59 seats |

The Conservatives, although having fewer seats than Labour, had a larger share of the vote:

| | *Votes* | *Share of vote* |
|---|---|---|
| Labour | 8,389,512 | 37.1% |
| Conservatives | 8,656,473 | 38.2% |
| Liberals | 5,308,510 | 27.7% |

This time, Baldwin, after contemplating meeting Parliament, decided to resign immediately. He told Stamfordham that 'He had appealed to the people to trust him, as in 1924, and they had refused. He was beaten and he accepts it and thinks this sporting attitude will count in his favour next time. If he hangs on they will say, "Here is this man clinging to office, he won't take his defeat, he is trying to prevent the Labour Party from enjoying their victory."' Yet there was also a political reason for Baldwin's immediate resignation. For if he had attempted to meet Parliament in 1929, it would have looked as if he was seeking to make terms with the Liberals, now led by Lloyd George, and this he was determined not to do. Thomas Jones, the Deputy Secretary to the Cabinet and a confidant of Baldwin's, describes Baldwin's process of thought:

On Friday afternoon, 31st, S.B., Mrs Baldwin, and Duff [i.e. Duff Cooper, a junior minister in the government] had gone down to Chequers to consider quietly whether he should resign at once, or wait for the meeting of Parliament under the Amendment to the Address to be moved by the Labour Leader. On Saturday several of his colleagues visited Chequers, including Davidson, Eyres-Monsell (the Chief Whip), Austen Chamberlain, and Sam Hoare. I arrived at 11.30 on Sunday morning in favour of his meeting Parliament. We talked it out in the study. I found him in a state of great nervous tension, the Ll. G. Obsession weighing heavily upon his mind. Austen was in favour of meeting Parliament; so was Winston. I said very little, but he spoke with great rapidity—most unusual with him, and only possible when roused by Ll. G. It was Ll. G. who had put the Socialists into office, and it was Ll. G. who throughout the day dominated our discussion. What would he do? As the day wore on I moved round to the view that the P.M. ought to resign straight away. Duff strongly held this opinion. What we all feared was that Ll. G. might keep S.B. in office for a week or a month, and humiliate him and his party in every conceivable way. S.B.'s instinct was to go out at once . . . If this were not done there would be a scream from Labour that S.B. was denying them the fruits of victory.

The discussion was hardly couched in constitutional terms, and there was no suggestion that Baldwin would be acting unconstitutionally if he were to meet Parliament. The discussion was a tactical one—how would Lloyd George and the Labour Party react? Had he not been so loath to enter into any kind of arrangement with Lloyd George, Baldwin might well have decided to meet Parliament. Instead he could afford to resign immediately, since, by contrast to 1923, he was not faced with any challenge to his leadership. Moreover, because the Conservatives were not the largest party in the Commons, there was no danger of the King calling another Conservative to the Palace who might, unlike Baldwin, be prepared to bargain with Lloyd George and construct a majority government.

Baldwin could, it seems, have decided to meet Parliament as he did in 1923 so as to place on the Liberals the onus of installing a Labour government, but, as the extract from Thomas Jones's diary shows, Baldwin did not trust Lloyd George to act as straightforwardly as Asquith had done. Asquith had immediately declared himself in 1923 as intending to turn the Conservatives out. Lloyd George, on the other hand, might allow the Conservatives to continue in government on sufferance extracting every last ounce of political advantage from the situation. As John Campbell has put it, Baldwin rated 'the fear of being humiliated by Lloyd George higher than the possible advantage to be gained by letting the Liberals be seen to install Socialism in office'.

The truth is that whether a Prime Minister decides to meet parliament or not in a situation in which no single party enjoys an overall majority depends not upon any abstract constitutional rules, but upon whether the Prime Minister wishes, for tactical reasons, to test the *grounds* on which the Opposition seeks to displace him. This was the course taken by Lord Salisbury after the general election of November 1885 which left him in a minority of 86 against the Liberals, with the Irish Nationalists also returning 86 members. He decided to meet Parliament so as to exhibit the fact that the Liberals could only come to power with the support of the Irish Nationalists. It was to lessen this tactical disadvantage that the

Liberals chose to defeat the Conservative government in January 1886, not on an Irish issue, but on the 'three acres and a cow' amendment, an issue of purely domestic policy. Similarly, in 1892, Lord Salisbury, although left in a minority of 40 against the Liberals and Irish Nationalists, decided to meet Parliament since he hoped to extract from Gladstone the particulars of the Home Rule Bill which he intended to introduce, and discover how it differed from the first version which had been defeated in the Commons in 1886.

In 1885, 1892, 1923/4 and 1929, the Prime Minister decided on political rather than constitutional grounds whether or not he should meet Parliament. Of course, one of the factors involved in making an estimate of the situation would be his judgment of whether meeting Parliament would make him appear 'unsporting' and unwilling to accept the verdict of the electorate. But that again is a political and not a constitutional argument.

[Bogdanor, *Multi-Party Politics*, 108–10.]

### (*e*) *February 1974*

| Party | Seats |
|---|---|
| Labour | 301 |
| Conservative | 297 |
| Liberal | 14 |
| Ulster Unionist | 11 |
| SDLP | 1 |
| SNP | 7 |
| Plaid Cymru | 2 |
| Others | 2 |

February 1974 produced an entirely new situation, in that neither of the two major parties could have reached a majority, even given the full support of the Liberals. In a House of 635, Labour had 301, the Conservative Party 296, the minor parties—Liberals, the Ulster Unionists (no longer automatically taking the Conservative whip) and the Scots and Welsh Nationalists and the Lincoln Social Democrat adding up to 37.

On the day following the polls, there was wide expectation that Edward Heath would tender the resignation of his Government, and that afternoon the Parliamentary Committee of the Labour

Party—the so-called 'shadow cabinet', intimated their 'availability', even though we proved to be eighteen short of an overall majority, that is, we had thirty-four less than the combined voting power of the other parties. In the event, Mr Heath spent the weekend trying to reach an accommodation with the Liberal leader, Jeremy Thorpe, and his party, offering Liberal participation in the government. By Monday, 4 March, these negotiations had broken down, and Mr Heath tendered his resignation. When I was called to the Palace the Queen asked me if I could form an administration. Answering yes, I was authorized to form a government, and in fact submitted the names of ten of the leading members of the Cabinet for the royal approval that evening.

Over this weekend there were suggestions that, as the Conservatives had fewer seats than Labour, and were having difficulty in securing allies, the Labour leader should have been invited to try. This would have been contrary to precedent. A prime minister was there—at Downing Street. If and when he resigned that would create a new situation. Alternatively, were he to face Parliament, without allies, and be defeated, he would then resign. As things were, there was no vacancy to fill.

The constitutional practice on a change of government is that the sovereign asks the party leader who has been called to the Palace whether he can form a government. There are two possible answers. One is for him to express assurance that a viable government can and will be formed. The other is a statement of willingness to hold the necessary consultations to find out *whether* a government can be formed.

In 1964, with an overall majority of four, I gave the first answer, and was in fact successful. In 1974, in a minority situation, I gave the same answer, and the minority government was formed. In 1963, on the other hand, though the Conservatives had an overall majority around ninety, Sir Alec Douglas-Home merely asked leave to go away and try, such was the disturbance in his party following the turbulent process of selecting a leader. Iain Macleod and Enoch Powell refused to serve, but Sir Alec's ability to form a government was confirmed by the decision of R. A. Butler and Reginald Maudling to join his Cabinet. R. A. Butler, in particular, received some criticism from opponents of Sir Alec's selection. In a letter to *The Times*, he explained his decision by his fear that, if Sir Alec failed to form a government, the Queen might have had no alternative but to send for Labour. I am sure that this view was ill-founded. The Conservatives still had an overall majority around ninety, and an alternative Conservative leader would almost certainly have been invited to accept the Queen's Commission.

[Wilson, *Governance*, 25–6.]

There was a Cabinet meeting on the evening of Friday 1 March. Ted Heath then went to the Palace to report on the situation. On Saturday 2 March he met Jeremy Thorpe and offered the Liberals seats in a coalition Government. He also offered that the Cabinet would support the establishment of a Speaker's Conference on electoral reform. After discussions between Thorpe and his colleagues on Sunday and on Monday morning the offer was rejected. A telegram was sent to the Ulster Unionists, led by Harry West, on Sunday 3 March, offering the Conservative Whip. There was a non-committal response. After the rejection of the coalition offer by the Liberals the Cabinet met twice in the course of 4 March. Ted Heath went to the Palace again to resign at 6.30 p.m.

As I held strongly to the views that I had already expressed in such extraordinary circumstances on television, I believed that this was the correct outcome. Certainly the immediate result was bad: a weak minority Labour Government; probably another general election within a year or so; and traumatic consequences for the Conservative Party and Ted Heath's leadership in particular. But if, as I maintained, the proposed coalition would have been regarded as wrong in principle by the British people, then it would have been most unpopular. It would therefore have been most unlikely to work in practice, even if—improbably—it held together when faced with contentious issues. If, as seemed likely, it ended in chaos, it would have had disastrous long-term consequences for the Conservative and Liberal Parties. As I reconsider these events today I remain profoundly of the same opinion.

[Lord Whitelaw, *The Whitelaw Memoirs* (London, 1989), 135.]

When the results were known on Friday 1 March, Heath, instead of resigning immediately, approached Jeremy Thorpe, the Liberal leader, and made an offer of coalition with full Liberal participation in government. Such a coalition would, of course, still not have commanded a majority in the Commons, for one of the peculiarities of the situation was that no two parties acting together (apart from

Labour and the Conservatives) could secure such a majority; but the Heath move would at least have made the Conservative/Liberal coalition the largest single grouping in the Commons. Negotiations continued until Monday 4 March when the Liberals rejected Heath's offer, and Heath resigned. Harold Wilson then formed a minority Labour government.

Heath's action in refusing to resign immediately once the election results were known was criticised as 'bordering on the unconstitutional' by Lord Crowther-Hunt (*The Times*, 4 March 1974), a Labour peer and Fellow in Politics at Exeter College, Oxford, shortly to become constitutional adviser to the Wilson government. Crowther-Hunt's reasoning was based on the fact that there was no twentieth-century case of a Prime Minister failing to resign after an election which left his party only the second largest in the Commons.

But it is doubtful whether one can build a constitutional principle upon the precedent of 1929. For, as we have seen, close examination of this precedent is insufficient to establish the conclusion that the Prime Minister is under any obligation to resign if his party is not the largest in the Commons; and there are contrasting, though admittedly earlier, precedents from 1885/6 and 1892.

Indeed, having once decided not to resign immediately, Heath might well have been better advised to meet Parliament. He would probably not have incurred much further criticism, and he might well have gained some tactical advantage by forcing the Liberals to be seen installing Labour in office. This had been the tactic adopted by Baldwin in 1924. Indeed, there was even the possibility, albeit a slim one, that Heath would not be defeated on a vote of confidence when the House met. This possibility is sufficient, surely, to dispose of Crowther-Hunt's assertion that Heath was acting unconstitutionally. For, so long as there was any uncertainty as to whether there was a majority against him, Heath was surely entitled to test the possibility. Whether meeting Parliament would have been politically wise is, of course, another question, and there is no doubt a case to be argued on both sides. But Heath's actual resignation immediately after the negotiations with the Liberals had failed, flowed from his political judgment and not from any constitutional necessity.

The negotiations with the Liberals may have had an important constitutional consequence. For Harold Wilson's minority Labour government faced the possibility of immediate defeat on an amendment to the Address on the Queen's speech. If that happened, would he be able to secure a dissolution, or would the Queen refuse a dissolution and summon Edward Heath, now Leader of the Opposition, to form a government?

In a speech at High Wycombe on 15 March 1974, ten days after his government was formed, Wilson warned the Conservative and Liberal Parties that, if they defeated him on the Address, they would face an immediate general election.

Frustrated and resentful at the advent of a Labour Government, the Opposition parties have, apparently, decided to continue the manoeuvering they first set in hand while the election results were still being declared . . . I believe that the British public . . . will be impatient of any further manoeuvering designed to put back into office the administration which almost had to be dragged from office 10 days ago.

As a realist I recognise that if the Opposition parties are determined to play around with the future of this nation they are in a position to do so.

I want to give this warning: That if *they* are realists they will recognise that they will do so at their electoral peril. The Labour Government will not emulate the Conservatives in a desperate attempt to hold on to office, for we believe the electorate will know how to respond. The British public will not lightly forgive politicians and parties who, having been rejected by the voters, seek to prevent the Labour Government from taking the measures necessary for the nation's survival . . . If Mr Heath and Mr Thorpe are determined to play the role of wreckers, it is the British people, in the first place, who will have to face a heavy bill for damages. But they and their parties will not be immune from the consequences of their own frivolous irresponsibility.

This masterly speech seems at first sight the opening shot in a new electoral campaign, but it also contained a veiled warning to the Opposition that Wilson had confidence in being granted a dissolution if he was forced to ask for one. It appears that this belief was conveyed by an informal and oblique channel—certainly not Wilson himself—to the Conservatives.

At any rate, the speech had its desired effect, and the Conservative threat to defeat him on the Address evaporated. For the Conservatives had no desire to precipitate a general election which they believed might be won by Labour with an overall majority. The Conservatives, therefore, failed to divide the House on an amendment which they themselves had tabled! . . .

[Bogdanor, *Multi-Party Politics*, 111–12.]

## (2) THE ROLE OF THE QUEEN

*After the return of each of the hung Parliaments this century, the party Leaders resolved the prime ministerial succession crisis. If, however, no political consensus emerged after a future inconclusive general election, the Queen might have to become involved. She is equipped to resolve such a crisis personally, using her own knowledge and experience, but advisers are to hand.*

### (*a*) *The Queen's Private Secretary*

It is perhaps characteristic of what foreigners are apt to regard as the inveterate tendency to 'amateurism' in the British Way of Life—a tendency which has, more than once, proved to be our salvation—that the British Constitution, which remained steadfastly silent as to the position of a Prince Consort and for forty years refused recognition of the office of Prime Minister, should be equally incognizant of so important a factor in its functioning as the Private Secretary to the Sovereign. The ponderous tomes of Anson and Dicey, the sparkling pages of Bagehot, the weighty treatises of Professor Berriedale Keith and Sir Ivor Jennings, though they have collectively illuminated to a very great degree our knowledge of what has been called 'the complicated metaphysics of limited monarchy', have shed but little light upon this vital link between the Crown and the Cabinet, between the Monarch and the machinery of government, and between the Sovereign and the Commonwealth.

The origin and growth of the office of Private Secretary to the Sovereign are in themselves amply illustrative of the advantages of an unwritten Constitution which, being a living organism, retains the power to adapt itself to necessities and the ability to accept the *de facto* with the same equanimity as the *de jure*: that genius for assimilation which has proved so vital in preserving the Monarchy, the Realm and the Commonwealth.

The Sovereign has always had his advisers. Originally these were the Lords of the Council assisted by clerks and secretaries. Secretaries of State emerged during the reign of Queen Elizabeth I, and, as the effective power of government passed from the Privy Council to Parliament, the Secretaries of State, as the executive committee of the Privy Council, became the Cabinet, bearing collective responsibility for the advice tendered to the Sovereign through their presiding officer and chief, the First Lord of the Treasury. It was customary for the King to attend the meetings of his Council, and though, for various reasons, George I and George II frequently absented themselves and left much of the transaction of the business of State to their First Ministers, George III gave assiduous attention to the affairs of the realm, not only conducting his own correspondence but keeping copies of his letters in his own hand.

The constitutional theory obtaining at this time was that the Secretary of State for the Home Department was the King's Private Secretary, and that it was both undesirable and irregular for anyone not a Privy Counsellor to have access to Cabinet secrets. In 1805, however, George III, having become almost totally blind, appointed, in defiance of tradition, Lieut.-General Sir Herbert Taylor to be his Private Secretary. This step, revolutionary in itself, was of the greater importance because, in addition to his blindness, the King's mental condition was rapidly deteriorating. General Taylor continued to give him valuable assistance until the final attack of insanity in 1810 resulted in the establishment of the Regency.

Parliament, which had been highly suspicious of the appointment of Sir Herbert Taylor, proved definitely hostile when the Prince Regent sought in 1812 to nominate Colonel McMahon as his Private Secretary at a salary of £2000 a year. The House of Commons raised a great clamour, one member declaring that the office of Private Secretary was 'dangerous and unconstitutional, rendering the person holding it the secret adviser of the Sovereign with a degree of influence over his mind totally at variance with the forms of Government in England . . . The office [he continued] would be destructive of a fundamental principle of the constitution, which was that no one ought to use the name of the Sovereign, give him advice, or be the bearer of his commands, unless he be one of the responsible ministers of the Crown, and answerable to Parliament.' In a division in a House of nearly three hundred members the appointment of the Prince Regent's Secretary was carried by seventy votes.

The Prince Regent retained Colonel McMahon's services for a while, creating him a Privy Counsellor, and subsequently a baronet. Later, however, the Regent circumvented the objections of the House of Commons by employing Sir William Knighton, an eminent physician, as Keeper of the Privy Purse, in which capacity he also served as Private Secretary. Sir William gave the Regent remarkably good advice not only on political matters but also in the highly complicated state of His Royal Highness's finances.

William IV recalled Sir Herbert Taylor from retirement and that tried veteran, who had been admitted to the Privy Council after serving as Ambassador in Berlin, gave patient and diplomatic counsel to his Sovereign during the period of agitation for Reform, in the course of which the King caused his Cabinet no little anxiety. This same experienced counsellor was summoned by Queen Victoria shortly after her accession to the Throne and consulted on the question of the appointment of a Private Secretary. 'Is Your Majesty afraid of the work?' Sir Herbert inquired, and on receiving the Queen's 'No', he continued: 'Then don't have a Private Secretary'. This advice the Queen followed, at least in form. Lord Melbourne combined the office of Prime Minister with that of private mentor and there followed the beneficent influence of Prince Albert as the Queen's chief adviser. Baron Stockmar acted in the capacity of Her Majesty's Private Secretary but was never so called, and it was not until after the death of the Prince Consort that the Queen appointed his former Private Secretary as her own—General Charles Grey, son of the Prime Minister of the Reform Bill.

General Grey served the Queen from 1861 to 1870 when he was succeeded by Colonel Henry Ponsonby. By this time the office of Private Secretary had become officially recognized, though Colonel Ponsonby was not sworn of the Privy Council until ten years after his appointment. On his death in 1895 he was in turn succeeded by Sir Arthur Bigge, later Lord Stamfordham.

King Edward VII on his accession appointed Sir Francis (later Viscount) Knollys, who had been his Private Secretary when Prince of Wales, in succession to Sir Arthur Bigge, who joined the Household of the Duke of Cornwall and York. When the latter came to the throne as King George V he recalled Sir Arthur, while still retaining Lord Knollys, and the office of Private Secretary was held in diarchy until the retirement of Lord Knollys in 1913. Lord Stamfordham continued to serve until his death in 1931.

Thereafter the Private Secretaries to the Sovereign have been as follows:

| | |
|---|---|
| George V | Sir Clive Wigram, 1931–1935 |
| Edward VIII | Major Alexander Hardinge, January–December 1936 |

| | |
|---|---|
| George VI | Sir Alexander Hardinge, 1936–1943 |
| | Sir Alan Lascelles, 1943–1951 |
| Elizabeth II | Sir Alan Lascelles, 1951–1953 |
| | Sir Michael Adeane, 1953– |

Though the office of Private Secretary to the Sovereign was officially accepted during the incumbency of General Grey, it is to Sir Henry Ponsonby and Lord Stamfordham, who between them occupied the office for over fifty years, that it owed the establishment of its prestige and importance. Theirs was the wisdom, the patience and the discretion which established the office, both in the mind of the Sovereign and in the mind of successive governments, as what Lord Rosebery did not hesitate to describe as being 'the most important in the public service',—a far cry from the criticisms raised in the House of Commons a hundred years before. Moreover—a development of equal importance—they set the pattern and example which their successors in office have followed so ably.

What, then, was this pattern of conduct for the Sovereign's Private Secretary, which has been handed down? It may be epitomized in the triple formula of the Sovereign's own prerogatives defined by Walter Bagehot—'the right to be consulted, the right to encourage and the right to warn'. These guiding principles may equally well apply to the Private Secretary, though, under the pressure of this modern period, too strict an interpretation of the 'right to be consulted' would be impossible.

The Private Secretary is the eyes and ears of his Sovereign. For, in order that the machinery of government may function smoothly, it is essential that the Sovereign must be fully informed on all current topics and on all basic issues. The Private Secretary plays a leading rôle, perhaps *the* leading rôle, in the maintenance of friendly relations between the Sovereign and the Ministers of the Crown; indeed, it is he more than anyone else who creates for the Sovereign the background of the régime, and from him, through his constant intercourse with all national leaders, that the general impression of the reign is largely drawn. He must owe loyalty to none but the Sovereign, whose complete confidence he must enjoy. Never must he be a Civil Servant in forced allegiance to the Government of the day. His complete independence of view must inspire confidence in the Opposition Party, which will show a good return when this party comes into power. He must know all that is going on and must be ready to advise upon all. Yet he must never so advise that he appears to influence the decision of the Sovereign in terms of the premise of his own thought.

Those who have read Lord Ponsonby's biography of his father and Sir Harold Nicolson's penetrating study of Lord Stamfordham in his biography of King George V will realize the degree to which these two men adhered in practice to the principles of their conception. Under their influence the office of Private Secretary attained the heights which it today maintains and to which so striking a tribute was paid by the late Professor Harold Laski in a review of Lord Ponsonby's book:

> . . . He [the Private Secretary] is the confidant of all Ministers, but he must never leave the impression that he is anybody's man. He must intrude without ever seeming to intrude. He must learn how to deflect the lightning from others. He must be able to carry the burden of the Sovereign's mistakes. He must not know the meaning of fatigue. He must take correction without being provoked to the humanity of remonstrance. He must accept condescension as a favour, and he must know when to be deaf and blind. He must have the art of translating attitudes into the gestures which make the royal relations possible. Receiving a thousand secrets, he must discriminate between what may emerge and what shall remain obscure. And he has to steer his way through the complicated labyrinth of anxious politicians, jealous courtiers, the mass of continental royalties, each of whom is on the watch lest a right be withheld or a claim denied.
>
> It is a life passed amid circumstances in which the most trifling incident may lead to major disaster. It is a life, too, which affords the maximum opportunity for the mischief-maker. The royal secretary walks on a tight-rope below which he is never unaware that an abyss is yawning. If the Monarch is lazy, like Edward VII, his very presence may almost become an error of judgment. If the Monarch is hard-working, like Queen Victoria, all his tact and discretion are required to keep firmly drawn the possible lines of working relations in a constitutional system. He has to be himself, since his sincerity is the crux of his position; but he must never be so insistently himself that Ministers are disturbed by his influence. It is vital that he be a judge of character; he has to thread his way through a host of influences the effective measurement of which is essential to the Monarch's position. He has to translate the obvious decisions of common sense into the elaborate formulae which the etiquette of the system requires. He must accept its pomps and ceremonies without fatigue; and he must be able to make the elegant minuet he is constantly performing capable of adaptation to a world which is constantly changing. Half of him must be in a real sense a

statesman, and the other half must be prepared, if the occasion arise, to be something it is not very easy to distinguish from a lacquey . . .

For he has to put aside his personal views; a private secretary to the Monarch who pushed his ideas might easily precipitate a crisis. He must be pretty nearly selfless; once private ambition begins to colour his horizons, his usefulness is over. He must move serenely amid all the events which move other men to passionate statement; he must seem, therefore, never to feel while he never appears to be without the power of sympathetic response. The secretary to the Monarch, in short, occupies to the Crown much the same position that the Crown itself in our system occupies to the Government; he must advise and encourage and warn. But whereas the Monarch can speak his mind—as we know from the royal letters of the last hundred years—the private secretary has no such luxury. He interprets as best he can a tradition which is never quite the same from one Monarch to another with the same Monarch . . .

. . . I do not think it is beyond the mark to say that a bad private secretary, one who was rash, or indiscreet, or untrustworthy, might easily make the system of constitutional monarchy unworkable unless the Monarch himself was a person of extraordinary wisdom. This is so because the system is built on compromises, accommodations, a process of half-measures, in which an attempt, on either side, to dominate might rapidly produce an explosive atmosphere. The Monarch, with us, has grown in influence as he has surrendered power and the very fact of that growth means that those who are playing for power will seek to capture his influence. To keep the Monarch nicely balanced in the delicate position he occupies is likely to call for a diplomatic talent of the first order.

This tribute of Professor Laski's, though directed primarily toward the conduct of Sir Henry Ponsonby, is entirely applicable to the office of Private Secretary in the present day. Within the last half-century there have been certain occasions in which, without his wise and tactful counsel, a situation might have developed in which the Crown might have become the arbiter of national destiny—a situation which it must ever be his object to prevent. Bad advice by Lord Stamfordham in 1923, when Mr Bonar Law resigned and the choice of a successor as Prime Minister lay between Mr Baldwin and Lord Curzon, or a year later, when the Labour Party first took office, might have induced a major political crisis. Similarly, an indiscretion by Sir Clive Wigram in the delicate and dangerous conditions which underlay the crisis of 1931, when King George V invited Mr MacDonald to form a National Government, might have provoked a political conflict of the first magnitude. There was the melancholy duty of Sir Alexander Hardinge in writing his famous letter to King Edward VIII in November 1936, in which he warned the Sovereign of impending crisis, and there were not infrequent occasions during the post-war years of King George VI's reign when a faulty judgment by Sir Alan Lascelles might have led to grave difficulties.

Complex and sensitive though the task of the Sovereign's Private Secretary has always been, it is increasingly so today and its importance is even more greatly enhanced. For upon his shoulders lies the major responsibility for maintaining the Crown as 'a dignified emollient', an essential and vital element in the metaphysics of constitutional monarchy. Nor is this all. With the emergence of the New Commonwealth the Private Secretary has become the sole link between the Sovereign and her Governors-General overseas, and between her Majesty and her Prime Ministers, not only in Westminster but also in Ottawa, Canberra, Wellington, Cape Town, Colombo and Accra. He must 'shape the whisper to the Throne' as it is spoken in not one but seven countries, for all have equal right of access to their Sovereign, and the channel of that access is the office of the Private Secretary.

Such is the task and the trust of one of the least known but most responsible officers of the Crown, for in his hands, more perhaps than in those of any other individual in the Commonwealth, lies the continued well-being of the Monarchy. As Sir Alan Lascelles informed the Select Committee on the Civil List in December 1947:

> Any Member of the Committee who may have read Sir Henry Ponsonby's letters, or an excellent article by Professor Harold Laski in the *Fortnightly* a year or two ago, will know what I mean when I say that life in that office is not by any means beer and skittles. His [the Private Secretary's] work, both in volume and in responsibility, is continually increasing . . .
>
> In my office at present we compare unfavourably with our relative opposite numbers in the Civil Service, as regards man-hours per day, as regards pay, and as regards leave. We serve, I may remind you, one of the very few men in this world who never gets a holiday at all and who, unlike the rest of us, can look forward to no period of retirement at the end of his Service, for his Service never ends.

[Sir John Wheeler-Bennett, *King George VI: His Life and Reign* (London, 1958), Appendix B.]

(*b*) *The outgoing Prime Minister*

*The Queen may seek the views of the outgoing Prime Minister, so long as this is not taken as being formal ministerial advice.*

## (3) THE SECOND DISSOLUTION

*If a government, formed after the return of a hung Parliament, were defeated on a vote of confidence, would the Prime Minister be entitled to obtain a dissolution of Parliament?*

(*a*) *No automatic dissolution*

It is generally agreed that there are at least some occasions on which the Queen is entitled to refuse to act on ministerial advice to dissolve Parliament. Mr Harold Macmillan indeed preferred to speak of 'requesting a dissolution' rather than 'advising' one, on the ground that 'advice in the long run the Crown must today accept'. It is not clear what he had in mind by 'the long run', but it seems unnecessary to treat ministerial 'advice' as if it meant 'binding advice' and better to suppose that there are degrees of freedom or discretion in complying with the advice offered by ministers.

A similar oddity about 'advice' is the notion that the Queen cannot act without advice and that for every act of the Crown some Minister is responsible. This presents difficulties both in relation to changes of government and to dissolution. When a Prime Minister resigns, his advice as to his successor is not treated as binding advice and indeed it is supposed that he is under no duty to volunteer it. Some writers used to suggest that the responsibility for appointment of an incoming Prime Minister fell (by a curious piece of constitutional acrobatics) on the succeeding Minister himself. Professor Berriedale Keith, for example, held that when a Minister accepts office 'he assumes therewith the duty of defending the formation of the new ministry', quoting Peel's remark after Melbourne's apparent dismissal in 1834 'I am by my acceptance of office responsible for the removal of the late government.' Sir Ivor Jennings disapproved of this notion as 'a pure fiction'. A similar view may be taken of the supposition that a new appointee may be held to have retrospectively authorized or advised the refusal of a dissolution to his predecessor. That might be thought an even more rarefied fiction. The fiction or allegation is plainly inconsistent with the labelling of some prerogative acts, including appointment of Ministers and dissolution of Parliament, as personal prerogatives. If that means anything, it means that they are taken on the Queen's own responsibility and not on ministerial advice.

The term 'personal prerogative' is perhaps not entirely a happy label for appointment, dissolution, and assent to legislation (though Sir Ivor Jennings in *Cabinet Government* devotes a chapter to the personal prerogatives under that name). In fact all three prerogatives are in the great majority of cases not exercised in accordance with any personal discretion. They only become personally exercised prerogatives in the few exceptional cases in which an independent judgment must be exercised in appointing a Prime Minister or refusing ministerial advice. But in those cases it cannot be said that the Queen's powers are exercised indirectly or remotely on retrospective advice. The responsibility must be the Queen's own. No British monarch in modern times has in fact dismissed a government or refused to assent to legislation or to dissolve Parliament, but where the so-called personal prerogative has been exercised in a Commonwealth country, it clearly has not been possible to avoid direct popular judgment of the Governor-General's actions by any supposition that they were retrospectively underpinned by ministerial advice.

What then of the possible occasions in the United Kingdom for a personal exercise of the prerogative to refuse a dissolution of Parliament? Some have argued that the prerogative is obsolete or should be made so. In 1938 Professor Harold Laski in his *Parliamentary Government in England* argued that after disuse for over a hundred years the prerogative of refusal could not be revived, and he expressed a similar view in his *Reflections on the Constitution* in 1951. In 1982 Mr Anthony Wedgwood Benn proposed that Parliament should transfer the Crown's prerogative in relation to appointment and dissolution to the Speaker of the House of Commons. In 1974 some Labour Members of Parliament argued that the Prime Minister had 'an absolute right to decide the date of the election and that the Queen was bound to grant a dissolution whenever the Prime Minister after discussion with his Cabinet colleagues requested it'. After the election of February 1974 no party had an absolute majority in the House of Commons and Mr Wilson's supporters may well have felt some apprehension that refusal of a request to dissolve Parliament might be the prelude to the formation of a Conservative–Liberal coalition. A situation in which a minority government is in office raises directly the question whether such a government is entitled at a time of its own choosing to appeal for a renewed electoral mandate, though its political opponents might be willing to assume office. Given the desirability of the Queen's remaining free from political involvement or partisan controversy, and given the certainty that installation of a Conservative or Liberal –SDP government by the Queen would attract violent criticism by the Labour Party, the prudential arguments for supposing that a General Election would present lesser evils seem obvious.

On the other hand, to admit an automatic right of any government to dissolve Parliament at any time would run counter to the views expressed by most constitutional authorities. That was conceded in 1974 by the Leader of the House of Commons, Mr Edward Short, whose reply to his back-benchers noted that 'Constitutional lawyers of the highest authority are of the clear opinion that the sovereign is not in all circumstances bound to grant a Prime Minister's request for a dissolution.' That view was stated categorically by Asquith in 1923 in discussing the entitlement of MacDonald's minority Labour Government to dissolve Parliament. Dissolution, he said, was not a mere feudal survival but a useful part of the Constitution. He added:

> It does not mean that the Crown should act arbitrarily and without the advice of responsible ministers, but it does mean that the Crown is not bound to take the advice of a particular minister to put its subjects to the tumult and turmoil of a series of general elections so long as it can find other ministers who are prepared to give it a trial. The notion that a Minister—a Minister who cannot command a majority in the House of Commons—is invested with the right to demand a dissolution is as subversive of constitutional usage as it would, in my opinion, be pernicious to the general and paramount interests of the nation at large.

Asquith was, of course, discussing the right of a minority government to appeal to the electorate. How far does his conclusion apply to a government that has a majority over all other parties? Can the existence of a prerogative power vary with the state of the parties? To that question the appropriate answer seems to be that whilst the existence of the legal prerogative is not affected, the conventional rules for its exercise are in fact different in situations of majority and minority government. There is perhaps one limitation that is generally perceived as applying even to a government with an overall majority; namely that a series of dissolutions aimed at securing successive increases in its majority would merit refusal. Repeated requests for dissolution would certainly be an improper putting of the country to the tumult and turmoil of General Elections. But it is so improbable a contingency that it has perhaps not been felt necessary to ask how the Queen could exercise the constitutional right to refuse advice even in the face of such an extreme course of action if the government could by its numerical support prevent the working of any alternative government.

The importance of that point became clear in 1950 when the Labour Government of Mr Clement Attlee took office. His 315 seats in the House of Commons gave him a majority over all other parties combined, though, being a majority of six, it was not one that was satisfactory to the Labour Party or one which in their opponents' view gave them a clear mandate to put their programme into effect. In his life of King George VI, Sir John Wheeler-Bennett noted that the majority was 'so narrow that it would not enable them to proceed nor justify them in trying to proceed'. A question was thus faced by the King as to his proper course of action if Mr Attlee should request an immediate dissolution of Parliament. Mr Winston Churchill in a letter to the King's Private Secretary asserted the principle that 'a new House of Commons has a right to live if it can and should not be destroyed until some fresh issue or situation has arisen to place before the electors'. This was perhaps reminiscent of earlier nineteenth-century views of dissolution that there should be some important political question at issue to justify an appeal to the electorate. But Sir Alan Lascelles's advice to the King rested on the different and more expedient ground that there did not seem any possibility of forming an alternative government. When Sir Alan later wrote to *The Times* (under the pseudonym 'Senex'), he suggested that a dissolution might be refused if (1) the existing Parliament was still vital and capable of doing its job, (2) a General Election would be detrimental to the national economy, and (3) the King could rely on finding another Prime Minister who could carry on his government for a reasonable period with a working majority in the House of Commons. Clearly the third consideration is the crucial one; and it was on that ground that the King was advised that though he would be 'perfectly entitled' to refuse a dissolution to Attlee if he were persuaded that the sitting Parliament had not exhausted its usefulness and that the country's interest demanded the postponement of a General Election, it was 'doubtful whether the argument is valid in present circumstances'. Perhaps a clearer way of summarizing the position would have been to say that in the absence of a viable alternative government the King was *not* constitutionally entitled to refuse a dissolution, whatever his views on the viability of Parliament or the need for a General Election. Sir Alan Lascelles's advice referred to the occasion in 1926 on which the then Prime Minister of Canada, Mr Mackenzie King, was refused a dissolution by the Governor-General. Lascelles remarked that it was questionable if this refusal did any good and that it left a considerable legacy of bitterness against the Crown. The relevant point about the Canadian precedent, however, was that the Governor-General was not able, as it turned out, to meet the third condition as to an alternative government capable of carrying on for a reasonable period. A refusal of dissolution to the Hertzog government in South Africa in 1939, on the other hand, was followed by the establishment of an alternative government under General Smuts. If that had happened in Canada, it might still have led to bitterness against the Crown and the Governor-General, but such criticism should presumably not in itself constitute a bar to the exercise of the prerogative in a proper case.

Clearly, situations in which there is no overall majority are those in which the possibility of finding alternative Ministers will occur. Asquith's declaration that a minority government does not have an automatic right to a dissolution does not distinguish between a government that has asked for a dissolution without having been defeated and a government that has been defeated either on a vote of confidence or on major legislative proposals. Nor is there anything in Lascelles's advice to George VI which turns on the question whether a government requesting dissolution has suffered defeat (since he was considering the likelihood of a request from Attlee's majority government). In summing up the conclusions of his study of the dissolution power, Dr Markesinis makes no distinction, saying that 'The Crown may under certain circumstances refuse a dissolution to a minority government (whether defeated or undefeated), provided an alternative government is possible and able to carry on with the existing House.' It is unclear whether in principle being undefeated should increase or diminish a government's entitlement to be allowed to dissolve. If a government were undefeated because an immediate request to dissolve had been made before the House had been allowed to meet, then absence of defeat would not enhance the government's claim. Moreover, a request that is made to avoid defeat or censure, or a request made whilst a motion of censure is under debate should equally not enhance a claim to dissolve.

In the future situations that are likely to arise if electoral reform or changes in the number and relationships of the parties produce a House of Commons in which no single party can take office with an overall majority, requests for dissolution are likely to come from either single-party minority governments or coalition governments that find their programme obstructed, or who are defeated on issues of confidence. Whether such a government should be allowed to appeal to the country for support, or whether positive efforts should be made by the Queen to enlist the support of other party leaders in forming an alternative government without an election, would present a difficult and delicate question for decision. A Social Democratic/Liberal government would not easily be replaceable by any conceivable combination of Conservative and Labour politicians. A Labour minority government might more easily be replaced by a formal or informal grouping of Conservatives and Liberals or Alliance members. It might or might not be the case that a different single party would be willing to take office as a minority government. But should the issue be raised by the Queen or, if raised by the parties, should the Queen respond? A Labour government that was refused a dissolution would almost certainly criticize the refusal as partisan, as the Liberals in Canada did in 1926, on the ground that the Crown would in due course be compelled to grant a dissolution to the alternative party or party grouping, having refused it to the government in office. That would not be a strong argument since the two refusals would be in different situations and on different grounds. Nevertheless the argument would certainly be used by critics of the Queen's action. It seems likely that if a government, whether minority or coalition, had been in office for a significant period and if some time had passed since the last General Election, the alternative of granting dissolution would present less difficulties and arouse less controversy than an attempt to send for an alternative Prime Minister or to issue invitations to opposition leaders to form a government (thus assuming the burden of judging whether any given combination of alternative office-holders could be assured of continuing support in the Commons). Nevertheless in other situations and if little time has passed since the last election, a difficult and controversial judgment by the Queen might still be required. There is also the possibility in an era of multi-party governmental groupings that requests for dissolution might be disputed or resisted within the governmental party or that the coalition leader might be held to be requesting dissolution to preserve his own position or for narrow party political reasons. (He might even have been removed from his leadership of the party by antagonistic party followers.) In these situations criticism of the Crown will be less if the conventions are clear. The last possibility suggests some consideration of the conventional rules governing the relationship of the Prime Minister and the Cabinet.

[Marshall, *Constitutional Conventions*, 35–42.]

### *Dissolution of Parliament*

In the absence of a regular term for the life of Parliament fixed by statute, the Sovereign may by the prerogative dissolve Parliament and cause a general election to be held. The Sovereign normally accepts the advice of the Prime Minister and grants a dissolution when this is requested. Since 1918, it has become established practice that a Cabinet decision is not necessary before the Prime Minister may seek a dissolution, although members of the Cabinet may be consulted before the Prime Minister makes his decision. The refusal of a dissolution when the Prime Minister had requested it would probably be treated by him as tantamount to a dismissal. Are there circumstances in which the Sovereign would be justified in refusing a dissolution or is it automatic that the Sovereign should grant a dissolution when requested?

It is doubtful whether there can be grounds for the refusal of a dissolution to a Prime Minister who commands a clear majority in the Commons. Our political practice accepts that a Prime Minister may choose his own time for a general election within the five-year life of Parliament prescribed by the Parliament Act 1911. If a Sovereign did refuse dissolution to a Prime Minister who commanded a majority in a House, and the Prime Minister then resigned from office with the other ministers, any other politician invited to be Prime Minister (for example, the leader of the Opposition) would presumably have no prospect of a majority at Westminster until an election had been held. The Sovereign would therefore be faced with an early request for a dissolution from the new Prime Minister and with inevitable criticism for political bias if he granted this request. Where a minority government holds office, the position is more complicated but here again it is for the Prime Minister rather than the Sovereign to choose the time for an election. Much would depend on the circumstances in which the minority government had come about and on how recently a general election had been held. Thus a Prime Minister who had been granted one dissolution and failed to get a majority at the ensuing election, could scarcely request a second dissolution immediately. His duty would be to resign and to give the leader of another party the opportunity of forming a government. Where a Prime Minister had been in office for a considerable period (for example, some months) since the previous election, and was then defeated on an issue of confidence in the House, he would then have a choice between resigning or, as MacDonald did in 1924, seeking a dissolution.

In 1950, during discussion of the problems caused by the Labour government's small majority after the 1950 election, it was submitted by the Private Secretary to George VI that the Sovereign could properly refuse a dissolution if he were satisfied that (a) the existing Parliament was still 'vital, viable, and capable of doing its job', (b) a general election would be detrimental to the national economy and (c) he could rely on finding another Prime Minister who could carry on his government for a reasonable period with a working majority. It will be seldom that all these conditions can be satisfied, and it might be argued that these are eminently matters for the Prime Minister in office to decide. It might be particularly difficult for the Sovereign to be reasonably certain that another Prime Minister could command a working majority in the House. Yet the Sovereign would be strongly criticised if having refused a dissolution to one Prime Minister he was faced with an early request from his successor for dissolution.

In the last 100 years there are no instances of the Sovereign having refused a dissolution in the United Kingdom, but there are two leading illustrations of the problem from the former Dominions where the prerogative was exercisable by the Governor-General. In 1939 the Governor-General of South Africa refused a dissolution to the Prime Minister, General Hertzog, whose proposal that South

Africa should be neutral in the Second World War had been defeated in Parliament, and he invited General Smuts to form a government which remained in power thereafter. But in 1926, the Governor-General of Canada, Lord Byng, refused a dissolution to the Liberal leader, Mackenzie King, and instead invited Meighen, the Conservative leader, to form a government believing that Meighen would be supported by a third party which held the balance of power. When that support failed within a matter of days, Meighen sought a dissolution of Parliament which was granted by Lord Byng: the ensuing election was won by the Liberals and the Governor-General was much criticised for his decisions.

The controversy between the 'automatic' and 'discretionary' views of the prerogative of dissolution was raised again in 1969. Although at that time Labour had a clear majority in the Commons, there were press reports of Labour dissension within the party. The question was raised whether a Prime Minister could use the weapon of dissolution to defend his own position against attempts within the party to dislodge him. In 1974, after the election in February 1974, when no party had an absolute majority, the question was raised whether Mr Wilson as Prime Minister was entitled to a dissolution if his government were defeated in the Commons by a combined opposition vote. Certain Labour M.P.s, who feared that a Liberal-Conservative coalition might be formed to govern the country, urged that the Sovereign was both constitutionally and morally bound to grant dissolution whenever the Prime Minister requested it. In reply, the Lord President of the Council, Mr Short, told them: 'Constitutional lawyers of the highest authority are of the clear opinion that the Sovereign is not in all circumstances bound to grant a Prime Minister's request for dissolution'; it was impossible to define in advance the circumstances in which the Sovereign's discretion to refuse a request for a dissolution might be exercised. There the matter had to rest, since the government refused to allow the matter to be debated in the Commons. In the event, when Mr Wilson sought a dissolution in September 1974, this was granted without question by the Sovereign.

That the Sovereign should not refuse a Prime Minister's request for dissolution except for very strong reason is obvious. In practice, the political significance of the Prime Minister's power to decide when Parliament should be dissolved is much greater than the possibility of the Sovereign's refusal of a dissolution. But the view that the Sovereign's reserve power may serve to restrain a Prime Minister who otherwise might be tempted to abuse his position is an argument for maintaining the reserve power as a potential weapon, not for abolishing it.

[Wade and Bradley, *Constitutional and Administrative Law* (London, 10th edn., 1985, by A. W. Bradley), 239–41.]

The decision [to hold the 1959 general election] had now been taken, and accordingly on 7 September, after first stopping at Aboyne where I had a talk with James Stuart,

> I went on to Balmoral, arriving about 6.15. Audience before dinner. The Queen was very gracious. I ventured to impress on her that a P.M. had no right to 'advise' a dissolution. 'Advice', in the long run, the Crown must today accept. The P.M. 'asks' for a dissolution, which the Crown can agree to or not. This, the last great prerogative of the Crown, must be preserved. It might be of vital importance at a time of national crisis.

The Queen formally agreed to my request. The date seemed to her well chosen.

[Macmillan, *Riding the Storm*, 750.]

April 29

Sir,

It is surely indisputable (and common sense) that a Prime Minister may ask—not demand—that his Sovereign will grant him a dissolution of Parliament; and that the Sovereign, if he so chooses, may refuse to grant this request. The problem of such a choice is entirely personal to the Sovereign, though he is, of course, free to seek informal advice from anybody whom he thinks fit to consult.

In so far as this matter can be publicly discussed, it can be properly assumed that no wise Sovereign—that is, one who has at heart the true interest of the country, the constitution, and the Monarchy—would deny a dissolution to his Prime Minister unless he were satisfied that: (1) the existing Parliament was still vital, viable, and capable of doing its job; (2) a General Election would be detrimental to the national economy; (3) he could rely on finding another Prime Minister who could carry on his Government, for a reasonable period, with a working majority in the House of Commons. When Sir Patrick Duncan refused a dissolution to his

Prime Minister in South Africa in 1939, all these conditions were satisfied: when Lord Byng did the same in Canada in 1926, they appeared to be, but in the event the third proved illusory.

I am, etc.,
SENEX

[Sir Alan Lascelles, Private Secretary to King George VI, writing as 'Senex' in a letter to *The Times*, 2 May 1950.]

### (*b*) *Possible ways forward*

One way out of this dilemma seems attractive. The Palace could intimate (during a time of political peace, when it could not be seen who might be advantaged or hurt by the decision) that a dissolution would be granted only when it was plain that there was no possibility of a majority government emerging from the current House. Such an intimation could, of course, come in response to a resolution from Parliament but, equally, it might be volunteered. The sovereign, without abandoning any formal prerogative, would be making plain the neutral way in which the umpire's role would be exercised. Just as the Speaker exercises his casting vote on principles laid down in Erskine May's *Parliamentary Practice* and escapes all suspicion of partiality, so the Palace, by setting out its mechanical decision rules in advance, can avoid embarrassing imputations.

One device, suggested in 1974, has its possibilities. A no confidence motion, or an Opposition amendment to the Queen's Speech, could contain within its wording a humble suggestion that, if it was carried, the Prime Minister should not be granted a dissolution or that another government was available. Formally the House of Commons has no authority over the sovereign and the use of the royal prerogative cannot be the subject of debate. But nothing in Standing Orders would prevent the House from expressing its desires, even if the passage of the motion could have no binding force on the sovereign.

This would not go so far as the rule in countries where the legislature can be dissolved before the statutory end of its four-year term only if there is a clear majority vote by its own members. If this were accepted practice in Britain, the sovereign would be freed from the possibility of having to exercise a potentially embarrassing discretion.

To refer all decisions over dissolution to the House of Commons does not guarantee a solution to all crises. It is hypothetically possible to conceive of a House of Commons that refused to vote for its own dissolution, even though it was unable to produce a viable government from its current membership. No set of rules can save a democracy from a totally obstinate refusal to compromise by its politicians. However, the dilemma envisaged here has not, in fact, been a problem in any of the Commonwealth or European countries with a comparable parliamentary system. Crises do get solved, usually fairly quickly, either by the emergence of a coalition or a minority government with a reasonable expectation of life, or by a dissolution. And politicians are always inhibited in criticizing a dissolution; what, after all, is a dissolution but the referring of a political problem to the decision of the politicians' ultimate 'sovereign'—the people?

[David Butler, *Governing Without a Majority* (London, 2nd edn., 1986), 132–3.]

(1) If a government continues in office as a minority administration after an inconclusive general election obtained by its Prime Minister and is immediately defeated on an amendment to the loyal address in reply to the Queen's Speech, there is no precedent for such a Prime Minister seeking a second dissolution; rather, there is ample precedent for him to resign. Baldwin resigned in just that circumstance in 1924. Any such request would be improper because it would smack of an attempt to get a recount of the electorate's first decision (a decision recorded at the Prime Minister's asking). If any such request were made, it would rightly be rejected. Such a refusal of ministerial advice could be said to involve the indirect dismissal of the government.

(2) If either a minority or coalition government is formed from a hung House of Commons and the new Prime Minister had not obtained the first dissolution, then a request by him at any time for a general election should be granted—although I will argue shortly that the alternative course of the Queen seeking another administration should not be ruled out. The first part of this proposition can be demonstrated from the 1974 hung Parliament. Harold Wilson clearly assumed that, since he had formed the minority Labour government in March 1974, a dissolution was his for the asking at the time of his choosing (and certainly if the opposition parties were to defeat his

government on a vote of confidence). That assumption, it is submitted, was entirely right. His predecessor Mr Heath had been granted the February 1974 dissolution, so that Mr Wilson's request would be his first; and Mr Heath and Mr Thorpe had shown in their abortive talks in February that a Conservative-Liberal coalition could not be formed from that House. A Prime Minister in a position similar to that of Harold Wilson would, like him, have a clearer right to a dissolution the longer the hung Parliament were to last, as that Parliament would have done its job for a period and there could be no convincing allegation that he was really seeking an improper recount. Equally, the Queen would not want to look for an alternative government in such a case.

(3) If a Prime Minister of either a minority or a coalition government in a hung Parliament were to ask for a general election, even for his first time, in order to forestall another majority and workable grouping supplanting his administration, then again refusal would be defensible if that alternative grouping in fact existed. Suppose that, after an inconclusive general election, a Conservative-third party coalition were formed but that eventually a disagreement on some central issue arose. Suppose further that the third party threatened to resign and join a willing Labour Party in a new majority coalition in return for an agreed programme. The Conservative-third party Prime Minister might recommend an immediate election to thwart the coup. The Queen would be required to reconcile two conflicting consitutional principles, the one being that she must accept ministerial advice (here, to dissolve), the other being that a person with a parliamentary majority behind him has the right to be Prime Minister (here, the head of the proposed new coalition). In favour of Her Majesty applying the second principle would be the facts that the Prime Minister would be seeking a dissolution with the improper motive of trying to prevent his ouster from office by an adverse parliamentary majority, and also that a new majority government could be installed without the need for a general election. If the Queen were to apply that second principle and refuse a dissolution, the government would resign and the new Labour-third party administration would take office.

Inherent in the second and third propositions is the question of the presence of an alternative majority government in the existing House of Commons. One major reason in favour of the 'automatic theory' of dissolution is the predictable allegation of bias which would be made against the Queen if she were to refuse a general election to the Prime Minister in the mistaken belief that another government could be formed, and could carry on without an election, when in the event that new government were forced to seek, and was granted, the very thing which had been denied its predecessor. I suggest that, as with the primary decision whether to commission a minority government or a coalition on the return of a hung Parliament, those party Leaders who were wanting to form a majority coalition (so as here to remove the need for dissolution) would have to make public an agreed and watertight package concerning the majority government in waiting. Nothing less than that would do if the Queen were to feel sufficiently confident to take the novel course of refusing a dissolution of Parliament and of bringing about a new administration. This would, in a way, be an example not of revolutionary royal interventionism but of the Queen giving effect to the wishes of Members of Parliament—it would once again be the proper recognition of political decisions, politically arrived at.

Events in Ontario in 1985 give significant support for my approach. Ontario has a system of government which, within the Canadian federation, is similar to Britain's. Elections to the 125-seat Legislative Assembly have to take place every four years, but earlier dissolution is possible. The Premier is appointed by the Queen's representative in the province, the Lieutenant-Governor, and is usually the Leader of the majority party in the Assembly: indeed, the Progressive Conservative Party had enjoyed such a majority for decades. In 1985 the Premier, Mr William Davis, asked for a dissolution from the Lieutenant-Governor, Mr John Black Aird, which was granted. The result gave the Progressive Conservatives fifty-two seats, the Liberals forty-eight, and the New Democrats twenty-five. Mr Davis decided to form a minority government; the Liberals and the New Democrats, meanwhile, formally agreed on a two-year programme of government, including an agreement that there should be no general election within that period. The Conservatives' Speech from the Throne was duly defeated and a motion of no confidence in Mr Davis's government was passed. The Lieutenant-Governor had caused it to be made clear informally that, if the Premier were to ask for a second dissolution, that request would be denied as there was a viable alternative government waiting in the Assembly which, as the result of its public pact, would have a very fair prospect of governing for at least two years. Not surprisingly, Mr Davis made no such request, but resigned, and the Leader of the Liberal Party was appointed Premier.

This Ontario episode shows, perhaps, in the British context that the 'automatic theory' of dissolution is dead (assuming that it ever lived); that a minority government, having received one dissolution, will not receive another dissolution, if beaten on an early vote of confidence; that a published copper-bottomed party pact on an alternative government can avoid any embarrassment of having to grant a dissolution to one head of government having refused it to his predecessor; and that an informal communication of the Queen's attitude, in response to the published agreement of some party Leaders prepared to take over the government without a dissolution, avoids, among other things, the general embarrassment of the tendering of formal ministerial advice and its formal rejection.

Of course it would be less controversial for the Queen to accept a request to dissolve Parliament than to seek an alternative. I have, however, posed three cases which could arise in a hung Parliament in which a royal refusal would be possible.

[Brazier, *Constitutional Practice*, 40–3.]

The government of Queensland is constituted by members of the National party of Australia. Members of the National party command a majority on the floor of the Legislative Assembly. The Hon. Sir J. Bjelke-Petersen K.C.M.G., M.L.A. had held the leadership of the party, and the office of Premier of Queensland since 1968. On November 24, 1987 a majority of the parliamentary members of the National party elected the Hon. M. J. Ahern, M.L.A. as the leader of the parliamentary party. Mr Ahern had just been dismissed from office as Minister for Health and Environment of Queensland; his appointment as a member of the Executive Council was also terminated. Two other ministers of the Crown had similarly been dismissed from office. It appears that the Premier had initially sought the removal from office of five ministers of the Crown. The Governor of Queensland, the Hon. Sir Walter Campbell Q.C., had agreed to terminate the appointment of three ministers. Under an

Act of 1987, members of the Executive Council of Queensland may be removed from office by the Governor. This statute restated earlier Letters Patent of 1986 which constituted the office of Governor. The appointments of the members of the Executive Council would have been terminated by the Governor under the Letters Patent as the statute was assented to on December 1, 1987.

After their election to the party leadership, Mr Ahern and his deputy informed the Governor of the fact of their election. Mr Ahern presented a memorandum to the Governor which was signed by all National party members of the Legislative Assembly except the Premier. The memorandum expressed confidence in the leadership of Mr Ahern. It is reported that the Governor declined to withdraw the Commission of the Premier. His Excellency considered that the matter should be determined by the Parliament, if the Premier declined to resign. It might be mentioned that a motion of no-confidence in the administration by the Premier of the government had been defeated a few weeks prior to these events. On December 1,1987 the Premier resigned his office as Premier. In these circumstances, the Governor commissioned Mr Ahern, the leader of the Parliamentary party, as Premier. It seems that the Governor would then have had regard to the memorandum of support. On December 2, 1987 the Legislative Assembly passed a motion of confidence in Mr Ahern.

The decision of the Governor not to initially withdraw the Commission of the Premier was in accordance with a Queensland precedent of the last century. In 1871 the government of Queensland was sustained in office by a majority of one. Twelve members of the parliamentary opposition addressed the Governor requesting him to intervene in the administration of the government. The Governor (the Marquis of Normanby) replied to the memorial by stating that he 'must decline to accept the opinion of twelve members as the decision of a house constituted of thirty-two representatives of the people.' However, the decision of the then Governor appears not to have been solely based upon the numerical strength of the petitioners. The decision appears to have also rested upon the appropriate forum which must determine such a question. His Excellency also stated, 'I shall always be found ready to pay the greatest deference to the opinion of parliament, but that opinion must be expressed by the majority of the Assembly in their legislative capacity, and not by a majority without the walls of the House of

Assembly.' These remarks have relevance to the present case, particularly in view of the fact that the former Premier had recently survived a motion of no-confidence.

[P. M. McDermott, 'Queensland Revisited' [1988] *Public Law*, 31–2.]

# [2]

# THE TRANSFER OF POWER

## Why Prime Ministers Resign

### 1. ELECTORAL DEFEAT

*If a government is defeated at a general election and one opposition party is returned with a majority of seats in the new House of Commons, the modern practice is for that government to resign without meeting Parliament. If a government is defeated on a vote of no confidence, the Prime Minister will recommend a dissolution of Parliament to the Queen.*

Mr Speaker, now that the House of Commons has declared itself, we shall take our case to the people. Tomorrow I shall propose to Her Majesty that Parliament be dissolved as soon as essential business can be cleared up, and I shall then announce as soon as may be—and that will be as soon as possible—the date of the Dissolution, the date of the election and the date of the meeting of the new Parliament.

[The Prime Minister, Mr James Callaghan, following a vote of no confidence in his government which had been carried by one vote: 965 H.C. Deb. 589 (28 March 1979).]

### 2. PERSONAL REASONS

*A Prime Minister may be forced to quit through illness (Campbell-Bannerman 1908, Bonar Law 1923, Eden 1957, Macmillan 1963), old age (Salisbury 1902, MacDonald 1935, Churchill 1955), or he may die, or he may voluntarily decide to retire (Baldwin 1937, Wilson 1976). His or her party will then elect a successor who will be appointed Prime Minister (see chapter 1).*

In March 1974 I decided that I would remain in office for no more than two years. I have not wavered in this decision, and it is irrevocable . . . I must, of course, inform my colleagues of my reasons. First, I have been Leader of this Party for over thirteen exciting and turbulent years—nearly eight of them in Government. My period as Prime Minister has been longer than that of any of my peacetime predecessors in this century . . . Second, I have a clear duty to the country and to the Party not to remain here so long that others are denied the chance to seek election to this post . . . Third, it is my view that my successor should be in post now, to impose his or her style and to work out the strategy for the remaining years of this Parliament . . . Fourth, there *is* a danger, to which I have been alerted all my working life. It is that, in times of rapid change, you may be faced with a decision which, perhaps in different conditions, you have faced before. If, on the earlier occasions you considered and rejected a particular course of action, there *is* a tendency to say you have been into that, so that you do not give the fresh consideration the circumstances may require. I am determined not to succumb to this danger. I want to make it quite clear . . . that these reasons represent the total explanation of my decision.

[Harold Wilson's statement to the Cabinet, 16 March 1976, having informed the Queen of his intention to resign. See *Final Term: The Labour Government 1974–1976* (London, 1979), 301–2.]

## 3. FORMATION OF A NEW GOVERNMENT

*The resignation of a Prime Minister and his immediate reappointment may take place to show that the whole political basis of the government is to change. There have been three examples this century.*

### (1) 1915: WAR COALITION

After much reflection, and consultation today with Lloyd George and Bonar Law, I have come decidedly to the conclusion that, for the successful prosecution of the war, the Government must be reconstructed on a broad and non-party basis.

*Asquith reached agreement on a coalition and was appointed Prime Minister of it.*

[Asquith's papers, 19 May 1915, quoted in Roy Jenkins, *Asquith* (London, Fontana edn., 1967), 403.]

### (2) 1931: 'NATIONAL GOVERNMENT'

At ten o'clock [on 24 August 1931 MacDonald] and the other two party leaders were received by the King. MacDonald said that he had the Cabinet's resignation in his pocket, but the King replied that he trusted that there was no question of the prime minister's resignation. He hoped that the prime minister would help in the formation of a National Government, which the King was sure would be supported by the Conservatives and the Liberals. The King assured the prime minister that, remaining at his post, his position and reputation would be much more enhanced than if he surrendered the Government of the country at such a crisis. The King's appeal turned the scales. By 10.35 it had been agreed that Baldwin and Samuel would serve under MacDonald in a National Government . . .

*MacDonald formally resigned later that day and was immediately appointed Prime Minister of the National Government.*

[David Marquand, *Ramsay MacDonald* (London, 1977), 636–7, 643.]

### (3) 1945: CARETAKER GOVERNMENT

At noon on Wednesday May 23, Churchill went to Buckingham Palace, where, in an audience with King George VI, he tendered his resignation . . . Then, driving back to Buckingham Palace at four o'clock that afternoon, he was invited to form a new administration.

*The caretaker Conservative government which Churchill then formed was heavily defeated at the 1945 general election.*

[Martin Gilbert, *Never Despair: Winston Churchill 1945–1955* (London, 1988), 22–3.]

## Formal Appointment of a Prime Minister

*The Prime Minister must be a Privy Councillor; he is invariably also appointed First Lord of the Treasury (the Ministerial and other*

*Salaries Act 1975, s. 1(1) and Schedule 1 link the two offices for salary purposes), and, since 1968, is also Minister for the Civil Service.*

On January 22nd [1924], Baldwin left office. At midday, MacDonald went to the palace to be sworn of the privy council . . . In the afternoon he returned to kiss hands as prime minister.

[Marquand, op. cit. 304.]

The Prime Minister accepts office by attending The Queen in private audience. The appointment—and as First Lord of the Treasury—takes effect from that moment. At the audience the new Prime Minister kisses hands. There are no other formalities.

[Memorandum of Mr Geoffrey de Deney, Clerk of the Privy Council, para. 7, reproduced in full below: see p. 133.]

*In unusual circumstances a Prime Minister may take another portfolio as well. Asquith was also Secretary of State for War during the Curragh crisis in 1914; Baldwin remained Chancellor of the Exchequer for five months after becoming Prime Minister in 1923 during the convalescence of Reginald McKenna; MacDonald was his own Foreign Secretary in 1924; and Churchill was also Minister of Defence throughout his war premiership and in 1951–2, as was Attlee for the first 17 months of his government. Harold Wilson took personal charge of the Department of Economic Affairs in 1967–68, but a Secretary of State remained at its head.*

I took over that responsibility last August because I was not satisfied with the co-ordination among the industrial departments on industrial work . . . I retain my present and previous responsibility for the co-ordination, not only of industrial matters, but of economic matters in general; and this will continue.

[Mr Harold Wilson explaining why he had taken charge of the Department of Economic Affairs: 762 H.C. Deb. 1582 (11 April 1968).]

## Choosing the Cabinet

*Any modern Cabinet will consist of some 18 to 24 Ministers, and all the main departments of state will be represented in it. A Prime*

*Minister will be constrained to include certain people in the Cabinet by virtue of their seniority in the government party and experience in office and opposition. New Cabinet Ministers will, in the main, be given the portfolio which they had shadowed in opposition. The Parliamentary Labour Party has standing orders which are designed to limit a Labour Prime Minister's choices.*

[See generally Rodney Brazier, 'The Constitutional Role of the Opposition' (1989) 40 *Northern Ireland Legal Quarterly* 131.]

## 1. MRS THATCHER'S CABINET IN 1990

*In 1990 the Cabinet contained the following ministers:*

Prime Minister, First Lord of the Treasury and Minister for the Civil Service
Lord President of the Council and Leader of the House of Commons
Secretary of State for Foreign and Commonwealth Affairs
Chancellor of the Exchequer
Lord Chancellor
Secretary of State for the Home Department
Secretary of State for Defence
Secretary of State for Employment
Secretary of State for Northern Ireland
Secretary of State for the Environment
Secretary of State for Trade and Industry and President of the Board of Trade
Chancellor of the Duchy of Lancaster
Secretary of State for Education and Science
Secretary of State for Health
Minister of Agriculture, Fisheries and Food
Secretary of State for Scotland
Secretary of State for Transport
Secretary of State for Social Security
Lord Privy Seal and Leader of the House of Lords
Secretary of State for Wales
Secretary of State for Energy
Chief Secretary to the Treasury

## 2. A LABOUR CABINET

In Opposition, the composition of the Parliamentary Committee shall be the four Officers of the PLP, eighteen members of the

Parliamentary Party having seats in the House of Commons, elected by the Members of the Party in the House of Commons; the Leader and Chief Whip of the Labour Peers and one member of the House of Lords all elected by the Labour Peers.

[Parliamentary Labour Party standing order F, No. 4.]

When the Party is in Office, the Cabinet shall continue to be appointed by the Prime Minister. On taking office as Prime Minister, the Leader shall appoint as members of his Cabinet those who were elected members of the Parliamentary Committee at the Dissolution and have retained their seats in the new Parliament.

[Parliamentary Labour Party standing order E.]

## 3. A NEW PRIME MINISTER FROM A CONTINUING GOVERNMENT

*When a Prime Minister resigns on personal grounds and is succeeded by a Cabinet colleague, the new Prime Minister may have a little more room for manoeuvre than if he had just formed a government following success at a general election.*

The post of Foreign Secretary had to be filled and in other times Roy Jenkins [the Home Secretary] would have been a natural successor . . . But the wounds had not healed since his resignation as Deputy Leader during the European Community battles, and as he had been the leading protagonist on one side, every action he would have taken as Foreign Secretary would have been regarded with deep suspicion by the anti-Marketeers on our benches . . . In any case there was another suitable candidate, in the person of Tony Crosland [the Environment Secretary].

*Mr Crosland was appointed Foreign Secretary by Mr Callaghan.*

[James Callaghan, *Time and Chance* (London, 1987), 399.]

I took a deliberate decision to replace some Ministers in their sixties by younger people who would enjoy some experience of Cabinet even if we were defeated in the near future . . . I therefore asked Willie Ross [the Secretary of State for Scotland], Bob Mellish [the

Chief Whip with a Cabinet seat] and Barbara Castle [the Social Services Secretary] to pass on the baton.

[Callaghan, *Time and Chance*, 402.]

## 4. THE SOVEREIGN'S INFLUENCE

*The Sovereign has the formal legal power to appoint and to dismiss Ministers by virtue of the royal prerogative. But she must act on the Prime Minister's advice at the formation of a new government as at any other time. On at least two occasions the Sovereign has required the Prime Minister to justify a proposed appointment, and on another probably caused the swapping of two planned Cabinet appointments.*

### (1) F. E. SMITH AS LORD CHANCELLOR 1919

But taking into consideration Sir Frederick's age, 47, and that he has only been Attorney General for between three and four years, His Majesty fears the appointment will come as somewhat of a surprise to the legal profession. The King knows that his career both at the bar and in Parliament has been very successful: but His Majesty does not feel sure that Sir Frederick has established such a reputation in men's minds as to ensure that the country will welcome him to the second highest post which can be occupied by a subject of the Crown. His Majesty however only hopes that he may be wrong in this forecast.

*Lloyd George persisted, and the King gave way.*

[The King's Private Secretary, Lord Stamfordham, writing to Lloyd George, quoted in Kenneth Rose, *King George V* (London, 1983), 233]

### (2) BEAVERBROOK AS MINISTER OF AIRCRAFT PRODUCTION 1940

. . . I would like to warn you of the repercussions, which I am sure will occur, especially in Canada, at the inclusion of [Beaverbrook]. You are no doubt aware that the Canadians do not appreciate him, and I feel that as the Air Training Scheme for pilots and aircraft is in

Canada, I must tell you this fact. I wonder if you would not reconsider . . . I fear that this appointment might be misconstrued.

*The King agreed to the appointment when Churchill pressed it.*

[Letter from George VI to Winston Churchill in 1940, objecting to Churchill's nomination of Beaverbrook as Minister of Aircraft Production, quoted in Martin Gilbert, *Finest Hour: Winston Churchill 1939–1941* (London, 1983), 316. For Churchill's account, see *The Second World War*, ii., *Their Finest Hour* (London, Penguin edn., 1985), 12.]

### (3) BEVIN AND DALTON IN 1945

Mr Attlee mentioned to the King that he was thinking of appointing Mr Dalton to be Foreign Secretary. His Majesty begged him to think carefully about this, and suggested that Mr Bevin would be a better choice.

[Memorandum by the King's Private Secretary, Sir Alan Lascelles, after Attlee's audience with the King, quoted in Ben Pimlott, *Hugh Dalton* (London, 1985), 414.]

It is impossible to know what was decisive [in making Bevin Foreign Secretary and Dalton Chancellor of the Exchequer]: but it is reasonable to suppose that the King's advice was an important factor.

[Pimlott, *Hugh Dalton*, 415.]

## Other Ministers

*The number of Ministers outside the Cabinet in 1990 were:*

| | |
|---|---|
| Law Officers | 4 |
| Parliamentary Secretary to the Treasury (Chief Whip) | 1 |
| Paymaster General | 1 |
| Ministers of State | 26 |
| Parliamentary Under-Secretaries of State | 32 |
| Whips and Assistant Whips | 20 |

*(See also chapter 5.) A Prime Minister has a freer choice of Ministers who are not to be in the Cabinet, although a Labour Prime Minister will have to have regard to Parliamentary Labour Party standing orders.*

The formation of a Government and the changes that from time to time become necessary are matters upon which it is very difficult to get advice, except to some extent from the Chief Whip of the day and perhaps the more senior members of the Private Office or the Cabinet Secretariat. It is difficult to discuss the merits or demerits of one colleague with another, especially where the higher posts are concerned. When it comes to the less vital but often equally perplexing task of filling up the junior ranks of administration, many considerations have to be borne in mind, apart from the merit or suitability of the candidate. It is important that different parts of the country should be represented, as well as different groups of opinion within the party. Loyalty should be rewarded, but remembering my own past I never felt that sincere disaffection should be held against a young Member. Senior Ministers are sometimes—and not unnaturally—insistent in pressing the claims of the young men who have served them. This makes the formation of a whole Administration, consisting of over eighty members, a difficult and complicated task not unlike a jigsaw puzzle. If one drops out, whether in the senior or the junior ranks, a whole series of alterations have to be made in the plan. Nevertheless, in this my first attempt, the chief objective was to make as little change as possible consistent with what seemed to me the needs of the moment. In all this I found Edward Heath, the Chief Whip, a most admirable assistant. Sir Norman Brook was always ready with advice when called on, and I had in Freddie Bishop, Principal Private Secretary, a tower of strength.

[Harold Macmillan, *Riding the Storm* (London, 1971), 191–2.]

. . . The junior appointments were made in a very unsystematic way, often almost as an afterthought. There are many junior posts to be filled and a Prime Minister may not always know who are the best candidates among the young MPs. In some cases he accepts the suggestions of a departmental Minister, especially if the latter is a powerful political colleague. (James Callaghan and Roy Jenkins effectively made their own junior appointments.) In March 1974 many of the other junior postings were chosen on the suggestions of Mr Wilson's personal staff at lunch.

[BERNARD DONOUGHUE, *Prime Minister: The Conduct of Policy Under Harold Wilson and James Callaghan* (London, 1987), 48.]

Junior Posts and Front Bench Spokespersons shall be appointed by the Leader but the list shall be submitted to the PLP for its approval and any change effected by the Leader shall be notified to the PLP at the earliest available opportunity. The total number of Front Benchers shall be of the order of one-fifth of the PLP.

[Parliamentary Labour Party, standing order G, No. 1.]

*The total number of salaried Ministers who may sit and vote in the House of Commons is controlled by statute.*

2.—(1) Not more than ninety-five persons being the holders of offices specified in Schedule 2 to this Act (in this section referred to as Ministerial offices) shall be entitled to sit and vote in the House of Commons at any one time.

(2) If at any time the number of members of the House of Commons who are holders of Ministerial offices exceeds the number entitled to sit and vote in that House under subsection (1) above, none except any who were both members of that House and holders of Ministerial offices before the excess occurred shall sit or vote therein until the number has been reduced, by death, resignation or otherwise, to the number entitled to sit and vote as aforesaid.

(3) A person holding a Ministerial office is not disqualified by this Act by reason of any office held by him ex officio as the holder of that Ministerial office.

[House of Commons Disqualification Act 1975.]

*Salaries may be paid to 105 Ministers. Occasionally a Minister takes office unpaid (such as Lord Young in Mrs Thatcher's Cabinet).*

1.—(1) Subject to the provisions of this Act—

(*a*) there shall be paid to the holder of any Ministerial office specified in Schedule 1 to this Act such salary as is provided for by that Schedule [as amended] . . .

[Ministerial and other Salaries Act 1975.]

MINISTERIAL SALARIES

*Office* — *Salary [Amounts not reproduced]*

PART I

Prime Minister and First Lord of the Treasury
Chancellor of the Exchequer
Secretary of State
Minister of Agriculture, Fisheries and Food
Any of the following offices for so long as the holder is a member of the Cabinet:

(*a*) Lord President of the Council;
(*b*) Lord Privy Seal;
(*c*) Chancellor of the Duchy of Lancaster;
(*d*) Paymaster General;
(*e*) Chief Secretary to the Treasury;
(*f*) Parliamentary Secretary to the Treasury;
(*g*) Minister of State.

PART II

1. Any of the offices listed at (*a*) to (*g*) in Part I above for so long as the holder is not a member of the Cabinet

2. Minister in charge of a public department of Her Majesty's Government in the United Kingdom who is not a member of the Cabinet, and who is not eligible for a salary under any other provision of this Act

3. Financial Secretary to the Treasury

PART III

Attorney-General
Lord Advocate
Solicitor General
Solicitor General for Scotland

PART IV

Captain of the Honourable Corps of Gentlemen-at-Arms
Parliamentary Secretary other than Parliamentary Secretary to the Treasury
Captain of the Queen's Bodyguard of the Yeoman of the Guard
Treasurer of Her Majesty's Household
Lord in Waiting
Comptroller of Her Majesty's Household
Vice-Chamberlain of Her Majesty's Household
Junior Lord of the Treasury
Assistant Whip, House of Commons

PART V

1. (1) The salary to be paid to the holder of any office mentioned above in this Schedule shall be of the annual amount stated in relation to that office in column 2 or, as the case may be, of such annual amount not more than the upper figure of less than the lower figure so stated as the First Lord of the Treasury may determine.

(2) The date on which the holder of any office listed at (*a*) to (*g*) in Part I above becomes or ceases to be a member of the Cabinet shall be notified in the London Gazette, and any such notification (whether before or after the passing of this Act) shall be conclusive evidence for the purposes of this Schedule.

2. In the case of the following offices a salary may be paid to more than one holder of the office at the same time, subject to the limitations expressed below, that is to say—

(*a*) Secretary of State, so long as not more than 21 salaries are paid at the same time in accordance with Part I above;
(*b*) Minister of State, so long as not more than 50 salaries are paid at the same time in accordance with Parts I and II above;
(*c*) Parliamentary Secretary other than Parliamentary Secretary to the Treasury, so long as not more than 83 salaries are paid at the same time in accordance with Parts I and II above taken together with salaries to any Parliamentary Secretary in accordance with Part IV above;
(*d*) Junior Lord of the Treasury, so long as not more than 5 salaries are paid at the same time;
(*e*) Assistant Whip, House of Commons, so long as not more than 7 salaries are paid at the same time;
(*f*) Lord in Waiting, so long as not more than 5 salaries are paid at the same time.

[Ministerial and other Salaries Act 1975, Schedule 1.]

*A Minister must have a seat in a House of Parliament (although the Solicitor-General for Scotland has frequently not had such a seat). The Lord Chancellor is always a peer, and the Ministerial and other Salaries Act 1975, s. 1(2) provides for his pay on the basis that part of it is received as Speaker of the House of Lords. The Chancellor of the Exchequer must, in practice, be an M.P. given the predominance of the Commons in financial matters. The Opposition always objects if a peer is made Foreign Secretary, but there is nothing improper in such an appointment provided that there is adequate Foreign and Commonwealth Office representation in the House of Commons.*

. . . Selwyn [Lloyd] and I agreed that the best solution would be himself at the Treasury and Alec Home at the Foreign Office. But we have to face the two difficulties of Alec's health and [his membership of] the House of Lords.

*Lord Home was made Foreign Secretary in 1960, with Mr Edward Heath as Lord Privy Seal in the Cabinet to represent him in the Commons.*

[Harold Macmillan, *Pointing the Way* (London, 1972), 230, quoting his diary.]

I was, therefore, delighted when invited to be Foreign and Commonwealth Secretary [in 1979]. And as counterweight to my membership of the Lords I was given first-class ministers to handle our business in the Commons—Ian Gilmour, in the Cabinet as Lord Privy Seal, was my number two, and I also had Peter Blaker, Richard Luce, Nick Ridley and Douglas Hurd, a splendid team.

[Lord Carrington, *Reflect on Things Past* (London, 1988), 280.]

## Formal Appointment of Ministers

Privy Council Office
Whitehall, London SW1A 2AT
10 September 1987

1. It is perhaps simplest to begin with the relinquishment of appointments. There is very little in the way of formalities connected with the giving up of Ministerial posts. Broadly speaking, the relinquishment is effected by a resignation, express or implied. The resignation of a Prime Minister—other than in his personal capacity—normally carries with it the resignation of the whole of his administration. A reshuffle may be prompted by a Ministerial resignation or resignations. When the initiative comes from the Prime Minister it is normally formalized by subsequent letters of resignation from those leaving office. In the case of a Minister leaving one office for another his resignation of the former is implicit. In the case of appointments for which the mechanics include Letters Patent or formal warrants the normal practice is for these instruments to include an express revocation of the previous

appointment. The Lord Chancellor and the Chancellor of the Duchy of Lancaster have the privilege of claiming a private audience with The Queen for the purpose of delivering up their seals. Formerly it was the practice for other Ministers who had seals to deliver up to do so at a private audience with the Sovereign. More recently, that practice has been discontinued. The Royal Household normally arrange individual private audiences with The Queen for outgoing Ministers. These audiences, however, are entirely a matter of courtesy and form no part of the machinery of relinquishing office. The seals of outgoing Ministers, other than the Great Seal and that of the Duchy of Lancaster, are now simply collected by this office in preparation for their delivery to their new holders.

2. The position with regard to appointments is much more complicated. Although taking the oath of office is properly a consequence of an appointment and not the appointment itself, it is helpful to deal first with the Promissory Oaths Act 1868. This prescribes, in section 3, the terms of the oath of office and section 5 requires that oath shall be tendered to and taken by each of the officers named in the first part of the Schedule of the Act as soon as may be after his acceptance of office. The Schedule directs that the oath to be taken by officers listed in the first part is to be tendered by the Clerk of the Council and taken in the presence of Her Majesty in Council or otherwise as Her Majesty shall direct. The power to direct otherwise has been exercised twice. First by the Order in Council, directing the manner in which the oath of allegiance and the official oath as to England shall be tendered and taken by certain officers, dated 9 August 1872; secondly by the Promissory Oaths Order S.I. 1939/916. The 1872 Order is now applicable only in relation to the Chancellor of the Duchy of Lancaster. For all other purposes the 1939 Order is now effective, its effect being to require the oath of office to be taken by members of the Cabinet before The Queen in Council and by those Ministers included in Part I of the 1868 Act Schedule but not in the Cabinet before another senior Minister, usually the Lord President. To take the oath in Council, the person concerned must be a member of the Council. Accordingly, on becoming a member of the Cabinet a Minister, if he is not one already, is made a Privy Counsellor. It would, in any case, be the normal practice for all members of the Cabinet to be made Privy Counsellors. The provisions of the 1868 Act make this invariable.

3. It is for this reason that, in rehearsing the provisions of

section 5 of the 1868 Act above, I omitted any reference to the oath of allegiance. This oath is one of the two oaths taken when a person is sworn into the Council. The swearing in of new Counsellors is the first item of business at any Council. A person who becomes a Cabinet Minister who was not previously a Privy Counsellor accordingly takes the oath of allegiance separately from and before taking the oath of office. The oath of allegiance, however, is taken only once. On appointment to a Cabinet post, therefore, unless the appointee is not already a Privy Counsellor, it will be unnecessary for him to take the oath of allegiance in addition to the appropriate oath of office. It is unusual, except on a change of Government, for those appointed to Cabinet posts not to be already members of the Council.

4. I have referred throughout above to swearing and the taking of oaths. There is, of course, provision for affirmation to be made by non-believers.

5. Before leaving the taking of oaths, I should mention kissing hands. This is a courtesy which follows the oath when that is taken before The Queen in Council. It is a practice which is invariably observed. It is not, however, a formality on which the appointment in any way depends.

6. Returning now to the actual mechanics of appointments, I have attached a summary at the end of this memorandum which sets out the details in tabular form.

7. The Prime Minister accepts office by attending The Queen in private audience. The appointment—and as First Lord of the Treasury—takes effect from that moment. At the audience the new Prime Minister kisses hands. There are no other formalities.

8. As regards other appointments, the general rule is that these take effect, in the absence of any other factor to the contrary, from the moment of The Queen's approval of the Prime Minister's list or lists of recommendations. Thus, although the Minister of Agriculture, Fisheries and Food, when in the Cabinet, is required to take the oath of office in Council, his appointment dates from the moment The Queen approves it and not from the Council at which he takes the oath and kisses hands. The same—that is that appointment dates from The Queen's approval—applies with nearly all other middle and junior rank Ministers.

9. The general rule is, however, displaced in various ways. The Lord President is so declared by The Queen in Council and his

appointment is effected by, and from the moment of, that declaration. In the case of all offices which have seals of office the appointment is effected by the delivery of those seals by the Sovereign to the holder of the office. This takes place, with one exception, in the Council at which the oath of office is taken and the appointee kisses hands. The exception is the Chancellor of the Duchy of Lancaster who, because of the personal character of the appointment, receives the seals in private audience, usually immediately after the Council at which the other appointments are made, and takes the oath and kisses hands in that audience.

10. It should be noted that, whilst the Prime Minister does not take an oath of office as such, he or she is required to take the oath of office in his or her capacity as First Lord of the Treasury. This oath is taken with the others in Council. There is, however, no seal associated with this office. As indicated above, therefore, the appointment as First Lord takes effect at the same moment as the appointment as Prime Minister.

11. The mechanics for some appointments include formal documents. Section 4 of the Paymaster General Act 1835 prescribes a warrant under the Royal Sign Manual as the method of appointment for this office. It is, accordingly, the warrant which is effective in making this appointment which dates from the date of the warrant and not from The Queen's approval of the Prime Minister's recommendation for the appointment.

12. In a number of other appointments Letters Patent are included as part of the machinery. This is the case with both the Lord Privy Seal and the Chancellor of the Exchequer. In these cases, however, the appointment dates from the delivery of the seal and not from that of the Letters Patent. It should also be noted that the Letters Patent involved in connection with the appointment of the Chancellor of the Exchequer are distinct from the Letters Patent appointing the Commissioners of the Treasury, of which the Chancellor is one, referred to in the following paragraph.

13. The position with the Commissioners of the Treasury is different again. Their appointment is by Letters Patent and is regulated by section 2 of the Consolidated Fund Act 1816. The appointments as Commissioners of the Treasury take effect from the date of these Letters Patent. Thus, the appointment of the Prime Minister as First Lord of the Treasury and of the Chancellor

of the Exchequer will normally take effect before they are formally appointed Commissioners of the Treasury. The Treasury Commission includes, of course, all the junior Treasury offices. In practice, it is not unusual for successive commissions to be issued so that the principal appointments are not held up by any delay in completing the list of junior appointments.

14. The offices of Attorney-General and Solicitor-General, which are not included in the Schedule of the 1868 Act, follow the general rule for Ministerial appointments. These two appointments are, however, confirmed by Letters Patent like the offices of Lord Privy Seal and Chancellor of the Exchequer.

15. There remain a number of 'phantom' appointments. Certain offices need to remain in being, usually because, for example, property is statutorily vested in the holder of that office. They are not held separately but are held by the occupant of another substantive office. Because of changes in allocation of Ministerial responsibilities, the identity of these offices varies from time to time and, as a result, it is impossible to give any exhaustive account of such appointments. Broadly, formalities in relation to these 'phantom' appointments are kept to a minimum. As regards appointment proper, the Presidency of the Board of Trade is the only one calling for particular mention. This office is held in conjunction with the Secretaryship of Trade and Industry (or of Trade when these two responsibilities are separately held). The Board of Trade is still, technically, a Committee of the Privy Council and its President is appointed by an Order in Council approved at the same time as the holder of the substantive office receives the seal and takes the oath of office. Some of these 'phantom' offices are included in the First Schedule, as amended, of the Promissory Oaths Act. This means that the holder of the substantive office with which they are held in conjunction, must also take the oath in respect of the 'phantom' office in accordance with the requirements of the Act and the Orders made under it.

16. The political appointments in the Royal Household follow the same rules as above. That is to say, they are all middle or junior Ministerial appointments and take effect when The Queen approves the Prime Minister's recommendations. The non-political appointments to the Royal Household proper are entirely a matter for The Queen. One or two of these appointments, however, are still

included in the first part of the Schedule of the 1868 Act, e.g. the Lord Chamberlain, and on his appointment he takes the oath of office before the Lord President.

Ministerial appointments

| Office | Procedure | Documents (if any) |
|---|---|---|
| Prime Minister | Received in private Audience and kisses hands | |
| First Lord of the Treasury | Takes oath of office, in Council, as First Lord of the Treasury and kisses hands | Treasury Commission—as member of Treasury Board—by Letters Patent |
| Lord President | Declared in Council and thereupon takes oath of office and kisses hands | |
| Lord Chancellor | Takes oath of office in Council, kisses hands and receives the Great Seal | |
| Lord Privy Seal | Takes oath of office in Council, kisses hands and receives the Privy Seal | Letters Patent |
| Secretaries of State | Take oath of office in Council, kiss hands and receive Seals | |
| Chancellor of the Exchequer | Takes oath of office in Council, kisses hands and receives Seal of Office | Letters Patent Treasury Commission—as member of the Treasury Board—by Letters Patent (distinct from above) |
| Chancellor of the Duchy of Lancaster | Takes oath of office *in private Audience* (usually after the Council), kisses hands and receives the Seal of Office | Warrant under the Sign Manual |
| Minister of Agriculture/ Paymaster General | If in Cabinet, takes oath of office in Council and kisses hands, otherwise sworn before Lord Chancellor or a Secretary of State | Warrant under the Sign Manual |

| | | |
|---|---|---|
| Law Officers | | Letters Patent |
| Other Treasury Ministers and Lords of the Treasury | | Treasury Commission—as members of the Treasury Board—by Letters Patent |
| 'Phantom' Offices | | |
| President of the Board of Trade | Appointee to substantive office, with which this is held, takes oath in respect of both offices | Order in Council approved at time oath of office is taken |
| Others | Oath of office is taken by holder of substantive office if required by Promissory Oaths Act and in accordance with procedure stipulated | |

No special procedure or documentation applies in the case of remaining Ministers, whose appointments take effect from the moment The Sovereign approves the relevant submission from the Prime Minister.

[Memorandum by the Clerk to the Privy Council, reproduced by his kind permission.]

# [3]
# THE PRIME MINISTER

## Personality and Style

*There is no such thing as an 'average' Prime Minister. Each brings his own personality and style of government to the office, and this will have an important effect on the ways in which the government is run.*

### 1. ATTLEE 1945–51

The main criticism of Attlee made in retrospect by his colleagues was that he was so remote. Though he always worked in the Cabinet Room, in the very central location of power, his ministers thought of him as living his life at a much greater distance away. The flat at the top of the house, in which he spent as much time as he possibly could with Vi, seemed to his colleagues to be psychologically on another planet. He made no effort to appear in touch. Yet, as can be seen from the prime ministerial minutes given in Appendix IV below, no problem was too small to interest him if brought to his notice, and nobody could take the risk of bypassing his authority on the grounds that the matter was not worthy of his attention. John Strachey wished to publish some poems. A colleague pointed out to him that Cabinet ministers could not publish a book without the Prime Minister's prior consent. Strachey wrote to Attlee that he proposed to publish a book, but that he did not think the Prime Minister would wish to see the book since it would consist of poems. Attlee asked to see it. Strachey complied. He heard nothing of the book for three weeks, so made a telephone call to the Prime Minister. Attlee came to the phone. 'You can't possibly publish. The lines don't scan.'

His remoteness was an imperfection in his premiership. He was an excellent listener, but was not good at exchanging views, especially embryonic views. He did not think aloud, and did not encourage the practice in others. Colleagues were expected to have done their thinking before they came to see him, and, as Harold Wilson said, 'You'd think twice before you *asked* to see him.' Some of his junior colleagues complained that he did not encourage them enough, that he behaved less as captain, more as umpire. Some liked his habit of handing out general ideas rather than specific directives, others were worried by this, since they might expect tart comments if their implementation went wrong. 'You felt that there was always a bad-tempered headmaster in the background,' said Strauss.

Yet many letters among Attlee's papers suggest that this was not a universal view—for example a note dated 2 August 1951 from a minister who was by no means close to him, Richard Stokes, then Lord Privy Seal: 'Thanks for your kind words of confidence in my efforts at the Cabinet yesterday. I will do my best.' When he addressed his new junior ministers after he had formed his government in 1945 he made a very good impression on them, especially when he said: 'One more thing: if I pass you in the corridor and don't acknowledge you, remember it's only because I'm shy.' If he was sometimes too shy to make contact, he was always sympathetic. In 1948 he asked Herbert Bowden, later Lord Aylestone, an assistant Whip, to move the Loyal Address. Just before Bowden went into the Chamber he found himself next to Attlee. 'How do you feel?' asked Attlee. 'Very nervous, Prime Minister.' 'Don't worry, I'm *always* nervous.'

As 1949 opened Attlee's public prestige was high, and his authority over his government widely recognized. On 9 January *The Observer* carried a profile of him, accompanied by a rather grim photograph which made him look like Lenin. The article was well-informed and perceptive; the opening paragraphs reflect the wonderment of many thinking people as they beheld the transformation of a mouselike little man into an outstandingly powerful prime minister.

> When Clement Richard Attlee became Prime Minister in 1945, it was commonly assumed that he would prove little more than the nominal head of his Cabinet, a competent and conciliatory chairman; holding office not by reason of positive qualities of his own but as an intermediary between Bevin and Morrison.
>
> Yet he is today the complete master of his Cabinet, and he has quietly carried through changes in Cabinet structure which place in his hand more of the strings of power than have ever before been held by a British Prime Minister in peacetime. Most of his colleagues stand somewhat in awe of

him. His prestige with the public has also risen steadily, and stands ahead of that of his Government as a whole . . .

The secret of Attlee's power is often sought in his great integrity. But integrity is not so rare a quality in our political life that its possession, even in a high degree, is sufficient to endow a man with leadership. The secret lies deeper. Mr Attlee's strength comes from a peculiar form of disciplined independence. Even Sir Stafford Cripps, with his monk's pride in his own asceticism, needs the sustenance of a few disciples. Attlee is completely self-sustained. He is not afflicted by unpopularity. He is, in fundamental decisions, even unaffected by the approval or disapproval of intimates, of whom indeed he has few.

Mr Attlee's appearance has been compared to that of Lenin. Wild as the comparison may seem, it is nevertheless true that he has something of that quality of private decision, that ability to follow his own analysis of events to its logical conclusion, unperturbed by the feelings of those around him, unperturbed, also, by his own feelings, fears, or vanities, that Lenin possessed.

But a politician, to manœuvre, also needs tactical skill and a quiet nimbleness. Here, again, Attlee is surprisingly well-equipped. He has successfully ridden every revolt in his party, chiefly by remarkable timing—by knowing when to remain quiescent and when to bring the issue to a climax. Those who have challenged him are never quite sure just how they were defeated. Moreover, he has, to a degree equalled only by Bevin, among the Labour leaders, an almost instinctive awareness of the reactions of the rank and file of his party and of the country at large.

When he came to power in 1945 he assembled and managed a team of ministers which carried out a programme of legislation so massive and so radical that, however controversial, it entitles him to be regarded as a great Prime Minister. The nationalization of the basic industries, the foundation of the Welfare State, and the establishment for the first time of the Labour Party as a plausible party of government had an impact on Britain and the world which no British government had made in the twentieth century. To do these things, he had in the first place to bring his party to power. That in itself was a great feat, and one which he thought was his most important achievement: 'to take a party intact into a coalition, keep it intact for five years, bring it out intact, and win an election with it when most people expected defeat. Not many precedents for that.' Moreover, it is inconceivable that any of the Labour Party leaders but Attlee could have controlled the Cabinet, led the party and satisfied the public opinion which was a prerequisite for the success of his legislative programme. Had any of the other possible leaders become prime minister—Bevan, Bevin, Morrison, Cripps, Dalton—there would have been conflicts, more likely than not because of personal clashes, that would have hampered the action and possibly have brought about a débâcle. Attlee's patience, self-control, self-effacement, sense of timing, feeling for what was possible, and his unique knowledge of party and governmental techniques gained in forty years of public work, were his strength—a combination of personal qualities and professional expertise which none of his colleagues could rival.

He was laconic and lacked charisma, yet his personality had a message which reached the people. He was respectable, solid and quiet, a happy family man who wore a business suit, a homburg hat, smoked a pipe and loved cricket. At a time when a socialist programme was being presented in all its might and range to a British middle class whose majority disliked and feared it, the prime minister who presented it could be seen as a symbol of middle-class moderation, decency, respectability and decorum. His very lack of rhetoric and colour was an indispensable contribution to his cause. He was so ordinary that many people accepted—however grudgingly—measures which expressed and executed by a man of passion would have been resisted, or rejected. And for many there was something uplifting about him and his rise to power. He was not 'a great man'; he was not exactly 'the common man'; he was, in fact, an ordinary middle-class figure, and yet he was now the leader of the country. If it could happen to him, it could happen to anybody.

[Keith Harris, *Attlee* (London, 1982), 409–10, 427–8, 567.]

## 2. CHURCHILL 1951–5

[During his peacetime government] details, however, bored him. He continued his wartime 'searchlight technique' of focusing his attention on particular policy matters, but the beam was dimmer and moved at a slower tempo . . . Highly selective in the areas that interested him, he contributed little to social policy apart from the support of the house-building programme . . .

He regarded the Cabinet as extremely important, even sacrosanct, and would rarely ride roughshod over it to get his way.

[Anthony Seldon, *Churchill's Indian Summer: The Conservative Government 1951–1955* (London, 1981), 30, 85.]

In Britain, and perhaps still more in other countries of the free world, the signal 'Churchill is back' carried some of the nostalgic appeal that it had for the Royal Navy on September 3rd, 1939. His name was a household word far beyond the shores of the British Isles. Roosevelt was dead; Stalin was now recognised to be an ogre; Churchill alone of the world's political leaders was placed by millions of people on a pedestal wearing a halo. His return to power seemed to many to presage the recovery of hopes tarnished by the dismal aftermath of the war.

If those hopes, like almost all human hopes, fell short of complete fulfilment, it is nevertheless true that in the three and a half years of Churchill's last administration, there was a shedding of austerity, a return to comparative prosperity and a temporary restoration of peace on earth. This was not so in the first year when, as my diary illustrates, the financial situation remained bleak and rationing was as severe as ever. However, late in 1952 the clouds began to lift and by the time of Queen Elizabeth II's Coronation in June 1953, the prospects were brighter than they had been for many years past.

The tones of Auld Lang Syne were gradually muted and in due course the Overlords, Field Marshal Alexander and Lord Cherwell thankfully departed. General Ismay became Secretary General of N.A.T.O. Sir Ian Jacob, to his great relief, returned to run the B.B.C. Lords Beaverbrook and Bracken, by this time inseparable allies, seldom crossed the threshold of 10 Downing Street, though Bracken's devotion to Churchill did not waver. The Korean war ended; the Coronation was an occasion for even greater national enthusiasm than the royal wedding six years before; Mount Everest was conquered by a British expedition; rationing was a misery soon forgotten; larger foreign travel allowances were granted; and though Churchill's last ambition, to bring the Cold War to an end after Stalin's death, was frustrated, the early 1950s do in retrospect seem like a golden summer.

All this is the more remarkable in that the new administration inherited both a war in the Pacific and an alarming economic crisis at home. It may not be altogether extravagant to suggest that the figure of Winston Churchill brooding benevolently over the scene and, as his eightieth birthday approached, as much cherished by the Labour Party and the Liberals as by his own side, made a significant contribution to the sense of well-being which briefly filled the hearts of men in the United Kingdom and far afield.

With the strain of war-time leadership relaxed, he was now less irascible and impatient than of old and readier to be convinced by argument, provided the right moment was chosen for the exercise. The charm and the lovable qualities were undiminished and at Chartwell, now a more frequent week-end resort than Chequers, he was a solicitous host.

At least until the midsummer of 1953 his mind was as clear and his reactions almost as prompt as in former days. He still dictated incisive minutes, though the menacing red labels, ACTION THIS DAY (carefully hoarded by the messengers at No. 10 and placed on the Cabinet Room table the very day of his return) were no longer in use. His speeches were heard with attention in the House of Commons, reported at length by the press and seldom interrupted except by cheers. He still dominated the Cabinet, now more like Buddha than Achilles, but not with the long monologues, product of weariness, which had irritated his colleagues during the last year of the war.

Like most elderly people, he was bad at remembering names. It had not been one of his more notable gifts ten years previously. When Sir Norman Brook brought Sir Thomas Padmore on to the scene as probationary Deputy Secretary to the Cabinet, Churchill persisted in referring to him as Potsdam; and he said to me one morning, 'I don't think much of that fellow Shorthorn.' It required ingenuity to discover that the object of his temporary dissatisfaction was General Sir Nevil Brownjohn.

If his memory had lost some of its sharpness, that was only by contrast with its unusual, indeed phenomenal, strength in former days. In lighter moments he could, and did, still quote verses of poetry, sing the music-hall songs of the 1890s and discourse learnedly on the American Civil War or the campaigns of Marlborough and Prince Eugene. He abandoned his war-time practices of an hour's sleep in the afternoon and perusing the first editions of the following day's newspapers before going to bed; but the number of cigars he smoked remained constant and, although he was never inebriated (or, indeed, drank between meals anything but soda-water faintly flavoured with whisky), he would still consume, without the smallest ill-effect, enough champagne and brandy at luncheon or dinner to incapacitate any lesser man.

As far as current affairs were concerned, he was as attentive to Parliament as ever, but in the ordinary day's business he concentrated his thought on those issues, mainly in the foreign field, that interested him. From time to time this led to clashes with the Foreign Secretary, Anthony Eden, who objected to Prime Ministerial interference in his diocese. Churchill was content to leave much of the rest, except where housing, food and labour relations were concerned, to Ministers and officials whom he no longer pursued on points of detail. He made greater use of his Private Office to handle relationships with his colleagues; he was influenced by the sensible and usually moderating opinions of his new son-in-law and Parliamentary Private Secretary, Christopher Soames; and he listened to the advice of the Secretary to the Cabinet, Sir Norman Brook, whose wisdom and diligence he esteemed and whose company he found so agreeable that he elected him to the Other Club. That was the highest personal honour he could confer, and not one offered to either of Norman Brook's predecessors.

[Sir John Colville, *The Fringes of Power: Downing Street Diaries 1939–1955* (London, 1985), 633–5.]

## 3. EDEN 1955–7

My position as Lord Privy Seal was anomalous. I had taken over, at Anthony's request, the chairmanship of what was called the Liaison Committee, a body consisting of government and party representatives which met weekly to plan the co-ordination of our publicity. For this reason perhaps, the Prime Minister paid me the compliment of expecting me, more than the Chairman of the party, to be responsible for Conservative success in the country. I was therefore at the receiving end of those innumerable telephone calls, on every day of the week and at every hour of the day, which characterized his conscientious but highly strung supervision of our affairs. At a time when there were few runs to be made on the home wicket, his lack of experience in any domestic Ministry was not a help . . .

[Lord Butler, *The Art of the Possible* (London, 1971), 183–4.]

Politics are what is called in the current jargon 'a high-stress profession' for all but the most callously ambitious and the most idle or ignorant. Reaction to this can take many forms, some beneficial, some malignant. Churchill took comfort in his home, his writing and his painting during his periods of what he called 'the black dog';

Baldwin, far more sensitive than he is usually depicted, had a profound feeling for the English countryside and literature; Neville Chamberlain had his fishing, his family and his passion for music. Eden indeed had his deep knowledge of art and books, and his as yet unrequited love affairs with the joys of country living, but he lacked a satisfying marriage, that inestimable boon given to Churchill, Baldwin and Chamberlain; and, in spite of the façade, he had constant money worries. His work became too large a part of his life, as he later realized, to his bitter regret; he drove himself too hard, as he often drove those who worked for and with him. Some found this exhilarating, others did not.

His relationships with his Permanent Under-Secretaries were not always easy. Vansittart patronized him as well as disagreeing with him; and Eden wrote of him (16 November 1936): 'I fear that he is not balanced and is in such a continual state of nerves that he will end up making would-be aggressors think the more of us as a potential victim.' Alexander Cadogan, beneath an impressive veneer of professional suavity, could be testy, as his diaries demonstrate, but he was later to write of Eden: 'I don't think any Secretary of State I served excelled him in finesse, or as a negotiator, or in knowledge of foreign affairs. When something had to be done, Anthony would long to do it. That quality was perhaps carried to a fault; but on the whole a good fault for a Foreign Secretary. No one worked harder.' This was very high praise from that very critical source.

One who came to know him officially very well once remarked of Eden that what struck him was that he had many political cronies but few real friends in politics. There is much truth in this, although not the whole truth, as his correspondence and diaries reveal so clearly. He did not spare much time for the 'club' aspect of the House of Commons, which Churchill so relished, and was not well equipped by temperament or intellect to endure fools gladly. None the less, his politeness was legendary, and he lost his urbanity only when provoked or in a dark mood. Very humanly, he preferred to have around him people he liked, but these were not invariably the most able or the most representative. This is very understandable, but it has its political drawbacks. One cannot choose one's parliamentary colleagues, and it is often necessary to work with people who are uncongenial; this was not one of the political virtues at which Eden shone, and he often overestimated those he liked and underestimated those he did not. Thus his real political following in the House of Commons and in the Cabinet was, in contrast with his public following, remarkably small, as events were to demonstrate. Where it existed was usually in the Labour Party, among whose members he was always popular and respected. A former Labour MP has written:

> Somehow, news that my stepfather had died reached Anthony Eden and he sent me a handwritten two-page letter of sympathy. In it he referred to his feelings at his own father's death. I was very moved. As a backbencher from the opposite side of the House, I felt the letter confirmed my belief that Eden really cared about people. As long as he lived, I remained one of his admirers and I hope history will be kinder to him than his contemporaries were . . .

For Anthony Eden belongs to that small group of British politicians who were regarded with deep and widespread affection as well as admiration, which have long survived his death, making his grave at Alvediston a place of pilgrimage for people from abroad as well as his fellow countrymen. It is unusual indeed to find anyone who speaks of him with rancour, and many who opposed him so vehemently over Suez almost invariably speak of it with regretful sadness, often mingled with incomprehension, rather than with anger.

What was the secret of this remarkable durability of popular regard and warmth? Those who disparage him ascribe it to good looks, blandness, and luck that eventually ran out, all surface and no substance. This will not do; there is far more to it.

As this biography has demonstrated, Anthony Eden was an exceptionally complex and sensitive man, of varying moods. Eden 'up' was a delight; Eden 'down' was less attractive, however short and explosive such occasions might have been. One of the best modern parliamentarians, it was in Office that he was most content. His relationship with the Conservative Party was always uneasy so far as the House of Commons was concerned, but not in Warwick and Leamington. Clarissa Eden wrote in her diary in February 1953: 'I'm not really a Conservative, A. says, I have more sympathy with the opposition. I am an old-fashioned Liberal.' In reality he was a Conservative whose real education had been in the First World War, the precursor and champion of modern One Nation Conservatism, and whose relationship with the Conservative Party had been as complex as that of Churchill, seeking to emphasize the best aspects and despising the worst.

Those who ascribed his success to good luck did not appreciate the extent to which he had experienced the reverse. The deaths of his brothers, the disaster that befell Windlestone, the sadness of his first marriage, the death of Simon, and, perhaps most important of all, the debilitating impact of poor health, may be especially cited; the responsibility for the ultimate failure over Suez, as I have demonstrated, should be apportioned more broadly, and he certainly had ill luck virtually throughout that melancholy episode.

It was especially ironical that the greatest source of Anthony Eden's ill luck had been Winston Churchill, the object of his scorn—and worse—as a schoolboy, soldier and young politician; his closest political friend and leader in the most terrible of all wars; and the man under whose shadow he had worked for so long. If Churchill had succumbed to any of his serious wartime ailments, Eden would have automatically succeeded him as Britain's leader; if Churchill had retired in 1945, Eden would have become the uncontested leader of the Conservative Party, and would have reached the political summit at the height of his powers; if he had not been so desperately ill himself, he would almost certainly have been Prime Minister in 1953. Instead, he did so under lowering circumstances that were, unhappily, stronger than he could survive.

Although Churchill had many supreme qualities that Eden lacked, Eden had others that Churchill did not have, which made them such a uniquely powerful combination in war, but which made Eden the stronger and more attractive in peace. With Churchill, one always had the vivid emotion of being carried back nostalgically to more glorious days; with Anthony Eden, one looked to a better future. But, when Churchill reluctantly departed in 1955, too much had happened to ensure a successful inheritance. It was not calculated, but it happened. If Churchill had acted differently, this biography would have had a very different ending. But Churchill acted as he did, and events occurred as they did.

The British people understood this much better than most politicians. From the beginning Eden had seemed different, as indeed he was. His kindness, his warmth and erudition were genuine, as was his shyness. He was also palpably honest and brave, with that precious, unusual, but crucial quality of sincerity. Historians may question some of his judgements and actions; but it will be difficult indeed for them to discover turpitude, even in the 1956 Anglo-French-Israeli agreement. This action can be criticized, but it was done sincerely in the national interest. Again, I am sure that this was also widely recognized, and the swiftly aborted venture in 1966 to reopen the Suez issue is good evidence of this.

Winston Churchill loved the phrase 'An English Worthy', his highest form of praise. It applies perfectly to Anthony Eden, for the 'secret' of his success and regard was that he was a highly intelligent, good, honest, sincere and decent man who was worthy of trust. Of all the honours he received, the greatest of all was the most rare of all—the confidence and love of the British people.

[Robert Rhodes James, *Anthony Eden* (London, 1987), 159–60, 621–2.]

## 4. MACMILLAN 1957–63

Harold Macmillan had been a stimulating political chief under whom to serve, and he managed to make the conduct of government interesting, agreeable and entertaining. He would enquire of Ministers how things were going from time to time, but would seldom interfere. If he wanted some course of action he would say so, and expect it to be done without constant supervision. He was easy to reach, and easy to talk to freely. We would therefore go to him for advice only when we really needed it, and we were sure of a ready and understanding hearing.

Lady Dorothy, too, kept open house, and the whole was a family affair. Harold was also incomparably amusing even on official occasions. I recall walking with him through the miles of statues which the Vatican houses, and arriving face to face with the ultimate reward which was the famous bust of Julius Caesar. He gazed upon it reverently, and twenty or thirty Italians waited hanging upon his words. He turned to me and said, 'It's terribly like Douglas Jay.' And that was all.

In Cabinet he deliberately used to illustrate his points with analogies from the shooting-field, which he knew nine-tenths of the members would not understand. I remember one such beginning, 'Of course if you brown into a covey of partridges—' He took an impish delight in the general bewilderment . . .

The secret of Macmillan's political success was his absolute mastery of every parliamentary occasion. It involved a lot of preparation, but it paid a high political dividend. As an historian, too, he had a finely developed sense of perspective.

If he had been given the health—even after the Profumo affair—I would not have put it past him to have led the Party to a fourth Conservative victory.

He was, apart from his great ability, a supremely successful showman. Years later, in a private house, when he was discussing politics among a group of friends, he said musingly, 'Of course, when a man becomes Prime Minister, he has to some extent to be an actor.' We kept our faces and behaved remarkably well.

[Lord Home, *The Way the Wind Blows* (London, 1976), 191–2.]

Harold Macmillan was not a reluctant prime minister. He savoured the office, its history and its place in the scheme of things. 'He seemed', wrote his early biographer Anthony Sampson, 'to see himself as part of a fashionable play.' His attention to the style of his premiership shone through even at the age of ninety, twenty years after his departure from No. 10, in a television interview with Ludovic Kennedy:

MACMILLAN I enjoyed Prime Minister because I found it much the most relaxed of the offices I held. I didn't work so hard.

KENNEDY Many people would find that surprising.

MACMILLAN Yes, but you didn't have to do the work of the departments. Oh, you had the Cabinet to run and all that. I found I read a lot of books and so on, I rested a lot. It's a great mistake to get yourself into a state of nervous excitement all the time . . . nobody should ever overdo it you know . . . you should read Jane Austen and then you'll feel better.

In fact he was a nervous man, particularly before making one of his unforgettable, mannered speeches whose flow continued into the mid-1980s. The unflappable image needed to be worked on—and he began as soon as he entered No. 10 in January 1957. He hung up a notice in his own writing bearing a quote from *The Gondoliers*:

Motto for Private Office and Cabinet Room.
Quiet, calm deliberation
Disentangles *every* knot.

His irreverent friend and Downing Street assistant (unpaid and unofficial), John Wyndham, added,

And remember, if it doesn't
You will certainly be shot.

The new relaxed Downing Street style was instantly picked up by the Cabinet and greatly appreciated. None had relished Eden's tendency to transmit his own nervousness to colleagues. The transformation was vividly recalled by the man Macmillan pipped for the premiership, R. A. Butler:

Eden would ring up, sometimes as often as a dozen times a day, to ask why there had been a certain speech made in the provinces by a member of the opposition, why an answer hadn't been given, and that sort of thing. When I came to Macmillan, it was with the greatest difficulty that I telephoned him at all. Because when you raised the telephone . . . he showed great irritation and pretended not to hear you, so that it immediately made you think that you'd been unwise to telephone at all.

Macmillan may have appeared to treat the premiership as if he were a Whig grandee running a great estate in the gaps between his private reading. In reality 'he had a firm business-like approach to running the Cabinet', according to John Barnes and Anthony Seldon. He made use of the Cabinet-committee structure as a filter for business, though he chaired very few committees himself (the main exceptions were the Economic Policy and Defence committees). He kept abreast of committee minutes and in close touch with the chairmen. Sometimes, if taking an initiative in an area he deemed crucial, he would take the chair, as he did at the Reflation Committee in 1958.

In the early years of his premiership he was very sharp, though, as Iain Macleod recalled, 'he could be maddeningly discursive—it was nothing to reach a decision on an enquiry into rating via the Greek Wars and Parnell'. He made Cabinet fun, as his successor, Lord Home, remembers: 'He was marvellously entertaining always. You did your business but it was great fun at the same time.' All the same, Home thought he was over-indulgent: 'Harold was very clever. He was one of those prime ministers in Cabinet who let everyone talk—too much sometimes.'

[Peter Hennessy, *Cabinet* (Oxford, 1986), 58–9.]

In addition to the Foreign Secretary and the Chancellor of the Exchequer, the Prime Minister should encourage individual Ministers to come to him with their problems and discuss them informally.

With the members of the Administration outside the Cabinet, whether Ministers or Under Secretaries, he should try to keep in as close touch as possible. It is a useful tradition that when the principal of a Department is away the Under Secretary comes in his place to the Cabinet, as of course do other Ministers not in the Cabinet when their particular subject is on the agenda.

Finally, Cabinet meetings should not be too solemn. A little humour can often act as a lubricant or even a solvent at tense moments. While I could not, of course, hope to rival Churchill, I had his example always in my mind . . .

The physical as well as the intellectual strain involved was certainly heavy. Although I had inherited a strong constitution it had undoubtedly been impaired by serious wounds in the First War and by subsequent illnesses and operations. I was in my sixty-third year when I became Prime Minister, and in my seventieth when I resigned. During all this period I found it only possible to carry out my duties by taking great care and resting as much as possible—doing a great deal of my work in bed. One rule I kept to—to read for at least an hour before going to sleep and usually old favourites —Jane Austen, Dickens, Thackeray and Trollope.

However responsible the position of the Minister in charge of one of the great Departments of State—the Foreign Office, the Treasury, the Ministry of Defence and the rest—to become Prime Minister makes a complete change in one's life. In a Department, the burdens, however onerous, are to some extent limited. As Prime Minister one is answerable for everything. In a Department, the ordinary life with one's colleagues and with the outside world goes on in a normal atmosphere and follows a more or less normal pattern. The Prime Minister's position is unique. Strangely enough it is also very lonely. I imagine a captain of a ship to have something of the same feeling. For example, I had soon noticed that people do not come and see you unasked—at least not the people that you want to see. Yet with this loneliness there is a complete lack of privacy. I had grown accustomed to being guarded by detectives when I was Foreign Secretary, but one could sometimes elude them. As Prime Minister this was quite impossible. Every moment of the day and night is planned out, recorded, watched. Indeed, during the summer of 1963 when the most fantastic charges were being thrown about in the Lobbies of the House of Commons and in the less reputable by-ways of Fleet Street, I remember saying laughingly to one of my colleagues, that I alone could rebut any accusations against my private life because I had none!

There is no respite and in effect no holiday. You go away for a few days. The staff goes with you and the Press photographers too. These seemed to take a special interest in my few relaxations—golf and shooting. But the telegrams and papers followed day by day, often hour by hour; even to the golf links or the grouse moor, and by some perverse arrangement there was always a crisis in August. The only method of getting a complete holiday was to hand over the Government, with the Queen's permission, to a colleague. But this was equally to deprive a hard-worked Minister of his hard-earned rest. This was an expedient to which I never had recourse, except during a long tour—for instance, a Commonwealth tour. Then I was fortunate in being able to entrust the management of affairs to Butler. Even so the messages came—and the crises—coupled with requests for advice and decision. Nevertheless, if it was hard work, it was great fun. No one has any sympathy with the self-pitying statesman, going about, like poor Ramsay MacDonald, complaining that he felt like 'a weary Titan'. After all, the answer is easy. Nobody asked you to hold up the world. If your shoulders are tired, there are others ready and anxious to sustain the burden.

[Harold Macmillan, *Pointing the Way* (London, 1972), 34, 42–3.]

Perhaps the two most hard-worked words in Macmillan's extensive vocabulary of jocularity were 'fun' and a 'bore'. Being Prime Minister was, whatever the pressures and problems, always 'fun'—and he determined from the very first day that working for him should be, too. The atmosphere of No. 10 adjusted itself accordingly.

In one of the very rare passages of his lengthy memoirs where Macmillan, briefly, lets drop the mask to reveal the man inside, he tells how—after the rush of the first week in No. 10 had passed—he found 'a short opportunity for reflection'. Was he really Prime Minister? *What* was he? 'There was certainly attached to the whole affair a certain atmosphere of unreality and even absurdity . . .' He reflected that one side of his personality was, by instinct and training:

what has been called 'a gown man'; a product of a system which was intended to supply in the Middle Ages 'clerks' as priests and administrators, and in later times men to serve the Empire in its vast responsibilities . . . and, in addition, to provide instructors of the next generation. Even my family business had close connections with this quiet world of literature and art.

But 'The First World War turned me unexpectedly into a "swords man". Action—harsh, brutal, compelling, ousted learning. The gown was exchanged for a tunic.'

Macmillan admitted that he had 'ever since been conscious of this duality'. On the whole it had been an advantage; it had enabled him to escape from the worst moments of anxiety into the world of books. With considerable effort at self-mastery over the agony of nervous apprehension within, he had contrived to acquire externally 'a certain calm'. Though on a humbler scale, he liked to bracket himself with his two great heroes, Disraeli and Churchill, who 'both had this combination of the thinker and the doer—the artist and the man of action'.

His admiration for the wartime *style* of Field-Marshal Alexander showed just how important 'artistry' was to Macmillan. Deliberately, he set about achieving it at No. 10. He started by replacing the atmosphere of frenzy and 'flap' that had permeated the place under Eden with one of studied calm. Unashamedly he let it be known that he read Trollope. He silenced the klaxon on the prime ministerial car, which Eden had used liberally, while on the green-baize door of the Private Secretaries' room he pinned a quotation—in his own handwriting—from *The Gondoliers*: 'Quiet calm deliberation disentangles every knot.' (To it Wyndham, the ineffable Wodehousian humorist, once appended: 'And if it doesn't, you'll probably be shot!') The self-assured, ebullient Macmillan of the war years, 1939–45, the triumphant 'Viceroy of the Mediterranean', began to take command.

Unlike Eden, constantly interfering in departmental management, in Cabinet Macmillan would right away agree to basics, then leave the responsible minister to get on with the task on his own, and back him to the hilt. 'This had a very good effect in Cabinet,' observed one of his senior ministers, Derick Heathcoat Amory: 'It was exactly what ministers liked, it gave you a feeling of greater confidence . . .' For all the light-hearted informality he encouraged in Cabinet, a firm check was nevertheless kept on any levity that might threaten his authority. David Eccles, for four years his Secretary of the Board of Trade, recalled how, in Eden's day, letter-racks stood on the Cabinet table and Macmillan would amuse himself (and others) by detaching paper from them and scribbling ribald notes to his neighbours during dull moments—often (and perhaps deliberately) to the irritation of Eden. 'The day Harold Macmillan took over, the racks all disappeared.'

For her part, Dorothy Macmillan, even though her first reaction, according to John Wyndham, had been one of horror—'I married a publisher; now look at what I've got!'—with the same uncontrived natural charm that had won the hearts of the voters at Stockton, immediately gained the affections of all, down to the humblest 'garden-room girl' typists. Her success here was unrivalled by any subsequent Prime Minister's wife. Although her attachment to Boothby evidently still continued, modified by middle age, the responsibilities of office now eclipsed the errant love affair of the 1930s. No one spoke of it any more. In contrast to the childless Edens, there was a constant presence of family, with 'bicycles, tricycles, scooters, as well as an occasional perambulator' making itself felt in the august hall of No. 10. Standing orders were issued to grandchildren that, if they wished to play draughts with the policemen, 'they should do so in a way which would never obstruct the arrival of ambassadors or Cabinet ministers'. Nevertheless Dorothy herself would often burst into the house unannounced with a vanload of vegetables and flowers from Birch Grove, as the cosy Queen Anne town-house possessed no back door. Always the passionate gardener, she was soon at work with a trowel in the garden. No. 10, Macmillan glowed, was 'very comfortable. I have a good room as a study, next to Dorothy's "boudoir". (She has arranged a working sitting room upstairs.) The house is rather large, but has great character and charm. It is very liveable . . .'

Chequers, despite the great mound in the grounds, reputed to have been the fortress of King Cymbeline, was less appealing to the Macmillans: 'It is certainly a fine house, but it has been rather spoilt . . . there seems to be too much of everything . . .' Dorothy felt like a temporary leaseholder there; there was no point working seriously on the garden when it would go to someone else—probably Mrs Gaitskell; so it seemed logical to let the unhappy Selwyn Lloyd have it. Consequently, the Macmillans spent most of their time at Birch Grove, or at No. 10.

Macmillan was not exaggerating when he claimed that all these factors had combined to provide 'a certain warmth and geniality to the new regime' in a very short time. Despite the loneliness at the top and the vast volume of work, his 'job-fulfilment' was manifest—and infectious. He enjoyed vastly his Tuesday evening audiences with the Queen, whom he found 'not only very charming, but incredibly well-informed'. (Less 'fun' were visits from the Archbishop of Canterbury, then Fisher: '. . . I try to talk to him about religion. But he seems quite uninterested and reverts all the time to politics . . .').

[Alistair Horne, *Macmillan 1957–1986* (London, 1989), 12–14.]

## 5. DOUGLAS-HOME 1963–4

In a sense, Lord Home was a landed version of Attlee. They are the only two post-war premiers to have had no time for the black arts of political news management and personal public relations. Both were frugal in their use of energy and time. Both practised political economy around the Cabinet table. Both were tough on the prolix. As we have seen, Home thought Macmillan, whom he liked and admired, lax in this respect. For Lord Home, in Cabinet 'the great thing is to be short. People can't bear—they've got enough to listen to already—and anybody who waffles is written off pretty quickly and, therefore, you lose your point . . . To be short and concise is the secret of making an impact in Cabinet.'

Another Home technique for reducing the burden on the premiership was to devolve, even in an area central to his and the Government's fortunes:

HENNESSY You were always very honest about the one area in which you lacked expertise, which was economics. Did you try and compensate for that by the way you set up your Cabinet-committee structure? Did you chair the Economic Policy Committee, can you remember?

HOME Oh no. No, no, I wouldn't. The Chancellor of the Exchequer did that. But I used to talk to him [Reginald Maudling] regularly, of course. I used to talk to him regularly about what he was up to. I was not familiar with economics. They had never come my way. Nor have I been encouraged ever since to think there's an exact science. But it was a weakness. If I had thought I was going to be Prime Minister, I would have taken more trouble to understand the various theories.

In No. 10 Lord Home relied on his Principal Private Secretary, Derek Mitchell, a Treasury man, for assistance in this area. 'He was very efficient. I never understood a word about economics and his strength was economics.' Lord Home, who possesses a degree of candour unusual in political life, is still ambivalent about his handling of economic policy. 'If I'd taken more trouble with economics I might have been more effective as Prime Minister. But then, on the other hand, I believe in devolving your economics to the Chancellor of the Exchequer. If he can't make a go of them, nobody can.'

In one area he did, reluctantly, take steps to improve upon his lack of natural gifts.

HENNESSY It seems to be a conventional wisdom that relations with the media are absolutely crucial for a prime minister. But you, with Mr Attlee, were thought to be the most unworldly of post-war prime ministers on that. You just behaved as you, in fact, naturally were and had no time for the black arts of propaganda. Is that right?

HOME Well, I was bored by the whole of presentation as far as television was concerned because I think television is bound to be superficial. I was wrong. Harold Wilson convinced me I was wrong because he trained himself very, very well to be a pretty good television performer, and I think it is necessary for the Prime Minister. I still regret it, but I'm afraid the Prime Minister has to appear a great deal on the media.

[Hennessy, *Cabinet,* 64–5.]

## 6. WILSON 1964–70; 1974–6

On Monday, 19th October, we held our first Cabinet. Apart from myself, only two of the twenty-three members had sat in a Cabinet before. Patrick Gordon Walker had been Commonwealth Secretary in Clem Attlee's Government, from February 1950 to October 1951 and for that same period Jim Griffiths—now appointed, at the age of seventy-four, as a kind of 'Charter' Secretary of State for Wales—had been Secretary of State for the Colonies. George Brown had been a senior departmental minister at the Ministry of Works, but not a member of the Cabinet.

I had to lay down the rules, and as far as possible, and to the best of my memory, I based them on those insisted on by Clem Attlee. Strict timekeeping: the Cabinet could not be kept waiting for one or two laggards. Circulation of documents in adequate time for colleagues to read: only in an emergency would I give authority for a paper to be circulated on the day before Cabinet met. Departmental disagreements should be thrashed out before Cabinet met: where possible an agreed statement should be submitted where more than one department was involved. Where disagreement remained, this should be clearly stated and the arguments set out either in joint or separate papers. Any proposals involving expenditure should be fully discussed with the Treasury first, and Treasury agreement—or disagreement—recorded. The cost to the public purse should be set out in the paper. The figure, agreed by the Treasury, should be shown, even if the Treasury opposed the expenditure. In subsequent years I insisted more and more that the cost, too, in terms of civil service manpower should also be set out; before the end of the Government I accepted a Conservative backbench suggestion that such estimates, in addition to statements of financial cost, should be attached to the explanatory memorandum which accompanies public Bills when they are presented to Parliament.

[Harold Wilson, *The Labour Government 1964–1970: A Personal Record* (London, 1971), 17.]

## 7. HEATH 1970–4

Every Cabinet is coloured primarily by the personality of the Prime Minister. Each Premier has a different style and induces a different atmosphere. The first Cabinet in which I sat was led by Alec Home. He was easy-going, urbane, very commonsensical and practical, and had little taste for speculative flights of fancy. He aroused considerable loyalty and where there is strong loyalty to a Premier within Cabinet that loyalty spreads laterally and members find it more natural to support each other.

Ted Heath was a different sort of leader. Certainly, he attracted loyalty. A somewhat lonely man, he needed friendship, yet found it hard to unbutton himself to the affection of others; but those who knew him best were loyallest to him and I always found him an agreeable and happy companion, and at Chequers as well as Downing Street a charming host. Later, when his leadership was challenged, I had no difficulty in saying publicly that I thought the party would be best served if it retained Heath as its chief. In my view he had vision and a sense of history superior to those of any other claimant. Of course people said there was friendship as well as genuine calculation in my support, but friendship is a relevant factor in politics and particularly in Government. In a Cabinet there should be friendship, a sufficient degree of friendship in the atmosphere. It cannot work well otherwise.

Heath could, as Prime Minister, be abrasive and sometimes contrived to seem at the same time both touchy and autocratic. But in my experience Prime Ministers tend to become autocratic. It is probably necessary. They also tend, after a honeymoon period with their party, to be criticized for not listening to others—Heath certainly was. In my view this was untrue. He certainly listened. He may not always have been persuaded by what he heard—but that is the top person's prerogative.

He was an indifferent steward of his own time, sometimes showing small capacity for concentrating on the right priorities, on always putting first things first. Nevertheless I had a high regard for Ted Heath and I believe that history will rate him as a Prime Minister, and his administration, a good deal higher than it does at present. He was delightful to work with. He was passionately devoted to his country, and he wanted to achieve specific things. He had no use for the game of politics as such—he was the sort of politician who is interested only in results and realities. He had a much broader view of what Britain could be than most leading politicians I have known. He had a strong, lucid mind. He was a man of wide interests and talents—sporting, artistic, cultured. He was extremely courageous. He had, when at the Foreign Office, led the way in devilling our negotiating position to join the European Community, an experience which had undoubtedly widened his understanding; and he was utterly convinced that in bringing Britain into the Community he was taking a step which was as essential as it was historic. He will increasingly be proved right. The Community was a great element in Ted Heath's political faith.

[Lord Carrington, *Reflect on Things Past* (London, 1988), 252–3.]

## 8. CALLAGHAN 1976–9

James Callaghan's premiership lasted only three years. So rocky was the first of them that few political observers expected him to complete a second, let alone a third. In that first year he faced the loss of his parliamentary majority, the public discipline of the IMF, and the death of the one senior colleague on whom he could have expected most to rely: Foreign Secretary Anthony Crosland.

Although his son-in-law Peter Jay claimed that he saw himself as a Moses leading his people in search of the Promised Land, Callaghan's style was better suited to the close huddle and the well-chosen word than to the wilderness and inspired leadership. The rival whom he had swiftly let go to Brussels, Roy Jenkins, who had described him to Crossman as a unique case 'where a man combined such a powerful political personality with so little intelligence', now sees his period in office more charitably:

'He had a great ability to nudge himself along a channel . . . He navigated not by sitting down in advance and working out his course with instruments but doing it very successfully by instinct.'

This was the only method Callaghan could use in negotiating the uncharted political waters in which he found himself: nudge the banks, and hope to get through. He believed that this caution would win him support when he had to submit himself to the electorate in his own right. One of his youngest cabinet ministers, William Rodgers, remembers that Callaghan used to muse:

'We can win the election if when I go into [it] people will say, "Jim Callaghan is the Prime Minister of this country, he's the able seaman, he's a man who understands the common man."'

Or, as Len Murray describes this common touch:

'He was best when he thought with his stomach. He had every strong intuition about what was possible in the field of politics.'

Such a leader does not put the highest priority on the views of his middle-class activists or their cherished aims. It was later to be a cause of rebuke from them that his government failed to deliver on its manifesto promises. In fact Callaghan's government continued the attempt of the Wilson cabinet to implement further social and employment legislation buttressing the Social Contract, and, in spite of a prolonged procedural rearguard action, nationalised the aircraft and shipbuilding industries. Failures included, in the end: devolution for Scotland and Wales, where the government strove mightily (see chapter 14); and pledges to introduce a wealth tax, reform of Official Secrets, and the reduction of the privileges of private education—in all of which the government strove not at all. Winning time, rather than winning the arguments, sometimes seemed to be its preoccupation. Time for the reduction of inflation to be appreciated. Time for the country to get over the falling sickness of 1976. The key to gaining this time was to win the support, or at least the acceptance, of the major groups in and out of Parliament who held the fate of a minority Labour government in their hands.

[Phillip Whitehead, *The Writing on the Wall* (London, 1985), 256–7.]

I did my work mainly in the Cabinet Room at No. 10, for I liked its sense of history. It also has the asset of being more airy and less claustrophobic than the Prime Minister's study on the first floor, and as the Private Secretaries live in the next room, it saves their legs. For the first day or two while I was making governmental changes there was a constant stream of Ministers coming and going, but once that was complete I sat back and realised I had nothing to do. Ministers were busy with their Departmental work; the telephone did not ring for, generally speaking, people do not telephone the Prime Minister—the Prime Minister telephones them; replies to hundreds of letters of congratulations were being drafted elsewhere; the Cabinet Secretariat was efficiently arranging the meetings of Ministerial committees and my next appointment seemed to be a meeting of the Cabinet in two days' time.

In all my previous Departments Private Secretaries would have arrived in the room as soon as I set foot in the door, bearing piles of official papers to read and files with urgent problems for immediate decision. For a brief period as I sat in the Cabinet Room I savoured the suspicion that as everyone else was doing the Government's work, I could be the idlest member of the Administration if I was so minded. It was of course an illusion, although I never went to the other extreme and believed that a Prime Minister must be a workaholic. There are several instruments at his hand whose purpose is to ease the load, and provided he understands what can safely be delegated, and has a politically sensitive network around him to ring alarm bells before matters go too far wrong in Cabinet, Parliament or Party, he need not be the hardest worked member of his Government.

In my experience the work-load was greater both as Chancellor and as Foreign Secretary. To a large extent the Prime Minister makes his own pace. It is the Prime Minister himself who takes the initiatives, who pokes about where he chooses and creates his own waves. Ideally he should keep enough time to stand back a little from the Cabinet's day-to-day work, to keep in touch with Parliamentary and outside opinion, and to view the scene as a whole, knowing full well that periods of crisis will occur when this will be impossible.

[James Callaghan, *Time and Chance* (London, 1987), 402–3.]

## 9. THATCHER 1979–

'Margaret Thatcher is courageous and resolute. She speaks for the people of Britain and is the first Prime Minister for decades to have the guts to do what is necessary to put the country back on its feet. She sticks up for the individual. She speaks for the moral values we have lost. She has put pride and purpose back into the nation. Francis Pym is ineffective and negative. He epitomises the willingness to compromise that has led Britain downhill. He has no practical alternatives to offer. All he does is whine about things he does not have the nerve to do himself.'

'Margaret Thatcher is a dangerous, doctrinaire demagogue. She has brought industrial disaster to the country because of an inflexible refusal to adjust her bogus ideology. She is determined to destroy the social services and to bring misery to working people. Francis Pym had the courage to stand up to this tyranny and look where it got him. He stands for the decent, compassionate side of Conservatism. He is a man of principle and integrity.'

Neither paragraph is a direct quotation, yet the flavour of each will seem familiar to anyone who reads the newspapers—especially the first, since it reflects the view of most Fleet Street proprietors. The public is presented with one of these stereotypes and told to agree with it. Failure to agree with the stated view, it is suggested, means acceptance of the opposite view, and look how ridiculous that is. No point in between is on offer.

Of all the arguments advanced in this book, the one I most want to communicate is that the habit of viewing life, politics and personalities in black and white terms is both false and dangerous. To reduce the complexities of life to two polarised contradictions on every issue is to contradict the nature of life itself. Anyone who approaches this book expecting either to agree or to disagree with everything it says will, I hope, be disappointed. We may need to simplify life in order to deal with it, but we should never assume that life is simple, that any one person's conclusions are the truth or that no alternatives exist.

Yet the spirit of the age encourages us to be absolutist. Margaret Thatcher is in tune with this spirit and has perhaps done more than anyone to create it. She likes everything to be clear-cut: absolutely in favour of one thing, absolutely against another. It is the opposite of my approach, which is no less decisive, but which is to say—yes, we should take this action, but we should do it in a particular way, because we must take into account the legitimate view of this group or that. It is a mode of thought that she dislikes: she prefers to go straight for her target.

Such an approach does not lack all merit: sometimes it is right and necessary and the only way to get things done. But it is not my preferred approach and not my style. I do not accept that proposed courses of action are totally good or totally bad. I do not accept that people are wholly right or wholly wrong. I do not accept that one set of policies will lead to unalloyed triumph, nor the other to unmitigated disaster. Yet this Government, more than most, presents itself in such a way and most newspapers echo the polarity. To be loyal means one hundred per cent acceptance of Government thinking: any dissent, or even the admittance of doubt, is treachery and treason. After nine years as party leader and five as Prime Minister, Margaret Thatcher still asks people the question, 'Are you one of us?', by which she means, 'Are you completely free of any doubt as to the utter rightness of everything we are doing?'

It will come as no surprise that I am not 'one of us'. I regard the viewpoints expressed in the opening paragraphs as caricatures. Both contain elements of the truth, but exaggerated to the point where they become untrue. Truth must involve balance, which both statements lack. Balance is tiresome. It means that one has to think about things, to see other points of view, to abandon the comforting crutch of certainty. How much simpler it is to declare one's own convictions to be the truth and to have done with all the difficulties. It is easy to fall victim to this process. Many people must think that, since I am not an unqualified admirer of the Government, I am its out and out critic. I am not. I admire a great deal about both the Prime Minister and the Government, but not everything. So I would ask the reader to give up all preconceptions at this point, to approach the book in a spirit of balanced enquiry and to acknowledge that the rich colours of life cannot be reduced to black and white.

The second point I want to make at the outset also concerns

balance. I believe that every positive characteristic has an opposite dimension and that the two are intrinsically related. If everything that I most dislike about the Government's approach was to be eradicated, much of what I most admire might well be eradicated also. The same is true of everyone and everything. The two sides of the coin may not be of equal value, but both sides exist. If one recognises this fact, one can find ways to obviate the weaknesses and enhance the strengths. In politics, I believe this argues the need for a Government—or any other group—which contains a range of complementary talents, rather than one with such similar talents that its collective weaknesses restrict its collective strengths. This belief, together with my sense of the overall balance of life, precludes me from seeing anything or anyone in wholly black and white terms. These attitudes colour the rest of the book.

[Francis Pym, *The Politics of Consent* (London, 1984), 1–3.]

The power of a modern Prime Minister is awesome, particularly when it comes to the power of appointment and dismissal of Ministers. But the Leader of any party in power will know that there has to be some sort of balance in a Cabinet, between right and left, youth and age, different backgrounds and so on.

The balance of the Cabinet looked better for our wing of the Party than I had dreamt possible. Looking round the table at our first Cabinet meeting, I saw that most of us had worked together in the Shadow Cabinet and had managed to restrain Margaret from pursuing her more extreme instincts.

The only major changes from the Shadow Cabinet were the introduction of Christopher Soames, Peter Walker, George Younger and Humphrey Atkins, who had been Chief Whip in Opposition and became Secretary of State for Northern Ireland following Airey Neave's assassination on the eve of the election campaign.

A number of us had experience of Government at the highest level and knew the difficulties and how hard it would be to bring about change. It wasn't that we were against changes which would lead to a free and more dynamic economy; but we were conscious of the need to seek to carry people with us so that the changes we made would stick. We knew as well that our problem would be compounded by a deepening world recession, which was bound to follow the further dramatic increase in the price of oil in 1979, from around \$13 per barrel at the start of the year to \$23 by February. By May, deals approaching \$40 per barrel were being reported.

I thought that we would at least be able to avoid most of the follies which new Governments tend to commit and that we wouldn't be stupidly right wing and doctrinaire about economic policy, as we had been between 1970 and 1972. It is often forgotten that *The Times*' leading articles in 1971 were arguing that the Heath Government was the most right wing government since the Second World War. In the same way, Labour Governments behave in a ridiculous left wing manner for the first two years before settling down and accepting the facts of life.

However, the composition of the economic team at the Treasury and the other economic Departments obviously showed she was going to have her own way as far as she possibly could. Margaret's main supporters at the outset in Cabinet were Geoffrey Howe, her Chancellor, Keith Joseph at Industry, John Nott at Trade, David Howell at Energy, Patrick Jenkin at Social Services, Angus Maude as Paymaster-General and John Biffen as Chief Secretary to the Treasury—not a very impressive bunch, and with little experience at the centre of Government. In addition, the three 'territorial' Ministers, Nick Edwards at the Welsh Office, George Younger at the Scottish Office, and Humphrey Atkins at Northern Ireland, in the early days all generally supported the Prime Minister's line.

I was the only Minister in the economic team with whom she was likely to have any difficulties. In some respects I was surprised to be offered Employment. After all, I had not had a very easy run with the Party in Opposition but I think Margaret felt to have changed me then would have signified too dramatic a shift in policy, and in any case what else was she likely to have offered me? The writing may already have been on the wall, but it did not seriously worry me to start with, because I assumed she would take things gradually, bearing in mind the experience of Ted's Government some five years before.

The dissenters in the Cabinet included Peter Carrington at the Foreign Office, myself at Employment, Peter Walker at Agriculture, Mark Carlisle at Education, Michael Heseltine at the Environment, Norman St John Stevas as Leader of the House, and Gilmour as Lord Privy Seal and Carrington's deputy.

This left a powerful foursome of Willie Whitelaw at the Home Office, Hailsham as Lord Chancellor, Francis Pym at Defence, and

Christopher Soames as Leader of the Lords, who were less openly in one camp or the other. This foursome nearly always split equally, with the former two supporting the Prime Minister.

In Cabinet, Quintin Hailsham, the Lord Chancellor, varied from being brilliant to being astonishingly off-beam. He is a man of enormous character, a splendid and convincing orator. He was always unpredictable, except where the judges were concerned: he would always defend them and their pay increases until he was beaten into the ground. I had great rows with him and he got the impression I was anti-lawyer: in fact, I was not against them, but I was against lawyers getting away with things they would never agree to other people getting away with.

Yet Quintin was a great ally in my 'step-by-step' approach on trade union reform. He did understand human nature, unlike Geoffrey Howe and the then Solicitor-General, Sir Ian Percival, who knew nothing about the shop floor and what made people tick.

Christopher Soames was the most interesting of the newcomers. He had not been associated with the liberal wing of the Party, and he was very much of the traditional centre, tending in some ways to be rather to the right. He was a man of very considerable authority and experience who had been in Cabinet at the time of Macmillan and Alec Home, then Ambassador in Paris and a Vice-President of the European Commission. Yet whenever he had an argument with Margaret, or if someone else was stating a policy with which he did not agree, he became in some strange way at a disadvantage. I think he disappointed himself by not being able to put his points as cogently or coherently as he would have wished.

Having wanted Christopher back because she thought that he would give strength and stability to her otherwise fairly inexperienced Cabinet, Margaret was disappointed and very quickly took the line that she could manage without him. No one had as much experience of the people or workings within the Commission of the Community as Christopher yet she deliberately avoided letting him play any part in discussion about it. Having made an inspired decision to bring him back into Government, she then failed to make use of him.

Peter Walker also returned, although he had been a rebel for a number of years. It was a clever appointment, because the Minister of Agriculture has to spend a great deal of time negotiating in Brussels, and Peter had never been a great supporter or admirer of the Community. He therefore found it quite easy to argue the toss with our European partners, and he was also kept away from the centre of Government decision-making.

Francis Pym had taken over responsibility for Foreign Affairs for a short while before the election. But it was clear that Peter Carrington would be Foreign Secretary. He was well versed in Foreign Affairs, had been Defence Secretary for most of Ted's Government, and was a director of Rio Tinto Zinc, which took him all over the world, particularly to Africa.

Peter's great advantage in Margaret's eyes was that he was a Lord, and therefore not a close rival for her job. She had a soft spot for the aristocracy, especially someone with Peter's charm and intelligence. I was delighted when she made him Foreign Secretary. With all his gifts, he proved a great advocate and ambassador for Britain. He was immensely popular with the Foreign Office at home and with his counterparts abroad.

In the early days of Margaret's Cabinet, Ministers often used to pass notes to one another during Cabinet. There were those which were meant to be amusing, or some private notes; there were those which were very private, which said: 'Wasn't he simply terrible?' or, 'She's got it all wrong.'

Peter Carrington was a great note-passer—his were all cryptic little remarks about what was being discussed or how dreadful someone was. I used to pass notes a lot to Peter Carrington, Christopher Soames and Ian Gilmour—although they were right down the other end of the table so it wasn't easy. Geoffrey Howe was also a great note-passer, and it was he who produced the anagram of Mugabe as 'E Ba Gum'.

Perhaps Peter's most celebrated note was the one he passed Margaret when they were having a meeting with the Chinese Prime Minister. It became clear that nothing could stop the latter talking, and Margaret was getting agitated and fed up. Peter sent her a note saying, 'Prime Minister, you are talking too much.'

Margaret had little experience of the higher levels of Government. She had always been cold-shouldered by Ted; she sat in Cabinet on his right side, carefully hidden by the Secretary of the Cabinet, who was always leaning forward to take notes. It was the most difficult place for anyone to catch the Prime Minister's eye, and I am sure that she was placed there quite deliberately.

The best position is one of the seats opposite the Prime Minister, which are occupied by the Chancellor, the Home Secretary, and the Foreign Secretary. I also sat facing Margaret, although not directly opposite. In those early days Margaret was better than Ted at allowing everyone to have a say—her Cabinet tended to be far more argumentative—and it was nothing like such a disadvantage to sit on the same side of the table as Margaret and on the far side of the Cabinet Secretary: for example, Peter Walker and Norman Tebbit both sat there.

Margaret found for the first time that she really did have the levers of power in her hands, and my goodness she was going to exercise them. From day one in Cabinet she was very much more determined and gave a far stronger lead than she ever gave in Opposition. The full extent of the power of a modern Prime Minister, who has the support of the Cabinet Office and Number Ten itself, is still not fully appreciated. Nothing really happens in Whitehall unless the central driving force of Number Ten or the Cabinet Office has approved it.

In Opposition, Margaret's tendency to the extreme had been tempered by her need to carry colleagues with her and her need not to frighten people into believing there would be chaos if she were elected. The belief then that Britain was ungovernable was never far below the surface. But, once in power, Margaret turned this belief to her advantage, for it could then be used to support her argument that strong government was what the country really needed. I am sure that by 1979 people were looking for new courage and a fresh determination in tackling Britain's problems. Margaret showed at once that she was tough and not likely to be shaken off once she had made up her mind. More than ever I think that has been her greatest asset.

Those of us in Cabinet who were out of sympathy with Margaret's views grossly under-estimated her absolute determination, along with Geoffrey and Keith, to push through the new right wing policies. We also under-estimated enormously the change in the whole philosophy of the right and the changes in the Conservative Party which were taking place. The fact that the Conservative Research Department was reduced to a nonentity following Chris Patten's departure to become an MP; that the Centre for Policy Studies was built up to rival and usurp it; and that the new right had a grip on the Press, with people like Paul Johnson and Andrew Alexander spouting extreme right wing views.

We didn't appreciate the degree to which the Party was becoming more and more doctrinaire in its approach and less and less pragmatic. And the doctrinaire people were in a strong position in that, although their own policies did not seem to fare particularly well at first, they were able to say the whole time that they had to be given a fair chance: after all, the pragmatic approach had been tried for the previous twenty or more years and could not be judged as an enormous success. Even the era of Macmillan and Butler was talked about as a disaster.

We pragmatists were on a very difficult wicket, because we could not prove in a short time that their ideas were wrong. We could not even say that ours had been particularly successful, because in the 1970s they undoubtedly had not succeeded. Only the passage of time would prove our point, but by then a great deal of damage could have been done to the country, and to our Party.

We made a number of fundamental mistakes in the way that we tried to deal with Margaret and her allies. We obviously weren't subtle enough; perhaps we weren't clever enough to take them on at their own game. But it was very much like the problems that the Conservative Opposition had when Wilson became Prime Minister in 1964. He was able to blame everything on the thirteen wasted years of Tory misrule. The thirteen 'wasted' years were the most successful years this country has ever had, but that could still not be proved for a few years, until things started to go wrong. But if someone is determined enough they can make anything that has gone before look rather silly for a time.

[James Prior, *A Balance of Power* (London, 1986), 114–19.]

On another topic, I am asked if Margaret Thatcher ever listens to points of view other than her own. This question, with its perception of her, angers me, for it is grossly unfair. I think she probably enjoys an argument more than most people, and the more vigorous it is, the better, as far as she is concerned. She is by nature a conviction politician and so has very strong views, yet she can certainly be swayed and influenced by good arguments in the final event. I wish the critics would realize that no one could have presided over such a successful team as Leader unless they had been prepared to take account of internal discussions. Of course it is not easy to convert her, but that should surely be the case with a powerful Leader. She is certainly the type of chairman who leads from the front and from the start of a discussion makes no secret of her own feelings and views. But all chairmen have their different methods, even if most successful ones like to get their way in the end. I know that I am totally different from Margaret Thatcher in the way that I handle meetings, and that some people regard me as too conciliatory. But I have to acknowledge the truth of the remark which Norman Tebbit alleges that I made to him: 'My image is emollient—and so I am, but only when I am getting my own way.'

[Lord Whitelaw, *The Whitelaw Memoirs* (London, 1989), 263.]

Margaret Thatcher is a person of striking firmness of purpose and integrity of character. She has been caricatured in the way that strong personalities often are, so that the whole world reckons it knows them well, and likes or loathes according to preference, with few indifferent. Such characters, and particularly if they are politicians, arouse powerful reactions of adulation or condemnation, and Margaret Thatcher has had her share of both. It may be a defect in my temperament that I find it much more natural to like than dislike people I work with or for. I may be irritated by characteristics but I generally sympathize with perceived difficulties and challenges. I could see why people criticized Ted Heath, but I thoroughly liked him and admired him, and I regretted his departure. In the same way but for different reasons I came to like and admire Margaret Thatcher too.

Margaret Thatcher's attitudes are not far from the historic Liberal Party in England with its emphasis upon self-help and individualism. She calls things by their proper names, she is unashamed of any of her views, she has an excellent mind and well-reasoned opinions and she knows her strengths. Margaret, from the first day of leading the party, made clear that she thought and felt we needed to take a new direction, that there was no hope for our country unless inflation was destroyed by strict monetarist measures (whose efficacy I suspect she exaggerated, but I have no desire for an economic dissertation in this book), no hope unless the possibility and the will for individual effort and reward were revived among the British, no hope unless the power of the state were sharply diminished, particularly in economic affairs, and unless the function of the trades unions was restored to representing their members' interests (as opposed to dictating to Governments which economic policies the TUC found acceptable). In all this there was no doubt she had the mood of the country increasingly with her. In all this—or in the specific policies her philosophy indicated—she was particularly supported and inspired by the studies led by Keith Joseph, a much misunderstood man whose intellect and goodness of heart were equally great, but perhaps greater than was his power of communication with ordinary people, despite his enormous kindness. Under Margaret Thatcher the Tory Party took a decisive turn—described as 'right wing', a somewhat imprecise term; or towards 'conviction politics'; or in many other laudatory or offensive terms, according to taste. The mood was for classical economic theory, for the self-regulatory efficiency of market forces, for wider ownership of property, for personal responsibility and inducement, and for strong, patriotic commonsense in addressing all manner of issues. I suspect much of this—and I hope the best of this—marks a permanent shift of emphasis.

The danger of such attitudes is that they can be applied to issues beyond their reach. It may be estimable to feel in a particular way about a certain relatively uncomplicated matter—robust commonsense and moral courage may be exactly the qualities required. In other fields, and notably in those where foreign policy is concerned, they may not suffice. The prejudices of others are often tedious and irrational—and may be contrary to their own best interests, too—but where they exist they are facts: and factors. The heart may urge in one direction but the head, tiresomely, may indicate another course. In foreign affairs, particularly, one has always to calculate the consequences, and shun the self-indulgence of reacting as instinct may suggest.

It is to Margaret Thatcher's credit that on such occasions—of which, later, I was to observe several—her heart was generally compelled by her to yield, albeit grudgingly, to her highly intelligent head; and this not under pressure from others but because she, a woman of integrity, could weigh evidence, perceive (no doubt often with irritation) what course would turn out best and, against natural impulse, decide to follow it. That takes a great deal of doing, not least when one has to shed some old friends as well as previous conceptions along the way. Later, some of her more assiduous admirers were quick to suppose that her instincts (assumed as combative) would always be in conflict with the advice of the

Foreign Office (presumed to be placatory). They may have sometimes supposed correctly, but they seldom appreciated that her judgement was capable of being superior to her—and their—instincts, and that genuine agreement could result.

[Carrington, *Reflect on Things Past*, 274–6.]

Mrs Thatcher is not a committee person, preferring to do things rather than to discuss them. Having decided upon her philosophical orientations, her aim was to operationalise them: discussion would be at best wasteful and was clearly potentially obstructive. From Cabinet ministers she desired unquestioning support. As Francis Pym observed, 'To be loyal means one hundred per cent acceptance of Government thinking: any dissent, or even the admittance of doubt, is treachery and treason.' After nine years as party leader and five as Prime Minister, Margaret Thatcher still asks people the question 'Are you one of us?', by which she means 'Are you completely free of any doubt as to the utter rightness of everything that we are doing?' In Cabinet, when the Prime Minister had to face expressions of doubt, she responded aggressively. Often she would present her viewpoint and then seek to defend it, being keen to intimidate and dominate, and if such a domineering style did not prevail, or if it was unlikely to prevail, then the tactic adopted was to prevent or postpone discussion. Clearly, Mrs Thatcher is not the chairman style of Prime Minister. When questioned in 1980 about the alleged difficulty that ministers have in expressing a viewpoint, she replied 'Oh no, if they want to speak, they can speak. I always look around to see whether anyone else wants to say anything.' The reductions noted by Peter Hennessy in the use of Cabinet meetings (about half the 1950s norm), in the submissions of discussion papers to Cabinet (about one sixth of the 1950s norm) and in the use of committees, are a clear indication that less discussion is taking place now than was the case in the past. Francis Pym in 1984 commented on the difficulty of expressing views in Cabinet and Michael Heseltine, at the time Secretary of State for Defence, in his resignation speech during the Westland affair, echoed this point. He suggested that Mrs Thatcher tried to get her own way as regards Westland, and when she could not do so, she prevented discussion in Cabinet. He also complained about the lack of accuracy of a Cabinet minute and that ministerial statements on Westland were to be cleared before publication. Such clearance systems are in fact normal procedure, and in so far as they ensure that ministers speak in accord, they protect both the minister and the doctrine of collective responsibility. As to the issue of the minute, guidance is provided by the rule book of ministerial conduct,'Questions of Procedure for Ministers'. On the conduct of Cabinet meetings, it states that the record of meetings 'is limited to the decisions taken and such summary of the discussion as may be necessary for the guidance of those who have to take action on them'. The non-recording of a discussion, and even more so the non-recording of a protest by a minister, which were the matters that Michael Heseltine made an issue of, may well not have been omissions under these criteria. Even the avoidance of discussion of an issue is provided for by these rules in that the Prime Minister controls the agenda. The problem with this analysis is that such powers are of great assistance to an autocratically-minded Prime Minister and, indeed, it was as a protest over the style of government that Michael Heseltine resigned.

The role of the Cabinet under Mrs Thatcher is to endorse rather than to make decisions. This was evident in a statement by Geoffrey Howe, Secretary of State for Foreign and Commonwealth Affairs since 1983, during an interview with the *Daily Mail* on the 6th February 1984. When asked whether or not the full Cabinet had discussed the decision to ban trade unions at the Government Communications Headquarters at Cheltenham, he replied, 'No. It was discussed, as almost every government decision is discussed, by the group of ministers most directly involved. There are very few discussions of government decisions by full Cabinet.' Mrs Thatcher favours decision making by means of informal ad hoc sessions at Number 10. The behaviour of a Cabinet committee, led by Lord Whitelaw, at the time Lord President of the Council and from 1979–83 Home Secretary, which was set up in 1985 to consider the teachers' pay dispute, is informative. Instead of making a report to the Cabinet, it reported back to the Prime Minister at a meeting she chaired at Number 10. James Prior, who was Secretary of State for Employment (1979–81) and Secretary of State for Northern Ireland (1981–4), tells us that the use of such groups developed gradually; that she used the formal machinery of Cabinet government at first, but then, 'after a few years, the formal Cabinet committees were very much downgraded and she began to operate much more in small groups dominated by her cronies'. He also suggests that it was the Falklands issue in 1982 which convinced her of the advantages of working with just five or six people and that in the years since 'she has adopted ad hoc groups as one of her main methods of government'. The Falklands crisis has been portrayed as a situation in which the Prime Minister had to consult with and carry the Cabinet. Peter Hennessy states that during the crisis 'she practised Cabinet government in something approaching the traditional form'. However, as a corrective to this, he notes the view of David Howell, Secretary of State for Energy (1979–81); for Transport (1981–3), 'the major issues of the Falklands War were more or less written in the stars. There wasn't actually a great sense of choice or option.' If Cabinet government is characterised by collective decision making, it seems to be a very poor example of it if there are in fact no decisions or choices to be made. Much of the above claims as to style of decision making are admitted by Mrs Thatcher herself. During a Panorama television documentary in February 1986 she stated that 'The idea that you could run things competently by having everything to Cabinet is nonsense. There are twenty-one members of Cabinet. On one issue if they all speak two minutes that's forty-two minutes. It's absolutely ridiculous that you can do things that way. Most things are done in Cabinet committee and then reported to Cabinet.' However, as James Prior pointed out, by making decisions in ad hoc groups, and not having discussions in Cabinet, you end up with Cabinet ministers 'who felt they were never told what was really going on'.

Mrs Thatcher attempts to make as many decisions as she can herself. As Francis Pym indicates, 'She would ideally like to run the major departments herself and tries her best to do so—not just in terms of overall policy, but in strategic detail.' This point had been made as early as September 1979 by the *Economist*. It stated that the Prime Minister had involved herself in policy, in virtually every department, to an unprecedented extent. David Watt also commented upon the level of control sought by the Prime Minister, 'It has been virtually impossible to talk to any minister or senior official outside the Cabinet office for many months without hearing another tale of woe—about prime-ministerial highhandedness, about Downing Street interference in detailed departmental matters and about the manipulative use of Cabinet committees and ad hoc working groups to ensure that decisions are taken in accordance with Mrs Thatcher's wishes.' This centralisation was indicated by

Mrs Thatcher herself when in 1984 she commented, 'I was re-elected with an overwhelming majority last year.' In the reliance on her own viewpoint, she is attempting resolutely to operationalise her philosophy, a situation summed up by her statement to senior colleagues, 'Don't tell me what, tell me how, I know what.'

Centralisation has also been apparent in relation to Mrs Thatcher's use of support staff at Number 10 and in the control she has exercised over the appointment of senior civil servants. In terms of the former, whilst she attempted in 1979 to manage with very few, expansion in numbers over the years amounted in Francis Pym's view to 'establishing a government within a government'. The aim in appointing these monetarist-orientated experts in the major policy areas was to provide support for the Prime Minister's attempts to implement spending cuts and policies. Support was required because of the opposition offered by departmental ministers and civil servants. Francis Pym commented upon this, 'I object to a system that deliberately pits Downing Street against individual departments, breeds resentment amongst ministers and civil servants and turns the Prime Minister into a President.' As to the civil service, Mrs Thatcher came as something of a culture shock. A notable feature of this was that the monetarist approach was generally not understood or supported. In order to increase the positive contribution of the civil service to her scheme of things and to minimise negative factors, Mrs Thatcher, as Prime Minister, took a more than usual interest in the appointment of senior officials. By vetting appointments, she could ensure the selection of those sympathetic to her policy aspirations. Such a politicalisation is clearly a breach of the established convention, that appointments should be for their ability to serve differently orientated administrations. Equally, this politicalisation and use of patronage by the Prime Minister confuses the conventional relationships between ministers and civil servants because it encourages the latter to view the Prime Minister rather than the departmental ministers as their political master.

From the evidence to date, it seems that Mrs Thatcher favours a restricted role for the Cabinet; her expressions of contempt for many of her Cabinet colleagues also suggest this. Simon Winchester noted the viewpoint of an undisclosed close acquaintance of the Prime Minister, 'She thinks of them as pretty useless baggage, the kind of dead weight a Tory leader has to carry along.' Hugh

Stephenson gave a less dramatic account of her attitude to her Cabinet colleagues, 'Her manner towards them was often that of a bossy hen-pecking wife, or a school-marm towards her intelligent but potentially delinquent charges'. Peter Riddell, more in line with Westminster's source, stated that 'In the early days of her administration Whitehall frequently buzzed with stories about the ministers she had told to shut up in front of officials, the ultimate loss of face in the mandarin world'. In similar vein Simon Hoggart reported: 'Once in front of a couple of dozen Tory Members of Parliament, she asked Francis Pym, who was then Defence Secretary, what he was doing about the Sea Eagle missile. He said that he had not made up his mind. "Then Clive and I will have to do it for you. We always do." she said rudely.' (Clive Whitmore was Permanent Secretary at the Ministry of Defence.) Bruce Arnold's account of the launch of the Conservative Party manifesto in 1983 is also instructive: 'The overriding impression given at that first encounter was of the party leader's complete dominance over her colleagues and the press. She gave a clear demonstration that she was running the show from beginning to end. She contradicted Francis Pym, virtually silenced William Whitelaw, took over one question from Sir Geoffrey Howe, and looked with indulgence only upon Norman Tebbit and Cecil Parkinson. (Norman Tebbit held Cabinet posts from 1981 to 1987 which included Secretary of State for Employment, whilst Cecil Parkinson was at the time Chancellor of the Duchy of Lancaster, and later Secretary of State for Trade and Industry.) It was her election, her party, her manifesto. And it was going to stay that way.' Hoggart also noted Norman Tebbit's privileged position and her contempt for others when he quoted a backbencher who knows her well, 'Basically she thinks that everyone is useless except Norman.' In short, Mrs Thatcher seemed to regard her ministers as obstacles rather than allies in the business of government, a point she made herself in an event referred to by Winchester. In 1981 she climbed on to a chair at a Downing Street reception to announce, 'You see before you a rebel amidst a government of squares.'

On the basis of the above the following conclusions can be offered: that Mrs Thatcher attempts to make a wide range of decisions herself in a centralisation of policy making; that she prefers decision making of an informal kind as the formal structure of the Cabinet may act as a constraint upon her; that the Cabinet is faced by an aggressive and manipulative Prime Minister who attempts to dominate those for whom she seems to have little respect —in short, that she attempted a prime-ministerial style of government. However, the strategies by which she attempted to dominate ministers did not go unopposed. As Hugh Stephenson pointed out, 'In foreign affairs, on trade union law, on energy policy, for example, she was faced with ministers who had, or soon developed, strong views of their own, for which they were prepared to fight.' The result was that in the period up to the autumn of 1981, during which she was in a minority in Cabinet, there was an extraordinarily high level of publicised dissent by ministers from the Thatcher strategy, particularly over economic policy. Analysis of this period provides reinforcement for the views on Mrs Thatcher's style expressed above, and also provides insights as regards the power of a Prime Minister in the face of considerable adversity.

[Michael Doherty, 'Prime-Ministerial Power and Ministerial Responsibility in the Thatcher Era' (1988) 41 *Parliamentary Affairs* 49 at 53–7.]

## A Prime Minister's Strengths

### 1. THE ELECTORATE'S CHOICE

A Prime Minister has the invaluable political authority of being the choice (directly or indirectly) of the electorate, an advantage which neither his party nor any other Minister can claim. A general election is today the machinery through which a Prime Minister is chosen. Since the 1945 general election at the latest voters have been offered a choice—sometimes stark—between very different party Leaders: they will vote to keep Mr A in office, or to put in Mr B in his stead. At some elections the personification of a government in its leader will be stronger (as for instance with Macmillan in 1959, or Mr Wilson in 1966, or Mrs Thatcher in 1983 and 1987) than at others (as, say, with Sir Alec Douglas-Home in 1964). But now that general elections are firmly established in the United States presidential mould and are projected to a mass television audience it is most unlikely that any party would now try to win an election by offering a collective leadership with its Leader buried somewhere in it. No party returned to power this century could claim with any justice that it had won despite its Leader—rather, the victorious political parties will acknowledge that, while the nation's boredom with the late government, perhaps exacerbated by that government's loss of steam, taken with the attraction of the successful party's alternative policies, all played their parts, the personalities of the Leaders were vitally important. That concentration of attention on the successful Leader can clearly be seen in most of the six general elections since 1945 at which there was a change of government, and in the 1970 contest a case has been made that Mr Heath won almost despite his party.

Even when someone becomes Prime Minister by succeeding a resigning colleague or at the formation of a coalition, he can still be regarded as the indirect choice of the electorate, for he must be able to count on the support of the existing House of Commons returned by that electorate. Since 1945 Eden, Macmillan, Sir Alec Douglas-Home, and James Callaghan did not come initially to office in the wake of electoral victory, but they became accepted quickly by the majority party in the Commons (and in Mr Callaghan's case he had been elected by a majority of the Parliamentary Labour Party). From his first moments in office, therefore, a Prime Minister is imbued with authority conferred personally (albeit sometimes indirectly) by the electorate.

[Rodney Brazier, *Constitutional Practice* (Oxford, 1988), 64–6.]

## 2. POWER OVER MINISTERS

*Patronage in relation to Ministers is the most important political power enjoyed by a Prime Minister. No one achieves ministerial office without his approval; his continuing favour is essential if a Minister is to retain office; the deference which this can cause is clear.*

### (1) CHAMBERLAIN AND THATCHER

Feeling that Churchill's inclusion [in Chamberlain's Cabinet] would be of immense advantage to the Government, Hore-Belisha had a talk with Chamberlain, but the Prime Minister was quite adamant in his refusal. 'If I take him into the Cabinet,' Chamberlain said, 'he will dominate it. He won't give the others a chance of even talking.' Churchill was not informed of this conversation, for Hore-Belisha hoped that in time he might succeed in wearing down Chamberlain's resistance. When he later broached the subject, the Prime Minister with renewed emphasis remarked: 'I won't have anyone who will rock the boat.'

[R. J. Minney (ed.), *The Private Papers of Leslie Hore-Belisha* (London, 1960), 130.]

Sacking is the ultimate weapon in any prime minister's hand, and this meeting persuaded Mrs Thatcher that she had no alternative but to use it. All cabinet reshuffles, of course, have to be carefully calculated. Some ministers are strong enough not to be removed with impunity. But after more than two years in office, the season of reshuffling already beckoned. And the experience of those two years had hardly suggested that any collection of wets, even wets embittered by loss of office, would be capable of summoning the will and the method to damage the Government from the back-benches. At any rate, it was a gamble worth taking, for a prize that would be great: a cabinet, at last, dominated by people she could call her own. The event of 23 July [1981] hardened her purpose, and probably extended the range of her butchery.

The new cabinet was announced on 14 September, after all concerned had had a summer holiday to think about it. The mordant Gilmour was the first target, sacked from the Foreign Office. He was accompanied into the wilderness by Mark Carlisle, the Education Secretary, and Lord Soames, so recently the hero of Zimbabwe, now despatched from his position as leader of the House of Lords. Carlisle and Soames, although not major figures, were to be found on the wrong side of most of the arguments she cared about. Unlike Gilmour, who came stylishly out of 10 Downing Street to tell the waiting reporters that the Government was 'heading for the rocks', their public responses were meek. But Soames did not go quietly. When summoned to be sacked, he turned upon Mrs Thatcher all the fury of the dispossessed grandee. Her Private Secretary, Whitmore, was dismissed from the room, while Soames assailed her for twenty minutes for her various shortcomings, including the way she had treated him as minister for the civil service, handling a very bitter civil service strike. He had never been spoken to by a woman, he told her, in the abusive way she had spoken to him then. His thunderous curtain-lines, it was said, could be heard out of the open window halfway across Horseguards Parade.

A rather different case was James Prior. He was held not to be so dispensable, but was, on the other hand, ripe for moving. He was allowed to know in early August that he might be offered a very particular move, to the post of Secretary of State for Northern Ireland. This signal was conveyed, as became a regular Thatcher style with reshuffles that were going to hurt somebody, by nods and winks from Downing Street. Prior chose to respond with a bold tactic, letting it be known by signals of a similar kind that he would not accept the post. He was determined to stay where he was, close to the centre of economic power. He would not accept demotion and exile, and he made this clear in many public ways.

Somehow it was fitting that the leader's final act in this completion of her ascendancy, after a thirty-month passage of arms with the Conservatism she was determined to uproot, should be to call Prior's bluff. And it was equally appropriate that he, a decent and well-meaning man, should let this happen to him, as he had let quite a lot happen before. He decided, when she did formally offer him the Irish post, that in all honour he could not refuse it. To do so would have looked like running away from gunfire. Besides, perhaps his particular qualities of goodwill and sweet reason and political ingenuity would be more welcome in the benighted province than they any longer were in Whitehall.

Prior would have made a good Industry Secretary. It was the job he was qualified for, having actually worked in industry, unlike most of his colleagues. He passionately wanted to be there, at the productive end of the economy; and, under a leader more interested in forming a ministry of all the talents than in marginalising or excluding those that caused her trouble, he would have got it.

Instead, Belfast was, in all the circumstances, a natural terminus for this apostle of the old paternalism . . .

[Hugo Young, *One of Us* (London, 1989), 220–1.]

## (2) CABINET PECKING ORDER AND TABLE PLACINGS

My own procedure was to rely on the order of precedence within the Cabinet, the so-called 'pecking-order', making clear that the second in the list chairs Cabinet and any Cabinet committee normally chaired by me, if I were absent, and also stands in for me in answering questions in Parliament. From 1964 to 1968 George

Brown, who was elected deputy leader of the Party, held this position; after his resignation he held on to the deputy leadership outside the Government, and I simply advanced Michael Stewart to second place in the list of Cabinet precedence.

[Harold Wilson, *The Governance of Britain* (London, 1976), 23.]

Margaret had little experience of the higher levels of Government. She had always been cold-shouldered by Ted; she sat in Cabinet on his right side, carefully hidden by the Secretary of the Cabinet, who was always leaning forward to take notes. It was the most difficult place for anyone to catch the Prime Minister's eye, and I am sure that she was placed there quite deliberately.

The best position is one of the seats opposite the Prime Minister, which are occupied by the Chancellor, the Home Secretary, and the Foreign Secretary. I also sat facing Margaret, although not directly opposite. In those early days Margaret was better than Ted at allowing everyone to have a say—her Cabinet tended to be far more argumentative—and it was nothing like such a disadvantage to sit on the same side of the table as Margaret and on the far side of the Cabinet Secretary: for example, Peter Walker and Norman Tebbit both sat there.

[Prior, *Balance of Power*, 117.]

One morning I came into the Cabinet room rather early and found the Cabinet Secretary, Sir Norman Brook (later Lord Normanbrook) changing all our places. I asked what had happened—Had there been a shuffle?—or had one of us died in the night? 'Oh no,' said Sir Norman, 'it's nothing like that. The Prime Minister cannot stand Enoch Powell's steely and accusing eye looking at him across the table any more, and I've had to move him down to the side.'

[Home, *The Way the Wind Blows*, 192.]

## (3) RESHUFFLES

The power of appointment is therefore one of the chief ways a Prime Minister keeps his control over his party and while there are some restrictions on a Premier taking office for the first time, he has much greater freedom when it comes to later rearrangements. This power applies not only at first appointment but at every stage up the hierarchy and can be used with great subtlety. A man whom the Prime Minister does not care for may be given a tough assignment so that if he fails, he is destroyed, but if he succeeds the government as a whole and its leader can take the credit. Observing the political scene Lord Woolton concluded that 'Prime Ministers are apt to be autocratic in the disposal of their ministers, and I can see no other way by which the practice could operate.' In his draft Introduction to the new Edition of Bagehot's classic, *The English Constitution*, Mr Crossman, after eighteen years in politics, included a sentence that the British Prime Minister can liquidate the political career of one of his colleagues as effectively as any of the leaders of the Soviet Union can remove rivals. His publishers protested and he removed the observation. In 1967 after three years in the Cabinet, the only thing he regretted about his Introduction was the omission of this sentence.

The way in which these powers are operated naturally differs from one Prime Minister to another. Stanley Baldwin shrank from episodes involving personal tension and had no strong views on policy which might have made him contemplate changes. His chief desire was to keep the Conservative Party strong and give no chances to Labour or Lloyd George. Thus he left Austen Chamberlain and F. E. Smith out of his Cabinet in May 1923 when it became clear that their appointment would cause more disruption than their exclusion. Although he had fought the 1923 election under the banner of protection, Baldwin appointed the turbulent free-trader, Churchill, as his Chancellor of the Exchequer in 1924 and endured him for five years. Baldwin did not, however, disguise his relief when the landslide of 1931 and the reduced number of posts available in the National Government allowed him to relegate all those whom he had found restless or uneasy colleagues. Neville Chamberlain, in contrast, had no such hesitations. When he appointed Lord Maugham (a complete stranger) as Lord Chancellor, he told Maugham that the office might have to be surrendered if he, the Prime Minister, needed it in a reshuffle. In May 1938 Chamberlain dismissed the Secretary of State for Air, Lord Swinton, although the latter had the confidence of the Cabinet and was evidently a successful administrator. Hore-Belisha, who had been active and efficient at the War Office and had had Neville Chamberlain's confidence till late in 1939, was asked, without any warning, to resign on January 4, 1940. The Prime Minister had been to France, found there was acute resentment against Hore-Belisha among the senior British officers and decided to change his Secretary of State for War. At various times in 1938 and 1939 senior ministers had urged Chamberlain to broaden the membership of his Cabinet, but he flatly refused to take in men like Churchill or Eden who had disagreed with him. 'I won't have anyone who will rock the boat.'

[John Mackintosh, *The British Cabinet* (London, 3rd edn., 1977), 439–40.]

(*a*) *Constraints on a Prime Minister*

At the heart of the Conservatives' concerns was the economy. Economic regeneration was the major electoral commitment, and it included, however deceptively, a pledge to cut the dole queues. This was the major point of the leader's own attacks on the Labour Government. 'Sometimes I've heard it said', she had stated in a party political broadcast in May 1977, when unemployment stood at 1.3 million, 'that Conservatives have been associated with unemployment. That's absolutely wrong. We'd have been drummed out of office if we'd had this level of unemployment.' James Callaghan, she also said, would go down in history as the prime minister of unemployment. He could not 'run away from the fact that our policies did not produce unemployment as his have'.

Now she had to put this to the proof. She did not promise any quick fixes. 'It contains no magic formula, and is not a recipe for an easy or a perfect life,' she cautioned when the 1979 manifesto was published. 'The recovery of our country' would take a long time to begin to bring about.

The making of her first cabinet reflected this economic imperative. Conscious of her weakness in the party, she was determined not to let it compromise the central economic programme. She was not able to dispose of the old guard of Heathites and other sceptics, but she didn't need to put them in charge of the departments that mattered most to her, where the break with the past was, she believed, most necessary. Although she insisted that the policy was based 'not on a dogma but on reason, on common sense', she ensured that believing dogmatists were placed in the economic departments, where the dogma of monetarism would prove the surest defence against the siren voices of old orthodoxies.

To the Treasury she sent Geoffrey Howe, her faithful servant for the past five years. This was not a foregone conclusion. Howe had given the party some anxiety as shadow chancellor. He was essentially a man of government not opposition, and in Parliament, where shadow ministers make or break their reputations, his plodding style scored few hits against the incumbent Chancellor, Denis Healey. Indeed, so vast was the discrepancy in their public performance that an innocent visitor to the House of Commons might well have supposed that it was the brilliant and brutal Healey who was the Opposition spokesman, and Howe, with his defensive, narcoleptic monotone, who faced the daily task of defending one of the most dismal economic records of any post-war government. When Healey likened an argument with Howe to the experience of being 'savaged by a dead sheep', Sir Geoffrey was not alone in being wounded by the thrust. Many Conservatives could see the truth of it.

The leader too was worried. A measure of the desperation around her was a suggestion, seriously canvassed late in 1978, that Keith Joseph should, after all, be given the Treasury. There was even another idea. Some advisers toyed with the notion of persuading Roy Jenkins back to British politics. Jenkins, who had proved himself an excellent disciplinarian Chancellor between 1967 and 1970 in the Government of Harold Wilson, was now President of the European Commission. He was known to be thoroughly disenchanted with his old party, and had ceased to refer to himself as a member of it. Although no direct approach was made to him, there was talk, as the election drew nearer and Howe stubbornly failed to impress, of luring him back from Brussels into a safe Conservative seat. Nothing came of it. But set beside the arrogant self-confidence later exhibited by Conservative economic policy-makers, including Howe himself, this usefully recalls a period of uncertainty. Before the election, the Thatcher leadership was far less settled or sure than it usually appeared afterwards.

So Howe got the job. The inexorable tortoise of late-twentieth-century Conservatism continued on his way. Howe was not the designer of economic Thatcherism. In fact he was rather looked down on by men whose past was cleaner than his of pragmatic intellectual compromise. He did not take an automatic place in what passed for the Thatcher circle, even when he lived next door at 11 Downing Street. But he became Thatcherism's chief mechanic, the indispensable overseer of the machine, whatever direction it took.

[Young, *One of Us*, 140–2.]

A re-disposition affecting a substantial number of ministers at all levels is like a nightmarish multidimensional jigsaw puzzle, with an almost unlimited number of possible permutations and combinations—including the complementary qualities between the senior and junior ministers in a given department. Sometimes, after hours of juggling with the pieces, the prime minister finds that the last consequential piece will not fit, as when I was once left with a Yorkshire lady minister and a vacancy as minister of state in the Welsh Office, and had to go back to the drawing-board.

[Wilson, *Governance*, 34.]

(*b*) *Attitude of Prime Ministers to reshuffles*

Lord Attlee has said that an important quality in a Premier is the capacity to dismiss inadequate ministers. When one such person was summoned and told to resign, he is reported to have hesitated, hoping for some words of condolence from Attlee, and as none were forthcoming, to have asked why he was being removed. 'Because I don't think you measure up to the job' was the answer. Senior ministers might, on occasion, press their views on Mr Attlee. Sir Stafford Cripps and others urged that Mr Shinwell should be removed from the Ministry of Fuel and Power in 1947 (this was done) and the Prime Minister discussed the question of Bevin's successor at the Foreign Office with Mr Morrison and with Bevin himself but in every case the final decision was made by Mr Attlee. Mr Churchill was not above repaying old scores and in 1951 he was reluctant to give places to those who had, from his point of view, let him down in the appeasement period. The most dramatic display of Prime Ministerial power occurred in July 1962. Then Mr Macmillan, with no warning, summoned and dismissed seven members of a Cabinet of twenty. He had heard alarming reports about the probable result in a by-election (after a series of reverses) and felt that unless the government presented a more youthful and vigorous image it would decline even further. In addition to this unprecedented action, he also made some spectacular promotions, such as that of Mr Michael Noble to be Secretary of State for

Scotland after being in the House only four years and making only a single speech. [He had served as a junior Whip.] Mr Wilson, perhaps because of the unhappy repercussions of Macmillan's action in 1962 but more because of his dislike of hurting people, has had regular minor rearrangements. Indeed a feature of his policy has been a reluctance to remove ministers, preferring to find them other posts rather than replace them on the back-benches. Yet he brought Mr Shore and Mr Varley into the Cabinet very rapidly, both having been close to him as his Parliamentary Private Secretaries. Mr Heath had a reputation for punishing personal disloyalty and, for far wider political reasons, he was always adamant that Mr Powell would not be given a place in any Cabinet under his leadership. After 1974, as has been said, Mr Wilson used the power of appointment with great care to hold together the various factions in the party and, in particular, to reconcile the Left to the adoption of pro-EEC and moderate domestic politics.

[Mackintosh, *British Cabinet*, 440–1.]

Even Clement Attlee concedes that he was not immune, despite his recorded statement that he always avoided a 'cushion', a comforting explanation: 'I don't think that's playing straight with a fellow. If he doesn't measure up to the job, you should tell him.'

I knew personally of a friend who, on being dropped, asked him why and was told 'You're not up to the job.' In a softer mood, his formula was, 'Well you've had a good innings. Time to go back to the pavilion and put up your bat.'

[Wilson, *Governance*, 34.]

But Cabinets, especially over a period of years, are necessarily subject to changes. These can take various forms. Naturally, in the course of a long Administration or a series of Governments of the same Party, there are a number of resignations for private and personal reasons. There are others that take place on public grounds. In the first few months I had an example of the latter in the resignation of Lord Salisbury, from the office of Lord President of the Council. This was a great grief to me, since he was an old friend from school and university days. We were also closely connected by marriage. The occasion was the decision of the Government to liberate Archbishop Makarios from prison. A year later I was faced with the resignation of the Chancellor of the Exchequer, Peter Thorneycroft, on the question of public expenditure. Other resignations had to be accepted not on any public issue, but for private reasons, such as those of Alan Lennox-Boyd after the election of 1959, and of Derick Heathcoat Amory in 1960. But these events, sad as they are, seldom leave any lasting wound behind them. A much more disagreeable task, but one which cannot be avoided, is when either a particular Minister needs to be replaced, or the situation demands a larger Government reshuffle. In the first instance, although others may have seen signs of loss of grip and authority, the individual concerned is seldom conscious of any deterioration. After long years of office, under the tremendous burden which falls on Ministers today, it is almost impossible for any man to hold any of the most responsible posts year after year without the risk of becoming a victim to overstrain. Then there is the continual pressure of the Press, the Party machine and the Party in the House of Commons, for changes. While this can be resisted in a Government only running a single Parliament, it becomes much more difficult to do so if a Government of the same political complexion lasts for three Parliaments, twelve or thirteen years in all. Moreover, as a Parliament draws to its close, it is very important to ensure that a proper proportion of the Ministers, both of Cabinet rank and outside the Cabinet, if they are in the Lower House, should be willing to stand for election again. Otherwise a defeated Party may face a period of Opposition with no experienced men available for the front bench. A Prime Minister, both in that position and in his capacity as Leader of the Party, must give great weight to this consideration. I remembered how frequently in the past following long periods of consecutive office, a Party has drifted slowly into decay and left behind it hardly a leading figure. It was naturally very distasteful for me to have to make these decisions. Sometimes I was accused of being too loyal to my Ministers and standing by them too obstinately. Sometimes I was accused of ruthlessness in my changes. Often a colleague would come to me month after month or week after week, assuring me that his place was available any time I wanted it. If I took him at his word, he might show an unexpected indignation, which he was not anxious to disguise from the world. Nor does the public quite realise another problem which confronts a Prime Minister, and is wholly different from that, let us say, of a Chairman of a great company. The precise date of the resignation of an important official in a company, even the General Manager or Managing Director, can be discussed in detail and fixed for some period ahead. It may be announced, for instance, in the summer that the General Manager is to retire at Christmas. But this is quite impossible in the case of a Minister. You cannot have a Chancellor of the Exchequer dealing with a crisis in July, who is known to be about to retire in December. You cannot have a Foreign Secretary playing out the last few months of a long tenure of office like an employee (or even a Civil Servant) working for his pension. This means that changes have to be made quickly, without hesitation, and apparently brutally.

[Macmillan, *Pointing the Way*, 32–3.]

As for the Government itself, I am now convinced that one of Harold's greatest mistakes is his constant reshuffling. Too many job changes in three years means a tremendous decline in the power of the politician over the Civil Service machine and a tremendous growth in the power of the Whitehall Departments, both to thwart central Cabinet control and to thwart departmental Ministers' individual control. The truth is that a Minister needs eighteen months to get real control of his Department. I had just about got it when I was moved from Housing and therefore I was deprived of the third and fourth year when I could really have achieved something. Harold has appointed Denis Healey for a five-year period and he probably has done a great deal to change the detailed running of Defence. But look at Transport where Barbara, having just got control of the Department and launched her Bill, was ripped out to go to Productivity and an unenthusiastic Dick Marsh was sent in. The Department takes over and does exactly what it likes. It's the constant fiddling with Ministers and shifting them round which has undermined the central strategy of this Government.

[Richard Crossman, *Diaries of a Cabinet Minister* (London, 1977), iii, 78.]

Whatever else may be said of it, my meeting with the Prime Minister on the evening of Friday, 10 June 1983 was brief and to the point. 'Francis', she said, 'I want a new Foreign Secretary.'

[Pym, *Politics of Consent*, p. ix.]

Ministers of the Crown generally have a quite short tenure of office. In the period from the formation of the first government after the First World War to the end of 1971, the average length of tenure for the holders of seven leading ministerial portfolios ranged from 22.6 months (Defence) to 36.7 months (Agriculture). The average tenure of office in the seven ministries taken together was 27.5 months. (Valentine Herman in V. Herman and J. E. Alt, *Cabinet Studies: A Reader* (1975), 55.) In the 1964–70 Labour Government there was an especially rapid turnover of ministerial office, the median tenure of Cabinet ministers being 19 months. (Bruce Headey, *British Cabinet Ministers: The Roles of Politicians in Executive Office* (1974), 95–6.) Donald Shell records that of 85 ministers appointed to departmental posts in 1979, 60 had been moved at least once by 1983: (1983) 36 *Parliamentary Affairs* 154. (See further the articles by R. K. Alderman and J. A. Cross in (1979) 9 *British Journal of Political Science* 41 and (1981) 29 *Political Studies* 425.) Few ministers bring to their departments an appropriate specialized knowledge, and few remain long enough to acquire it.

[Colin Turpin, *British Government and the Constitution: Text, Cases and Materials* (London, 1985), 128–9.]

## (4) DISMISSAL OF MINISTERS

*When a Prime Minister wants a ministerial colleague to go, the language of dismissal is rarely used: rather, a Minister is asked for his resignation. No one is fooled. The following is Selwyn Lloyd's letter to Macmillan after the Prime Minister had sacked him as Chancellor of the Exchequer in 1962.*

You have told me that you would like me to resign, and this I willingly do.

I realize that the policies with which I have been associated have been unpopular. On the other hand I believe that they have been right and have had a considerable measure of success. In my view our currency is stronger and our economic prospects on a firmer basis than for some time, and we are in a better position to face any difficulties which may come.

I am also glad to have been associated with certain new departures, such as the development of an incomes policy and the creation of the National Economic Development Council. My primary aim has been to strengthen the country's competitive power and lay the foundation for sound growth.

I know that you are well aware of my concern that these policies should be continued, and also of my anxiety that the growth of public expenditure, so much of it highly desirable in itself, should not outstrip our resources.

I am very grateful to you for the many personal kindnesses which you have shown me.

*Two junior Ministers since 1945 have been formally dismissed (rather than any euphemism being employed): Mr Eric Heffer in 1975, and Mr Keith Speed in 1981.*

## (5) CONTROL OVER CABINET MEETINGS

### (*a*) *The agenda*

*Preparation of business for Cabinet and Cabinet Committees*

9. The Secretary of the Cabinet (or in the case of a Cabinet Committee the Secretary of the Committee) shall be given seven days' notice of any business (including business to be raised orally) which a Minister wishes to bring before the Cabinet or a Cabinet Committee; and memoranda shall be circulated at least two working days before they are to be discussed. It is of the utmost importance that this '48-hour rule' should be observed if Ministers are to have a proper opportunity of considering the issues involved. Ministers who fail to comply with the rule should not be surprised if their papers are not placed on the agenda. When the subject is of major importance Ministers should as a general rule be given more than the minimum time to consider papers before they are discussed and wherever possible such papers should be circulated at least seven days before the meeting at which they are to be considered.

10. Ministers' Private Secretaries can help the Secretary of the Cabinet (or, in the case of a Cabinet Committee, the Secretary of that Committee) by indicating, when asking for a subject to be placed on the agenda, which Ministers other than members of the Cabinet or Committee are likely to be concerned, so that arrangements may be made for their attendance.

11. Proposals which involve expenditure or affect general financial policy should be discussed with the Treasury before they are submitted to the Cabinet or to a Ministerial Committee; and the results of those discussions together with the best possible estimate (or estimates, if the Department's figures cannot be reconciled with the Treasury's) of the cost to the Exchequer, should be indicated in the memorandum. Where proposals affect United Kingdom obligations

or interests as members of the European Community this should be clearly explained; and where those obligations or interests are not affected this should be made clear. If the memorandum contains proposals which make demands on manpower or may give rise to problems of recruitment, these should be clearly stated after consultation with the Civil Service Department. Attention should also be drawn to any accommodation problems, after consultation with the Property Services Agency. No memorandum should be circulated to the Cabinet unless any legal implications which it raises have been cleared, or at least clarified, with the Law Officers. The Cabinet Office will not normally accept a memorandum for circulation to the Cabinet or a Ministerial Committee unless these steps have been taken.

12. These rules do not limit the right of Ministers to submit to the Cabinet memoranda setting out their views on general issues of policy.

13. Memoranda for the Cabinet and Committees of the Cabinet should be as clear and as brief as possible, not exceeding two pages at maximum. Time spent in making a memorandum short and clear will be saved many times over in reading and in discussion; and it is the duty of Ministers to ensure that this is done by personal scrutiny and, where necessary, revision of memoranda submitted to them by their officials. The model memorandum explains at the outset what the problem is, indicates briefly the relevant considerations, and concludes with a precise statement of the decisions sought. It is sometimes useful to include a summary of the main points brought out in the body of the memorandum, but such a summary should never exceed a few lines. Prefatory covering notes should be avoided. To facilitate reference in discussion, paragraphs should be numbered.

14. When a Minister wishes to raise a matter orally at the Cabinet, the Prime Minister's consent should be sought through the Secretary of the Cabinet.

*Cabinet conclusions and Cabinet Committee minutes*

15. The record of Cabinet and Cabinet Committee proceedings is limited to the decisions taken and such summary of the discussion as may be necessary for the guidance of those who have to take action on them. The Cabinet Office are under instructions to avoid, so far as practicable, recording the opinions expressed by particular

Ministers. Matters of exceptional secrecy or political sensitivity may be recorded in a Limited Circulation Annex.

16. Any suggestions for amendment of Cabinet Conclusions or Cabinet Committee minutes must reach the Secretary not later than 24 hours after the circulation of the minutes.

[*Questions of Procedure for Ministers* (1976 version), paras. 9–16.]

In assessing the relations of the Premier and his colleagues, the former's control over the machinery of the Cabinet must be taken into consideration. Meetings of the Cabinet are held twice a week during the parliamentary session but the Prime Minister arranges the order of business and can keep any item off the agenda indefinitely. It is regarded as quite improper for a minister to raise any matter which has not previously been accepted for the agenda by the Prime Minister. For instance, on June 29, 1927, Neville Chamberlain wanted to discuss the dispute over the reform of the House of Lords. It was not on the agenda and though he did try to bring it up at the end of the listed business, Baldwin rose and walked out of the room, thus ending the Cabinet. The more important foreign despatches are only sent to those members of the Cabinet who must have the information and the Prime Minister has to give his consent before there are any departures from the rule. In March 1938 Duff Cooper wrote a paper advocating the end of the system whereby the Service departments' finances were rationed out but the Chancellor of the Exchequer and Chamberlain stopped it going any further. Hore-Belisha wanted to circulate memoranda advocating partial mobilisation and conscription on April 15, 1939. Neville Chamberlain refused, though he later permitted Hore-Belisha to raise the matter verbally.

[Mackintosh, *British Cabinet*, 449.]

In the eighteenth century it was the practice of any minister who desired to lay a matter before the Cabinet to summon it for that purpose. The regularisation of business made for regular Cabinets, and for many years the Cabinet met weekly during the parliamentary session. Since 1945 it has usually met twice a week. Additional meetings are summoned by the Prime Minister when they are necessary. The question of the right of the Prime Minister to refuse to summon a Cabinet is perhaps of some theoretical interest. As a matter of practice, it never arises. If a matter is of great urgency, it is inconceivable that the Prime Minister will not recognise it as such. If a dispute has arisen between the Prime Minister and a minister, that alone is a question of urgency upon which the Prime Minister himself will desire an immediate decision.

Normally, a proposal is submitted to the Cabinet by the minister concerned in the form of a written memorandum. Copies of these memoranda are produced, usually by the Cabinet Office, and are circulated by that Office. If a memorandum is of any considerable length it generally concludes with a summary prepared in order that ministers who are not specially conversant with the subject may readily inform themselves of what is proposed. But the insistence on memoranda, which is an elementary rule of business, does not prevent an item being placed, with the Prime Minister's approval, on the agenda without a memorandum. Moreover, it is of course open to the Prime Minister to allow questions not mentioned on the agenda to be raised as matters of urgency.

Before the war of 1939–45 there was a Cabinet instruction, renewed by each Cabinet, that memoranda, draft Bills and other constituents of Cabinet agenda were not to be circulated until after their subject-matter had been fully examined between the departments from which they emanated, the Treasury, the Law Officers where contentious Bills were involved, and any other departments concerned. The post-war rule is apparently not so detailed, but it is still the rule that proposals affecting other departments must not be submitted to the Cabinet until they have been thoroughly discussed with those departments at the official level and, if necessary, between ministers. Where there is a conflict of interest between departments, it should never come to the Cabinet until the possibilities of securing agreement at lower levels have been fully explored and exhausted.

As a result of attempts made in 1919 to secure proper financial control it was also laid down that no proposal involving finance should be circulated until the sanction of the Chancellor of the Exchequer had been obtained: but this rule disappeared during the war and has been replaced by the rule, already quoted, requiring preliminary consultation, which necessarily applies *a fortiori* to the Treasury. Moreover, the general practice of consultation, to which reference has already been made, makes formal instructions less necessary.

The Prime Minister can always refuse to have a question discussed until, in his opinion, it is ripe. In January 1919 Mr Churchill, as Secretary of State for War, concocted a scheme for the armies of occupation with Field-Marshal Sir Henry Wilson. It was based on the continuance of compulsory service, and was strongly objected to by Mr Lloyd George, who was in Paris. Mr Lloyd George refused to have it brought before the War Cabinet in his absence, and Mr Bonar Law, who presided over the Cabinet, refused to allow a decision to be taken. But next day Churchill, Wilson and Haig saw Lloyd George, who then allowed it to be brought beore the Cabinet.

It is an instruction to the Secretary, subject to the power of the Prime Minister to waive the requirement, that no proposal shall be placed upon the Cabinet agenda until a period of two clear days has elapsed since the circulation of the appropriate memoranda. These memoranda are circulated daily, and more often if necessary. At the end of each week a programme of Cabinet business for the following week is issued, with the sanction of the Prime Minister, for the guidance of the departments, so that they may have advance notice of the subjects likely to be raised. The final agenda papers are issued later, though still a day or two in advance of the meeting. These name the ministers other than members of the Cabinet who are invited to be present for particular items, and specify the time at which they are to attend. At the first of the weekly meetings the traditional order of business is followed and the first item is 'Foreign Affairs (if any)'. This enables the Secretary of State to give any general explanation that he thinks fit, and enables any minister to call attention to any matter of importance set out in the Foreign Office despatches and telegrams of the week. At the second meeting of the week it is usual to discuss the parliamentary business for the next week, which is announced in the House of Commons that afternoon. The agenda is, however, invariably submitted to the Prime Minister, and he can change the order, or direct the deletion of items, or add new items. The agenda, in short, is as much under the control of the Prime Minister as it was when there was no formal circulated agenda. Each item refers, however, to the relevant Cabinet papers. Thus, a minister's private secretary can gather together the necessary documents, attach them to the agenda, and so enable the minister to prepare himself for the Cabinet discussions.

If, after the agenda has been circulated, questions of urgency arise, the Prime Minister can always authorise a supplementary agenda paper. This is circulated as quickly as possible and is, if necessary, laid on the table. It is the recognised right of a minister to have circulated as a Cabinet document any remarks which he may desire to make on a Cabinet proposal. When Mr Balfour circulated his memorandum on fiscal reform in 1903, for instance, Mr Ritchie and Lord Balfour of Burleigh circulated reasoned statements against its conclusions. But it appears that normally, and apart from departmental memoranda, ministers may prefer to make orally such statements on general policy. It has to be remembered, in this connection, that the Cabinet minutes will contain a reference to the memorandum and the memorandum itself will be preserved in the Cabinet Office, unless the Cabinet otherwise directs. If, on the other hand, the minister states his case orally, the minutes will not as a rule indicate which minister put forward these arguments. In other words, the minister who circulates a memorandum is putting his views on record.

The items on the agenda are usually concerned with questions of departmental policy upon which the ministerial head of a department desires a Cabinet decision. Wider political questions, not of a departmental nature, would normally be raised by the Prime Minister. It is generally understood by the departments that their documents should be as complete as possible, and should contain the various arguments in favour of the proposal and the criticisms which might be brought against it. But, probably, the purpose of this rule is effectively secured by the requirement, already mentioned, that no proposal should be circulated until it has been submitted to the interested departments, especially the Treasury in respect of financial matters, or to the Law Officers in respect of legislative proposals. In any case, the Cabinet does not like to be confronted with technical inter-departmental questions of minor importance. It considers that the ministers concerned should themselves settle such matters.

[Sir Ivor Jennings, *Cabinet Government* (Cambridge, 3rd edn., 1959), 245–9.]

The agenda for Cabinet and for all Cabinet committees chaired by the prime minister is approved by the prime minister in consultation with the secretary of the Cabinet. (The forward programme of Cabinet and its committees—irrespective of who chairs them—is masterminded by an informal meeting of the prime minister, lord president, chancellor, foreign and commonwealth secretary, chief whip and Cabinet secretary each Friday morning, when the issues coming up for decision are surveyed for a period of roughly a fortnight ahead.)

It has been suggested that the prime minister is in unique control of the agenda.

> Meetings of the Cabinet are held twice a week [sic] during the Parliamentary session but the Prime Minister arranges the order of business and can keep any item off the agenda indefinitely. It is regarded as quite improper for a minister to raise any matter which has not previously been accepted for the agenda by the Prime Minister.

In theory of course, he is in charge as chairman, but this is not how things are done.

In any case, ministers are free to raise matters under 'Parliamentary Affairs' or 'Foreign and Commonwealth Affairs'. If a minister (or ministers) is worried about an issue that is disturbing MPs he can raise it under the former item, or if he is concerned over some development in, e.g., Eastern Europe, or Rhodesia, he can ask about it. The appropriate minister would then explain how things stood, or he or the prime minister could say that this was coming up the following week in Cabinet, or was being currently considered by the relevant committee. There is no rigidity of style in Cabinet: the best style is the one that gets the boat along fast and in the right direction.

[Wilson, *Governance*, 47–8.]

### (*b*) *Summoning of Cabinet*

*Only the Prime Minister has the authority to summon a meeting of the Cabinet.*

The Chancellor came to see me again; he had no more news from Washington, except that the meeting had adjourned for lunch. Nothing was expected before 11.00 p.m. our time. I told him that we were trying to find George Brown. Roy Jenkins said he was due to meet George at ten o'clock to outline his Budget thinking to him, but Foreign Office messages suggested he was unlikely to turn up.

At 10.40 p.m. Secretary Fowler came through on the phone to the Chancellor, who told me he had had a 'bad call'—the line was far from clear—but that Fowler sounded 'battered'. All he could understand was that the Americans wanted us to close down the London gold pool, and that William Martin was talking to the Governor at the same time. Sir Leslie O'Brien would immediately come round to the Treasury to report. At 11.00 p.m. Sir Leslie arrived at No. 11 and Roy brought him in.

It was true, he said, that the Americans wanted us to close the gold pool, and they were calling a meeting in Washington on the Saturday of central bankers and finance ministry representatives of all the gold pool countries. At that meeting, we understood, the Americans were going to advance their 'two-tier proposal'. We were ready to close the gold pool, but this meant that the London foreign exchange must also be closed. This would mean a bank holiday, which in turn, we were advised, would mean an Order in Council, and a Privy Council that night.

I sent Michael Halls over to the House to tell the Lord President of the Council, Dick Crossman, who was fully involved in an all-night session on a guillotine motion on Barbara Castle's Transport Bill. Clearly there could not be a Council without his knowledge, but in all the circumstances I offered to stand in for the customary pre-Council Audience with the Queen.

By this time, with no precedents to guide us, we had sorted out the arrangements for the bank holiday. Bank branches would remain open to cash cheques—for example, those required for paying wages—but there were to be no inter-account settlements. This would be sufficient to prevent foreign exchange transactions. But we were concerned about what might happen to sterling on markets remaining open in other capitals. We decided to let the rate go on all the European markets but felt it essential to see that it was maintained in New York. The Chancellor and I agreed to close the gold pool and the gold market but only on condition that the Americans supported sterling on the New York market, which was remaining open. The deputy-Governor suggested that the New York Federal Bank could be asked to buy and hold guaranteed sterling. I pointed out sharply that sterling must be guaranteed in terms of dollars, not gold. This was agreed. The Governor said that, while the Federal Reserve chairman had hinted at support, he could not say that any firm assurance had been given. I said that we could not agree to take action on all the other steps we had been asked to take, including the closure of the gold pool itself, until the assurance was given. The Governor put a call through to Washington. It was not until 12.05 a.m., or soon thereafter, that we were in the clear, and I asked the Clerk to the Privy Council to go ahead with the Council for 12.15 a.m., or as soon afterwards as possible. At this point, having heard that George Brown had surfaced, I sent a senior secretary over to the House to tell him what was happening. A few minutes earlier Peter Shore, who had heard rumours that something was afoot, had telephoned to ask what was going on. I could not tell him anything but, realising we should have to assemble with all speed a quorum for the Council, sent a message asking him to come over. It was an afterthought with cataclysmic results.

After the Council, the Chancellor prepared a public statement and brought it to me at about 1.00 a.m. Shortly afterwards George Brown came through on the telephone in a great state. He had apparently assembled a meeting of ministers in his room and, with a choice of language I should not normally associate with him, demanded my presence there at once. I said that if a meeting were desired, he and they should come over to No. 10 for a properly convened one. This they did, in a very anxious mood. I asked the Chancellor to give a résumé of the facts from 6.00 p.m. that night, to explain what had been done and the acute danger—at least until we knew that markets were to close—of holding a ministerial meeting. This they fully accepted and agreed with the steps we had taken; agreeing, too, that we had had no alternative. Not so George Brown. He was not concerned with the facts and instead of listening to the Chancellor kept up a running commentary, mainly directed to the accusation that Peter Shore had been involved from the outset. He was told that Peter knew nothing of it until sent for; he had learnt the facts only in the Chancellor's car on the way to the Palace. The decibels grew with the strength of the accusations, with all the ministers who had come over with him telling George to control himself.

(I should not have thought it necessary to recount these matters had George not published in the autumn of 1970 a highly tendentious account of the night's events: omitting many relevant facts, some of which he had not known, others of which he must have forgotten. I am drawing, as I said, entirely on the note I dictated at the time.)

[Wilson, *The Labour Government*, 508–9.]

(*c*) *Frequency of meetings*

Take first the raw statistics of Cabinet business. It is rare for Mrs Thatcher to have more than one meeting of the full Cabinet per week. Allowing for parliamentary recesses, that adds up to between forty and forty-five Cabinet meetings a year—not a particularly significant statistic if more business is being taken in committees, of which more in a moment. Attlee and Churchill, however, logged twice that figure . . . The flow of Cabinet papers is well down, moreover. The CP (84) series, as the 1984 collection will be classified in the Cabinet Office's Confidential Library, includes only sixty to seventy papers, about one sixth of the annual totals accumulated in the late forties and early fifties . . . Sir Robert Armstrong, incidentally, for all his protestations about open government, refused to release under Section 5(1) of the Public Records Act, 1958 (which permits declassification ahead of the thirty-year rule), statistics on the number of Cabinet meetings and papers since 1955. He argued that 'It would be entirely contrary to longstanding conventions in these matters to publish this sort of information.'

Judged by the frequency of meetings and flow of formal Cabinet papers, full Cabinet activity under Mrs Thatcher is at an historical low. So, too, is the workload being devolved to Cabinet committees. On entering No. 10 in May 1979, Mrs Thatcher made it clear to the Whitehall machine that she was not a Cabinet-committee person. She would do business with her fellow ministers free of the curse of committees. 'Events', as one insider put it, 'soon took care of that'. As we have seen from the blueprint of Mrs Thatcher's Engine Room . . . she now presides over some 160 of the hated things, though not, naturally, in the literal sense of chairing the lot.

[Hennessy, *Cabinet*, 99–100.]

Through most of the nineteenth century the normal day of meeting was Saturday. With the coming of the week-end habit at the turn of the century, Wednesday became the regular day with Monday kept for extra meetings if needed. Attlee's Cabinets generally met on Mondays and sometimes on Thursdays as well. Under Conservative Prime Ministers the regular days were Tuesdays and Thursdays. Mr Harold Wilson had as a rule one Cabinet a week, usually on Thursdays, sometimes on Tuesdays: but a considerable number of further meetings was held. Sometimes these came with great frequency when a critical issue arose—such as the sale of arms to South Africa or the threat of war between Egypt and Israel. Alongside normal meetings, a series of Cabinets was sometimes devoted to a particular issue with no other business on the agenda. One example was the succession of Cabinets on the question of entry into the Common Market: these met about twice a week between March and May 1967; and considered papers on such matters as mobility of labour; regional, immigration, social policies; and constitutional issues. Another example was the half-dozen Cabinet meetings on cuts in government expenditure in January 1968. This useful practice was, I think, an innovation by Mr Harold Wilson.

[Patrick Gordon Walker, *The Cabinet* (London, revised edn., 1972), 101.]

*The Cabinet meets less frequently than in earlier times partly because of the increased use of Cabinet committees and informal ministerial meetings: see below, pp. 265–85.*

(*d*) *Prime Minister's summing up*

Summing-up is vital: it is the fine art of Cabinet government. The great improvement over the past thirty years is due not only to the style of Clement Attlee: the consistent improvement in the service provided by the Cabinet Secretariat is itself a guarantee of clarity.

Ex-prime ministers have confirmed—as I can—that in reaching a decision Cabinet does not vote, except to save time, on minor procedural matters. On many issues, discussion is confined to one or two, or very few ministers; and, perhaps after suggesting a formula which appears to command assent, the prime minister asks 'Cabinet agree?'—technically a voice vote, sometimes just a murmur. On a major issue it is important not only to give the main protagonists their heads, but to ensure that everyone expresses an opinion, by going round the table to collect the voices. The prime minister usually keeps a tally of those for and against, after which he records his assessment of the predominant view—or occasionally puts forward a suggestion of his own which all, or nearly all, can support. Sometimes on a minor issue where all the arguments are known—perhaps they have been discussed at an earlier Cabinet—

and no arguments are likely to make converts, it saves time to go quickly round the table and take the sense of Cabinet.

[Wilson, *Governance*, 55.]

(*e*) *Cabinet minutes*

A few days before Richard Crossman went to America to deliver his Godkin Lectures at Harvard on 'Bagehot Revisited', he thought I ought to look at them. His main thesis, in support of his doctrine of 'prime ministerial government', was that Cabinet was controlled by a conspiracy between the prime minister and the secretary of the Cabinet, who sat down the day after the meeting virtually to cook the Cabinet Conclusions. He was incredulous when I told him that, not only had I never seen them before circulation, but that it was only very rarely that I would read them after they were circulated—only then for purposes of refreshing my memory, if the subject came up again. He duly re-wrote the lectures, though I doubt if I fully convinced him. Perhaps, recalling the view he took of most senior civil servants, he was content to believe—wrongly—that the Cabinet secretary was capable of doing the necessary cooking without my help. The Cabinet minutes are immaculately conceived.

This doctrine is, of course, pure fantasy. It is the rarest occurrence for any of those who do pore over the Conclusions, officials as well as ministers, to query their accuracy or fairness.

[Wilson, *Governance*, 56.]

After Cabinet I went to see Burke Trend because I had something to put to him about the text of the Cabinet minutes of the previous Thursday. I had read them with special attention because I wanted to compare them with my own note of the meeting and I had been struck by the sentence in which Harold was stressing the importance of the British Government centring its attention on the prevention of nuclear proliferation. I noticed that in the minutes a second aim was added, the aim of satisfying the nuclear aspirations of the Federal German Government. As soon as I saw this I was sure that Harold had never said it and that, if he had said it, he would have caused a stormy row with at least Tony Greenwood and Frank Cousins. In fact, the impression he had left was that he was determined to frustrate the nuclear aspirations of the Federal

German Government. So I pointed this out to Burke Trend and I said, 'Harold can't have said this.' To which he replied, 'Ah, of course he never said it, we never do give verbatim what people say. We précis the sense and give the substance of what they say.' To which I replied, 'This is not the substance of what he said, and if it had been the substance he would have divided the Cabinet.' 'Well,' said Burke Trend, 'what would you like? Would you like me to have "deal with" instead of "satisfy"?' I replied that this indeed would change the whole tone of the passage and its meaning. 'I don't mind giving you "deal" instead of "satisfy",' said Burke airily and friendlily.

I should round this off perhaps by an incident which occurred next day when I ran into Burke and he asked me whether I was content with the minutes of the Cabinet dealing with the Beeching incident. I said I was, and he twinkled. What all this shows is the importance of being the kind of awkward Cabinet Minister who reads Cabinet minutes carefully. But it also shows that it's important not to raise the issue in Cabinet but to raise it verbally after Cabinet with the Secretary, so as not to embarrass him publicly, and then having done that to mention it to the Prime Minister.

[Richard Crossman, *Diaries*, i, 103–4.]

## 3. THE HIGHEST PROFILE; PATRONAGE; DISSOLUTION

### (1) HIGHEST PROFILE

A Prime Minister's power is greater than the sum total of his powers, and a significant reason for this is that his profile is higher than any other Minister's. In Parliament, he answers Prime Minister's Questions every Tuesday and Thursday, whereas other Ministers have a chance to shine only once every three to five weeks. His skill at such frequent gladiatorial contests can enhance his prestige with Ministers and back-benchers—and, through television and radio news reports (and the occasional live radio broadcast), with the general public. The Prime Minister will also decide when to intervene in debates, unlike all other Ministers who will normally only speak in debates touching their departmental responsibilities. In that sense a Prime Minister has no portfolio and every portfolio and can put his personal prestige behind an issue or a particular Minister. In the country, the Prime Minister can frequently be news: his visits and speeches, these days carefully arranged into 'photo opportunities' for newspaper photographers and television cameramen, concentrate attention on his doings and sayings. If he wishes to make an announcement over television or radio by ministerial broadcast, he can do so. Abroad, Prime Ministers have represented the country in personal attempts to improve international relations, a development started with Chamberlain's visits to Hitler and accelerated by the onset of easy air travel. The epitome was Harold Macmillan, who during his premiership clocked up a tour of the Commonwealth, a visit to Moscow, meetings with Presidents Eisenhower and Kennedy, and the 1960 Paris summit; others, since, have made similar though not such extensive journeys. Today, if the Prime Minister wants to discuss an issue at length with the President of the United States, it is taken for granted that he will fly to see him. At the many regular international gatherings, too, the Prime Minister will represent the United Kingdom—the biennial Commonwealth heads of government meetings, European Council gatherings, economic meetings of the western industrialized nations, and so on. Additionally, important visitors from abroad are received personally by the Prime Minister. The electorate must be forgiven if it concludes that the Prime Minister *is* the government, a conclusion which the Prime Minister might not wish to correct.

[Brazier, *Constitutional Practice*, 79–80.]

## (2) PATRONAGE

Mr Canavan asked the Prime Minister whether he will list all the public appointments for which he is responsible, the names of the present holders of these appointments and their salaries and allowances.

THE PRIME MINISTER The list below shows the paid appointments on which it is my duty to advise the Queen. It also includes the Police Complaints Board whose members are appointed by me. The list excludes ministerial and ecclesiastical appointments and also a number of Civil Service appointments whose holders are recruited through normal Civil Service channels. I am also responsible for a number of unpaid appointments, notably to the boards of trustees of certain museums and galleries.

*British Broadcasting Corporation*
Chairman
Vice-Chairman
National Governor for Wales
National Governor for Northern Ireland
National Governor for Scotland
Governors

*Crown Estate Commission*
First Commissioner
Part-time Commissioners

*Development Commission*
Chairman

*Forestry Commission*
Chairman
Part-time Commissioners

Lord Chief Justice of England
Master of the Rolls
President of the Family Division
Lords of Appeal in Ordinary
Lord Justices of Appeal
Lord Justice General and Lord President of the Court of Session in Scotland
Lord Justice Clerk
Comptroller and Auditor-General
Parliamentary Commissioner for Administration
Health Service Commissioner for England, for Scotland and for Wales
Clerk of the Parliaments
Clerk of the House of Commons
Royal Commission on the Press Chairman
Royal Commission on the Distribution of Income and Wealth: Chairman
Members

*Police Complaints Board*
Deputy Chairmen
Members

First Church Estates Commissioner

*Cambridge University*
Regius Professor of Modern History
Regius Professor of Civil Law
Regius Professor of Physic
King Edward VII Professor of English Literature
Master of Trinity College
Master of Churchill College

*Oxford University*
Regius Professor of Greek
Regius Professor of Modern History
Regius Professor of Civil Law
Regius Professor of Medicine
Regius Professor of Hebrew
Provost of Eton
Principal of King's College, London

*Bank of England*
Governor
Deputy Governor
Directors

[The Prime Minister, Mr James Callaghan, 932 H.C. Deb. *232–6* (written answers 19 May 1977). *The names and salaries are not reproduced above.*]

*The Prime Minister also advises the Queen on whom to appoint to senior positions in the Church of England (currently some 384), and to many other public offices as well.*

## (3) DISSOLUTION

The major right acquired by the Prime Minister—considerably later than the others—was that of advising the Crown on his own authority to dissolve Parliament. The implicit or open threat to use this power became the most potent instrument in his hand for maintaining discipline in his Parliamentary party. The threat is normally conveyed to M.P.s by the Government Whips. In January 1968 Mr Harold Wilson used the menace of a dissolution at a meeting of the Parliamentary Labour Party.

[Gordon Walker, *Cabinet*, 82.]

An older method of control has been cited by the late Lord Morrison. He considered that 'governments are often saved from parliamentary defeat by the back-benchers' fear of a dissolution.' In January 1968 Mr Wilson told a meeting of the Parliamentary Labour Party that numerous abstentions could force a general election and the same threat was used several times after the Labour Party returned to office in 1974. However, in modern conditions the use of this threat is limited. In the mid-nineteenth century, when Members paid their own election expenses and fought more or less single-handed for their seats, there was a genuine abhorrence of premature elections. But if abstention or cross-voting is being considered nowadays, what worries a Member is loss of patronage or standing in the party or the risk of expulsion or refusal or renomination by the local constituency party rather than any fear of having to fight an election campaign as an accredited party candidate. Indeed, an election is just the time when politicians pull together and no parliamentary leader is likely to play into the hands of his opponents by asking the public to defeat troublesome members of his own party. Any party leader with a desire to survive will settle or smooth over a rebellion before going to the country and while Mr Wilson in the instance just quoted may have been stating a fact—too many abstentions could theoretically have led to a defeat, his resignation, a Conservative Government and an immediate election—none of the Parliamentary Labour Party took this seriously as a disciplinary threat. One situation in which a Premier might consider a dissolution as an aid to discipline is when he is confident of winning and wishes to show grumblers that his policies have popular support. In December 1938, Neville Chamberlain 'was wondering whether he could ever shake down with this "uneasy and disgruntled House" without an election.' But there is no sign that he had to use such a threat to save himself from defeat. The other case where this fear still has some validity is when the majority is very narrow. Then members who might have allowed themselves the luxury of abstention on one or two issues over which they felt strongly might hesitate in case the position of the Government was seriously prejudiced by a defeat. This is why the Labour Government was able simply to order the 37 abstainers of March 1976 to reverse their votes a few nights later.

[Mackintosh, *British Cabinet*, 606–7.]

*The Prime Minister, by convention, now has the right to recommend a dissolution at a time which seems most propitious for him. A threat to dissolve (see above) is not very convincing, given that the electorate would see a government party in disarray. The legitimacy of the Prime Minister's sole right to recommend a dissolution without the collective advice of the Cabinet, is now entrenched—but it has been challenged.*

The manner in which the Prime Ministerial theory of dissolution came into existence in Britain deserves examination. In 1918 Mr Bonar Law made a remarkable statement in the House of Commons which is possibly the starting-point of the present received belief. At the end of 1918, suggestions of a dissolution were in the air, but in the House of Commons on 7 November Mr Bonar Law spoke of a General Election as being decided by the 'head of the Government'. 'In my belief,' he said, 'there is no custom more clearly defined than that what advice on this matter should be given to the Sovereign is a question not for the Cabinet but for the Prime Minister.' Mr Lloyd George, he said, agreed with him on this. When challenged on the point, he added that the doctrine as he had stated it had always been the regular practice; that he had himself known of recent cases where no intimation had been given to the Cabinet; and that members would recall the action of Mr Gladstone in 1874 when his colleagues received the intimation of the coming election from the public press.

A remark in a letter which he had received from Balfour several weeks before may conceivably have suggested this formulation. In October 1918 Balfour, writing to Bonar Law about the timing of the election, had written that responsibility for it 'in fact' rested with the

Prime Minister and that on some previous occasions the Prime Minister of the day 'had not even gone through the form of consulting his colleagues'. But wherever it originated, each part of Bonar Law's statement was open to question. Morley's account of the 1874 dissolution does not support it. Gladstone in January 1874 wrote to the Queen that he was about 'to recommend his colleagues humbly and dutifully to advise an immediate dissolution' and (two days later) that he 'laid before the Cabinet a pretty full outline of the case . . . and . . . the Cabinet unanimously concurred, upon a review of its grounds, in the wisdom of the proposed measure.' What again were the recent cases of which Mr Bonar Law knew? The three previous dissolutions were in 1906 and 1910. If Mr Asquith's word is to be accepted each of those resulted from Cabinet decisions. Mr Asquith was particularly clear on the point: 'Such a question as the Dissolution of Parliament is always submitted to the Cabinet.' In a survey of the eleven dissolutions between 1868 and 1910 in *Fifty Years of Parliament*, he could find no exception to this rule. Why then did Bonar Law and Balfour assert the contrary in 1918? The most plausible reason seems to be that they may have had in mind a quite different question about dissolution which had been raised in 1916. In December 1916, Bonar Law had had an interview with the King after the resignation of Mr Asquith. At this interview the question of dissolution of Parliament had been discussed. George V, being reluctant to contemplate a General Election in wartime, had consulted Lord Haldane upon the question whether Mr Bonar Law or any proposed successor to Asquith might properly make a dissolution of Parliament a condition upon which he would accept office. Lord Haldane had advised that the King could not entertain any such bargain with a *possible* Prime Minister not yet in a position to give advice as a responsible Minister of the Crown. Unfortunately the memorandum which Haldane sent to Lord Stamfordham summarized this position by the words 'The only minister who can properly give advice as to a dissolution of Parliament is the Prime Minister.' It rather looks as if Lord Haldane here unwittingly helped to originate the misunderstanding which Bonar Law in the heat of a Commons debate subsequently amplified and handed on to his post-war successors. Clearly Haldane, who had sat in Mr Asquith's Cabinet, did not mean to deal in his 1916 memorandum with the internal relationships of an administration in office. His mind was not directed to that issue. What he had been asked to advise upon, as the memorandum—printed in Sir Harold Nicolson's biography of George V—makes plain, was the right of a *potential* Prime Minister to advise or bargain for dissolution *before* assuming office. His categorical phrase 'The only minister who can properly give advice . . .' was meant only to emphasize the right of the King to decline to guarantee in advance a particular use of the prerogative to a potential incumbent who, not yet being in office, would not be constitutionally entitled to proffer advice on anything. It was not intended to prejudge the quite different question, not then in issue, of a Cabinet's collective rights as against a Prime Minister.

Subsequent opinion seems, then, to have rested upon the plainly mistaken assertion about previous practice made in 1918 in a confused party situation, when Bonar Law, and possibly others, wished to leave the responsibility for dissolving Parliament to Lloyd George. Balfour, as we have seen, concurred in the prime ministerial prerogative doctrine, but whether he got it from George Wyndham and gave it to Bonar Law, or whether Bonar Law was confused by the different issue raised in 1916 is less certain. Lloyd George, perhaps not surprisingly, agreed with Bonar Law's statement of Lloyd George's rights. In the debate on 7 November 1918 Bonar Law said that 'In the Prime Minister's view and in my view the question of deciding whether or not there should be an election is the duty of the Prime Minister.' This certainly seems to be the point in time at which the Prime Ministerial heresy gained acceptance. Mr Bonar Law, however, could not be compared as a constitutional authority with Mr Asquith, and why his opinion should have been adopted as the popular view remains mysterious. It may be that the better view should, if possible, be reinstated? Whatever has been recently believed and acted upon, there seems no adequate constitutional foundation for the view that the discretionary power to dissolve and hold a General Election is a peculiar personal perquisite of the office of Prime Minister. It may perhaps be felt by some that the Prime Ministerial view is the more realistic and that it is in any event too firmly established to be overthrown. Neither point is persuasive. Constitutional conventions are established through the medium of belief and conviction, both of which can be changed. As to realism, it could be urged that the more realistic and down-to-earth view lies with the recognition that a decision to hold a General Election is no less a piece of political decision-making than any other issue of cabinet policy.

[Geoffrey Marshall, *Constitutional Conventions* (Oxford, 1984), 48–51.]

*The modern practice is for the Prime Minister to consult senior Ministers about a possible election date, then to inform the Cabinet of the chosen date, followed by an audience of the Queen and a public announcement. This preserves the Prime Minister's sole right to select a date, but also implicates Ministers in the choice in case the government loses the election.*

By the time of the local elections on 7 May the momentum for an election was almost irresistible. Indeed Margaret herself seemed to make no effort to cool the election fever. As in 1983 Keith Britto and his team at Central Office had prepared a computer programme to analyse the local election results and offer a range of forecasts for a general election on various assumptions about the possible movement of opinion during the election. These were more elaborate than in 1983, even calculating a factor to correct the mismatch between the opinion poll measurement of support for the parties and the support actually given at the general election of 1983 and at the local elections of 1987. Our statistics were not only more detailed and comprehensive but more quickly fed into a more sophisticated computer programme than those of any other party or the TV companies. Results, ward by ward, across the country were telephoned, faxed or rushed by road to be fed into the computer. From the central computer they were even fed to me through my own personal terminal as I sat in the television studio commenting on the local election results that night. When we met at Chequers on the Sunday morning I had already supplied Margaret with our findings and unlike 1983 there was no drama as I presented my conclusions. June it was to be, and 11 June the date.

Although our analysis pointed to a majority of 98 I told the others that my central forecast was for one of 50 to 60. The over-all arithmetic had always been pretty clear. If we could achieve 40 per cent or more of the votes and lead Labour by 3 per cent then we would achieve another victory. If our share fell below 38 per cent then at best it would be a hung parliament.

The Prime Minister's decision was welcomed by the Cabinet next morning and I outlined the strategy of the campaign to those who had not yet seen the War Book. The need to clear up parliamentary business dictated a longer campaign than I would have ideally preferred, but it gave us some leeway to complete our preparations. The 'Campaign Guide', our compendium of political facts (published for sale and used by all political parties and journalists) was already printed and available. The printing of the manifesto, however, was badly delayed and we missed the peak demand, although David Young assured the Cabinet that we would have enough to satisfy the press, if not the public, by publication day.

[Norman Tebbit, *Upwardly Mobile* (London, 1988), 260–1.]

I began to receive advice [about a possible general election] and opinions from many quarters. Michael Foot came to see me and urged that we should put the idea of an autumn election out of our minds and concentrate on preparing for the next session. The Chief Whip, Michael Cocks, came separately and also expressed a strong preference for embarking upon another session. He said we would have a bumpy ride, but he believed we could reach the journey's end. He reported that the Whips' Office had met privately to discuss the options for the timing of the election, and by a clear majority (I believe it was seven votes to two) had declared against an autumn election. Among the diverse opinions they garnered were that Scotland and Wales were safe, but the English marginal seats still remained to be won, and they could not see any substantial Labour gains either in the North or in the Midlands in the autumn. Some thought that the electors might believe that an autumn election meant the Government was 'running away' before the situation worsened, but others argued that if there was no autumn election, we would be said to be 'hanging on' without cause.

Those in favour of going to the country argued that Parliamentary defeats, even on small issues, would be damaging and that the prospect of uncertainty about the behaviour of the unions during the winter meant it was preferable to go to the country while things were in reasonable shape, even though our prospects were uncertain. In terms of whether or not we could win votes in Parliament, the Deputy Chief Whip, Walter Harrison, who was a genius at conjuring majorities out of thin air, was characteristically robust.

'We have lived on next to nothing for years and should have a go at carrying on.'

Amongst my advisers there was general agreement that Party morale was good and that an autumn election would find our active supporters in good heart. But welcome news though this was, it would not necessarily be sufficient for victory. I found myself recalling an earlier election in 1959 when the Party fought with great enthusiasm and went through the campaign believing we had a splendid chance of victory, but when the results were declared we found the Conservatives had gained a number of seats, and the Labour vote had actually fallen. One reason for this was the Party's attitude at the time of Suez in 1956 which still rankled three years later with some of our own supporters and this had cost us votes.

Action should have been taken earlier to offset the five-fold increase in the price of Middle East oil in 1973, but for the first two years until 1975 we had sought, by borrowing abroad, to stave off the effects. In due course in 1976 came the recourse to the IMF and although that loan was being steadily repaid and the inflation rate was lower than when the Conservatives had left office, it seemed to me that not enough time had elapsed for the traumas of 1976 to sink into the background of the public memory. There is usually a time gap between current economic reality and public awareness of it and this was such an occasion. The text which every Government should pin up in the Cabinet Room is: 'Take the disagreeable medicine as soon as you come to power. The sweets can follow later.'

A number of Cabinet colleagues wrote to tell me their views. Most were in favour of an appeal to the country although their letters conveyed very little conviction that we could win outright. They based themselves on such arguments as the prospect of defeats in the House sapping our morale: the damage if we appeared to be 'hanging on'; we would have no reliable allies in the House; (flatteringly) my personal reputation was high: industrial problems were awaiting us: the Party workers were ready to go and in the case of Scotland, were enthusiastic. But while all these arguments were important, only one member of the Cabinet expressed a belief that we could win. Even he hedged his bet: 'We cannot be certain of winning. But we would start at least evens and I believe we would pull ahead during the campaign.' This was hardly a trumpet call, especially as he added that in his judgement the conclusive argument was that the Government could not survive the Parliamentary scene until the spring.

Bernard Donoughue sent me a summary of the pollsters' figures. They showed that the Conservative lead over Labour in the early months of 1978 had dwindled, although they were still ahead by a small margin. They also indicated that the incomes policy was still popularly approved by 66 per cent of the electorate with no more than 24 per cent dissatisfied.

I continued taking soundings during the first fortnight of August 1978, consulting a number of colleagues in different parts of the country by telephone; they were generally agreed that our electoral situation was much better than it had been a year earlier. Opinions differed, but a realistic view came from the West Midlands where I was warned that Labour's results in Council bye-elections, although showing a dramatic recovery from our low point, were not good enough to hold on to a number of the Parliamentary seats that we had won in 1974.

I did my own amateur calculations and came up with 303 Labour seats and 304 Conservatives—which if I were anywhere near being right would have left us with a small loss of seats, but with a Conservative gain of more than twenty. Such a result would have been a tremendous psychological fillip for the Tory Party and the situation would have resembled 1950/51 when a Tory Party with its tail up because of its gains in the 1950 election, harried the Attlee Government until it lost its authority and fell. My estimate was that the most probable result would be another 'hung' Parliament, a prospect I did not relish. While I would have been ready to carry on at the head of a government with a reasonable majority, I had no wish to undergo once again the frustration and uncertainty of having no Parliamentary majority. Moreover, the polls showed that as the country began to understand what we were trying to do, an increasing number liked what they saw. There was still another twelve months to run before the life of Parliament must come to an end. Why run the risk of a very doubtful election result in October 1978 if we could convert it into a more convincing majority in 1979? I made up my mind. The Government should aim to consolidate the progress we had made and then ask the country to confirm us in office on a progressive manifesto in the spring. I looked at the 1979 calendar. A new electoral register would come into force in February; British Summer Time would begin on 18 March; Good Friday was on 13 April. I drew a ring around Thursday 5 April 1979, the last day of the income tax year. This seemed as auspicious as any other day. Having decided, I telephoned the Chancellor who was my near neighbour in Sussex and invited myself to tea on Friday 18 August. I recall it was a lovely summer's afternoon, and we sat in the garden while I told him what I had decided. We then reviewed the winter's prospects.

Before the Cabinet had dispersed for the summer recess, I had informed them that they would be the first to know my decision and we had arranged to hold a Cabinet Meeting on 6 September, which was the first occasion when we should all be in the country at the same time. Before that meeting I had an earlier engagement to address the Congress of the TUC at Brighton and I took the opportunity to invite the 'Neddy 6' to dinner at the farm on Friday 1 September. They came, David Basnett, Geoffrey Drain, Terry Duffy, Moss Evans and Lionel Murray, led by the Chairman Lord Allen. My wife's reputation as a cook was well known and she presided over a splendid table at which our guests were served by my eldest granddaughter, Tamsin Jay. Now that the August holidays were over and with the approach of the TUC Congress, the press had resumed its speculation about an autumn election, and it was obvious that my guests had convinced themselves that it must be held in October. Without revealing my decision, I argued the alternative case for the spring quite strenuously, but apparently not convincingly.

Afterwards I heard that some members of the General Council felt they had been misled about the date, but no one who was present at dinner on that evening has ever said as much to me, and I doubt if they would, in view of my vigorous advocacy that a genuine alternative did exist, for which valid reasons could be advanced. But I made a mistake in allowing the speculation to build up to an almost feverish crescendo without uttering a word to cool it. My reason was my promise to the Cabinet that they should be the first to hear, but on reflection, I could have found a means of informing most of them earlier and so killed the speculation before it had become a 'certainty' in the mind of the media. When I finally made the announcement, the astonishment and in some places (like Conservative Central Office, which had already spent a lot of money on propaganda) the consternation, I was told, was awesome.

I met the Cabinet on Thursday morning 7 September and informed them of the announcement to be made later that day. They received the news in a matter of fact way and at once turned to government business. Later in the day I made a television broadcast:

The benefit the country is experiencing today is a result of your efforts and the Government has eased the situation because we thought the economy could stand it and for no other reason.

This can be a lasting, not a temporary, improvement if we follow through with consistent policies, so I am not proposing to seek your votes because there is some blue sky overhead today. Obviously all parties want to win a General Election when it comes, but let us think for a moment of the great domestic issues the country faces now, and ask ourselves whether a General Election now would make it any better this winter.

Would a general election now make it easier to prevent inflation going up once more? Would unemployment be any less this winter? Would a general election now solve the problem of how to deal with pay increases during the next few months? Would it bring a sudden dramatic increase in productivity? No. There are no instant solutions. Advertising slogans are no substitute. The Government must and will continue to carry out policies which are consistent and determined, which do not chop and change and which have brought about the present recovery in our fortunes.

We shall face our difficulties as we come to them. I can already see some looming on the horizon. I cannot, and do not, promise we shall succeed. I can say we shall deserve to. Basically, I want to say we go on because we are doing what is best for Britain. So, I shall not be calling for a general election at this time. Instead, I ask every one of you to carry on with the task of consolidating the improvements now taking place in our country's position. Let us see it through together.

After people had recovered from their surprise it was apparent that the decision had done us no harm. Indeed, if the polls were to be believed, Labour was riding high in November 1978 after the season of party conferences had been held, when our standing had so far improved that we had drawn ahead with a lead of 5.5 points over the Conservatives.

Taking one month with another, the Opinion Polls were oscillating, pointing in no consistent direction, but it seemed not unreasonable to assume that the Government, having made such a remarkable recovery in public estimation from our abysmal showing of two years earlier, would have good hopes of consolidating public confidence by the spring of 1979 and even prospects of scoring an outright victory.

But the winter of discontent intervened, and I must retrace my steps and give some account of those events that were to shatter our hopes and antagonise the country beyond recall.

[Callaghan, *Time and Chance*, 514–18.]

By April 1983, Margaret was trying to decide on the date for the general election. She consulted Cabinet by summoning us in small groups. I saw her with Peter Walker, George Younger and Nick Edwards.

I went to our meeting thinking that the last thing in the world she would want would be an early election, because it was against all her instincts. I was absolutely amazed to find that she had virtually decided to go in June: she put all the arguments for an early election, and hardly any for an October one.

All of us were in favour of the early election. The discussion then focussed on whether it should be the 9th, 16th or 23rd. It was a question of whether she could afford to be away at the Economic Summit during the campaign. We thought she could. The Social Democrats had failed to get off the ground at the Darlington by-election earlier that year. If they had done well there, it would have put our thoughts about an election in a totally different perspective.

[Prior, *Balance of Power*, 149.]

## 4. THE DIRECTION OF DEPARTMENTS

*A Prime Minister will, depending on his personality and style, exercise his authority within Ministers' own departments to a greater or lesser degree. Some Prime Ministers (like Baldwin) have scarcely interfered at all; others (like Eden or Thatcher) have intervened to a considerable extent; others have intervened for a particular purpose or for a limited period.*

Having chosen his team, and where necessary laid down certain lines of policy, Baldwin never stood at his colleagues' backs. He would have laid no claim himself to pre-eminence as an administrator. 'After he left the Treasury, he took very little interest in the concrete details of legislation,' Lord Davidson wrote, and Eustace Percy, in his memoirs, went further: 'it would almost be true to say that he trusted his colleagues for all executive action and himself only for expounding their policies to the country in terms which public opinion would understand and approve.' Individual cases disprove the rule: but he was content to leave great areas of policy and sweeping, imaginative changes to individual ministers like Neville Chamberlain and Churchill. In this Government, these two and, to a lesser extent, Cunliffe-Lister, Amery, Steel Maitland and Joynson Hicks—whose work for penal reform is too often overlooked—made up, by any standards, an outstanding team of administrators. Their innovations, though conservative and perhaps cautious, were far-reaching both at home and abroad. But the story of 1925–9 has shown that none of them could have carried out their policies without the support and encouragement of the Prime Minister.

[Keith Middlemas and John Barnes, *Baldwin* (1969), 482–3.]

So long as he [Baldwin] was in Downing Street he was always accessible to his ministers and was on terms of easy familiarity with them. What is more, he was intensely loyal to them and they could always be sure of his support. On the other hand, he was rarely of much assistance to them when they needed advice. A Prime Minister like Mr Balfour would listen carefully to a long exposition of a problem, pick on the weak points on each side of it, and produce a masterly summary which usually led the departmental minister to the right conclusion. Mr Baldwin had no such capacity. Sir Austen Chamberlain explained to the present writer that when the preliminaries of the Locarno Pact were under discussion at the Foreign Office he took the whole problem to the Prime Minister, since any further steps in the negotiations would necessarily bind His Majesty's Government to take some steps, at least, to meet the German point of view. Mr Baldwin listened carefully, but at the end his remark was: 'Well, Austen, do what you think fit and I will support you.' This was no doubt gratifying to Sir Austen, but what he wanted was a second opinion on the scheme which was being worked out by the Foreign Ministries; and this Mr Baldwin was unable or unwilling to give him. Sir Austen's biographer has made the same point, though somewhat less emphatically:

> It was always the custom of Mr Baldwin to allow his Ministers a free hand, and a Foreign Secretary in his Cabinet was particularly favoured in this respect, for the Prime Minister had little knowledge of, or interest in, international affairs. Austen enjoyed, for example, far more freedom both

in the initiation and execution of his policy than had been allowed to Sir Edward Grey by Mr Asquith, but he could also count, as experience was to prove, on Mr Baldwin's loyal support in a crisis.

[Jennings, *Cabinet Government*, 189.]

She would ideally like to run the major Departments herself and tries her best to do so—not just in terms of overall policy, but in strategic detail. This is neither practical nor desirable. Policy and decision-making require a full and careful understanding of many facts and considerations. Margaret Thatcher may have a retentive grasp of detail, but she cannot know enough to dictate the policy of each Department, as she has gradually discovered. Her response has been to expand the Downing Street staff to include experts in every major area, thus establishing a government within a government. In most cases, people have been chosen who reinforce her point of view rather than challenge it, which produces a greater rigidity of outlook than that encountered in the Civil Service.

[Pym, *Politics of Consent*, 17.]

I was now to be concerned with an equally serious but much more delicate and unpleasant question—the personal factor. The preparation, and even the launching, of large policies is an agreeable exercise enjoyed by all politicians and their friends. But matters of high ministerial posts, above all when changes in the Cabinet itself are concerned, involving many old and tested friendships—all these throw upon the head of an administration an uncongenial and often almost intolerable burden. A talk with Lord Cromer, the Governor of the Bank of England, convinced me that there was a real risk of a world deflation.

This makes . . . an effective 'incomes policy' more important. At present we dare not re-inflate, because our system is open at both ends—wages, and imports. Increased wages mean (without increased productivity) more imports and less exports.

On 21 June, while I was turning over all these questions in my mind, Butler came to lunch—as always calm and helpful.

He feels that the present grave political situation is due entirely to the bad handling of the economic problem (or rather its bad presentation) by the Chancellor of the Exchequer and the Treasury. He felt that drastic action was necessary to save the situation. This means the problem (an immense human and political problem) of replacing the Chancellor of the Exchequer.

On 22 June there was a preliminary talk with some of my colleagues on the Incomes Policy paper which I had now circulated.

A very good but very critical discussion. We shall have to do a lot more work on it. This makes me all the more angry with the Treasury and the Chancellor for their delay and lack of initiative. A whole year gone, and then the P.M. has to do it himself, at the last minute.

[Harold Macmillan, *At the End of the Day* (London, 1973), 88–9.]

I had two days more in Scilly before returning to London. Michael Stewart was there for a holiday and I discussed my ministerial plans with him. He had done a painstaking and thorough job at DEA and had brought order and a sense of system to its work. The view was much put about that, under his direction, the department seemed to be losing authority as against the Treasury. This was not so. But though, on his appointment, I had transferred responsibility for individual price and income cases to the executive departments, he remained bogged down in general incomes policy to a point where, in Whitehall and more widely, this seemed to be DEA's only role. Nevertheless, during these criticial months he had succeeded in holding down cost inflation more successfully than at any time for years past and in marked contrast to the record of some of our principal industrial competitors. And he had pioneered new and successful incentives for regional development.

But I now wanted Michael for a full-time co-ordinating role—previously discharged by Douglas Houghton—and it was time to give Patrick Gordon Walker a department. I doubted whether Michael would last very long in that role, however; it could only be a matter of time before one of George's late-night resignations stuck and I would want Michael back at the Foreign Office.

Although a great deal had been done in modernising and re-structuring industry, I was not satisfied with the pace. While as Prime Minister I interested myself closely in modernisation plans, it had to be largely at second remove or by chairing ministerial committees over some interdepartmental dispute. I did not want us to go on to the end of our term relying on purely monetary measures and demand management; my whole strategy from the time of my Swansea speech in January 1964 had been aimed at strengthening the competitive base of British industry so that sustained growth without balance of payments repercussions could be possible. I therefore told Michael that I would propose myself to take charge of DEA with a Secretary of State to assist me. In addition I would take over the chairmanship of the National Economic Development Council and strengthen contacts with industry at the highest level.

[Wilson, *The Labour Government*, 426.]

*The Prime Minister must have his own sources of information in order to discharge his responsibilities, and especially so as to assess the advice which he receives from individual Ministers and departments.*

Another of the Prime Minister's levers was the Policy Unit headed by Dr Bernard Donoughue (now Lord Donoughue), who was my Senior Policy Adviser. This was one of Harold Wilson's effective creations which I was happy to inherit. It was staffed by specialists from outside the Civil Service and was more overtly political than the Think Tank. It provided me with systematic policy analysis distinct from that of the Departments, and thus supported by facts and figures, I was in a stronger position to challenge Departmental proposals—especially those from the Treasury, which usually fired the heaviest guns. I had considerable respect for the Treasury's intellectual fire-power, but I also knew how they could spread confusion in the fog of battle and disperse and destroy their opponents one by one. Bernard Donoughue's task was to clear away the fog. He has a keen political insight and employed his unit for the purpose of what the Americans call an 'overview' of the Government's progress. He helped me in my effort to stand back and view developments as a whole. The unit proposed new initiatives from time to time where gaps existed and would call my attention to inconsistencies in Government policies. Its thinking was unorthodox and refreshing and it had considerable influence when I launched the so-called Great Debate on education.

The Private Office, whose room is the only one that opens directly into the Cabinet Room, is in every sense closer to the Prime Minister than the Think Tank, the Policy Unit or even the Secretary to the Cabinet. It is small in numbers, staffed on secondment by civil servants drawn from a number of Departments, with the Treasury and the Foreign Office always supplying at least one apiece. Normally the Prime Minister is given a list of the high-fliers in the main Departments and he makes his own choice of Private Secretaries from this, often interviewing them personally before they join his staff. Their tasks are limitless, bounded only by the number of hours in the day and the curiosity and energy of the Prime Minister. But a prime task is to sort out essential items for him to consider from the flood of reading matter that reaches the office in the form of Cabinet memoranda, correspondence from colleagues, resolutions from the Party, letters from the public, pleas from industrialists, seekers of honours, foreign telegrams and so on, in a never-ending forest of paper.

The Private Secretaries are the focal point for the Prime Minister's activities: they coordinate his engagements; take responsibility for assembling material for his speeches and usually have an important hand in drafting them; ensure he is properly briefed before Cabinet and other meetings at home and when paying official visits overseas; act as eyes and ears by maintaining a close liaison with other Ministers' Private Offices; act as the link with the Queen's Private Secretary; and act as a filter through which those who wish to see the Prime Minister must pass. They need to be diplomatic enough to pacify the untimely visitor—once it was Earl Mountbatten who received the treatment when he called unannounced at No. 10, choosing a moment when it was impossible for me to see him.

The Private Secretaries are among the few who may walk in to the Prime Minister's room at any time, and if he is wise enough to strike up a trusting relationship with these young men and women, he will benefit greatly by being offered the frank opinions of three or four of the best and most intelligent members of their generation. They understand the mysterious ways of the Whitehall machine and how to make it respond, and are almost certainly destined to rise to the top of their profession. They act as though they share your successes and care about your failures, and as you all face the music together a corporate spirit develops. I place on record my debt to all my Private Secretaries, headed by Sir Kenneth Stowe who like the others has gone on to higher things and is Permanent Secretary at the Department of Health and Social Security. Perhaps the best illustration I can give of our close relationship is that although the No. 10 team has long been dispersed, some serving abroad as Ambassadors or in high positions at home, we still enjoy a regular reunion to renew our friendship and exchange our news. I may add in passing that because I had served a government at periods since 1947 there was a time while I was Prime Minister when no fewer than four Permanent Secretaries and a brace of Ambassadors had acted as my Private Secretary in one Department or another in the past.

Another lever at the Prime Minister's hand is his Political Office. This is made up entirely of non-civil servants recruited from among Party members and paid for by funds that the Prime Minister has to find for himself. This Office was headed by Tom McNally, at one time the Secretary of the International Department of the Labour Party, whom I had recruited while at the Foreign Office and took with me to Downing Street. His task was to maintain constant contact with the officers and National Executive Committee of the Labour Party. He dealt with local constituency parties, and kept in touch with the senior officers of the trade unions. He fulfilled an indispensable liaison role, and made sure I was informed about Party developments, alerted me to signs of dissatisfaction from the National Executive Committee, suggested visits to factories and different areas of the country and generally made certain that in carrying out the absorbing tasks of government I did not overlook the foundation upon which it all rested—namely, the support of the Party in the country.

Tom had a fertile mind, and was adept at ensuring that I was constantly reminded of the party political background against which Ministers' Departmental programmes should be judged. He was very ingenious in suggesting courses of action and then in carrying them through. Naturally the Political Office did not work in isolation either from the Policy Unit or the Private Office, and all of them had close links with the Press Office under Tom McCaffrey. There was much cross-fertilisation and through this we endeavoured to secure an integrated approach, though sometimes there was overlapping. Tom McCaffrey was also an old friend who had been the Press Officer at the Home Office several years earlier during my period there. When we won the election of 1974, I asked the Home Office if he could join me at the Foreign Office and they agreed. Later, he was to come with me to No. 10 and when I left No. 10 he too left and resigned from the public service. I admired his fierce Scottish integrity and his candour, of which I had been the victim when I had been at the Home Office for only a few weeks and he told me bluntly that I was not living up to the high expectations with which the Home Office had greeted me. These traits not only gained him my respect; the press and other media trusted him, for while he sometimes could not tell them the whole truth, he made it a point of principle never to mislead them or lay false trails. It was thanks to him that I enjoyed a less barbed relationship with the press than I might have done, for his patience and modesty were greater than mine. Like the Private Office staff, Tom McCaffrey could see me at all times.

All these levers are directly under the Prime Minister's eye and are very personal to him and his requirements, but there is another and more powerful lever at one stage removed. The conventional role of the Cabinet Office is to serve all members of the Cabinet, but if the Prime Minister chooses, as nearly all of them do, to work closely with the Secretary to the Cabinet, then it becomes an instrument to serve him above the others. Its work has been often described and I will not repeat it here, except to emphasise the importance of its central role in coordinating the work of the Cabinet, which in turn puts it in a powerful position to exert influence over the rest of the Civil Service. The Cabinet Secretary prepares the agenda for Cabinet meetings, so he is in a position to influence what shall be discussed and when, although the final decision rests with the Prime Minister. All papers prepared by Ministers for the Cabinet's consideration are first sent to the Cabinet Office for circulation, which in turn gives the Prime Minister the chance to defer it by asking a Minister to think again or alternatively to accelerate its discussion. At inter-Departmental meetings of Civil Servants it is the Cabinet Secretary or one of his assistants who will frequently take the Chair, with all the opportunities for influence over the discussion that such a position bestows. And if, as in Mrs Thatcher's Administration, the Cabinet Secretary is also the Head of the Civil Service, the holder of the dual office is in a unique position to shape appointments as well as influence policy and so enables the Prime Minister to control the Government's actions with considerable economy of effort. It is not, however, an arrangement I recommend.

I have set out this catalogue of levers at the Prime Minister's hand because from time to time there is discussion about the need for a formal Prime Minister's Department and such talk frequently overlooks the instruments he already has. He is able to provide himself with his own sources of information; he can send up a trial balloon or fire a sighting shot across a Ministerial bow without directly involving his own authority or publicly undermining that of the Minister; and he has the necessary facilities to take a decisive hand in policy-making at any moment he chooses to intervene.

The establishment of a formal Prime Minister's Department, with the Prime Minister's representatives attending Cabinet Committees, would not only add an unnecessary layer of administration, but could have the political disadvantage, when contentious issues were under discussion, that his or her representatives would be forced to take a line too early and thus restrict room for manoeuvre later on. For, despite current fashion, reconciliation and compromise between contending groups in a well-ordered system of Cabinet Government will continue to be an important function of the Prime Minister, as well as the need to give a clear lead when the occasion demands.

[Callaghan, *Time and Chance*, 404–8.]

The final broad area which is important in determining the degree of the Prime Minister's influence on policy concerns the kind of advice which he receives, the expertise that is at his disposal, providing facts and figures and shaping arguments. This matters because the exercise of government is not a question of the Prime Minister simply issuing instructions. The conduct of British government involves a process of continual inter-departmental debate which frequently turns into intense and protracted trench warfare. Protagonists in these policy battles need a good supply of the ammuniton of facts, figures and arguments. This is particularly true in battles with the Treasury, which is well armed with economists and statisticians prepared to provide the numerical arguments for any policy position. Unless the Prime Minister is able to argue with the Treasury using his own well-researched statistics, thus being able to point out that the Treasury case can be seen in a different light and that alternative policies can be.supported statistically, he usually will not win. The Prime Minister not only has to deal with the Treasury but also with the various other Whitehall departments which themselves have thousands of troops servicing their current policy positions. A Prime Minister who inclines to take a different view is therefore inevitably under-powered. The British Prime

Minister does not have a separate, permanent department of his own, unlike the American and French Presidents or the German Chancellor. To some extent the modest servicing of the British Prime Minister compared to that of his international counterparts simply reflects a lack of space. No. 10 Downing Street is a relatively small building composed of two back-to-back town houses. Its five floors contain various offices, four reception rooms, the Cabinet room, the Prime Minister's study and flat, and some bedrooms under the roof. In total there is space for a little over a hundred working people. The majority of these are secretaries, messengers and police officers. The number of people in senior advisory positions is inevitably limited, and there are no more than a dozen in all, with a similar quota of junior advisers.

The advisory staff are nearly all divided into four functional groups which service the Prime Minister's main roles . . . (Cabinet, party, parliamentary, media). The respective offices servicing these prime ministerial roles in Downing Street are: (i) the Private Office secretaries who are temporarily loaned to No. 10 by other Whitehall departments and who conduct the Prime Minister's official relations with Whitehall, Parliament and the public in his capacity as executive head of government; (ii) the Press Office, which handles the Prime Minister's relations with the media; (iii) the Political Office, which conducts the Prime Minister's affairs in his capacity as a Member of Parliament and as leader of a political party; and (iv) the Policy Unit which advises the Prime Minister on all areas of government policy.

The staff of the Private Office are always permanent civil servants, whereas those of the Political Office are always temporary outsiders. The Press Office has regular civil service information officers but it may be led either by an outsider, as with Harold Wilson bringing in Joe Haines, or a regular civil servant, as with Tom McCaffrey working for James Callaghan or Bernard Ingham for Mrs Thatcher. The Policy Unit which I ran between 1974–9 was composed entirely of temporary recruits from the outside world, although under Mrs Thatcher there has been some colonisation by the regular civil service.

The Prime Minister's Private Office is the single most important section of the administrative support services in No. 10. It is the communications centre of Downing Street, and is in regular contact with all the ministerial private offices. Virtually all official communications to or from the Prime Minister, written or verbal, are channelled through the Private Office. The Private Secretaries sift through the flow of papers and decide—based upon their experience of central government and upon their knowledge of a particular Prime Minister's interests and priorities—which to put before him urgently, which to delay, and which not to bother him with but to answer themselves. They fill the Prime Minister's red boxes for his nightly or his weekend reading. The Senior Secretaries will periodically sit with him in the study or in the flat discussing how to respond on certain issues. Usually a close bond of trust builds up between the Prime Minister and his Private Office, which organises the whole routine of his governmental working day. Few people, inside or outside government, enjoy such a devoted and such an efficient service. The danger is that Prime Ministers become entranced by and dependent on the support, which gives the Private Secretaries great potential power to influence. After leaving Downing Street most Prime Ministers feel deprived and may find it difficult to adjust once more to organising their own political lives.

The Private Secretaries occupy two high, crowded rooms next to the Cabinet room. The Principal Private Secretary sits in the smaller room of the two with his desk beside the large double doors guarding the side entrance into the Cabinet room. When we arrived in office in March 1974 the occupant of this powerful seat and the boss of the Downing Street administration machine was Robert Armstrong. A man of formidable intellect and authoritative bearing, he appeared to me quite daunting in our opening discussions on the role of the Policy Unit. He was undoubtedly concerned that the internal lines of communication to the Prime Minister in Downing Street should not be confused or his own status diminished. However, we rapidly established not only an excellent working relationship but also a personal friendship of mutual respect which has survived many changes of circumstances. He is a warm, complex and very sensitive man and comes professionally from the best civil service tradition of integrity and public duty. He was a Rolls Royce in Whitehall. His successor, Kenneth Stowe, was an easier and simpler man, entirely without side. He gave the Policy Unit every possible assistance and we worked closely and comfortably together. His great virtues were his calmness, his openness and his directness. Mr Callaghan thought the world of him and I could quite see why. He was a marvellous team member.

With the Principal Private Secretary sits the Foreign Affairs

Private Secretary, usually a Foreign Office official who is expected to rise high in the ranks of the Diplomatic Service. In my time the three occupants of the post were Lord Bridges (son of a former Head of the Civil Service and later to be Ambassador to Rome), Bryan Cartledge (subsequently a predictably hawkish Ambassador to Moscow) and Patrick Wright, a marvellously amusing colleague who deservedly became head of the Diplomatic Service. These Foreign Service Secretaries all seemed a little set apart from the rest of us in No. 10. Perhaps it was simply because they were the only ones who were not members of the Home Civil Service. But it seemed to be more than that. Somehow they never ceased to be the Foreign Office representatives to the Prime Minister. The other Private Secretaries were unreservedly the Prime Minister's men.

The larger room is occupied by a group of younger Private Secretaries, each with a distinct specialisation. One, usually from the Treasury, concentrates on economic matters. While I was there a second domestic post was established to cover the rest of social policy. One secretary dealt with parliamentary affairs, specialising in predicting the wicked intentions behind the most innocent looking Commons questions. The Prime Minister's daily diary also required the full-time attention of a secretary (although under Mrs Thatcher this job was for a time carried out by a personal staff member and not by a regular civil servant). In practice any one of these secretaries might cover the field of an absentee and one of them always had to be available at the weekend. Finally, squeezed in one corner was a duty clerk who handled the multitude of routine office tasks and was on duty to take telephone calls and process any business which arose throughout the night.

The administrative quality of these young Private Secretaries was in my time extremely high. They were selected from the cream of their departments and with the help of their Downing Street experience were expected to rise to the top positions in the civil service. The three secretaries from the Treasury with whom I worked—Robin Butler, Nigel Wicks and Tim Lankester—were very impressive. Indeed, Robin Butler was the most outstanding civil servant with whom I ever had to deal, at any level. It was very important to the success of the Policy Unit that we should get on well with the Private Secretaries, especially those covering the economic field. They were a vital source of information for us. It was also helpful if their advice to the Prime Minister did not entirely conflict with ours.

A Prime Minister is more likely to be impressed by a united No. 10 view. For this reason we worked very closely with the Private Secretaries and during some of the most stressful crises their support was absolutely essential.

The Policy Unit was the newest part of the Downing Street machine. Previous Prime Ministers had employed individual advisers. However, until Harold Wilson created the Policy Unit in 1974 there was no systematic policy analysis separate from the regular civil service machine and working solely for the Prime Minister. These are the three characteristics which distinguished the Policy Unit from what had existed before: it was systematic, it was separate from the Whitehall machine and it was solely working to the Prime Minister. This strengthening of the supportive mechanisms serving the Prime Minister has proved an important reform among the several contributions which Harold Wilson made to the effectiveness of British central government. It is significant that not only did James Callaghan retain the Policy Unit, but his Tory successor, Margaret Thatcher, continued and strengthened it.

Harold Wilson described the proposed Policy Unit as his 'eyes and ears' when asking me to create it in March 1974. I worked frantically during the early weeks interviewing and recruiting members. Our target was to have six to eight policy specialists together with a couple of research assistants. The recruitment was not always an easy procedure as candidates had little idea of how the new institution would work and some had observed the unhappy treatment of outside advisers previously admitted to Whitehall. Nor could they be offered much security. Special advisers are temporary civil servants and their appointments terminate automatically when their Minister leaves office—hence I received letters of dismissal in advance of the general elections of October 1974 and May 1979, and on 16 March when Harold Wilson announced his resignation. At first we were offered no redundancy terms but I subsequently negotiated some compensation for special advisers related to their years of service. However, in the spring of 1974, with another election expected soon, it was not possible to offer much security of tenure. Fortunately people of the highest ability are rarely motivated by a strong desire for security, and I was able to recruit a group of distinguished policy experts who worked in our three cramped rooms situated up the corridor from the Cabinet room and the Private Offices and directly opposite the locked green baize door to the Cabinet Office—through which I could see from my desk Sir John Hunt, the Cabinet Secretary, frequently bustle, clutching his precious key. By the summer I was assisted by Andrew Graham, Fellow in Economics from Balliol College, Oxford; Gavyn Davies, a young economist also from Balliol; David Piachaud, a lecturer in social policy from the London School of Economics; Catherine Carmichael, lecturer in social administration at the University of Glasgow; Richard Graham, Manager of Domestic Trunks Services with British Airways; and Richard Kirwan, a housing economist from the Centre for Environmental Studies. They were later joined by Richard Smethurst and David Gowland, economists from Oxford and York Universities respectively, by Jim Corr from the World Bank and by Elizabeth Arnott from Transport House's social policy research staff. Often assisted by Mr Wilson's outstanding Press Secretary, Joe Haines, they constituted an intellectual power house with wide policy expertise and strong political awareness. Whipped into line by my personal assistant, Brenda Haddau, a brilliant young civil service administrative assistant, they made a formidable team without which I could have achieved very little.

The press release on the new Policy Unit issued from Downing Street stated that the Unit would 'assist in the development of the whole range of policies contained in the Government's programme, especially those arising in the short and medium term'. This was an attempt to distinguish it from the Central Policy Review Staff (CPRS), based in the Cabinet Office which was more, although not exclusively, orientated to longer-term policy horizons. Members of the Unit were specifically enjoined to maintain regular liaison with the CPRS, with other special advisers working for individual departmental Ministers, with the chairmen of policy committees of the parliamentary Labour party and with policy specialists in party headquarters. An internal memorandum to Unit members, drafted by myself and cleared by Mr Wilson, described the Unit's functions in detail: 'The Unit must ensure that the Prime Minister is aware of what is coming up from departments to Cabinet. It must scrutinise papers, contact departments, know the background to policy decisions, disputes and compromises, and act as an early warning system. The Unit may feed into the system ideas on policy which are not currently covered, or are inadequately covered . . . The Unit should feed in "minority reforms" which departments may overlook, or which fall between departmental boundaries, or which are the subject of worthy but unsuccessful Private Members Bills. This is especially the case with issues which concern ordinary people (and of which Whitehall may be unaware).' The political dimension in its work was underlined: The Prime Minister has assumed

> responsibility as custodian of the Labour manifesto. The Unit must assist in that role, making sure that the manifesto is not contravened, nor retreated from, without proper discussion and advance warning . . . Throughout its policy work the Unit will clearly be aware of the political dimension in Government. It must maintain good relations with the party organisation. The individual Ministries must not become isolated from the Government as a whole and lapse into traditional 'departmental views'.

My next most important task after recruiting its members was to negotiate the Unit's working arrangements within Whitehall—and above all its rights to access to the decision-making process based on the jungle of committees. Without access one is impotent in Whitehall. I had prolonged and strenuous talks with the then Cabinet Secretary, Sir John Hunt. His concern, quite properly, was that the Unit advisers should not replace the normal Private Office channels of communication between No. 10 and Ministers on official business, which I accepted. In return he readily conceded that, as departmental Ministers did not have matching special advisory *cabinets*, the Unit would have to make direct links with officials. We were therefore authorised to be in immediate contact with other departments in order to discover 'official thinking on departmental policies'. Most important were our relations with the central committee system and the Cabinet Office itself, and to this end I negotiated with Sir John a carefully drafted list of 'ground rules' which were circulated to senior officials towards the end of April 1974. It enjoined the Cabinet Office, the CRPS and the Central Statistical Office to assist the Unit 'with advice and information to the maximum extent possible'. The outline stated that I would not normally be a member of official committees but that if I wanted myself or my staff to attend or receive papers 'there should be a disposition to say yes'. (In practice I attended not only any official committees I chose, but also all Cabinet Committees with the Prime Minister in the Chair, many Cabinet Committees with other Ministers in the Chair, and some full Cabinets. I also attended the weekly meetings of Deputy Secretaries in the Cabinet Office to determine the Government's future programme—but I never managed to get into the weekly mandarin summit of Permanent Secretaries held every Wednesday morning under the chairmanship of the then head of the Civil

Service, Sir Douglas Allen.) In return for these very important concessions concerning the Unit's access to the Whitehall machine, I was formally required to promise that I would not 'show papers of Official Committees to the Prime Minister or report the views of individual officials to him'. This was 'not just to preserve the freedom of official discussion of issues at a preliminary stage but more importantly to respect the position of departmental Ministers' and I always respected that condition. The Cabinet Secretary was also very concerned that the Policy Unit's role should not affect his personal channels of communication to the Prime Minister or his function of providing a steering brief for the Prime Minister as Chairman of Cabinet Committees. He therefore issued instructions that copies of Cabinet Office briefs should not be sent to me. In fact I could always slip down to Private Office to read them and if necessary add my own covering brief—and the Private Secretaries often alerted me when a controversial Cabinet Office brief had arrived and they felt that something extra from the Policy Unit would be helpful to the Prime Minister. The agreement which Sir John and I reached concluded with a statement from him to his officials that 'we must therefore work closely together and make a success of it'. Both sides did their utmost to ensure this. The formal access guaranteed by this document was a major advance on anything achieved before. However, it was a privilege conceded only to members of the Downing Street Policy Unit and did not apply in every respect to other departmental special advisers working to individual Ministers in Whitehall. The latter were more restricted in access and were limited in number to two per Minister after December 1974. There was a proposal from the Minister responsible for the Civil Service in April 1974 to appoint me formally as head of all the special advisers in Whitehall; but I declined on the basis that it would give me responsibility for people over whom I had no control.

The most important contribution of the Policy Unit to central government was that it increased the Prime Minister's capacity for effective intervention in other Ministers' policy areas, for which more than mere personal will-power and the status of Downing Street is required, especially in the field of economic policy. It is simply not possible to maintain a sustained influence over economic policy without conducting a long, high-level and successful debate with the Treasury. Prime Ministers do, of course, have the ultimate power to overrule the Chancellor and insist on particular policies, which Mr Wilson did in 1975 when rejecting the Treasury's proposals for a statutory pay policy and Mr Callaghan did in 1976 when insisting on his own modest IMF package; Mrs Thatcher also is reported to have intervened on several occasions, particularly when amending the Treasury's 1981 budget. Under democratic Cabinet government, however, such an arbitrary approach is not one that a prudent Prime Minister would for long pursue, or a self-respecting Chancellor for long allow. Following such a path, a Prime Minister would soon consume his capital reserves of goodwill with his Cabinet colleagues. In Britain, as in the United States and most electorally accountable democracies, government involves a lengthy process of argument. In establishing the Policy Unit in Downing Street, Harold Wilson added significantly to the Prime Minister's fire-power in the policy-making process, and, indeed, the Policy Unit played a central role in the prime ministerial interventions in the crises of 1975, 1976 and 1979. This was only possible because the staff supporting me were of outstanding calibre. Each was required to have a rare combination of intellectual and political skills. As a single adviser covered one departmental policy area, the work-load on individuals was enormous. They needed the knowledge and intelligence to monitor and combat a whole department. (Our battles with the Treasury were basically conducted over those five and a half years by three remarkable economists, Gavyn Davies, Andrew Graham and David Piachaud.) I always recruited acknowledged policy experts of intellectual distinction because otherwise departments would not respect them or bother to include them in policy discussions. In addition they needed to have good political instincts, as the political dimension was one which mattered greatly to the Prime Minister; such instincts the regular civil service might either lack or, for professional reasons, prefer to leave to those with overt political commitments. The ultimate difference between us special advisers and the regular civil servants was that we alone were held directly responsible for the Prime Minister's policies in the sense that we shared his electoral fate if they failed—as indeed happened to me after the 1979 general election when I joined the ranks of the unemployed for five months.

I shall not write at length about either the Press Office or the Political Office because I had no direct professional experience of working in either. Under Harold Wilson I worked very closely with his Press Officer, Joe Haines. Joe was the toughest, funniest and most loyal colleague I have ever known and he is a man of total integrity. He knows the Fleet Street press inside out and handled them in exactly the way Harold Wilson wanted—which was quite roughly at times. However, his role in No. 10 went further than just dealing with the media. He possessed remarkable political insight and judgment and for most of the 1974–6 period he was effectively the Prime Minister's main political adviser. In my time he also wrote nearly every word of virtually all of Harold Wilson's public (as opposed to his parliamentary) speeches. But each Press Secretary in Downing Street, together with his half a dozen staff, does the job in his own way. Joe Haines's successor when James Callaghan took office, Tom McCaffrey, was more the civil servant, keeping a lower profile and not attempting to have the same political or policy influences with Mr Callaghan which Joe had enjoyed with Mr Wilson. Under Mrs Thatcher, Bernard Ingham has allegedly played a strong role in trying to manipulate the media and has even at times given the impression of being an independent source of political decision-making inside No. 10. It is very difficult to generalise about the Press Office as its methods reflect the different wishes of various Prime Ministers and the different styles of numerous Press Secretaries. There is, however, no doubt about its importance. All Prime Ministers, whatever they say in public, care passionately about how they are treated in the media. As far as they are concerned, the Press Secretary is a most important servant who has ready access at any time.

The Political Office can likewise be run in different ways, although much of its work concerns relations with the Prime Minister's party, at national and parliamentary and at constituency level, and is therefore not always visible to other officials within Downing Street. The Political Office is important because it reflects the crucial fact that the Prime Minister is still a partisan leader as well as head of the nation's government and he has to ride both horses at the same time. It is politically imprudent for a Prime Minister to be beguiled by the calls of national interest into completely abandoning his party political base—he must never forget that without the party he would never have reached Downing Street in the first place. The job of Political Secretary requires good political contacts at all levels, an ability to keep open many lines of party communication, and skill in protecting the Prime Minister's weak spots. Under Mr Callaghan, Tom McNally managed this successfully, as well as maintaining most amiable relations with the rest of No. 10. In addition, he often participated constructively in the discussions of the Policy Unit.

There are, of course, extra arms to the Prime Minister's advisory capability which are situated outside Downing Street. The Central Statistical Office—created by Harold Wilson after the 1964 election to improve the numeracy of the regular civil service—is part of that central capability. However, most important of the services provided to the Prime Minister from outside No. 10 are those from the Cabinet Office.

[Bernard Donoughue, *Prime Minister: The Conduct of Policy under Harold Wilson and James Callaghan* (London, 1987), 16–26.]

## A Prime Minister's Weaknesses

### 1. TEMPORARY GOVERNMENTS

Longevity of Prime Ministers since 1902

| Name | Years and months in office |
|---|---|
| M. Thatcher | 10–8 (to January 1990) |
| H. Asquith | 8–8 |
| *W. Churchill | 8–8 |
| *H. Wilson | 7–9 |
| *S. Baldwin | 6–10 |
| *R. MacDonald | 6–9 |
| H. Macmillan | 6–9 |
| C. Attlee | 6–2 |
| D. Lloyd George | 5–10 |
| E. Heath | 3–8 |
| A. Balfour | 3–5 |
| J. Callaghan | 3–1 |
| N. Chamberlain | 2–11 |
| Sir H. Campbell-Bannerman | 2–4 |
| Sir A. Eden | 1–9 |
| Sir A. Douglas-Home | 1–0 |
| A. Bonar Law | 0–7 |

*indicates not a consecutive period

[Source: David Butler and Gareth Butler, *British Political Facts 1900–1985* (London, 6th edn., 1986), 84.]

*Leaving the present incumbent out of account, the average period in office of Prime Ministers since 1902 has been 4 years and 9 months—less than a full Parliament. A Prime Minister will be exceptional if he enjoys more than 8 years in power—less than two full Parliaments.*

## 2. DEPENDENCE ON LUCK

### (I) EDEN

*Eden had been Churchill's heir apparent for 13 years when he became Prime Minister in 1955. The Suez affair and the collapse of his health led to his resignation after only 21 months in power.*

As this biography has demonstrated, Anthony Eden was an exceptionally complex and sensitive man, of varying moods. Eden 'up' was a delight; Eden 'down' was less attractive, however short and explosive such occasions might have been. One of the best modern parliamentarians, it was in Office that he was most content. His relationship with the Conservative Party was always uneasy so far as the House of Commons was concerned, but not in Warwick and Leamington. Clarissa Eden wrote in her diary in February 1953: 'I'm not really a Conservative, A. says, I have more sympathy with the opposition. I am an old-fashioned Liberal.' In reality he was a Conservative whose real education had been in the First World War, the precursor and champion of modern One Nation Conservatism, and whose relationship with the Conservative Party had been as complex as that of Churchill, seeking to emphasize the best aspects and despising the worst.

Those who ascribed his success to good luck did not appreciate the extent to which he had experienced the reverse. The deaths of his brothers, the disaster that befell Windlestone, the sadness of his first marriage, the death of Simon, and, perhaps most important of all, the debilitating impact of poor health, may be especially cited; the responsibility for the ultimate failure over Suez, as I have demonstrated, should be apportioned more broadly, and he certainly had ill luck virtually throughout that melancholy episode.

It was especially ironical that the greatest source of Anthony Eden's ill luck had been Winston Churchill, the object of his scorn—and worse—as a schoolboy, soldier and young politician;

his closest political friend and leader in the most terrible of all wars; and the man under whose shadow he had worked for so long. If Churchill had succumbed to any of his serious wartime ailments, Eden would have automatically succeeded him as Britain's leader; if Churchill had retired in 1945, Eden would have become the uncontested leader of the Conservative Party, and would have reached the political summit at the height of his powers; if he had not been so desperately ill himself, he would almost certainly have been Prime Minister in 1953. Instead, he did so under lowering circumstances that were, unhappily, stronger than he could survive.

Although Churchill had many supreme qualities that Eden lacked, Eden had others that Churchill did not have, which made them such a uniquely powerful combination in war, but which made Eden the stronger and more attractive in peace. With Churchill, one always had the vivid emotion of being carried back nostalgically to more glorious days; with Anthony Eden, one looked to a better future. But, when Churchill reluctantly departed in 1955, too much had happened to ensure a successful inheritance. It was not calculated, but it happened. If Churchill had acted differently, this biography would have had a very different ending. But Churchill acted as he did, and events occurred as they did.

The British people understood this much better than most politicians. From the beginning Eden had seemed different, as indeed he was. His kindness, his warmth and erudition were genuine, as was his shyness. He was also palpably honest and brave, with that precious, unusual, but crucial quality of sincerity. Historians may question some of his judgements and actions; but it will be difficult indeed for them to discover turpitude, even in the 1956 Anglo-French-Israeli agreement. This action can be criticized, but it was done sincerely in the national interest. Again, I am sure that this was also widely recognized, and the swiftly aborted venture in 1966 to reopen the Suez issue is good evidence of this.

Winston Churchill loved the phrase 'An English Worthy', his highest form of praise. It applies perfectly to Anthony Eden, for the 'secret' of his success and regard was that he was a highly intelligent, good, honest, sincere and decent man who was worthy of trust. Of all the honours he received, the greatest of all was the most rare of all—the confidence and love of the British people.

[Robert Rhodes James, *Anthony Eden*, 621–2.]

## (2) MACMILLAN

*Macmillan—'Supermac' from 1957 to 1962—was hit, from 1962, by security lapses, by-election losses, failure of his attempt to join Britain to the European Community, the Profumo scandal (on which see below p. 361), and what he termed 'the stroke of fate'—an emergency operation followed by his resignation in 1963.*

On looking back upon these two or three weeks of hesitation I am surprised and shocked at my vacillation. I was not accustomed, even in the most difficult circumstances of my life, to shilly-shally or to seek unnecessarily the advice of others. During all this period—that is from after my return from Yorkshire at the beginning of September—I felt nervous, uneasy and with a curious lack of grip, combined with a tendency to drowsiness at inconvenient moments. This I put down to fatigue and did little about it. But I have no doubt that these weaknesses were symptoms of my coming illness. My doctor, Sir John Richardson, was on holiday, and I did not want to bring him back, nor did I consult any other physician. Nevertheless, when I had finally reached, after these unusual procrastinations and hesitations, the decision to continue and fight the Election, I felt immensely relieved. Naturally, my wife fully agreed. Although she had been doubtful of my physical strength (perhaps she had watched this strange apathy coming on me), she now seemed relieved at my new determination.

> I went to bed last night determined to inform the Cabinet that I had now decided to stay on and fight the General Election and to ask for the full support of my colleagues. I would say that I fully realised the difficulties, but that I felt they could be overcome.

Since much has been written, often inaccurately, about the events which followed, it is necessary for me to give the detailed story. It seemed indeed almost incredible that on the very day that I decided, and received the full support of the Cabinet, to continue my work, I was struck down. Some commentators thought the sequence of events scarcely believable. One famous columnist, Cassandra, alleged that I had invented my illness. I could only hope that he would never undergo anything so disagreeable himself. On the night of 7 October, I had determined to remain Prime Minister and seek again the suffrage of the people. Twenty-four hours later I was in hospital and had already undergone the preliminary attentions of the surgeons.

In the middle of the night (or rather earlier in the evening while our agitated discussions were going on) I found it impossible to pass water and an excruciating pain when I attempted to do so. I was seized by terrible spasms . . . Dorothy came to my help and got a doctor—Dr King-Lewis (Sir John Richardson was on holiday in Windermere). He finally arrived about 4 a.m. and managed to give me relief by inserting an instrument to drain the water out of the bladder. Unfortunately, the bladder kept filling up, and by about 8 a.m. it was worse. Dr K.-L. came again and helped. He promised me that he would get Mr [A.W.] Badenoch, the greatest surgeon in this line of business, by 1 p.m.

Cabinet at 10. A large number of items—rating relief, Robbins's educational report, etc., etc. At noon, I stopped further items; asked Cabinet Secretariat to leave (except Sir Burke Trend) and explained shortly the problem to the Cabinet and announced my plan. Since I realised (I said) that there could be no free discussion in my presence, I withdrew. (The 'plan', of course, was to announce at Blackpool that I would lead in the General Election.) At this point, I had no reason to think (from what Dr King-Lewis had said) that my trouble would be very serious. He hoped that normal passing of water might be re-established in a few hours. Any treatment of a more radical character would be perhaps avoided or postponed. Of course, Dr K.-L. was quite right to keep me quiet at the time and had no idea of the issues involved. He thought it only a question of going to Blackpool for the speech on Saturday. But during the Cabinet, I had to go out twice with spasms, and felt pretty bad. At 12.45 p.m. Mr Badenoch came. He re-inserted the instrument and drained the bladder. After consultation with Dr K.-L., he told me that the cause was the inflammation of the prostate gland (by either a benign or malignant tumour) and that it would have to be dealt with. Sir J.R. had been told by telephone and would be in London by 4 p.m. or so. It was agreed that there should be a meeting at 6 p.m. to decide on a course of action. Meanwhile, I heard (at about 1.30) from Chief Whip that the Cabinet had (with one exception) agreed to back me to the full if I decided to go on through the General Election . . .

The afternoon went on, with coming and going, some pain and some moments of relief. We were giving a party to our staff, to celebrate the return to No. 10, at 6.30–8 p.m. I managed to appear at this, *after* the doctors' conference and verdict. The decision was to go to hospital at once, for the operation.

The rest of the evening was rather confused. I telephoned to Lord Poole (at Blackpool). Butler came in to see me. I had talks with Maurice and my daughters.

At 9 p.m. I went to the Hospital (King Edward's Hospital for Officers) in excruciating pain. Mr Badenoch came and I was taken at once to the operating theatre, where he put in a catheter, to drain the bladder. This gave me relief.

After the usual hospital doings, I was put to bed and got to sleep about 11.30 p.m.

Before I had left No. 10 on the night of 8 October, Harold Evans rightly insisted that the true story be given to the Press. In the morning, therefore, it was 'headline news'. During the course of the next day, the Foreign Secretary and the Lord Chancellor came to see me. It so happened that Lord Home would take the chair at Blackpool as President of the National Union for the year. With their help and with that of my admirable private staff, we got a lot of work done.

1. Letter for Alec to read out on Friday, which makes it clear that although I had decided to go on through the Election, this is now impossible.
2. *Approval* of this letter by the Queen.
3. Letter in general terms about situation to the Queen.
4. I have had—before getting ill—a wonderful letter from the President about my part in getting the Test Ban. Could it be read to the Conference? Or published in some other way? David Gore will ask President. (It was read: 15 October)
5. Some general plans about date of my retirement and successor taking over. If Hailsham is to be a competitor, he must at once give up his peerage and find a constituency.

I managed in the course of the day to finish all the outstanding routine work. Dorothy came in afternoon, Maurice in the morning.

A parade of doctors, etc., at 6.30 tonight—two surgeons, two physicians, a house doctor, an anaesthetist. Also during the day, blood test, heart test, lungs x-rayed, etc., etc., which was rather painful, since any movement is rather painful.

In the middle of the day the tube got blocked—either by a clot of blood or some impurity or by some technical hitch—and I had to have another rather tiresome clearing of it—which the house doctor did (and very well, I thought).

Wrote up the diary. Read Bible . . .

This unhappy stroke of fate could not have come at a worse moment. Had it been a month earlier, the whole matter of succession might have been settled quietly in accordance with past precedents, without any reference to the Party Conference and all the excitement that was caused at Blackpool. Had it been a month later, the

Party Conference would have been satisfactorily past; I would have announced my intention to continue; and on being struck down my resignation would again have followed in an orderly way. Finally, had there been any certainty as to the succession, such as was the case with Churchill and Eden, even this unfortunate timing might have produced no real trouble. But the combination of these events combined to cause the maximum of confusion and excitement and, alas, corresponding injury to the Party. This was, and has remained, a great source of grief to me. Political death is always uncomfortable; but in my case it could not have been more untimely.

[Macmillan, *At the End of the Day*, 500–3, 505.]

## (3) DOUGLAS-HOME

*On succeeding Macmillan in 1963, Sir Alec Douglas-Home had only one year in which to reverse the Conservative government's fortunes before the 1959–64 Parliament came to an end. He was fortunate to keep the Labour government's majority as low as 5. He realised that, as Leader of the Opposition, he was no match for Harold Wilson as Prime Minister, and resigned the Leadership in 1965.*

## (4) WILSON

*Wilson's misjudgement of the electorate's mood in 1970—by offering them a Baldwinesque 'safety first' campaign—on top of the enforced devaluation in 1967 and repeated economic and financial crises all contributed to his loss of the general election.*

## (5) HEATH

It had been agreed that as Chairman of the Contingencies Unit I should keep in close contact with Ted over Christmas. It was important that we should be seen to be in control of events. The country might be on holiday, but the Government had many problems and there was a national emergency in force. I had reported to him by phone, and he then suggested that I should visit him at Chequers, not so much to get through a lot of work as for appearance's sake.

I travelled down to see Ted at Chequers on December 27. His hospitality was, as always, generous. We did no serious work. He was rightly relaxed, and no doubt contemplating how he would play his hand over the ensuing weeks. It was quite clear that he did not wish to become embroiled with me over questions of a possible election.

Every time I got round to the need to prepare a manifesto the subject was changed. It was almost as if he wished to be incommunicado as far as decisions on election preparations were concerned, although both Peter Carrington and myself were becoming convinced that it was the only answer. We couldn't face yet another humiliating climb-down with the miners, the Party was only just recovering from the 1972 débâcle. We had unwittingly played ourselves into a corner and an appeal to the public on who governed Britain looked the best answer.

After lunch there was not much point in my staying any longer, but I decided not to leave too early as this would create the wrong impression. I was asked whether I would like to see a film, so after lunch I sat in solitary state and watched *The Belstone Fox*. It tells the story of a fox which is kept and mothered as a pet by the huntsman's family, and when put back into the wild draws the hounds across a railway line where many are slaughtered. I sense now, looking back on it, that Joe Gormley was proving himself to be the wily old fox. And we were soon to chase him to our own disaster.

This frame of mind in Government explains how we missed an opportunity which came on January 9 at the regular monthly meeting of the National Economic Development Council attended by Ministers, industrialists and union leaders. Sydney Greene, the NUR leader and then chairman of the TUC's economic committee, put forward the TUC's offer to restrain other pay demands if the miners could be made a special case. But we spurned them.

Len Murray had very recently succeeded Vic Feather as TUC General Secretary, and Willie Whitelaw, who had only just taken over at Employment, had not had time to get to know the union leaders. As a result the Government had no inkling beforehand of the TUC's proposition. The usual practice, before suggesting such a major initiative at a forum like Neddy, would have been to discuss the idea privately first, so that all concerned could take the necessary soundings. It has been said that the idea was kept under wraps for fear that it would leak, but if that was so I am sure it was a mistake and should have been handled differently.

Tony Barber, chairing the Neddy meeting as Chancellor, did

nothing to encourage the TUC to believe that their offer would be taken up. But he didn't rule out the idea altogether and immediately consulted Ted and others. Given our attitude by this stage, it is perhaps not surprising that the offer was rejected. The TUC had talked of 'special cases' many times in the past, but were never able, or willing, to hold the line.

Around this time Frank Chapple, the power workers' leader, came to see me, and in his usual forthright way made it clear that, if the miners were a special case, so were his members. We thus urged Ted to stick to a tough line. With hindsight, however, our rejection of the TUC offer was clearly a missed opportunity. It would have got us off the hook and put the unions on best behaviour—had their self-restraint failed, we would then have been in a much stronger position to take whatever steps might have been necessary.

Late in the afternoon of Thursday, January 17, the day on which we would have had to announce an election for polling on February 7, I went to see Ted at Number Ten: 'If it's any consolation, I'd like you to know that all the Labour Members were coming up to me in the tea room to tell me that we have let them off the hook. They're throwing their hats in the air—they haven't been in that kind of mood for weeks.'

Ted retorted, 'It's all your bloody fault. If you hadn't allowed Central Office to steam this thing up, we would never have got into this position.'

'If you had told us definitely that you were against an election, it wouldn't have been steamed up,' I replied. We had already marched the Party's troops up the hill, ready for combat, and then had to march them down again; it would be much harder to march them up a second time.

Within a week the miners had voted 81 per cent in favour of an all-out strike and in the end Ted felt there was nothing else he could do but go to the country. We had no room for manoeuvre, any opportunities to find a settlement had been lost, the miners were going on an all-out strike and the world economy had been thrown into turmoil by the oil crisis.

I was guest speaker at a Press Gallery lunch at the Commons on Wednesday, February 6. My comment that 'the miners have had their ballot, perhaps we ought to have ours' was the signal that the hawks' view had finally, perhaps belatedly, prevailed. The next day,

Ted called the election for February 28, three weeks later than we hawks had wanted.

At my last business questions I announced the dates of the reassembly of the new Parliament. There then followed a few minutes of party political banter. Andrew Faulds, the Labour MP and an actor, asked me whether I would 'make speedy arrangements to have erected on one of the plinths . . . in the Members' Lobby a rubber statue of the imminently ex-Prime Minister, bearing the words, carved in stone: "The wrecker".' I had been longing to have a go at Faulds for months and replied that I hoped he would have 'a good chance to go back to the job which he occupied before and take part in another film such as *Young Winston*, in which he played the part of a mounted Boer'. As I walked out of the House, Harold Wilson stopped me to say that he wished he had thought of making that remark to Faulds.

[Prior, *Balance of Power*, 91–3.]

## (6) CALLAGHAN

Strangely enough, when the result [of the vote of no confidence] was declared there was no wild outburst of joy from the Opposition benches—only a muted cheer. It was as if they knew they had delivered a blow against pay moderation. I at once rose to face a crowded and expectant House and declared that in view of this narrow defeat on an important issue, I would place the future of the Government in the hands of the House. I would put down a vote of confidence at once which would be debated on the next day. I did this in order to make the Scottish Nationalists face the consequences of their actions, for they knew that if the Government lost the vote of confidence and a general election took place, the result would be to postpone the referendum on Devolution for which they had been eagerly waiting, and might indeed lead to its abandonment. This move had the expected effect: on the following day the Scottish National Party changed sides. We emerged with a majority of ten.

During my speech in the confidence debate, I defended the Government's policy as the best way to hold down inflation and to prevent a rise in unemployment, and once again I repeated my forecast that if the policies of the Conservative Party were adopted they would lead to a multitude of bankruptcies and would put tens of thousands of men and women out of work. Experience was to show that this estimate was a modest one.

The CBI came to see me to thank the Government for dropping the threat of using sanctions against their members, adding that there would not be a pay explosion in the private sector of industry provided the Government was resolute in resisting excessive pay claims from the public sector. This was all very well, but even as they spoke road haulage and oil tanker drivers, with encouragement from the TGWU, were striking in support of 25 to 30 per cent pay increases. Moss Evans washed his hands of any responsibility for the long-term effect of his actions, affirming, 'My responsibility is to look after my members' pay claims', and made the strike official, thus ensuring that it would be a long struggle.

The next downwards step was for the shop stewards to enforce secondary picketing—a pernicious system that brought pressure to bear on workers in industries totally unconnected with the original dispute, calling on them to cease work themselves in solidarity. Some pickets even had the effrontery to issue so-called permits to owners and drivers, with the pretence of authorising what goods could or could not be moved. Mrs Thatcher exploited this attempted usurpation of authority with gusto and the leaders of the TGWU could not have been surprised at the growing dislike they engendered.

There was alarmist talk of a shortage of food, some of which was exaggerated for political advantage and led to panic buying, but John Silkin, the Minister in charge of food supplies, kept a cool head throughout and was justified in his denials of rumours. The contagion spread to other industries and services, and during January 1979 unofficial strikes erupted every week, with workers in one industry inflicting hardship on their fellows in other industries. Public service workers were in the van. Some union officials did nothing to discourage them although we were actively discussing with their leaders means of relieving their members' grievances through the medium of those same comparability studies which the Government had suggested earlier and which the TUC had then rejected. Even with the passage of time I find it painful to write about some of the excesses that took place. One of the most notorious was the refusal of Liverpool grave-diggers to bury the dead, accounts of which appalled the country when they saw pictures of mourners being turned away from the cemetery. Such heartlessness and cold-blooded indifference to the feelings of families at moments of intense grief rightly aroused deep revulsion and did further untold harm to the cause of trade unionism that I, like many others, had been proud to defend throughout my life. What would the men of Tolpuddle have said? My own anger increased when I learned that the Home Secretary Merlyn Rees had called upon Alan Fisher, the General Secretary of NUPE, to use his influence to get the grave-diggers to go back to work, and Fisher had refused.

Merlyn was Chairman of the Cabinet's Contingencies Unit and was a tower of strength and commonsense, but as the pressure grew during January and February he needed assistance and I detached Gerald Kaufman, one of Labour's rising stars, from his work at the Department of Industry, to be full-time in the Cabinet Office. Together with Bill Rodgers, the Secretary for Transport, he worked with considerable success to ensure that essential supplies continued to move.

Indeed, the only redeeming features that I could discern throughout the whole affair were the remarkable ingenuity with which those affected set about improvising arrangements to beat its adverse effects, and the stoicism with which the general public met the hardship and inconvenience to which they were subjected. Ministers considered whether we should declare a state of emergency. My instinct was in favour of doing so as a demonstration of our determination, but it was argued that it was very uncertain whether a declaration would do much practical good. The Conservative Government of 1970–4 had declared five such states of emergency, and it was pointed out that none of them had made any significant difference.

After a time signs began to appear that the fever was running its course. The TGWU grew apprehensive at the backlash of public opinion against the excesses of some of their shop stewards, and told the Home Secretary that if the Government would inform them where essential foodstuffs or other materials were held up, they would try to unblock the channels.

During the dispute the TUC had stood by helplessly watching, the influence of the General Council washed away by the tide of industrial irresponsibility, but Ministers had kept in touch with their officials and by the end of January they judged that the time had come to pick up the threads once again . . .

The margin of defeat could not have been smaller—311 votes to 310—but one was enough and a general election was inevitable. I left the Chamber with my Parliamentary Private Secretary, Roger Stott, who had been my constant companion, advisor and eyes and ears during the previous three years. He seemed more depressed than I as we sat talking in my room until nearly midnight, quietly reviewing the prospects. I had seen many setbacks in earlier years but it was hard for him as a younger man to see our hopes dashed. However, he has great resilience and later became a most effective front bench Spokesman for the Party. For my part, I slept well that night, for the uncertainty was over and the die was cast.

Even if the vote had gone in our favour I did not expect the election to be long delayed. Since Christmas the Government had suffered severe set-backs on incomes policy and on Devolution, and we could command a majority in the House of Commons for neither. On the morning after our defeat, I called the Cabinet together to fix the date of the general election, which was complicated by the forthcoming Local Authority elections and by the first election of Members of the European Parliament. Our meeting concluded, I went immediately to Buckingham Palace to acquaint the Queen formally of the position and seek a dissolution of Parliament to be followed by a general election on 3 May.

The Government's defeat had been the first time since 1924 that a Government had lost a confidence vote. That occasion had seen the ending of a short-lived minority Labour Government and its replacement by a big Conservative majority.

Contrary to the myths which have sprung up since 1979, Labour did not lose support in the general election—our national vote was in fact slightly higher than it had been nearly five years earlier in October 1974, when we had won more seats than the Tories. It demonstrated how much steady understanding and support existed for what we had tried to do. But, tempted by promises of lower taxation and with memories of the winter, the abstaining Tories of 1974 had flocked back to their Party's colours and this gave Mrs Thatcher a large majority of seats.

It was a miracle that we had governed as long and effectively as we had and carried out as much of our programme. The Labour Government of 1974 to 1979 had no reason to feel ashamed, and much to be proud of.

[Callaghan, *Time and Chance*, 536–8, 563–4.]

## 3. RIVALS IN THE CABINET

The Cabinet is not a body of twenty or so politicians unquestioningly committed to the Prime Minister's success. At any time there will be up to five overlapping elements in the Cabinet which can weaken a Prime Minister's authority.

There will be, first, the potential successors who must demonstrate their own departmental successes and (within the limits of collective responsibility) distance themselves from the Prime Minister in anything which smacks of political failure. Sometimes the number of potential successors will be greater than at other times, so that, for example, in the last Wilson Cabinet from 1974 to 1976 there were several, whereas in his first 1964 Cabinet there had been initially none (if previous ministerial experience and position in the party were taken as the main criteria). Secondly, there will be those who will never themselves be contestants for the premiership but who will none the less put the success of the party above the unquestioned continuance of any particular Prime Minister. Such a grouping is easier to discern in the Conservative Party—the grandees, or the 'magic circle'. Thirdly, some senior members of any Cabinet will owe their membership of it not to the Prime Minister's patronage but to their position in the party or to their indispensability to the Prime Minister. Thus the Deputy Leader of the Party in a Labour Cabinet, defeated rivals in a Party Leadership contest, and senior figures in a Cabinet of any colour could not realistically be excluded, and none of them necessarily owes any personal loyalty to the Prime Minister. Fourthly, some members of a Cabinet will have a different political philosophy or will represent a different strand of party opinion from the Prime Minister. They may believe that the Prime Minister's time will eventually run out and that their time will come—not necessarily through a particular individual succeeding to the premiership but perhaps by means of their political position once more becoming mainstream government philosophy. It is for instance clear that Mrs Thatcher's 1979 Cabinet was a coalition in economic policy terms, of monetarists and the so-called 'wets'. The latter might have hoped that their outlook would carry the Cabinet, but in that particular case the monetarists were triumphant by the time of the 1981 reshuffle. Lastly, there will be those—probably a majority of every Cabinet—who want to survive politically, so that as long as things go well they will support the Prime Minister to the limit; but if things go wrong, if the Prime Minister starts to lose his grip, or if the opinion polls swing away from the government and stay away, they will become the more ready to question and on occasion challenge the Prime Minister. Those five groups will thus usually give a Prime Minister conditional support at best. They will be prepared when it is in their interests to do so to act to overrule the Prime Minister on particular issues or to force a change of style of government. The Cabinet in that case will assert itself: Cabinet government, at least for a time, may again rival government by Prime Minister.

[Brazier, *Constitutional Practice*, 89–90.]

## 4. ULTIMATE DEPENDENCE ON THE PARLIAMENTARY PARTY

*Even peacetime Prime Ministers enjoying a parliamentary majority have, in effect, realised that they must resign because the continued support of the parliamentary party could no longer be guaranteed: Churchill's resignation in 1955 is an example. Even had Eden been fit, it is unlikely that Conservative MPs would have allowed him to continue as Prime Minister after Suez. Lloyd George was forced out in 1922 after the Conservative Party had voted at the Carlton Club to withdraw from the coalition. In wartime, Asquith in 1916 and Chamberlain in 1940 resigned when it became clear that their parliamentary bases had gone.*

# [4]
# THE CABINET

## The Cabinet Office

*The following descriptions of the organization and work of the Cabinet Office under the 1974–9 Labour government are probably still largely accurate today.*

The Cabinet Office is directly adjacent to No. 10, although its main entrance is in Whitehall. There is a door between the two buildings which is kept locked—only the Cabinet Secretary on the one side and the No. 10 Private Office on the other have keys. The Cabinet Office's basic task is to co-ordinate and ensure the smooth running of Whitehall's official policy-making and administrative machinery. It also currently has the main responsibility for administering the civil service since Mrs Thatcher abolished the elephantine Civil Service department, dividing the responsibility between the Cabinet Office and (for pay and rations) the Treasury. Whether the Cabinet Secretary as the Prime Minister's most senior personal adviser should also run the civil service is seriously questionable—although it must be admitted that in my time the Civil Service Department was an equally imperfect solution.

The Cabinet Office existed originally simply to service the mechanics of government policy-making, including providing the secretariat for Cabinet and Cabinet meetings, issuing agendas and producing minutes. The Cabinet Secretary is the only person who institutionalises and reconciles the legitimate departmental conflicts of interest and differences of policy view which inevitably exist in Whitehall. This vital function of organising the machinery of central government is still conducted. Early in each week the Cabinet Office Secretariat issue the Cabinet Secretary with their proposals for Cabinet and Cabinet Committee business over the following fortnight. (This is supplemented periodically by what is called a 'Forward Look' which carries the same exercise forward for a period of up to six months.) Later in the week—usually on Thursday mornings during Cabinet—the Private Secretary to the Cabinet

Secretary goes to No. 10 and establishes a programme in discussion with the two Private Secretaries who work on the Prime Minister's personal and parliamentary diaries. This constitutes the provisional programme of Cabinet business and Cabinet Committees to be chaired over the next two or three weeks. This draft programme is then discussed at a meeting which I and the Principal Private Secretary from Downing Street normally attended in the Cabinet Office under the Cabinet Secretary's chairmanship with his Deputy Secretaries late on Thursday or early on Friday. In the light of that discussion the Cabinet Secretary produces a forward programme of Cabinet, Cabinet Committee and official committee business which is sent to the Prime Minister, who in turn normally discusses it with his advisers and his Chief Whip on Friday morning. The Prime Minister's comments and conclusions are embodied in the specific arrangements which are then made for government business in the following week.

Apart from this purely administrative role, however, the Cabinet Office has over the years, perhaps inevitably, acquired an independent policy-making function. This tendency was accelerated during the Second World War when a section of economic advisers was located in the Cabinet Office; and again in the 1970s when Mr Heath established the Central Policy Review Staff (regrettably abolished by Mrs Thatcher in 1983) to carry out independent policy analysis for the Cabinet.

At the head of the Cabinet Office is the Cabinet Secretary who is usually the single most powerful official in Whitehall or indeed in the country. Although technically, and still often in practice, servicing the Cabinet, the Cabinet Secretary naturally works closely with the Prime Minister and, as such, and being a senior Permanent Secretary, he was, and still is, the most senior official working directly to the Prime Minister, as nobody in No. 10 in my time was above the level of Deputy Secretary. Under both Mr Wilson and Mr Callaghan the Cabinet Secretary was Sir John, now Lord, Hunt, who was impressively efficient and very effective at ensuring that the Whitehall machine delivered what the Prime Minister wanted.

There are certain ambiguities in the Cabinet Secretary's responsibilities which emerged clearly during the Labour Governments of the 1970s. First was the uncertainty already referred to, as to whether the Cabinet Office should be concerned simply with administration—with making the wheels of Whitehall turn smoothly

—or whether it had an independent policy role. In practice, led by an ambitious Cabinet Secretary, backed by a swelling staff of over 500, and particularly aided by the CPRS, the Cabinet Office clearly exercised policy influence. This influence may be seen daily in the briefing papers which the Cabinet Secretary submits to the Chairmen of Cabinet Committees, and especially to the Prime Minister as Chairman of Cabinet. These briefs contain skilful advice on how to conduct the meeting, bearing in mind the interests and preferences of ministerial members. However, they have also increasingly contained arguments steering the Prime Minister towards one policy conclusion rather than another (usually prefaced by appropriate courtesies such as 'you may wish to . . .'). This is why the Policy Unit often found it necessary to submit its own briefing relating to the Cabinet Secretary's briefs. The increase in the policy influence of the Cabinet Office caused displeasure to some departmental Ministers who often complained to me about the intrusion of this extra policy arm. There were even occasional tensions between the Cabinet Office and the Policy Unit.

A similar ambiguity arose concerning whether the Cabinet Secretary's prime responsibility lay to the Cabinet as a collective whole or personally to the Prime Minister, on whose right hand he always sits in Cabinet. It can be argued that there should be no problem here since the Prime Minister is both Chairman and part of the Cabinet. However, political life is not as simple as that. At times the Prime Minister has personal interests which do not necessarily coincide with those of all his Cabinet colleagues. The Prime Minister might wish to restrain the policy activities of certain Cabinet colleagues, in which case he would want to influence the pace and way in which these were handled by the Whitehall machine. He might even wish to keep these issues from coming to Cabinet and also to influence which departments were or were not represented on the Cabinet Committees which discussed them. He would then use the Cabinet Secretary to achieve this—as Tony Benn periodically complained of during 1974–9. The Cabinet Secretary is, of course, supposed to serve the whole Cabinet but, in practice, where there is a conflict between the Prime Minister's interests and a Cabinet Minister's interests, he is always tempted to give priority to his final master and centre of power, the Prime Minister, who in any case might be said to be the ultimate definer of what is in the Cabinet's true interest.

This leads naturally into the third ambiguity, concerning the

Cabinet Secretary, which is whether he, or the Principal Private Secretary who runs the Downing Street Private Office, is actually the Prime Minister's primary official adviser. Certainly the Cabinet Secretary, Sir John Hunt, had ambitions and claims to be Mr Wilson's and Mr Callaghan's chief adviser. He was a senior Permanent Secretary, the only senior Permanent Secretary within the Prime Minister's central capability. He ranked above everybody in No. 10 and he commanded the Whitehall machine. However, although he had the status, he was not based at No. 10 and he did not therefore have automatic access to the Prime Minister. The Cabinet Secretary by convention had to telephone the Principal Private Secretary in order to receive clearance to come through the locked door to No. 10. On the other hand, the Principal Private Secretary—who in 1974–9 was first Robert Armstrong and then Kenneth Stowe—was always either an Under-Secretary or a Deputy Secretary. He therefore had the access but not the seniority. Watching the relations between the distinguished Cabinet Secretary and the rising Principal Private Secretary was absolutely fascinating. It was a game about territory. Some of the boundaries were clearly defined, not least by the locked green baize door between the two offices. But there was a grey area of common land which each sought to occupy. This led to subtleties of behaviour and finesse of language which aroused my amused admiration: the total courtesies of address; the softly veiled hints of status from the Cabinet Secretary when telephoning to say 'I am coming through to see the Prime Minister about a highly important and secret issue, but of course I am phoning to let you know'; the politely deferential tone of the Principal Private Secretary to his senior, while even so sometimes stating, 'This is not a convenient time but I will give you a ring when he is ready to see you.' Only the authors of the television series 'Yes, Prime Minister' could fully convey the delightful nuances of some of these exchanges. On the important issues, of course, these officials usually worked together in impressive tandem, serving both of my Prime Ministers to their great satisfaction. However, the status relationships and ambiguities at the margin led to perennial tension, which Mr Wilson always relished and seemed occasionally to provoke.

[Bernard Donoughue, *Prime Minister: The Conduct of Policy under Harold Wilson and James Callaghan* (London, 1987), 26–30.]

The conventional role of the Cabinet Office is to serve all members of the Cabinet, but if the Prime Minister chooses, as nearly all of them do, to work closely with the Secretary to the Cabinet, then it becomes an instrument to serve him above the others. Its work has been often described and I will not repeat it here, except to emphasise the importance of its central role in coordinating the work of the Cabinet, which in turn puts it in a powerful position to exert influence over the rest of the Civil Service. The Cabinet Secretary prepares the agenda for Cabinet meetings, so he is in a position to influence what shall be discussed and when, although the final decision rests with the Prime Minister. All papers prepared by Ministers for the Cabinet's consideration are first sent to the Cabinet Office for circulation, which in turn gives the Prime Minister the chance to defer it by asking a Minister to think again or alternatively to accelerate its discussion. At inter-Departmental meetings of Civil Servants it is the Cabinet Secretary or one of his assistants who will frequently take the Chair, with all the opportunities for influence over the discussion that such a position bestows. And if, as in Mrs Thatcher's Administration, the Cabinet Secretary is also the Head of the Civil Service, the holder of the dual office is in a unique position to shape appointments as well as influence policy and so enables the Prime Minister to control the Government's actions with considerable economy of effort. It is not, however, an arrangement I recommend.

[James Callaghan, *Time and Chance* (London, 1987), 407.]

## Matters not for the Cabinet

### 1. THE PREROGATIVE OF MERCY

*The prerogative of mercy is exercised by the Sovereign on the Home Secretary's advice. Only in exceptional circumstances has the Cabinet been involved in formulating that advice.*

Before Ireland could be entirely tucked back under the carpet, there remained one further matter for the Cabinet to settle. This was the question of Casement's execution. After his arrest on the coast of Kerry, Casement had been brought to London for trial. On

June 29th [1916], with F. E. Smith prosecuting, he was convicted of high treason and sentenced to death. The case was taken to the Court of Criminal Appeal on July 17th and 18th, but his appeal was there rejected by a panel of five judges. Smith declined to give his fiat for a further appeal to the House of Lords. All that remained, therefore, was for the Home Secretary to decide whether or not he should exercise the prerogative of mercy. Exceptionally, he did not attempt to decide this for himself. Casement's execution was a Cabinet matter even before the Court of Appeal had given its decision. At the end of the meeting of July 5th it was decided to submit his now famous homosexual diaries to an 'alienist,' as the word then was. 'Several members of the Cabinet (including Sir E. Grey and Lord Lansdowne),' Asquith wrote, 'were strongly of opinion that it would be better (if possible) that he should be kept in confinement as a criminal lunatic than that he should be executed without any smirch on his character and then canonized as a martyr both in Ireland and America.'

On July 12th the Cabinet received the alienist's report and noted that it declared him 'to be abnormal but not certifiably insane.' On July 19th, the day after the Court of Appeal decision, Asquith told the King that 'it was the unanimous decision of the Cabinet that (Casement) should be hanged.' On July 27th it was decided that the Foreign and Home Offices should co-operate in drawing up a statement of the Government's reasons for proceeding with the execution. Since the previous meeting Asquith had received strong representations for a reprieve from Bryce (who had been both Chief Secretary and Ambassador to Washington), Dillon and Devlin. On August 2nd:

> The greater part of the sitting was occupied in a further and final discussion of the Casement case, in view of some further material and the urgent appeals for mercy from authoritative and friendly quarters of the US. The Cabinet was of the opinion that no ground existed for a reprieve, and Lord Grey drew up a statement of reasons to be shown by Sir C. Spring-Rice to Senator Lodge and others.

On August 3rd Casement was hanged. There can be few other examples of a Cabinet devoting large parts of four separate meetings to considering an individual sentence—and then arriving at the wrong decision. The effect in the United States was as bad as it could have been. In Ireland, Casement became a martyr. And even in

England the effects of the case reverberated on for forty years or more. Asquith himself would have preferred a reprieve based on medical evidence, but in the absence of this he did not feel it right to treat Casement more leniently than his supposed followers had been treated by Maxwell.

[Roy Jenkins, *Asquith* (London, Fontana edn., 1967), 452–4.]

Similarly before the abolition of capital punishment, the Home Secretary was solely responsible for deciding whether to grant a reprieve, and the Colonial Secretary had the same right in cases arising in the colonies. But when, for example, the death sentence was passed on young Cypriots for offences during the struggles for independence in the late 1950s, the Cabinet might well have broken through the convention to consider the effect of executions on world opinion or on negotiations about the future of the island.

[John Mackintosh, *The British Cabinet* (London, 3rd edn., 1977), 414.]

## 2. THE DECISION TO PROSECUTE

*The Attorney-General's consent is required by law before certain prosecutions may be started; he may enter a* nolle prosequi *to stop any prosecution. He is expected to exercise an independent judgement in these matters, and should not be directed by the Cabinet or any ministerial colleague.*

This is what Lord Birkenhead said, talking of the duties of the Attorney-General in relation to a particular case, and a case only brought to his attention by the Public Prosecutor:

When I was the Attorney-General, the then War Cabinet, of which I was not a member, directed me to prosecute a certain person for sedition, and entered this direction upon the minutes of the Cabinet. The Director of Public Prosecutions brought this minute to me and asked for my directions. I told him that I would not even consider the question of instituting a prosecution upon its merits until the unconstitutional minute had been excised. Nor did I do so.

[The Attorney-General, Sir Patrick Hastings, 177 H.C. Deb. 614 (8 October 1924).]

It seems to have been denied that in a case where the public interest may conflict with the strict exercise of his duty, the Attorney-General is not only entitled to, but, if he does his duty must, go to the Executive Government to know what the public interest is. For instance, does a lawyer anywhere or any lawyer in the House say that an Attorney-General would be acting wrongly if he said this: 'This is a case of sedition, in which I think there ought to be a prosecution, but I desire the opinion of the Government whether one should be taken or not'? Does any ex-Law Officer say that that would be wrong? . . . I am going to read to the House one letter which was written on 31st January, 1919, to the Director of Public Prosecutions . . .

My dear Director,

There can be no doubt, I think, that this speech is seditious and that a prosecution may properly follow, but it appears to me that the real question is one of policy, and therefore is a question in the first instance for the Home Secretary and the Minister of Labour.

Yours sincerely,
Gordon Hewart

I think every Law Officer would agree that Sir Gordon Hewart was right [to proceed in that way].

[The Attorney-General, Sir Patrick Hastings, 177 H.C. Deb. 598–9 (8 October 1924).]

Meanwhile, a more dangerous storm had begun to gather in a different quarter. Its origins lay in a series of blunders and equivocations two months earlier. On July 25th [1924], an article had appeared in the *Workers' Weekly*, the official organ of the Communist Party, calling on soldiers in the British Army 'to let it be known that neither in the class war nor in a military war, will you turn your guns on your fellow workers'. On July 30th, the director of public prosecutions brought the article to the notice of the attorney general, Sir Patrick Hastings. Hastings was a brilliant advocate, but a novice in Labour politics; he appears to have given no thought to the effect which a prosecution might have on the Labour movement. He decided that the article was an incitement to mutiny, and he instructed the director of public prosecutions to bring such proceedings under the Incitement to Mutiny Act as he thought fit. The following Saturday, a warrant was granted for the arrest of the editor, John Campbell. The news was reported in the press; and on August 6th, Hastings had to answer questions about it in the House of Commons. There were angry protests from the Labour benches. Maxton asked whether the prime minister had read the article and whether he was aware that the point of view expressed in it was shared by a large number of Labour members; Buchanan pointed out that the article expressed 'the views and findings of Labour party conferences'; Scurr and Lansbury threatened to raise the matter in the debate on the Appropriation Bill. After questions, Hastings saw Maxton and some of his colleagues in his room at the House. They told him that Campbell was only the acting editor, and that he had an excellent war record; it can be assumed that they also told him that if he persisted with the prosecution, he would incur bitter hostility from the left wing of his own party.

What happened next is less clear. MacDonald had not been consulted formally about the case, and had learned about it by accident from Ammon, the parliamentary secretary to the Admiralty. Ammon told him that the War Office and the Air Ministry had both agreed to the prosecution, and that the Admiralty had been asked for its views. Ammon himself was opposed to the prosecution, and had written a minute to that effect; MacDonald told him to add that the prime minister must be informed before any action was taken. According to a letter which he wrote to Lord Stamfordham on August 22nd, however, MacDonald heard nothing more until the news of Campbell's arrest appeared in the press. When he saw it, he was 'furious', and, as he put it to Lord Stamfordham.

> I sent for the Attorney-General and the Public Prosecutor and gave them a bit of my mind . . . They replied that the whole matter could be dropped. I told them that, as they had begun, they had to go through with it. Later on I was informed that the editor was prepared to write a letter which would amount to an apology for what he had done. I agreed that, if he did that, the matter might be dropped.

Hastings's account is slightly different. According to him, it was his conversation with Maxton which made him think that a prosecution might, after all, be ill-advised. He had made his reputation as a defence counsel, and he asked himself how he would conduct the defence if some other attorney general singled out for prosecution as a dangerous Communist a man 'who had had both his feet almost blown off in the war, who had fought through the war from beginning to end, and who had been decorated for exceptional gallantry'. After talking to Maxton, he therefore sent for the director of public prosecutions. The director was away, but the assistant director, Sir Guy Stephenson, came instead; and it was from him that Hastings learned that Maxton's story was true. The conversation between Hastings and Stephenson took place in MacDonald's room at the House of Commons, but at first MacDonald was not present. When he came in, he made it clear, according to Hastings, that he thought the prosecution 'ill-advised from the beginning'.

At six o'clock that evening, the question came before the Cabinet. Hankey was away, and his deputy, Tom Jones, acted as secretary instead. Jones's notes of the remarkably muddled and incoherent discussion which followed were filed with the Cabinet minutes and have since been published; although they are not as clear as they might be, they make it possible to reconstruct at least the broad outlines of what must have taken place. The proceedings began with an unseemly bout of mutual recrimination, summarized in Jones's notes as follows:

> PRIME MINISTER: First I heard in House of Commons, Ammon said he'd had a minute from Admiralty. War Office agreed. Air agreed and Admiralty asked for views. He minuted against it. But I said 'It will not be begun until I know'. You add 'PM must be informed before action taken'. In papers I read it—done.
>
> SNOWDEN: Had been done then.
>
> PM: I sent for Assistant Director Public Prosecution. I asked him to take files on which he acted. Hastings said he did not authorise action. He was asked and said article criminal. Gave legal view. Assistant Director saw me—he produced Minute: S. of S. agrees to go on with prosecution.
>
> HENDERSON: No. We agreed to transfer letters we'd received to the Director of Public Prosecutions . . . Nothing about prosecution. I asked A-G if he'd authorised proceedings. He agreed with you. He is under A-G not under me.
>
> PM: I misread Minute also.
>
> HENDERSON: My Secretary has known for a week that I was opposed to prosecution.

After more crying over spilt milk, Hastings came in. He accepted full responsibility for what had happened, and made it clear that he still thought that proceedings should be taken. He also told the

Cabinet, however, that Campbell had only taken on the editorship temporarily, while the editor was on holiday, and that this would provide a 'possible way out' if the Cabinet wished to drop the case. Jones's notes continue:

PRIME MINISTER: Settled that no one else will be arrested—I'd rather go through once started than show white feather. If you stop prosecution you will be asked all round what going to do. Editor is known—why not arrest him.

WALSH: Worst article I've ever read. One paragraph atrocious. I thought it would come before Cabinet. It would be peculiarly weak action if we abandoned prosecution having regard to all the circumstances . . .

PRIME MINISTER: If put to me I should not have sanctioned it. I know the men and the game. Now in press and House of Commons. Answer given.

J. H. THOMAS: Don't withdraw now in view of House of Commons . . .

ATTORNEY-GENERAL: No debate tonight or tomorrow. Man arrested prepared to write letter to say he was only few days.

J .H. THOMAS: Real fight will start two months hence.

ATTORNEY-GENERAL: I'll accept his letter—reply being we had to take cognisance reluctantly.

HENDERSON: More questions tomorrow.

ATTORNEY-GENERAL: Steps have been taken. Nothing to add.

(Attorney-General authorised).

These unhappy proceedings were then summarized by Jones in an official minute. Like most Cabinet minutes in this period, it was fairly brief, and did not name the participants in the discussion or give a full account of the arguments which had been put forward. The attorney-general, said the minute, told the Cabinet that 'inasmuch as it transpired that the person charged was only acting temporarily as editor and was prepared to write a letter to that effect steps could be taken not to press the prosecution in the circumstances against this particular offender, if the Cabinet so desired.' The Cabinet, it concluded, agreed:

(*a*) That no public prosecution of a political character should be undertaken without the prior sanction of the Cabinet being obtained;

(*b*) That in the particular case under review the course indicated by the Attorney-General should be adopted . . .

. . . There could be no doubt that Hastings was entitled to consult the Cabinet, and, having done so, to decide that the prosecution should be withdrawn. But, although Hastings was entitled to withdraw the prosecution, the Cabinet was not entitled to instruct him to do so. In fact, as Jones's notes make clear, the Cabinet did not instruct him. The suggestion that the prosecution should be withdrawn came from Hastings, not from the Cabinet; and the meeting ended with Hastings informing the Cabinet of the steps he intended to take. But, although this is clear from Jones's notes, it is not at all clear from the minute which he wrote the following day. On the contrary, the minute, by lumping the conclusion on the Campbell case together with the conclusion on the general issue of prosecutions of a political character, suggests, if anything, that the Cabinet had taken the decision on both and had illegitimately given the attorney general instructions on a matter over which it had no proper jurisdiction . . .

On August 13th, the prosecution was duly withdrawn . . .

[David Marquand, *Ramsay MacDonald* (London, 1977), 365–9.]

I would like to make a statement on my decision to prosecute Mr Ponting [under section 2 of the Official Secrets Act 1911). On 13 August 1984 certain facts were drawn to the attention of the Director of Public Prosecutions by the Ministry of Defence. In my absence, the Director consulted my hon. and learned Friend the Solicitor-General the same day. On 16 August 1984 a report by the Ministry of Defence police was sent to the Director. [The Solicitor-General] and the Director considered that report on 17 August, and both formed the view that this was a serious breach of duty and trust by a senior civil servant. They decided to consult me and I was telephoned the same day. The facts as represented to the Director were explained to me. The nature of the documents which had been communicated was described and I was told that the Director and the Solicitor-General advised a prosecution. Having considered the facts myself I, too, decided that the case fell within my published guidelines and that there should be a prosecution. Neither I nor the Solicitor-General nor any of my officials sought the view of or consulted any other Minister, nor was the view of any other Minister conveyed to us before the decision was taken.

[The Attorney-General, Sir Michael Havers, 73 H.C. Deb. 180 (12 February 1985).]

. . . Questions of prosecutions are never discussed collectively between Ministers . . . [The Attorney-General] does not consult his colleagues—indeed, he debars himself from consulting his colleagues on any matter relating to a prosecution.

*None of those assertions is correct.*

[The Home Secretary, Mr Douglas Hurd, 109 H.C. Deb. 823 (3 February 1987).]

## 3. THE BUDGET

*The Cabinet is informed of the contents of the Chancellor of the Exchequer's Budget as a* fait accompli *only a few hours before he is to deliver it to the House of Commons. This is justified by the claim that only such a procedure ensures that secrecy be maintained; it places economic and financial matters which are to be dealt with in the Budget firmly in the hands of the Chancellor and the Prime Minister. Cabinets have protested about this procedure from time to time; occasionally the Budget Cabinet has forced (usually minor) changes on the Chancellor.*

This tendency affects not only specific Ministerial responsibilities, but collective Cabinet responsibility as well. The 1981 Budget was rigidly deflationary and thus highly controversial at a time of deep recession, yet the strategy behind it was never discussed in Cabinet and was only revealed to the full Cabinet on Budget Day itself. One can guess the reason: the Chancellor and the Prime Minister concluded that the Cabinet might well insist on some changes. But that is why the Cabinet exists—to make collective decisions on important issues that face individual Departments, and thus affect the Government as a whole. Collective responsibility is based on collective decision-making. Margaret Thatcher is not the first Prime Minister to circumvent her colleagues, nor will she be the last, but this habit is not the sign of a happy or healthy Government.

[Francis Pym, *The Politics of Consent* (London, 1984), 18.]

As the recession deepened and unemployment soared the argument between 'wets' and 'dries' was whether further cuts in public expenditure had become self-defeating. This argument led to the deep divisions over the March 1981 budget. The Treasury had failed in the autumn of 1980 to secure the large cuts in public spending that it had sought.

Amongst the proposed savings was a plan to remove that year's indexation of state pensions—in other words, the basic old age pension would not even have been increased in line with prices. But I went to Cabinet armed—as was Patrick Jenkin, the Social Services Secretary—with copies of Geoffrey Howe's and Keith Joseph's own personal election addresses in their constituencies at the 1979 election, in which they had specifically pledged to protect pensioners against inflation. So that idea was soon thrown out—Margaret was too good a politician to allow that to happen.

[James Prior, *A Balance of Power* (London, 1986), 130.]

He had no inkling of the furore that was to erupt at the pre-Budget Cabinet on Saturday 7 April [1962]. The main point at issue was the abolition of Schedule A (the Party Conference at Scarborough in October 1960 had passed a motion calling for the ending of this tax on privately owned houses so resented by the owner-occupier), but there was also concern about the political presentation. Selwyn wrote in his diary:

At the Cabinet on Sat 7 April, strong criticisms were made of my proposals. Hailsham said the Budget was unsaleable. Eccles said that the 'economic balance' was right but the methods were wrong, and others joined in. Not one of those whom I had consulted supported it. Rab, Maudling, Erroll, Macleod, Hill who knew what was in it, kept quiet—a lot of talk about Schedule A—I promised to reconsider.

I had lunch at the US Embassy and on my way back looked in at No. 10. I saw Harold and Rab. They were disposed to leave it to me. Rab said Harold thinks that you are very upset about this morning. I told him you are not!! I told Rab that he was absolutely right . . . Next morning, after thinking it over, I came to the conclusion that I would not hold to Schedule A against the party's wishes. If therefore I was in any case going to lose, say at the end of July, it was much better to make a virtue of necessity and yield now. I did realise that the legal complications were considerable and we might satisfy only a proportion of householders but I felt that it could be done and therefore I should not oppose the collective wisdom of my colleagues.

Selwyn then went to the Treasury after seeing Macmillan. He was in a considerable state of depression. The pre-emptive strike of the *fait accompli* that Chancellors are traditionally supposed to enjoy had been denied him and he was in no doubt that his standing had been damaged. 'We've got to do something else', he told his secretary Tom Caulcott. It was an unprecedented defeat for a Chancellor on the eve of a Budget and the pre-printed Budget Red Book (available in the vote office after the Chancellor has sat down) proved on the Monday to be only a partial summary of the proposals. Selwyn decided that he should announce his intention to abolish Schedule A (at a cost to the Exchequer of £60m in a full year), a change introduced by his successor, Reginald Maudling, in 1963. From the Treasury Selwyn travelled to Windsor for an audience of the Queen at 6.30 p.m., but because of the changes that needed to be incorporated into his speech returned to Chequers for dinner. He was acutely aware of how much the party expected him to lift their electoral fortunes; but he was even more aware of how important it was to get the economy on a sound footing.

[D. R. Thorpe, *Selwyn Lloyd* (London, 1989), 333–4.]

The Public Records Office history of the Cabinet Office sets out the practice, and the traditional form of minuting:

> The Chancellor of the Exchequer communicated to the Cabinet particulars of the proposals in the forthcoming Budget.
>
> In accordance with precedent, details are not recorded in the Cabinet conclusions.

This formula is still used today. The Cabinet Office history on the basis of the pre-1945 practice regards it as axiomatic that 'there was insufficient time to make changes in his plans.' In fact, Hugh Gaitskell was forced by Cabinet objection to drop a proposal for a differential fuel tax.

[Harold Wilson, *The Governance of Britain* (London, 1976), 59.]

Geoffrey Howe's deflationary Budget in the spring of 1981 polarised the divisions in the Cabinet. It was the one occasion on which two of the other leading wets and I deliberately made issue together.

Geoffrey asked me to see him late in the afternoon of the Monday, the day before the Budget. When he told me the main outline of the Budget I told him that I thought it was awful and absolutely misjudged: it was far too restrictive, the PSBR was being cut by far too much, and it would add to unemployment. I couldn't say anything bad enough about it.

Geoffrey was cross and said that he was surprised that I had taken this line because he had seen Willie Whitelaw, Peter Carrington and Francis Pym, who had all seemed to think it was quite all right.

I went home and said to Jane: 'Either my judgment has gone totally haywire, or I'm right about this Budget and all the others are wrong.' Next morning we had the pre-Budget meeting, and there was no doubt that Geoffrey received overwhelming support. Ian Gilmour, Peter Walker and myself were critical. Peter Carrington, Francis Pym and even Willie Whitelaw were not very pleased, but they took the line that we had to support the Chancellor and, if he said we had to have tough measures to stick to our policy, that was that.

Peter, Ian and I met for breakfast the next morning and tried to decide what action we could take. The Budget had been announced in the House, so in effect we were already beaten.

I felt so desperately about it that I was willing to chuck in my hand. Although it is enormously difficult to leave a government, with accusations of rocking the boat and letting your colleagues down, I would have been prepared to face all that. But there are other ties of loyalty—a lot of people in my own constituency had supported me loyally over issues which they didn't really think too much of, and they would see their MP, almost at the first whiff of gunfire in Government, quitting to make critical speeches from the back benches. It is not a role I would choose for myself.

I came very close to resigning, and a year or so later regretted very much that I hadn't, but at the time I felt that the resignations of the three of us would not have made much mark. Peter was beginning to recuperate after having been on the back benches for four years, from 1975 to 1979, and was not at that time a very powerful figure. It was also known that Ian Gilmour had been protected by Peter Carrington in the January 1981 reshuffle. Therefore our quitting wouldn't have made much difference. A lot of people also said that I would be sacrificing myself unnecessarily.

Once you think of resignation you have to decide whether you will have more influence from outside than inside the Government. Most experience shows that you have more influence within, although I am now less certain. This was one of the major factors in my thinking, not because I had any major qualms about leaving my

Department, as by then my industrial relations reforms, about which I write in the next chapter were on the Statute Book and consultations were under way on the Green Paper on Trade Union Immunities. My concern was to stay in a position to try to influence economic policy.

There were, however, perhaps two beneficial consequences of my row over the 1981 Budget. With support from Ian, Peter and the others who had not been too happy about the Chancellor's severity, we did establish for the first time that Cabinet had to have the opportunity for a full discussion on economic policy in January or early February each year, before the Chancellor goes into purdah to reach his Budget judgment. There would be a further Cabinet economic session in the summer before the start of Whitehall's annual review of public spending. This was at least a concession by Margaret, although its practical value was limited.

[Prior, *Balance of Power*, 140–1.]

## 4. THE DISSOLUTION OF PARLIAMENT

*This was examined in the previous chapter: see above, pp. 205–16.*

## Cabinet Committees and Ministerial Meetings

## 1. CABINET COMMITTEES: DEVELOPMENT

So far the discussion has been in terms of the Cabinet itself. No modern Cabinet could function for a month without the extensive infrastructure of Cabinet committees. Most ministers, including the prime minister, spend more time in such committees each week than in Cabinet.

Cabinet committees are not new. There was a Crimean Committee in the Aberdeen Government in 1855, and a Cabinet committee to draft the abortive Reform Bill of 1854. Lloyd George made great use of them in World War I. There was later a corresponding cutting back of the Cabinet committee system. (Sir Warren Fisher, permanent secretary to the Treasury, strenuously tried to merge the Cabinet Office in the Treasury; it continued as an independent organization, though severely reduced, particularly from 1923.)

The committee system and the Cabinet Office were both greatly strengthened in World War II. These changes are recorded by the Public Records Office in *The Cabinet Office to 1945*, which sets out the principal committees serviced by the Cabinet Office between December 1916 and May 1945, as well as the number of committees and committee meetings.

The contrast between the period after World War I, particularly after 1923, and the years after 1945 owes something to the degree of state intervention in World War II, something also to a public determination not to suffer the earlier scandals of demoralization and the mass unemployment of the early twenties, but more to the difference between the 'Back to Normalcy' ideologues who swept into power in the Khaki Election, and Clement Attlee—together with Ernest Bevin, who had master-minded the successful and smooth 1945–6 demobilization, with a minimum of transitional unemployment.

The success of wartime Cabinet committees was another important fact. Sir John Anderson's successful chairmanship of the Lord President's Committee—later chaired by Clement Attlee—directing economic affairs, and that of other Cabinet committees by Herbert Morrison and Lord Woolton, helped to create an administrative revolution.

Sir John Anderson, while still a member of the wartime government, wrote an internal report recommending the retention of the Cabinet Office and, by implication, the system of Cabinet committees after the war.

Clement Attlee retained the system. As he recorded in his memoirs, 'I had a good deal of responsibility for arranging committees during the war-time Government and the experience so gained stood me in good stead when making arrangements for Government machinery in the Labour Administration.' He experimented in particular with a number of strategic economic committees, mainly chaired by Herbert Morrison and Sir Stafford Cripps, until the 1947 crisis led the Prime Minister to chair a still more high-powered one. As an economic minister I was on a number of these, and since the Board of Trade was regarded as neutral and uncommitted in the struggle to the death between the Ministries of Agriculture and Food, I had to spend what seemed years as one of the 'independent' members of such exciting committees as White Fish, and Farm Gate Prices, both of which had to settle the precise boundary where Agriculture handed over its produce and Food took over. Eventually, under Winston Churchill, the two departments merged in November 1954 and, inevitably, it became a virtual takeover by Agriculture. (In 1974, as a believer in creative tension between contesting departments based on interest, I gave the consumer a champion once more by appointing Shirley Williams as secretary of state for prices and consumer protection.)

During the thirteen years of unbroken Conservative rule from 1951 to 1964, the committee system, so far from being weakened, was strengthened and developed. The Conservatives of those days had a number of experienced administrators well qualified to take the lead, such as Lord Woolton (in the early years), Harold Macmillan, R. A. Butler, Derik Amory and Iain Macleod. Harold Macmillan's highly revealing autobiography, based on a very full diary, shows his faith in the system, which equally benefited from the growing strength and quality of the Cabinet Office. The process had begun when Sir Edward Bridges relinquished the secretaryship of the Cabinet, which was taken by Sir Norman Brook. It was Harold Macmillan, towards the end of his premiership, who completed the process of separation by creating the modern system by ending the unitary control, where the permanent secretary of the Treasury, aided by deputies, was at one and the same time the head of the Treasury as the principal economic department, and head of the Civil Service. Harold Macmillan, following the Plowden Report, created three virtually equal-ranking officers at senior permanent secretary level, separating the secretary of the Cabinet, while the Treasury and Civil Service functions were directed by two co-equal joint permanent secretaries. The operation was completed by me in 1968, following the report of the Fulton Committee on the Civil Service. I set up the Civil Service Department, with the prime minister as minister for the Civil Service, assisted by the lord privy seal and leader in the Lords, and now by a minister of state as well, and with the joint permanent secretary to the Treasury for the Civil Service in a separate command as permanent secretary to the Civil Service Department and head of the Civil Service.

The undoubted success of the Macmillan reform owes a great deal to Lord Plowden and the then Prime Minister, but no less to the fact that the civil servants who have been appointed include some of the best—indeed, the best—I have known in thirty-six years of close and intimate knowledge of the machine and its leading personalities.

We have seen that the development of Cabinet committees has been used by adherents of the Crossman school to suggest that the power of the prime minister is enhanced thereby. This is a facile view: what it does is to make the whole government more effective, and to shield Cabinet from over-absorption in detail. Business coming before Cabinet is reduced to the extent that it puts its work, so to speak, into commission, by committees with power to act. The principal checks on over-delegation, or lack of co-ordination with other sectors of the government, are, first, the right of any minister to ask for the matter to go to Cabinet on appeal, or at least be reported there; second, the ability of the prime minister to direct that such and such an issue shall go straight to Cabinet, or a committee decision be reported to the senior body, for confirmation or second thoughts—a power very rarely used in my recent experience; and, third, where the membership of an established committee seems inappropriate for a particular reference, a decision to make it more representative, *or* to create a special *ad hoc* committee to deal with this particular issue, a so-called MISC (jargon for 'miscellaneous'). The Government does not publish the names or number of Cabinet committees, but there are currently about 25. *The Times* profile of the Cabinet Office also records some 118 official sub-committees.

But it is fanciful to suggest that by these means the prime minister's power is enhanced at the expense of that of the Cabinet. For one thing, it would be extremely difficult for even a megalomaniac prime minister (who would not last long) to plan to set aside an agreed, or substantially agreed, decision of a powerful committee consisting of seven or eight of his Cabinet colleagues. His role is to see that the committee system, as an indispensable part of the Cabinet machine, works satisfactorily—by delegating enough to the committee and giving them authority, but also by being suffi ciently politically and administratively sensitive to know when to respond to an appeal by a dissatisfied minority, or to spot the case that ought to go straight to Cabinet. But when this is what he decides he must make this clear in advance, not weaken counsel and the standing of his ministerial colleagues by invoking Cabinet to reverse a decision they have taken.

Another positive duty he has is to ensure that the principal Cabinet committees, including *ad hoc* groups set up for a specific problem, are not packed with adherents of a particular departmental or political viewpoint. It is for him to ensure that a Cabinet committee is the Cabinet *in parvo*, a microcosm of the Cabinet itself.

On the question of 'appeals' to Cabinet, a tendency developed in the 1960s for a defeated minister almost automatically to seek for a rerun at Cabinet, even if he was in a minority of one. This threatened to congest the work of Cabinet, and to weaken the authority of the committees and their chairmen. I had to direct—and make public—that no appeal to Cabinet could hope to succeed unless it had the backing of the chairman of the committee. Under any government, committee chairmen are experienced ministers who have enough *nous* to know when, for administrative or political reasons, the matter should be taken higher, irrespective of their own views on the decision reached.

A better judgment than that of the confrontation school is that of Lord Blake: . . . It is by no means clear that this procedure, [i.e. the greater use of Cabinet committees] makes the Prime Minister a more dominant force. It could be equally well argued that it strengthens—by making more efficient—the Cabinet itself.'

When the prime minister, through Cabinet or a senior Cabinet committee, moves in and takes a subject over, it can well be for the purpose not of weakening Cabinet control, but of strengthening it against action by an individual department which is striking a discordant note against the orchestrated harmony which it is the purpose of Cabinet government to aim at, and the duty of the prime minister to ensure.

To take an example, which, unless millions of copies of national newspapers are regarded as secret documents, is public property. There were the anxieties in the summer of 1974 that work on the manifesto commitments on the National Enterprise Board and Planning Agreements was, in the first place, going too slowly for announcement by the Government before the planned October election, and, secondly, that there seemed to be some departure from the precise manifesto language, in favour of an earlier National Executive Committee document, which had not been adopted as an election programme, and which had in fact not been approved by the Labour Party Conference in 1973. I had insisted that, since legislation could not possibly be introduced before the October election—and 'industrial regeneration' was bound to be a central issue on the hustings—there must be a government White Paper setting out the policy, and saying precisely not only what we were going to do, but what we were not going to do. As the draft was unsatisfactory, I put it into commission—to a Cabinet committee representative of all shades of opinion—with myself in the chair. The White Paper was produced on time, and was the basis for the legislation introduced after the general election, enacted in the 1974–5 parliamentary session, receiving the Royal Assent on 12 November 1975.

An act of prime ministerial authority? Or the assertion of Cabinet supremacy? It has a potential for unending academic argument: but this was an assertion by Cabinet, on prime ministerial initiative, of its collective authority. It also illustrated the duty of the prime minister to enforce a time-table as well as his duty arising out of his position as political, as well as administrative, head of government.

For the reasons I have given, the use of the Cabinet committee system, serviced by the Cabinet Office on behalf of the Cabinet as a whole, has increased, is increasing, and ought not to be diminished—give or take the removal from the list of Cabinet committees of one or two which have served their purpose, and rarely if ever now meet. If the system had not existed, it would have had to be invented. The enormous increase in the work load on ministers, senior officials and the machine itself following the oil crisis and the problems of world inflation, world depression and world payments imbalance, if it could be statistically measured, must be, I would estimate, between thirty and fifty per cent. This, together with the volume of legislative and other action required of a reforming government elected on a specific manifesto, means collective delegation from the Cabinet to bodies deriving their authority from the Cabinet and answering to it.

This is not to say that there are no problems. The sheer weight of business in the departments and at inter-departmental level means that at important committees junior ministers have sometimes to stand in, lacking the authority of their secretaries of state. It is more difficult for the chairman, however experienced, to collect a sense of the meeting; and decisions by voting or counting of heads are utterly wrong in such meetings. One cannot equate the voice of the foreign secretary or chancellor with that of the most recently recruited parliamentary under-secretary.

Another problem arises when the issue under discussion involves public expenditure. At any Cabinet committee there is a danger that the chief secretary, or other Treasury representative, is in a minority of one. (Strangely, while spending ministers in Cabinet hardly ever form a bloc against the chancellor, in Cabinet committees there is a tendency to do so.) In recent months decisions have had to be taken to obviate this danger. The public expenditure decisions announced to Parliament in Cmnd 6396 are overriding by Cabinet directive. The contingency fund for the current year is not up for grabs at a committee: all claims on it must be tabulated, assembled, assessed and brought to Cabinet for decision.

I have referred to junior ministers. On occasion, following Clement Attlee's example, I have found it useful on an important but not crucial issue to set up committees consisting entirely of junior ministers. One such was responsible for the reorganization and strengthening of the Government's statistical service. I set up a committee under the chairmanship first of Peter Shore, later of Edmund Dell, which also included the principal heads of statistical departments, though I chaired the first meeting to show that I meant business and received regular reports from the Chairman (and from the head of the Government's statistical service, Sir Claus Moser) on the progress recorded. This, incidentally, was a mixed committee, including junior ministers and officials (mainly from the Central Statistical Office and departmental statistical branches). Mixed committees are a practice I would normally deprecate.

Looking back, I regret that I did not set up more committees of junior ministers; no less than I did not follow Clement Attlee's precedent of calling groups of young ministers at all levels to meet under his chairmanship to discuss fresh ideas for the future. The work some of us—particularly Fred Lee—did in 1950–1 opened up a great deal of new thinking. Lee's work foreshadowed new thinking on industrial democracy; my own contribution prepared for thinking that paved the way after many years for the philosophy that produced the Industrial Reorganisation Corporation (IRC) and the NEB.

[Wilson, *Governance*, 62–8.]

7. The Cabinet is supported by a system of Ministerial Committees which has a two-fold purpose. First, it relieves the pressure on the Cabinet itself by settling as much business as possible at a lower level; or failing that, by clarifying the issues and defining the points of disagreement. Second, it buttresses the principle of collective

responsibility of the Government by ensuring that, even though an important question may never reach the Cabinet itself, the decision will be fully considered and the final judgment will be sufficiently authoritative to ensure that the Government as a whole can be properly expected to accept responsibility for it.

8. When there is a conflict of interest between Departments, it should not be referred to the Cabinet until all other means of resolving it have been exhausted, including personal correspondence or discussions between the Ministers concerned. If the Ministerial Committee system is to function effectively, appeals to the Cabinet must clearly be infrequent and the Chairmen of Committees must be free to exercise their discretion in deciding whether to advise the Prime Minister to allow them. The Prime Minister will not entertain appeals to the Cabinet except after consultation with the Chairman of the Committee concerned. Departmental Ministers should normally attend in person meetings of Committees of which they are members or to which they are invited; unless a Minister can make it possible for his colleagues to discuss with him personally issues which he considers to be important, he cannot—except where his absence is due to factors outside his control—expect them to agree that he should have a right to appeal against their decision if it goes against him in his absence.

[*Questions of Procedure for Ministers* (1976 version), paras. 7–8.]

## 2. CABINET COMMITTEES: DEFINITION

*A Cabinet committee is a committee of Ministers (which can include non-Cabinet and junior Ministers) established by the Prime Minister (whether or not chaired by him), having formal procedures and servicing by the Cabinet Office.*

### (1) STANDING CABINET COMMITTEES

*Every government will have a number of standing Cabinet committees which will endure for the life of that government. Examples will be the Economic Strategy Committee, the Home and Social Affairs Committee, the Legislation Committee, and the Defence and Oversea Policy Committee.*

I have established four standing committees of the Cabinet: a defence and oversea policy committee and an economic strategy committee, both under my chairmanship; a home and social affairs committee under the chairmanship of my right hon. Friend the Home Secretary; and a legislation committee under the chairmanship of the Lord Chancellor. Attendance at these committees will vary according to the subject under discussion. Where appropriate, sub-committees of the standing committees will be established. Membership and terms of reference of the standing committees or the sub-committees will remain confidential.

[The Prime Minister, Mrs Margaret Thatcher, 967 H.C. Deb. *179* (written answers 24 May 1979).]

These broad issues engage the collective responsibility of Ministers. Subject to the supreme authority of the Prime Minister and the Cabinet, they will be dealt with by a Committee on Defence and Oversea Policy, which will meet under the chairmanship of the Prime Minister and will normally include the First Secretary of State, the Foreign Secretary, the Chancellor of the Exchequer or the Chief Secretary to the Treasury, the Home Secretary, the Secretary of State for Commonwealth Relations and the Colonies, and the Secretary of State for Defence. Other Ministers will be invited to be present as necessary. The Chief of the Defence Staff and the Chiefs of Staff will be in attendance as the nature of the business requires. Other officials, such as the Permanent Under Secretaries of State or the Chief Scientific Adviser to the Secretary of State for Defence, will also attend as required. The Committee will be supported by a Committee of senior officials.

[Central Organization for Defence, Cmnd. 2097 (1963), para. 16.]

## (2) AD HOC COMMITTEES

Ad hoc committees meet to handle a single issue such as Trident, or are convened spasmodically (an example is MISC 62, the so-called 'Star Chamber', which gathers each year in early autumn in an attempt to force economies on reluctant spending departments).

[Peter Hennessy, *Cabinet* (Oxford, 1986), 31.]

## (3) OTHER COMMITTEES

### (*a*) *Official committees*

. . . In addition to the Cabinet Committees which only Ministers normally attend, there is a full network of official committees [of civil servants]; and the work of the Ministers is therefore strictly and completely paralleled at the official level. This means that very often the whole job is pre-cooked in the official committee to a point from which it is extremely difficult to reach any other conclusion than that already determined by the officials in advance; and if agreement is reached at the lower level of a Cabinet Committee, only formal approval is needed from the full Cabinet. This is the way in which Whitehall ensures that the Cabinet system is relatively harmless.

[Richard Crossman, *Diaries of a Cabinet Minister* (London, 1975), i, 198.]

### (*b*) *Mixed committees*

However, as the monetarist approach moved to the centre stage of government thinking, so the machinery of government was forced to respond. The Treasury raised the seniority of its own officials on the monetary side (incidentally setting up tensions with the Bank over where the primacy lay). But the key question was how to involve Ministers. Because the government's economic success or failure might be determined by what its monetary policies were, it seemed to us necessary to involve Ministers in determining their own fate. The No. 10 advisers, initiated by the very able Principal Private Secretary, Kenneth Stowe, discussed which new procedures would be appropriate. A conventional Cabinet Committee was ruled out, as questions of proposed actions on interest rates or on sterling exchange rates were too sensitive to be discussed in a wide committee with circulation of papers. Instead, a secret committee called 'The Seminar' was formed, in which normal rights of ministerial attendance did not apply. It was a small 'mixed' committee, containing ministers and officials, under the chairmanship of the Prime Minister. Others who regularly attended were the Chancellor, the Permanent Secretary and the External Finance Second Secretary from the Treasury, the Governor of the Bank of England, Harold Lever (then Chancellor of the Duchy of Lancaster), the Secretary to the Cabinet, the Principal Private Secretary and myself. Occasionally the President of the Board of Trade or other officials would attend if their presence was relevant to the agenda. It was interesting that the Bank of England regularly attended a meeting of Cabinet Ministers—rather in the way that the Chiefs of Staff attended the Cabinet Defence Committee.

This 'Seminar' committee met regularly in 1977–9 in order to discuss the major decisions on interest rates and sterling. During this time the Prime Minister was particularly concerned to prevent sterling from rising and so creating unemployment, but all attempts to 'cap' sterling failed because the Government's overall economic and monetary policy was so successful during 1977 and 1978 (it was not even necessary fully to implement the second year's IMF cuts). The general confidence about the economy fed through to sterling and foreigners became once again willing to buy. It was also clear that the Bank of England was very happy to have a strong currency operating against inflation. The Prime Minister often put pressure on the Governor, Gordon Richardson, but refused to allow the committee to issue him with instructions. These two men always treated one another with considerable respect; after one particularly sharp discussion, when the Governor was being at his most impressively and courteously obstinate, Mr Callaghan said to me: 'He has to do his job. I either back him or sack him, and I am certainly not going to sack him.' Although it is presumably conducted in a different style, the 'Seminar' machinery for considering monetary questions was continued by Mrs Thatcher after 1979, when monetarism reached its brief period of excessive influence. For Mr Callaghan it became one more area of central government in which during 1977–8 he exercised his dominance over the conduct of policy. The IMF crisis had given him the opportunity he needed to establish that dominance.

[Donoughue, *Prime Minister*, 101–2.]

The powers in the EPA 1920 have been invoked on twelve separate occasions, all concerned with industrial disputes in key undertakings . . . The decision to invoke has typically been at Cabinet level founded on recommendations from an Emergencies Committee of the Cabinet, composed of ministers and senior officials from relevant departments, spawning sub-committees shadowed by official sub-committees closely monitoring the particular dispute. Advice has also been taken from the security services on the nature of the dispute. Recurring issues have been: the dilemma of if and when to invoke; the need to act quickly but to avoid provocative action; whether troops should be used; possible roles for civilian volunteers; which regulations should be prepared—regulations peculiar to that dispute or a more general code; whether subversive elements hide behind genuine industrial grievances and manipulate them for their own ends. In terms of running the show, the present structure dates from 1972, when an internal review by Lord Jellicoe and the then Cabinet Office Deputy Secretary, John Hunt, led to 'a refashioned, streamlined emergencies organisation, the Civil Contingencies Unit (CCU), located in the Cabinet Office and having the status of a standing Cabinet committee.' It is a mixture of ministers and officials, usually chaired by the Home Secretary when ministers are present. Apparently, over the years since 1920, officials and military men have by and large acted as a moderating influence on some of the 'wilder notions' of their political masters in governments of varying political complexion. The CCU has a central role in planning the response to possible disputes and in so managing operations during them as to avoid, if possible, the necessity for resort to emergency powers or, if not, to be best able to judge when to invoke them.

[David Bonner, *Emergency Powers in Peacetime* (London, 1985), 29–30.]

## 3. MRS THATCHER, CABINET COMMITTEES, AND MINISTERIAL MEETINGS

. . . There are very few discussions of government decisions by the full Cabinet.

[The Foreign Secretary, Sir Geoffrey Howe, interview in the *Daily Mail*, 6 February 1984.]

Judged by the frequency of meetings and the flow of formal Cabinet papers, full Cabinet activity under Mrs Thatcher is at an historical low. So, too, is the workload being devolved to Cabinet committees. On entering No. 10 in May 1979, Mrs Thatcher made it clear to the Whitehall machine that she was not a Cabinet-committee person. She would do business with her fellow ministers free of the curse of committees. 'Events', as one insider put it, 'soon took care of that.' As we have seen from the blueprint of Mrs Thatcher's Engine Room . . . she now presides over some 160 of the hated things, though not, naturally, in the literal sense of chairing the lot.

Yet, she *is* running the slimmest Cabinet machine since before the Second World War. As we have seen, Attlee accumulated 148 standing and 313 ad hoc groups in six and a quarter years, and Churchill 137 and 109 respectively in three and a half years. The figures for Eden are incomplete, and those for Macmillan and Home remain a mystery which the current Cabinet Secretary refuses to resolve. Thanks to Mrs Castle's Diary, we have some intelligence on Wilson Mark I. Elected in October 1964, he had by early 1969 (i.e. after four and a quarter years) reached his 236th ad hoc group. The Heath era is another unknown. Wilson Mark II, between March 1974 and March 1976, ran up a total of somewhere around 120 ad hoc groups. Callaghan in the three years between April 1976 and April 1979 commissioned about 160 ad hoc committees, a similar growth rate to Attlee's. Judging by the Cabinet-committee criterion, Mrs Thatcher has done exceedingly well. Under her, there have been 30–35 standing-committees and just over 120 ad hocs in six and a half years. So Cabinet *and* Cabinet-committee discussion is down.

Does that indicate that the load has diminished in parallel? Has Britain against the odds re-entered a period of small government? In philosophical terms the answer is probably 'Yes'; in practical terms 'No.' The reason has been stated frequently by Sir John Hoskyns. In the short run, disengaging from state activity is just as difficult and time-consuming as getting into it—if not more so. Privatization, like nationalization, imposes a stiff workload and absorbs a great deal of parliamentary time.

So, where is the business being done? A fair amount is conducted by ministerial correspondence, a perfectly acceptable method in constitutional terms. The Franks Report on the Falklands gives an indication of just how much this goes on. One reason, for example, why the Falklands issue figured so infrequently on the agenda of the Cabinet's Oversea and Defence Committee before the Argentine invasion of April 1982 is that Lord Carrington, then Foreign and Commonwealth Secretary, disliked bringing Foreign Office business before committee meetings of his colleagues. Another swathe of high-level business is tackled by Mrs Thatcher in ad hoc groups which fall outside Sir Robert Armstrong's Cabinet Committee Book.

[Hennessy, *Cabinet*, 100–1.]

When in 1956, though not yet a member, I was first able to view a working Cabinet at fairly close range, it was undoubtedly an institution greatly changed from that which my father had joined in 1924. Cabinets met only twice a week, and it is worth noticing in passing that Mrs Thatcher's Cabinet meets normally once, and Cabinet papers for controversial discussion have since become something of an exception rather than the rule. It is obvious that, in the time usually available, say 10.00 a.m. to lunchtime on a Tuesday or a Thursday, no body of about twenty people can successfully dispose of the longer term issues of policy. A discussion of current Parliamentary business, and the week's events in international affairs inevitably account for most of the time available, and where a financial decision is required or a Cabinet paper on some other contentious topic requires decision, one other item is usually the most that can be managed before one o'clock. Ministers then disperse for lunch and take their seats on the front benches of their separate Houses at 2.30 or 3.00 p.m. The Cabinet is at an end till the following Thursday, when the process is repeated. It is obvious, therefore, that only a few of the most important decisions are made in Cabinet at all.

This has meant that, beneath the Cabinet structure, a network of Cabinet Committees, usually chaired by the appropriate Cabinet Minister, take some and perhaps most of the important decisions. Not all Cabinet Ministers are permanent members of any one of these, and of this minority some at least are often represented by Junior Ministers sitting in their place. Talking of Junior Ministers, these themselves form an important element in the structure and stability of Cabinet Government. It is here that future Cabinet Ministers are trained, largely by the Civil Service, in the actual working of the Government machine. Unlike myself, who learned much of what it is essential for a minister to know by working as a Staff Officer during the War, this is virtually the only technical training which a Minister receives. To this extent at least we remain a Government of amateurs. I do not regard this as an altogether unmixed blessing. It might be as well if all Ministers received, on appointment, in addition to the paper containing the so-called Prime Minister's rules, a short course on Ministerial practice, staff duties and collegiate responsibilities. Some, at least, of recent resignations might thus have been avoided. As it is, Ministers are simply given a document to read embodying some of the more important conventions they are expected to observe.

As a slight but not unimportant parenthesis, the sub-Cabinet structure of Junior Ministers does require a word of expansion. Their very numbers affect the balance of power within the House of Commons, and form an added weapon at the disposal of the Prime Minister and the Whips. Together with the unpaid Parliamentary private secretaries, the corps of those members of either House directly in the service of Government, and therefore bound, on pain of resignation, irrespective of the merits, to record their votes in its support on contentious issues, is by no means an insignificant factor in the stability of Cabinets. In the House of Commons alone, where they are most important, this 'pay roll vote', as it has come to be called, usually amounts to something between one hundred and twenty and one hundred and thirty favourable votes as they move obediently through the lobbies. Considering that an average Government (if there is such a thing) depends on mustering something a little more than three hundred on a three-line whip (making some allowance for absentees on both sides), this cohesive group, not available in the same form to oppositions, must play a significant part in the calculations of the Whips in the case of any threatened revolt amongst Government supporters . . .

It has become increasingly the habit of successive Prime Ministers, Conservative certainly, but I believe Labour also, to summon groups of Ministers under their own Chairmanship to deal with particular issues (or related issues of a particular class) outside the formal Cabinet Committee structure and which continue to exist in parallel with them for routine business, thus prejudging discussion in Cabinet and avoiding the necessity for the regular attendance, sometimes by Junior Ministers, of the Departments represented at the regular Cabinet Committees. To some extent the existence of these bodies has now become formalised. Some have regular designations as subcommittees (in name but not in reality) of the regular Committees or of the Cabinet itself. Some are grouped together under a designation indicating their miscellaneous character, but the fact that there have now been very much more than a hundred of these with the same generic but separate numeration shows that we are in the presence of a semipermanent, and, I believe, novel development in Cabinet Government.

The new system has manifest advantages. To begin with, though it has certain features in common with them, it is constitutionally vastly superior to the so-called kitchen cabinets which are said to have become a notorious peculiarity of some Labour administrations. It is flexible, confined to Senior Ministers, and presents an easy and convenient method of disposing of day to day business not requiring the presence of large numbers, and of dealing with the unexpected and extremely diverse incidents and accidents which characterise the life of any executive government. It is among the factors which have rendered it possible to hold one single weekly, usually Thursday, Cabinet and thus render unnecessary the extremely onerous burden of holding Cabinet twice a week on Tuesdays and Thursdays, with long, and at times inconclusive, discussions between Ministers not always well acquainted with the detailed matters under debate. One group, at least, of these bodies has substituted a business-like and more decisive control of the conduct of industrial disputes in the public sector, which greatly weakened the control of inflation during the Macmillan Government.

Yet I think it would be impossible to deny that, like all gradual developments which have come partly by chance, and even by inadvertence, there are, or at least may be, important constitutional implications in what has happened. Obviously the collegiate character of the Cabinet has been to some extent weakened by less frequent meetings and less personal involvement in many of the important decisions of Government. Equally obviously the frequent participation of the Prime Minister in the chair of the ad hoc meetings will have strengthened his or her position, not indeed in the direction of Presidential government, which is impossible so long as Ministers have to face the Houses of Parliament across the floor, but, at any rate, at the expense of the collegiate responsibility of the full Cabinet. Moreover the very handiness of the small group, although well served and advised by the Cabinet secretariat, to some extent favours rapid and not always well thought out decisions, and the occasions when small groups are chaired by trusted deputies in place of the Prime Minister inevitably tend to create a hierarchy within the collegiate body which cannot be recognised in any constitutional or formalised way, except by the creation, seldom resorted to in peacetime, of a formally appointed deputy Prime Minister.

[Lord Hailsham of St Marylebone, Granada Guildhall Lecture 1987, 'Will Cabinet Government Survive?', 6–7, 9–10.]

In her early years as Prime Minister, Margaret adhered closely to the traditional principles and practice of Cabinet government. She operated very strictly through the Cabinet committee system, with the Cabinet Office taking the Minutes.

In Ted's Government, Margaret had been left out from the ad hoc committees which were set up. Any Secretary of State for Education is always stuck in rather an isolated department. She had, however, proved herself a disruptive influence on one Cabinet Committee, the Science Committee, where she had complained that Solly Zuckerman and Victor Rothschild were only officials and had no right to speak. They in their turn had complained about her.

I always thought she would stick closely to the official committee system because she had resented being excluded from the small ad hoc groups set up by Ted. I felt that her views were right. After all, if you are a Cabinet Minister with collective responsibility, you ought to know what is going on. Too often Cabinet Ministers don't know, and this causes resentment.

Unfortunately, after a couple of years, the formal Cabinet committees were very much down-graded and she began to operate much more in small groups dominated by her cronies. I suppose this was inevitable, but for all that it was also regrettable. Even before 1981 she had one small group who met her for breakfast and which was kept very hush-hush. It included Nigel Lawson, Norman Tebbit —neither of whom was then in the Cabinet—and John Biffen. I fancy it was disbanded after John proved himself a rather less reliable supporter. This cosy arrangement was later superseded by her close relationship with Cecil Parkinson.

The operation of a small 'war Cabinet' during the Falklands crisis in 1982 also convinced her that it was far easier to settle issues with just five or six people.

In the years since, she has adopted ad hoc groups as one of her main methods of government. This had obvious advantages for those few on the 'inside track', who come to regard meetings with their other colleagues as increasingly unnecessary and time-wasting. But it is not at all good for the many, including Cabinet Ministers, who are on the outside and who believe ad hoc groups can be weighted against them in the way Cabinet cannot. Keith Joseph and Margaret had become bitter at their sense of being excluded by Ted but Margaret stored up more trouble for herself with colleagues who felt they were never told what was really going on.

Margaret would give as her reason for working increasingly in small groups that she couldn't rely on her colleagues to respect her authority. I regret to say that this was true.

But the coining of the term 'wet' itself hardly presaged an inclination towards teamwork or mutual trust. Margaret was responsible for pinning this name on to her opponents. It was effective for a time and rather unnerving. In due course it became a badge of honour, but it was hardly conducive to loyalty in Cabinet.

We must have been the most divided Conservative Cabinet ever. There was a deep division on economic and social policy, and members were not prepared to be put off from giving their own views.

[Prior, *Balance of Power*, 133–4.]

Other ad hoc groups beyond the reach of the MISC series can have a considerable impact, even though they may only meet once or twice. For example, Mrs Thatcher convened a meeting of ministers to consider the now legendary minute entitled 'It Took a Riot' prepared for her by Michael Heseltine, then Secretary of State for the Environment, based on his experience in Merseyside following the inner-city riots of July 1981. It proposed an ambitious programme of investment and the designation of Cabinet colleagues as ministers for various decaying areas. Mr Heseltine had evangelized Whitehall on behalf of his cause like a latter-day John the Baptist. He held a secret dinner at Locket's restaurant in Westminster for several influential permanent secretaries, including Sir Robert Armstrong. They were impressed.

The Prime Minister, however, prevailed. In September 1981 she convened an ad hoc group on inner cities and stacked it against Heseltine. It consisted of herself, Heseltine, Sir Geoffrey Howe, Chancellor of the Exchequer, Sir Keith Joseph, Secretary of State for Industry, and William Whitelaw, then Home Secretary. Whitelaw, concerned as ever to be the mediator, strove to find a middle way between Heseltine and those who did not want a penny extra for the cities for fear of being seen to reward rioters. Heseltine was isolated. There was an increase in the urban programme but on nothing like the scale he wanted. On this occasion, he succumbed to the verdict of a loaded ministerial group.

[Hennessy, *Cabinet*, 102.]

## 4. SECRECY AND CABINET COMMITTEES

*More secrecy surrounds Cabinet committees than the Cabinet itself. The most comprehensive justification for this state of affairs was made by Mr James Callahan when Prime Minister: it is challenged in Rodney Brazier,* Constitutional Practice *(Oxford, 1988), 110–11.*

Consistently with the practice of all former Prime Ministers I have always refused to publish details of Cabinet Committees or to answer Questions in the House about them . . . There is, however, now some evidence that Select Committees would like to interest themselves in the Committee system and may be seeking to erode the present convention. I have therefore been considering the case for taking the initiative and disclosing details of the Committee structure.

I accept that the present convention has certain disadvantages for us. In particular non-disclosure makes it difficult to answer charges that the Government's policies are not properly co-ordinated. For example the Select Committee on Overseas Development has recommended the establishment of a Cabinet Committee to co-ordinate political, trade and aid policies towards the developing world largely because the Ministry for Overseas Development were not able to disclose that such a committee (RD) already exists. It is also arguable that non-disclosure is inconsistent with a policy of greater openness. In any case some parts of the Committee structure are quite widely known outside Government: in these cases what is at issue therefore is a refusal to admit publicly what a lot of people know about privately.

It is important therefore to understand the reasons for the current practice of non-disclosure. They are as follows: the Cabinet Committee system grew up as the load on the Cabinet itself became too great. It allows matters of lesser importance to be decided without troubling the whole Cabinet: and major issues to be clarified in order to save the time of the Cabinet. The method adopted by Ministers for discussing policy questions is however essentially a domestic matter: and a decision by a Cabinet Committee, unless referred to the Cabinet, engages the collective responsibility of all Ministers and has exactly the same authority as a decision by the Cabinet itself. Disclosure that a particular Committee had dealt with a matter might lead to argument about the status of the decision or demands that it should be endorsed by the whole Cabinet. Furthermore publishing details of the Committees would be both misleading and counter-productive. The existence of some could not be disclosed on security grounds: others are set up to do a particular job and are then wound up. The absence of a Committee on a particular subject (e.g. agriculture or poverty) does not mean that the Government do not attach importance to it: and the fact that a particular Minister is not on a committee does not mean that he does not attend when his interests are affected. Publication would almost inevitably lead to pressures for both more and larger Committees, and for disclosures of information about their activities.

I do not believe that we could in any event disclose the existence of the [*ad hoc*] groups. This is partly because of their ephemeral nature and partly because disclosure would often reveal either that very sensitive subjects were under consideration or that we had something in train about which we were not ready to make an announcement. Disclosure of the main standing Committees would thus give a partial picture only. Moreover having gone as far as this I do not believe that it would be possible for me to hold the line and refuse to answer any further questions about the composition and activities of the Committees. At the minimum we would be under pressure to reveal the names of the Chairmen. This would make it harder for me to make changes: and it would have implications for the responsibilities of Departmental Ministers since Select Committees would try to summon the Chairmen of Cabinet Committees to give evidence in addition to the responsible Minister. I should also be under continuing pressure to say that a committee was considering a particular subject (and often it would be a GEN group): and there would be questions about when Committees were meeting, the work they were doing, whether particular Ministers are on them, the details of under-pinning Official Committees, etc.

I have therefore decided that we should not change our stance on this matter. The present convention is long established and provides a basis on which we can stand. Any departure from it would be more likely to whet appetites than to satisfy them. I ask my colleagues therefore to rest on the position that the way in which we co-ordinate our decisions is a matter internal to Government and not to answer questions about the Cabinet Committee system.

[The Prime Minister, Mr James Callaghan, *Disclosure of Cabinet Committees, New Statesman,* 10 November 1978; Colin Turpin, *British Government and the Constitution: Text, Cases and Materials* (London, 1985), 138–9.]

## Confidentiality

### 1. LEGAL RESTRAINTS

#### (1) THE OFFICIAL SECRETS ACT 1911, S. 2

(1) If any person having in his possession or control [any secret official code word, or pass word, or] any sketch, plan, model, article, note, document, or information which relates to or is used in a prohibited place or anything in such a place, or which has been made or obtained in contravention of this Act, or which has been entrusted in confidence to him by any person holding office under His Majesty or which he has obtained [or to which he has had access] owing to his position as a person who holds or has held office under His Majesty, or as a person who holds or has held a contract made on behalf of His Majesty, or as a person who is or has been employed under a person who holds or has held such an office or contract,—

(*a*) communicates the [code word, pass word,] sketch, plan, model, article, note, document, or information to any person, other than a person to whom he is authorised to communicate it, or a person to whom it is in the interest of the State his duty to communicate it, or,

[(*aa*) uses the information in his possession for the benefit of any foreign power or in any other manner prejudicial to the safety or interests of the State;]

(*b*) retains the sketch, plan, model, article, note, or document in his possession or control when he has no right to retain it or when it is contrary to his duty to retain it [or fails to comply with all directions issued by lawful authority with regard to the return or disposal thereof] [or

(*c*) fails to take reasonable care of, or so conducts himself as to endanger the safety of the sketch, plan, model, article, note, document, secret official code or pass word or information:]
that person shall be guilty of a misdemeanour.

[1A] If any person having in his possession or control any sketch, plan, model, article, note, document, or information which relates to munitions of war, communicates it directly or indirectly to any foreign power, or in any other manner prejudicial to the safety or interests of the State, that person shall be guilty of a misdemeanour.

(2) If any person receives any [secret official code word, or pass word, or] sketch, plan, model, article, note, document, or information, knowing, or having reasonable ground to believe, at the time when he receives it, that the [code word, pass word,] sketch, plan, model, article, note, document, or information is communicated to him in contravention of this Act, he shall be guilty of a misdemeanour, unless he proves that the communication to him of the [code word, pass word,] sketch, plan, model, article, note, document, or information was contrary to his desire.

(3) . . .

*(Section 2 was repealed by the Official Secrets Act 1989, s. 16(4) and Schedule 2: see below, p. 290. Section 2 did not, however, restrain Ministers as a matter of law from publishing Cabinet secrets.)*

This afternoon I was having a highly technical meeting of Coventry shop stewards when Robin Wendt came down to the House to say that the Prime Minister urgently wanted to see me. I rushed up and found him sitting in his room (I rarely go there now) and I saw he had in front of him my review, with another long piece of paper attached to it. Harold said, 'Now this is quite a thing. It seems to me that first of all we have Gordon Walker on *The Cabinet* and then Macleod's review of Gordon Walker, then Crossman on Macleod and now Burke Trend on Crossman.' He threw across a five-page review of my article from Burke Trend's office. It was the most extraordinary stuff, a kind of public school, prim, pious critique of Crossman as an easy-going person who didn't appreciate the meaning of collective responsibility. It was a picture of the non-loyal member of the team, who is using his position in an improper way, and about whom nothing can be done.

Among this there was a proper criticism saying that I had mentioned three times that members of the Cabinet had got away with writing books violating the Official Secrets Act. Harold said this was highly embarrassing not only because this week such a prosecution is going on, but also because Ministers can't be prosecuted in this way. He said, 'For God's sake, can't you get the Official Secrets Act out and substitute "collective responsibility"?' I said, 'Of course I can't. It doesn't fit.' But to my amazement I found it did. I had learnt something staggeringly important. Burke and Harold admit that the Official Secrets Act, which is really the only threat against a Cabinet Minister, doesn't operate. No one can be prosecuted under it, so there is therefore no sanction against a Cabinet Minister at all. He must be allowed to have access to the documents, he writes what he likes and then it is a matter of whether the Secretary of the Cabinet and the Prime Minister of the day can manage to persuade him to leave out things they think improper. In fact it is a question of whether sufficient sense of collective responsibility is instilled into you to ensure that, after you leave office, you will in your book-writing still feel enough of a member of the team, a part of the Cabinet system, to behave properly. That is all they rely on. It may sound obvious now I have said it but I certainly hadn't known it before. I had thought the ultimate sanction was the threat of prosecution.

It made me realize that Burke can be two-faced. He has never indicated in any possible way that he disapproves of me but I now know that he does. He actively distrusts me, mainly because I am not a reliable member of the team and when I get the chance I am liable to write a book which will say more than should be said and which he therefore won't approve. Burke knows this and I now think it is quite right that I should do it.

[Crossman, *Diaries*, iii, 898–9.]

No prosecution under the Official Secrets Acts has been instituted against a Minister or ex-Minister.

[Report of the Radcliffe Committee on Ministerial Memoirs, Cmnd. 6386 (1976), para. 26.]

Nevertheless governments do regularly reveal a great deal of official information. These disclosures do not contravene section 2 . . . Actual practice within the Government rests heavily on a doctrine of implied authorisation, flowing from the nature of each Crown servant's job . . . Ministers are, in effect, self-authorising. They decide for themselves what to reveal.

[Report of the Franks Committee on Section 2 of the Official Secrets Act 1911, Cmnd. 5104 (1972), para. 18.]

### (2) BREACH OF CONFIDENCE

The Cabinet is at the very centre of national affairs, and must be in possession at all times of information which is secret or confidential. Secrets relating to national security may require to be preserved indefinitely. Secrets relating to new taxation proposals may be of the highest importance until Budget day, but public knowledge thereafter. To leak a Cabinet decision a day or so before it is officially announced is an accepted exercise in public relations, but to identify the Ministers who voted one way or another is objectionable because it undermines the doctrine of joint responsibility.

It is evident that there cannot be a single rule governing the publication of such a variety of matters. In these actions we are concerned with the publication of diaries at a time when 11 years have expired since the first recorded events. The Attorney-General must show (*a*) that such publication would be a breach of confidence; (*b*) that the public interest requires that the publication be restrained, and (*c*) that there are no other facts of the public interest contradictory of and more compelling than that relied upon. Moreover, the court, when asked to restrain such a publication, must closely examine the extent to which relief is necessary to ensure that restrictions are not imposed beyond the strict requirement of public need.

Applying those principles to the present case, what do we find? In my judgment, the Attorney-General has made out his claim that the expression of individual opinions by Cabinet Ministers in the course of Cabinet discussion are matters of confidence, the publication of which can be restrained by the court when this is clearly necessary in the public interest.

The maintenance of the doctrine of joint responsibility within the Cabinet is in the public interest, and the application of that doctrine might be prejudiced by premature disclosure of the views of individual Ministers.

There must, however, be a limit in time after which the confidential character of the information, and the duty of the court to restrain publication, will lapse. Since the conclusion of the hearing in this case I have had the opportunity to read the whole of volume one of the Diaries, and my considered view is that I cannot believe that the publication at this interval of anything in volume one would inhibit free discussion in the Cabinet of today, even though the individuals involved are the same, and the national problems have a distressing similarity with those of a decade ago. It is unnecessary to elaborate the evils which might flow if at the close of a Cabinet meeting a Minister proceeded to give the press an analysis of the voting, but we are dealing in this case with a disclosure of information nearly 10 years later.

It may, of course, be intensely difficult in a particular case, to say at what point the material loses its confidential character, on the ground that publication will no longer undermine the doctrine of joint Cabinet responsibility. It is this difficulty which prompts some to argue that Cabinet discussions should retain their confidential character for a longer and arbitrary period such as 30 years, or even for all time, but this seems to me to be excessively restrictive. The court should intervene only in the clearest of cases where the continuing confidentiality of the material can be demonstrated. In less clear cases—and this, in my view, is certainly one—reliance must be placed on the good sense and good taste of the Minister or ex-Minister concerned.

In the present case there is nothing in Mr Crossman's work to suggest that he did not support the doctrine of joint Cabinet responsibility. The question for the court is whether it is shown that publication now might damage the doctrine notwithstanding that much of the action is up to 10 years old and three general elections have been held meanwhile. So far as the Attorney-General relies in his argument on the disclosure of individual ministerial opinions, he has not satisfied me that publication would in any way inhibit free and open discussion in Cabinet hereafter.

It remains to deal with the Attorney-General's two further arguments, namely, (*a*) that the Diaries disclose advice given by senior civil servants who cannot be expected to advise frankly if their advice is not treated as confidential; (*b*) the Diaries disclose observations made by Ministers on the capacity of individual senior civil servants and their suitability for specific appointments. I can see no ground in law which entitles the court to restrain publication of these matters. A Minister is, no doubt, responsible for his department and accountable for its errors even though the individual fault is to be found in his subordinates. In these circumstances, to disclose the fault of the subordinate may amount to cowardice or bad taste, but I can find no ground for saying that either the Crown or the individual civil servant has an enforceable right to have the advice which he gives treated as confidential for all time.

For these reasons I do not think that the court should interfere with the publication of volume one of the Diaries, and I propose, therefore, to refuse the injunction sought but to grant liberty to apply in regard to material other than volume one if it is alleged that different considerations may there have to be applied.

[*Attorney-General* v. *Jonathan Cape Ltd.* [1976] Q.B. 752 at 770–2, per Lord Widgery L.C.J.]

## (3) THE OFFICIAL SECRETS ACT 1989

7.—For the purposes of this Act a disclosure by—

(*a*) a Crown servant; or

(*b*) a person, not being a Crown servant or government contractor, in whose case a notification for the purposes of section 1(1) above is in force,

is made with lawful authority if, and only if, it is made in accordance with his official duty.

(2) For the purposes of this Act a disclosure by a government contractor is made with lawful authority if, and only if, it is made—

(*a*) in accordance with an official authorisation; or

(*b*) for the purposes of the functions by virtue of which he is a government contractor and without contravening an official restriction.

(3) For the purposes of this Act a disclosure made by any other person is made with lawful authority if, and only if, it is made—

(*a*) to a Crown servant for the purposes of his functions as such; or

(*b*) in accordance with an official authorisation.

(4) It is a defence for a person charged with an offence under any of the foregoing provisions of this Act to prove that at the time of the alleged offence he believed that he had lawful authority to make the disclosure in question and had no reasonable cause to believe otherwise.

(5) In this section 'official authorisation' and 'official restriction' mean, subject to subsection (6) below, an authorisation or restriction duly given or imposed by a Crown servant or government contractor or by or on behalf of a prescribed body or a body of a prescribed class.

(6) In relation to section 6 above 'official authorisation' includes an authorisation duly given by or on behalf of the State or organisation concerned or, in the case of an organisation, a member of it.

8.–(1) Where a Crown servant or government contractor, by virtue of his position as such, has in his possession or under his control any document or other article which it would be an offence under any of the foregoing provisions of this Act for him to disclose without lawful authority he is guilty of an offence if—

(*a*) being a Crown servant, he retains the document or article contrary to his official duty; or

(*b*) being a government contractor, he fails to comply with an official direction for the return or disposal of the document or article.

or if he fails to take such care to prevent the unauthorised disclosure of the document or article as a person in his position may reasonably be expected to take.

(2) It is a defence for a Crown servant charged with an offence under subsection (1)(*a*) above to prove that at the time of the alleged offence he believed that he was acting in accordance with his official duty and had no reasonable cause to believe otherwise.

(3) In subsections (1) and (2) above references to a Crown servant include any person, not being a Crown servant or government contractor, in whose case a notification for the purposes of section 1(1) above is in force.

(4) Where a person has in his possession or under his control any document or other article which it would be an offence under section 5 above for him to disclose without lawful authority, he is guilty of an offence if—

(*a*) he fails to comply with an official direction for its return or disposal; or

(*b*) where he obtained it from a Crown servant or government contractor on terms requiring it to be held in confidence or in circumstances in which that servant or contractor could reasonably expect that it would be so held, he fails to take such care to prevent its unauthorised disclosure as a person in his position may reasonably be expected to take.

(5) Where a person has in his possession or under his control any document or other article which it would be an offence under section 6 above for him to disclose without lawful authority, he is guilty of an offence if he fails to comply with an official direction for its return or disposal.

(6) A person is guilty of an offence if he discloses any official information, document or other article which can be used for the purpose of obtaining access to any information, document or other article protected against disclosure by the foregoing provisions of this Act and the circumstances in which it is disclosed are such that it would be reasonable to expect that it might be used for that purpose without authority.

(7) For the purposes of subsection (6) above a person discloses information or a document or article which is official if—

(*a*) he has or has had it in his possession by virtue of his position as a Crown servant or government contractor; or

(*b*) he knows or has reasonable cause to believe that a Crown servant or government contractor has or has had it in his possession by virtue of his position as such.

(8) Subsection (5) of section 5 above applies for the purposes of subsection (6) above as it applies for the purposes of that section.

(9) In this section 'official direction' means a direction duly given

by a Crown servant or government contractor or by or on behalf of a prescribed body or a body of a prescribed class.

12.–(1) In this Act 'Crown servant' means—

(*a*) a Minister of the Crown;

(*b*) a person appointed under section 8 of the Northern Ireland Constitution Act 1973 (the Northern Ireland Executive etc.);

(*c*) any person employed in the civil service of the Crown, including Her Majesty's Diplomatic Service, Her Majesty's Overseas Civil Service, the civil service of Northern Ireland and the Northern Ireland Court Service;

(*d*) any member of the naval, military or air forces of the Crown, including any person employed by an association established for the purposes of the Reserve Forces Act 1980;

(*e*) any constable and any other person employed or appointed in or for the purposes of any police force (including a police force within the meaning of the Police Act (Northern Ireland) 1970);

(*f*) any person who is a member or employee of a prescribed body or a body of a prescribed class and either is prescribed for the purposes of this paragraph or belongs to a prescribed class of members or employees of any such body;

(*g*) any person who is the holder of a prescribed office or who is an employee of such a holder and either is prescribed for the purposes of this paragraph or belongs to a prescribed class of such employees.

(2) In this Act 'government contractor' means, subject to subsection (3) below, any person who is not a Crown servant but who provides, or is employed in the provision of, goods or services—

(*a*) for the purposes of any Minister or person mentioned in paragraph (*a*) or (*b*) of subsection (1) above, of any of the services, forces or bodies mentioned in that subsection or of the holder of any office prescribed under that subsection; or

(*b*) under an agreement or arrangement certified by the Secretary of State as being one to which the government of a State other than the United Kingdom or an international organisation is a party or which is subordinate to, or made for the purposes of implementing, any such agreement or arrangement.

(3) Where an employee or class of employees of any body, or of any holder of an office, is prescribed by an order made for the purposes of subsection (1) above—

(*a*) any employee of that body, or of the holder of that office, who is not prescribed or is not within the prescribed class; and

(*b*) any person who does not provide, or is not employed in the provision of, goods or services for the purposes of the performance of those functions of the body or the holder of the office in connection with which the employee or prescribed class of employees is engaged,

shall not be a government contractor for the purposes of this Act.

[Official Secrets Act 1989, ss. 7, 8, 12.]

## 2. CONVENTIONAL RESTRAINTS

*Ministers keep secrets for conventional, rather than legal, reasons—the weight of tradition, loyalty to their colleagues, a desire not to inhibit future frank discussion, and the threat of dismissal. The Privy Councillor's oath does not provide a legal basis for confidentiality. That oath is as follows.*

You do swear by Almighty God to be a true and faithful Servant unto the Queen's Majesty, as one of Her Majesty's Privy Council. You will not know or understand of any manner of thing to be attempted, done, or spoken against Her Majesty's Person, Honour, Crown, or Dignity Royal, but you will lett and withstand the same to the uttermost of your Power, and either cause it to be revealed to Her Majesty Herself, or to such of Her Privy Council as shall advertise Her Majesty of the same. You will, in all things to be moved, treated, and debated in Council, faithfully and truly declare your Mind and Opinion, according to your Heart and Conscience; and will keep secret all Matters committed and revealed unto you, or that shall be treated of secretly in Council. And if any of the said Treaties or Counsels shall touch any of the Counsellors, you will not reveal it unto him, but will keep the same until such time as, by the

Consent of Her Majesty, or of the Council, Publication shall be made thereof. You will to your uttermost bear Faith and Allegiance unto the Queen's Majesty; and will assist and defend all Jurisdictions, Pre-eminences, and Authorities, granted to Her Majesty, and annexed to the Crown by Acts of Parliament, or otherwise, against all Foreign Princes, Persons, Prelates, States, or Potentates. And generally in all things you will do as a faithful and true Servant ought to do to Her Majesty.

SO HELP YOU GOD

1. The conventions currently governing the publication by former Ministers of memoirs and other works relating to their experience as Ministers were laid down in a statement made in the House of Commons on 1 August 1946 on behalf of the Prime Minister (Mr Attlee) by the Lord President of the Council (Mr Herbert Morrison). This was based on a memorandum by the Secretary of the Cabinet, Sir Edward Bridges, which Mr Attlee's Cabinet had approved. (Paragraphs 13, 14, 41, 42.)

2. The conventions established in 1946 have been maintained under successive Administrations and the Committee do not recommend modification of the principles then advocated. They do however draw out of the conventions certain specific working rules: and make recommendations as to the administrative structure which should condition the clearance of the ex-Minister's intended memoirs. The conventions are to be regarded as concessions made to the author, rather than as restrictions imposed on him. (Paragraphs 19, 38, 43.)

3. The author should be free to use his ministerial experience for the purpose of giving an account of his own work, subject to restrictions on three separate categories of information:

1. He must not reveal anything that contravenes the requirements of national security operative at the time of his proposed publication.
2. He must not make disclosures injurious to this country's relations with other nations.
3. He must refrain from publishing information destructive of the confidential relationships on which our system of government is based. In particular—

(*a*) In dealing with the experience that he has acquired by virtue of his official position, he should not reveal the opinions or attitudes of colleagues as to the Government business with which they have been concerned. That belongs to their stewardship, not to his. He may, on the other hand, describe and account for his own.

(*b*) He should not reveal the advice given to him by individuals whose duty it has been to tender him their advice or opinions in confidence. If he wishes to mention the burden or weight of such advice, it must be done without attributing individual attitudes to identifiable persons. Again, he will need to exercise a continuing discretion in any references that he makes to communications received by him in confidence from outside members of the public.

(*c*) He should not make public assessments or criticisms, favourable or unfavourable, of those who have served under him or those whose competence or suitability for particular posts he has had to measure as part of his official duties.

He may, however, regard the obligations concerned with confidential relationships (but not those concerned with national security and international relations) as lifted after the expiry of 15 years from the relevant events, though even beyond that point he should not reveal the advice tendered by individuals who are still members of the public services nor make public assessments or criticisms of them. (Paragraphs 45–7, 83, 85, 86.)

4. These restrictions leave him a wide latitude for the writing of an account of his stewardship. (Paragraph 87.)

5. The established principles of law do not provide a system which can protect and enforce those rules of reticence that the Committee regard as called for when ex-Ministers compose their memoirs of ministerial life. (Paragraph 65.)

6. Nor does legislation offer the right solution. (Paragraph 69.).

7. There can be no guarantee that, if the burden of compliance is left to rest on the free acceptance of an obligation of honour, there will never be an occasional rebel or an occasional breach; but so long as there remains a general recognition of the practical necessity of some rules and the importance of observing them, the Committee do not think that such transgressions, even though made the subject

of sensational publicity, should be taken as having shattered the fabric of a sensible system. (Paragraph 69.)

8. A Minister on taking and leaving office should have his attention drawn explicitly to his obligations in relation to memoirs. (Paragraphs 71, 72.)

9. A former Minister proposing to publish a work relating to his ministerial experience should submit the manuscript to the Secretary of the Cabinet. (Paragraphs 73–7.)

10. The Secretary of the Cabinet, acting at the request of the Prime Minister and on his behalf, should have duties of two kinds in relation to such a manuscript. (Paragraphs 77, 78.)

1. *To have it examined in respect of national security and the preservation of international relations and to transmit any objections to the author.* The author should have a right of reference to the Prime Minister but should accept the latter's decision as final. (Paragraph 79.)

2. *To offer views on the treatment of confidential relationships in the manuscript.* The author should pay careful attention to this advice but must take upon his own shoulders the responsibility for deciding what he is going to say. If he decides to publish material in spite of advice from the Secretary of the Cabinet, he should let the Secretary know what he proposes to do so that before publication there may be time for the Prime Minister to bring his own direct influence to bear upon the dispute, if he wishes to do so. (Paragraph 80.)

11. A former Minister who has kept a diary of his ministerial experience should give testamentary instructions to ensure that its publication does not flout the current understandings that his own ex-colleagues are likely to be observing. (Paragraph 99.)

12. Former members of the public services should be under the same obligation as former Ministers to submit their manuscripts for scrutiny with regard to national security and international relations, and to defer to the judgement of those carrying the immediate responsibilities in these fields. In the matter of confidential relationships, the principles which the Committee enunciate concerning publications by ex-Ministers, the obligations which they suggest should rest upon them, and the periods for which these obligations should be maintained, should all be reflected also in the rules governing the publication of memoirs and other works relating to

their official experience by former members of the public services. (Paragraphs 92, 93.)

[Appendix 2 of the Report of the Radcliffe Committee of Privy Councillors, Cmnd. 6386 (1976).]

THE PRIME MINISTER: The Report of the Committee of Privy Counsellors on Ministerial Memoirs, under the chairmanship of Lord Radcliffe, which was submitted to me at the end of December 1975, is being published today as Cmnd. 6386. I should like to express to Lord Radcliffe and his colleagues my appreciation of the careful and thorough study they have made and of the distinguished report which has emerged from it.

The Report makes comprehensive recommendations as to the rules and procedures which should govern the publication by former Ministers of memoirs relating to their period of office. The recommendations are firmly based on the present conventions as they have developed over the years, which the Committee argue should properly be regarded as concessions made to the author rather than as restrictions imposed upon him.

The Committee recommends that an author should be free to use his ministerial experience for the purpose of giving an account of his own work, subject to restrictions on three categories of information. The first two consist of information relating to national security and to this country's relations with other countries. In these areas, the Committee considers that information must be withheld from publication for however long may be necessary and that authors must be prepared to accept as final the judgment of the current Prime Minister as to what material it would be harmful to publish.

The third category consists of information destructive of the confidential relationships upon which our system of government is based. It includes information about the opinions or attitudes of colleagues regarding any Government business; advice tendered to Ministers in confidence by individual officials; and personnel matters.

The Committee recommends that authors should regard themselves as precluded from publishing information in these categories for a period of 15 years after the relevant events, or, in the case of advice by individual officials or comments upon their capabilities, until the persons concerned have completed their official careers if that is the longer period.

It would of course be open to former Ministers to publish memoirs at any time providing that they did not contain information falling within any of the three categories identified in the Report.

As regards enforcement of the proposed rules, the Committee does not consider that satisfactory machinery is provided by the law as it now stands. It does not recommend the enactment of legislation establishing a series of new offences, and instead recommends that compliance should be allowed to rest on the free acceptance by the individuals concerned of an obligation of honour. It proposes, however, that a Minister, on taking and leaving office, should have his attention drawn explicitly to his obligations in relation to memoirs; and that, as now, a former Minister proposing to publish a work relating to his ministerial experience should submit the manuscript to the Secretary of the Cabinet who, acting on behalf of the Prime Minister, should ascertain whether it conformed to the proposed rules.

The Committee also recommends that the principles it has enunciated concerning publications by ex-Ministers should be reflected in the rules governing the publication of memoirs and similar works by former members of the public services.

The Government, having considered the Report, have decided to accept the Committee's recommendations in full. They trust that they will also command general acceptance and observance. They agree that a voluntary code of conduct is preferable to new legislation on this matter, although, as the Committee noted, the sanctions of the Official Secrets Act or any legislation which may supersede it, and, in an exceptional case, of the civil law, will continue to be available. I shall be arranging for all present Ministers to be informed of the new arrangements and, as recommended in the Report, shall invite them to sign an appropriate declaration.

[The Prime Minister, Mr Harold Wilson, 903 H.C. Deb. *521–3* (written answers 22 January 1976).]

## 3. LEAKS

*Ministers frequently want their views to be known publicly so as to mobilize support for their views or so as to distance themselves from decisions with which they disagree. They achieve this by leaking information to journalists on condition that the source of the story is not named. 'Briefing' of journalists about government policy is supposed to be something different and acceptable.*

Briefing is what I do and leaking is what you do.

[Mr James Callaghan, evidence to the Franks Committee on Section 2 of the Official Secrets Act 1911, Cmnd. 5104 (1972), iv, 187.]

. . . The notorious leaks have emanated as much from Downing Street as from anywhere else. The press receives a very good service from Number 10, which is perhaps why so much of it is so uncritical.

[Pym, *Politics of Consent*, 18.]

Norman St John Stevas was regarded by Margaret as the chief leaker and he paid the penalty by getting the sack in her first reshuffle in January 1981. Number Ten let it be known that one of the reasons for his dismissal was these alleged indiscretions or breaches of confidence, an impression which Margaret appeared to reinforce in a television interview the next day. These comments prompted a letter from Norman, in which he sought 'to clarify' the position. Margaret then had no choice but to contradict the Downing Street version in her reply to Norman.

Shortly after this incident I had a long talk with her about the state of the Government. It was one of many efforts to try to get back into a reasonable working relationship. As I was leaving I said to her: 'I know you think I leak things to the Press, and yes I sometimes do, deliberately at times and by mistake on others. But, of course, so do you.'

'Oh no, Jim, I never leak.'

'Well, if you tell me that I must accept it, but in that case your officials and press people certainly leak for you.'

'Oh, that is quite wrong: they never know anything, so how could they leak?'

Either she was incredibly naive, which I have no reason to believe, or she thought I was, and I frankly doubt that. I believe she really didn't think in terms of 'leaks' herself at all—if she said it, then it had to be right: how could there be any question of a leak?

Although on many occasions I have heard her use strong invective against both press and broadcasting, she was undoubtedly the most adept Prime Minister at handling the right wing Press since the war. She had a marvellous press, they kept on her side right the way through in a way which no other Conservative Government had experienced. Both press and people found her new, refreshing and interesting. Her good looks, the fact that she was a woman—absolutely no doubt that women were proud of her—and her candour and directness appealed in a way others have not managed.

I think Margaret was mistaken to hand out honours to so many working broadcasters and journalists, and they were even more mistaken to accept. I cannot believe that it is good for a free and independent press or TV and radio service.

Margaret was very well served by Bernard Ingham, her press secretary. He had been in the Department of Employment, and was a former Labour council candidate. Everyone was surprised and delighted with this appointment. I cannot help feeling though that he was another of the left like Paul Johnson who, having decided to change sides, has moved right across the political spectrum. However, he certainly did not qualify as an intellectual: he was more in the mould of a political bruiser.

Margaret developed a technique of getting the right wing popular press to have a major lead story on some matter coming up for decision on Cabinet that morning. The headline would be along the lines of 'Battling Maggie Under Attack from Wets'. The issue would then be unfolded in terms of being pro- or anti-Maggie. The Cabinet would hold its discussion and everyone would say how shocking it was that there had been a leak that morning, which simply must not be repeated. An edict would go out that no one, but no one, was to give any indication of the decision which had been taken.

But, if the *Standard* didn't carry a headline that evening, the morning papers would certainly do so. In October 1980, at the time of the Cabinet discussion on public spending, the *Sun* proclaimed: 'Premier Margaret Thatcher routed the "wets" in her Cabinet yesterday in a major showdown over public spending. She waded into attack . . . .' This was not what had happened. So much for creating a united and cohesive team. When the *Sun* finally reported a month later that the Prime Minister and her Treasury team had not secured the cuts they had sought, its headline typified the view that Margaret was somehow separate from her own Government: 'Maggie At Bay: Tories baffled as the battle for £2 billion extra cuts is lost.'

[Prior, *Balance of Power*, 134–5.]

LORD JENKINS OF HILLHEAD: My Lords, the general case for this amendment has been most powerfully and persuasively made by the noble Lord, Lord Mishcon, and by my noble friend Lord Hutchinson of Lullington. I intervene briefly to make a single adjacent point. This amendment is even more tightly drafted than the equivalent amendment that I moved in Committee. I was struck when I moved that amendment by the solidity with which the Benches opposite upheld the importance of secrecy in certain affairs of government.

I have been away for some time and I was even more amazed last Saturday evening when, sitting in a foreign airport, I picked up for the first time for two or three days a copy of the *Independent*. I read an account of what had happened at Thursday's Cabinet meeting when the Secretary of·State for Wales Mr Peter Walker, having indulged in a rather controversial statement recently, had tried to intervene but had deliberately not been called by the Prime Minister. This struck me as very odd indeed. However, one knows that there can be leaks wholly unauthorised by any official source. In what was the well equipped airport lounge, I also picked up *The Times*, the *Daily Telegraph* and the *Guardian*. I read exactly the same story. This can only happen when there has been what is politely called 'briefing' but what might brutally be called leaking from a central official source; in other words, the spokesman for the Government.

It was a most extraordinary affair. I have known leaks from the Cabinet. We all have. Those leaks—even from Cabinets we have sat in—have indicated different views. But to have an officially presented commentary, almost as if it were a sporting event, of who tried to do such at what time, was not called, and why, is something that I have never known in the history of Cabinet government.

I hope that the Leader of the House the Lord Privy Seal, when he replies, will comment on this rather extraordinary state of affairs and that he will reassure us. The thought arises in my mind that there is a certain hypocrisy about a government being very concerned to impose great discipline upon relatively minor officials and yet using leaking on a scale which is unprecedented in our political history when it happens to suit the powers-that-be.

[506 H.L. Deb. 713–14 (18 April 1989).]

## 4. FORMER MINISTERS' MEMOIRS

### (1) THE RADCLIFFE GUIDELINES

[see above, p. 295]

### (2) CROWN COPYRIGHT IN CABINET PAPERS

*Cabinet documents are the property of the Crown. Reproduction of them can, therefore, breach the Crown's copyright.*

### (3) ACCESS TO CABINET PAPERS

How then is there any continuity of policy or any profiting from past experience?

In the first place, there are three categories of papers which are generally regarded as excepted from the convention:

(i) Papers which, even if not publicly available can be deemed to be in the public domain, e.g. letters sent by former Ministers to trade associations, trade unions, etc., or to Members of Parliament about constituency cases, or to members of the public.

(ii) Papers, other than genuinely personal messages, dealing with matters which are known to foreign governments, *e.g.* messages about inter-governmental negotiations.

(iii) Written Opinions of the Law Officers, which are essentially legal rather than political documents.

Papers in all three categories may, if necessary in the interests of continuity, be shown to succeeding administrations. That does, however, leave a large area where the national interest requires some continuity of policy (or at least knowledge of what has happened before) and where it would be unreasonable to expect new Ministers to start with a clean sheet . . .

Since, as I say, the conventions are neither a matter of law nor static, no formal or exact definition of them exists. A careful reading of the debate in the House of Commons on July 8 and other publicly available sources suggests that a current formulation would be as follows:

(i) Current Ministers may not see the Cabinet papers of former Ministers of a different political party. Nor may they see other papers (except in a few well-defined categories) giving the unpublished views or comments of their predecessors or the advice submitted to them.

(ii) Current Ministers may normally see the papers of former Ministers of the same political party provided the need to do so arises in the course of their current ministerial duties. There could be exceptional circumstances in which it might be appropriate first to seek the agreement of the former Prime Minister concerned.

(iii) Before affording access to the Cabinet papers or other ministerial documents of a previous Government (whether of the same political party or not) to anyone not otherwise entitled to see them, the current Prime Minister would seek the agreement of the former Prime Minister concerned or, if he were not available, the current leader of his party.

Furthermore, since documents of a previous Administration are retained in Government departments subject to these conventions, it follows that:

(*a*) Former Ministers may have access to, but not retain, any documents which they saw when in office;

(*b*) officials have a duty to provide present Ministers with all relevant information about departmental policy or past events subject to not disclosing the personal views or comments of previous Ministers or the advice submitted directly to them.

[Lord Hunt of Tamworth, 'Access to a Previous Government's Papers' [1982] *Public Law* 514 at 516–18.]

# [5]

# MINISTERS AND DEPARTMENTS

## Ministers

### 1. WHAT IS A 'MINISTER'?

#### (1) STATUTORY DEFINITION

In this Act—

'Minister of the Crown' means the holder of an office in Her Majesty's Government in the United Kingdom, and includes the Treasury, the Board of Trade and the Defence Council.

[Ministers of the Crown Act 1975, s. 8(1).]

#### (2) GENERAL DEFINITION

*A Minister is a Member of Parliament or peer who is a member of the party (or one of the parties) which forms the government of the day and who is appointed to and removed from political office by the Sovereign on the Prime Minister's advice (or, in the case of junior Ministers, by the Prime Minister directly).*

### 2. GROUPS OF MINISTERIAL TITLES

#### (1) THE HISTORICAL OFFICES

*This group includes the offices of Prime Minister (on which see chapter 3), Lord Chancellor, Lord President of the Council, Lord Privy Seal, Chancellor of the Duchy of Lancaster, and Paymaster General. It also includes the office of Secretary of State.*

The Lord Chancellor (Rt Hon The Lord Mackay of Clashfern) is responsible for promoting general reforms in the civil laws for the procedure of the civil courts and for the administration of the Supreme Court (Court of Appeal, High Court and Crown Court) and county courts in England and Wales; the Lands Tribunal; the Pensions Appeal Tribunal; the Special Commissioners of Income Tax; the Social Security Commissioners; the VAT Tribunals; the Immigration Appellate Authorities and for the legal aid scheme. He is responsible for advising the Crown on the appointment of judges and certain other officers and is himself responsible for the appointment of Masters and Registrars of the High Court, District and County Court Registrars and Magistrates. He is responsible for ensuring that letters patent and other formal documents are passed in the proper form under the Great Seal of the Realm, of which he is the custodian . . .

The Lord President of the Council and Leader of the House of Commons (Rt Hon John Wakeham MP) has responsibility for the work of the Privy Council Office. As Leader of the House of Commons, he is responsible for planning and supervising the Government's legislative programme. He upholds the rights and privileges of the House as a whole, and in this capacity it falls to him to move Motions relating to the procedure of the House . . .

The Lord Privy Seal and Leader of the House of Lords (Rt Hon The Lord Belstead JP DL). As Leader of the House of Lords, he is responsible for the arrangement of Government business in the House and has a responsibility to the House itself to advise it on procedural matters and other difficulties as they arise . . .

The Chancellor of the Duchy of Lancaster and Minister of Trade and Industry (Rt Hon Antony Newton OBE MP). The Chancellor speaks for the Department in the House of Commons and has responsibility for the conduct of Departmental business in the House of Commons. He is the Cabinet Minister most concerned with: Inner Cities; the market for iron, steel and other industrial materials; engineering markets; consumer markets; vehicle markets (except for the sale of Rover shares); European R and D issues; intellectual property; regional policy, inward investment and financial assistance under the Industry Act; general policy towards nationalised industries; policy on British Steel (except privatisation), British Shipbuilders, British Technology Group and the Post Office; consumer protection and information; the Estate Agents Act; consumer safety; trading standards and trade descriptions; weights and measures; hallmarking; Nationalised Industries Consumer Councils; Citizens Advice Bureaux; advertising and public relations. In addition to his Departmental responsibilities, the Chancellor of the Duchy has overall responsibility supporting the Prime Minister for the co-ordination and presentation of the Government's inner cities policy. He is also responsible for Duchy of Lancaster business . . .

The Paymaster General (Rt Hon Peter Brooke MP) deals with European Community business, including UK Membership of the Budget Council; Civil Service Pay, personnel management, recruitment and industrial relations; the Royal Mint; the Central Computer and Telecommunications Agency; the Paymaster General's Office; Profit-related pay; charities (non-tax aspects); Treasury interest in general accounting issues not covered by specific responsibilities of other Ministers; and assistance to the Chief Secretary on public sector efficiency matters.

*The responsibilities of the Chancellor of the Duchy were altered in July 1989 when the holder, again, was made Chancellor of the Conservative Party Organization.*

[*List of Ministerial Responsibilities* (Cabinet Office, 1989, 13, 16, 19, 22.]

5.—In any Act, unless the contrary intention appears, words and expressions listed in Schedule 1 to this Act are to be construed according to that Schedule.
. . . 'Secretary of State' means one of Her Majesty's Principal Secretaries of State . . .

[Interpretation Act 1978, s. 5 and Schedule 1.]

*The office of a new Secretary of State can be created by an act of the royal prerogative, but the usual practice is to legislate by statutory instrument to make him a corporation sole, and to provide for his powers and duties (see below, p. 337.) The total number of paid Secretaries of State cannot exceed 21: Ministerial and other Salaries Act 1975, s. 1(1)(a) (see below, pp. 320, 323).*

## (2) THE LAW OFFICERS

The Attorney General (The Rt Hon Sir Patrick Mayhew, QC, MP) has overall responsibility for the work of the Departments (the

Treasury Solicitor's Department, the Crown Prosecution Service, the Serious Fraud Office and the Legal Secretariat to the Law Officers). He has a specific statutory duty to superintend the discharge of their duties by the Director of Public Prosecutions (who is the head of the Crown Prosecution Service) and the Director of the Serious Fraud Office. The Director of Public Prosecutions for Northern Ireland is also responsible to the Attorney General for the performance of his functions.

The Attorney-General is the Government's principal legal adviser; he deals with questions of law arising on Bills, and with issues of legal policy; he is concerned with all major international and domestic litigation involving the Government; and he has specific responsibilities for the enforcement of the criminal law.

The Solicitor General (Sir Nicholas Lyell QC MP) is responsible for such matters as the Attorney General delegates to him from time to time, and shares with him the handling of matters referred to the Law Officers by Members of Parliament.

The Law Officers answer in the House of Commons on matters for which the Lord Chancellor is responsible . . . and the Lord Chancellor answers in the House of Lords on matters for which the Law Officers are responsible.

[*List of Ministerial Responsibilities*, 12.]

'I hope', said Harold Macmillan, 'that you may consider joining my administration as Solicitor General.' I opened my mouth to reply. He raised his hand, a pale hand with long sensitive fingers, its palm toward me.

'But before you give me your answer I must remind you of the special position of the Law Officers, who are the last, the sole survivors in the long line of public servants of the Crown who sit in the House of Commons.' I swallowed back my words of acceptance and was honoured by a scholarly review of mediaeval office holders, a review which flowed into the sixteenth and seventeenth centuries, embraced approvingly the career of Samuel Pepys, and concluded with the admonition that the loyalties of a Law Officer must be first to the Crown, second to Parliament, and only thirdly, almost incidentally, to the administration. And now, concluded the Prime Minister, would I do him the honour of joining his administration as Solicitor General?

I certainly would . . .

In government the pressure of events is always so great that there is never time to stand aside and reflect. It is only when 'recollected in tranquillity' that it is possible to assess what actually happened or, more important, what ought to have happened. Only much later, looking back after nearly twenty years, can I now see that the historical and traditional concept of the Law Officers' role on which Harold Macmillan had lectured me in 1962 was, even in my time, coming to the end of its long and honourable life. Recent developments have confirmed that the ancient conception of the office no longer accords with the style and the demands of modern government.

The traditional role of the Attorney General was that of Counsel to the government. In the nineteenth century he still came from his chambers in the Temple to the Cabinet and gave his advice. He would then withdraw and return to his private law practice. He and not the Lord Chancellor was, as he still remains, the constitutional adviser on law to the Cabinet. He held only a retainer from the Crown and he still engaged in private practice. That custom ended earlier this century, but it was only after the Second World War in Hartley Shawcross's time that the Attorney began to be paid a full ministerial salary in lieu of the retainer and brief fees which he had hitherto received for appearing for the Crown in court and for the legal Opinions which he gave to ministers.

For the Law Officer faithfully to execute his responsibilities to the Crown, as opposed to those required of him by the administration of which he is a member, he must be regularly in court. But when he is in court he is not immediately available for consultation by ministers, and they find that inconvenient. Even in the early 1970s it was beginning to be put about that the Attorney, like all ministers, should put the convenience and the interests of the administration before that of any other. Even in those years irritation if not exasperation used to be delicately conveyed down the wire from Whitehall to my chambers in the Law Courts whenever I as Attorney was in court and not at immediate beck and call. Over the past decade and a half that attitude within government has grown, with more and more talk about the need to shift the priorities in the Attorney's duties from their Crown to their ministerial character. To mark this change it was suggested that the Law Officers' Department should leave its present quarters in the Royal Courts of Justice in the Strand and be brought to an office in Whitehall, a move which would not only be administratively convenient but would also significantly mark the definitive change in the character of the office . . .

The less and less frequent appearances of the Law Officers in the courts over the past fifteen years confirms the change in the service which they are now required to provide. This withdrawal from regular appearance in the courts signifies the end to the old tradition. In these circumstances, the Attorney ought, in this new situation, to retire from his position as titular Head of the Bar and if he has become merely a ministerial legal adviser who no longer appears in court, he has no intrinsic need even to hold the rank of Queen's Counsel. He would then necessarily have to give up his quasi-judicial responsibility for criminal prosecutions and his task as the guardian of the public interest. In effect the old office will have been abolished . . .

That all this has gone unchallenged must have been greeted with immense satisfaction in Whitehall. Quietly and without fanfare, there has been brought about not so much reform as revolution in the role of the traditional Law Officers of the Crown. For Whitehall has at last succeeded in clearing the way to transform them into ministerial legal servants, government legal eunuchs. The post of Lord Chancellor has become that of just another political bureaucrat in the Cabinet which is open in the future to any minister with some knowledge of law, while those of the Attorney and Solicitor Generals have been transformed into that of tame legal consultants to their master or mistress, the Prime Minister. It has been neatly accomplished, and without any debate either in Parliament or the profession over whether the eunuchs will give a better service to the administration of the law. But sooner or later this part of the Thatcher revolution in government will require to be legitimized. Over the political horizon, for better or for worse, there must now loom the spectre of a unified Ministry of Justice, with its ministerial head just another post for political careerists . . .

[Lord Rawlinson, *A Price Too High* (London, 1989), 4, 237, 238, 241.]

## (3) MINISTERS OF STATE

9.—(1) In this Act—

'Minister of State' means a member of Her Majesty's Government in the United Kingdom who neither has charge of any public department nor holds any other of the offices specified in Schedule 2 to this Act or any office in respect of which a salary is payable out of money provided by Parliament under section 3 (1) (*b*) of the Ministerial and other Salaries Act 1975 . . .

[House of Commons Disqualification Act 1975, s. 9(1).]

*In 1990 there were 24 Ministers of State. Many have been accorded 'courtesy titles' so as to indicate more clearly what their day-to-day departmental duties entail.*

Minister of State, Privy Council Office (Minister for the Arts)
Ministers of State, Foreign and Commonwealth Office
  Minister for Overseas Development
Ministers of State, Home Office
Minister of State, Welsh Office
Ministers of State, Ministry of Defence
  Minister of State for Defence Procurement
  Minister of State for the Armed Forces
Minister of State, Department of Employment
Minister of State, Northern Ireland Office
Ministers of State, Department of the Environment
  Minister for Local Government
  Minister for Housing, Environment and Countryside
  Minister for Water and Planning
Minister of State, Department of Trade and Industry
  Minister for Trade
Minister of State, Department of Education and Science
Minister of State, Department of Health
Ministers of State, Scottish Office
Minister of State, Department of Transport
  Minister for Public Transport
Minister of State, Department of Social Security
  Minister for Social Security
Minister of State, Department of Energy

[Source: *Hansard*.]

## (4) PARLIAMENTARY UNDER-SECRETARIES OF STATE

In this Act—

. . .

'Parliamentary Secretary' includes a person holding Ministerial office (however called) as assistant to a Member of Her Majesty's Government in the United Kingdom, but not having departmental responsibilities.

[House of Commons Disqualification Act 1975, s. 9(1).]

*Parliamentary Under-Secretaries of State (so styled if the ministerial head of department is a Secretary of State) or Parliamentary Secretary (if his chief is not a Secretary of State) give parliamentary and departmental help to a Minister of State; most Parliamentary Under-Secretaries are given responsibility for particular areas of government.*

## (5) GOVERNMENT WHIPS

*Every government will have about 20 Whips. Whips are nominally either part of the Treasury team or part of the Queen's Household. The titles are as follows:*

*Commons*
Parliamentary Secretary to the Treasury (Chief Whip)
Lords Commissioners of the Treasury (Government Whips; currently 5)
Treasurer of H.M.'s Household
Comptroller of H.M.'s Household
Vice-Chamberlain
Assistant Whips (currently 5)

*Lords*
Captain of the Honourable Corps of Gentlemen at Arms (Chief Whip)
Captain of the Queen's Bodyguard of the Yeomen of the Guard
Lords in Waiting (Whips; currently 5)

## 3. MINISTERIAL ASSISTANTS

### (I) PARLIAMENTARY PRIVATE SECRETARIES

39. Parliamentary Private Secretaries occupy a special position which is not always understood by the general public, either at home or abroad. They are not members of the Government, and should be careful to avoid being spoken of as such. They are Private Members, and should therefore be afforded as great a liberty of action as possible; but their close and confidential association with Ministers necessarily imposes certain obligations on them, and has led to the generally accepted practice set out in the following paragraphs.

40. Ministers choose and appoint their own Parliamentary Private Secretaries. The Chief Whip should, however, be consulted about the choice of a Parliamentary Private Secretary; and in view of the special position which Parliamentary Private Secretaries occupy in relation to the Government, the Prime Minister's approval should also be sought before any such appointment is offered or announced.

41. Each Minister is responsible for ensuring that his Parliamentary Private Secretary is aware of the principles governing his behaviour in the House of Commons, as set out in the remainder of this paragraph. Parliamentary Private Secretaries should not make statements in the House or put Questions on matters affecting the Department with which they are connected. They should also exercise great discretion in any speeches or broadcasts which they may make outside the House, taking care not to make statements which appear to be made in an official or semi-official capacity, and bearing in mind at the same time that, however careful they may be to make it clear that they are speaking only as Private Members, they are nevertheless liable to be regarded as speaking with some of the authority which attaches to a member of the Government. Generally they must act with a sense of responsibility and with discretion; and they must not associate themselves with particular groups advocating special policies.

42. Since Parliamentary Private Secretaries are not members of the Government, official information given to them should be limited to what is strictly necessary for the discharge of their Parliamentary and political duties. They should not have access to

secret establishments or information graded secret or above except on the personal authority of the Prime Minister.

[*Questions of Procedure for Ministers* (1976 version), paras. 39–42.]

*There are currently over 40 P.P.S.s.*

## (2) PERSONAL ADVISERS

The general doctrine is of course that Ministers take political decisions and civil servants carry them out. Why then do we want political advisers? What can they do that Ministers cannot?

There are two reasons which have caused us to experiment in this way.

The first is the pressure of work on Ministers. In less hectic days Ministers were their own political advisers. To a large extent this is still true. A politician with decades of experience and accountable to his electors can only survive if he can scent the changes of mood in the country and in his Party. But the burdens of modern government as developed in our country, the immense volume of papers, the exhausting succession of departmental committees, of Party gatherings and meetings with outside interests make it almost impossible for him to carry out his departmental and political responsibilities and at the same time sustain a detailed analysis of all the various political nuances of policy. If he can keep on top of his own department's work he is doing very well, but he finds it increasingly difficult to play a constructive part in the collective business of the Government as a whole.

The second is the nature of our Civil Service. The British Civil Service takes a pride in its political impartiality. As a result—unlike for example the United States—political change does not mean drastic changes in the Civil Service. This gives our system a degree of continuity and stability which is often admired. The ability of senior civil servants to change and often reverse policies is achieved both by a genuine wish to serve the Government of the day to the best of their ability and also by a certain amount of contingency planning in a pre-electoral period based on a careful on-going study of the proposals of potential Governments.

This system has not been without its critics however. There are those who say that the social and educational background of senior Civil Servants remains too narrow and that the 'Whitehall mandarin', coming as he does from such a background and guaranteed stability and continuity in his office, can become isolated from changes of mood and structure in our society.

We have tried to meet these problems in two ways.

First we have established a Central Policy Review Staff—or think-tank as it is often called—to assist the Government in the identification and evaluation of priorities. It works mainly on issues submitted to it by the Cabinet, but has sufficient spare capacity to work on issues which it chooses for itself. It is involved in regular presentations to the Cabinet of synoptic views of Government strategy and detailed analysis of selected particular issues. The CPRS tries to divide its work between both short-term and long-term issues but has to struggle with Gresham's Law that consideration of today's problems drives out consideration of tomorrow's.

The CPRS is a small unit (15–20). It was set up by our predecessors but we have found it very valuable and have continued it.

Members of the CPRS are *not* political appointments. Half are civil servants secured for a short term of duty and half are outside appointments, again for a short number of years, recruited on a non-political basis and subject to strict civil service rules and disciplines. They are a young staff, drawn from the widest possible range of civil service departments and outside disciplines and experiences. They work with departments rather than separately but their papers and their conclusions are independently arrived at. Uniquely, they put their papers directly to Cabinet Committee meetings without going through the Minister, and are invited to speak to their papers.

The CPRS is located in the Cabinet Office and serves all Ministers collectively. Thus it helps greatly over the problem of busy departmental Ministers who have little time to think about their colleagues' policies. It projects an independent, objective analysis—and often an alternative view. But it is in no sense a 'party' organisation.

Accordingly when we came into office in March 1974 I authorised the appointment by Cabinet Ministers of Political Advisers. This is not of course a wholly new concept—previous administrations had brought in advisers from outside, normally chosen from political sympathisers—and even now we have only 30 such advisers spread around 15 departments. The increase is however of considerable significance and Political Advisers now play a definite role in our affairs.

Since a Political Adviser is the personal appointment of his Minister his specific role within any particular department will vary to some degree or another. His role will also depend on his particular background and experience.

Examples however are:

1. As a 'sieve' examining papers as they go to Ministers, drawing attention to problems and difficulties, especially ones having Party political implications or electoral considerations, and looking for 'landmines'—especially in politically sensitive areas.

2. As a 'deviller' chasing up Ministerial wishes, checking facts and research findings outside Whitehall, spotting obstacles and ensuring that particularly sensitive political points are dealt with in an appropriately sensitive way.

3. Medium- and long-term planning. Since the Adviser is not under the same pressure of political, Parliamentary or constituency work he has the time to prepare 'think pieces' for his Minister which can generate long-term policy thinking within the Department.

4. Contributions to policy planning within the Departments. Most Departments have planning groups looking at medium- and long-term problems. A Political Adviser is eminently suitable to contribute ideas at this early planning stage, particularly ones which are new, or at least outside the mainstream, originating from outside the Government machine, and perhaps running contrary to long-established departmental views. The Adviser can thus extend the range of options available to a Minister.

5. Liaison with the Party. This is an important function if Party and Government are not to 'grow away' from each other. Such liaison will involve close co-operation with the Party's own research departments.

6. Outside interest groups. The Adviser can ease the Minister's burden in contact with outside interest groups.

7. Speech writing and research.

It is for the Minister to decide what papers the Political Adviser sees and what work he does. Much depends on the Political Advisers' background. Some are 'ideas men' or academics: others are former Party officials with specialist knowledge of their areas: and others are recent graduates and young Party activists. They do not however normally see papers of a high security classification and their contributions are made within their departments. They do not attend interdepartmental official committees.

I have set up a special Policy Unit in my own office. This team, which I have deliberately kept small (now 7), is made up of people with expert knowledge of the fields of economic, industrial and social policy. They advise me directly on the immediate decisions to be made, whether in Cabinet or elsewhere, and on longer term issues and developments. They work closely with my Private Office staff as well as with the network of Special Advisers serving other Ministers and with the CPRS and Cabinet Secretariat, and keep in touch with thinking outside Government through contacts in universities, industry, trade unions and pressure groups.

The purpose of this Policy Unit is not only to bring in experts to extend the range of policy options from which the Government—and particularly the Prime Minister as head of the Government—has to choose. The Policy Unit was set up, and its members were selected, to provide a team with strong political commitment to advise on, propose and pursue policies to further the Government's political goals. For policies without politics are of no more use than politics without policies.

To sum up. The Political Adviser is an extra pair of hands, ears and eyes and a mind more politically committed and more politically aware than would be available to a Minister from the political neutrals in the established Civil Service. This is particularly true for a radical reforming party in government, since 'neutralism' may easily slip into conservatism with a small 'c'.

Problems have arisen, but much less than some predicted. They are usually problems:

(i) of relationships—with civil servants and, surprisingly perhaps more delicate, with other ministers—and
(ii) of confidentiality since not all Special Advisers are accustomed to Civil Service reticence with the media.

We are still in the early stages of this experiment and, in a typically British way, prefer to work out the problems as we go along. But we can say at this stage that these developments are worth-while. Three dozen Political Advisers are not going to overturn our powerful government machine—nor should we want them to. They can however make a distinctive contribution. The reason why they are successfully doing that is that the nature and value of that contribution—and its limitations—has been recognised by all concerned. Indeed, most regular senior Civil Servants have openly welcomed the experiment and are co-operating to make it a success.

[Harold Wilson, *The Governance of Britain* (London, 1976), Appendix V.]

THE PRIME MINISTER: Since May 1979 the following have served or are serving as special advisers or political advisers to Ministers:

*Special Advisers*

| | |
|---|---|
| Mr J. Hoskyns | Head of the No. 10 Policy Unit (and subsequently to the Secretary of State for Transport) |
| Mr N. Strauss | Special Adviser to the Prime Minister |
| Professor A. Walters | Economic Adviser to the Prime Minister |
| Mr F. Mount | Head of the No. 10 Policy Unit |
| Sir Anthony Parsons | Foreign Affairs Adviser to the Prime Minister |
| Mr J. Redwood | No. 10 Policy Unit (currently Head of the Policy Unit) |
| Sir Percy Cradock | Foreign Affairs Adviser to the Prime Minister |
| Mr P. Shipley | No. 10 Policy Unit |
| Hon. C. Monckton | No. 10 Policy Unit |
| Mr O. Letwin | No. 10 Policy Unit |
| Mr D. Hobson | No. 10 Policy Unit |
| Mrs C. Ryder | Personal Assistant to the Prime Minister |
| Dame Felicity Yonge | Chief Whip |
| Mr D. Howe | Paymaster General (and subsequently to Lord President of the Council) |
| Mr G. Cardona | Financial Secretary, Treasury |
| Mr P. Cropper | Chief Secretary, Treasury (and subsequently to Paymaster General) |
| Mr R. Shepherd | Secretary of State for Employment (and subsequently Secretary of State for Northern Ireland) |
| Professor R. Dyson | Secretary of State for Social Services |
| Mr I. Heggie | Secretary of State for Transport |
| Mr D. Young | Secretary of State for Industry |
| Mr D. French | Chief Secretary, Treasury |
| Mr S. Sherbourne | Secretary of State for Industry |
| Mr E. Berman | Secretary of State for the Environment |
| Dr L.Rouse | Secretary of State for Energy (and subsequently Financial Secretary, Treasury) |
| Miss A. Ward | Chief Whip |

| | |
|---|---|
| Mr R. Lord | Chief Secretary, Treasury |
| Mr M. Portillo | Financial Secretary, Treasury |
| Mr A. Ridley | Chancellor of the Exchequer |
| Mrs K. Ramsay | Secretary of State for Transport |
| Mr C. G. Mockler | Secretary of State for the Environment |
| Sir R. Cooke | Secretary of State for the Environment |
| Mr N. True | Secretary of State for Social Services |
| Mr R. D. R. Harris | Home Secretary |
| Mr E. Bickham | Secretary of State for Northern Ireland |
| Mr J. Houston | Secretary of State for Foreign and Commonwealth Affairs |
| Mr S. Sexton | Secretary of State for Education and Science |
| Mr M. Dobbs | Secretary of State for Trade and Industry |
| Mr C. Butler | Secretary of State for Wales |
| Professor Sir Sam Edwards | Secretary of State for Energy |
| Mr J. Sterling | Secretary of State for Trade and Industry |
| Mr R. Ehrman | Secretary of State for Employment |
| Mr T. Baron | Secretary of State for the Environment |

Special advisers are civil servants and their terms of appointment are similar to those of other civil servants and they are subject to the same rules of conduct (including paragraphs 9870 and 9874 of the Civil Service code) apart from certain exceptions which reflect the special nature of their role.

## *Political Advisers*

### *No. 10 Downing Street*

| | |
|---|---|
| Mr D. Wolfson | Chief of Staff |
| Mr R. Ryder | Political Secretary |
| Mr S. Sherbourne | Political Secretary |
| Professor Sir Douglas Hague | Political Adviser |
| Miss C. M. Stevens | Personal Assistant |

### *Department of Employment*

Mr R. Gilbert (part-time)

Political advisers are not civil servants and are not paid from public funds. Although the provisions of the Civil Service code are not generally appropriate, political advisers are required to avoid conflicts of interest between their work for Ministers and their private and business affairs.

*Efficiency Adviser*

In addition, Lord Rayner and Sir Robin Ibbs have held the appointment of adviser on efficiency.

[The Prime Minister, Mrs Margaret Thatcher, 58 H.C. Deb. *155–6* (written answers 10 April 1984).]

## 4. MINISTERS' PAY

1.—(1) Subject to the provisions of this Act—

(*a*) there shall be paid to the holder of any Ministerial office specified in Schedule 1 to this Act such salary as is provided for by that Schedule; and

(*b*) there shall be paid to the Leaders and Whips of the Opposition such salaries as are provided for by Schedule 2 to this Act.

(2) There shall be paid to the Lord Chancellor a salary (which shall be charged on and paid out of the Consolidated Fund of the United Kingdom) at such rate as together with the salary payable to him as Speaker of the House of Lords will amount to £20,000 a year, but so that the salary payable to a Lord Chancellor under this subsection shall be abated by the amount of any pension payable to him in respect of any public office in the United Kingdom or elsewhere to which he had previously been appointed or elected.

(3) There shall be paid to the Speaker of the House of Commons a salary (which shall be charged on and paid out of the Consolidated Fund of the United Kingdom) of £13,000 a year; and on a dissolution of Parliament the Speaker of the House of Commons at the time of the dissolution shall for this purpose be deemed to remain Speaker until a Speaker is chosen by the new Parliament.

(4) Her Majesty may from time to time by Order in Council substitute another figure for that given by subsection (2) or (3) above or by Schedule 1 or 2 to this Act as the annual amount, or as the case may be the maximum or minimum annual amount, of any salary; but no recommendation shall be made to Her Majesty to make an Order in Council under this subsection unless a draft of the Order has been approved by resolution of each House of Parliament or, if it relates only to the salary to be paid to the Speaker of the House of Commons under subsection (3) above, by resolution of that House.

(5) A person to whom any salary is payable under subsection (1) above shall be entitled to receive only one such salary, but if he is the holder of two or more offices in respect of which a salary is so payable and there is a difference between the salaries payable in respect of those offices, the office in respect of which a salary is payable to him shall be that in respect of which the highest salary is payable . . .

3.—(1) The salaries payable under section 1(1)(*a*) of this Act shall be paid out of money provided by Parliament and, in the case of those payable in respect of the following offices, that is to say—

(*a*) Treasurer, Comptroller and Vice-Chamberlain of Her Majesty's Household; and

(*b*) Captain of the Honourable Corps of Gentlemen-at-Arms, Captain of the Queen's Bodyguard of the Yeomen of the Guard and Lord in Waiting;

shall be paid out of money so provided as part of the expenses of the Treasury.

(2) The sums payable out of money provided by Parliament in respect of the salary of the Chancellor of the Duchy of Lancaster shall be reduced by the amount of the salary payable to him otherwise than out of moneys so provided in respect of his office.

(3) The salaries payable under section 1(1)(*b*) of this Act shall be charged on and payable out of the Consolidated Fund of the United Kingdom . . .

## SCHEDULE 1

### MINISTERIAL SALARIES

*Office* — *Salary [Amounts not reproduced]*

Part I

Prime Minister and First Lord of the Treasury
Chancellor of the Exchequer
Secretary of State
Minister of Agriculture, Fisheries and Food
Any of the following offices for so long as the holder is a member of the Cabinet:

(*a*) Lord President of the Council;
(*b*) Lord Privy Seal;

(*c*) Chancellor of the Duchy of Lancaster;
(*d*) Paymaster General;
(*e*) Chief Secretary to the Treasury;
(*f*) Parliamentary Secretary to the Treasury;
(*g*) Minister of State.

Part II

1. Any of the offices listed at (*a*) to (*g*) in Part I above for so long as the holder is not a member of the Cabinet

2. Minister in charge of a public department of Her Majesty's Government in the United Kingdom who is not a member of the Cabinet and who is not eligible for a salary under any other provision of this Act

3. Financial Secretary to the Treasury

Part III

Attorney-General
Lord Advocate
Solicitor General
Solicitor General for Scotland

Part IV

Captain of the Honourable Corps of Gentlemen-at-Arms
Parliamentary Secretary other than Parliamentary Secretary to the Treasury
Captain of the Queen's Bodyguard of the Yeoman of the Guard
Treasurer of Her Majesty's Household
Lord in Waiting
Comptroller of Her Majesty's Household
Vice-Chamberlain of Her Majesty's Household
Junior Lord of the Treasury
Assistant Whip, House of Commons

Part V

1.—(1) The salary to be paid to the holder of any office mentioned above in this Schedule shall be of the annual amount stated in relation to that office in column 2 or, as the case may be, of such annual amount not more than the upper figure or less than the lower figure so stated as the First Lord of the Treasury may determine.

(2) The date on which the holder of any office listed at (*a*) to (*g*) in Part I above becomes or ceases to be a member of the Cabinet shall be notified in the London Gazette, and any such notification (whether before or after the passing of this Act) shall be conclusive evidence for the purposes of this Schedule.

2.—In the case of the following offices a salary may be paid to more than one holder of the office at the same time, subject to the limitations expressed below, that is to say—

(*a*) Secretary of State, so long as not more than 21 salaries are paid at the same time in accordance with Part I above;
(*b*) Minister of State, so long as not more than 50 salaries are paid at the same time in accordance with Parts I and II above;
(*c*) Parliamentary Secretary other than Parliamentary Secretary to the Treasury, so long as not more than 83 salaries are paid at the same time in accordance with Parts I and II above taken together with salaries to any Parliamentary Secretary in accordance with Part IV above;
(*d*) Junior Lord of the Treasury, so long as not more than 5 salaries are paid at the same time;
(*e*) Assistant Whip, House of Commons, so long as not more than 7 salaries are paid at the same time;
(*f*) Lord in Waiting, so long as not more than 5 salaries are paid at the same time.

## SCHEDULE 2

### OPPOSITION LEADERS AND WHIPS

### Part I

| *Position* | *Salary* *[Amounts not reproduced]* |
| --- | --- |
| In the House of Commons— | |
| Leader of the Opposition | |
| Chief Opposition Whip | |
| Assistant Opposition Whips | |
| In the House of Lords— | |
| Leader of the Opposition | |
| Chief Opposition Whip | |

### Part II

1. The salary to be paid to any of the persons mentioned above in this Schedule shall be of the annual amount stated in relation to that person in column 2.

2. In the case of the Assistant Opposition Whips in the House of Commons, salaries may be paid to not more than 2 at the same time.

3. No salary shall be payable in accordance with this Schedule to a person who is in receipt of a pension under section 26 (1) (past Prime Ministers) of the Parliamentary and other Pensions Act 1972.

[Ministerial and other Salaries Act 1975, ss. 1, 3, Schedules 1, 2.]

*The Ministerial and other Salaries Order 1989, S.I. 1989 No. 1000, and the Lord Chancellor's Salary Order 1989, S.I. 1989 No. 1088, are the current Orders. The effect of them is as follows:*

| Title | Total annual salary (£) |
|---|---|
| Prime Minister | 66,851 |
| Lord Chancellor | 91,500 |
| Cabinet Minister (Commons) | 55,221 |
| Cabinet Minister (Lords) | 44,591 |
| Minister of State (Commons) | 44,951 |
| Minister of State (Lords) | 39,641 |
| Parliamentary Secretary (Commons) | 38,961 |
| Parliamentary Secretary (Lords) | 33,241 |
| Attorney-General | 57,421 |
| Solicitor-General | 50,701 |
| Lord Advocate | 44,661 |
| Solicitor-General for Scotland | 39,109 |
| Government Chief Whip | 49,331 |
| Government Whips | 36,091 |

*Note:* Mrs Thatcher draws the same salary as a Cabinet Minister.

## Departments

### 1. DEFINITION

*A department of state is headed by a Minister, is staffed by civil servants, and is charged, through the Minister, with recommending policies to the Cabinet; and when those policies have been approved there (and perhaps by Parliament) the department has the task of implementing the details of those policies.*

## (1) DEPARTMENTS MERGED SINCE 1900
(dates of creation in parentheses)

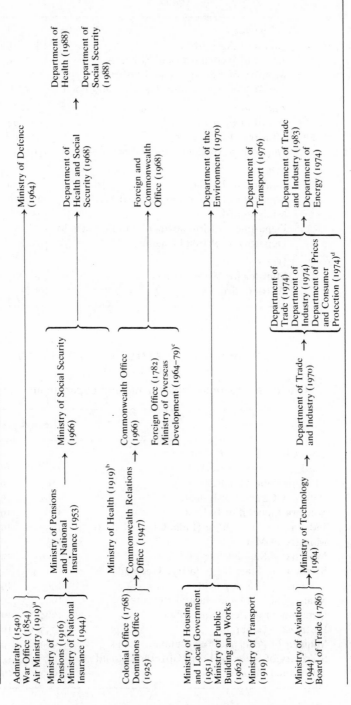

| | | | | | |
|---|---|---|---|---|---|
| Admiralty (1540)<br>War Office (1854)<br>Air Ministry (1919)[a] | → | | | Ministry of Defence (1964) | |
| Ministry of Pensions (1916)<br>Ministry of National Insurance (1944) | → Ministry of Pensions and National Insurance (1953) | → Ministry of Social Security (1966) | | → Department of Health and Social Security (1968) | → Department of Health (1988)<br>Department of Social Security (1988) |
| | Ministry of Health (1919)[b] | | | | |
| Colonial Office (1768)<br>Dominions Office (1925) | → Commonwealth Relations Office (1947) | → Commonwealth Office (1966)<br>Foreign Office (1782)<br>Ministry of Overseas Development (1964–79)[c] | | → Foreign and Commonwealth Office (1968) | |
| Ministry of Housing and Local Government (1951)<br>Ministry of Public Building and Works (1962) | → | | | Department of the Environment (1970) | |
| Ministry of Transport (1919) | → | | | Department of Transport (1976) | |
| Ministry of Aviation (1944)<br>Board of Trade (1786) | → Ministry of Technology (1964) | → Department of Trade and Industry (1970) | → Department of Trade (1974)<br>Department of Industry (1974)<br>Department of Prices and Consumer Protection (1974)[d] | → Department of Trade and Industry (1983)<br>Department of Energy (1974) | |

[a] Air Board (1917); Air Council (1918)
[b] Local Government Board to 1919.
[c] Merged into FCO 1979.
[d] Merged into DTI 1979.

## (2) CHANGES IN TITLES OF UNMERGED DEPARTMENTS SINCE 1900

| | |
|---|---|
| *Agriculture* | |
| Board of Agriculture | 1889–1903 |
| Board of Agriculture and Fisheries | 1903–19 |
| Ministry of Agriculture and Fisheries | 1919–55 |
| Ministry of Agriculture, Fisheries and Food | 1955– |
| *Education* | |
| Board of Education | 1900–44 |
| Ministry of Education | 1944–64 |
| Department of Education and Science[a] | 1964– |
| *Employment* | |
| Ministry of Labour | 1916–39 |
| Ministry of Labour and National Service | 1939–59 |
| Ministry of Labour | 1959–68 |
| Department of Employment and Productivity | 1968–70 |
| Department of Employment | 1970– |
| *Wales* | |
| Minister for Welsh Affairs | 1951–64 |
| Welsh Office | 1964– |

[a] Minister for Science 1959–64.

## (3) MAIN DEPARTMENTS AND TITLES ABOLISHED

(excluding wartime departments and departments merged)

| | Created | Abolished |
|---|---|---|
| Lord Chancellor of Ireland | 1801 | 1922 |
| Lord Lieutenant of Ireland | 1801 | 1922 |
| Chief Secretary for Ireland | 1801 | 1922 |
| Attorney-General of Ireland | 1801 | 1922 |
| Solicitor-General of Ireland | 1801 | 1922 |
| India and Burma Office (India Office 1858–1937) | 1837 | 1948 |
| Ministry of Materials | 1951 | 1954 |
| Ministry of Supply | 1939 | 1959 |
| Secretary of State for Industry, Trade and Regional Development | 1963 | 1964 |
| Ministry of Land and Natural Resources | 1964 | 1967 |
| Department of Economic Affairs | 1964 | 1967 |
| Postmaster-General | 1655 | 1969 |
| Minister of Posts and Telecommunications | 1969 | 1970 |
| Secretary of State for Local Government and Regional Planning | 1969 | 1970 |

### *1. A New Style of Government: Aims*

This Administration has pledged itself to introduce a new style of government. More is involved than bringing forward new policies and programmes: it means resolving the issue of the proper sphere of government in a free society; and improving the efficiency of the machinery intended to achieve the aims it sets itself within that sphere.

2. This Administration believes that government has been attempting to do too much. This has placed an excessive burden on industry, and on the people of the country as a whole, and has also overloaded the government machine itself. Public administration and management in central government has stood up to these strains, but the weakness has shown itself in the apparatus of policy formulation and in the quality of many government decisions over the last 25 years.

3. The Government intend to remedy this situation. The review of governmental functions and organisation which has been carried out over the last four months is intended to lay the necessary foundations. The aims in that review have been:

(i) To improve the quality of policy formulation and decision-taking in government by presenting Ministers, collectively in Cabinet and individually within their departments, with well-defined options, costed where possible, and relating the choice between options to the contribution they can make to meeting national needs. This is not confined to new policies and new decisions, but implies also the continuing examination, on a systematic and critical basis, of the existing activities of government.

(ii) To improve the framework within which public policy is formulated by matching the field of responsibility of government departments to coherent fields of policy and administration.

(iii) To ensure that the government machine responds and adapts itself to new policies and programmes as these emerge, within the broad framework of the main departmental fields of responsibility.

The fulfilment of these aims will improve the efficiency of government. This does not mean an increase in State power, nor any sacrifice of humanity and compassion in public administration.

Indeed, the systematic formulation of policy and the presentation to Ministers of defined options for decision provides them with the opportunity for greater openness in government, and more responsiveness to the needs and wishes of the community and of individuals —in short, a new and better balance between the individual and the modern State. The Civil Service itself, as it is given clearer objectives and more sharply defined responsibilities, will find that the work of public administration will again become more satisfying and that relations with the public it serves will improve.

4. The Government also recognise that the enhanced degree of efficiency in government which will be achieved raises the issue of the effectiveness of the system of Parliamentary scrutiny. In this context, they intend to publish in the near future a Green Paper setting out their proposals for a revision of the structure of the Select Committee system.

5. This review differs fundamentally both in the depth of its aims and in the breadth of its scope from previous piecemeal changes in the pattern of departmental responsibilities. It has been concerned not merely with departmental boundaries but with the central mechanism by which public policy is made and carried out. The results will therefore be longer lasting and will remove the need for continual changes for a considerable period in the future. The product of this review will be less government, and better government, carried out by fewer people. Less government, because its activities will be related to a long-term strategy aimed at liberating private initiative and placing more responsibility on the individual and less on the State. It will be better government, because the tasks to be done will be better defined and fewer in number, requiring fewer Ministers and fewer civil servants to carry them out.

### *II. The Reorganisation of Government: Principles*

6. To translate these broad aims into applied principles of organisation entails changes both in the methods of operation between government departments and within departmental organisation itself.

#### The analytical approach

7. The basis of improved policy formulation and decision-taking is rigorous analysis of existing and suggested government policies, actions and expenditure. This analysis must test whether such

policies or activities accord with the Government's strategic aims and, indeed, whether they are suitable for government at all. And it must test whether they are of greater or lesser priority than other policies or activities at present carried out, or likely to be proposed in the future; what is the most efficient means of execution; and whether their long-term effects are likely to accord with Government priorities and policies as they develop.

The functional approach

8. Using the same approach to deal with the issue of the organisation of government departments, the object has been to ensure that the broad framework of the central machinery in terms of Ministerial and departmental functions complies with the Government's strategic policy objectives. In practical terms, this means the application of the functional principle as the basis for the allocation of responsibilities: government departments should be organised by reference to the task to be done or the objective to be attained, and this should be the basis of the division of work beween departments rather than, for example, dividing responsibility between departments so that each one deals with a client group.

9. The basic argument for this functional principle is that the purpose of organisation is to serve policy. And policy issues which are linked should be grouped together in organisational terms. Furthermore, such grouping of related functions clarifies the lines of demarcation between responsibilities and saves duplication of effort between departments. It achieves economies of scale and avoids the diffusion of expert knowledge and the difficulty of co-ordination which organisation by area or by client group would involve. This grouping of related functions in unified departments has become the more important with the increasing complexity of modern society and, therefore, of government.

10. The acceptance of the functional principle of organisation does not mean that there can be no departure from it if there are strong reasons for moderating its application. Thus, the functional principle does not invalidate the existing pattern whereby Scotland and Wales are treated separately. That they should have policy objectives as specific to them as to England is generally recognised in a number of fields. But within the Scottish Office and the Welsh Office the same functional principle for the division of work applies.

The unification of functions

11. The outcome of the Government's review, in terms of departmental organisation, is set out in paragraphs 18–42 below. The emphasis is on the grouping of functions together in departments with a wide span, so as to provide a series of fields of unified policy. This continues the trend towards unification of functions which has evolved in recent years and which may be seen, for example, in the Ministry of Defence and the Foreign and Commonwealth Office.

12. This offers a number of advantages:

(i) A capacity within such unified departments to propose and implement a single strategy for clearly defined and accepted objectives.

(ii) A capacity to explore and resolve conflicts both in policy formulation and executive decision within the line of management rather than by inter-departmental compromise.

(iii) A capacity to manage and control larger resource-consuming programmes, in terms both of formulation and administration, within departmental boundaries, making possible in turn more effective delegation of executive tasks.

(iv) The easier application of analytic techniques within large and self-contained blocks of work and expenditure.

(v) More direct identification to the community of the Ministers and departments responsible for defined functions, programmes and policies, more open communication between government and the public about these, and better opportunities to discuss and challenge them.

(vi) A capacity to contribute more effectively to the formulation and development of the Government's overall strategy.

13. But these advantages will be offset if issues which warrant inter-departmental discussion are decided within the new unified departments without collective discussion by Ministers. This places an additional responsibility on departments, as well as on those in the central staffs, to ensure that the collective responsibility of Ministers is not eroded. Indeed, the two issues go together. The advantages of the unification of functions set out above are largely aspects of a single concept—the desirability of the comprehensive approach in government organisation. A department unifying a group of functions will be less open to the risk of being parochial and will, therefore, be more answerable to Parliament and the commun-

ity at large. Equally it will have less need to fear for and defend its interests against other interests so that in the formative stages of policy it must and will be ready to discuss issues with other departments. In this way, the full range of facts and issues will be presented to Ministers for their collective decision.

14. The Government recognise that the mere aggregation of functions into a series of large departments would lead to problems of management because of the size and complexity of the top organisational apparatus. But these problems will be reduced by defining clearly the boundaries of the functional wings which will make up the large departments and the responsibilities, both Ministerial and official, of those who work in them. There will be a sustained effort to ensure that among those functions which remain a necessary part of central government, executive blocks of work will be delegated to accountable units of management, thus lessening the load on the departmental top management. These are, however, major changes and will take some time to bring about. Special attention will also be paid to the need to create within these large departments a satisfactory organisation for handling career planning and staff management.

### The decision-taking process

15. The Government have also considered the machinery for decision-taking at the centre. It is here that changes are necessary to assist Ministers in assessing the relative priorities of departmental programmes and policies. Such changes must be designed to remedy the major difficulty which faces government in a modern complex society, which cannot be solved by good administration and management alone. It is the problem of policy formulation and decision-taking: how Ministers can have before them at the right time all the necessary information and the analysis to enable them to take decisions. Thus, the necessary basis for good government is a radical improvement in the information system available to Ministers.

16. To provide this essential basis it is important that there should be a capability at the centre for assessment of policies and projects in relation to strategic objectives, and the steps the Government are taking to improve their machinery for this purpose are set out in paragraphs 43–52 below: they mark an important stage in the introduction of techniques which will assist Ministers in taking

decisions, with the presentation to them of the information on a basis free from purely departmental considerations as the essential feature.

Stability

17. The considerable changes of government organisation outlined below will provide a firm basis on which the new techniques and the new approach to government can be applied to questions of policy and administration. The Government do not foresee a further prolonged period of change and disturbance in the central machinery of government once the remaining issues outlined in later paragraphs of this White Paper are resolved. A period of stability is of the highest importance if the machinery and the staff who constitute it are to work efficiently and well. No organisational form remains valid for ever; but the main departmental structures as now outlined are intended and expected to remain valid for a long time to come. The further review of work by each department referred to in paragraphs 53–54 below will be assisted by the structural changes now being introduced.

[The Reorganization of Central Government, Cmnd. 4506 (1970), paras. 1–17.]

*The White Paper was followed by the setting up of the Department of Trade and Industry, the Department of the Environment, and the merger of the Ministry of Overseas Development into the Foreign and Commonwealth Office.*

## 3. MACHINERY OF GOVERNMENT: THE LAW

1.—(1) Her Majesty may by Order in Council—

(*a*) provide for the transfer to any Minister of the Crown of any function previously exercisable by another Minister of the Crown;

(*b*) provide for the dissolution of the government department in the charge of any Minister of the Crown and the transfer to or distribution among such other Minister or Ministers of the Crown as may be specified in the Order of any functions previously exercisable by the Minister in charge of that department;

(*c*) direct that functions of any Minister of the Crown shall be exercisable concurrently with another Minister of the Crown, or shall cease to be so exercisable.

(2) An Order in Council under this section may contain such incidental, consequential and supplemental provisions as may be necessary or expedient for the purpose of giving full effect to the Order, including provisions—

(*a*) for the transfer of any property, rights and liabilities held, enjoyed or incurred by any Minister of the Crown in connection with any functions transferred or distributed;
(*b*) for the carrying on and completion by or under the authority of the Minister to whom any functions are transferred of anything commenced by or under the authority of a Minister of the Crown before the date when the Order takes effect;
(*c*) for such adaptations of the enactments relating to any functions transferred as may be necessary to enable them to be exercised by the Minister to whom they are transferred and his officers;
(*d*) for making in the enactments regulating the number of offices in respect of which salaries may be paid or in section 2 of, and Schedule 2 to, the House of Commons Disqualification Act 1975 (which regulate the number of office holders who may be elected, and sit and vote, as members of the House of Commons), such modifications as may be expedient by reason of any transfer of functions or dissolution of a Department effected by the Order;
(*e*) for the substitution of the Minister to whom functions are transferred for any other Minister of the Crown in any instrument, contract, or legal proceedings made or commenced before the date when the Order takes effect.

(3) No modifications shall be made by virtue of paragraph (*d*) of subsection (2) above, in any of the enactments mentioned in that paragraph, so as to increase the amount of any salary which may be paid, or the aggregate number of persons to whom salaries may be paid, under those enactments or the aggregate number of persons capable thereunder of sitting and voting as Members of the House of Commons.

(4) Where by any Order made under this section provision is

made for the transfer of functions in respect of which any Minister may sue or be sued by virtue of any enactment, the Order shall make any provision which may be required for enabling the Minister to whom those functions are transferred to sue or be sued in like manner.

(5) A certificate issued by a Minister of the Crown that any property vested in any other Minister immediately before an Order under this section takes effect has been transferred by virtue of the Order to the Minister issuing the certificate shall be conclusive evidence of the transfer.

Changes in departments of office of Secretary of State, or in their functions

2.—(1) Her Majesty may in connection with any change in the departments of the office of Secretary of State, or any change in the functions of a Secretary of State, by Order in Council make such incidental, consequential and supplemental provisions as may be necessary or expedient in connection with the change, including provisions—

(*a*) for making a Secretary of State a corporation sole,
(*b*) for the transfer of any property, rights or liabilities to or from the Secretary of State,
(*c*) for any adaptations of enactments relating to a Secretary of State, or to the department of a Secretary of State,
(*d*) for the substitution of one Secretary of State, or department of a Secretary of State, for another in any instrument, contract or legal proceedings made or commenced before the date when the Order takes effect.

(2) A certificate issued by a Minister of the Crown that any property vested in any other Minister immediately before an Order under this section takes effect has been transferred by virtue of the Order to the Minister issuing the certificate shall be conclusive evidence of the transfer.

(3) This section applies only to changes after 27th June 1974, and to the creation (in that year) of the Departments of Energy, Industry, Trade, and Prices and Consumer Protection.

Transfer of property etc. by or to Secretary of State

3.—(1) This section applies where any enactment (including an order under this Act) provides that a named Secretary of State and his successors shall be a corporation sole, and applies whether or not the office of corporation sole is for the time being vacant.

(2) Anything done by or in relation to any other Secretary of State for the named Secretary of State as a corporation sole shall have effect as if done by or in relation to the named Secretary of State.

(3) Without prejudice to the preceding provisions of this section, any deed, contract or other instrument to be executed by or on behalf of the named Secretary of State as a corporation sole shall be valid if under the corporate seal of that Secretary of State authenticated by the signature of any other Secretary of State, or of a Secretary to any department of a Secretary of State, or of a person authorised by any Secretary of State to act in that behalf.

Change of title of Ministers

4. If Her Majesty is pleased by Order in Council to direct that any change shall be made in the style and title of a Minister of the Crown, the Order may contain provisions substituting the new style and title—

(*a*) in the enactments (including those mentioned in section 1(2)(*d*) above) relating to the Minister;

(*b*) in any instrument, contract, or legal proceedings made or commenced before the date when the Order takes effect.

Supplementary provisions as to Orders

5.—(1) No Order in Council which provides for the dissolution of a government department shall be made under this Act unless, after copies of the draft thereof have been laid before Parliament, each House presents an Address to Her Majesty praying that the Order be made.

(2) An Order in Council under this Act, not being an Order made in pursuance of such an address as aforesaid, shall be laid before Parliament and shall be subject to annulment in pursuance of a resolution of either House of Parliament.

(3) Any Order under this Act may be varied or revoked by a subsequent Order thereunder made in the like manner and subject to the like conditions, so however that the variation or revocation of an Order providing for the dissolution of a government department shall not affect the dissolution thereof.

(4) No provision in any Act passed before 6th March 1946 shall be construed as limiting the powers conferred by this Act.

(5) Nothing in this Act shall prejudice any power exercisable by virtue of the prerogative of the Crown in relation to the functions of Ministers of the Crown.

(6) Any reference in the foregoing provisions of this Act to a Minister of the Crown shall include a reference to Ministers acting jointly.

Provisions applying to certain Ministers and their departments

6.—(1) The provisions of Schedule 1 to this Act shall apply to any Minister eligible for a salary under head 2 of Part II of Schedule 1 to the Ministerial and other Salaries Act 1975.

(2) The provisions of Schedule 1 to this Act (which re-enacts Schedule 1 to the Ministers of the Crown Act 1964) shall apply to the Secretary of State for Social Services, the Minister for the Civil Service and the Minister of Aviation Supply, and (where appropriate) to their departments, as the corresponding provisions of Schedule 1 to the said Act of 1964 applied immediately before the passing of this Act . . .

Interpretation, consequential amendment and repeals

8.—(1) In this Act—

'functions' includes powers and duties;

'Minister of the Crown' means the holder of an office in Her Majesty's Government in the United Kingdom, and includes the Treasury, the Board of Trade and the Defence Council.

(2) For the purpose of this Act any functions in respect of which a direction is given in an Order in Council made under Section 1(1)(*c*) above shall be treated as functions transferred; and any reference in this Act to the transfer of functions shall be construed accordingly.

(3) In section 6 (5) of the Decimal Currency Act 1967 (which defines 'Minister of the Crown' by reference to the Ministers of the Crown (Transfer of Functions) Act 1946) for the words '(Transfer of Functions) Act 1946' there shall be substituted the words 'Act 1975.'

(4) The enactments specified in Schedule 3 to this Act are hereby repealed to the extent specified in the third column of the Schedule . . .

## SCHEDULE 1

PROVISIONS APPLYING TO CERTAIN MINISTERS AND THEIR DEPARTMENTS

1. The Minister shall take the oath of allegiance, and the official oath, and the Promissory Oaths Act 1868 shall have effect as if the name of the Minister were included in Part I of the Schedule to that Act.

2. The Minister may appoint such secretaries, officers and servants as he may with the consent of the Minister for the Civil Service determine.

3. There shall be paid to the secretaries (other than any Parliamentary Secretary), officers and servants appointed by the Minister such salaries or remuneration as the Minister for the Civil Service may determine.

4. The expenses of the Minister, including any salaries or remuneration payable under paragraph 3 of this schedule, shall be defrayed out of money provided by Parliament.

5. The Minister shall for all purposes be a corporation sole, and shall have an official seal, which shall be authenticated by the signature of the Minister or of a secretary of the Ministry or of any person authorised by the Minister to act in that behalf.

6. The seal of the Minister shall be officially and judicially noticed, and every document purporting to be an instrument made or issued by the Minister and to be sealed with the seal of the Minister authenticated in the manner provided by a secretary to the Ministry or any person authorised as aforesaid, shall be received in evidence and be deemed to be so made or issued without further proof, unless the contrary is shown.

7. A certificate signed by the Minister that any instrument purporting to be made or issued by him was so made or issued shall be conclusive evidence of that fact.

8. The Documentary Evidence Act 1868 shall apply to the Minister as if his name were included in the first column of the Schedule to that Act, and as if he or a secretary to the Ministry or any person authorised by him to act on his behalf were mentioned in the second column of that Schedule, and as if the regulations referred to in that Act included any document issued by the Minister.

[Ministers of the Crown Act 1975, ss.1–6, 8 and Schedule 1.]

1.—(1) This Order may be cited as the Transfer of Functions (Health and Social Security) Order 1988.

(2) In this Order—'the new Departments' means the Department of Health and the Department of Social Security, and any reference to 'the new Secretaries of State' is a reference to the Secretaries of State for those Departments; 'health and personal social services functions' means such of the functions of the Secretary of State as, immediately before 26th July 1988 (the

date on which the new Secretaries of State were appointed) were entrusted to the Secretary of State for Social Services, other than his social security functions; 'social security functions' means such of the following functions of the Secretary of State, that is to say—

(*a*) his functions under the enactments and instrument specified in Schedule 1 to this Order; and

(*b*) the functions transferred to him from the Minister of Social Security by the Secretary of State for Social Services Order 1968 or subsequently conferred upon him in the exercise of any function so transferred, as, immediately before 26th July 1988, were entrusted to the Secretary of State for Social Services.

(3) This Order shall come into force on 28th November 1988.

2.—(1) The functions of the Secretary of State for Social Services under the enactments specified in Part I of Schedule 2 to this Order are hereby transferred to the Secretary of State for Health.

(2) All functions of the Secretary of State for Social Services which—

(*a*) are exercisable under local Acts or instruments passed or made before the making of this Order, and

(*b*) are similar to any health and personal social services functions or any functions transferred by paragraph (1) above,

are hereby transferred to the Secretary of State for Health.

(3) There are hereby transferred to the Secretary of State for Health all property, rights and liabilities to which the Secretary of State for Social Services is entitled or subject, at the coming into force of this Order, in connection with any health and personal social services functions or any functions transferred by this Article.

(4) Subject to Articles 5(3) and 6(4) below, any instrument, contract or other document made before the coming into force of this Order shall have effect, so far as may be necessary in connection with the entrusting of the health and personal social services functions to the Secretary of State for Health, or for the purposes of or in consequence of the transfer of functions, property, rights or liabilities effected by this Article, as if any reference to the Secretary of State for Social Services or the Department of Health and Social Security or an officer of his were a reference to the Secretary of State for Health.

3.—(1) The functions of the Secretary of State for Social Services under the enactments specified in Part II of Schedule 2 to this Order are hereby transferred to the Secretary of State for Social Security.

(2) All functions of the Secretary of State for Social Services which—

(*a*) are exercisable under local Acts or instruments passed or made before the making of this Order, and

(*b*) are similar to any social security functions or any functions transferred by paragraph (1) above, are hereby transferred to the Secretary of State for Social Security.

(3) There are hereby transferred to the Secretary of State for Social Security all property, rights and liabilities to which the Secretary of State for Social Services is entitled or subject, at the coming into force of this Order, in connection with any social security functions or any functions transferred by this Article.

(4) Subject to Articles 5(3) and 6(4) below, any instrument, contract or other document made before the coming into force of this Order shall have effect, so far as may be necessary in connection with the entrusting of the social security functions to the Secretary of State for Social Security or for the purposes of or in consequence of the transfer of functions, property, rights or liabilities effected by this Article, as if any reference to the Secretary of State for Social Services or the Department of Health and Social Security.

4.—(1) The person who, at the coming into force of this Order, is the Secretary of State for either of the new Departments and his successors shall be a corporation sole (with a corporate seal) by the name of the Secretary of State for Health or, as the case may be, the Secretary of State for Social Security.

(2) The corporate seal of the Secretary of State for either of the new Departments shall be authenticated by the signature of a Secretary of State, or of a Secretary to that Department, or of a person authorised by a Secretary of State to act in that behalf.

(3) The corporate seal of the Secretary of State for either of the new Departments shall be officially and judicially noticed, and every document purporting to be an instrument made or issued by the Secretary of State for that Department, and to be sealed with that seal authenticated in the manner provided by paragraph (2) above, or to be signed or executed by a Secretary of State to that Department, or a person authorised as above, shall be received in evidence and be deemed to be so made or issued without further proof, unless the contrary is shown.

(4) A certificate signed by the Secretary of State for either of the new Departments that any instrument purporting to be made or

issued by him was so made or issued shall be conclusive evidence of that fact.

5.—(1) The Documentary Evidence Act 1868 shall apply in relation to each of the new Secretaries of State—

(*a*) as if references to orders and regulations included references to any document, and

(*b*) as if the officers mentioned in column 2 of the Schedule included any officer authorised to act on behalf of the Secretary of State.

(2) . . .

(3) Except in regulation 2 of the Health Services (Notification) Regulations 1980, where the reference to an office of the Department of Health and Social Security shall be construed as a reference to an office of the Department of Health, any reference in any statutory instrument to such an office shall be construed as a reference to an office of the Department of Social Security.

(4) Schedule 3 to this Order, which contains consequential amendments, shall have effect.

6.—(1) This Order shall not affect the validity of anything done by or in relation to the Secretary of State for Social Services before the coming into force of this Order, and anything (including legal proceedings) which is then in the process of being done by or in relation to him may—

(*a*) if it relates to health and personal social services functions or to functions, property, rights or liabilities transferred by Article 2 above, be continued by or in relation to the Secretary of State for Health, or

(*b*) if it relates to social security functions or to functions, property, rights or liabilities transferred by Article 3 above, be continued by or in relation to the Secretary of State for Social Security.

(2) Any authority, appointment, determination, approval, consent or direction given or made or other thing whatsoever done, or having effect as if given, made or done, by the Secretary of State for Social Services shall, if in force at the coming into force of this Order, continue in force and have effect—

(*a*) if it relates to health and personal social services functions or to functions, property, rights or liabilities transferred by Article 2 above, as if given, made or done by the Secretary of State for Health, or (*b*) if it relates to social security functions or to functions, property, rights or liabilities transferred by Article 3 above, as if given, made or done by the Secretary of State for Social Security.

(3) Documents or forms printed or duplicated for use in connection with any health and personal social services functions or any social security functions or any functions transferred by this Order may be so used notwithstanding that they contain references to the Secretary of State for Social Services, and those references shall be construed—

(*a*) in relation to any health and personal social services functions or any functions transferred by Article 2 above, as references to the Secretary of State for Health, or

(*b*) in relation to any social security functions or any functions transferred by Article 3 above, as references to the Secretary of State for Social Security, and similarly with references to the Department of Health and Social Security or an officer of the Secretary of State for Social Services.

(4) Any power of appointing trustees conferred on the Secretary of State for Social Services by a trust instrument shall be exercised by either of the new Secretaries of State, and the trust instrument shall be construed accordingly.

[Transfer of Functions (Health and Social Security) Order 1988, S.I. 1988 No. 1843. Schedules not reproduced.]

*If the Prime Minister wants to create a new department (as distinct from merely transferring existing functions to it) with a 'Minister' at its head rather than a Secretary of State, the Ministers of the Crown Act 1975 does not apply, and a statute must be passed for the purpose. The last such statute was the Ministers of the Crown Act 1964.*

## 4. THE USE OF NON-DEPARTMENTAL MINISTERS

*The Lord President of the Council and the Lord Privy Seal often also act as Leader of each House. The Chancellor of the Duchy of Lancaster and any Minister without Portfolio are given duties by the Prime Minister ad hoc. More recently, the Chancellor of the Duchy has been appointed as deputy to a departmental Minister. More controversial is the use of a non-departmental Minister (or occasionally a departmental Minister) as Chairman of the Conservative Party Organization.*

I do not wish, in this, to seem to denigrate the work of some Party Chairmen in Opposition, or to imply that their task was easy. Far from it. Woolton did a wonderful job rebuilding the shattered ranks of Conservatives afer the demoralizing and unexpected defeat of 1945: I witnessed that, and greatly admired. Peter Thorneycroft did an excellent job. So did Tony Barber. But I reiterate that the task when in Government is both different and particularly difficult—probably Quintin Hailsham did it most successfully and most resoundingly between 1957 and 1959, a period when I was in Australia but which passed into legend. When in Government the party's supporters are prone to unease. All the mid-term—to say nothing of the more terminal—problems which beset any Government infect the confidence of its supporters in the country and of the people who try to enthuse them, organize, rally them. Even Quintin had found the going tough. I found it very tough indeed.

I accepted the charge with mixed feelings. Ted thought that I knew a lot of people in the party, that I had a good deal of experience, had been around a long time and was relatively senior. He obviously thought me a good choice. I doubted this. I was a hereditary peer, which makes things more difficult—although this had not, it was true, particularly handicapped some effective holders of the job in the past: nevertheless, I was always conscious that it was possible to say to me, 'What do you know about it? You've never faced a Selection Committee or fought an Election.' More importantly, I was extremely busy in the Ministry of Defence, with the additional time-load of international conferences, visits and tours which the post involved. I questioned whether the chairmanship should, ideally, be combined with one of the great Departments of State; and in the event the Ministry of Defence tended to think I spent too much time being Party Chairman, and the party officials certainly reckoned I devoted too many hours to being Secretary of State for Defence. I have not changed my mind on this—the combination is undesirable. Of course the party want, as Chairman, someone sufficiently senior to have the Prime Minister's ear, somebody in the inner counsels of Government, someone with status—that is natural, and to disregard it is to make the party itself feel disregarded, with bad consequences. But, I reiterate, combination with a major Department is bad for the party: bad for the Government; and bad for the country. Inevitably, however, I accepted. Most people feel they must do what a Prime Minister requests, defer to his or her judgement in such matters.

[Lord Carrington, *Reflect on Things Past* (London, 1988), 259–60.]

I was very pleased that when I was appointed Chairman of the Party the Prime Minister also made me Chancellor of the Duchy of Lancaster, a post whose history goes back to 1399. Many of its holders were forgettable and have been forgotten. Four of them met untimely ends. Thomas More was martyred by Henry VIII, another died on the scaffold, a third awaited trial in the Tower, a fourth was assassinated. On the other hand four became Prime Minister including both Churchill and Spencer Perceval—who was the one assassinated. The Chancellor's duties cover the appointment and discipline of the magistracy in the County Palatine of Lancaster, and, separately, he has the role of non-executive chairman of what is in effect a property and investment company managing the estates of the Duchy which are personal to the Queen and separate from the Crown Estates. Those matters are dealt with by a highly professional staff under the direction of the Council of the Duchy, in effect a non-executive board.

My work as a non-departmental Minister was managed from a delightful office overlooking the Horse Guards parade ground only minutes away from my attic flat. To my delight, Andrew Lansley, one of my private office team from the DTI, volunteered to come and organise my staff there and provide a link to the Duchy but principally to brief me on the tremendous range of Government matters in which I had an interest. I had a role in the Cabinet and its committees which, like that of Willie Whitelaw, extended very widely at times, and often put us in the position of non-executive directors or a court of appeal for unhappy colleagues . . .

Clearly I had no more influence over the general course of government than I had as a Secretary of State. My job was in that respect to persuade colleagues to think of the political impact of what they were doing, to present it more skilfully and above all to use the resources of Central Office to plan that political impact—not as a fire-fighting team to dampen down fires of resentment after a political explosion.

However I could do something to harmonise and focus the presentation of policies. I was ready to try new ideas and to experiment, not least through Party Political Broadcasts (six ten-minute peak-viewing-time slots each year) and constituency campaigns. I could also involve our activists more closely in our national campaign, and set about bringing resources of cash, equipment and personnel into the key constituencies to build up support ready for the general election.

Within weeks I had categorised every constituency in Britain, distinguishing between those where only a political earthquake would unseat the party holding the seat, the Conservative seats at risk in a tightly fought election and the Labour and Liberal seats we might expect to win if things went reasonably well. Our 1983 majority of 144 was unlikely to be repeated unless the split of Labour and Alliance votes was to be so near perfect for us again. My first priority was to achieve a good working majority. That meant identifying and putting our efforts into the key seats which we had to hold.

[Norman Tebbit, *Upwardly Mobile* (London, 1988), 241, 243.]

# [6]
# MINISTERIAL CONDUCT

## Collective Responsibility

### 1. DEFINITIONS

22. Decisions reached by the Cabinet or Cabinet Committees are binding on all members of the Government. They are however normally announced and defended by the Minister concerned as his own decisions. There may be rare occasions when it is desirable to emphasise the importance of a decision by stating specifically that it is the decision of Her Majesty's Government. This, however, should be the exception rather than the rule.

[*Questions of Procedure for Ministers* (1976 version), para. 22.]

There are three traditional branches of the collective responsibility convention: the confidence rule, the unanimity rule, and the confidentiality rule. The first is to do with the conditions on which a government holds office; the others with the way in which its members behave whilst in office. If we look at each branch of the convention we seem to see some changes. It sometimes used to be said that a prime non-legal rule of the Constitution was that governments defeated by the House on central issues of policy were obliged to resign. But only one Prime Minister has resigned as the result of a defeat in the House in the twentieth century and that was immediately after being deprived of his majority by a General Election (Baldwin in January 1924). MacDonald was defeated on a confidence issue in 1924 and Callaghan in 1979, but neither resigned. Both fought the subsequent General Elections as leader of a government, having advised dissolution.

So the rule about a government that loses the confidence of the House seems to be that it must *either* resign *or* advise dissolution. Its right is only to advise, not to have, dissolution; since dissolution can, as we have seen, in some circumstances be refused. Resignation might therefore follow as the result of such a refusal (by the Queen), but that has not happened. As to what constitutes a loss of confidence there seems also to have been a development in doctrine. The books used to say that defeat on major legislative measures or policy proposals as well as on specifically worded confidence motions was fatal to the continuance of the government. But this no longer seems to be believed or acted on. In 1977 *The Times* propounded the view that 'there is no constitutional principle that requires a government to regard any specific policy defeat as evidence that it no longer possesses the necessary confidence of the House of Commons'. Some were greatly shocked by this doctrine and Professor Max Beloff wrote to *The Times* to say that it was inconsistent with the principles of the Constitution as hitherto understood. Sir Ivor Jennings, he pointed out, had said in *Cabinet Government* that the government must go if the House failed to approve its policy. What provoked the disagreement was that the Labour Government had just failed to carry a budget proposal about the rate of income tax and was proposing to remain in office in defiance of Sir Ivor Jennings's view of the established convention. Sir Ivor Jennings was of course dead, which is supposed to augment the authority of a textbook writer by allowing his views to be cited more freely in the course of litigation. Unfortunately there is a countervailing disadvantage in that his works may go out of print and are no longer constantly perused by Ministers, who are thereby enabled to fall into lax habits and disregard established constitutional conventions. In the 1960s and 1970s, in any event, governments seem to have been following a new rule, according to which only votes specifically stated by the Government to be matters of confidence, or votes of no confidence by the Opposition are allowed to count. Just conceivably one can imagine amongst recent Prime Ministers those who might have felt it their duty to soldier on in the general interest even in the face of such a vote.

If we turn to the second meaning or branch of the collective responsibility principle, namely the unanimity or solidarity of the Cabinet, we see further change and uncertainty. The doctrine of collective responsibility in this second sense was treated roughly in 1975 when Mr Harold Wilson suspended it before the EEC referendum in order to allow free play to the convictions of the Labour Cabinet's anti-Common Marketeers. The reasons offered for the suspension were that it was necessary for a fair and free debate to take place and that the issue was one on which both political parties and 'many families and households' were divided. The 'divided parties and households' argument seemed unimpressive since neither parties nor families are Cabinets. Free and fair debate is certainly a good thing, but it is unclear why the debate would have been unfree and unfair if the opponents of cabinet policy had followed the normal practice and campaigned against it from outside the Cabinet. So the reasons given seemed suspect and the parallels drawn with the 1932 Coalition agreement to differ seemed not obviously applicable to a single-party government. It does not follow, however, that the Wilson Government were guilty of constitutional impropriety. Possibly Mr Wilson did not need to supply reasons for changing the Cabinet's customary practice. It may be that the custom of unanimity, like that of cabinet secrecy, is not a duty-imposing constitutional convention, though undoubtedly a historically observed and politically convenient practice. It is acknowledged that the Prime Minister may decide to which members of a government the rule of unanimity extends and to what times and places; for example to party meetings such as the Labour Party's national executive committee. But perhaps the principle in its entirety is a matter for the Cabinet and the Prime Minister between them to apply or not as they wish. The first sense of collective responsibility (resigning or dissolving after defeat on a confidence issue) is undoubtedly a duty-imposing convention since it entails an obligation or a duty to the House of Commons. Cabinet solidarity, on the other hand, is the subject matter of a right inhering in the Prime Minister correlative to a duty in his colleagues. It is not necessarily a right inhering in the House of Commons correlative to a duty in the Cabinet and Prime Minister. It has been said by some to be a duty to the Crown. But the traditional rationale for Cabinet solidarity rather makes against that notion since it developed historically not as a right of the Crown but as a partial shield against the Crown to avoid the penalizing or attempted dismissal of particular Ministers for their opinions. So if a Cabinet and Prime Minister do not mind exposing their internal differences of opinion, is that course unconstitutional or a breach of convention, as distinct from being politically imprudent or tactically risky? In nineteenth-century Cabinets, subjects that excited keen disagreement, such as Catholic emancipation, women's suffrage, and tariff reform were treated as 'open questions'. Those who now esteem open government ought perhaps to encourage open disagreements, openly arrived at.

Similar considerations affect the third aspect of collective responsibility, namely confidentiality. Disclosure and briefing of the Press by Ministers has always taken place when they have felt it to be in their interest. The rules respecting exercises in communication by individual Ministers, however were significantly modified by Mr Richard Crossman whose *Diaries of a Cabinet Minister* were published after an unsuccessful attempt to prevent their appearance by the Attorney-General in 1976. In the course of the proceedings a number of witnesses gave evidence about the nature of collective responsibility, including the Secretary of the Cabinet, Sir John Hunt. The Crossman manuscript had been submitted for security clearance to the Cabinet Secretary who had set out for Crossman's guidance a number of restrictive rules or 'parameters' (a term new to constitutional theory) . . .

[Geoffrey Marshall, *Constitutional Conventions* (Oxford, 1984), 55–8.]

'Bye the bye, there is one thing we haven't agreed upon, which is, what are we to say? Is it to make our corn dearer, or cheaper, or to make the price steady? I don't care *which*: but we had better all tell the same story.'

The essence of Lord Melbourne's cynical observation holds good today. For the doctrine of collective ministerial responsibility requires that all Ministers, and usually Parliamentary Private Secretaries, must accept Cabinet decisions, or dissent from them privately while remaining loyal to them publicly, or dissent publicly and resign, unless collective responsibility is waived by the Cabinet on any given occasion. If a Minister does not resign over an issue of policy or procedure he will be collectively responsible for it, in the sense that he will have to support it publicly through his votes in Parliament and through his speeches. It will be no defence or excuse for him to say that the decision was taken without his knowledge (because, for example, he was a mere Parliamentary Under-Secretary of State not privy to Cabinet discussions, or because he was absent from the relevant meeting), for the doctrine binds all members of the government from the lowest to the highest: it is for that reason misleading to refer to it as collective *Cabinet* responsibility.

There are many examples of Ministers of all ranks resigning or being required to resign because they could not accept collective responsibility for some decision or other—Cabinet Ministers, Ministers of State, Chief Whips, and Parliamentary Secretaries.

[Rodney Brazier, *Constitutional Practice* (Oxford, 1988), 129–30.]

## 2. SAFETY VALVES

*A number of 'safety valves' exist which help to maintain the concept of collective responsibility.*

### (1) LEAKS

*Leaks were considered above: see p. 299. Through an unattributable leak a Minister who is out of step with government policy can tell the press and public of his opposition, while retaining his job and maintaining the façade of collective responsibility.*

### (2) RELIANCE ON PRIME MINISTERIAL TOLERANCE

*A Minister may publicly distance himself from government policies in the knowledge or hope that the Prime Minister will not discipline him.*

There have been an increasing number of instances of this kind of reservation in recent years. Mr Frank Cousins, while in the Cabinet publicly expressed his 'delight' at resolutions by his Union condemning Government policies on prices and incomes and on the war in Vietnam. Although Mr Enoch Powell never openly criticised the policies of Conservative administrations of which he was a member, his extreme reverence for the operation of 'the free market' was well known and most observers appreciated how deeply he disagreed with the regional development and planning policies adopted in the last years of Mr Macmillan's Government. Mr Callaghan spoke against the Labour Cabinet's proposals in the White Paper, *In Place of Strife* at a meeting of the Labour Party's National Executive Committee and this was reported in the Press. Mr Wilson . . . did not call for his resignation but dismissed him from the Parliamentary

Committee or inner Cabinet. The possibility of allowing sections of the Cabinet to repudiate the policies of the majority had only been adopted once, in 1931, when three Liberals joined Ramsay MacDonald's National Government on the explicit understanding that they had 'permission to disagree' with the Cabinet's retreat from free trade. But these ministers came from a particular party, their views were well known and they joined a coalition from which they soon resigned.

[John Mackintosh, *The British Cabinet* (London, 3rd edn., 1977), 532.]

(*a*) Following is the text of a statement on the collective responsibility of ministers in all circumstances, with special reference to the National Executive Committee of the Labour Party, read to Cabinet on 3 April 1969, and authorized by Cabinet to be released to the press.

The Prime Minister said that there had for some time been a growing tendency for some Ministers to act in ways which called in question the collective responsibility of the Cabinet, in so far as they had apparently felt free, in their personal dealings both with members of the PLP and with the Press, to dissociate themselves from certain of the Government's policies and to allow this to be known to outside bodies, particularly the Trade Unions, with whom their colleagues were often conducting difficult and delicate negotiations in the name of the Government as a whole. Before a decision was reached on any item of Government policy a Minister was entitled to defend his own point of view within the Cabinet as strongly and persuasively as he wished. But once a decision had been taken the principle of collective responsibility required every member of an Administration to endorse it and to defend it to any outside body on any occasion, whether private or public. This remained true even if the Minister was himself a member of the outside body concerned. There was no objection in principle to Ministers retaining affiliations of this kind provided that no conflict of interest or allegiance resulted. But this proviso was especially important in the case of Ministers who were members of the National Executive Committee of the Labour Party (NEC), where any clash of loyalties was liable to be particularly embarrassing. It had to be recognised that the NEC's concept of its relationship to the Parliamentary Party had changed since the Labour Party became the Government Party. During the Labour Government of 1945–51 the Executive would never have sought to enforce a decision of the annual conference of the Party on the Government. And even in 1960, when the Labour Party were in Opposition, the Executive had refused to try to impose the decisions of the conference on the PLP. Now, however, it was seeking to assert a right to withhold support from the Government on issues on which the annual conference had not yet expressed a view.

It would be unfortunate if circumstances developed, perhaps later in the year, in which it proved impossible to deal with this situation except by means of a ruling that no member of the Cabinet might offer himself for election to the NEC. He himself would greatly regret it if he were forced to give such a ruling, since the result would be not only to weaken the links between the Government and the NEC but also to reduce the latter to a body which was competent merely to discuss and to protest but not to exercise influence or to accept responsibility. Nevertheless, this situation could be avoided only if Ministers themselves recognised and accepted that, where any conflict of loyalties arose, the principle of the collective responsibility of the Government was absolute and overriding in all circumstances and that, if any Minister felt unable to subscribe to this principle without reservation, it was his duty to resign his office forthwith.

14 May 1974

(*b*) In 1974 the issue arose again in relation to Chile and other matters. I wrote the following letter, which was published at the time, to three ministers who were members of the NEC. After some little difficulty, satisfactory assurances were received.

In my minute of 14 May 1974 I reminded Ministers of the principle of collective responsibility, as it applies to Ministers in their dealings with the Labour Party and in particular to Ministers who are members of the National Executive Committee. I attach a copy of that minute herewith.

That minute restated the rule that, where any conflict of loyalties arises, the principle of the collective responsibility of the Government is absolute and overriding in all circumstances and that, if any Minister feels unable to subscribe to this principle without reservation, it is his duty to resign his office forthwith.

I reminded all members of the administration at the Eve of Session Reception at 10 Downing Street as recently as Monday of this week of their duty to comply with the requirements of collective responsibility. I made it clear that it is inconsistent with the principle of collective responsibility for a Minister who is a member of the National Executive Committee to speak or vote in favour of a resolution of that body which is critical of Government policies or actions, or which seeks to impose on the Government views or decisions which are manifestly inconsistent with Government policy.

Your vote in support of the Simonstown resolution at yesterday's meeting of the National Executive Committee was clearly inconsistent with the principle of collective responsibility. You will be well aware of the embarrassment which this has created for your colleagues.

I must ask you to send me in reply to this minute an unqualified assurance that you accept the principle of collective responsibility and that you will from now on comply with its requirements and the rules that flow from it, in the National Executive Committee and in all other circumstances. I must warn you that I should have to regard your failure to give me such an assurance, or any subsequent breach of it, as a decision on your part that you did not wish to continue as a member of this administration. I should of course much regret such a decision; but I should accept it.

[Wilson, *Governance*, Appendix I.]

*Mr Peter Walker was appointed to the Cabinet in 1979. He survived annual Cabinet reshuffles despite being a 'wet' on economic and social issues, and despite making numerous public speeches arguing the case for 'wetter' policies.*

### (3) AGREEMENTS TO DIFFER

In this century the convention of collective responsibility has twice been expressly waived for a few months. The first occasion was in January 1932, and at the time the country had a national government, a Cabinet about half the normal size comprising Labour, Conservative and Liberal Ministers. In *The Times*, of August 26, 1931, it was argued that 'the government will have to exact the most undeviating loyalty from its supporters if its actions are to be as comprehensive and as swift as the situation demands.' When only a few months later the Cabinet, unable to agree on the 'Free Trade v. Protection' issue confronted the country with this constitutional innovation of freedom to disagree, there was much discussion in the press and Parliament. The criticism ran as follows: This was the first major departure from collective responsibility in the 100 years or so of its history and many saw it as 'breaking the honourable tradition.' It was also a 'deep shock to the constitutional sense of the country.' In the House of Lords, Lord Banbury criticised the lack of 'political-business' sense in this move to permit dissension. He considered the dire consequences if a great railway company (an analogy to the Government) decided that its directors could advise shareholders in different ways. The shareholders would be in a quandary, the shares on the Stock Exchange could well slump. The fate of this disunited Government, he postulated, might follow a similar path. Lord Ponsonby argued that the agreement to differ was a reflection of a complacent government obsessed with the idea of its indispensability. The National Government was virtually saying that it preferred to stay in power rather than accede to the conventional constitutional machine which provides that where a government cannot maintain unity in its ranks or parliamentary support it resigns. The 1932 Government was emasculating the constitutional safeguard of an alternative government ready to take its place. This argument is a little suspect in the light of the unusual facts of 1932. The Government, a coalition, was in power at a most critical time for the economy. Could such a situation justify the departure from collective responsibility? Lord Peel argued 'no', stating that 'the unity of a government is more necessary when several parties are combined in it, because everybody will imagine that there is no unity in that combined party government.' The freedom to disagree included a right to speak and vote against the proposals of the Government in the House of Commons as well as to speak freely in the country. Lord Peel suggested that 'if we are to have a great campaign in the country, and Ministers use the Cabinet as an entrenchment for attacks against their colleagues, I do not think the system will be long tolerated.' Lord Ponsonby, however, suggested that in the long term the 'overly rigid adherence' to collective responsibilty should be modified, but concluded that at the time the idea of collective responsibility was still very much a reality. The force of the argument in 1932 by those who opposed the agreement to differ indicated that collective responsibility was felt by many to still be a binding convention.

The arguments for the opposite view, that the Government be permitted to openly disagree were as follows: That the doctrine had become a myth and that the Government had full discretion as to how it conducted its administration. One of the few who presented this radical contention was the Lord Privy Seal (Lord Snowden) who stated: 'I am not in the least interested in constitutional authorities. . . . All human progress has been made by ignoring precedents.' The test he would apply had nothing to do with the notion of a binding convention, only with questions of expedience based on special circumstances, namely: Was it prudent? Was it necessary? He considered the answer was 'yes' in both cases and this gave the Government all the authority it needed for an agreement to differ. Viscount Sankey L.C. argued that when Cabinets had been smaller and dealing with a smaller range of subjects, collective responsibility had been an ideal which could be attained. Changes in Cabinet operation meant that collective responsibility assumed a type of mythical status where though it still remained, it remained as an ideal to be aimed at, 'but not always to be attained.'

Another argument, less damaging to collective responsibility, is that there was an actual 'agreement' within the Cabinet that they should differ on the Free Trade issue. This 'agreement' to disagree was itself said to be a manifestation of collective responsibility, so that Ministers could not turn around and say that they were not responsible for the suspension of the doctrine. The same argument was propounded by Sir John Hunt in relation to the 1975 agreement to differ when he stated: 'I would not regard the recent referendum as breaching collective responsibility because this was a decision by the Cabinet as a whole to waive collective responsibility on one particular issue for a limited time. It was not a decision which any Minister took unilaterally.' At the very most this is only a partial defence since the *reductio ad absurdum* is that collective responsibility could be argued to apply even it future operation of the doctrine is indeterminately suspended. This would be solely because the initial decision to suspend is protected by the rule of Cabinet unanimity.

In my submission the correct understanding of the 1932 agreement to differ would restrict this episode to its particular facts, minimising the damage to collective responsibility. It was contended at the time that the fact that the Government could adapt itself to the realities of the disagreement would strengthen Britain's position abroad, since people would see that even these fiscal difficulties, which were 'matters of common notoriety' were not able to defeat the British Cabinet. The idea that the Government were in agreement on all other issues was continually emphasised and it was stated that this was evidenced by a steadying influence in the country. A flagrantly eager return to party politics and the rigours of collective responsibility would have seriously unsettled the economy—a move the public would have been slow to forgive.

The motion of censure against the Government was overwhelmingly defeated in the Commons. However, if the experiment is considered on the basis of whether it maintained Cabinet solidarity, then it must be judged a failure. Eight months later the dissenting ministers resigned on the associated issue of Imperial Preference.

The evidence until the 1970s was that there was no real development of any practice of open disagreement on issues, or the allowing of 'free votes'. Evidently the words of Baldwin in 1932 had been essentially heeded to the effect that: 'had the precedent been made for a party government it would have been quite new and it would have been absolutely dangerous for that party.' Though a free vote was permitted among MPs including Cabinet Ministers on the issue of capital punishment in 1956, the move was severely criticised. When the Government proposed a free vote on the most controversial clauses of the Street Offences Bill 1959, the objections from its own backbenchers were so numerous that it altered its decision and imposed a two-line whip.

However, in 1975 the Government, Parliament and the Press showed little reluctance in accepting that once negotiations on entry to the Common Market were complete the Government would make their own recommendations, while allowing Ministers the right to dissent. A *Times* editorial soon after the decision was announced stated that 'nobody will be surprised to hear that . . . individual ministers will be allowed to disagree; Cabinets are bound to take account of political realities.' This editorial evidences just how weak collective responsibility was considered at that time.

The terms of this agreement to differ were not quite as extensive as in 1932. In a written answer in Parliament Harold Wilson spelt out the arrangement as follows:

(i) The freedom did not extend to parliamentary proceedings and official business.
(ii) Government business in Parliament would continue to be handled by all ministers in accordance with government policy.
(iii) Ministers dealing with European affairs who differ from the Government's recommendation were to state the Government's attitude without criticism.
(iv) If necessary questions were to be transferred to other ministers.
(v) At meetings of the Council of Ministers of the European Community and at other such meetings the Government policy was always to be followed.

Thus collective responsibility was not in full suspension as it had been in 1932, since restrictions were lifted only outside Parliament. The doctrine still had a potent aspect as was shown for example when Eric Heffer insisted in the House of Commons on opposing Britain's membership of the EEC. As a result he was required to resign his office as a Minister. Peter Shore, as one of the Cabinet Ministers opposed to membership also had difficulties when it came to answering parliamentary questions on EEC policy. At one stage the following comment was directed at him by a backbencher: 'In expressing the belief that it would be possible to negotiate a satisfactory free trade agreement . . . the word "we" was used. Who is "we"? Is it Her Majesty's Government or is it the anti-Market group?'

In the Commons, Harold Wilson justified this constitutional manipulation by many of the arguments rehearsed in 1932. The agreement to differ was dictated by unique circumstances; it was a constitutional innovation which nobody would regard as a precedent; it concerned matters crossing party lines; the Cabinet was united on all other issues; the only precedent—a 'sound one'—was devised by the Liberals in 1932. Whilst the circumstances in 1932 can be said to have justified the suspension of collective responsibility, in 1975 the issue was far less clear cut. One is tempted to wonder why Harold Wilson did not ride rough shod over the views of the minority as is the general style of the British Cabinet. There were apparently seven Ministers who wished Britain out of the Common Market, as against 16 supporters in the Cabinet. Harold Wilson, faced with a similar situation in 1969, had tried to rely on collective responsibility to force the White Paper *In Place of Strife* through a divided Cabinet and failed. Was there perhaps another reason why Harold Wilson was prepared to take the precarious step of moving outside the realms of collective responsibility while still maintaining a particular government policy? It must be remembered that at the time the N.E.C. did not support staying in. By permitting a free vote to Cabinet members, Harold Wilson pre-empted the necessity of an annual conference decision that would be binding on all members; in effect a plot by Wilson to thwart the N.E.C. My submission is that once again the N.E.C. policy caused an attack on the reality of collective responsibility, even though it occurred in an indirect fashion.

What then was the practical effect of this six months agreement to differ on collective responsibility? Harold Wilson has argued that: 'As soon as the votes had been counted, the party and the government thereafter were stronger, not weaker, more united, not divided, as a consequence of the agreement to differ and that there was a return to full collective responsibility.' Whilst I concede that the experiment was successful in that there was no mass ministerial resignation forcing the Government out of power, I think this result is a long way from proving that all was well as regards Cabinet unity and the general good health of collective responsibility.

The very fact that no immediate crisis resulted from allowing open disagreement evidences that collective responsibility is not always required to maintain a Government in power. The 1932 failure might have deterred potential followers of the example. Wilson's Government has shown that an openly divided one-party cabinet dealing with a very critical issue can survive. In other words, it will probably not be 40 or so years before the next attempt to follow this latest precedent. Recent parliamentary experience has shown that there is a willingness to see more open government by affording Ministers the freedom to vote according to their consciences.

In the House of Commons, the then Prime Minister, James Callaghan, announced that the White Paper on Direct Elections to the European Assembly would set out a choice among different electoral systems, but would make no specific recommendation. Accordingly, there was to be a 'free vote' in both Houses. In July 1977 *The Times* reported the true extent of this breach of collective responsibility. The Second Reading debate on the European Assembly Elections Bill produced the unedifying object of Ministers going off in different directions—in fact, six Cabinet Ministers and 26 Junior Ministers voted against a measure honouring a government obligation.

[D. L. Ellis, 'Collective Ministerial Responsibility and Collective Solidarity' [1980] *Public law* 367 at 383–8.]

The last and uncommon and derided but in my view attractive device for holding a government together is the agreement to differ. The only three examples of such agreements this century are well known and will not be rehearsed in any detail here. They were the 'National Government's' agreement to differ in 1932 over the introduction of a general tariff (without which four free-trade Cabinet Ministers would have resigned); the Labour Cabinet's decision to suspend collective responsibility 'in the unique circumstances' of the 1975 referendum campaign (on whether the United Kingdom should continue to be a member of the European Economic Community) so that Ministers who dissented from the Cabinet's recommendation to vote to remain in could say so publicly—although outside Parliament; and the further suspension in 1977 so that Ministers who could not support the introduction of direct elections to the European Assembly could vote against the second reading of the European Assembly Elections Bill. These suspensions are usually regarded as some sort of affront to our system of government, not to be spoken of in polite society. Sir Ivor Jennings, for instance, wrote that the 1932 agreement was a 'strange device', but that 'no harm was done by the precedent of 1932 provided that it is not regarded as a precedent'. MacDonald's resort to an agreement to differ is usually described as a failure. Now, partly no doubt because of their rarity, agreements to differ look bad. The contrast between government A, which keeps its disagreements discreetly private, and government B, which openly announces a disagreement, is sharp and provides political ammunition for the latter's opponents. And James Callaghan's announcement at the time of the 1977 suspension— '. . . I certainly think that the doctrine [of collective responsibility] should apply, except in cases where I announce that it does not'—was seen by some as a cynical exploitation of prime ministerial power. I find these objections unimpressive. The 1975 and 1977 suspensions were not only undoubted successes for the governments concerned—the two administrations held together, which is the main aim of the exercise—but also the issues before Ministers and the country (particularly in 1975) were more fully aired and argued than otherwise would have been the case. Even the 1932 experiment bought the coalition government an extra eight months of continued free-trade support (both National Liberal and National Labour) which it otherwise would have forfeited, at a time when the maximum national solidarity was desirable. More fundamentally, why in a mature democracy do we still insist on the maintenance of the fiction that all Ministers are agreed on everything all the time—or at least that they all loyally fall in unreservedly behind majority decisions? That they do not is eloquently attested to by leaks—themselves an accepted but dishonest ruse, more objectionable in my view than an occasional and open agreement to differ. Governments should be readier to announce majority decisions and should use suspensions of the obligations of collective responsibility more often. The electorate would see more of the reality of political life, and there would be some increase in public debate of major issues. Naturally, there would have to be limits: every government must officially hold together on essentials—monetarism (or whatever is the appropriate label) rather than traditional liberal Conservative orthodoxy in the 1980s, for example; and too many suspensions could be politically dangerous. Subject to that, I accept Dr Geoffrey Marshall's injunction in the same spirit in which it is offered, that 'Those who now esteem open government ought perhaps to encourage open disagreements, openly arrived at.'

[Brazier, *Constitutional Practice*, 132–4.]

## 3. RESIGNATIONS

*Resignations since 1960 on grounds of collective responsibility*

| Name | Post | Reason and date |
|---|---|---|
| C. Mayhew | Minister of State, Defence | Defence cuts (1966) |
| F. Cousins | Minister of Technology | Incomes policy (1966) |
| M. Herbison | Minister of Social Security | Social security policy (1967) |
| Ld. Longford | Lord Privy Seal | Education policy (1968) |
| W. Howie | Government Whip | Party discipline (1968) |
| G. Brown | Foreign Secretary | P.M.'s style (1968) |
| R. Gunter | Minister of Power | Government policies (1968) |
| J. Bray | Parliamentary Secretary, Technology | Permission to publish (1969) |
| E. Taylor | Parliamentary Under-Secretary, Scotland | Entry into EEC (1971) |
| J. More | Government Whip | Entry into EEC (1971) |
| N. Buchan | Minister of State, Agriculture | Agriculture policy (1974) |
| E. Heffer | Minister of State, Industry | Terms of agreement to differ (1975) |
| J. Hart | Minister of Overseas Development | P.M.'s style (1975) |

*cont./*

| Name | Post | Reason and date |
|---|---|---|
| R. Hughes | Parliamentary Under-Secretary, Scotland | Incomes policy (1975) |
| J. Lestor | Parliamentary Under-Secretary, Education | Education cuts (1976) |
| R. Prentice | Minister of Overseas Development | Government policies (1976) |
| J. Ashton | Assistant Government Whip | Government's handling of a power dispute (1977) |
| R. Cryer | Parliamentary Under-Secretary, Industry | Industrial policy (1978) |
| A. Stallard | Assistant Government Whip | Extra N.I. seats (1979) |
| K. Speed | Parliamentary Under-Secretary, Defence | Cuts in naval spending (1981) |
| N. Bugden | Assistant Government Whip | N.I. policy (1982) |
| I. Gow | Minister of State, Treasury | Anglo-Irish Agreement (1985) |
| M. Heseltine | Secretary of State for Defence | Westland: P.M.'s style; 'censorship' of ministerial statements |
| N. Lawson | Chancellor of the Exchequer | P.M.'s economic adviser (1989) |

## Individual Responsibility

### 1. DEFINITION

*A Minister is responsible for his private conduct, the general conduct of his department, and acts done (or left undone) by civil servants in his department.*

### 2. PERSONAL CONDUCT

27. All Ministers should be concerned to protect both the Government's reputation for integrity and the confidentiality of its proceedings which is the essential basis of collective responsibility. Ministers should therefore take care to conduct themselves, both in public and in private, in such a way as to avoid becoming involved in any circumstances which could either damage the Government's

good name by provoking scandalous speculation or be used against them as a means of pressure by hostile intelligence agents. On first appointment and, in certain cases, on appointment to a subsequent Ministerial office, Ministers will be briefed by the Security Service, who will explain both the basic threat to our security and the system of protection against it. They will also be invited to sign a declaration that they have read the relevant provisions of the Official Secrets Acts.

[*Questions of Procedure for Ministers* (1976 version), para. 27.]

## (1) MR JOHN PROFUMO 1963

THE SECRETARY OF STATE FOR WAR (MR JOHN PROFUMO): With permission, Sir, I wish to make a personal statement.

I understand that in the debate on the Consolidated Fund Bill last night, under protection of Parliamentary Privilege, the hon. Gentlemen the Members for Dudley (Mr Wigg) and for Coventry, East (Mr Crossman) and the hon. Lady the Member for Blackburn (Mrs Castle), opposite, spoke of rumours connecting a Minister with a Miss Keeler and a recent trial at the Central Criminal court. It was alleged that people in high places might have been responsible for concealing information concerning the disappearance of a witness and the perversion of justice.

I understand that my name has been connected with the rumours about the disappearance of Miss Keeler.

I would like to take this opportunity of making a personal statement about these matters.

I last saw Miss Keeler in December, 1961, and I have not seen her since. I have no idea where she is now. Any suggestion that I was in any way connected with or responsible for her absence from the trial at the Old Bailey is wholly and completely untrue.

My wife and I first met Miss Keeler at a house party in July, 1961, at Cliveden. Among a number of people there was Dr Stephen Ward, whom we already knew slightly, and a Mr Ivanov, who was an attaché at the Russian Embassy.

The only other occasion that my wife or I met Mr Ivanov was for a moment at the official reception for Major Gagarin at the Soviet Embassy.

My wife and I had a standing invitation to visit Dr Ward.

Between July and December, 1961, I met Miss Keeler on about half a dozen occasions at Dr Ward's flat, when I called to see him and his friends. Miss Keeler and I were on friendly terms. There was no impropriety whatsoever in my acquaintanceship with Miss Keeler.

Mr Speaker, I have made this personal statement because of what was said in the House last evening by the three hon. Members, and which, of course, was protected by Privilege. I shall not hesitate to issue writs for libel and slander if scandalous allegations are made or repeated outside the House.

[Mr John Profumo, 674 H.C. Deb. 809–10 (21 March 1963).]

Unhappily, another wave of painful and damaging rumours had begun to circulate. This time, however, although cloaked under the cover of security, they were moving into the realm of scandal. This was the beginning of a strange and even fantastic episode of which it is almost impossible, many years later, to give any coherent account. I do not propose to weary my readers with the detailed story of the 'Profumo case'. Much has been written and published, accurately and inaccurately. It is only necessary for me to give the broad outline of this sad series of events in order to explain the still stranger sequel, a general attack launched on the probity and moral character of almost the whole body of Ministers, with a ruthlessness and disregard for all semblance of truth unequalled since the days of Titus Oates.

On 4 February 1963, on my return from an official visit to Italy, I was informed by my Private Office that while I was away a newspaper had reported to us a 'story' involving an important, though not a Cabinet, Minister. It appeared that Jack Profumo, then Secretary of State for War, had, in the language of the police, 'compromised himself' with a girl of doubtful reputation, whom he met at a somewhat raffish party at Cliveden, to which she had been brought by a Mr Ward. She had sold or was about to sell her story to the Press. It had, or was to be given, a security angle, for the lady in question was said to share her favours with the Russian Naval Attaché, a certain Ivanov. My Private Secretary, Tim Bligh, had in my absence passed this information to the Security Service, and it had been agreed that Profumo should be asked whether there was any truth in it. Bligh and the Chief Whip accordingly saw Profumo. He admitted having been acquainted with the woman involved, a

Miss Christine Keeler, during 1961 and knew of her approach to the newspapers. But he denied all allegations of impropriety and said that on the advice of his solicitors he was awaiting the opportunity to take legal action to refute them if anything were published on which he could issue a writ. On the question of security, Profumo explained that he had been warned in 1961 to see as little as possible of Stephen Ward, because there was a security problem involved, and he had heeded that advice. I was satisfied with these assurances. No doubt Profumo had frequented circles in which, in my youth, it would have been thought inappropriate for a Minister to move. But times had changed, and although I had not myself much knowledge of this new social world I recognised that the distinctions which had ruled in the past no longer obtained. Respectable and disreputable people now seemed to be all mixed up together.

On 14 March the name of the lady in the case was mentioned in the courts. She had been cited as a prosecution witness in the trial of a West Indian accused of trying to murder her, but had failed to appear. Not unnaturally, in view of the charge, the police regarded her as an important element in obtaining a conviction. Her disappearance, therefore, began to be talked about in the whispering galleries of London which enjoys this kind of scandal as proof of her having been spirited away by powerful protectors. The 'romantic' element in this story was particularly appealing.

> I was forced to spend a great deal of today over a silly scrape [over a woman] into which one of the Ministers has got himself. It's Jack Profumo—Secretary of State for War. It would not matter so much if it was just an affair of morality. But unfortunately, among the frequenters of this raffish and disreputable set, which centres round Lord Astor (Bill Astor), was the Russian Military Attaché! This is the new Cliveden set! . . . I must decide what I ought to do . . . All this is very bad for the reputation of the Party and of the Government.

I had not forgotten the case of Galbraith, impugned by rumour, whom I felt I had allowed to suffer some injustice. I was determined not to let this happen again . . .

On 21 March, during a debate on the imprisonment of the two journalists for contempt of court, George Wigg, a Labour M.P., who had by then begun to take upon himself the role of unofficial keeper of morals and protector of security, made a definite charge, which he alleged it was his duty to do since the Press were muzzled by the Vassall Tribunal. He declared that rumours were going round which involved a member of the Government, who ought to admit or deny the accusation made against him. I was not present during this part of the debate. Wigg's speech was made on the Consolidated Fund Bill, on which, according to our rules, any matter could be raised without notice, and I had already left the House.

The M.P.s who raised the matter in Debate really helped Profumo. Conferences were held in the middle of last night and early this morning I was asked to approve a 'personal' statement after the House met (at 11 a.m.) today. I went through text with Attorney General and Chief Whip and went to the House to give Profumo my support. His statement was clear and pretty convincing. He had met ward at Cliveden originally and had called at Ward's flat where the girl was living. He (and his wife) had been friends with both, but he had actually not seen the girl since the end of 1961. Profumo has behaved foolishly and indiscreetly, but not wickedly. His wife (Valerie Hobson) is very nice and sensible. Of course, all these people move in a raffish, theatrical, bohemian society, where no one really knows anyone and everyone is 'darling'. But Profumo does not seem to have realised that we have—in public life—to observe different standards from those prevalent today in many circles.

Profumo's declarations were more specific than I recorded in my diary. He had not seen Miss Keeler since December 1961; he had first met her in July 1961 and again on half a dozen occasions between then and December 1961; he had nothing to do with her absence from the Old Bailey; there had been no impropriety in their behaviour, and he would issue a writ for libel and slander if any such allegations were made outside the House. This categorical statement in my eyes settled the matter . . .

My confidence in Profumo was strengthened by two libel actions which he immediately brought against *Paris-Match* and the Italian paper *Il Tempo*, and their distributors in London. In the first, the defendant retracted immediately; in the second, costs and damages were awarded. Had I any doubts about Profumo's integrity, I could hardly believe he had both misled the House of Commons and perjured himself in the courts . . .

On 29 May, I had a visit from the Head of the Security Service, who told me that, according to Miss Keeler, Ward had asked her to find out from Profumo some information concerning atomic secrets. But she denied having acted on his instructions. The evidence was too slender to permit of a prosecution of Ward. Indeed, it seemed a ridiculous story, for Profumo had no information on 'atomic secrets' and it was doubtful whether Ward was really an 'agent'. The police were convinced that Ward was not a spy—he was a disreputable man and probably a pimp, but he was far too open and lax in his methods to be an agent. Nevertheless, I did not feel that these new developments could be wholly disregarded. I therefore asked the Lord Chancellor to look further into the matter, and informed Wilson, who continued to press me, of my action.

Dorothy and I then left for a short holiday in Scotland.

> I am handing over to Butler for a week (the first time I have done so since I became PM, except for my longer visits abroad). I am to get only the minimum of telegrams and papers. It should be a real rest.

Alas! the few days of repose were quickly and rudely ended.

> When I was at Oban, I was told by telephone that Profumo had admitted that he had lied to me, to the House, and to the courts. Although we managed to finish our Scottish holiday and go to Iona and Gleneagles as planned, from the day I got back till now (when there is a slight pause) there has been a serious and at times dangerous crisis, which seemed likely to involve the fall of the Government as well as my resignation.
>
> I do not remember ever having been under such a sense of personal strain. Even Suez was 'clean'—about war and politics. This was all 'dirt'.

What had happened was simple. On 4 June Profumo suddenly 'came clean'. Over-burdened no doubt by a guilty conscience, he confessed to the Chief Whip and Bligh that Miss Keeler had been his mistress and that, in this respect, his statement to the House had been untrue.

This was unforgivable. Profumo had definitely, purposefully, and after careful warning from his friends and colleagues, lied both to the House of Commons and in the Courts of Law. I accepted his resignation by letter the next day. Since Parliament was not sitting, I did not think it necessary to return immediately.

[Harold Macmillan, *At the End of the Day* (London, 1973), 436–41.]

## (2) LORDS LAMBTON AND JELLICOE 1973

The Prime Minister

*Report of the Security Commission, July 1973*

1. In your letter of 4 June, 1973, you asked the Security Commission to verify that security was not endangered as a result of the incidents referred to in the statement you made in the House of Commons on 24 May, 1973, or by the actions of the persons involved. You pointed out:

(1) that this was intended to enable the Commission to deal with the possibility that there might have been a potential danger to security in what went on, even if it did not materialise in the event; and

(2) that, taken in conjunction with the general terms of reference with which we were appointed, this would empower the Commission not only to look into the facts of these particular matters but also to consider whether departmental security procedures were properly employed and whether, in the light of recent events, they need to be changed.

The questions involved

2. The incidents referred to in your statement in the House of Commons were the recent association of two Ministers, Earl Jellicoe and Lord Lambton, with prostitutes and, in the case of Lord Lambton, the possibility of his being involved with dangerous drugs. This had led to their resignation from their offices in the Government which each had held since June 1970, Lord Jellicoe from those of Lord Privy Seal and Leader of the House of Lords, Lord Lambton from that of Parliamentary Under-Secretary of State for Defence for the Royal Air Force.

3. We regard your letter as inviting us to inquire into three questions:

(1) 4. The first is whether as a result of those incidents any classified information, *viz.* information the disclosure of which might be harmful to the safety of the United Kingdom or its allies, was in fact communicated directly or indirectly to the intelligence service of any potentially hostile power.

5. This is a question about what did happen. As a result of our inquiries we can answer it categorically: No.

(2) 6. The second question is whether, if Lord Jellicoe and Lord Lambton had remained in their Ministerial offices and had continued to associate with prostitutes in the same sort of way as they had in the period before their resignations, there would have been any risk that classified information would be communicated to the intelligence service of a potentially hostile power.

7. This is a question about what might have happened. It cannot be answered categorically. Whenever any person is in possession of classified information there is always *some* risk of accidental or even intentional disclosure which may result in its coming to the knowledge of the intelligence service of a potentially hostile power. What 'security' is concerned with is whether the risk is so slight as to be acceptable. This depends upon the value of the information to such an intelligence service, and is reflected in the grading of classified information as RESTRICTED, CONFIDENTIAL, SECRET or TOP SECRET. The criterion of acceptability of risk which we have adopted for the purpose of answering the second question is: whether, with the knowledge of the facts relating to the conduct of the two Ministers which we have obtained in the course of our inquiry, we should ourselves have recommended in the interests of security that they should be denied access to information classified in the two highest categories SECRET and TOP SECRET.

8. In answering this question we find it necessary to differentiate between the cases of Lord Jellicoe and Lord Lambton. In the case of Lord Jellicoe we should not have considered it necessary on security grounds that he should be denied further access to SECRET and TOP SECRET information. In the case of Lord Lambton we should have felt compelled to recommend that he should be denied such access.

(3) 9. The third question requires us to review the adequacy of the existing departmental security procedures as they affect Ministers and also to consider whether, without prejudice to the question of their adequacy, they were properly employed in the cases of Lord Jellicoe and Lord Lambton.

10. In our consideration of this question, our inquiries have ranged more widely than was needed to enable us to answer the first two questions. They have brought to light some respects in which we think the existing procedures could be improved. These we deal with in paragraphs 35–43 of our Report. They have, however, no

bearing on the incidents referred to in your statement in the House of Commons. So in effect our Report is dealing with two separate subject matters.

11. We would emphasise that in answering the first two questions our concern is limited to security. It is no part of our function as the Security Commission to express opinions on the political or moral aspects of the matters we have investigated, nor would we regard ourselves as an appropriate body to do this. Still less is it our function to satisfy curiosity as to the private behaviour of men with distinguished records of public service, except to the extent that disclosure of details is necessary to a proper understanding of any risk to security which this behaviour may have involved.

[Report of the Security Commission, July 1973, Cmnd. 5367 (1973), paras. 1–11.]

### (3) MR CECIL PARKINSON 1983

After it was over I stayed on for a chat with Cecil Parkinson, partly to apologise for being late, but I had noticed he looked worried. I asked if anything was wrong and he told me he had 'a personal problem.' I invited him to share it, as perhaps I could help, and he told me that his secretary, Sara Keays, with whom he had had an affair, had told him she was pregnant. I told him to say nothing to anyone and do nothing except to play for time and we would talk about it again shortly . . .

A few days later I saw Cecil who told me that he and his wife Ann were determined to stay together. Miss Keays was determined that an end be put to the rumours by an announcement being made. In despair, Cecil told me he had no option but to resign: 'I will be gone by the morning.' I implored him not to do so. More politicians than him had had affairs outside their marriages. A good number had deserted their wives, married their mistresses and continued in office; why should he resign because his marriage had outlasted his mistress? He said it was better to resign than be hounded out of office. 'No,' I said, 'and not just for your sake. If they get you, they'll want to go on and drag someone else down. They're like wolves behind the sledge—if they drag one of us off, the blood-lust will be worse and they'll be after the rest. You've got to stay.'

I had to see the Prime Minister later in the day and I told her of

Cecil's mood, offering my opinion that she should ask him to stay as Secretary of State but stand down as Party Chairman, to avoid difficulties at the Party Conference. She had arranged to see him following our meeting and by mutual consent I stayed on. Margaret was wonderfully supportive, and Cecil left, still as Secretary of State . . .

The Parkinson story had still not broken in the press when the next evening (the 7th) the Chief Whip, John Wakeham, telephoned from Chequers to sound me out on who should succeed Cecil as Chairman of the Party. I suggested we needed someone who would not be compared with Cecil—perhaps a good peer or businessman who would concentrate on organisation and not the political role. The problem, however, was who?

Despite protracted telephone conversations with Margaret we were unable to identify a candidate for the chairmanship who answered this specification, and with more and more risk of the Parkinson story breaking she decided that John Gummer's presentational skills and his youthfulness made him the best candidate for the job. I had my reservations as I thought he would be unfairly criticised for being too young and too junior, perpetually suffering by contrast with Cecil. However it was arranged that John would go to see the Prime Minister at two o'clock on Tuesday to be told his fate. I asked him to come and see me when he returned, to tell him I thought he had a very difficult time ahead and to offer him some advice . . .

Within days, however, the Parkinson story broke in the press, posing more than enough problems for us. The Sunday papers were pretty hard on Cecil, the most damaging article was a human and perceptive piece by Simon Hoggart in the *Observer* because it focused on his apparent changes of mind. It was a bad start to our conference but my part at least went well. With the theme, 'We are a party of trades unionists now,' I proclaimed our intention to give by law to trade unionists the rights they had been denied by their own leaders. Industrial relations reform used to be seen as a minefield but Jim Prior and I had gone through the minefield step by step without treading on a mine. 'Indeed the only casualties so far have been on the TUC side. They have been left hanging on the barbed wire of their own defences', I said. My reforms, I claimed, would lead to better industrial relations and thereby more jobs. It was a mixture of toughness, humour and a determinedly cautious approach that went down very well indeed. I returned to the platform to hear and support Cecil Parkinson who made a good speech although he was clearly very tense. That night I believed he could survive the Keays affair.

We were up early next morning and on the road to London soon after 8 a.m. I had decided to miss the Prime Minister's speech as it was Lord Mayor's Prizegiving Day at the City of London School in which our son William as Head Boy played a major part, including his first public speech, and we had promised William we would be there. By 10 a.m. we heard on the car radio that Cecil Parkinson had resigned. Not long after returning from William's prizegiving I received a call from a television producer telling me that the *Sun* newspaper was publishing a story that Cecil had spoken bitterly of the failure of his colleagues to support him, and quoting him as saying, 'but my worst enemy in the Cabinet over these weeks has been Norman Tebbit.' It was supposed to have been said to the editor of the *Daily Express,* but the Express carried no such story. I was deeply upset and phoned several friends for advice, then suddenly I made up my mind—I would go to see Cecil. It was already 10.30 p.m. and my Margaret said she wanted to come—I said no but agreed to take William with me for company. Cecil's home was surrounded by press men so I drove past, parked a little way away and sent William armed with a note to Cecil and a copy of the next day's *Sun* which we had bought in Fleet Street. William returned to say Cecil would of course be pleased to see me, and the pair of us walked quickly through the photographers and into the house. Cecil was pretty miserable. He did feel he had been badly let down, but assured me he had not only not said I had been an enemy but knew I had been a friend. We talked about his future, whether he would stay in politics or not. He was preparing to go abroad for a holiday and we agreed to meet on his return—before he made any irrevocable decisions. Well after midnight William and I pushed through the press men outside and headed for home.

Late next day, Saturday the 13th, the Prime Minister rang from Chequers to ask me to replace Cecil at the Department of Trade and Industry.

[Norman Tebbit, *Upwardly Mobile* (London, 1988), 205, 208–11.]

## 3. CONDUCT OF DEPARTMENT

### (1) LORD CARRINGTON 1982

On Thursday 1 April I was back at my desk. Certain British forces had now been put at notice. On Friday 2 April Argentina invaded the Falkland Islands. On Monday 5 April I surrendered to the Queen at Windsor my seals of office as Foreign and Commonwealth Secretary.

It was a difficult as well as a painful decision and it was entirely my own. There was a good deal of pressure on me to remain at my post. I was grateful for the confidence and kindness this implied but I could not agree that it would be right. It was a great additional sadness to me that Humphrey Atkins, Lord Privy Seal and my number two in the Foreign Office, as well as Richard Luce, decided they should go as well.

As to the responsibility for the invasion itself, in the sense of having left undone something we should have done which would have pre-empted it, I could not with honesty and soul-searching feel much. To have prepared and sailed the sort of military force which could physically have prevented invasion, which could have defeated the attempt, was not a decision it was at any time rational for the Government to have taken before the event on the information they possessed. Had it, by some extraordinary stroke of intuition, been taken—say in late February—it might well have prevented an invasion in April, but we would never have known that there was to have been such an invasion: there was no conceivable argument by which such a force could be kept in the South Atlantic indefinitely: the Argentines would certainly have refused to negotiate 'under the threat of force'; and the subsequent withdrawal of the force would have exposed us to precisely the charge of 'sending the wrong signals' to Argentina, that must be the principal case to answer in the circumstances that actually occurred.

On the question of wrong signals, I will add only this. The right signals, for us and for previous British Governments, were to my mind to combine a clear readiness to negotiate with an equally clear determination to defend the islands if need arose. We could perhaps have done better on both counts in the areas I have touched upon; but I think that the fundamental difference between us and previous

British Governments of either party was not in the signals we were sending, but in the fact that we were faced with a Government in Buenos Aires determined on action whatever the realities of the situation.

As to whether we might—or British intelligence might—have discerned earlier the actual intention to invade, I doubt it. Plans, even detailed plans, are one thing: firm decisions quite another. It was rumoured afterwards that American satellite Intelligence had disclosed everything, and been rejected by us—rumours without a breath of truth. Lord Franks and his colleagues opined that from mid-March we were inadequately sensitive to a change and hardening in Argentinian attitudes. I believe that we were fully aware of this change, and appropriately disturbed by it: it was the background to my appeals to Al Haig. Nevertheless it doesn't appear that the junta's final decision to invade was taken until very shortly before the event, and there was force, however mistaken with hindsight, in the argument that overreaction could precipitate a crisis while calm might defuse it.

Stories which were later given currency that we in the Foreign Office ignored warnings from our Embassy in Buenos Aires were totally without foundation. The basic criticism levelled at us was, of course, miscalculation—we miscalculated that the Argentinians would invade. Certainly we did: we miscalculated Argentine folly. And history will record that the fundamental miscalculation was General Galtieri's.

It was not a sense of culpability that led me to resign—a subjective judgement, of course, but one which was later to find confirmation in the Franks Report. The logic of my resignation was different, and I had two principal reasons, one general and one more particular.

The general reason was my sympathetic understanding that the whole of our country felt angry and humiliated. I felt the same myself. British territory had, without warning, been invaded. There were hysterical outbursts in Parliament and yells of 'betrayal', and although these were inaccurate and offensive they were understandable. Inhabitants of a British colony—men and women of British blood—had been taken over against their will. Diplomacy had failed to avert this. Military reinforcement had not been tried. Deterrence had been exposed as a bluff. Our hand had apparently been called. There was never the slightest doubt that, with Margaret Thatcher at the head of the Government, we wouldn't take this lying down, and we didn't. But the first shock and fury were felt throughout Britain, and in those circumstances—with people very naturally turning on the Government and accusing it of mismanagement—it is right, in my judgement, that there must be a resignation. The nation feels that there has been a disgrace. Someone must have been to blame. The disgrace must be purged. The person to purge it should be the minister in charge. That was me. I was also very aware that my membership of the Lords was at that moment an embarrassment to the Prime Minister, and a weakness. In the Commons Humphrey Atkins was first-class, as was Richard Luce, but when there's a real political crisis it is in the House of Commons that the life and death of Government is decided and I bitterly regretted that I could not face that House at Margaret Thatcher's side.

The more particular reason was my awareness that the Government was in for a hard time and that my presence would make it not easier but harder. We were now assembling a task force and sailing it to the South Atlantic—an action with which I wholeheartedly agreed. During the time it would take—a matter of weeks not days—it was going to be difficult to keep Parliament and country sufficiently united behind our actions, and unity is essential in war. My departure would put a stop to the search for scapegoats. It would serve the cause of unity and help turn the eyes of all from the past to the immediate future. With John Nott, I had attended a fairly disagreeable meeting of the 1922 Committee and although nobody shouted for my resignation I knew that within the Conservative Party itself my remaining in office was not going to help the Prime Minister with her own supporters.

*Sir Ian Gilmour and Mr Richard Luce also resigned as Foreign Office Ministers.*

[Carrington, *Reflect on Things Past*, 368–71.]

### (2) MR NICHOLAS FAIRBAIRN 1982

The Solicitor-General for Scotland (Mr Nicholas Fairbairn):

With your permission, Mr Speaker, I should like to repeat a statement being made in another place by my right hon. and learned Friend the Lord Advocate.

Before reading that statement, may I make a personal apology to the whole House? Certain remarks attributed to myself were reported in the press yesterday and repeated this morning. Any remarks that I made were made before matters developed to the point when it was obviously the wish of hon. Members that a statement should be made in Parliament about the case. If anything that I may have said showed any disrespect to the House, I wish to apologise unreservedly as that was furthest from my intention. I shall now read the statement . . .

*Mr Fairbairn had explained to the press why no public prosecution would be forthcoming in a rape case. He later resigned.*

[16 H.C. Deb. 423 (21 January 1982).]

## 4. CIVIL SERVANTS' CONDUCT

### (1) SIR THOMAS DUGDALE 1954

In 1937 the Air Ministry had compulsorily acquired as an experimental bomb site some land near Crichel in Dorset. In 1950, under the previous Government, that Ministry had decided it had no further use for the land. The Ministry of Agriculture, however, was interested in it as a site for two new farm holdings and since the land had been acquired by Government for its own purposes it was simply transferred from one Ministry to another. That was the situation we inherited. We received independent advice from the Land Commission that from the point of view of production it would be best to keep the land which had been acquired together in two units as proposed. I was sent to inspect. I agreed with the Land Commission.

Some of the land, known as Crichel Down, had been bought from Lord Alington—just under half the total. His daughter, his heiress, had married Commander Toby Marten; and the Martens protested at the transfer of what had been their family land from one Ministry to another. They pointed out that there had always been assurances given to landowners from whom land had been acquired for wartime purposes that, if it were no longer required by Government, land-owners would be given the chance to repurchase. The matter turned, of course, on whether land acquired for one purpose could be retained by Government for a different purpose without breach of those assurances. The case dragged on amid a good deal of (mostly unfavourable) publicity. Eventually an Inquiry was held, Sir Andrew Clarke QC conducting it. The Inquiry's finding was that our Department had acted in an arbitrary manner. Officials were criticized by name and the minister faced a sceptical meeting of Conservative backbenchers. Eventually there was a long debate on the proceedings of the Inquiry, during which Dugdale said, stoutly, that he did not take so poor a view of the conduct of his officials as the Inquiry had: it was true, he said, that they had failed to make clear to him that the original purchase of the land had been under threat of compulsion, but he did not regard that as the dominant factor. Nevertheless he recognized, with dignity, the mood of the House and since he was an honourable man and his Department had been criticized by an Inquiry and, in effect, by Parliament, he reckoned there could only be one outcome. The Martens got their land. Tom Dugdale resigned.

Myth has collected around the Crichel Down case. Its upshot has been thought of as a triumph over bureaucracy, talked about as demonstrating the irresponsible and despotic power which civil servants can—and in wartime sometimes did—arrogate to themselves; as a failure of successive ministers to control their men; as, ultimately, a vindication of the subject against the Crown. It was not in the least like that. There was a certain amount of incompetence and administrative bungling involved in the run-up to the Crichel Down affair but at the heart of it was the point with which I began this chapter—a failure to appreciate that there was, in our country, a new spirit, a new situation. The material national interest, the need to maximize farm production and to use the power of Government where desirable to promote this, was like a charted line on a graph. It had been at its highest point when we had been under siege. It had continued high in the hungry aftermath of war. Now it was following a downward curve, and was approaching the point of convergence and then the crossing of another charted line—the line of individual rights of property, the line of ordinary personal and economic freedom. This second line had been at its lowest during the war, when all personal rights and privileges had been subordinated to winning and to survival. But now this line was on a rising curve—and rightly so. The advent of the Conservative Government in 1951 had the desired effect of making it rise more steeply still. Crichel Down showed that the two lines had crossed.

Personal rights mattered, and their restoration was more important than a Government Department's perception of how, one day, our land might marginally produce a little more.

Neither our civil servants in the Department, nor Tom Dugdale, nor I realized, at the time, that those lines had crossed. Dick Nugent did. He was always perfectly clear in his mind that the Martens should be offered back the land which had been theirs before Government took it from them. He was consistent in this opinion, although the fact was not always to be guessed from the rudeness with which he was on occasion described by those who criticized our Department's conduct most virulently. Dick realized that the lines had crossed and that people now saw such matters in a different way.

The Crichel Down case was disagreeable. It was my first job in Government and my first experience not only of being an object of public criticism but of coming to the conclusion that my judgement had been at fault and much of the criticism justified. Some people reckoned I had been let off lightly by the Inquiry, and said so: Sir Richard Acland, Labour MP for Gravesend, spread himself in the Commons debate on this particular theme.

I thought Tom Dugdale right to resign. Then Dick Nugent decided he should go too. I said, 'If you go, I go.' We wrote letters of resignation to the Prime Minister, who replied that there was no need for the step. Dick and I compared notes. We thought this private exchange inadequate and we still felt we ought to follow our chief and go. We asked to see Churchill and we saw him together. He peered at us.

'Do you both *want* to resign?'

We told him that an independent Inquiry had been critical of the Department and I pointed out that I had played a leading role in the business. We knew that the Prime Minister himself thought our Ministry had been on the wrong side, that Government policy had been led by us in a mistaken direction; and, obviously, the whole Government had been weakened as Governments always are if an Inquiry slates a Department.

Churchill grunted. Then he said, 'I think you had better carry on,' adding, 'What do you *want*?'

We settled for a published exchange of letters, and we agreed to stay. Churchill was not an easy person for young men to gainsay. I had asked the advice of Bobbety Salisbury earlier.

'I'm the worst possible person to talk to,' he said. 'I'm a resigner by nature!'

I have often been taunted about withdrawing my resignation. These things are hard and the path often obscure. Whether I was right or wrong to stay I do not know.

[Carrington, *Reflect on Things Past*, 90–3.]

## (2) THE VEHICLE AND GENERAL CASE

(8). Mr Jardine failed to guide or control the Insurance Branch of the Department in its dealings with the Company. He did not display initiative or imagination in considering the Company's affairs. The ultimate responsibility for the failure of the Department to take action against the Company lies with him. His conduct as a whole fell below the standard of competence which he ought to have displayed and constitutes negligence. (Chapter VIII, paragraph 341).

(9). Mr Homewood's concentration on the actuarial method of checking the reserves of a motor insurance company caused him to ignore danger signals about the Company's position. In consequence he did not advise that action should be taken against the Company. His conduct deserves criticism but does not amount to negligence. (Chapter VIII, paragraphs 338 to 339).

(10). Mr Steel inherited a vast and complex problem about the Company which in the light of the policy which he inherited from Mr Homewood caused him to hesitate and to be indecisive. In consequence he did not advise that action should be taken against the Company at a time when the known facts called for action. His conduct deserves criticism but does not amount to negligence. (Chapter VIII, paragraph 340).

(11). There was no negligence by any person in the service of the Crown other than Mr Jardine. (Chapter VIII, paragraphs 323, 328 to 344).

[Report of the Tribunal of Inquiry on the Vehicle and General Insurance Company, H.C. 133 (1971–2), Summary of Findings, paras. (8)–(11).]

*No Minister considered that he should resign following the criticism of civil servants in the Department of Trade and Industry.*

## 5. RESIGNATIONS SINCE 1960 ON GROUNDS OF INDIVIDUAL RESPONSIBILITY

| Name | Post | Reason and date |
|---|---|---|
| T. Galbraith | Parliamentary Under-Secretary, Scotland | Security: later exonerated (1962) |
| J. Profumo | Secretary of State for War | Lying to House of Commons (1963) |
| R. Maudling | Home Secretary | Poulson investigation (1972) |
| Ld. Lambton | Parliamentary Under-Secretary, Defence | Associating with prostitutes (1973) |
| Ld. Jellicoe | Lord Privy Seal | Associating with prostitutes (1973) |
| Ld. Brayley | Parliamentary Under-Secretary, Defence | Former business interests (1974) |
| N. Fairbairn | Solicitor-General for Scotland | Handling of a prosecution (1982) |
| Ld. Carrington | Foreign Secretary | Foreign Office failure over the Falklands (1982) |
| H. Atkins | Lord Privy Seal | Foreign Office failure over the Falklands |
| R. Luce | Minister of State, Foreign Office | Foreign Office failure over the Falklands |
| C. Parkinson | Secretary of State for Trade and Industry | Affair with his secretary (1983) |
| L. Brittan | Secretary of State for Trade and Industry | Leaking of Solicitor-General's letter (1986) |

## 6. NON-RESIGNATIONS

### (1) MR ALAN LENNOX-BOYD 1959

In addition, the Government had to face a number of critical situations, sometimes unexpected and unpredictable, sometimes arising from deep-rooted causes.

Among the former was a tragic incident following the suppression of the Mau Mau rebellion in Kenya. By the end of 1956 this terrible tale of barbarity was brought to a final conclusion, and the military were able to restore full responsibility for law and order to the civil authorities. In the course of the 'emergency', which caused dreadful loss of life to Europeans, Asians and Africans alike, 88,000 members of the Kikuyu tribe had been detained in custody. But by the beginning of 1959 all had been released except 4,000, who were serving prison sentences, and 1,000 'hard-core' incorrigibles held in special camps.

In one of these, named Hola, eleven prisoners died on 3 March. The inquest revealed that death was due to 'multiple bruising'. This story was widely reported in the British Press, and the Opposition immediately threatened a vote of censure. I felt particular concern for Alan Lennox-Boyd, the Colonial Secretary, whose deep sympathy for all African peoples had won him not only their respect, but their affection. A full enquiry into this regrettable event was held by W. H. Goudie, the Senior Resident Magistrate. There seemed to be no doubt that the fact that responsibility for the detention camps was shared between two Ministers in the Governor's Council had resulted in a failure to provide efficient control by either. My colleagues were at first somewhat divided as to whether to accede to an Opposition's demand for a public enquiry, but the publication of the White Paper on 10 June brought a good reaction.

> This morning's Press, following publication of the White Paper, has been pretty good. *The Times* (perhaps an *amende honorable*) wrote a very sensible leader.

The enquiry had been full and explicit. It was clear that only the most nominal responsibility could be attributed to the Colonial Secretary and little to the Governor, Sir Evelyn Baring.

On 16 June the matter was fully debated in the House of Commons.

> The debate has gone off 'as well as could be expected', but it has been an anxious day. Soskice (ex-Attorney-General) opened for the Opposition with a clever and well constructed speech, based largely on the Coroner's report. He ended with a bitter, but not ineffective, personal attack on Sir Evelyn Baring and the Colonial Secretary. Perhaps this was rather too highly coloured—for everyone on both sides of the House respects Lennox-Boyd and knows how much sympathy and devotion he has brought to his task. Colonial Secretary followed. His speech was very long, but in the main succeeded in its purpose. He frankly admitted the mistakes and

muddles of the Hola tragedy. But by giving the whole story of Mau Mau, and particularly by a vivid story of how the original 80,000 detainees had been brought down to under 1,000 by the 'rehabilitation' work, he did succeed in putting this unhappy incident in its proper perspective.

Nevertheless the Colonial Secretary thought it his duty to offer his resignation, which he pressed on me both in conversation and by letter. Although I respected his honourable sentiments, I went into great detail in my reply both as to the precedents in other departments and the special relationship between the Secretary of State and the Governor in the Colonial Office. More directly,

I kept telling him that it would be a fatal mistake and quite uncalled-for. But (with all his extraordinary charm and real ability) he is a highly-strung, sensitive, and rather quixotic character. I tell him that to resign now over this affair would (*a*) be a great blow to Her Majesty's Government at the most critical period before the General Election, when all is going well otherwise; (*b*) would be a very sad end to his splendid career as Colonial Secretary; (*c*) would upset the whole Colonial Service, whose loyalty and devotion he can command; (*d*) would have very bad—even dangerous—effects in Kenya and Africa . . . (*e*) that it would involve Sir Evelyn Baring's resignation. This would really be a tragic end to a fine career of voluntary service in Africa.

*Mr Lennox-Boyd did not resign.*

[Harold Macmillan, *Riding the Storm* (London, 1971), 733–4.]

### (2) MR WILLIAM WHITELAW 1982

On Friday 9 July a man called Fagan was arrested in Buckingham Palace after entering the Queen's bedroom. Mercifully, the Queen was totally unharmed and indeed showed remarkable courage and calm in dealing with this extraordinary incident.

My first reaction on being told the news was one of intense relief that the Queen was unharmed. Indeed, that feeling so dominated my mind that I did not at first appreciate the full horror of the whole affair. On Saturday 10 July I was due to go to Glenalmond School in Perthshire to attend the annual school prize-giving. I was looking forward to this as a somewhat special occasion, for my father had been in the school and I had never visited it. All my emotional feelings at never having known my father were aroused and so I was preparing my speech with special care. I became so absorbed in this immediate event that I doubt if anyone present on that Saturday afternoon could have realized the other preoccupations on my mind.

Anyway, all the necessary police action had been taken and police inquiries had been set in hand. There was really nothing else immediately to be done. It seemed likely that the story would leak in the Press over the weekend, but it was clear to me that if it did not, then I should have to give the news to Parliament on Monday. Clearly the terms of any such announcement needed discussion between the Palace and my Home Office officials in the first case.

In fact the story did not break until Monday morning. Over the weekend I began to feel in turn both amazed and furious that such a failure in the security surrounding Her Majesty should have occurred. But it was not until the news broke in the Monday morning papers that the full horror of the incident hit me. Then I felt deeply distressed that I personally, as Home Secretary, should have failed the Queen so dismally. I kept on contemplating the awful possibility that Her Majesty might have been injured in some way. Indeed, my feelings of dismay were such that I felt I must immediately go and see the Prime Minister, and I asked my Private Secretary to arrange the meeting as soon as possible. The Prime Minister's office confirmed that she would see me at once, and so I drove from the Home Office to No. 10, at that time utterly determined to resign at once.

As always on such occasions, the Prime Minister was kind and reassuring. She and all those around her told me that any such action would be absurd. Above all, the Queen was unharmed. And anyway the Home Secretary could not be regarded as directly responsible for the operational action of members in the organizations for which he had overall responsibility. Similar arguments had been put to me earlier by my Ministers and officials at the Home Office. My feelings of utter shame and misery were not assuaged, but I accepted their general advice and resolved to face Parliament and the Press furore which would certainly follow. When it did, I was much comforted by a message from one of my friends. It said, 'Don't be silly and resign. After all, if the Queen and the Prime Minister had wanted a Home Secretary who would be quick and agile in patrolling the Palace grounds and in pursuing and catching intruders, you would have been one of the last people that they would have considered. Thank goodness that is not your job.'

In Parliament I was at least able to tell the House that the Commissioner, David McNee, had immediately on the Friday appointed Deputy Assistant Commissioner Dellow to conduct an urgent inquiry. Furthermore, Mr Dellow had already submitted an interim report and had promised a further one later in the week. I told the House that I would also make a further statement at that time. The reaction in the House was predictably one of relief at the Queen being safe, and at the same time one of complete shock that such an appalling failure of the security arrangements surrounding Her Majesty could have occurred.

The next day there were some demands for my resignation in the Press, particularly of course from those who anyway wanted to get rid of me. Some parliamentary Press writers also stated that they were dissatisfied with my statement in the House, and one said that it had not 'lived up to the level of events'. I met him shortly afterwards and asked him if he would tell me what words in the English language would actually have met his criteria. Of course there was no answer. Sometimes it is quite easy to be a parliamentary critic from the gallery.

It was without doubt the unhappiest moment in my parliamentary career, but my friends in all parts of the House were understanding and their kindness did much to improve my morale. I knew that I would continue to be harshly criticized and derided by some sections of the Press and that I would have to face another important test when I came to make a full report later. Little did I know that before that happened I would have suffered another severe embarrassment.

[Lord Whitelaw, *The Whitelaw Memoirs* (London, 1989), 211–13.]

## (3) MR JAMES PRIOR 1983

On 25th September 1983, a Sunday I happened to be on duty in Northern Ireland, Jane and I had just been walking round the garden at Hillsborough at about 4 o'clock when I noticed a helicopter in the sky. I commented to Jane that I hoped it did not mean something was wrong.

Within ten minutes Noel Cornick, my private secretary, was on the phone to tell me that there had been a break-out by thirty-eight Republican prisoners from the Maze; a prison officer had been killed; ten prisoners had been quickly recaptured but the rest were still on the loose . . .

Immediately after the break-out I of course offered Margaret my resignation. She refused to accept it. She was naturally as furious as I was, but felt that the escape was a risk that was inherent in the unique conditions of Northern Ireland's prisons.

The discussion with the Prime Minister, with whom I agreed the lines of a statement I would make to the House, convinced me that it would be wrong for me to press my resignation. My statement included the broad terms of reference of the full report which I commissioned on the break-out from Sir James Hennessy, the Chief Inspector of Prisons. For me to have resigned straightaway would have played into the hands of all the troublemakers. It would have been seen as again giving way to pressure from irresponsible Unionist MPs. Above all it would have added another immense boost to the already heightened morale of the IRA.

The question of my resignation was one of many I had to answer in the House. To what extent is a Minister responsible for everything that happens in his Department, even down to the day-to-day operation of the prisons? I took the view that I should not resign unless it was clear from the Report, which would take some months to complete, that a policy change or directive had been the direct cause of the escape—for example, if we had denied resources to the prison or given ill-advised orders about the way in which discipline should be enforced.

During the course of the inquiry, we were criticised by the prison officers on the grounds that the prime cause had been new rules introduced at the end of the hunger strike on the wearing of prison clothes and allowing prisoners to associate more freely within the block. But the accusation was quickly refuted, as owing to the prisoners' intransigence we had refused to relax the rules on greater association at that time.

A much more serious charge was that the reforms that we had granted at the end of the hunger strike had undermined the authority of the prison staff. They alleged that this was a moral victory for the republican prisoners which had sapped morale so seriously that their own discipline had suffered to the point of permitting the break-out.

Apart from the accusations of inefficiency in the prison service, every charge under the sun was laid against the RUC and the Army for not capturing more of the prisoners who had escaped. In the circumstances of Northern Ireland there are always people who will hide terrorists on the run and then in time get them safely across the border to the South, where they can lie low; as indeed most of them have done ever since—although a few have returned to terrorist activity.

When the Hennessey Report on the break-out was finally published in January 1984, it showed that no policy decisions contributed to the escape. But it was extremely critical of many aspects of security at the Maze, and I therefore had to decide whether to take action against the Governor, who must carry ultimate responsibility for the state of the prison. If I had done nothing, undoubtedly I would have been told that the whole inquiry was a whitewash. On the other hand, when I asked him to resign and leave the service early—although we fully safeguarded his pension—I was accused of trying to push the blame on to him when it properly resided with me. Politicians in the Province were particularly quick to do this. It is much easier for them to blame British Ministers and the Northern Ireland Office than to accept any responsibility for what goes wrong within Northern Ireland themselves . . .

Of course the public wanted to be assured that a gaol-break of this kind would not happen again and that the escaped prisoners would be recaptured as fast as possible. It was understandable that they felt an example should be made of whoever was responsible, whether it was the prison Governor, a junior Minister, or me. But I still think that both in principle and in practice my decision to remain was right, although I was certainly not unaware of the constitutional dilemma.

[James Prior, *A Balance of Power* (London, 1986), 230–33.]

## Ministers' Personal Financial Affairs

### *VIII Acceptance of Gifts and Services*

63. It is a well-established and recognised rule that no Minister or public servant should accept gifts, hospitality or services from anyone which would, or might appear to, place him under an obligation.

64. This is primarily a matter which must be left to the good sense of Ministers. But if any Minister finds himself in doubt or difficulty over this, he should seek the Prime Minister's guidance.

65. There may be difficulty in refusing a gift from another Government (or Governmental organisation) without the risk of apparent discourtesy. In deciding whether to accept or to offer gifts of this kind Ministers should where possible consult their Permanent Secretaries, who will be able to advise them about the rules applicable to civil servants in analogous circumstances; and in any case of doubt they should seek the Prime Minister's views. If however such a gift is accepted the following rules apply:

(*a*) Its receipt should, in all cases, be reported to the Permanent Secretary.

(*b*) Gifts of small value (currently this should be put at £30) may be retained by the recipient.

(*c*) Gifts of a higher value should be handed over to the Department for disposal, except that

(i) if the recipient wishes to purchase the gift at its cash value (abated by £30), he may do so;

(ii) if the recipient wishes to reciprocate with a gift of equivalent value out of his own pocket, he should be allowed to retain the gift that he receives;

(iii) the gift may be displayed or used in the Department where this is appropriate;

(iv) if the disposal of the gift would cause offence or if it might be appropriate for the recipient to use or display the gift on some future occasion as a mark of politeness, then the gift should be retained in the Department for this purpose for a period of up to five years.

### *IX Ministers' Private Interests*

66. The principles which should guide Ministers in deciding whether they may properly continue to hold Company Directorships and similar offices have been stated from time to time in the House of Commons. The conventions at present to be observed are set out below.

67. It is a principle of public life that Ministers must so order their affairs that no conflict arises, or appears to arise, between their private interests and their public duties.

68. Such a conflict may arise if a Minister takes an active part in any undertaking which may have contractual or other relations with a Government Department, more particularly with his own Department. It may arise, not only if the minister has a financial interest in such an undertaking, but also if he is actively associated with any body, even of a philanthropic character, which might have negotiations or other dealings with the Government or be involved in disputes with it. Furthermore Ministers should be free to give full attention to their official duties, and they should not engage in other activities which might be thought to distract their attention from those duties.

69. Each Minister should normally decide for himself how the principles apply to him. Over much of the field, as is shown below, there are established precedents. Where there is a doubt it will almost always be better to surrender the interest but in such cases the Prime Minister of the day must be the final judge, and Ministers should submit any such case to him for his decision.

70. Where it is proper for a Minister to retain any private interest, it is the rule that he should declare that interest to his colleagues if they have to discuss public business in any way affecting it, and that he should entirely detach himself from the consideration of that business.

Public appointments

71. Ministers should on assuming office give up any other public appointments they may hold. Where it is proposed that such an appointment should be retained, the Prime Minister must be consulted.

Directorships

72. Ministers must on assuming office resign any directorships which they may hold, whether in public or in private companies and whether the directorship carries remuneration or is honorary. The only exception to this rule is that directorships in private companies established for the maintenance of private family estates, and only incidentally concerned in trading, may be retained subject to this reservation—that if at any time the Minister feels that conflict is likely to arise between this private interest and his public duty, he should even in those cases divest himself of his directorship. Directorships or offices held in connection with philanthropic under-

takings should also be resigned if there is any risk of conflict arising between the interests of the undertakings and the Government.

Partnerships

73. Ministers who are partners in professional firms, as, e.g., solicitors, accountants, etc., should, on assuming office, cease to play any part in the day-to-day management of the firm's affairs. They are not necessarily required, however, to dissolve their partnership or to allow e.g., their annual practising certificate to lapse. Beyond this it is not possible to lay down precise rules applicable to every case; and any Minister who is in doubt about his personal position in this respect should consult the Prime Minister.

Shareholdings

74. Ministers cannot be expected, on assuming office, to dispose of all the investments they may hold. But if a Minister holds a controlling interest in any company, considerations arise which are not unlike those governing the holding of directorships; and, if there is any danger of a conflict of interest, the right course is for the Minister to divest himself of his controlling interest in the company. There may also be exceptional cases where, even though no controlling interest is involved, the actual holding of particular shares in concerns closely associated with a Minister's own Department may create the danger of a conflict of interest: where a Minister considers this to be the case, he should divest himself of the holding. There may also be less clear-cut cases where a Minister would feel it appropriate to place his holding in the hands of trustees.

75. Ministers should scrupulously avoid speculative investments in securities about which they have, or may be thought to have, early or confidential information likely to affect the price of those securities.

'Names' at Lloyds

76. A Minister cannot properly continue to be a 'name' at Lloyds while holding office as Prime Minister, Chancellor of the Exchequer or Secretary of State for Trade. In each case he is required to suspend his underwriting activities. As regards other Ministers who, on appointment to office, are 'names', it is clearly inappropriate that they should take an active part in the management

of the affairs of the syndicates of which they are members; and there may be cases in which, because of the emphasis of a syndicate's business, any continued participation in it must be regarded as inconsistent with the holding of a particular Ministerial office. All Ministers are therefore required, on appointment whether to their first or to any subsequent Ministerial office, to obtain the permission of the Prime Minister before continuing a connection with Lloyds, however nominal, which they had established before appointment or establishing any such connection during their term of appointment. Before granting permission, the Prime Minister will need to be satisfied that the conditions indicated above will be met.

Nominations for international awards, etc.

77. From time to time, the personal support of Ministers is requested for nominations being made for international prizes and awards, e.g., the annual Nobel prizes. Ministers should not sponsor individual nominations for any awards, since it would be inevitable that some people would assume that the Government was itself thereby giving its sponsorship.

78. For the same reason Ministers invited to become signatories of open appeals or open letters or to attend a rally or other function to which publicity is to be given should consult the Prime Minister before agreeing to do so . . .

117. Ministers should not accept payment for official broadcasts on radio or television.

Press articles

118. Ministers are precluded from the practice of journalism including the contribution of regular weekly or fortnightly articles to local newspapers in their constituencies.

119. This rule need not debar a Minister from contributing to a book, journal or newspaper (including a local newspaper in his constituency), on occasion, for the purpose of supplementing other means of informing the public about the work of his Department, provided that publication will not be at variance with his obligations to Parliament and his duty to observe the principle of collective Ministerial responsibility. It may be appropriate on occasion for such articles to be expanded to cover broader issues of Government policy. In cases of doubt, and in all cases where a Minister is

contemplating the contribution of an article going beyond the strict confines of his Departmental responsibility, the Prime Minister should be consulted, preferably before work has begun and in any case before any commitment to publish is entered into. In all cases where an article contains material which falls within the Departmental responsibility of another Minister, that Minister must be consulted. Ministers should not accept payment for such writings.

120. It is not in general desirable for Ministers to engage in controversy in the correspondence columns of either the home or the overseas Press. Ministers are not debarred from writing letters to newspapers; but the Prime Minister's authority should be obtained beforehand . . .

*XIII Ministerial Memoirs and Other Writings*

127. The prohibition on the practice of journalism by Ministers does not extend to writings of a literary, artistic, musical, historical, scientific, philosophical or fictional character which do not draw directly on their Ministerial experience.

128. The principle of collective responsibility and the need to safeguard national security and our relations with other countries impose certain obligations on former Ministers who are contemplating the publication of material based upon their recollection of the conduct of Government business in which they took part. They are required to submit their manuscript to the Secretary of the Cabinet and to conform to the principles set out in the Radcliffe Report of 1976 (Cmnd. 6386).

129. A Minister who is keeping a diary of his Ministerial experience may judge it advisable to leave testamentary instructions to ensure that any arrangements for its subsequent publication conformed with the requirements of the previous paragraph.

[*Questions of Procedure for Ministers* (1976 version), paras. 63–78, 117–120, 127–9.]

# [7]

# THE OPPOSITION

## The Leader of the Opposition

### 1. SUCCEEDING TO THE OFFICE

*A party Leader will become Leader of the Opposition either (a) if he loses a general election as Prime Minister but remains Leader of his party which is the largest in opposition, or (b) if he is elected to be Leader of his party in succession to the Leader of the Opposition.*

| Leader of the Opposition | Dates | Reason he succeeded |
|---|---|---|
| Winston Churchill | 1945–51 | Loss of 1945 election |
| Clement Attlee | 1951–5 | Loss of 1951 election |
| Hugh Gaitskell | 1955–63 | Succeeded Attlee |
| Harold Wilson | 1963–4 | Succeeded Gaitskell |
| Sir A. Douglas-Home | 1964–5 | Loss of 1964 election |
| Edward Heath | 1965–70 | Succeeded Douglas-Home |
| Harold Wilson | 1970–4 | Loss of 1970 election |
| Edward Heath | 1974–5 | Loss of 1974 election |
| Margaret Thatcher | 1975–9 | Succeeded Heath |
| James Callaghan | 1979–80 | Loss of 1979 election |
| Michael Foot | 1980–3 | Succeeded Callaghan |
| Neil Kinnock | 1983– | Succeeded Foot |

### 2. IDENTITY OF THE LEADER OF THE OPPOSITION

2.—(1) In this Act 'Leader of the Opposition' means, in relation to either House of Parliament, that Member of that House who is for the time being the Leader in that House of the party in opposition to Her Majesty's Government having the greatest numerical strength in the House of Commons; and 'Chief Opposition Whip' means, in relation to either House of Parliament, the person for the time being nominated as such by the Leader of the Opposition in that House; and 'Assistant Opposition Whip', in relation to the House of Commons, means a person for the time being nominated as such, and to be paid as such, by the Leader of the Opposition in the House of Commons.

(2) If any doubt arises as to which is or was at any material time the party in opposition to Her Majesty's Government having the greatest numerical strength in the House of Commons, or as to who is or was at any material time the leader in that House of such a party, the question shall be decided for the purposes of this Act by the Speaker of the House of Commons, and his decision, certified in writing under his hand, shall be final and conclusive.

(3) If any doubt arises as to who is or was at any material time the Leader in the House of Lords of the said party, the question shall be decided for the purposes of this Act by the Lord Chancellor, and his decision, certified in writing under his hand, shall be final and conclusive.

[Ministerial and Other Salaries Act 1975, s. 2.]

## 3. FUNDING THE LEADER OF THE OPPOSITION

The Lord President of the Council (Mr Wakeham): The current annual cost to public funds of staff and benefits in kind provided to the official Opposition in addition to the moneys provided under the scheme for financial assistance to Opposition parties ('Short money') is estimated to be as follows:

| Opposition Whips' Office (Commons) | Estimated cost (£) |
|---|---|
| 4 staff | 55,000 |
| Office equipment | 1,500 |
| Postal services | 15,000 |

| Opposition Whips' Office (Lords) | Estimated cost (£) |
|---|---|
| Postal services | 12,000 |
| HMSO supplies | 1,500 |

In addition, a car is available to the Leader of the Opposition from the Government car service. The cost of this in the current financial year is estimated to be about £36,000.

[127 H.C. Deb. 657 (written answers 17 February 1988).]

## 4. CONSTITUTIONAL DUTIES OF THE OPPOSITION LEADER

The paramount constitutional duty of the Leader of the Opposition is to be ready to take office as Prime Minister. All his actions in opposing the government are taken with the aim of being required to assume that duty, which is characterized by a number of rights and obligations.

(i) After a general election in which his party has secured an overall majority of seats in the House of Commons, the Leader of the Opposition is entitled to be appointed Prime Minister on the resignation of the outgoing Prime Minister. That entitlement is so absolute that the transfer of power in that circumstance is as well-drilled as the changing of the Guard.

(ii) In that clear case, it is the Leader of the Opposition's right to succeed to power forthwith, with no delay either from the defeated Prime Minister or from the Sovereign. No Prime Minister who has been defeated at the polls has waited to meet Parliament to have his fate sealed there since Baldwin in 1924. Procrastination by him would be pointless, given that party disciplines are such that the accumulation of seats under each party's banner at the polls can be guaranteed to be translated into firm party arithmetic in the new House of Commons. No Sovereign would seek to delay the fruits of victory to the Leader of the Opposition. He must not be put even to the theoretical risk of exclusion from power through the Sovereign taking advice before sending for him. If she were to consult anyone else in this clear parliamentary situation it could only be for the purpose of thwarting the Leader of the Opposition. No modern monarch would contemplate trying to put the clock back to Queen Victoria's occasional attempts to circumvent the will of the electorate.

(iii) On the return of a hung Parliament, however, the Leader of the Opposition has no automatic expectation either of the Prime Minister's immediate resignation or of his own summons to form a government. So, for example, Mr Edward Heath acted perfectly properly after the February 1974 general election had produced a hung Parliament by staying in office as Prime Minister for a few days to try to negotiate a coalition with the Liberal Party. The then Leader of the Opposition, Mr Harold Wilson, subsequently acknowledged the propriety of Mr Heath's course of action. When Mr Heath's attempt at coalition-making failed, he resigned—four days after the election—and Mr Wilson was appointed to succeed him, forming a minority Labour government.

(iv) In the different case of the retirement of the Prime Minister, or of his death, leaving a majority government, the Leader of the Opposition has no constitutional task to perform. The government party will elect a new Leader, and the Queen will appoint him Prime Minister.

Most of the daily burden on a Leader of the Opposition does not, of course, consist of taking part in the transfer of power, but in leading his party in Parliament and in the country. It is inappropriate to dilate here on the party political duties of the Leader of the Opposition. Through his questioning of the Prime Minister in the House of Commons every Tuesday and Thursday, in leading for his party in major debates, in harrying the government, and in seeking to portray the strengths of himself and of his party in the House of Commons, on television, and up and down the country, he is, in part, discharging his duty of preparing himself and his colleagues to take over the government, by working for the electoral defeat of their opponents.

[Rodney Brazier, 'The Constitutional Role of the Opposition' (1989) 40 *Northern Ireland Legal Quarterly* 131 at 132–3.]

## 5. CO-OPERATION WITH THE PRIME MINISTER

### (1) MEETINGS ON PRIVY COUNCILLOR TERMS

*(a) Membership of Privy Council*

*A new Leader of the Opposition, if not already a Privy Councillor, will be made a member of the Privy Council. This allows,* inter alia, *briefings by Ministers on Privy Councillor terms, that is, on condition that that information communicated to him will not be revealed without permission.*

*(b) Pre-general election facilities*

Whitehall is always well prepared for a change of Government. In July 1964, the civil service mandarins were clearly expecting a Labour victory and wanted to be prepared for it. At the suggestion of Lord Plowden, an eminent public figure with close Whitehall contacts—he had been responsible for the Macmillan reforms in the senior levels of the civil service—I was invited to dine with Sir Laurence Helsby, the joint permanent secretary of the Treasury, whose duties included the responsibility for the home civil service and for the machinery of government. When I was invited to meet Sir Laurence, I asked whether this proposal had the assent of the then Prime Minister. I was told that he was prepared to agree to this meeting provided, quite fairly, that I did not announce it as an indication that he was conceding in advance the result of the General Election and that the meeting would not take place until the last week of July, which, since we were near the end of the statutory life of the 1959 Parliament, effectively meant at the end of the sittings of that Parliament. He was concerned lest questions might be raised in Parliament if news of our secret dinner party were to leak. I accepted these conditions.

At that dinner with Sir Laurence I indicated some of my ideas for changes in departmental responsibilities. In fact, I had underrated the civil service. Earlier in the year I had recorded an interview with Dr Norman Hunt for the BBC Third Programme. The recording had lasted for over an hour. The programme was in the event cut for transmission to twenty-five minutes. The text of the broadcast itself was reprinted in the *Listener*. Sir Laurence showed the most intimate knowledge of my broadcast and I suspected that he had had the sixty-minute and not the twenty-five-minute version. He gave me his advice on a number of ideas I had, and also his own proposals for adding overseas shipping and civil aviation to the trade and tourist responsibilities of the Board of Trade. He raised no argument against my proposals either for a Department of Economic Affairs or my proposed Ministry of Technology.

[Harold Wilson, *The Labour Government 1964–1970: A Personal Record* (London, 1971), 4.]

Looking back, it seems that my own thinking may have gone farther ahead than that of the Prime Minister and some of my other colleagues, and it is possible that I made assumptions in my mind which the others did not, in fact, share. But at that time I believed that we were all agreed on the necessity of having a major government department to deal with economic affairs in ways which would not be subservient to the Treasury.

With the approval, or at any rate with the knowledge of, the then Conservative Ministers, I began to discuss things informally with senior Civil Servants—not only to help us, but also because of the obvious value to them in making their contingency plans against the possible return of a new Government. I tried to work out how a Department of Economic Affairs, such as I envisaged, might be established and staffed, what its relationships with the Treasury should be, what should be the lines of communication, and so on.

I had discussions not only with Civil Servants, but with economists, newspaper writers, trade unionists and industrialists, local authority people, and with all kinds of academics from the universities. We formed a large collection of overlapping study groups, and gradually our ideas emerged and clarified, though they were never, as it were, put together on one piece of paper. I think it is a pity that we didn't produce a 'blueprint' setting out precisely what we were trying to achieve. That would have been a valuable exercise in itself, and a useful source of reference when some of our ideas were questioned later. But everybody was always so busy that things just didn't get done in that way.

To do such things you need an elaborate secretariat, and the problem in the Labour Party always has been—and still is—that we run our administrative and research departments on the most ridiculous shoestring. In those vital days I, as Deputy Leader of the Party, Chairman of the Home Policy Committee and heaven knows what else, had to work in a tiny office in the House of Commons with just one secretary for all attempts at co-ordinating policy, plus my constituency work, plus my parliamentary work. The wonder is that anything got done at all.

Finally, we took our whole collection of ideas to a meeting at the St Ermin's Hotel, at which the Leader, Harold Wilson, and I were both present, together with all the other people concerned with policy-making and strategy for the coming election. Our meeting was followed by a dinner, from which those of us who were M.P.s had to go to a division in the Commons. Harold Wilson and I travelled together in a taxi, and it was on that ride to the House that we decided firmly to set up a Department of Economic Affairs, and that I should head it. That is the origin of the much-told story that the D.E.A. was born in a taxi—true, but not by any means the whole truth. From then on the establishment of the D.E.A. became a settled part of the official Labour policy.

One of the great problems was who was to be the Civil Service head of the new department, its Permanent Secretary, and here I probably made a grave misjudgement.

Among the people with whom I discussed the question was Sir William Armstrong, then Joint Permanent Secretary to the Treasury. I spent some time with Sir William, going over with him the potential work of the new department, and discussing the personalities to be reckoned with in making it work. What I failed to consider was whether Sir William might have been interested in heading the D.E.A. himself.

I never asked him about this, but I have the feeling now that had I pressed him to consider moving to the D.E.A. he might well have done so. If this had happened, events almost surely would have turned out very differently; and to say this is no reflection on the man who actually took on the job. Had I been even more conscious than I was of the battle that would have to be fought between the entrenched Treasury and our new department which was going to usurp some of its functions, the appointment of Sir William as the head of the D.E.A. might have resulted in that battle's being won before it started.

But I didn't ask Sir William, and instead considered all the other names that he and other people had suggested. In the end the decision was settled by a fortuitous meeting whilst visiting New York. I saw walking towards me along Fifth Avenue our then recently appointed Economic Minister to Washington, Sir Eric Roll. He was one of those whose names we were considering, and I thought, 'Given his experience, here is the very man for the D.E.A.!'

We talked there and then, and later in London. With all the appropriate proprieties observed towards the then Conservative Government, Sir Eric became very much involved in our planning. Sir Donald MacDougall, who had been Economic Director of the National Economic Development Council since 1962, had already agreed to join us as Director-General. Anthony Crosland had come to be accepted as the probable Deputy Minister, and our discussions began to take more formal shape.

[George Brown, *In My Way* (London, 1972), 88–90.]

*This courtesy is probably offered routinely to the Leader of the Opposition before every general election. In 1987 it was offered to Dr David Owen and Mr David Steel as well.*

### (c) *Other briefings*

#### (i) *Constitutional affairs*

Even so, it was obvious to Asquith that the time had come when he should try to talk to the Unionist leaders. Even if agreement proved impossible (and he was much less sanguine than Churchill) it was important to show the King, and even some members of the Cabinet, that he had at least tried. Accordingly, he wrote from Balmoral on October 8th:

Dear Mr Bonar Law,

Churchill has reported to me the substance of a conversation he had with you here last month.

You will probably agree with me that anything in the nature of a 'Conference' (as proposed for instance by Lord Loreburn) between the leaders of parties is under existing conditions out of the question, whatever may be the case hereafter.

I understand, however, the suggestion thrown out by you to Churchill to be that an informal conversation of a strictly confidential character between yourself and myself—with perhaps another colleague on either side—might be useful as a first step towards the possible avoidance of danger to the State, which all responsible statesmen must be equally anxious to avert.

I write, therefore, to say that (if you are still in the same mind) I should be happy to take part without delay in a conversation so conditioned.

I shall be back in London on Friday night and shall remain there for the best part of a week. Perhaps you would kindly address your reply to Downing Street.

Yours very truly,
H. H. Asquith

The coolness of tone was accounted for by the fact that Asquith hardly knew Bonar Law, and had no great liking for what he knew. The caution of the proposal (combined with a determination to pin upon Law the responsibility for the initiative) arose from Asquith's conviction that any compromise plan must be suggested by the opposition and not by himself. The Government's bill, supported by a majority in the House of Commons, was on the table. It was not for him to tell the opposition what he would give them for threatening to break the law—particularly as he thought they would always ask for more. But if the opposition chose to state what provisions, within a general Home Rule framework, would meet the Ulster problem, that was a different matter. This fencing to avoid the initiative was an important factor in the negotiations of the next few months.

Bonar Law, after consulting Lansdowne, agreed to the meeting and suggested Cherkley Court, 'the house of a friend of mine, Sir Max Aitken' as an appropriate rendezvous. 'It is about an hour by motor from London,' he added, 'it is quite isolated and the only risk of publicity would be through the servants which in this case would not be great.' Asquith agreed to the arrangement, and after luncheon on Wednesday, October 14th, he drove out to meet the leader of the opposition. 'He arrived,' so Mr Robert Blake informs us, 'to find Bonar Law, characteristically, engaged in a game of double dummy with his host—the need for secrecy precluding a four.

[Roy Jenkins, *Asquith* (London, Fontana edn., 1967, 320–1.]

Birkenhead pressed, therefore, for an early commission [on the future government of India] which a Conservative government could control in the hope of obtaining a cautious report. The choice of Simon, the Liberal 'elder statesman', as chairman was calculated to this end. The selection of a 'Liberal' sounded encouraging to those progressive Indians and British who were not aware that Simon had denounced the General Strike as illegal, and since then had moved further and further to the right. He was known by Birkenhead and Baldwin to have returned from a visit to India with the view that Indian reform should proceed very slowly indeed. The other six commissioners were chosen with the object of getting a 'sober' report. Four of them were Conservatives. Lord Burnham, a diehard Tory, was the owner of the *Daily Telegraph*. Lord Strathcona was a close friend of Baldwin. George Lane Fox was a fox-hunting Tory MP with a background similar in some respects to that of his fellow Yorkshireman and brother-in-law, the Viceroy—Lord Irwin, later Lord Halifax. Edward Cadogan was much esteemed for his public work, especially by Attlee, because of his work for discharged Borstal boys. The two Labour members named were

Attlee and Stephen Walsh. Soon after his appointment Walsh withdrew on grounds of ill health; his place was taken by Vernon Hartshorn, according to Attlee 'the ablest of the South Wales miners in the House'.

For Labour representation on the commission, Birkenhead had consulted MacDonald. Walsh and Hartshorn were both safely orthodox figures. Why MacDonald chose Attlee is not clear. By the end of 1927 Attlee had established a reputation in the House as hardworking and well informed, but he had no Indian experience; his expertise was 'gas-and-water' socialism in Britain. Attlee had no wish to leave Vi for several months when she had two small babies to look after, and another child on the way. He did not think the job would benefit his political career, and went to some trouble to ascertain from MacDonald that his absence from Britain would not affect his chances of office in the next Labour government. MacDonald may have chosen Attlee because he knew that Birkenhead wanted the kind of report which was bound to be unpopular with the Labour Party, and he did not wish a shadow minister of the first rank to be associated with it. Nor would MacDonald have wanted a Labour man on the Statutory Commission who would come home and provide ammunition with which the extremists of the party would try to commit the leadership to immediate Home Rule. Attlee would have fitted these requirements admirably.

[Kenneth Harris, *Attlee* (London, 1982), 76–7.]

Unknown to anyone but Neville Chamberlain, [Baldwin] called Attlee [Leader of the Opposition], Sinclair [Leader of the Liberal Party] and Churchill to No. 10 on the morning of the 25th to put the question to them—would they be for or against the Government if it came to resignation [over its advice to Edward VIII about his proposed marriage to Mrs Simpson]? Attlee and Sinclair pledged loyalty and said that they would not form a Government if asked. Churchill replied that, though his attitude was a little different, he would certainly support the Government.

[Keith Middlemas and John Barnes, *Baldwin* (London, 1969), 999.]

But when I thought about the crucial part that the Lords might be forced to play in a situation of real danger—in the sort of situation, however far-fetched it might appear to recall it, which had overtaken the German Reichstag in 1933—when I reflected that this, although it might never have to be invoked, was the ultimate justification for a second Chamber with power to restrain and to force a pause; then I realized, as I think I had always realized, that the existing composition of the House of Lords was not simply hard to defend in political theory—it was actually dangerous. A House which in effect appealed to the people by blocking the House of Commons had to have some sort of demonstrable authority. Our House consisted of hereditary peers, of first creations or of life peers; and, of course, of bishops. The first category were legislators because of the performance or fortune of their forebears: the second two categories were there on the recommendation of a Prime Minister —in effect they were nominees, however meritorious. I did not believe the House of Lords, unless reformed, could play what might be its most essential role in history: it could not play it with the necessary support of the nation.

My conclusion was not exactly novel. The preamble to the Parliament Act of 1910 referred to the problem of the composition of the Lords as being so urgent 'as to brook no delay'. Over fifty years later I felt the same, and nearly eighty years on I feel so even more. But the problem then as now was easier to state than to solve, for any change in the composition of the Lords which strengthened its position in the country—and it was that which was required—inevitably aroused the hostility of at least part of the House of Commons. A reformed House of Lords could and undoubtedly would use its enhanced status to play a more energetic part in the parliamentary process, and the House of Commons could feel diminished thereby, challenged in its authority as sole representative Chamber. There had always, therefore, been more disposition to grumble about the Lords than to agree on what should replace it. There were, of course, the extremes: the abolitionists who wanted a single Chamber and the traditionalists who would have no change. Most people, however, were in between, but organizing a consensus for reform was a different matter.

I was determined to try: obviously both main parties needed to be associated with the attempt and I welcomed a Government initiative which led to a sequence of talks. The Leader of the House was Shackleton and the Leader of the Commons was Dick Crossman. I was supported by George Jellicoe, my deputy, who had followed me at the Admiralty, and Iain Macleod held a watching brief for the

Conservative Opposition in the Commons. The five of us were, I think, at least agreed on the basic object, on the framework of our conferences. We all wanted a second Chamber which could be recognized as having a right to play its proper and most important part in the constitution. We all thought that this was incompatible with a House consisting of inheritors and nominees. We all recognized that the existing House did its job perfectly well in practice—it was its theoretical basis which could be mortally attacked at the critical moment. And we none of us wanted that.

[Lord Carrington, *Reflect on Things Past* (London, 1988), 206–8.]

*The Prime Minister will also consult the Leader of the Opposition on the lists of new working peers and on Dissolution Honours Lists: see below pp.502–3.*

*(ii) Foreign affairs and defence*

Meanwhile, [Baldwin, as Leader of the Opposition] grew personally closer to MacDonald [as Prime Minister]. At the Junior Carlton Club [Baldwin] had proposed a truce of fair play on foreign policy—as MacDonald had done for him in 1923. Throughout 1924, [Baldwin] received a selection of Foreign Office papers and telegrams and the continuity of policy was, except with regard to Russia, carefully preserved.

[Middlemas and Barnes, *Baldwin*, 268.]

Opposition and government are carried on alike by agreement. The minority agrees that the majority must govern, and the majority agrees that the minority should criticise. The process of parliamentary government would break down if there were not mutual forbearance. The most important elements in parliamentary procedure are the discussions 'behind the Speaker's Chair' or 'through the usual channels'. The Prime Minister meets the convenience of the leader of the Opposition and the leader of the Opposition meets the convenience of the Government. The respective whips, in consultation with the respective leaders, settle the subjects to be debated, the time to be allowed and, sometimes, the information to be provided and the line of attack. The Government agrees that a vote of censure be moved on Monday provided that a Bill be given a second reading on Tuesday. The Opposition assents to its inevitable defeat at 6.30 p.m. in order that it may move a resolution for the rest of the evening and suffer its inevitable defeat at 10 p.m.

Sometimes, indeed, it agrees not to oppose. This is particularly true of foreign affairs. For the enmity within is as nothing compared with the enmity without. The suggestion that the nation is divided gives encouragement to enemies abroad. From the outbreak of war in 1914 until the formation of the Coalition Government in 1915 the Opposition did not oppose in public but made representations in private. The Government in its turn communicated paraphrases of secret cables—paraphrases in case the documents should fall into enemy hands and so disclose the ciphers—to the Opposition 'Shadow Cabinet'. Mr Austen Chamberlain, as the former Conservative Chancellor of the Exchequer, assisted the Liberal Chancellor of the Exchequer on the financial questions of the war. Agreement was especially necessary where secret promises were made which might have to be carried out by a subsequent Government, as with the promise to allot Constantinople to Russia. In January 1918 the Liberal leaders were informed of the Government's peace proposals. Throughout the period of crisis from early 1938 to the fall of his Government in 1940 Mr Neville Chamberlain kept the Opposition leaders informed of his actions, though they did not always agree with him. The notion that it is 'unpatriotic' to oppose a foreign policy or a 'little war' is, however, a perversion of this doctrine. It is always difficult for Government supporters, especially Conservatives, to distinguish between what is right and what they think to be right. There are, unfortunately, no agreed criteria of right and wrong, except under dictatorships. If the Opposition considers a policy to be wrong it must say so, within whatever discretionary limits that the national interest seems to them to require. In the Suez crisis of 1956 the Labour party were not the 'friends of Nasser' but the critics of Sir Anthony Eden.

[Sir Ivor Jennings, *Cabinet Government* (Cambridge, 3rd edn., 1959), 500–2.]

Some conflicting ideas about the respective responsibilities of Government and Opposition were broached in March and April of 1958 when approaches were made by the Prime Minister to the Leader of the Opposition envisaging the possibility of joint talks between himself and Mr Gaitskell on defence matters. The suggestion was declined, and it was suggested that the arrangement was incompatible with the fulfilment by the Opposition of its constitutional function of criticism. The imparting of confidential information to Opposition leaders might clearly in many circumstances place them in an inhibiting and embarrassing position in relation to back-bench members of the Opposition party. Both party leaders, however, were in agreement that the disclosing of information to a Committee of the House was not an alternative which they were prepared to support.

A number of arguments were advanced in criticism of these attitudes. Amongst them was the suggestion that the Opposition has a responsibility to the Crown which cannot be discharged if information which would aid them in their duties is refused, and that the duties of the Opposition could not be construed as merely being to oppose until such time as a change of government took place. It was urged in addition that the leaders of parties in office are frequently in possession of information which they cannot disclose to their followers and that the ultimate responsibility of Ministers for the advice given to the Crown would not in this sphere be fatally undermined by consultation or even 'the educative device of a special Parliamentary Committee'. What could or would be disclosed to such a committee clearly depends more upon the particular degree of mutual trust between party leaders at any one time than upon constitutional convention. The absence of consultation in October 1956 was not caused by the lack of an appropriate parliamentary forum for it.

[Geoffrey Marshall and G. C. Moodie, *Some Problems of the Constitution* (London, 5th edn., 1971), 138.]

THE PRIME MINISTER (MRS MARGARET THATCHER): As a matter of normal practice I do not propose to confirm or deny whether briefings [for the Leader of the Opposition] are envisaged or have taken place.

[143 H.C. Deb. *345* (written answers 9 December 1988).]

## Constitutional Duties of the Opposition

### 1. TO OPPOSE

Democratic government thus demands not only a parliamentary majority but also a parliamentary minority. The minority attacks the Government because it denies the principles of its policy. The Opposition will, almost certainly, be defeated in the House of Commons because it is a minority. Its appeals are to the electorate. It will, at the next election, ask the people to condemn the Government, and, as a consequence, to give a majority to the Opposition. Because the Government is criticised it has to meet criticism. Because it must in course of time defend itself in the constituencies it must persuade public opinion to move with it. The Opposition is at once the alternative to the Government and a focus for the discontent of the people. Its function is almost as important as that of the Government. If there be no Opposition there is no democracy. 'Her Majesty's Opposition' is no idle phrase. Her Majesty needs an Opposition as well as a Government . . .

It is not untrue to say that the most important part of Parliament is the Opposition in the House of Commons. The function of Parliament is not to govern but to criticise. Its criticism, too, is directed not so much towards a fundamental modification of the Government's policy as towards the education of public opinion. The Government's majority exists to support the Government. The purpose of the Opposition is to secure a majority against the Government at the next general election and thus to replace the Government. This does not imply that a Government may not be defeated in the House of Commons. Nor does it imply that parliamentary criticism may not persuade the Government to modify, or even to withdraw, its proposals. These qualifications are important; but they do not destroy the truth of the principle that the Government governs and the Opposition criticises. Failure to understand this simple principle is one of the causes of the failure of so many of the progeny of the Mother of Parliaments and of the supersession of parliamentary government by dictatorships . . .

Attacks upon the Government and upon individual ministers are the function of the Opposition. The duty of the Opposition is to oppose. It adopts Sir Toby's advice, 'So soon as ever thou seest him, draw; and, as thou drawest, swear horrible.' That duty is the major check which the Constitution provides upon corruption and defective administration. It is, too, the means by which individual injustices are prevented. The House of Commons is at its best when it debates those individual acts of oppression or bad faith which can never completely be overcome in a system of government which places responsibility on such minor officials as police officers. It is the public duty of the Opposition to raise such questions. It is a duty hardly less important than that of government. 'Her Majesty's Opposition' is second in importance to 'Her Majesty's Government'. The apparent absurdity that the Opposition asks for parliamentary time to be set aside by the Government in order that the Opposition may censure the Government, or that the Government is asked to move a vote of supplies for the Ministry of Labour in order that the Opposition may attack the Minister of Labour, is not an absurdity at all. It is the recognition by both sides of the House that the Government governs openly and honestly and that it is prepared to meet criticism not by secret police and concentration camps but by rational argument.

There is a duty to oppose in another sense; perhaps it may be described as a duty to accept defeat. It is so obvious a duty, so much an ordinary part of parliamentary democracy, that we are apt to forget its importance. The parties believe, with a fervour which ordinary 'cross-bench' people find puzzling, in the rightness of their respective causes, though they do not always believe what they put into speeches and election addresses. When they are defeated ignorance or malevolence or fraud has triumphed and the truth has been trampled on by mass prejudice. Nevertheless, there they are every day, sitting on the Opposition benches, asking their questions, making their speeches, pretending that it is all such fun; and before they catch the late buses home they tramp through the lobbies, knowing that the vote is a foregone conclusion. There are countries in which there are no minorities because they might become majorities; and there are countries where the minorities have taken to the barricades because they could not win votes. Only once since 1832 has such action been threatened in the United Kingdom, when Ulster started arming against Home Rule. That occasion was unique, and no doubt it had unusual causes. Even then the rebels were not the Conservative party, but only some of the least worthy of the Unionists. The Conservative party as such remained to act as His Majesty's Opposition, though it did once shout down the Prime Minister.

The best example, however, is the Labour Opposition of 1931. Defeated at an election in which defeat was inevitable, and by methods which were unnecessarily offensive—though it cannot be alleged that the Labour candidates themselves treated their 'renegades' with studied politeness—a small band of fifty-two survivors took their seats on the Opposition benches, led by two relics of the former Labour Government, neither of whom was very experienced or very able. They kept the machinery of Opposition working, and their principal opponent recognized it: 'They might have sulked, they might have seceded, and they never thought of it. When the history of Parliament is written, see that Lansbury gets his due.' So said Mr Baldwin.

[Jennings, *Cabinet Government*, 15–16, 427, 499–500.]

From time to time the Opposition put down a motion on the [order] paper expressing lack of confidence in the Government—a 'vote of confidence' as it is called. By established convention the Government never fails to accede to the demand from the Leader of the Opposition to allot a day for the discussion of such a motion. In allotting a day for this purpose the Government is entitled to have regard to the exigencies of its own business, but a reasonably early day is invariably found. This convention is due to the recognized and responsible position of the Opposition as a potential Government—a position which guarantees the legitimacy of such an interruption of normal business. For its part, the Government has everything to gain by meeting such a direct challenge to its authority at the earliest possible moment.

[Erskine May, *Parliamentary Practice* (London, 21st edn., 1989), 272.]

## 2. TO QUESTION AND TO DEBATE

*The Leader of the Opposition questions the Prime Minister every Tuesday and Thursday. The Opposition (currently through the Shadow Leader of the House) initiates business questions to the Leader of the House every Thursday.*

13.—(2) Twenty days shall be allotted in each session for proceedings on opposition business, seventeen of which shall be at the disposal of the Leader of the Opposition and three of which shall be at the disposal of the leader of the second largest opposition party; and matters selected on those days shall have precedence over government business provided that—

(*a*) two Friday sittings shall be deemed equivalent to a single sitting on any other day;

(*b*) on any day other than a Friday, not more than two of the days at the disposal of the Leader of the Opposition may be taken in the form of four half days, and one of the days at the disposal of the leader of the second largest opposition party may be taken in the form of two half days; and

(*c*) on any such half day proceedings under this paragraph shall either—

(i) lapse at seven o'clock if not previously concluded, or

(ii) be set down for consideration at seven o'clock and, except on days on which private business has been set down for consideration under the provisions of paragraph (5) of Standing Order No. 16 (Time for taking private business), shall be entered upon at that time:

Provided that on days on which business stands over until seven o'clock under the provisions of Standing Order No. 20 (Adjournment on specific and important matter that should have urgent consideration) proceedings under this sub-paragraph shall not be entered upon until such business has been disposed of, and may then be proceeded with for three hours, notwithstanding the provisions of Standing Order No. 9 (Sittings of the House).

[House of Commons Standing Order 13(2).]

## 3. TO PROVIDE CHAIRMEN

*By convention Opposition M.P.s chair important select committees of the House, such as those on Public Accounts, on the Parliamentary Commissioner for Administration, and on Statutory Instruments. They also chair about half the departmental select committees.*

## 4. TO OBSERVE COLLECTIVE RESPONSIBILITY

*Opposition spokesmen willingly accept the obligation of collective responsibility—at the time of their appointment, at any rate. This is necessary if a Shadow Cabinet and administration are to look like an alternative government. Resignation or dismissal may follow if the obligation proves unacceptable. Some recent examples follow.*

| Name | Reason and date |
|---|---|
| N. Buchan (arts spokesman) | Future ministerial arrangements for broadcasting: dismissed 1986 |
| A. Clwyd (education spokesman) | Voting against the defence estimates: dismissed 1988 |
| C. Short (employment spokesman) | Voting against terrorism legislation: dismissed 1988 |
| A. Bennett (education spokesman) | Voting against terrorism legislation: dismissed 1988 |
| D. Davies (Shadow Defence Secretary) | Leader's development of defence policy without consultation: resigned 1988 |
| A. Mitchell (trade & industry spokesman) | Taking job as interviewer on Sky tv: dismissed 1989 |

## The Shadow Government

### 1. HISTORICAL BACKGROUND

This task of deciding policy, providing leadership and, to a lesser extent, of planning tactics in Parliament also had to be performed by the opposition. As the parties became more organised and the struggle for power more intense, ex-Cabinets or as they were termed by some in the 1880s Shadow Cabinets met more regularly. By March 1868 Gladstone was emerging from his mood of aggrieved defeatism and Argyll, Granville, Fortescue, Cardwell, Brand and Glynn met at his house to consider the terms of his resolutions on the Irish Church. Similar meetings of up to seven ex-ministers and two Whips took place regularly in May to discuss tactics, though more frequent informal contact was kept up with a smaller group. In 1875 the Liberal ex-Cabinet met to determine such matters as its attitude to the government's refusal to allow slaves to take refuge on British warships, though there was no great unity or vigour. The machinery was just strong enough to prevent a serious split over Gladstone's resolutions condemning the government's Near Eastern policy in 1877. One was modified, three were dropped, and pressure from Hartington persuaded most of the Liberal rank and file to support their leaders in the division. Indeed, if the ex-Cabinet was not operating, this was a sign of serious divisions in the party and no very effective opposition could be maintained in the House. Gladstone was determined to keep a free hand after he left office in 1885 and refused to call his ex-colleagues together despite requests from Harcourt. He appreciated that a meeting was not likely to produce agreement or even a measure of unity. This situation was a reflection of divisions in the recent Liberal Cabinet and foreshadowed the cleavage that was to occur when his decision to take up Home Rule became known. In fact the former Cabinet was falling into several groups, soon to consolidate and form the Liberal and Liberal Unionist front benches. Gladstone had been consulting Spencer and Granville, and a radical group met to prosecute 'the Unauthorised Programme,' while Selborne, Northbrook, Hartington, Derby, Carlingford and Lord Monk-Bretton agreed that they would oppose any move towards Home Rule. Similarly, the divisions of 1894–1896 made it hard for Rosebery and then Harcourt to convene the ex-Cabinet, and yet failure to do so prevented any concerted opposition.

Conservative and Unionist Shadow Cabinets had worked fairly smoothly in the early 1880s and between 1892 and 1895, but after 1906 there were difficulties. Middleton records that 'constant meetings were held of the ex-Cabinet, in which the divisions of opinion as to throwing out the Budget were only less acrimonious than those which ensued on the Parliament Act.' Balfour pointed out one difficulty: 'Had it been a real Cabinet, one of two things would have followed. Either the dissentient minority would have resigned, or they would have silently acquiesced in the decision of the majority. There could, of course, be no question in the case of a Shadow Cabinet of resignation. There certainly has been no silent acquiescence.' The former point was not strictly true. Rosebery, Harcourt and Morley had all ceased attendance at Liberal Shadow Cabinets at various points in the late 1890s while Long had threatened to resign from the Conservative front bench in 1907. But it was also true that elements often remained or tried to gain entry in the hope that they might capture the Shadow Cabinet before the next ministry was formed. Thus Harcourt and his radical allies had tried to force their way into Liberal meetings in the 1870s, the Liberal Imperialists refused to leave in the 1890s and after 1906, under Balfour, neither the Protectionists nor their opponents would abandon the field. Obtaining agreement among the Shadow Cabinet was so difficult that Balfour acted on his own in giving the Albert Hall pledge in late 1910, meetings being virtually suspended during the crisis over the leadership in 1911. After his selection, Bonar Law, taking Balcarres' advice, tried to call meetings as rarely as possible, only doing so when controversial issues came up and some authoritative party pronouncement had become imperative.

Modern writers have sometimes suggested that the tactics of opposition in this period were to attack the government from every angle simply aiming to discredit it, there being no attempt to present a coherent series of alternatives. Nothing could be further from the case. At a time when the opposition expected to be in office with the next electoral swing and political memories were longer than they are today, great care was taken to advocate only what could be put into practice. Gladstone may have failed to alter all the policies he had condemned in his Midlothian campaigns, but he had spoken in good faith. Pledges were held to be binding, and Gladstone assumed that front bench support for a motion by Trevelyan (in the late 1870s) for household suffrage in the counties committed the next Liberal Cabinet to such a measure. Queen Victoria urged Forster 'when out of office . . . to be very cautious *not* to *pledge* himself *strongly* to *any particular* cause, and to particular measures for they invariably hamper a statesman who takes office.' The whole point of the struggles over imperialism in the Liberal Shadow Cabinet and over protection among Conservatives arose from the Opposition's need to present a viable and consistent alternative to the policy of the existing Cabinet.

[John Mackintosh, *The British Cabinet* (London, 3rd edn., 1977), 259–61.]

## 2. LABOUR SHADOW CABINET

### *F. The Parliamentary Committee*

1. There shall be a Parliamentary Committee which when the Party is in Government shall have the following membership: the four Officers of the PLP; six Back-Bench Members of the House of Commons, who shall be elected by the Back-Bench

Members of the Party in the House of Commons; one elected Back-Bench Member of the House of Lords: four other members of the Government, one being from the House of Lords and the other three from the House of Commons of whom one, if he or she is not an Officer, shall be the Leader of the House; the remainder being selected by the Prime Minister or appointed or elected by a method decided by the Prime Minister.

2. In Government, the Parliamentary Committee shall be chaired by the Chairman of the PLP. The Deputy Chairman shall be that Member elected with the largest number of votes in the Sessional Ballot.
3. In Government, the Chief Whip in the House of Lords (if not a Member of the Committee) shall have the right to attend meetings of the Parliamentary Committee.

. . .

4. In Opposition, the composition of the Parliamentary Committee shall be the four Officers of the PLP, eighteen members of the Parliamentary Party having seats in the House of Commons, elected by the Members of the Party in the House of Commons; the Leader and Chief Whip of the Labour Peers and one member of the House of Lords all elected by the Labour Peers.
5. In Opposition, the Leader and Deputy Leader of the Party shall act as Chairman and Deputy Chairman of the Parliamentary Committee.

. . .

6. The Secretary of the PLP shall be Secretary to the Committee.
7. After a General Election, the Officers and members of the Parliamentary Committee who have retained their seats in the House of Commons shall retain their respective positions in the new Parliament until fresh elections can take place.
8. The General Secretary of the Party shall have the right to attend meetings of the Parliamentary Committee.
9. Casual vacancies shall be filled by by-elections.
10. The Parliamentary Committee is the executive authority of the Parliamentary Labour Party. Its functions are:
    (i) Deciding when Party meetings are to be called and the subjects to be discussed.
    (ii) Ensuring the effective function of the regional groups and departmental committees.

(iii) Easing any difficulties which may arise between individual Members and the Whips' Office.

(iv) Ensuring proper liaison between the Parliamentary Party and the National Executive Committee, including appropriate representation of the Parliamentary Party on the Party's policy-drafting working-parties and study groups.

(v) Dealing with the Business of the House and in Government maintaining an effective two-way channel of communication between the Government and Back-Benchers in both Houses.

11. The Committee shall meet once a week whilst Parliament is in session, and at such other times as may be determined.

12. The Committee shall make regular reports to the Parliamentary Party at the weekly meeting of the PLP and by a written report circulated with the weekly Whip.

13. The Committee's term of office shall expire on the election of a new Committee at the commencement of each Parliamentary session unless otherwise determined by the Parliamentary Party.

[Parliamentary Labour Party Standing Order No. F.]

. . . 5. The Parliamentary Committee

The eighteen Commons Members of the Committee shall be elected in accordance with the following procedure:

(i) nominations shall be invited by Notice given to all Members of the Party with seats in the House of Commons;

(ii) if more than eighteen nominations are made ballot papers shall be issued;

(iii) ballot papers must not record more votes than there are places to be filled;

(iv) the eighteen candidates receiving the highest number of votes shall be declared elected, but in the event of a tie for the last place a further ballot shall be taken to decide which of the candidates concerned shall fill the remaining place.

(v) casual vacancies shall be filled by election.

[P.L.P. Standing Order No. I, para. 5.]

*A Labour Leader of the Opposition may also invite other colleagues to attend Parliamentary Committee meetings. So, for example, Mr Martin O'Neill and Mr Kevin McNamara were invited to be Shadow*

*Defence and Northern Ireland Secretaries respectively by Mr Kinnock even though neither had been elected to the Committee.*

## 3. CONSERVATIVE SHADOW CABINET

The manner in which Churchill ran the Opposition was conspicuously haphazard. The idea of 'shadow' ministers and a 'shadow' Cabinet with allocated subjects had not yet dawned, and Churchill's front-bench team was expected to turn itself to any task or issue that arose. Churchill liked to keep the great occasions for himself, but, although he asked Eden to watch foreign affairs for him, Eden also found himself asking questions and making speeches on a very wide range of subjects. Churchill gave regular lunches for his front-bench team at the Savoy, which were very jolly occasions, but there was a conspicuous absence of coherent thinking or even tactics. Brendan Bracken, who had been re-elected to the Commons, not at all convincingly, for Bournemouth, was given the job of opposing the nationalization of gas, which he undertook with much gusto, at one point reducing the minister responsible, Hugh Gaitskell, to tears. Butler was always thoughtful and effective, the two Olivers, Lyttelton and Stanley, much enjoyed discomfiting ministers over a broad range, and among the younger men Quintin Hogg, Peter Thorneycroft and Selwyn Lloyd were conspicuously eager and able; Harry Crookshank was a particularly good gadfly, and the return to the Commons of Harold Macmillan (for Bromley) was a particularly welcome reinforcement. There was no shortage of talent and experience; what was lacking was any strategy, or even a philosophy. What was the Conservative Party *for*? As Eden, Butler and others realized at once, blood-and-thunder Churchillian anti-Socialism was not enough.

[Robert Rhodes James, *Anthony Eden* (London, 1986), 317–18.]

*A Conservative Leader of the Opposition has a discretion whom to appoint to the Shadow Cabinet—or to the Leader's Consultative Committee as it is formally known. But in 1964 greater formality was introduced, including making each member responsible for shadowing a particular department.*

## 4. THE SHADOW ADMINISTRATION

*Because every modern government will consist of some hundred Ministers, a Shadow Cabinet of 20 people must be supplemented by additional spokesmen. Attlee introduced this concept of a shadow administration in 1955, and every Leader of the Opposition since has adopted it. Mr Kinnock currently has 80 shadow spokesmen.*

### *G. Junior Posts in Government and Front Bench Spokespersons in Opposition*

1. Junior Posts and Front Bench Spokespersons shall be appointed by the Leader but the list shall be submitted to the PLP for its approval and any change effected by the Leader shall be notified to the PLP at the earliest available opportunity. The total number of Front Benchers shall be of the order of one-fifth of the PLP.
2. In respect of areas outside their own portfolios, non-elected Front Benchers may take part in Question Time, Statements, debates and other proceedings in the Chamber, and may submit written Questions subject to the following guidelines:
   (i) the non-elected Front Benchers should, wherever possible and certainly where a regular or frequent participation is intended, clear this with the senior Front Bench spokesperson for the area concerned.
   (ii) where a Question Time, Statement or debate is oversubscribed and there are plainly more back-benchers wishing to intervene or to speak, the non-elected Front Benchers should not seek to intervene on a supplementary to a question not their own, or to speak except where he or she has a compelling constituency or regional interest; and
   (iii) non-elected Front Benchers should not depart from the policy line of the senior spokesperson for the area.

[P.L.P. Standing Order No. G.]

## Shadow into Substance

### 1. A LABOUR GOVERNMENT

*E. The Cabinet*

When the Party is in Office, the Cabinet shall continue to be appointed by the Prime Minister. On taking office as Prime Minister, the Leader shall appoint as members of his Cabinet those who were elected members of the Parliamentary Committee at the Dissolution and have retained their seats in the new Parliament.

[P.L.P. Standing Order No. E.]

*That standing order, together with S.O. No. G (see above), purport to restrict the freedom of a Labour Prime Minister in the appointment of his entire government. The standing orders were adopted in 1981, and so have not been tested.*

### 2. A CONSERVATIVE GOVERNMENT

#### (1) 1951

*Churchill's very loose shadow arrangements from 1945 allowed him considerable room to manoeuvre when he formed his 1951 government, and he made a number of surprise appointments.*

On that first night of the new administration, Lord Ismay, who from 1940 to 1945 had been head of Churchill's Defence Office, went to bed early. He was fast asleep when the telephone rang, rousing him from his slumbers. As he later recalled:

> I was told that Mr Churchill wanted to speak to me. There were many people sitting by their telephones that night, hoping, and perhaps praying, that the new Prime Minister might have something to offer them, but these were problems which were no concern of mine.
>
> The conversation was brief. 'Is that you, Pug?' 'Yes, Prime Minister. It's grand to be able to call you Prime Minister again.' 'I want to see you at once. You aren't in bed, are you?' 'I've been asleep for over an hour.' 'Well, I only want to see you for five minutes.'

I put my head under a cold tap, dressed in record time, and was at 28, Hyde Park Gate within a quarter of an hour of being wakened. Mr Churchill was alone in his drawing-room, and told me, without any preliminaries, that he wanted me to be Secretary of State for Commonwealth Relations. I thought that the cold tap had failed to do its work and that I was still dreaming, but Mr Churchill brushed aside my doubts and hustled me into the dining-room, where I found Mr Eden, Lord Salisbury, Sir Norman Brook, and a bevy of secretaries working away on a variety of drafts.

The years rolled back. It was like old times.

Thus Ismay, who only a few weeks earlier had been helping Churchill with the final volume of his war memoirs, now joined the Government.

[Martin Gilbert, *Never Despair: Winston Churchill 1945–1965* (London, 1988), 653–4.]

## (2) 1970 AND BEYOND

*Since 1964 the Conservatives in opposition have had a formal system of shadowing Ministers. As a result, a new Conservative Prime Minister will in general appoint to the Cabinet most of those who had been in the Shadow Cabinet, and also appoint them to the jobs which they had been shadowing in opposition.*

| Date | Size of Cabinet | Number of Shadow Cabinet members not included | Number included in Cabinet who had not been in Shadow Cabinet |
|---|---|---|---|
| 1970 | 21 | 2 | 2 |
| 1979 | 22 | 3 | 3 |

# [8]

# CONSTITUTIONAL MONARCHY

## Introductory

*The Sovereign's role in the appointment of the Prime Minister has been considered above (see p. 15), as has her function in the formation of a new government (see p. 127), and the circumstances in which she might refuse a request for a dissolution of Parliament (see p. 205).*

*Prime Ministers have written of the Queen's assiduity, knowledge of national and international problems, and her accumulated political knowledge and experience—all of which became apparent to them at the Prime Minister's weekly audience of the Queen. Some examples of those writings follow.*

This duty was always conscientiously performed. All Cabinet papers, all departmental papers, all foreign telegrams are sent to [the Queen], and carefully studied by her. All the Cabinet's decisions, which under the Cabinet secretarial system are rapidly and accurately circulated, are available to her immediately. All great appointments under the Crown must never be a matter for formal approval. In these, as in matters of policy, it is true that the monarch must in the end yield to the formal advice given by Ministers. But the Queen has the absolute right to know, to criticise, to advise—or, as a great authority has put it, 'to advise, to encourage, and to warn'. We are fortunate that these duties, which are always so important, and may well in a critical situation become vital, are so scrupulously performed. Moreover, as the years pass, the Queen will necessarily accumulate more political experience and knowledge than most of her advisers. I shall have occasion to recount later in this volume the incident of the Queen's visit to Ghana in 1961, which showed her to be at once courageous and determined.

Since her accession the Queen has made it a practice to receive her Prime Ministers at a weekly audience, generally on Tuesday afternoons. I found these at first somewhat difficult, for when making my report I could not help remembering Queen Victoria's description of Mr Gladstone addressing her as if she were a public meeting. I, therefore, adopted the plan of sending her, whenever possible, before the audience a note about the main points which it would be my duty to raise. This made discussion easier and avoided preliminary explanations. Throughout she adopted the practice of allowing her Prime Ministers to sit rather than to stand, which made for ease of conversation. At the risk of impertinence I must pay tribute to the width and depth of the Queen's knowledge and the assiduity with which she read and absorbed the vast mass of documents circulated. I must also record with gratitude her invariable graciousness and understanding.

[Harold Macmillan, *Pointing the Way* (London, 1972), 30.]

There is one recurring engagement of which it is safe to say that every Prime Minister has the happiest of recollections. It is the weekly audience during the parliamentary sessions with the Sovereign. The Queen, after twenty-five years of her reign, knows almost every Head of State and Leader of Government in foreign countries; while as Head of the Commonwealth she has an intimate knowledge of the leading political personalities and of their ways.

Her experience is readily put at the disposal of the Prime Minister and is invaluable to him. Few realize the exacting nature of the work which it is necessary for the Sovereign to do, if she is to keep abreast of events all over the world which are of interest to her country. Her Private Secretaries are doubtless skilled in the selection and presentation of telegrams, but there remains a mass of fact and information which needs to be absorbed if Her Majesty is to meet Ministers of the Crown and foreign visitors on their own ground. The Queen, as I and my predecessors and successors can readily testify, is always up to date and fully versed in the niceties of every national and international problem.

[Lord Home, *The Way the Wind Blows* (London, 1976), 201.]

It was at this juncture, while I was considering what to do next [about Rhodesia], that by chance I had an opportunity of talking with the Queen.

She had been present at a performance at Covent Garden of

Rossini's opera *La Cenerentola*, conducted by La Scala's principal conductor, Claudio Abbado. The occasion was a visit to London by Signora Leone, the wife of the President of Italy, and I was among the guests. The Italian Ambassador invited us to supper at his residence in Grosvenor Square when the performance was over and kindly placed me next to the Queen. During supper I described to her Lord Greenhill's visit to Rhodesia and the aftermath, and discussed the alternative courses of following the matter up, or of letting it simmer for the time being, adding that I had not yet decided which would be better. After supper we met other guests among whom I was particularly glad to make the acquaintance of Toscanini's daughter, as Audrey and I had followed this great conductor with rapt attention during the late 1930s when he conducted the BBC Orchestra in a series of Beethoven's symphonies in the old Queen's Hall in London. The Queen departed at about midnight and the rest left shortly afterwards.

The next afternoon a letter was handed to me from Sir Martin Charteris, the Queen's Private Secretary. He said that the Queen had told him how much she enjoyed our conversation about Rhodesia. She had reflected on our talk and 'she recognises that any initiative you take may prove ineffective, but none the less believes it would be worthwhile to make the effort. Her Majesty sends you her best wishes for your efforts in dealing with this intractable problem.'

Inevitably the Queen's opinion was enough to tip the scales, for she is an authority on the Commonwealth and I respected her opinion: I decided to go ahead. Two years before, when I became Foreign and Commonwealth Secretary, I had told the Queen's Private Secretary of my hope to build stronger links with the Commonwealth and his reply at the time, as well as the Queen's comments on other occasions, left me in no doubt of the keenness with which she followed Commonwealth affairs and of her genuine concern for its well-being. Her very perceptive understanding comes not only from many years spent reading Foreign Office documents, but also from her numerous meetings with successive Commonwealth leaders and her regular overseas tours. These have given her a knowledge of Commonwealth politicians and politics unequalled by any member of the Diplomatic Service or any British politician. I should also add that she is extremely careful to separate her duty as Queen of the United Kingdom from her responsibility to individual

Commonwealth countries and to the Commonwealth as a whole, and long experience enables her to reconcile her various roles with wisdom and tact.

On receipt of the Queen's letter, I called a meeting with the other Ministers at the Foreign Office, Roy Hattersley and Ted Rowlands, without telling them of the Private Secretary's communication. We agreed that I should send a message to Smith, telling him that in the view of Her Majesty's Government the spread of guerrilla activity meant that if he was willing to give a public commitment to majority rule and to hold elections on this basis within the next eighteen months to two years, Her Majesty's Government would be willing to play a constructive part in negotiations between him and the African leaders in order to prevent chaos and loss of life, and to reach a settlement satisfactory to both Europeans and Africans. As part of a settlement Britain would be ready to contribute towards compensation for those adversely affected, and to give financial aid for development and African education. We would also recommend that sanctions be lifted by the United Nations.

At this point the negotiations which had been taking place betwen Smith and Nkomo broke down, leaving a political vacuum that was filled by increasing guerrilla activity. I decided that in view of the deteriorating situation I should convey our proposals not only to Smith but also to Parliament and this I did on 22 March 1976. Reggie Maudling, the Shadow Foreign Secretary, and members on both sides of the House urged Smith to accept the broad principle of my approach; the level of approval was so high that I said that I hoped 'the several expressions of view of the Opposition benches will convince Mr Smith that in this approach there is a great deal of unity in the House of Commons'.

Shortly after this I left the Foreign Office and as history records, Smith did not agree. In later years, while he clung to power, the prospects of any settlement were undermined by visits to Salisbury by right-wing Conservative MPs who encouraged him to believe that if he hung on, the eventual return of a Conservative Government would improve his prospects. Again, history shows that they were wrong.

Harold Wilson had announced his resignation only a few days before my statement to the House and a handful of cynics scornfully claimed that I made the intervention only as a play to assist my campaign to become Leader of the Party and Prime Minister. They were not aware of the events that led up to it, but I do not suppose it would have made any difference had they known.

I had always thought since that the Queen's initiative on Rhodesia was a perfect illustration of how and when the Monarch could effectively intervene to advise and encourage her Ministers from her own wide experience and with complete constitutional propriety.

[James Callaghan, *Time and Chance* (London, 1987), 380–2.]

## The Sovereign's Usual Powers

### 1. MINISTERIAL ADVICE

The part to be played by the Crown, in such a situation as now exists, has happily been settled by the accumulated traditions and the unbroken practice of more than 70 years. It is to act upon the advice of the Ministers who for the time being possess the confidence of the House of Commons, whether that advice does or does not conform to the private and personal judgment of the Sovereign. Ministers will always pay the utmost deference, and give the most serious consideration, to any criticism or objection that the Monarch may offer to their policy; but the ultimate decision rests with them; for they, and not the Crown, are responsible to Parliament. It is only by a scrupulous adherence to this well-established Constitutional doctrine that the Crown can be kept out of the arena of party politics.

It follows that it is not the function of a Constitutional Sovereign to act as arbiter or mediator between rival parties and policies; still less to take advice from the leaders on both sides, with the view to forming a conclusion of his own. George III in the early years of his reign tried to rule after this fashion, with the worst results, and with the accession of Mr Pitt to power he practically abandoned the attempt. The growth and development of our representative system, and the clear establishment at the core and centre of our Constitution of the doctrine of Ministerial responsibility, have since placed the position of the Sovereign beyond the region of doubt or controversy . . .

[The Prime Minister, H. H. Asquith, minute to King George V, December 1910, quoted in Colin Turpin, *British Government and the Constitution: Text, Cases and Materials* (London, 1985), 76–7.]

We have now a well-established tradition of two hundred years, that, in the last resort, the occupant of the Throne accepts and acts on the advice of his ministers . . . He is entitled and bound to give his ministers all relevant information which comes to him; to point out objections which seem to him valid against the course which they advise; to suggest (if he thinks fit) an alternative policy. Such intimations are always received by ministers with the utmost respect and considered with more respect and deference than if they proceeded from any other quarter. But, in the end, the Sovereign always acts upon the advice which ministers, after (if need be) reconsideration, feel it their duty to offer. They give that advice well knowing that they can, and probably will, be called upon to account for it by Parliament.

The Sovereign undoubtedly has the power of changing his advisers, but it is relevant to point out that there has been, during the last 130 years, one occasion only on which the King has dismissed the Ministry which still possessed the confidence of the House of Commons. This was in 1834, when William IV (one of the least wise of British monarchs) called upon Lord Melbourne to resign. He took advantage (as we now know) of a hint improvidently given by Lord Melbourne himself, but the proceedings were neither well-advised nor fortunate. The dissolution which followed left Sir R. Peel in a minority, and Lord Melbourne and his friends in a few months returned to power, which they held for the next six years. The authority of the Crown was disparaged, and Queen Victoria, during her long reign, was careful never to repeat the mistake of her predecessor . . .

Nothing can be more important, in the best interests of the Crown and of the country, than that a practice, so long established and so well justified by experience, should remain unimpaired. It frees the occupant of the Throne from all personal responsibility for the acts of the Executive and the legislature. It gives force and meaning to the old maxim that 'the King can do no wrong'. So long as it prevails, however objectionable particular Acts may be to a large section of his subjects, they cannot hold him in any way accountable. If, on the other hand, the King were to intervene on one side, or in one case—which he could only do by dismissing ministers in *de facto* possession of a Parliamentary majority—he would be expected to do the same on another occasion, and perhaps for the other side. Every Act of Parliament of the first order of importance, and only passed after acute controversy, would be regarded as bearing the personal *imprimatur* of the Sovereign. He would, whether he wished it or not, be dragged into the arena of party politics; and at a dissolution following such a dismissal of ministers as has just been referred to, it is no exaggeration to say that the Crown would become the football of contending factions.

This is a constitutional catastrophe which it is the duty of every wise statesman to do the utmost in his power to avert.

[The Prime Minister, H. H. Asquith, memorandum to King George V, 1913, quoted in Sir Ivor Jennings, *Cabinet Government* (Cambridge, 3rd edn., 1959), 336–7, 408.]

## 2. THE RIGHTS TO ADVISE, TO ENCOURAGE, AND TO WARN

To state the matter shortly, the sovereign has, under a constitutional monarchy such as ours, three rights—the right to be consulted, the right to encourage, the right to warn. And a king of great sense and sagacity would want no others. He would find that his having no others would enable him to use these with singular effect. He would say to his Minister: 'The responsibility of these measures is upon you. Whatever you think best must be done. Whatever you think best shall have my full and effectual support. *But* you will observe that for this reason and that reason what you propose to do is bad; for this reason and that reason what you do not propose is better. I do not oppose, it is my duty not to oppose; but observe that I *warn*.' Supposing the king to be right, and to have what kings often have, the gift of effectual expression, he could not help moving his Minister. He might not always turn his course, but he would always trouble his mind.

[Walter Bagehot, *The English Constitution* (London, 1963 edn.), 111.]

## (I) ENCOURAGEMENT

### (*a*) *Of Chamberlain*

King George was very deeply a man of peace. The prospect of the peoples of his Commonwealth and Empire being plunged into war shocked and appalled him. To him the counsels of patience and reason were ever more welcome than those of precipitance, and, whereas he viewed with horror the more bestial aspects of the dictatorships, he was at one with his Prime Minister in believing that no reasonable effort must be spared to prevent the dictators from involving the world in a general conflagration. Moreover, he had boundless confidence in Mr Chamberlain, whose personality he found agreeable and assuring, and he was convinced of the wisdom of a policy which, if it was not finally successful in preserving peace, would at least make abundantly clear to the world with whom lay the responsibility for war . . . The intrepid initiative of Mr Chamberlain [to fly to meet Hitler], which fired the imagination of all Englishmen and appealed to their sense of sportsmanship, took hold upon him also, and he waited anxiously for the Prime Minister's return. A letter in the King's own hand awaited Mr Chamberlain on his arrival at the airport on the evening of September 16, 1938.

My dear Prime Minister,

I am sending this letter to meet you on your return, as I had no opportunity of telling you before you left how much I admired your courage and wisdom in going to see Hitler in person. You must have been pleased by the universal approval with which your action was received. I am naturally very anxious to hear the result of your talk, and to be assured that there is a prospect of a peaceful solution on terms which admit of general acceptance. I realize how fatigued you must be after these two very strenuous days, but if it is possible for you to come and see me either this evening or tomorrow morning, at any time convenient to yourself, I need hardly say that I shall greatly welcome the opportunity of hearing your news.

Believe me,<br>
Yours very sincerely,<br>
George R.I.

[Sir John Wheeler-Bennett, *King George VI: His Life and Reign* (London, 1958), 328, 349.]

(*b*) *Of Churchill*

This situation, however, was of but brief duration. The eminent good sense of the King and his keen appreciation of greatness; the grandeur and the charm of Mr Churchill; the very gravity of the danger to nation and Commonwealth with which both were jointly confronted in the leadership of the State, were all conducive to a close relationship of collaboration, which waxed rapidly into a friendship of mutual affection and admiration. It was not long before the King was regarding the Prime Minister's audiences with pleasurable anticipation. He found them fruitful opportunities for a common unburdening of mind, and by September the formal audiences had been replaced by regular Tuesday luncheons at which the King and his Prime Minister, serving themselves from a side-table, would transact State business undisturbed save by an occasional air raid. 'As a convinced upholder of constitutional monarchy,' wrote Mr Churchill, 'I valued as a signal honour the gracious intimacy with which I, as first Minister, was treated, for which I suppose there has been no precedent since the days of Queen Anne and Marlborough during his years of power.'

By the New Year the relationship between Sovereign and Minister had passed the initial test. 'I could not have a better Prime Minister', the King wrote in his diary . . .

[Wheeler-Bennett, *King George VI*, 446–7.]

(*c*) *Of Attlee*

But whatever King George's personal misgivings may have been, he did not permit them to affect his relations with his new Ministers, with whom he worked in a remarkable degree of friendship, help and co-operation. Their relative lack of governmental experience, however, materially increased his own burden of responsibility. 'You will find that your position will be greatly strengthened', Lord Mountbatten had written to him soon after the Election results had been announced, 'since you are now the old experienced campaigner on whom a new and partly inexperienced Government will lean for advice and guidance', and this was indeed true. The audiences which followed in the latter months of 1945 and the beginning of 1946 provided both Sovereign and Ministers with an opportunity for increased mutual respect and enlightenment. His advisers learned to appreciate the King's innate probity, his selflessness of character and his remarkable capacity of knowing in detail exactly what he was talking about, while he grew to appreciate their very considerable qualities.

With his new Prime Minister the King was well acquainted. Mr Attlee is an example of those who have come into public life by the way of 'good works'. Haileybury and University College, Oxford, had prepared him for a legal career but, following the strong family tradition of social service, he combined his practice of the law with work in the East End of London, first at the Haileybury College Club and later at Toynbee Hall, of which he became secretary in 1910. His experience of social conditions and his desire to reform them caused him to enter local politics in Stepney and to become a member of the Independent Labour Party. On his return from the First World War he was elected Stepney's first mayor in 1919 and in 1922 entered the House of Commons as Member for Limehouse, a seat which he retained for the next eighteen years.

Owing, in part, to the general respect for his integrity and ability and, in part, to the warring personalities of his colleagues, Mr Attlee became leader of the Labour Party in 1935, and in this capacity he had entered the Coalition Government in 1940 as deputy to the Prime Minister, proving himself a wise and loyal colleague to Mr Churchill throughout the war. In the difficult years of his own premiership, though a curiously elusive figure to the public, he exercised great gifts of judgment and leadership within his Cabinet, holding together what was perhaps a difficult team, of which the chief figures were men of such diverse individualism as Mr Herbert Morrison, Mr Ernest Bevin, Sir Stafford Cripps, Dr Hugh Dalton and Mr Aneurin Bevan.

Mr Attlee's personal relationship with King George was at first not easy. Both were essentially shy men and the initiation of conversation did not come easily to either of them. At the outset the Prime Minister's audiences were not infrequently marked by long silences. This, however, quickly wore off. Both persevered—and with success. The King writes in his diary later of 'long talks' with Mr Attlee, in the course of which he was able, apart from conducting the business of the day, to put to the Prime Minister some of the aspects of thought which were current at the time, not infrequently surprising him by the extent, detail and accuracy of his information. 'I told Attlee', he wrote on one occasion, 'that he must give the people here some confidence that the Government was not going to stifle all private enterprise. Everyone wanted to help in rehabilitating the country but they were not allowed to', and again:

> We discussed Housing & Clothing. I told him I had heard that Local Authorities had had their plans turned down & were unable to build any houses because they could not get a permit from Health. Papers he had read showed a good improvement in approved permits to build now. But where are the houses, I asked? The delay is very worrying. Private building contractors had done well. As to Clothing the P.M. told me all available suits etc. go to the Demobilised Men, & the Women's clothes stocks are much exaggerated. I said we must all have new clothes & my family are down to the lowest ebb.

On the subject of strikes also the King was emphatic with his Prime Minister. A stoppage of work by gas employees, which had not been accorded official Trade Union recognition, caused considerable inconvenience during the winter of 1945 and Mr Attlee expressed the hope that it would be settled quickly. King George commented that 'the liberty of the subject was at stake if a strike interfered with home life. Essential services such as gas, electricity and water should never be used for those purposes in an unofficial strike. He & I could easily go on strike. He would send me no papers and if he did I would not sign them. But we don't!'

[Wheeler-Bennett, *King George VI*, 650–2.]

## (2) ADVICE AND WARNING

### (*a*) *MacDonald*

As an example of the King's desire that the new Prime Minister should not be embarrassed through ignorance of customary usage, the following Memorandum may be quoted, summarising, for Mr MacDonald's information, the procedure to be followed in matters requiring the Sovereign's approval.

House of Commons

A letter is written to the King every day during the Session by the Leader of the House of Commons, describing the proceedings of the House. A telegram briefly reporting any outstanding particulars in the proceedings is sent every evening by one of the Whips.

Cabinet

1. No change is made in the constitution of the Ministry until the King's approval has been obtained.

2. No mention should be made publicly or privately of any matters which have transpired in Cabinet, without the approval of His Majesty being first obtained.

3. Before a Minister goes abroad he should acquaint the King of his intention to do so.

Foreign Office

All important Foreign Office Despatches are submitted to His Majesty before being sent abroad.

Ecclesiastical preferment.

A very important responsibility. The Archbishop of Canterbury will be found very fair and liberal-minded with a wide knowledge of the personnel of the Church and always ready to advise. It is important that the letters which convey the offer of important preferment should be written by the Prime Minister himself.

Honours and appointments

It is hoped that a firm hand will be kept on the distribution of Honours. With the exception of the last Government, the bestowal has been extravagant. Especial care should be taken with regard to appointments to the Privy Council. Mr Gladstone said that a Privy Councillorship used to be regarded as a greater honour than a Peerage.

Before any person is offered an Appointment under the crown, or an Honour, the King's approval should be obtained, until which time the individual in question should not be approached on the subject.

All recommendations for Honours are submitted in conjunction with the Prime Minister with the exception of the Order of Merit and the Royal Victorian Order (which are made on the King's initiative).

Except in very special cases, Submissions for Honours are only made twice a year, i.e. New Year's Day and the King's Birthday.

The number of names submitted on each occasion for Baronetcies and Knighthoods, other than those for the Dominions, should not respectively exceed 8 and 24.

The King deprecates the bestowal of Honours on Ministers while in Office.

[Sir Harold Nicolson, *King George V* (London, 1952), 388–9, footnote 1.]

A more detailed version of his historic audience is contained in the memorandum written by Lord Stamfordham, at the time:

Tuesday, 22nd January 1924

Today the King saw Mr Ramsay MacDonald and entrusted to him the formation of a new Government, which he undertook.

He assured the King that, though he and his friends were inexperienced in governing and fully realised the great responsibilities which they would now assume, nevertheless they were honest and sincere and his earnest desire was to serve his King and Country. They may fail in their endeavours: but it will not be for want of trying to do their best.

The King told Mr Ramsay MacDonald that he might count upon his assistance in every way. His Majesty only asked for frankness between them. The King referred to recent utterances of Mr Lansbury, in which he went out of his way to express a threat and a reminder of the fate which had befallen King Charles I. His Majesty was not affected by these personal attacks but did take exception to Mr Lansbury's basing his remarks upon the idea of intrigues at Court. The King said Mr Ramsay MacDonald might be certain that—with the exception of his Private Secretary, part of whose duty was to keep His Majesty informed as to the views of the men in the various schools of political opinion, and of the Assistant Secretaries—he did not discuss these matters with anyone else but formed his own judgment.

His Majesty went on to say that, little expecting to occupy his present position, he served in the Navy for 14 years—and thus had opportunities of seeing more of the world and mixing with his fellow creatures than would otherwise have been the case: while during the past 14 years he had naturally gained much political knowledge and experience of the working of the machinery of Government under 4 different Prime Ministers. He always follows Foreign Affairs with especial interest and is inclined to wonder whether Mr Ramsay MacDonald had fully considered the heavy responsibilities and duties incurred by undertaking the office of Secretary of State for Foreign Affairs in addition to that of Prime Minister. The King referred to the case of Lord Salisbury who, in spite of his great knowledge of Foreign Affairs, found it difficult to carry on the duties of both offices: indeed he did very little of the work of the Prime Minister, whereas now-a-days the latter position in itself and its heavy responsibilities must be a serious tax upon anyone holding that office. Mr Ramsay MacDonald explained that for the moment he had no one to appoint to the Foreign Office, but perhaps later on he might be able to hand it over to someone else.

The King spoke of the recognition of Russia. Mr Ramsay MacDonald said that he had heard from Monsieur Benes himself that Monsieur Poincaré had asked him to go to Russia and arrange for the recognition of the Government by France. Signor Mussolini was on the point of recognising Russia and if we were left out we should find that other countries had forestalled us in all business enterprises. The King said he was sure that Mr Ramsay MacDonald would understand how abhorrent it would be to His Majesty to receive any representative of Russia who, directly or indirectly, had been connected with the abominable murder of the Emperor, Empress and their family, the King's own first cousin, and His Majesty hoped that the representative might be a Minister and not an Ambassador.

The King referred to the unfortunate incident at the recent Meeting at the Albert Hall, presided over by Mr Ramsay MacDonald, at which the *Marseillaise* and the *Red Flag* were sung. Mr Ramsay MacDonald spoke very openly and said he was sure the King would be generous to him and understand the very difficult position he was in *vis-à-vis* to his own extremists; and he could assure His Majesty that, had he attempted to prevent the *Red Flag* being sung on that occasion, a riot would inevitably have ensued. Moreover there was a very serious possibility on Monday night of the *Red Flag* being sung in the House of Commons and it had required all his influence and that of his moderate and immediate friends to prevent this taking place: they had got into the way of singing this song and it will be by degrees that he hopes to break down this habit.

Later in the afternoon, after the House of Commons had sat and adjourned, the King saw Mr Ramsay MacDonald who kissed hands on appointment and gave His Majesty a list of his Government and discussed the qualifications of the respective Members.

[Nicolson, *King George V*, 384–6.]

(*b*) *Churchill*

On the morning of Friday, June 2, I set out in my train for our siding by Eisenhower's headquarters near Portsmouth, with Field-Marshal Smuts, Mr Ernest Bevin, General Ismay, and my personal staff. Just before we started a further letter arrived.

Buckingham Palace
June 2, 1944

Mr dear Winston,

I want to make one more appeal to you not to go to sea on D Day. Please consider my own position. I am a younger man than you, I am a sailor, and as King I am head of all these Services. There is nothing I would like better than to go to sea, but I have agreed to stay at home; is it fair that you should then do exactly what I should have liked to do myself? You said yesterday afternoon that it would be a fine thing for the King to lead his troops into battle, as in old days; if the King cannot do this, it does not seem to me right that his Prime Minister should take his place.

Then there is your own position. You will see very little, you will run a considerable risk, you will be inaccessible at a critical time, when vital decisions might have to be taken, and however unobtrusive you may be your mere presence on board is bound to be a very heavy additional responsibility to the Admiral and Captain. As I said in my previous letter, your being there would add immeasurably to my anxieties, and your going without consulting your colleagues in the Cabinet would put them in a very difficult position, which they would justifiably resent.

I ask you most earnestly to consider the whole question again, and not let your personal wishes, which I very well understand, lead you to depart from your own high standard of duty to the State.

Believe me,
Your very sincere friend,
George R.I.

Meanwhile my train lay just outside Southampton, and we were soon connected by telephone with Eisenhower's headquarters. That afternoon we paid him a visit. His tents and caravans were very well concealed in a wood near by. His Majesty was concerned at not having had a reply from me to his letter. At 11.30 p.m., in response to inquiries, I spoke to Lascelles at Windsor Castle on the scrambler telephone, and said that I had cancelled my arrangements in deference to His Majesty's desire. I wrote the following letter in the small hours of the morning and sent it at once by dispatch-rider to Windsor.

June 3, 1944

Sir,

I must excuse myself for not having answered Your Majesty's letter earlier. It caught me just as I was leaving by the train, and I have been in constant movement ever since. I had a dispatch-rider standing by in order to take it to you to-night.

Sir, I cannot really feel that the first paragraph of your letter takes sufficient account of the fact that there is absolutely no comparison in the British Constitution between a Sovereign and a subject. If Your Majesty had gone, as you desire, on board one of your ships in this bombarding action it would have required the Cabinet approval beforehand, and I am very much inclined to think, as I told you, that the Cabinet would have advised most strongly against Your Majesty going.

On the other hand, as Prime Minister and Minister of Defence I ought to be allowed to go where I consider it necessary to the discharge of my duty, and I do not admit that the Cabinet have any right to put restrictions on my freedom of movement. I rely on my own judgment, invoked in many serious matters, as to what are the proper limits of risk which a person who discharges my duties is entitled to run. I must most earnestly ask Your Majesty that no principle shall be laid down which inhibits my freedom of movement when I judge it necessary to acquaint myself with conditions in the various theatres of war. Since Your Majesty does me the honour to be so much concerned about my personal safety on this occasion, I must defer to Your Majesty's wishes, and indeed commands. It is a great comfort to me to know that they arise from Your Majesty's desire to continue me in your service. Though I regret that I cannot go, I am deeply grateful to Your Majesty for the motives which have guided Your Majesty in respect of

Your Majesty's humble and devoted servant and subject,

Winston S. Churchill

[Winston Churchill, *The Second World War*, v. (London, 1985 Penguin edn.), 549–50.]

## 3. CONFIDENTIALITY BETWEEN SOVEREIGN AND MINISTERS

Letters to the Press from the Queen's Private Secretary are rare events and worthy of record. In May 1950 Sir Alan Lascelles wrote a letter to *The Times* setting out some principles governing the Crown's right to refuse a dissolution of Parliament. The letter was written under the pseudonym 'Senex' (though the author's identity must have been put about in some way, since everybody seems to have known who he was). On 28 July 1986, Sir William Heseltine wrote to *The Times* under his own name, possibly feeling that 'Senex' or anything similar was unsuitable to the present age, or else that his name would be revealed by the Press in any event and perhaps attributed to a Palace 'mole'.

The occasion for Sir William's letter was the appearance of an article in the *Sunday Times* newspaper on July 20 which stated that the Queen was dismayed by an 'uncaring Mrs Thatcher.' 'Sources close to the Queen' were quoted as saying that the Queen had misgivings about the dispute within the Commonwealth over Britain's attitude towards South Africa, which was threatening Commonwealth unity, and also about the Prime Minister's handling of the miners' strike and the United States raid from British bases on Libya. Somewhat similar reports had appeared in other newspapers. None of them however had chosen to raise a constitutional question or to reveal the sources, if any, of their information. The

*Sunday Times* by contrast made a news story of its own news story. That originally appeared in a feature article by one of its investigative journalists, whose copy, the *Sunday Times* asserted, had been checked with official sources, later claimed to be 'within the Palace and at the highest level' (though the number of sources subsequently appeared not to have exceeded one). On the night that this story appeared the Buckingham Palace Press Office issued a statement saying that 'reports purporting to be the Queen's opinion of Government policies are entirely without foundation.' This statement the editor of the *Sunday Times* refused to print on the grounds that he believed his journalist's story to have been checked in detail with the sources (not then named) mentioned in the article. He added that if the Palace's statement were not retracted he would make further revelations . . .

There must be a lesson here for the Queen's advisers. The assertion by the editor of the *Sunday Times* that the Buckingham Palace Press Office is the official voice of the Queen and speaks authoritatively about her should not be accepted. If there is to be such an office at all, should its incumbent's role not be confined to supplying information of a routine factual or logistical kind, and not for offering guidance of the sort that has become familiar in the running of government departments and of government in general? An official holding Mr Shea's office should not allow himself to be asked about the Queen's opinions or about matters of politics or policy and if asked should not answer. In government generally, it may be that the relations between ministers or between ministers and civil servants are not seriously prejudiced by the rigmarole of 'sources close to the Prime Minister' or lobby briefings, or guidance on an unattributable basis. But the confidentiality mentioned in Sir William Heseltine's third principle, that governs the relationship between Crown and ministers, though it may not be absolute, is different in purpose and character from that between ministers, and it must be damaged by exercises of the kind seen last summer.

[Geoffrey Marshall, 'The Queen's Press Relations' [1986] *Public Law* 505–6, 508.]

Sir,

In the debate about the supposed revelations of the Queen's opinions about Government policies, I take three points to be axiomatic:

1. The Sovereign has the right—indeed the duty—to counsel, encourage and warn her Government. She is thus entitled to have opinions on Government policy and to express them to her chief Minister.
2. Whatever personal opinions the Sovereign may hold or may have expressed to her Government, she is bound to accept and act on the advice of her Ministers.
3. The Sovereign is obliged to treat her communications with the Prime Minister as entirely confidential between the two of them. This was central to the statement issued by the Buckingham Palace Press Office on July 19, as soon as the original *Sunday Times* articles appeared.

After 34 years of unvarying adherence to these constitutional principles, it is preposterous to suggest that Her Majesty might suddenly depart from them. No sensible person would give a moment's credence to such a proposition.

It is equally preposterous to suggest that any member of Her Majesty's Household, even supposing that he or she knew what Her Majesty's opinions on Government policy might be (and the Press Secretary certainly does not), would reveal them to the Press.

It is the business of the Press Secretary and other members of his office to deal with Press enquiries to the Palace; and in the process to comment on, or refuse to comment on, propositions put to them by journalists. There is nothing in any way improper about that and there is no secret about it either.

I am assured that, in the several exchanges between the Press Secretary and Mr Simon Freeman before the *Sunday Times* articles were published, the Press Secretary said nothing which could reasonably bear the interpretation put upon it by the writers of the article on the front page in the edition of July 20 . . .

The publication of the original articles was clearly bound to call in question the constitutional relationship between the Sovereign and the Prime Minister, and this without any attributable source and without any attempt by the Editor himself to verify the story. The subsequent claim that the unnamed *sources* were 'within the Palace and at the highest level' constitutes an unjustified slur on the impartiality and discretion of senior members of the Royal Household.

In short, I repeat what the Buckingham Palace Press Office said on the night the original story was published, and which the Editor of the *Sunday Times* refused to print:

> 'As with all previous Prime Ministers, the Queen enjoys a relationship of the closest confidentiality with Mrs Thatcher, and reports purporting to be the Queen's opinions of Government policies are entirely without foundation.
>
> Yours faithfully,
> William Heseltine
> Palace of Holyroodhouse
> July 27 [1986]

[The Queen's Press Secretary, Sir William Heseltine, letter to *The Times*, 29 July 1986.]

## 4. CIRCUMSTANCES IN WHICH MINISTERIAL ADVICE UNNECESSARY

What had prompted Mr Powell to raise the constitutional doctrine of ministerial responsibility in his Leicester speech in the first place was precisely that purpose of avoiding direct personal criticism of the Queen for the performance of one of her public acts. The act in question was the Queen's 1983 Christmas Day broadcast. The content of this broadcast had to his mind, and according to the press to a number of Conservative M.P.s, addressed itself too enthusiastically to the problems of countries abroad, and to 'a vociferous minority of newcomers' at home, to the detriment of the broad mass of her Christian subjects within the United Kingdom; all this being 'pregnant with peril for the future'. By raising the doctrine that the Sovereign always acted and spoke upon the advice of ministers, he could claim that his criticism of what she had said 'can no more involve disrespect or disloyalty to the Sovereign than to question or to criticise any of the other advice to the Crown upon which the government of the kingdom is carried on.' Furthermore, he spoke of the special 'duty' of Privy Councillors (of which he is one) arising from their oath of fealty, which rendered them 'reluctant beyond others to remain silent' if they believe they see cause to speak.

However, Mr Powell had raised the one occasion when Commonwealth politicians agree that the Queen is acting free from any notion of ministerial responsibility both in theory and practice. This is because, when delivering her Christmas Day broadcast, it is not a broadcast to any particular State of which she may or may not be Queen, but to the Commonwealth collectively, and the sole capacity in which she is said to be acting is that of 'Head of the Commonwealth.' Neither is the Commonwealth an organisation which has any representative council of ministers or governing group to whom she is in any way accountable, except perhaps in the last resort in practice to all the Heads of Government collectively at their biennial meetings.

This is to be contrasted with all other occasions, save for similar speeches at Commonwealth Day or Conferences, when the Queen acts in the twofold capacities of Head of the Commonwealth and monarch of a particular State. When at home, or travelling outside the Commonwealth, or in a Commonwealth country that is a republic or has its own monarchy, the Queen is monarch of the United Kingdom and she therefore acts upon the advice and responsibility of her U.K. ministers. When within a Commonwealth country where she is retained as monarch, she acts upon the advice and responsibility of the Prime Minister of that country. Lord Blake reiterated these conventions in a later letter to *The Times* and completely supported the exception that 'The Queen's Christmas broadcast and Commonwealth Day message in March are the only occasions when she speaks without ministerial responsibility. This has always been the convention.'

[R. W. Blackburn, 'The Queen and Ministerial Responsibility' [1985] *Public Law* 361 at 364–6.]

*The conferment of peerages on members of the Royal Family (such as the Dukedom of York) and on former Prime Ministers probably does not require ministerial advice. Nor does conferment of the Orders of the Garter and of the Thistle, the Order of Merit, and the Royal Victorian Order, all of which are in the Queen's personal gift.*

## The Sovereign's Reserve Powers

*If the Queen were to reject ministerial advice, she would be using her formal legal power to the exclusion of the cardinal convention of the constitution that the Sovereign only acts on such advice.*

The previous chapter shows that, while the Queen has in normal circumstances 'the right to be consulted, the right to encourage, the right to warn', she must, in the last resort, give way to the advice of the Cabinet. There are, however, certain prerogative powers which she exercises on her own responsibility, and which may fitly be called 'the personal prerogatives'. Exactly what they are is by no means clear; for there are differences of opinion in respect of several of them. There is no controversy that she need not accept advice as to the appointment of a Prime Minister or as to the creation of peers so as to override the opposition of the House of Lords. There is controversy as to whether she can dismiss a Government or dissolve Parliament without advice, or whether she can refuse to dissolve Parliament when advised to do so.

There have indeed been suggestions that other personal prerogatives survive. William IV seems to have suggested in 1834, after the burning of the Palace of Westminster, that he could summon Parliament to meet where he pleased. Lord Melbourne replied:

> There can be no question that, as your Majesty states, it is your Majesty's undoubted prerogative to appoint the meeting of your Parliament, but this place of meeting has been upon the present spot so unvariably for so many years—ever since the time of Charles II, who summoned one Parliament under very peculiar circumstances at Oxford—that, without adverting to the possibility of the House of Commons not sanctioning any arrangement made at present by voting the sums necessary to defray the expense of it, it appears to Viscount Melbourne that it would be highly inadvisable, and in some degree ungracious, to exercise this prerogative except after full consultation with the two Houses of Parliament.

He accordingly suggested that the Government should draw up a plan for submission to Parliament. Lord Melbourne's reply was a polite and constitutionally correct intimation that the question was one between the Government and Parliament . . .

[Jennings, *Cabinet Government*, 394–5.]

## 1. REFUSAL OF A DISSOLUTION

*This was examined above: p. 205.*

## 2. INSISTENCE ON A DISSOLUTION

*In the wholly unlikely events of a government losing a vote of confidence in the House of Commons but refusing either to recommend a dissolution or to resign, or of a government which tried improperly to extend the life of Parliament beyond the statutory maximum of five years, the Queen would be justified in insisting on an immediate dissolution. There has been royal insistence on a dissolution twice this century in the context of the Prime Minister's request to create peers so as to coerce the House of Lords: in both cases the Prime Minister unreservedly acquiesced.*

### (1) EDWARD VII

'He began by saying,' Nash recorded, 'that the King had come to the conclusion that he would not be justified in creating new Peers (say 300) until after a second general election and that he, Lord K., thought you should know of this now, though, for the present he would suggest that what he was telling me should be for your ear only. The King regards the policy of the Government as tantamount to the destruction of the House of Lords and he thinks that before a large creation of Peers is embarked upon or threatened the country should be acquainted with the particular project for accomplishing such destruction as well as with the general line of action as to which the country will be consulted at the forthcoming Election.'

[Note made on 15 Dececember 1909 of a conversation between Asquith's secretary, Vaughan Nash, and the King's Private Secretary, Lord Knollys, quoted in Roy Jenkins, *Asquith* (London, Fontana edn., 1967), 225.]

### (2) GEORGE V

Mr Asquith did not ask for an immediate reply. It seems, however, that King George and his private secretary misunderstood the purport of the discussion. Mr Asquith intended to prepare the King for the advice which he would subsequently receive from the Cabinet, while the King thought that no guarantee for the creation of peers would be sought before the election. Three days later Lord Knollys discovered that the King was mistaken, and Sir Arthur

Bigge was instructed to telegraph that it would be impossible for the King to give contingent guarantees. The King 'much resented the implication' that in the event of a Liberal Government being returned he might fail to act constitutionally; and he considered that Mr Asquith was seeking to use his name to secure a Liberal victory. On 15 November the Cabinet gave the following advice in a formal minute:

> An immediate dissolution of Parliament—as soon as the necessary parts of the Budget, the provision of old age pensions, and one or two other matters have been disposed of. The House of Lords to have the opportunity, if they demand it, at the same time, but not so as to postpone the date of the dissolution, to discuss the Government Resolution. H.M. Ministers cannot, however, take the responsibility of advising a dissolution unless they may understand that in the event of the policy of the Government being approved by an adequate majority in the new House of Commons, H.M. will be ready to exercise his constitutional powers (which may involve the prerogative of creating peers) if needed, to secure that effect shall be given to the decision of the country.
>
> H.M. Ministers are fully alive to the importance of keeping the name of the King out of the sphere of party and electoral controversy. They take upon themselves, as is their duty, the entire and exclusive responsibility for the policy which they will place before the electorate. H.M. will doubtless agree that it would be inadvisable in the interest of the State that any communication of the intentions of the Crown should be made public unless and until the actual occasion should arise.

Mr Asquith and Lord Crewe (as leader of the House of Lords) saw the King on the following day. The King, after much discussion, 'agreed most reluctantly to give the Cabinet a secret understanding that, in the event of the Government being returned with a majority at the general election, I should use my prerogative to make peers if asked for. I disliked having to do this very much, but agreed that this was the only alternative to the Cabinet resigning, which at this moment would be disastrous.'

The 'secret understanding' was due only to Mr Asquith's unfortunate speech of 14 April. He was thought to have pledged himself to secure guarantees or resign. The 'secret understanding' was a compromise. It would enable Mr Asquith to say afterwards that they had not recommended a dissolution except on the conditions specified on 14 April. On the other hand the secrecy would meet the King's objection that the purpose of the guarantee was to make use of his name for catching votes. In other words, it was a device to save Mr Asquith's face.

The King insisted that the Parliament Bill should be submitted to the House of Lords before the election. To this Mr Asquith agreed, and the Bill was read a first time and discussed on second reading in the House of Lords before the dissolution. The elections then proceeded on the issue raised by the Bill, and the Government's position was substantially unchanged. At no time was any public announcement or private communication made that the King had consented to a creation of peers, if necessary.

[Jennings, *Cabinet Government*, 440–1.]

*A mass creation of peers is not, in fact, an expeditious way of converting an obstructive House of Lords into a co-operative one: see Rodney Brazier,* Constitutional Practice *(Oxford, 1988), 153.*

## 3. REFUSAL OF ROYAL ASSENT

*The government might* recommend *refusal of royal assent (a) to a Bill which had been introduced by one government and had been passed by both Houses, at which time that government had been succeeded without a general election by a new administration which opposed the Bill; and (b) to a Private Member's Bill which had passed both Houses against the government's wishes.*

Perhaps an 'automatic' theory is most obviously justified in relation to the giving of assent to legislation that has received the assent of the Commons and the House of Lords. That the Royal Assent should not be refused in such circumstances is perhaps the least controvertible application of the general convention that prerogative powers are exercised on ministerial advice. This conclusion rests on a clear negative precedent, that no such Bill has failed to receive the Royal Assent since 1707 when Queen Anne refused assent to a Militia Bill. Normally, of course, ministerial advice here coincides with, and is reinforced by, that of the Queen's advisers in the assembled Houses. There could of course be circumstances of an unusual kind in which the two did not coincide. A Private Member's Bill perhaps might be given the approval of both Houses and the government not wish it to be enacted into law. Should the advice of Ministers be complied with when it is clearly not supported by a majority in Parliament?

Leaving aside such cases, however, can it be concluded that the power to refuse assent to legislation is now a dead letter? Under present constitutional arrangements it may well be so. But there are conceivable constitutional changes that might raise further questions about the Royal Assent. Suppose, for example, that a Bill of Rights were to be introduced and protected against repeal by a special legislative procedure requiring a specified majority in one or both Houses. Alternatively, suppose that a similar constitutional entrenchment were to require that some particular legal change was to be submitted to a referendum before being enacted into law. Though provisions of this kind have been enacted in some Constitutions in the Commonwealth, their effectiveness in the United Kingdom is a matter of debate. If such provisions were introduced and subsequently disregarded by a government that believed them to be ineffective and did not wish to be bound by them, it might be that the Queen would have to consider whether such a government's advice to assent to legislation should be refused if the legislation had not been submitted to the previously prescribed procedure. A decision by the courts would be the most appropriate way of deciding an issue of this kind but it might be that there would be procedural difficulties inhibiting a judicial remedy to restrain an improper presentation of a Bill for assent. A decision might therefore at some point have to be taken by the Queen and her advisers independently of Ministers.

[Geoffrey Marshall, *Constitutional Conventions* (Oxford, 1984), 21–3.]

## 4. DISMISSAL OF THE GOVERNMENT

No Government has been dismissed by the Sovereign since 1783. The general impression in 1834 was that Lord Melbourne's Government was, to use Palmerston's expression, 'turned out neck and crop'. The facts now available do not substantiate this conclusion, though they do not deny that William IV might have dismissed his ministers if he had so pleased. The Whigs had already been weakened by the resignation of Lord Grey, Mr Stanley, and Sir James Graham, when the death of Earl Spencer transferred Lord Althorp to the House of Lords. Lord Melbourne had made Lord Althorp's adhesion a *sine qua non* to his acceptance of office on the resignation of Lord Grey, owing to the weakness of the Government in the House of Commons. The removal of the party leader in that House might be regarded as the removal of the foundation upon which the Government was built . . .

The question did not become practical in England until 1913, when the Conservatives, enraged by their impotence against a Government which was imposing the Home Rule Act on them under the Parliament Act 1911, tried to find an ally in the Crown. Professor A. V. Dicey then wrote:

> I entirely agree that the King can do nothing except on the advice of Ministers. I totally disagree with the doctrine drawn from this principle that he can never dismiss Ministers in order that he may ascertain the will of the nation. Of course, the incoming ministers must, like Sir Robert Peel, accept responsibility for the change of Ministry. No one need be ashamed of following the principle set by Pitt and Peel.

In the course of his memorandum on the King's position in relation to the Home Rule Bill, Mr Asquith wrote:

> The Sovereign undoubtedly has the power of changing his advisers, but it is relevant to point out that there has been, during the last 130 years, one occasion only on which the King has dismissed the Ministry which still possessed the confidence of the House of Commons. This was in 1834, when William IV (one of the least wise of British monarchs) called upon Lord Melbourne to resign. He took advantage (as we now know) of a hint improvidently given by Lord Melbourne himself, but the proceedings were neither well-advised nor fortunate. The dissolution which followed left Sir R. Peel in a minority, and Lord Melbourne and his friends in a few months returned to power, which they held for the next six years. The authority of the Crown was disparaged, and Queen Victoria, during her long reign, was careful never to repeat the mistake of her predecessor . . .
>
> Nothing can be more important, in the best interests of the Crown and of the country, than that a practice, so long established and so well justified by experience, should remain unimpaired. It frees the occupant of the Throne from all personal responsibility for the acts of the Executive and the legislature. It gives force and meaning to the old maxim that 'the King can do no wrong'. So long as it prevails, however objectionable particular Acts may be to a large section of his subjects, they cannot hold him in any way accountable. If, on the other hand, the King were to intervene on one side, or in one case—which he could only do by dismissing ministers in *de facto* possession of a Parliamentary majority—he would be expected to do the

same on another occasion, and perhaps for the other side. Every Act of Parliament of the first order of importance, and only passed after acute controversy, would be regarded as bearing the personal *imprimatur* of the Sovereign. He would, whether he wished it or not, be dragged into the arena of party politics; and at a dissolution following such a dismissal of ministers as has just been referred to, it is no exaggeration to say that the Crown would become the football of contending factions.

This is a constitutional catastrophe which it is the duty of every wise statesman to do the utmost in his power to avert.

To these observations George V replied:

While you admit the Sovereign's undoubted power to change his advisers. I infer that you regard the exercise of that power as inexpedient and indeed dangerous.

Should the Sovereign *never* exercise that right, not even, to quote Sir Erskine May, 'in the interests of the State and on grounds which could be justified in Parliament'? Bagehot wrote, 'The Sovereign too possesses a power according to theory for extreme use on a critical occasion but which in law he can use on any occasion. He can *dissolve* . . .

Mr Asquith replied that for the King to dismiss ministers might entail consequences 'very injurious to the authority of the Crown'. Lord Esher, while denying that the King could refuse assent, considered that 'the King still possesses the power of dismissing his Ministers, but not of dictating policy, whether in the form of a dissolution of Parliament or otherwise'.

In February 1914, the King and Mr Asquith discussed the consequences of a failure in the negotiations proceeding among the parties. The King suggested that a general election would clear the air, would show whether the Government possessed a mandate, and would in any case relieve the King and the Prime Minister of responsibility for what followed. Mr Asquith replied that a general election would settle nothing and that, whatever the consequences, the responsibility would rest not with the King but with his ministers.

The King replied that, although constitutionally he might not be responsible, still he could not allow bloodshed among his loyal subjects in any part of his Dominions without exerting every means in his power to avert it. Although at the present stage of the proceedings he could not rightly intervene he should feel it his duty to do what in his own judgment was best for his people generally.

Mr Asquith expressed his surprise and hoped that the King was not thinking of refusing assent, which would 'inevitably prove disastrous to the Monarchy'. The King could dismiss his ministers, but if so it should be done at once. The King replied that he had no intention of dismissing his ministers, though his future action must be guided by circumstances.

Reasons have been given above for asserting that the precedent of 1834 is no precedent for the dismissal of ministers in modern conditions. Mr Asquith's memorandum, so far as it goes, is incontrovertible. It does not, however, meet the point which was made by Unionists in 1913 and mentioned by their most expert constitutional lawyer, that the King has the right to dismiss ministers if he has reason to believe that their policy, though approved by the House of Commons, has not the approval of the people. Such an argument, it must be confessed, is an argument for a dissolution and not for a dismissal of ministers. If the King believes that the Government has lost its majority, and if it is any concern of his, his obvious step is to ascertain whether his assumption is correct and to insist upon a dissolution. If ministers refused to 'advise' the dissolution in Council they would resign; and if they did not resign he could dismiss them.

But is it his duty to make such an assumption? Is he sufficiently in touch with public opinion to be able to form a judgment? It is suggested that the answer to the second question is in the negative. Though his 'splendid isolation' makes him more impartial than most, it also keeps him away from the movements of opinion. He can judge only from newspapers, from by-elections, and from his own entourage. Of the first, it is enough to say that even the unanimous opposition of London newspapers would be no criterion. Of the second it can be said that by-elections (as Mr Disraeli discovered) are apt to prove deceptive, especially to one far removed from them. Of the third it must be asserted that it is always more biased and less well-informed then the King himself.

Nor is it his business to anticipate the decision of the electorate. Every Government takes decisions which would not be approved by the electorate. It is neither practicable nor desirable that an election should be held whenever it is suspected that a particular decision is not approved. The electorate is asked to approve not a particular decision but a course of policy. It is asked to approve such policy at intervals of four or five years, if not more frequently. If the King selects decisions which seem to him to be important, his selection must depend upon his subjective notions, which it is his duty, as an impartial Sovereign, to ignore. If he selects because of the vehemence of the Opposition, he invites all Oppositions to be vehement.

The Home Rule Bill differed from some other Government decisions in that, once accepted, its policy could hardly be reversed. It would not have been practicable for the Conservatives to have abolished Home Rule if the war had not intervened and they had taken office in 1915. In this it was not so exceptional as was sometimes argued. Nearly every decision of foreign policy or of Commonwealth or colonial policy, every constitutional change, and even such a matter of internal policy as the imposition of a general tariff or a fundamental modification of the system of taxation, is of a kind that cannot immediately be reversed. Home Rule had been a policy of the Liberal party from 1886 to 1910 even if, as the Conservatives alleged, it was not specifically submitted to the country in 1910. But, even if a fundamental change of policy is made without a 'mandate', all the considerations urged by Mr Asquith suggest that it is not for the King to intervene, except by warnings and protests. It is inevitable that a Sovereign who dismisses ministers or compels them to resign should be regarded as the ally of the Opposition, and as such be made the subject of attack.

George V did his very best in 1913–14 to exercise his functions impartially; but he was not impartial because, like everybody else in his kingdom, he was affected by the strong emotions prevailing. His principal advisers, Lord Stamfordham and Lord Esher, were in all essentials Conservatives and the latter quite openly. They agreed with Mr F. E. Smith that 'Ulster will fight', and they were by no means certain that he was wrong to add 'and Ulster will be right'. Both the King and Mr Asquith admitted the right to dismiss ministers and, as a matter of right, it cannot be denied: but if there had been neither agreement between the parties nor war and the King had dismissed ministers, there would probably have grown up a strong republican party.

The Queen's function is, it is suggested, to see that the Constitution functions in the normal manner. It functions in the normal manner so long as the electors are asked to decide between competing parties at intervals of reasonable length. She would be justified in refusing to assent to a policy which subverted the democratic basis of the Constitution, by unnecessary or indefinite prolongations of the life of Parliament, by a gerrymandering of the constituencies in the interests of one party, or by fundamental modification of the electoral system to the same end. She would not be justified in other circumstances; and certainly the King would not have been justified in 1913.

[Jennings, *Cabinet Government*, 403, 407–12.]

# [9]
# THE HOUSE OF COMMONS

## Parliaments, Members, and Parties

### 1. LIFE OF A PARLIAMENT

#### (1) MAXIMUM DURATION

This present Parliament and all Parliaments that shall at any time hereafter be called, assembled, or held, shall and may respectively have continuance for five years, and no longer, to be accounted from the day on which by the writ of summons this present Parliament hath been, or any future Parliament shall be, appointed to meet, unless this present or any such Parliament hereafter to be summoned shall be sooner dissolved by his Majesty, his heirs or successors.

[Septennial Act 1715, as amended by the Parliament Act 1911, s. 7.]

#### (2) DISSOLUTION

LORD DENHAM: My Lords, it may be for the convenience of your Lordships to know that . . . the Prime Minister has today asked Her Majesty the Queen to proclaim the Dissolution of Parliament. Her Majesty has been graciously pleased to signify that she will comply with this request. Parliament will be dissolved on Monday 18 May. The general election will take place on Thursday 11 June. The new Parliament will be summoned on Wednesday 17 June . . .

*Ironically, no such equivalent statement was made to the House of Commons.*

[Statement by the Government Chief Whip in the Lords: 487 H.L. Deb. 422 (11 May 1987).]

### (3) SUMMONING

From henceforth a Parliament shall be holden once in three years at the least.

*In practice, of course, Parliament meets every year in annual session.*

[Meeting of Parliament Act 1694.]

### (4) PROROGATION

*The end of each parliamentary session is marked by prorogation, with a brief Queen's Speech outlining the work of that session. The main practical effect of prorogation is to cause all public Bills which have not completed all stages to lapse. Customarily, a prorogation ceremony also took place before dissolution, but there was no such ceremony before the 1979, 1983, or 1987 dissolutions.*

To most outside observers, the question of pre-dissolution procedures may seem largely inconsequential, but it raises points of constitutional interest. The change to adjournment has diminished the role of the Monarchy in the parliamentary ceremony. Furthermore, it may seem illogical that a Sovereign's speech is now delivered at the end of every session except the last; or, put another way, at the end of some sessions but not others. A more important point is that, given that prorogation before dissolution was such an ancient practice, and given also the declared intention in 1967 for the related ceremony of Royal Assent by Commission to be held at least once in every session, it is extraordinary that the change has never been properly debated, and still remains to be explained by a minister in Parliament.

For persons in doubt as to who is responsible for making the decision, an illuminating feature of the Speaker's utterances on May 12 and 14, 1987 will be the stress he gave to the fact that the decision was not his, and therefore by implication not that of the House of Commons on whose authority he acts. The decision rests with Her Majesty's Government, and ultimately with the Prime Minister, who is responsible for advising the Sovereign upon the prerogatives of prorogation and dissolution. Undoubtedly, before 1991 or such date as the next dissolution occurs, the relevant officials and ministers, particularly the Leaders of both Houses, in tendering their own respective advice to the Prime Minister, will take note of Mr Weatherill's opinion and also any further representations made by members, and also perhaps peers. But in the democratic era, it remains strange that matters relating to the life of Parliament do not belong to Parliament itself.

[R. Blackburn, 'Prorogation and Adjournment Before a Dissolution of Parliament' [1987] *Public Law* 533 at 542.]

## 2. QUALIFICATIONS TO BE AN MP

### (1) AGE

. . . No person hereafter shall be capable of being elected a member to serve in this or any future Parliament who is not of one and twenty years . . .

[Parliamentary Elections Act 1695, s. 7.]

### (2) BRITISH CITIZENSHIP

. . . No person born out of the kingdoms of England Scotland or Ireland or the dominions thereunto belonging . . . shall be capable to be of the privy council or a member of either House of Parliament . . .

*Citizens of the Republic of Ireland are not aliens for this purpose: British Nationality Act 1981, s. 50(1).*

[Act of Settlement 1701, s. 3.]

### (3) ABSENCE OF DISQUALIFICATION

Our conclusion on this branch of the case accordingly is that, if the respondent has in fact succeeded to the Viscounty of Stansgate, and it is open for us so to find, he became by that succession disqualified from being a candidate at the election or from sitting in the House of Commons notwithstanding that he had not applied for or received a writ of summons to attend the House of Lords.

We think it right to say that this conclusion seems to us to be in accordance with sound constitutional doctrine. So long as the hereditary principle is maintained as part of the fabric of the constitution—and we express no opinion as to whether it should be so maintained—it would seem to us to be wholly inconsistent with that principle that the successor to a hereditary peerage should have a free option as to which House he desires to sit in. By the fact of succession he has entered a particular class of persons upon whom the duty of attending the House of Lords (unless granted leave of absence) is imposed by law and immemorial usage; and no modern constitutional convention to the contrary has in our view been established.

[*In re Parliamentary Election for Bristol South East* [1964] 2 QB 257 at 288–9, per Gorman J.]

Not long afterwards my father died suddenly, and I was transferred automatically to the House of Lords. We were at dinner in the House of Commons when I received the news. I had left some notes in the Chamber, and unthinkingly went in to fetch them. I learned later that someone had reported me to the authorities for breaking a rule, which of course I had done, for I was already a peer.

[Lord Home, *The Way the Wind Blows* (London, 1976), 100–1.]

(*a*) *Bankruptcy*

427.—(1) Where a court in England and Wales or Northern Ireland adjudges an individual bankrupt or a court in Scotland awards sequestration of an individual's estate, the individual is disqualified—

(a) for sitting or voting in the House of Lords,
(b) for being elected to, or sitting or voting in, the House of Commons, and
(c) for sitting or voting in a committee of either House.

(2) Where an individual is disqualified under this section, the disqualification ceases—

(a) except where the adjudication is annulled or the award recalled or reduced without the individual having been first discharged, on the discharge of the individual, and
(b) in the excepted case, on the annulment, recall or reduction, as the case may be.

(3) No writ of summons shall be issued to any lord of Parliament who is for the time being disqualified under this section for sitting and voting in the House of Lords.

(4) Where a member of the House of Commons who is disqualified under this section continues to be so disqualified until the end of the period of 6 months beginning with the day of the adjudication or award, his seat shall be vacated at the end of that period.

(5) A court which makes an adjudication or award such as is mentioned in subsection (1) in relation to any lord of Parliament or member of the House of Commons shall forthwith certify the adjudication or award to the Speaker of the House of Lords or, as the case may be, to the Speaker of the House of Commons.

(6) Where a court has certified an adjudication or award to the Speaker of the House of Commons under subsection (5), then immediately after it becomes apparent which of the following certificates is applicable, the court shall certify to the Speaker of the House of Commons—

(a) that the period of 6 months beginning with the day of the adjudication or award has expired without the adjudication or award having been annulled, recalled or reduced, or

(b) that the adjudication or award has been annulled, recalled or reduced before the end of that period.

(7) Subject to the preceding provisions of this section, so much of this Act and any other enactment (whenever passed) and of any subordinate legislation (whenever made) as—

(a) makes provision for or in connection with bankruptcy in one or more parts of the United Kingdom, or

(b) makes provision conferring a power of arrest in connection with the winding up or insolvency of companies in one or more parts of the United Kingdom,

applies in relation to persons having privilege of Parliament or peerage as it applies in relation to persons not having such privilege.

[Insolvency Act 1986, s. 427.]

(*b*) *Imprisonment*

1.—A person found guilty of one or more offences (whether before or after the passing of this Act and whether in the United

Kingdom or elsewhere), and sentenced or ordered to be imprisoned or detained indefinitely or for more than one year, shall be disqualified for membership of the House of Commons while detained anywhere in the British Islands or the Republic of Ireland in pursuance of the sentence or order or while unlawfully at large at a time when he would otherwise be so detained.

2.—(1) If a person disqualified by this Act for membership of the House of Commons is elected to that House his election shall be void; and if such a person is nominated for election as a member of that House his nomination shall be void.

(2) If a member of the House of Commons becomes disqualified by this Act for membership of that House his seat shall be vacated.

[Representation of the People Act 1981, ss. 1, 2.]

MR SPEAKER: I have to inform the House that I have received a letter dated 16 June 1987 from the Clerk of Petty Sessions, in Enniskillen, in the following terms.

> 'At Enniskillen Magistrates' Court on Monday 15 June 1987, Mr Kenneth Maginnis MP appeared to answer to a Summons charging him with failing to tax his car . . . A warrant of commitment was issued forthwith committing him to prison for a period of 7 days.'

I shall cause the text of the letter to be printed in the *Official Report*.

*During a sentence of less than one year an MP may not sit or vote. Any sentence for treason automatically disqualifies.*

[118 H.C. Deb. 36–7 (25 June 1987).]

(*c*) *Detention in a mental hospital*

141.—(1) Where a member of the House of Commons is authorised to be detained on the ground (however formulated) that he is suffering from mental illness, it shall be the duty of the court, authority or person on whose order or application, and of any registered medical practitioner upon whose recommendation or certificate, the detention was authorised, and of the person in charge of the hospital or other place in which the member is authorised to be detained, to notify the Speaker of the House of Commons that the detention has been authorised.

(2) Where the Speaker receives a notification under subsection (1) above, or is notified by two members of the House of Commons

that they are credibly informed that such an authorisation has been given, the Speaker shall cause the member to whom the notification relates to be visited and examined by two registered medical practitioners appointed in accordance with subsection (3) below.

(3) The registered medical practitioners to be appointed for the purposes of subsection (2) above shall be appointed by the President of the Royal College of Psychiatrists and shall be practitioners appearing to the President to have special experience in the diagnosis or treatment of mental disorders.

(4) The registered medical practitioners appointed in accordance with subsection (3) above shall report to the Speaker whether the member is suffering from mental illness and is authorised to be detained as such.

(5) If the report is to the effect that the member is suffering from mental illness and authorised to be detained as aforesaid, the Speaker shall at the expiration of six months from the date of the report, if the House is then sitting, and otherwise as soon as may be after the House next sits, again cause the member to be visited and examined by two such registered medical practitioners as aforesaid, and the registered medical practitioners shall report as aforesaid.

(6) If the second report is that the member is suffering from mental illness and authorised to be detained as mentioned in subsection (4) above, the Speaker shall forthwith lay both reports before the House of Commons, and thereupon the seat of the member shall become vacant.

(7) Any sums required for the payment of fees and expenses to registered medical practitioners acting in relation to a member of the House of Commons under this section shall be defrayed out of moneys provided by Parliament.

[Mental Health Act 1983, s. 141.]

### (*d*) *Expulsion*

Resolved, That the article written by Mr Allighan, and published in *World's Press News* on 3 April 1947, in its general tone, and particularly by its unfounded imputations against unnamed Members of insobriety in the precincts of the House, is an affront to this House; and that both Mr Allighan, as the writer of the article, and Arthur Heighway, the editor and publisher of *World's Press News*, are guilty of a gross contempt of this House.

Resolved, That Mr Allighan, in persistently misleading the Committee of Privileges in his evidence, and in seeking to cast suspicion on others in respect of the very matter of which he knew himself to be guilty, has committed a gross contempt of this House . . .

Resolved, That Mr Allighan, for his gross contempts of the House and for his misconduct, be expelled from this House.

*Mr Heighway was, at the House's direction, admonished by the Speaker.*

[443 H.C. Deb. 1110, 1111, 1197 (30 October 1947).]

## (4) RESIGNATION

### (*a*) *Chiltern Hundreds*

Constitutionally, a Member of Parliament has no power of voluntary retirement. A resolution of the House on 2nd March 1623 laid down that 'a man, after his is duly chosen, cannot relinquish'; and this remains in force. Death, elevation to the Peerage, dissolution or expulsion are the only causes, apart from legal disqualification, by which a Member's seat can be vacated. Therefore a Member wishing to resign has to disqualify himself by going through the process of applying for an office of profit under the Crown, which legally allows him to vacate his seat and obliges the House to order a new writ.

The prohibition of resignation, established by Resolution of the House in 1623, may have come about because serving in Parliament was often regarded, like holding parish or county office, as an obligation to be accepted only reluctantly, not an honour eagerly to be sought. To have allowed resignation would have opened the door to those who served reluctantly too easily to have relinquished their burden.

Acceptance of a paid office of the Crown, from the late 17th century, was reckoned to incapacitate a Member from continuing to serve, presumably because a Member receiving a salary from the Crown could not be expected properly to exercise his duty of disinterestedly scrutinising actions of the Crown or the Crown's government. This was applied obliquely to Ministers, in that on their acceptance of office up to 1919 they were disqualified from sitting, and had to submit to a fresh election. Acceptance of certain paid offices (*e.g.* as a judge) still disqualifies (the last Member to give up his seat from appointment to an actual paid office was Sir Thomas Williams, appointed a circuit judge on 1 June 1981). Details of these will be found in Schedule 1 of the House of Commons Disqualification Act 1975.

The Crown had at one time many sinecure offices at its disposal to which appointments could be made. All these offices no doubt at one time had actual duties, but over the centuries these had become lost or were farmed out. Two of them have been retained as purely normal offices of profit—no salary actually attaches to them.

The two offices now used for this purpose are that of Crown Steward and Bailiff of the three Chiltern Hundreds of Stoke, Desborough and Burnham, and that of the Manor of Northstead. Both these used formerly to be offices of profit, and are still retained as nominal offices of profit by tradition because of their usefulness and to meet the requirements of the House of Commons Disqualification Act 1975.

A Member wishing to retire thus applies to the Chancellor of the Exchequer for one of the offices, which he retains until the Chancellor appoints another applicant or until the holder applies for release from it. (Every new warrant issued expressly revokes the grant to the last holder). For symmetry, it is usual to grant the offices alternately; it also enables two Members to retire at precisely the same time. Indeed on 17 December 1985, 15 Ulster Unionist MPs resigned on the same day.

[House of Commons Public Information Office, *Factsheet* No. 34.]

(*b*) *Acceptance of other disqualifying office*

1.—(1) Subject to the provisions of this Act, a person is disqualified for membership of the House of Commons who for the time being—

- (a) holds any of the judicial offices specified in Part I of Schedule 1 to this Act;
- (b) is employed in the civil service of the Crown, whether in an established capacity or not, and whether for the whole or part of his time;
- (c) is a member of any of the regular armed forces of the Crown;

(d) is a member of any police force maintained by a police authority;
(e) is a member of the legislature of any country or territory outside the Commonwealth; or
(f) holds any office described in Part II or Part III of Schedule I.

(2) A person who for the time being holds any office described in Part IV of Schedule 1 is disqualified for membership of the House of Commons for any constituency specified in relation to that office in the second column of Part IV.

(3) In this section—

'civil service of the Crown' includes the civil service of Northern Ireland, Her Majesty's Diplomatic Service and Her Majesty's Overseas Civil Service;

'police authority' means any police authority within the meaning of the Police Act 1964 or the Police (Scotland) Act 1967, or the Police Authority for Northern Ireland; and 'member' in relation to a police force means a person employed as a full-time constable;

'regular armed forces of the Crown' means the Royal Navy, the regular forces as defined by section 225 of the Army Act 1955, the regular air force as defined by section 223 of the Air Force Act 1955, the Women's Royal Naval Service, Queen Alexandra's Royal Naval Nursing Service and Voluntary Aid Detachments serving with the Royal Navy.

(4) Except as provided by this Act, a person shall not be disqualified for membership of the House of Commons by reason of his holding an office or place of profit under the Crown or any other office or place; and a person shall not be disqualified for appointment to or for holding any office or place by reason of his being a member of that House.

[House of Commons Disqualification Act 1975, s. 1.]

(*c*) *Ordination*

No person having been ordained to the office of priest or deacon, or being a minister of the Church of Scotland, is or shall be capable of being elected to serve in Parliament as a member of the House of Commons.

[House of Commons (Clergy Disqualification) Act 1801, s. 1.]

No person in holy orders in the Church of Rome shall be capable of being elected to serve in Parliament as a member of the House of Commons; and if any such person shall be elected to serve in Parliament as aforesaid such election shall be void . . .

[Roman Catholic Relief Act 1829, s. 9.]

## 3. M.P.s' PAY AND CONDITIONS

### (1) PAY

Resolved, That . . . (a) the salaries of Members . . . shall, in respect of service in 1988 or any subsequent year, be at a yearly rate equal to 89 per cent of the rate which on 1 January in that year represents the maximum point on the main national pay scale for grade 6 officers in the Home Civil Service . . .

*The rate of pay in 1990 was 26,701 a year.*

[120 H.C. Deb. 336 (21 July 1987).]

### (2) ALLOWANCES

(*a*) *Office costs allowance*

*M.P.s may claim an office costs allowance for general office expenses, secretarial assistance, and research assistance. It was fixed at £20,140 a year in 1987, but it rises automatically each year by the same percentage increase in salary as that which is received by a senior personal secretary in the Home Civil Service. See 120 H.C. Deb. 338–9 (21 July 1987).*

(*b*) *Other privileges and allowances*

*M.P.s are entitled to free stationery and inland telephone and postal services; they may claim reimbursement for journeys on parliamentary business (and their spouses and children are entitled every session to 15 free return journeys each from their constituencies to Westminster); they may claim up to £8000 a year for London accommodation (or £1000 a year as a London supplement if they represent an inner London constituency.)*

### (3) PENSION AND RESETTLEMENT GRANT

*Pensions are payable under the Parliamentary and other Pensions Act 1972, the Parliamentary and other Pensions Act 1976, the Parliamentary Pensions etc. Act 1984, and the Parliamentary and other Pensions Act 1987. Examples of amounts payable are given at 112 H.C. Deb* 628–30 *(written answers 19 March 1987.)*

MR WAKEHAM (LEADER OF THE HOUSE): At the 1987 general election resettlement grants totalling £702,630 were paid to Members who retired and £372,220 to Members who lost their seats . . .

[136 H.C. Deb. *313* (written answers 30 June 1988).]

### (4) ACCOMMODATION

MR WAKEHAM (LEADER OF THE HOUSE): A total of 283 right hon. and hon. Members occupy single rooms, 230 share a room with one other right hon. or hon. Member, 36 share a room with two other hon. Members and 95 share a room with three or more right hon. or hon. Members.

[143 H.C. Deb. *578* (written answers 14 December 1988).]

The 1987 Services Committee report recommended that by 1995 every hon. Member should have a room of their own, if they wanted one. The building work which is currently under way, and the proposed building under consideration today, should go some way towards this.

[Mr Wakeham: 142 H.C. Deb. 966 (2 December 1988).]

### (5) THE REGISTER OF MEMBERS' INTERESTS

The purpose of the Register is to provide information of any pecuniary interest or other material benefit which a Member may receive which might be thought to affect his conduct as a Member or influence his actions, speeches or vote in Parliament and Members are required to have this general purpose in mind when determining what interests should properly be declared. They may, if they think it right and relevant, disclose interests beyond those set out below.

The scope of the Register, devised by the Select Committee and adopted by the House, seeks to balance, on the one hand, what should be publicly known about Members of Parliament with, on the other, the proper degree of privacy to which they and their families are entitled. They are not required to disclose the amount of any remuneration or benefit they may have, nor the interests of spouses or children, except in certain circumstances relating to shareholdings.

It is left to individual Members, with or without the advice of the Registrar, to give the required information, and any inconsistencies of style or content that are apparent in the Register spring from that fact. Each Member is responsible for what is recorded about himself here, as each is answerable to his fellow-Members and the public.

The nine specific classifications under which Members have been required to register their interests are:

1. remunerated directorships of companies, public or private.
2. remunerated employments or offices. Ministerial office and membership of the European Parliament, Council of Europe, Western European Union and the North Atlantic Assembly do not need to be registered.
3. remunerated trades, professions or vocations.
4. the names of clients when the interests referred to above include personal services by the Member which arise out of or are related in any manner to his membership of the House. These services include as well as any action connected with any proceedings in the House or its Committees, the sponsoring of functions in the Palace, making representations to Ministers, Civil Servants and other Members, accompanying delegations to Ministers and the like.
5. financial sponsorships, (a) as a parliamentary candidate where to the knowledge of the Member the sponsorship in any case exceeds 25 per cent of the candidate's election expenses, or (b) as a Member of Parliament, by any person or organisation, stating whether any such sponsorship includes any payment to the Member or any material benefit or advantage direct or indirect. This subsection includes gifts in relation to a Member's parliamentary duties, other than those received from abroad to which category 7 applies. Such gifts include services: for example the full or part-time services of a research assistant

or secretary by an external organisation (see below). It is, however, not necessary for a Member to register the fact that he is supported by his local constituency party.

6. overseas visits relating to or arising out of membership of the House where the cost of any such visit has not been wholly borne by the Member or by public funds. Overseas visits undertaken on behalf of the Inter Parliamentary Union, the Commonwealth Parliamentary Association, the Council of Europe, the Western European Union and the North Atlantic Assembly, or by any institution of the European Economic Communities need not be registered.
7. any payments or any material benefits or advantages received from or on behalf of foreign Governments, organisations or persons.
8. land and property of substantial value or from which a substantial income is derived. The requirement is to register the general nature of the interest rather than a detailed list of the holdings. A Member's home need not be declared, unless he also receives an income from it.
9. the names of companies or other bodies in which the Member has, to his knowledge, either himself or with or on behalf of his spouse or infant children, a beneficial interest in shareholdings of a nominal value greater than one-hundredth of the issued share capital.

*There is further elaboration of what should be declared at 89 H.C. Deb. 256–7 (17 December 1985).*

[The Register of Members' Interests on 10 January 1989, H.C. 105 (1988–9), iii–iv.]

## 4. THE OPPOSITION

*See chapter 7.*

# 5. PARTIES IN THE HOUSE

## (1) ARRANGEMENT OF COMMONS BUSINESS

13.—(1) Save as provided in this order, government business shall have precedence at every sitting.

[House of Commons standing order No. 13(1).]

The expression 'through the usual channels' is used primarily in relation to the arranging of business. It is concerned with the regular management and smooth running of the business of the House with a tacit understanding that, however important the rights of the Opposition may be, the Government must be allowed to govern and to get through its essential legislation. Where some of the fiercest clashes occur is when a Government is alleged by its critics not to represent a majority of the electors and to be introducing legislation, the justification for which the Opposition does not accept. Broadly, however, it still remains true, as stated by Sir Courtenay Ilbert, that 'the existence of every Government, and especially of every constitutional Government, depends on the observance of understandings which proceed on the assumption of a general desire to make the machine work. If these understandings are not observed, the wheels of the machine are stopped and the machinery may be brought to a standstill'. The usual channels work on the general assumption that it is mutually desirable that the machinery should work.

[Donald Wade, *Behind the Speaker's Chair* (London, 1978), 24.]

## (2) THE WHIPS

### (*a*) *'The whip'*

*Each party sends its M.P.s a weekly whip—a document in which forthcoming Commons business is underlined once, twice, or three times to denote how imporant is attendance. The parties claim that the whip is an order to attend, but it carries an implicit instruction to vote with the party.*

### (*b*) *Functions of the Whips*

*The Whips convey back-bench opinion to the party leaderships, and vice versa; they keep Members informed through the weekly whip;*

*they supervise pairs with M.P.s from other parties so that paired absences do not affect the results of divisions; they make recommendations of back-benchers for promotion; and they help to maintain party discipline. They also form an important element in 'the usual channels'.*

## (3) PARTY ORGANIZATION IN THE HOUSE

### (a) *The Conservative 1922 Committee*

*The 1922 Committee—so named after the meeting of Conservative M.P.s at the Carlton Club in 1922 which decided to end the Lloyd George coalition—is made up of all Conservative M.P.s who are not in the government or the Shadow Cabinet. It is an important focus of opinion, and the 1922 Committee elects the party Leader (see above, p. 1).*

### (b) *The Parliamentary Labour Party*

#### *A. Weekly Party Meetings*

1. There shall normally be two meetings of the Party each week when the House is in session.
2. The main Party Meeting shall be on Wednesdays from 11.30 a.m.–1.00 p.m. except on the fourth Wednesday of each month when the NEC meeting is held:

   The agenda shall read as follows:
   - (i) Parliamentary Committee Report
   - (ii) Report of any TUC/Labour Party Liaison Committee meeting
   - (iii) Report of any NEC/Parliamentary Committee joint meeting
   - (iv) Report of any Departmental Committee
   - (v) Motions
   - (vi) Any Other Business
3. All Motions shall be tabled in sufficient time for inclusion with the Party Whip one week in advance of discussion and all Amendments tabled forty-eight hours before the meeting. Amendments shall receive written circulation at the meeting itself.

4. A meeting shall also be held each Thursday at 6.00 p.m. with the sole item of Business being:

   (i) Next Week's Business in the House

5. A record of Proceedings consisting of a note of the decisions taken at the weekly meetings PLP shall be circulated with the Whip.

[P.L.P. standing order No. A.]

(*c*) *The Social and Liberal Democrats*

9.1. The Parliamentary Party in the House of Commons shall consist of all Members of that House in receipt of the Party's whip. Its Leader shall be the Leader of the Party elected as provided in Article 10. It shall be entitled to make such regulations (not being inconsistent with this Constitution) as it thinks fit for the conduct of its own proceedings. In particular, these regulations shall make provision for a Chief Whip and, if thought fit, a Deputy Leader of such Parliamentary Party.

9.2. The Parliamentary Party in the House of Lords shall consist of all members of that House in receipt of the Party's whip. It shall be entitled to make such regulations (not being inconsistent with this Constitution) as it thinks fit for the conduct of its own proceedings, which shall make provision for a Leader and a Chief Whip of such Parliamentary Party.

[Social and Liberal Democrat *Constitution*, article 9.]

## (4) FORMULATION OF PARTY POLICY

(*a*) *Conservative*

*The Conservative Leader has, in effect, the final say on party policy and complete control of the party's election manifesto—although of course he will seek advice from party committees and colleagues.*

(*b*) *Labour*

(1) The party conference shall decide from time to time what specific proposals of legislative, financial or administrative reform shall be included in the party programme.

No proposal shall be included in the party programme unless it has been adopted by the party conference by a majority of not less than two-thirds of the votes recorded on a card vote.

(2) The National Executive Committee and the Parliamentary Committee of the Parliamentary Labour Party shall decide which items from the party programme shall be included in the manifesto which shall be issued by the National Executive Committee prior to every general election. The joint meeting of the two committees shall also define the attitude of the party to the principal issues raised by the election which are not covered by the manifesto.

[Labour Party *Constitution*, clause V.]

(*c*) *Social and Liberal Democrat*

5.1. The Federal Party shall determine the policy of the Party on issues having implications for Great Britain or the UK as a whole and shall do so in accordance with the following provisions of this Article.

5.2. The State Parties shall by their respective internal procedures determine the policy of the Party on issues of specific concern to that State which do not have substantial implications for Great Britain or the UK as a whole and are accordingly not issues of solely federal, or concurrent, concern.

5.3. On issues of concurrent concern (ie issues which have implications for Great Britain or the UK as a whole but which also have a distinct and specific impact on a particular State) policy shall be determined wherever possible by agreement between the Federal Party and the relevant State Party. If such an agreement cannot be reached the policy of the Party shall be determined by the Federal Party. Any dispute as to whether a particular issue is a matter of concurrent concern may be determined as provided by Article 14.

5.4. Any policy-making body that is not entitled to make policy on any issue may discuss it on a consultative basis.

5.5. The Federal Policy Committee ('FPC') shall be responsible for commissioning, preparing, publishing and submitting to the Federal Conference:

(*a*) interim policy proposals ('Green Papers'), including options where appropriate;
(*b*) definitive policy proposals ('White Papers'), including options where appropriate; and
(*c*) motions and amendments (including emergency or topical motions and amendments).

Motions and amendments may also be submitted by members of the Federal Conference (in accordance with its Standing Orders), State Parties in accordance with their internal procedures, Regional Parties in England, Local Parties and Specified Associated Organisations: provided that none of them may submit more than two motions for any one meeting of the Conference.

5.6. The Federal Conference may propose additions to, modifications of or deletions from a Green Paper. The FPC shall consider any such proposals and any comments submitted in the course of the consultations under Article 5.10(*b*), and shall prepare a White Paper which shall (unless circumstances make this inappropriate) be submitted to the next meeting of the Conference. Any revised proposals in the White Paper shall, so far as time permits, be subject to further consultation under Article 5.10(*b*) before submission to the Conference.

5.7. If a White Paper does not incorporate a proposal passed by the Federal Conference in the debate on the Green Paper, that proposal may be raised again in the debate on the White Paper and, if passed, shall be incorporated into the final version of the White Paper. Other amendments to a White Paper may be submitted, either as ordinary amendments or (where circumstances have changed shortly before the debate) as emergency amendments, but such amendments will be subject to the provisions of Article 5.8.

5.8. The FPC shall have the power to require that a motion or an amendment tabled at the Federal Conference (other than pursuant to the first sentence of Article 5.7 or the last sentence of this Article 5.8) shall, unless rejected by the Federal Conference, be referred to the FPC, in which case the FPC shall be obliged, following the consultations specified below, to prepare and submit to the next following meeting of the Federal Conference a motion or a definitive policy proposal on the related topic. The movers of the original motion or amendment so referred shall have the right to submit to the Federal Conference at the same time the substance of their original motion or amendment by way of amendment to the proposals of the FPC.

5.9. Subject to the foregoing procedure, all definitive policy proposals and motions approved by the Federal Conference shall thereby become the policy of the Party and shall, in the event of conflict, prevail as against policy determined by a State Party or a Regional Party in England other than under Article 5.2.

5.10 The FPC shall:

(*a*) consider policy proposals submitted to it by State Parties, Regional Parties in England, Local Parties, Associated Organisations and individual members of the Party; and

(*b*) consult with State Parties, Regional Parties in England, Local Parties and (on matters of special interest to the Associated Organisation concerned or on which it has special knowledge or expertise) Associated Organisations on Green Papers; on any revised proposals intended for inclusion in White Papers; and on proposed responses to references under Article 5.8.

5.11 The FPC shall prepare (and from time to time revise) statements as to the policy of the Party as produced by the foregoing process.

[Social and Liberal Democrat *Constitution*, article 5.]

## Commons Confidence in the Government

### 1. 'ELECTIVE DICTATORSHIP'

The two theories are the theory of centralized democracy, known to me as elective dictatorship, and the theory of limited government, in my language the doctrine of freedom under law . . . Between the two there can be no compromise. Both may depend upon universal adult suffrage. But the one [elective dictatorship] will assert the right of a bare majority in a single chamber assembly, possibly elected on a first past the post basis, to assert its will over a whole people whatever that will may be.

[Lord Hailsham, *The Dilemma of Democracy: Diagnosis and Prescription* (London, 1978), 9–10.]

## 2. DEFEAT OF A MAJORITY GOVERNMENT

Whereupon Motion made, and Question put, That Item A be reduced by £100, in respect of the salary of the Secretary of State [for War].

[34 H.C. Deb. 1712 (21 June 1895).]

*The motion was carried by seven votes. This was the last occasion on which a government with a Commons majority was defeated on a vote which had been accepted by the government to be a vote on a matter of confidence. The vote to reduce Campbell-Bannerman's salary was based on an alleged shortage of ammunition and cordite—the 'cordite vote'. The Prime Minister recommended a general election, which the government lost.*

## 3. VOTES OF NO CONFIDENCE

The Labour Government will go out if it is defeated upon substantial issues, issues of principle, issues which really matter. It will go out if the responsible leaders of either party or any party move a direct vote of no confidence, and carry that vote . . . If the House on matters non-essential, matters of mere opinion, matters that do not strike at the root of the proposals we make, and do not destroy fundamentally the general intentions of the Government in introducing legislation—if the House wish to vary our propositions, the House must take the responsibility for that variation—then a division on such amendments and questions as those will not be regarded as a vote of no confidence.

[The Prime Minister, Ramsay MacDonald, 169 H.C. Deb. 749–50 (15 January 1924).]

The government intend to treat with suitable respect, but not with exaggerated respect, the results of any snap vote or any snap division . . . In case of a Government defeat . . . the Government will not be forced to go to the country except in a situation in which every Hon. Member of the House was voting knowing the full consequences of his vote. It is a vote of confidence about which I am speaking . . . In other words, we shall provide a recount.

[The Prime Minister, Harold Wilson: 870 H.C. Deb. 71–2 (12 March 1974).]

*Governments with even large Commons majorities will suffer defeats on its legislation from time to time. If it is defeated on a formal vote of confidence (for an example, see above, p. 467) the Prime Minister will recommend a dissolution. Defeat on any other major matter may cause the government to ask the House to approve a motion of confidence, and to recommend a dissolution if that were lost.*

MRS THATCHER (LEADER OF THE OPPOSITION): On a point of order, Mr Speaker. The Government have been decisively defeated and discredited on a matter central to their whole economic policy. Such a defeat is unprecedented in modern times. In the light of the decision of the House of Commons, I call upon the Government to resign, or to seek a vote of confidence forthwith . . .

(907 H.C. Deb. 565–6 (10 March 1976).]

*The government's expenditure plans had failed to be approved by 284 votes to 256. The government arranged for a debate on its economic policy the following day, which was technically on the adjournment but which the government described as a vote of confidence. It won that vote with a majority of 17. See 907 H.C. Deb. 634–758 (11 March 1976).*

## Members' Influence on the Government

### 1. PRECEDENCE OF GOVERNMENT BUSINESS

13.—(1) Save as provided in this order, government business shall have precedence at every sitting.

[House of Commons standing order No. 13(1).]

## (1) THE CLOSURE

35.—(1) After a question has been proposed a Member rising in his place may claim to move, 'That the question be now put,' and, unless it shall appear to the chair that such motion is an abuse of the rules of the House, or an infringement of the rights of the minority, the question, 'That the question be now put,' shall be put forthwith.

(2) When a question 'That the question be now put' has been decided in the affirmative, and the question consequent thereon has been decided, a Member may claim that any further question be put which may be requisite to bring to a decision any question already proposed from the chair, and if the assent of the chair, as aforesaid, be not withheld, any question so claimed shall be put forthwith.

(3) This order shall apply in committee only when the Chairman of Ways and Means or either Deputy Chairman is in the chair.

36. If a division be held upon a question for the closure of debate under Standing Order No. 35 (Closure of debate) or for the proposal of the question under Standing Order No. 28 (Powers of chair to propose question), that question shall not be decided in the affirmative unless it appears by the numbers declared from the chair that not fewer than one hundred Members voted in the majority in support of the motion.

[House of Commons standing order Nos. 35, 36.]

## (2) THE GUILLOTINE

80. There shall be a committee, to be called the Business Committee, consisting of the Chairman of Ways and Means, who shall be chairman of the committee, and not more than eight other Members to be nominated by Mr Speaker in respect of each bill to which this order applies. The quorum of the committee shall be four. The committee—

(*a*) shall, in the case of any bill in respect of which an order has been made by the House, allotting a specified number of days or portions of days to the consideration of the bill in committee of the whole House or on report, divide the bill into such parts as it may see fit and allot to each part so many days or portions of a day so allotted as it may consider appropriate; and (*b*) shall report its resolution (or resolutions) to the House, and on a motion being made for the consideration of such report the question thereon shall be put forthwith and on consideration of the said report the question 'That this House doth agree with the committee in its resolution (or resolutions)' shall be put forthwith and, if that question be agreed to, any such resolution shall have effect as if it were an order of the House.

Proceedings in pursuance of this sub-paragraph, though opposed, may be decided after the expiration of the time for opposed business.

81. If a motion be made by a Minister of the Crown providing for an allocation of time to any proceedings on a bill Mr Speaker shall, not more than three hours after the commencement of the proceedings on such a motion, put any question necessary to dispose of those proceedings.

*Six government bills were guillotined in the 1987–8 session.*

[House of Commons standing order Nos. 80, 81.]

## 2. PARLIAMENTARY QUESTIONS

### (1) MACHINERY

17.—(1) Notices of questions shall be given by Members in writing to a Clerk at the Table or to the Table Office.

(2) Questions shall be taken on Monday, Tuesday, Wednesday and Thursday, after private business has been disposed of, and not later than a quarter to three o'clock.

(3) No question shall be taken after half-past three o'clock, except questions which have not been answered in consequence of the absence of the Minister to whom they are addressed, and questions which have not appeared on the paper, but which are in Mr Speaker's opinion of an urgent character, and relate either to matters of public importance or to the arrangement of business.

(4) A Member who desires an oral answer to his question shall distinguish it by an asterisk, but subject to paragraph (5) of this order notice of any such question must appear at latest on the notice

paper circulated two days (excluding Sunday) before that on which an answer is desired.

(5) Questions received at the Table Office before half-past two o'clock on a Monday or Tuesday on which the House is sitting may, if so decided by the Member, be put down for oral answer on the following Wednesday or Thursday respectively:

Provided that this paragraph shall not apply to questions received on the first day of a session nor to questions received on the day on which the House first meets pursuant to Standing Order No. 12 (Earlier meeting of House in certain circumstances).

(6) Notice of a question shall not be given for oral answer on a day later than ten sitting days after the date of notice.

(7) If a Member does not distinguish his question by an asterisk, or if he is not present to ask it, or if it is not reached by half-past three o'clock, the Minister to whom it is addressed shall cause an answer to be printed in the Official Report of the Parliamentary Debates, unless the Member has before half-past three o'clock signified his desire to postpone the question. A Member who, while not desiring an oral answer to his question, desires that the answer to it shall be printed in the Official Report on the day for which notice has been given, shall distinguish it with the letter W, and the Minister shall cause the answer to be so printed:

Provided that the minimum notice for such a question shall be the same as that prescribed for questions for oral answer.

[House of Commons standing order No. 17(1)–(7).]

### (2) COST

MR BIFFEN (LEADER OF THE HOUSE): The cost in officials' time of replying to questions varies considerably, but the current average cost is estimated at £75 for oral answers and £45 for written answers . . .

[115 H.C. Deb. *56* (written answers 27 April 1987).]

### (3) THE ROTA

Ministers are questioned on a rota agreed by the Government and Opposition parties through the 'usual channels'. Each major Department is allocated to a particular day of the week, together with three or four others. When at the top of the rota, its Minister will be questioned first and is likely to be questioned for the whole of the time available. In the following week he will be at the bottom of the rota; and in each successive week he rises a place, so that after three or four weeks he is back at the top. Thus he can usually expect to answer Questions for the best part of an hour once a month.

The main exception to this routine is the Prime Minister, who answers Questions every Tuesday and Thursday from 3.15 p.m. to the end of Question-time soon after 3.30 p.m. Thus the Prime Minister will answer Questions for about two hours a month, compared with about one hour's questioning of each of his or her chief colleagues . . .

Other exceptions to the normal workings of the rota are Ministers with special responsibilities or at the head of minor Departments, such as the Attorney General or the Lord Privy Seal, who answer questions for a short period beginning at 3.10, 3.15 or 3.20 p.m. on a particular day at regular intervals, usually every four weeks or so. Private Members are also included in the rota, in their capacities as the Members answering for the Church Commissioners, the House of Commons Commission, or the Public Accounts Commission.

[House of Commons Public Information Office *Factsheet* No. 46, 4.]

### (4) PRIME MINISTER'S QUESTIONS

*See also above, p. 406.*

One evening I found Churchill at the Cabinet table . . . 'What are you doing, Prime Minister?' I asked. 'Oh, parliamentary questions. Preparing improvisations! Very hard work!'

[Harold Macmillan, *Tides of Fortune* (London, 1969), 496.]

### (5) ADMISSIBILITY

[Questions] should relate to the public affairs with which [Ministers] are officially connected, to proceedings pending in Parliament, or to matters of administration for which they are responsible.

[Erskine May, *Parliamentary Practice* (London, 21st edn., 1989), 285.]

(6) REFUSAL TO ANSWER

. . . Attorney-General

Details of investigations by the Director of Public Prosecutions.
Day to day administration of the Legal Aid Scheme . . .

. . . Defence

Details of arms sales
Operational matters
Contract prices
Costs of individual aircraft etc.
Details of research and development
Numbers of foreign forces training in the United Kingdom
Accident rates for aircraft

. . . Exchequer

Economic and budgetary forecasts
Exchange Equalization Account
Government borrowing
Sterling balances
Tax affairs of individuals or companies
Day to day matters of the Bank of England

. . . Home

Telephone tapping
Names of prohibited immigrants
Regional seats of government
Security service operations
Operational matters of the police

. . . Prime Minister

Telephone tapping
Cabinet Committees
Cost of the 'hot line'
Security arrangements at Chequers
Detailed arrangements for the conduct of government business
List of future engagements . . .

[Memorandum by the Principal Clerk of the Table Office: Matters about which successive administrations have refused to answer questions, Appendix 9 to the Report from the Select Committee on Parliamentary Questions, H.C. 393 (1971–2).]

## (7) DISPROPORTIONATE COST

MR SIMS: To ask the Chancellor of the Exchequer whether he has any proposal to raise the advisory cost limit of £200 for answering parliamentary questions.

MR PETER BROOKE: Yes. The advisory figure of £200 was introduced in 1982 as the level at which the likely cost of a full reply to a parliamentary question should be drawn to the attention of Ministers. This figure is now out of date. It is accordingly being raised as from today to £250.

This does not alter the discretion of individual Ministers to decide that a particular question should be answered partially or in full regardless of cost.

[129 H.C. Deb. *429* (written answers 14 March 1988).]

## (8) POPULARITY WITH M.P.S

*Over 70,000 questions were put down for answer by M.P.s in the 1987–8 session.*

Question Time . . . comes right at the beginning of the daily business, the Chamber is much fuller than for most of the rest of the day and it is a convenient time for the Press reporters, some answers even being early enough to appear in the evening papers. There is something for everybody at Question Time—a Minister may shine or be caught out and forty or fifty Members have a chance of getting on their feet and uttering a few words in the Chamber, a rare event for most of them . . . The fact that most of the information could have been obtained by way of written answer, that few Members are particularly brilliant at asking supplementaries and that few Ministers are caught napping by them still makes it a special occasion. Above all it is not given over to lengthy frontbench speeches, it is largely a backbenchers' affair, and Ministers are there to answer to even the newest and humblest Member of the House . . .

Thus a large number of [a minister's] own supporters will see how he performs, whether he appears to be on top of his job and gives an air of confidence, and what his attitude is to this or that facet of the work of his department . . .

It must also be remembered that a Minister personally handles very few of the day-to-day decisions which are taken by his civil servants in his name. These decisions are, of course, made in a way which the official thinks conforms to ministerial policy. A Question about one of these decisions brings the case on to the Minister's desk. The decision may have been taken at quite a low level in the department. It now is looked at by the senior members of the department, even the Permanent Secretary as well as the Minister and one or more Parliamentary Secretaries. The PQ file (each Question is normally given its own file) will normally contain not only a draft answer but also any relevant facts. The Minister has no excuse for not going into the case and satisfying himself that the departmental decision was correct and conformed to his policy. When he examines it he may be surprised, even shocked, and make a different decision or clarify or redefine the policy to be followed in future. This is the internal reality of the public answerability of the Minister.

[Sir Norman Chester, 'Questions in the House', in S. A. Walkland and M. Ryle (eds.), *The Commons Today* (London, 1981 edn.), 188–9.]

## 3. ADJOURNMENT DEBATES

*A 30-minute adjournment debate is the last item of each day's business. One M.P. may raise his chosen topic; a junior Minister replies. A ballot is held weekly to select Members who will introduce the debates.*

## 4. CONSOLIDATED FUND AND APPROPRIATION BILL DEBATES

54.—(1) On any day on which the second reading of a Consolidated Fund or an Appropriation Bill stands as the first order of the day, the question thereon shall be put forthwith upon the reading of that order, no order shall be made for the committal of the bill and the question for third reading shall be put forthwith.

(2) At the conclusion of proceedings on a Consolidated Fund or an Appropriation Bill, a member of the Government may move

'That this House do now adjourn', the motion shall not lapse at ten o'clock, or be interrupted at that hour save for the purpose of moving a motion pursuant to paragraph (2) of Standing Order No. 14 (Exempted business), may be proceeded with at any hour, though opposed, and if proceedings have not been concluded by nine o'clock in the morning at that sitting, the motion shall lapse at that hour:

Provided that if the sitting shall have commenced on a Thursday, the motion shall lapse at eight o'clock in the morning.

*The adjournment debate which ensues gives M.P.s opportunities to raise any topics, and a junior Minister replies to each one.*

[House of Commons standing order No. 54.]

## 5. RECESS ADJOURNMENT DEBATES

22.—Whenever a motion shall have been made by a Minister of the Crown for the adjournment of the House for a specified period or periods, any questions necessary to dispose of proceedings shall be put three hours after they have been entered upon, if not previously concluded.

*During the three-hour debate M.P.s may raise any topic, and at the end of the debate the Leader of the House replies to them all.*

[House of Commons standing order No. 22.]

## 6. OPPOSITION DAYS

13.—(2) Twenty days shall be allotted in each session for proceedings on opposition business, seventeen of which shall be at the disposal of the Leader of the Opposition and three of which shall be at the disposal of the leader of the second largest opposition party; and matters selected on those days shall have precedence over government business provided that—

(*a*) two Friday sittings shall be deemed equivalent to a single sitting on any other day;

(*b*) on any day other than a Friday, not more than two of the days at the disposal of the Leader of the Opposition may be taken in the form of four half days, and one of the days at the disposal of the leader of the second largest opposition party may be taken in the form of two half days; and

(*c*) on any such half day proceedings under this paragraph shall either—

(i) lapse at seven o'clock if not previously concluded, or

(ii) be set down for consideration at seven o'clock and, except on days on which private business has been set down for consideration under the provisions of paragraph (5) of Standing Order No. 16 (Time for taking private business), shall be entered upon at that time:

Provided that on days on which business stands over until seven o'clock under the provisions of Standing Order No. 20 (Adjournment on specific and important matter that should have urgent consideration) proceedings under this sub-paragraph shall not be entered upon until such business has been disposed of, and may then be proceeded with for three hours, notwithstanding the provisions of Standing Order No. 9 (Sittings of the House).

(3) For the purposes of this order 'the second largest opposition party' shall be that party, of those not represented in Her Majesty's Government, which has the second largest number of Members elected to the House as members of that party.

[House of Commons standing order No. 13(2), (3).]

## 7. PRIVATE MEMBERS' MOTIONS

(7) Private Members' notices of motions and private Members' bills shall have precedence, in that order, over government business on ten Fridays in each session to be appointed by the House.

(8) On four days other than Fridays in each session to be appointed by the House private Members' notices of motions shall have precedence until seven o'clock and, if not previously concluded, the proceedings thereon shall lapse at that hour and the House shall then proceed with government business.

(9) Ballots for private Members' notices of motions shall be held after questions on such Wednesdays as may be appointed by the House in respect of motions having precedence on Fridays; and on such days as may be appointed by the House in respect of motions

having precedence on days other than Fridays. Notice of a subject to be raised on any motion for which a ballot is held in pursuance of this paragraph may be given at the Table or in the Table Office not less than nine days before the day on which the notice of motion is to have precedence.

*A ballot is held through which successful back-benchers are enabled to challenge and criticize the government during debates on these motions.*

[House of Commons standing order No. 13(7)–(9).]

## 8. PRIVATE MEMBERS' BILLS

*In the 1987–8 session, 11 private Members' Bills passed into law—but 115 had been introduced.*

### (1) BALLOT

(4) Private Members' bills shall have precedence over government business on ten Fridays in each session to be appointed by the House.

(5) On and after the seventh Friday on which private Members' bills have precedence, such bills shall be arranged on the order paper in the following order:

> consideration of Lords amendments, third readings, consideration of reports not already entered upon, adjourned proceedings on consideration, bills in progress in committee, bills appointed for committee, and second readings.

(6) The ballot for private Members' bills shall be held on the second Thursday on which the House shall sit during the session under arrangements to be made by Mr Speaker, and each bill shall be presented, by the Member who has given notice of presentation or by another Member named by him in writing to the Clerks at the Table, at the commencement of public business on the fifth Wednesday on which the House shall sit during the session.

*In recent sessions twelve Fridays have been set aside for this purpose.*

[House of Commons standing order No. 13(4)–(6).]

### (2) TEN-MINUTE RULE

19.—(1) On Tuesdays and Wednesdays, and if given by a Minister of the Crown, on Mondays and Thursdays, notices of motions for leave to bring in bills, and for the nomination of select committees, may be set down for consideration at the commencement of public business. Mr Speaker, after permitting, if he thinks fit, a brief explanatory statement from the Member who makes and from a Member who opposes any such motion respectively, shall put either the question thereon, or the question, 'That the debate be now adjourned'.

(2) With respect to a private Member's motion for leave to bring in a bill under this order—

(*a*) notice shall be given in the Public Bill Office by the Member in person or by another Member on his behalf, but on any one day not more than one notice shall be accepted from any one Member;

(*b*) no notice shall be given for a day on which a notice of motion under this order already stands on the paper;

(*c*) no notice shall be given for a day earlier than the fifth or later than the fifteenth sitting day after the day on which it is given;

(*d*) not more than one such notice shall stand on the paper in the name of any one Member for a day within any period of fifteen sitting days.

[House of Commons standing order No. 19.]

### (3) PRESENTATION AFTER GIVING NOTICE

58.—(1) A Member may, after notice, present a bill without previously obtaining leave from the House to bring in the same.

(2) When a bill is presented either in pursuance of an order of the House or under the provisions of paragraph (1) of this order, the bill shall be read the first time without any question being put, shall be ordered to be read a second time on such day as the Member presenting it shall appoint, and shall be ordered to be printed.

(3) If a Member informs the Clerks at the Table of his intention to take charge of a bill which has been brought from the Lords, the bill shall be deemed to have been read the first time on the day on

which the Member so informs the Clerks, and to have been ordered to be read a second time on such day as he shall appoint, and shall be recorded in the Journal of the House as having been read the first time and ordered to be read a second time on the day so appointed, and shall be ordered to be printed.

[House of Commons standing order No. 58.]

### (4) NO SUCH BILL MAY AUTHORIZE A CHARGE

48.—(1) A bill (other than a bill which is required to be brought in upon a ways and means resolution) the main object of which is the creation of a public charge may either be presented, or brought in upon an order of the House, by a Minister of the Crown, and, in the case of a bill so presented or brought in, the creation of the charge shall not require to be authorised by a resolution of the House until the bill has been read a second time, and after the charge has been so authorised the bill shall be proceeded with in the same manner as a bill which involves a charge that is subsidiary to its main purpose.

(2) The provisions of paragraph (1) of this order shall apply to any bill brought from the Lords, of which a Minister of the Crown has informed the Clerks at the Table of his intention to take charge.

[House of Commons standing order No. 48.]

This study of private members' bills clearly indicates that the procedure is not one through which controversial issues can be resolved. Perhaps the most significant fact of all those we have produced is that no private members' bill which has had a vote on the floor of the House has passed since 1959, unless it has been granted time by the Government. At the same time Governments are less willing to grant time now than in the past. This means that most of the bills passed in recent years have been minor, technical and uncontentious. In fact most have been Government bills in all but name.

Of course one might argue that this does not matter, that private members' bills serve other purposes, and/or that in the British parliamentary system the executive does, and should, control legislation. Certainly, as we have seen, many MPs introduce bills with no hope of success. Their purpose is to publicise an issue in order, they hope, to persuade Government to introduce legislation directly, or influence the public to press for reform which the Government may take up at a later date. This does sometimes happen although it is rare. In fact the most plausible defence of the current system is probably that, even if it results in minor, technical, Government-initiated bills it gives back-bench MPs experience of piloting a bill through Parliament and dealing with civil servants. As such it provides a training ground, offering experience useful to MPs when, and if, they become ministers.

Despite all this it is clear to us that the nature and limitations of the private-members'-bill procedure is merely a reflection of executive dominance in the British system which is itself a reflection of the view of democracy which underpins the institutions and processes of British Government. Any fundamental change in the procedure would only result from a change in the nature of executive-legislative relations which itself would necessitate a move towards a more participatory view of democracy.

[D. Marsh and M. Read, *Private Members' Bills* (Cambridge, 1988), 184.]

## 9. EMERGENCY DEBATES

20.—(1) On Monday, Tuesday, Wednesday and Thursday a Member rising in his place at the commencement of public business may propose, in an application lasting not more than three minutes, to move the adjournment of the House for the purpose of discussing a specific and important matter that should have urgent consideration. If Mr Speaker is satisfied that the matter is proper to be so discussed, the Member shall either obtain the leave of the House, or, if such leave be refused, the assent of not fewer than forty Members who shall thereupon rise in their places to support the motion, or, if fewer than forty Members and not fewer than ten shall thereupon rise in their places, the House shall, on a division, upon question put forthwith, determine whether such motion shall be made.

(2) If leave is given or the motion is so supported or the House so determines that it shall be made the motion shall stand over until the commencement of public business on the following day (or, on Thursdays, until the commencement of public business on the following Monday) when proceedings upon it shall be interrupted

after three hours, or, if Mr Speaker directs that the urgency of the matter so requires, until seven o'clock on the same day.

(3) A Member intending to propose to move the adjournment of the House under the provisions of this order shall give notice to Mr Speaker by twelve o'clock, if the urgency of the matter is known at that hour. If the urgency is not so known he shall give notice as soon thereafter as is practicable. If Mr Speaker so desires he may defer giving his decision upon whether the matter is proper to be discussed until a named hour, when he may interrupt the proceedings of the House for the purpose.

(4) In determining whether a matter is proper to be discussed Mr Speaker shall have regard to the extent to which it concerns the administrative responsibilities of Ministers of the Crown or could come within the scope of ministerial action. In determining whether a matter is urgent Mr Speaker shall have regard to the probability of the matter being brought before the House in time by other means . . .

*Such applications are only rarely successful: in the 1987–8 session, 87 were made but only one was allowed by the Speaker.*

[House of Commons standing order No. 20.]

## 10. DEPARTMENTAL SELECT COMMITTEES

### (1) BACKGROUND

5.15. . . . The House should no longer rest content with an incomplete and unsystematic scrutiny of the activities of the Executive merely as a result of historical accident or sporadic pressures, and it is equally desirable for the different branches of the public service to be subject to an even and regular incidence of select committee scrutiny into their activities . . .

5.18. We have concluded that the [select] committee structure should in future be based primarily on the subject areas within the responsibility of individual government departments or groups of departments. We have taken this view partly because we believe that one of the main responsibilities of the committees should be to continue and develop the work of the Expenditure Committee and its sub-committees in examining the expenditure and administration of the civil and public service . . . and partly because any division of governmental activities into subject areas will in any case, with certain exceptions, reflect the division of responsibilities between government departments . . .

5.20. We have . . . concluded that the terms of reference of the new committees should be widely drawn and that provision should be made for liaison and cooperation between them to allow joint inquiries and consultation . . .

[1st Report from the Select Committee on Procedure, H.C. 588–I (1977–8).]

130.—(1) Select committees shall be appointed to examine the expenditure, administration and policy of the principal government departments set out in paragraph (2) of this order and associated public bodies, and similar matters within the responsibilities of the Secretary of State for Northern Ireland.

(2) The committees appointed under paragraph (1) of this order, the principal departments of government with which they are concerned, the maximum numbers of each committee and the quorum in each case shall be as follows:

| Name of committee | Principal government departments concerned | Maximum numbers of Members | Quorum |
|---|---|---|---|
| Agriculture | Ministry of Agriculture, Fisheries and Food | 11 | 3 |
| Defence | Ministry of Defence | 11 | 3 |
| Education, Science and Arts | Department of Education and Science | 11 | 3 |
| Employment | Department of Employment | 11 | 3 |
| Energy | Department of Energy | 11 | 3 |
| Environment | Department of the Environment | 11 | 3 |
| Foreign Affairs | Foreign and Commonwealth Office | 11 | 3 |
| Home Affairs | Home Office | 11 | 3 |
| Scottish Affairs | Scottish Office | 13 | 5 |
| Social Services | Department of Health and Social Security | 11 | 3 |
| Trade and Industry | Department of Trade and Industry | 11 | 3 |
| Transport | Department of Transport | 11 | 3 |
| Treasury and Civil Service | Treasury, Management and Personnel Office, Board of Inland Revenue, Board of Customs and Excise | 11 | 3 |
| Welsh Affairs | Welsh Office | 11 | 3 |

(3) The Foreign Affairs Committee, the Home Affairs Committee and the Treasury and Civil Service Committee shall each have the power to appoint one sub-committee.

(4) There may be a sub-committee, drawn from the membership of two or more of the Energy, Environment, Trade and Industry, Scottish Affairs, Transport, and Treasury and Civil Service Committees, set up from time to time to consider any matter affecting two or more nationalised industries.

(5) Select committees appointed under this order shall have power—

(*a*) to send for persons, papers and records, to sit notwithstanding any adjournment of the House, to adjourn from place to place, and to report from time to time;

(*b*) to appoint specialist advisers either to supply information which is not readily available or to elucidate matters of complexity within the committee's order of reference;

(*c*) to report from time to time the minutes of evidence taken before sub-committees;

(*d*) to communicate to any other such committee its evidence and any other documents relating to matters of common interest; and

(*e*) to meet concurrently with any other such committee for the purposes of deliberating, taking evidence, or considering draft reports;

and the sub-committees appointed under this order shall have power to send for persons, papers and records, to sit notwithstanding any adjournment of the House, and to adjourn from place to place, and shall have a quorum of three.

(6) Unless the House otherwise orders, all Members nominated to a committee appointed under this order shall continue to be members of that committee for the remainder of the Parliament.

[House of Commons standing order No. 130.]

## (2) LORD CHANCELLOR'S DEPARTMENT AND LAW OFFICERS' DEPARTMENT

*These two departments are excluded from select committee supervision, despite the recommendation of the Select Committee on*

*Procedure that they should be supervised by the Home Affairs Committee.*

I am sure that the House will agree that the new Committees should not be allowed to threaten either the independence of the judiciary or the judicial process.

[Mr Norman St John-Stevas, Leader of the House: 969 H.C. Deb. 38–9 (25 June 1979).]

. . . In practice the [Home Affairs] Committee has been scrupulous in avoiding comment on matters before the courts, and has in any case decided not to concern itself with individual cases; the departments, on their side, have not been unhelpful . . . [But] the House cannot claim that its oversight of the public service by select committees is complete; an annual sum of £360 million . . . is currently going unexamined, . . . and major matters such as legal aid and the administration of the courts are unsusceptible to close parliamentary scrutiny. We recommend that in the next Parliament the terms of reference of the Home Affairs Committee should be extended to include those departments.

[1st Report from the Liaison Committee, The Select Committee System, H.C. 92 (1982–3), para. 24.]

### (3) LIAISON COMMITTEE

131.—(1) A select committee shall be appointed, to be called the Liaison Committee—

(*a*) to consider general matters relating to the work of select committees, and

(*b*) to give such advice relating to the work of select committees as may be sought by the House of Commons Commission.

(2) The committee shall report its recommendations as to the allocation of time for consideration by the House of the estimates on any day or half day which may be allotted for that purpose; and upon a motion being made that the House do agree with any such report the question shall be put forthwith and, if that question is agreed to, the recommendations shall have effect as if they were orders of the House.

Proceedings in pursuance of this paragraph, though opposed, may be decided after the expiration of the time for opposed business.

(3) The committee shall have power to send for persons, papers and records, to sit notwithstanding any adjournment of the House, and to report from time to time.

(4) Unless the House otherwise orders, each Member nominated to the committee shall continue to be a member of it for the remainder of the Parliament . . .

[House of Commons standing order No. 131.]

## (4) ATTENDANCE AND QUESTIONING OF MINISTERS AND CIVIL SERVANTS

There need be no fear that departmental Ministers will refuse to attend Committees to answer questions about their Departments or that they will not make every effort to ensure that the fullest possible information is made available to them.

I give the House the pledge on the part of the Government that every Minister from the most senior Cabinet Minister to the most junior Under-Secretary will do all in his or her power to co-operate with the new system of Committees and to make it a success.

[Mr Norman St John-Stevas, Leader of the House: 969 H.C. Deb. 45 (25 June 1979).]

[The select committees'] powers have been used responsibly and flexibly. Committees undoubtedly have an unqualified power to summon witnesses. If one refuses to appear, he may be summoned formally. Failure to attend can then be reported to the House which will consider what future action is necessary. Similarly, a witness who refuses to answer questions properly put to him may be reported to the House. In either case the individual concerned may be held guilty of contempt and punished accordingly.

[1st Report from the Liaison Committee, The Accountability of Ministers and Civil Servants to Select Committees of the House of Commons, H.C. 100 (1986–7), para. 2.]

If a Select Committee has been given by the House the power to send for persons, papers and records, its power to secure the attendance of an individual *named* civil servant is unqualified . . .

[4th Report from the Defence Committee, Westland plc: The government's decision-making, H.C. 519 (1985–6), para. 228.]

We have faced much more serious difficulties over the Civil Service Memorandum of Guidance for Officials appearing before Select Committees, under which at the hearing on 12 March the Permanent Secretary and officials from the DTI refused to answer a whole series of detailed questions . . . The principal basis of the refusal to answer appears to have been that section of the Memorandum which states that 'in order to preserve the collective responsibility of Ministers, the advice given to Ministers by their Departments should not be disclosed'.

[2nd Report from the Employment Committee, H.C. 305 (1985–6), para. 10.]

15. The general principle to be followed is that it is the duty of officials to be as helpful as possible to Committees, and that any withholding of information should be limited to reservations that are necessary in the interests of good government or to safeguard national security. Departments should, therefore, be as forthcoming as they can (within the limits set out in this note) when requested to provide information . . . Because officials appear on behalf of their Ministers, Departments might want to clear written evidence and briefing with Ministers. It may only be necessary for Ministers to be consulted should there be any doubt among officials on the policy to be explained to the Committee. However, Ministers are ultimately responsible for deciding what information is to be given and for defending their decisions as necessary, and Ministers' views should always be sought if any question arises of withholding information which Committees are known to be seeking . . .

25. Officials should not give evidence about or discuss the following topics:

(i) In order to preserve the collective responsibility to Ministers, the advice given to Ministers by their Departments should not be disclosed, nor should information about interdepartmental exchanges on policy issues, about the level at which decisions were taken or the manner in which a Minister has consulted his colleagues. Information should not be given about Cabinet Committees or their discussions . . .

(ii) Advice given by a Law Officer . . .

(iii) The private affairs of individuals or institutions on which any information . . . has been supplied in confidence . . .

Officials should also, where possible, avoid giving written evidence about or discussing the following matters . . .

(iv) Questions in the field of political controversy . . .

(v) Sensitive information of a commercial or economic nature, e.g. knowledge which could affect the financial markets, without prior consultation with the Chancellor of the Exchequer; sensitive information relating to the commercial operations of nationalised industries, or to contracts; commercial or economic information which has been given to the Government in confidence, unless the advance consent of the persons concerned has been obtained . . .

(vi) Matters which are, or may become, the subject of sensitive negotiations with governments or other bodies, including the European Community, without prior consultation with . . . the Ministers concerned . . .

(vii) Specific cases where the Minister has or may have a quasi-judicial or appellate function, e.g. in relation to planning applications and appeals, or where the subject-matter is being considered by the Courts, or the Parliamentary Commissioner . . .

[Memorandum of Guidance for Officials appearing before Select Committees, Cabinet Office, 1980.]

In February 1985, with the consent of the Prime Minister, I issued a note of guidance restating the general duties and responsibilities of civil servants in relation to Ministers. That note was reproduced in a Written Answer by the Prime Minister to a Parliamentary Question on 26 February 1985 (OR 26 February 1985, columns *130* to *132*). In the light of the subsequent discussion, including observations of the Treasury and Civil Service Select Committee and the Defence Committee of the House of Commons and comments from the Council of Civil Service Unions, I have expanded the note of guidance, and a revised version is now issued. As previously, the note is issued after consultation with Permanent Secretaries in charge of Departments and with their agreement. As with the earlier version, this revised version is issued with the consent of the Prime Minister, and will be reported by her to the House of Commons.

2. This note is concerned with the duties and responsibilities of civil servants in relation to Ministers. It should be read in the wider context of Ministers' own responsibilities, which were set out in the Government's reply to the Seventh Report from the Treasury and Civil Service Committee (Cmnd. 9841):

> The Government believes that Ministers are well aware of the principles that should govern their duties and responsibilities in relation to Parliament and in relation to civil servants. It goes without saying that these include the obligations of integrity. They include the duty to give Parliament and the public as full information as possible about the policies, decisions and actions of the Government, and not to deceive or mislead Parliament or the public. In relation to civil servants, they include the duty to give fair consideration and due weight to informed and impartial advice from civil servants, as well as to other considerations and advice, in reaching policy decisions; the duty to refrain from asking or instructing civil servants to do things which they should not do; the duty to ensure that influence over appointments is not abused for partisan purposes; and the duty to observe the obligations of a good employer with regard to terms and conditions of service and treatment of those who serve them.

3. Civil servants are servants of the Crown. For all practical purposes the Crown in this context means and is represented by the Government of the day. There are special cases in which certain functions are conferred by law upon particular members or groups of members of the public service; but in general the executive powers of the Crown are exercised by and on the advice of Her Majesty's Ministers, who are in turn answerable to Parliament. The Civil Service as such has no constitutional personality or responsibility separate from the duly constituted Government of the day. It is there to provide the Government of the day with advice on the formulation of the policies of the Government, to assist in carrying out the decisions of the Government, and to manage and deliver the services for which the Government is responsible. Some civil servants are also involved, as a proper part of their duties, in the processes of presentation of Government policies and decisions.

4. The Civil Service serves the Government of the day as a whole, that is to say Her Majesty's Ministers collectively, and the Prime Minister is the Minister for the Civil Service. The duty of the individual civil servant is first and foremost to the Minister of the Crown who is in charge of the Department in which he or she is serving. The basic principles of accountability of Ministers and civil servants are as set out in the Government's response (Cmnd 9916) to the Defence Committee's Fourth Report of 1985–86:

—Each Minister is responsible to Parliament for the conduct of his Department, and for the actions carried out by his Department in pursuit of Government policies or in the discharge of responsibilities laid upon him as a Minister.
—A Minister is accountable to Parliament, in the sense that he has a duty to explain in Parliament the exercise of his powers and duties and to give an account to Parliament of what is done by him in his capacity as a Minister or by his Department.
—Civil servants are responsible to their Ministers for their actions and conduct.

5. It is the duty of civil servants to serve their Ministers with integrity and to the best of their ability. In their dealings with the public, civil servants should always bear in mind that people have a right to expect that their affairs will be dealt with sympathetically, efficiently and promptly.

6. The British Civil Service is a non-political and professional career service subject to a code of rules and disciplines. Civil servants are required to serve the duly constituted Government of the day, of whatever political complexion. It is of the first importance that civil servants should conduct themselves in such a way as to deserve and retain the confidence of Ministers, and to be able to establish the same relationship with those whom they may be required to serve in some future Administration. That confidence is the indispensable foundation of a good relationship between Ministers and civil servants. The conduct of civil servants should at all times be such that Ministers and potential future Ministers can be sure that that confidence can be freely given, and that the Civil Service will at all times conscientiously fulfil its duties and obligations to, and impartially assist, advise and carry out the policies of, the duly constituted Government of the day.

7. The determination of policy is the responsibility of the Minister (within the convention of collective responsibility of the

whole Government for the decisions and actions of every member of it). In the determination of policy the civil servant has no constitutional responsibility or role distinct from that of the Minister. Subject to the conventions limiting the access of Ministers to papers of previous Administrations, it is the duty of the civil servant to make available to the Minister all the information and experience at his or her disposal which may have a bearing on the policy decisions to which the Minister is committed or which he is preparing to make, and to give to the Minister honest and impartial advice, without fear or favour, and whether the advice accords with the Minister's view or not. Civil servants are in breach of their duty, and damage their integrity as servants of the Crown, if they deliberately withhold relevant information from their Minister, or if they give their Minister other advice than the best they believe they can give, or if they seek to obstruct or delay a decision simply because they do not agree with it. When, having been given all the relevant information and advice, the Minister has taken a decision, it is the duty of civil servants loyally to carry out that decision with precisely the same energy and good will, whether they agree with it or not.

8. Civil servants are under an obligation to keep the confidences to which they become privy in the course of their work; not only the maintenance of the trust between Ministers and civil servants but also the efficiency of government depend on their doing so. There is and must be a general duty upon every civil servant, serving or retired, not without authority to make disclosures which breach that obligation. This duty applies to any document or information or knowledge of the course of business, which has come to a civil servant in confidence in the course of duty. Any such unauthorised disclosures, whether for political or personal motives, or for pecuniary gain, and quite apart from liability to prosecution under the Official Secrets Acts, result in the civil servant concerned forfeiting the trust that is put in him or her as an employee and making him or her liable to disciplinary action including the possibility of dismissal, or to civil law proceedings. He or she also undermines the confidence that ought to subsist between Ministers and civil servants and thus damages colleagues and the Service as well as him or herself.

9. Civil servants often find themselves in situations where they are required or expected to give information to a Parliamentary Select Committee, to the media, or to individuals. In doing so they should be guided by the policy of the Government on evidence to

Select Committees, as set out in memoranda of guidance issued from time to time, and on the disclosure of information, by any specifically departmental policies in relation to departmental information, and by the requirements of security and confidentiality. In this respect, however, as in other respects, the civil servant's first duty is to his or her Minister. Thus, when a civil servant gives evidence to a Select Committee on the policies or actions of his or her Department, he or she does so as the representative of the Minister in charge of the Department and subject to the Minister's instructions, and is accountable to the Minister for the evidence which he or she gives. As explained in paragraph 2, the ultimate responsibility lies with Ministers, and not with civil servants, to decide what information should be made available, and how and when it should be released, whether it is to Parliament, to Select Committees, to the media or to individuals. It is not acceptable for a serving or former civil servant to seek to frustrate policies or decisions of Ministers by the disclosure outside the Government of information to which he or she has had access as a civil servant . . .

[The Duties and Responsibilities of Civil Servants in relation to Ministers: A Note by the Head of the Home Civil Service 1987, reproduced at 123 H.C. Deb. 572–5 (written answers 2 December 1987).]

So if in the course of an inquiry a Select Committee were to discover evidence that called in question the 'conduct' of an individual named civil servant, the understanding is that the Select Committee should not pursue their own investigation into the 'conduct' of the person concerned or act as a disciplinary tribunal, but should pursue the matter with the Minister . . .

[Government Response to the 1st Report from the Liaison Committee, Cm. 78 (1987), Annex para. 5.]

## (5) EVALUATION

All this increased activity [of the select committees] has made great demands on Members, but it is our view that it has considerably extended the range of the House's activity, strengthened its position relative to that of the Government, and deepened the quality of its debates . . .

[1st Report from the Liaison Committee, The Select Committee System, H.C. 92 (1982–3), para. 6.]

The House's reliance on a select committee system is of long standing, but the addition to it of the departmentally-based select committees in 1979 can now be seen as a major, successful, Parliamentary reform . . .

[1st Report from the Liaison Committee, The Select Committee System, H.C. 363 (1984–5), para. 1.]

MR WAKEHAM: A total of 565 reports have been published by the departmental Select Committees since 1979. During the same period, 60 reports from departmental Select Committees have been referred to on the Order Paper as relevant to debates in the House in accordance with the views expressed by the Liaison Committee. Sixteen reports have been debated in relation to the consideration of the Estimates; four on motions for the Adjournment; and six reports have been named in substantive motions. Votes were taken on four of these substantive motions.

[122 H.C. Deb. *702* (written answers 20 November 1987).]

# [10]

# THE HOUSE OF LORDS

## Acquiring and Losing Membership

### 1. MEMBERSHIP

The following, if not under the age of twenty one, are members of the House of Lords:

The Prince of Wales;

Hereditary Peers of England, Scotland, Great Britain and the United Kingdom who have not disclaimed their peerages under the Peerage Act 1963;

Lords Spiritual: the two Archbishops; the Bishops of London, Durham and Winchester; and twenty-one other diocesan Bishops of the Church of England according to seniority of appointment to diocesan sees;

Lords created under the Appellate Jurisdiction Act 1876 (as amended);

Life Peers created under the Life Peerages Act 1958.

[House of Lords standing order No. 2.]

#### (1) HEREDITARY PEERS

| Rank | Number |
|---|---|
| Royal dukes | 5 |
| Dukes | 24 |
| Marquesses | 36 |
| Earls | 191 |
| Viscounts | 125 |
| Barons | 463 |
| Lords Spiritual | 26 |
| Law Lords | 21 |
| Life peers | 360 |

[Source: Roll of the Lords Spiritual and Temporal, H.L. 1 (1988–9).]

*Peerages created since 1801 are peerages of the United Kingdom. Peers of Scotland whose peerages were created before the Act of Union 1707, and female hereditary peers, have been entitled to sit in the Lords as of right since 1963; peers in the Irish peerage cannot sit at all.*

The holder of a peerage in the peerage of Scotland shall have the same right to receive writs of summons to attend the House of Lords, and to sit and vote in that House, as the holder of a peerage in the peerage of the United Kingdom; and the enactments relating to the election of Scottish representative peers shall cease to have effect.

[Peerage Act 1963, s. 4.]

A woman who is the holder of a hereditary peerage in the peerage of England, Scotland, Great Britain or the United Kingdom shall (whatever the terms of the letters patent or other instrument, if any, creating that peerage) have the same right to receive writs of summons to attend the House of Lords, and to sit and vote in that House, and shall be subject to the same disqualifications in respect of membership of the House of Commons and elections to that House, as a man holding that peerage.

[Peerage Act 1963, s. 6.]

If your Lordships agree with the opinion which I have expressed, I think that the Report of the Committee to the House could be based on the facts that, by virtue of the provisions of the Union of Ireland Act, 1800, 28 Irish representative peers sat in this House on the part of Ireland, each being elected for life: that on the death of an Irish representative peer an election of a successor was held in the manner provided by the said Act: that no such election has been held since 1919: that those Irish peers who had been so elected continued to sit as members of the House until their respective deaths and that the last Irish peer so elected died in 1961: and on the opinion of the Committee that the provisions of the said Act relating to the election of Irish representative peers ceased to be effective on the passing of the Irish Free State (Agreement) Act, 1922: and that the right to elect Irish representative peers no longer exists.

[*Re Earl of Antrim's Petition* [1967] 1 AC 691 at 717–8, per Lord Reid.]

The holder of a peerage in the peerage of Ireland shall not by virtue of that peerage be disqualified—

(*a*) for being or being elected as a member of the House of Commons for any constituency in the United Kingdom; or

(*b*) for voting at elections for that House whether or not he is a member of that House.

[Peerage Act 1963, s. 5.]

## (2) LIFE PEERS

*Life peerages were first introduced in 1958.*

(1) Without prejudice to Her Majesty's powers as to the appointment of Lords of Appeal in Ordinary, Her Majesty shall have power by letters patent to confer on any person a peerage for life having the incidents specified in subsection (2) of this section.

(2) A peerage conferred under this section shall, during the life of the person on whom it is conferred, entitle him—

(*a*) to rank as a baron under such style as may be appointed by the letters patent; and

(*b*) subject to subsection (4) of this section, to receive writs of summons to attend the House of Lords and sit and vote therein accordingly,

and shall expire on his death.

(3) A life peerage may be conferred under this section on a woman.

(4) Nothing in this section shall enable any person to receive a writ of summons to attend the House of Lords, or to sit and vote in that House, at any time when disqualified therefor by law.

[Life Peerages Act 1958, s. 1.]

## (3) LORDS SPIRITUAL

The Lords Spiritual are the archbishops and bishops of the Church of England having seats in Parliament by ancient usage and by statute. In 1847, on the creation of the bishopric of Manchester, it was enacted that the number of bishops sitting in Parliament should not be increased in consequence, and a similar provision has been made in the case of bishoprics which have been created subsequently.

The bishops now having seats in Parliament are the two archbishops (of Canterbury and York) and twenty-four of the English bishops. Whenever any one of the sees of Canterbury, York, London, Durham, or Winchester becomes void, the vacancy in the House of Lords is supplied by the issue of a writ of summons to the bishop elected to the see; and a similar writ is issued to any bishop already sitting in the House of Lords who is translated to another see. If a vacancy among the bishops sitting in Parliament is caused by the avoidance of any other see than the five already mentioned, such vacancy is supplied 'by the issue of a writ of summons to that bishop of a see in England who, having been longest bishop of a see in England, has not previously become entitled to such writ'. A bishop may, under section 2 of the Bishops (Retirement) Measure 1951, resign his see, and therewith his seat in the House of Lords, when the vacancy is filled up in the same manner as if he were dead.

[Erskine May, *Parliamentary Practice* (London, 21st edn., 1989), 9.]

THE EARL OF ONSLOW: My Lords, I beg leave to ask the Question standing in my name on the Order Paper.

The Question was as follows: To ask Her Majesty's Government whether Lords Spiritual have the right to vote in parliamentary elections.

THE PARLIAMENTARY UNDER-SECRETARY OF STATE, HOME OFFICE (LORD ELTON): My Lords, Lords Temporal are disqualified from voting at parliamentary elections at common law. The question of whether Lords Spiritual can vote at parliamentary elections has never been expressly considered by the courts.

THE EARL OF ONSLOW: My Lords, after 800 years of the existence of your Lordships' House (or is it 700? I am not quite sure) is it not time that this particular point was clarified? Is my noble friend aware that I would agree—I hope he is aware that I would agree, but, if not, is he so aware—that 26 votes are not going to have a catastrophic influence upon the outcome of a parliamentary election? Furthermore, is it not verging on the irresponsible to take it upon oneself to produce a new piece of constitutional law—which, I believe, took place in the electoral district of Vauxhall at the last election?

LORD ELTON: My Lords, I agree with the first inference of my noble friend's supplementary question: that the votes of the entire Bench of Bishops would not reverse what would otherwise be the outcome of any general election. I therefore feel that the outcome of any other inquiries is of academic rather than constitutional significance.

LORD SHINWELL: My Lords, the noble Lord the Minister has just stated that the matter of Lords Spiritual voting in general elections has never been considered by the courts. Is it a matter to be considered by the courts? Is it not a matter to be decided by the House? Could this matter not be decided by a simple vote? If there is no one prepared to do that, then I am prepared to move that in future Lords Spiritual be precluded from voting in parliamentary elections unless every one of us is entitled to the same privilege.

LORD ELTON: My Lords, I recognise the enthusiasm of the noble Lord to defend constitutional propriety. I understand that the courts became the proper arbiters of electoral procedure some time towards the end of the last century, although I am open to correction on the date. It is also generally accepted that it is not up to Members of this House to determine the composition of another place. However, as I said before, the impact of 26 widely scattered votes is hardly likely to do that.

THE LORD BISHOP OF DERBY: My Lords, while thanking the noble Lord the Minister for his interesting replies, and speaking as one who since becoming a Member of this House has always regarded himself as a disqualified person—and who has been helped along the path of sanity and virtue by seeing the letter 'L' against his name in the register of voters and by not receiving a polling card—may I ask whether the noble Lord the Minister is aware that neither the most reverend Primate the Archbishop of Canterbury nor any other Lord Spiritual has any desire or intention to take this matter any further, and nor will any of us in future knowingly go against tradition and custom in this matter?

[443 H.L. Deb. 242–3 (29 June 1983).]

Furthermore, since the courts have not specifically addressed the question, their judgments regarding the absence of voting rights of peers cannot necessarily be read as conferring voting rights on Lords Spiritual. Rather, a general historical perspective would indicate that the rationale underlying the exclusion in the case of Lords Temporal is equally applicable to that of Lords Spiritual, namely, that all Lords of Parliament are accorded a specific role in the legislative process by virtue of their membership in that House, and that that membership should disentitle them from interfering in any manner in the affairs of the other House, whether by virtue of voting in elections for that House or by attempting to obtain election to that House whilst still entitled to sit in the House of Lords. Since Lords Spiritual are full members of the House of Lords and as such are entitled to vote on all matters be they spiritual or temporal, the exclusion from voting in the election of members of the House of Commons would logically seem to apply. Indeed, this reasoning is clearly reflected in a standing order of the House of Commons adopted in 1802 which read: '. . . it is a high infringement of the liberties and privileges of the Commons of the United Kingdom for any lord of parliament or other peer *or prelate* . . . to concern himself in the election of members to serve for the Commons in parliament . . .'

Whilst welcoming the assurance of the Bishop of Derby that Lords Spiritual will refrain from voting in the future, it would be desirable for the constitutional role of Lords Spiritual to be more clearly delineated.

[Philippa Hughes and Stephanie Palmer, 'Voting Bishops' [1983] *Public Law* 393 at 395.]

### (4) LORDS OF APPEAL IN ORDINARY

For the purpose of aiding the House of Lords in the hearing and determination of appeals, Her Majesty may . . . by letters patent appoint . . . qualified persons to be Lords of Appeal in Ordinary.

A person shall not be qualified to be appointed by Her Majesty a Lord of Appeal in Ordinary unless he has been at or before the time of his appointment the holder for a period of not less than two years of some one or more of the offices in this Act described as high judicial offices, or has been at or before such time as aforesaid, for not less than fifteen years, a practising barrister in England or Ireland, or a practising advocate in Scotland.

Every Lord of Appeal in Ordinary shall hold his office during good behaviour, and shall continue to hold the same notwithstanding the demise of the Crown, but he may be removed from such office on the address of both Houses of Parliament.

. . .

Every Lord of Appeal in Ordinary, unless he is otherwise entitled to sit as a member of the House of Lords, shall by virtue and according to the date of his appointment be entitled during his life to rank as a Baron by such style as Her Majesty may be pleased to appoint, and shall . . . be entitled to a writ of summons to attend, and to sit and vote in the House of Lords; his dignity as a Lord of Parliament shall not descend to his heirs.

On any Lord of Appeal in Ordinary vacating his office, by death resignation or otherwise, Her Majesty may fill up the vacancy by the appointment of another qualified person.

A Lord of Appeal in Ordinary shall, if a Privy Councillor, be a member of the Judicial Committee of the Privy Council, and, subject to the due performance by a Lord of Appeal in Ordinary of his duties as to the hearing and determining of appeals in the House of Lords, it shall be his duty, being a Privy Councillor, to sit and act as a member of the Judicial Committee of the Privy Council.

[Appellate Jurisidiction Act 1876, s. 6.]

The expression 'high judicial office' as defined in the twenty-fifth section of the Appellate Jurisdiction Act, 1876, shall be deemed to include the office of a Lord of Appeal in Ordinary and the office of a member of the Judicial Committee of the Privy Council.

[Appellate Jurisdiction Act 1887, s. 5.]

The maximum number—

(*a*) of Lords of Appeal in Ordinary shall be eleven; . . .

[Administration of Justice Act 1968, s. 1(1)(*a*).]

## 2. CREATION OF PEERAGES

### (1) FORMAL CREATION; TAKING OF SEATS

*Nowadays peerages are formally created by the issue of Letters Patent by the Sovereign. New peers by creation must be formally introduced into the House of Lords before they may sit or vote; peers who have inherited their titles merely take their seats.*

Writs of Summons are issued by direction of the Lord Chancellor from the Office of the Clerk of the Crown in Chancery.

New Writs are issued before the meeting of each Parliament to all Lords spiritual and temporal who have established their right to them. Writs in a slightly different form are also issued to all Lords who are newly created or who, having succeeded to a peerage, establish their right to them during the course of a Parliament.

In order to receive a Writ, a Peer on succession makes application to the Lord Chancellor, producing such evidence of his claim as may be required; if the Lord Chancellor is satisfied, the Writ is issued. If the Lord Chancellor has any doubts, he declines to issue the Writ. The Peer may then petition the Crown, and the matter may then be referred, like other peerage claims, to the Committee for Privileges.

Writs are not issued to Peers who are disqualified for sitting.

An Archbishop, on appointment or translation, and a Bishop who has become entitled to sit, or who, having already a seat, has been translated to another See, should apply for the issue of his Writ to the Office of the Clerk of the Crown and produce such evidence as the Lord Chancellor may require.

Writs (called Writs of Assistance or Writs of Attendance) are also sent to the following: the Attorney General, the Solicitor General, the Lord Chief Justice, the Master of the Rolls, the President of the Family Division, the Lords Justices of Appeal, and the Justices of the High Court. The attendance of the judges was formerly frequent but is now confined to the State Opening of Parliament.

[Sir John Sainty (Clerk of the Parliaments), *Companion to the Standing Orders of the House of Lords* (London, 15th edn., 1984), 5.]

The following must be ceremonially introduced before taking their seats in the House:

(1) Newly created Peer (or an hereditary Peer if no previous holder of the title has been introduced).
(2) Peer advanced in degree.
(3) Peer called up in a barony held by his father.
(4) Newly appointed Lord of Appeal in Ordinary, who is not already a member of the House.
(5) Archbishop, on appointment, or on translation.
(6) Bishop, on first receiving a Writ of Summons or, if already a member of the House, on translation to another See.

When a Writ has been issued to any such Peer or Lord Spiritual, the Lord Chancellor fixes a day (often a Wednesday) for his introduction. Introductions may not take place on the first day of a new Parliament. Usually not more than two introductions take place on any one day. Lords are supported on introduction by two Lords of their own degree in the House. No Lord may act as supporter at the introduction of another Lord without having first taken the Oath.

Lords of Appeal in Ordinary are normally introduced at a sitting for Public Business. They may, however, be introduced at a judicial sitting during prorogation, and also at a judicial sitting during a recess, if it is in the interest of the despatch of judicial business . . .

A Peer who succeeds by descent (unless no previous holder of the title has been introduced) requires no introduction and, on receiving his Writ, can take his seat and the Oath of Allegiance without any ceremony. He is then recorded in the Minutes of Proceedings and Journals as having 'sat first in Parliament' after the death of his predecessor.

No Peer may be charged fees by the Heralds upon his first coming or his introduction into the House.

A Lord may not use the facilities of the House, other than the right to sit on the steps of the Throne, before he has taken his seat for the first time.

[Sainty, *House of Lords Standing Orders*, 7–8.]

## (2) SIX LISTS OF PEERS

A person will receive a peerage today through one of six entirely separate lists. First, a list of working peers is drawn up, usually once a year, consisting of new peers who are expected to take a full part in the parliamentary work of the House and who should see their peerages as a means to that end rather than primarily as honours. Such peers belong to a political party and sit with the peers of that party in the House of Lords. The list of working peers announced in February 1987 contained eleven names, six Conservative and five Labour, recommended by the Prime Minister after informal consultation with the Leader of the Opposition—although not with any other party Leader. These annual working peer lists are the largest regular source of new recruits to the Lords. Secondly, new peers may be included in the Queen's Birthday and New Year Honours

Lists, again on the Prime Minister's recommendation. Inclusion in them signifies mainly the bestowal of an honour, although of course such peers may take part in the proceedings of the House if they choose to do so. Thirdly, a Dissolution Honours List is issued early in the life of each new Parliament, primarily to honour former Ministers and MPs of all parties who did not seek re-election. Former Cabinet Ministers will normally receive a life peerage in that list. The Prime Minister is, again, responsible for the list, and there will be consultations with other party Leaders. If the government changes as a result of the general election the new Prime Minister will take responsibility for his predecessor's list. In the 1987 Dissolution Honours List, by way of example, nineteen life peerages were announced; eleven went to former Conservative Cabinet Ministers, six to former Labour Ministers and MPs, one to a former Liberal MP, and one to Mr Roy Jenkins on the nomination of the Leader of the SDP. Additionally, four other former MPs received knighthoods, and Mr Norman Tebbit (who had retired from the Cabinet after the general election but who remained Chairman of the Conservative Party and an MP) was made a Companion of Honour. Fourthly, when a Prime Minister resigns other than following a general election, he will compile a Resignation Honours List, consisting only of members of his party and others who have served him, which his successor will recommend without amendment. It will normally contain a number of peerages. Fifthly, special creations may be made infrequently and not necessarily on the Prime Minister's advice, though no doubt with his knowledge. Members of the royal family who receive peerages may be so classified—such as Prince Andrew's creation as Duke of York in 1986, or Mr Armstrong-Jones's ennoblement in 1961 as Earl of Snowdon—and so may the peerages customarily conferred on former Prime Ministers. Since 1900 only six former Prime Ministers have remained commoners. All the rest (apart from three) have received earldoms, the most recent being Attlee in 1955, Eden in 1961, and Harold Macmillan, who became Earl of Stockton in 1984 on his ninetieth birthday, twenty years after he had left the House of Commons. Sir Alec Douglas-Home was made a life peer on his retirement from the Commons in 1974, the only rank of peerage he could by law receive as he had disclaimed his hereditary peerages in 1963. Harold Wilson and James Callaghan were created life peers in the 1983 and 1987 Dissolution Honours Lists respectively, although they might of course both have declined hereditary peerages as they had recommended no such creations while Prime Minister. The attitude of the potential recipient and perhaps the personal intervention of the Sovereign in relation to the rank of peerage offered and accepted may be important, and it seems safe to conclude that a former Prime Minister is entitled to be made an earl or a countess if that is what he or she wishes. Sixthly and lastly the Prime Minister may recommend a peerage for someone without a seat in either House in order that he may become a Minister. Thus Macmillan procured a peerage for Percy Mills on his being brought into the Cabinet from industry as Minister of Power in 1957, and Mrs Thatcher obtained a peerage for David Young on joining the Cabinet as Minister without Portfolio in 1984.

[Rodney Brazier, *Constitutional Practice* (Oxford, 1988), 198–200.]

### (3) PEERAGES RECOMMENDED BY PRIME MINISTERS

| Prime Minister | Con. | Lab. | Lib./SDP | Ind. | Total |
|---|---|---|---|---|---|
| Macmillan & Home 1958–64 | 17 | 29 | 1 | 18 | 65 |
| Wilson 1964–70 | 11 | 78 | 6 | 46 | 141 |
| Heath 1970–74 | 23 | 5 | 3 | 15 | 46 |
| Wilson & Callaghan 1974–79 | 17 | 82 | 6 | 34 | 139 |
| Thatcher 1979–87 | 64 | 38 | 9 | 32 | 153 |
| Totals | 142 | 232 | 25 | 145 | 544 |

[Source: D. Shell, *The House of Lords* (Deddington, 1988), 31.]

## 3. LOSING MEMBERSHIP

### (1) DISCLAIMER

1.—(1) Subject to the provisions of this section, any person who, after the commencement of this Act, succeeds to a peerage in the peerage of England, Scotland, Great Britain or the United Kingdom may, by an instrument of disclaimer delivered to the Lord Chancellor within the period prescribed by this Act, disclaim that peerage for his life.

(2) Any instrument of disclaimer to be delivered under this section in respect of a peerage shall be delivered within the period of twelve months beginning with the day on which the person disclaiming succeeds to that peerage or, if he is under the age of twenty-one when he so succeeds, the period of twelve months beginning with the day on which he attains that age; and no such instrument shall be delivered in respect of a peerage by a person who has applied for a writ of summons to attend the House of Lords in right of that peerage.

(3) The foregoing provisions of this section shall apply to a person who has succeeded to a peerage before the commencement of this Act as they apply to a person who succeeds to a peerage after the commencement of this Act, but subject to the following modifications:—

(*a*) the period within which an instrument of disclaimer may be delivered by such a person shall be twelve months beginning with the commencement of this Act or, if he is then under twenty-one years of age, twelve months beginning with the day on which he attains that age; and

(*b*) an instrument of disclaimer may be delivered by such a person notwithstanding that he has applied before the commencement of this Act for a writ of summons to attend the House of Lords.

(4) In reckoning any period prescribed by this section for the delivery of an instrument of disclaimer by any person no account shall be taken of any time during which that person is shown to the satisfaction of the Lord Chancellor to have been subject to any infirmity of body or mind rendering him incapable of exercising or determining whether to exercise his rights under this section.

(5) The provisions of Schedule 1 to this Act shall have effect with respect to the form of instruments of disclaimer under this section, and the delivery, certification and registration of such instruments.

2.—(1) Where a person who succeeds to a peerage to which section 1 of this Act applies is a member of the House of Commons when he so succeeds, any instrument of disclaimer to be delivered by him under that section in respect of that peerage shall be delivered within the period of one month beginning with the date of his succession, and not later; and until the expiration of that period he shall not, by virtue of that peerage, be disqualified for membership of the House of Commons whether or not he has delivered such an instrument:

Provided that—

(*a*) a person who is exempt from disqualification for membership of the House of Commons by virtue only of this subsection shall not sit or vote in that House while so exempt; and

(*b*) if any such person applies for a writ of summons to attend the House of Lords in right of the peerage in question, this subsection shall cease to apply to him.

(2) Where a person who succeeds to such a peerage as aforesaid has been or is nominated as a candidate at a parliamentary election held in pursuance of a writ issued before his succession, he shall not (unless he applies for such a writ of summons as aforesaid) be disqualified by virtue of that peerage for election to the House of Commons at that election, and if he is so elected subsection (1) of this section shall apply to him as if he had succeeded to the peerage immediately after the declaration of the result of the election.

(3) Where an instrument of disclaimer is delivered under this Act by a person to whom this section applies, a copy of that instrument shall be delivered to the Speaker of the House of Commons.

(4) In reckoning any period prescribed by this section in relation to any person no account shall be taken—

(*a*) of any time during which proceedings are pending on any parliamentary election petition in which the right of that person to be elected or returned to the House of Commons is in issue;

(*b*) of any time during which that person is shown to the satisfaction of the Speaker of the House of Commons to have been subject to any such infirmity as is mentioned in subsection (4) of section 1 of this Act; or

(*c*) of any time during which Parliament is prorogued or both Houses of Parliament are adjourned for more than four days;

and if Parliament is dissolved during that period the foregoing provisions of this section shall cease to apply to that person in respect of the peerage in question.

3.—(1) The disclaimer of a peerage by any person under this Act shall be irrevocable and shall operate, from the date on which the instrument of disclaimer is delivered,—

(*a*) to divest that person (and, if he is married, his wife) of all right or interest to or in the peerage, and all titles, rights, offices, privileges and precedence attaching thereto; and

(*b*) to relieve him of all obligations and disabilities (including any disqualification in respect of membership of the House of Commons and elections to that House) arising therefrom,

but shall not accelerate the succession to that peerage nor affect its devolution on his death.

(2) Where a peerage is disclaimed under this Act, no other hereditary peerage shall be conferred upon the person by whom it is disclaimed, and no writ in acceleration shall be issued in respect of that peerage to the person entitled thereto on his death.

(3) The disclaimer of a peerage under this Act shall not affect any right, interest or power (whether arising before or after the disclaimer) of the person by whom the peerage is disclaimed, or of any other person, to, in or over any estates or other property limited or settled to devolve with that peerage.

(4) The reference in the foregoing subsection to estates or other property limited or settled to devolve with a peerage shall, for the purposes of the application of this Act to Scotland, be construed as including a reference to estates or other land devolving as aforesaid under an entail or special destination, or the beneficial interest in which so devolves under a trust.

[Peerage Act 1963, ss. 1–3.]

## *Peerage Act 1963*

Whereas I, The Right Honourable Sir Alexander Frederick Douglas-Home, Knight of the Most Ancient and Most Noble Order of the Thistle, succeeded to the peerages described in the Annex hereto on the date specified in that Annex, and desire to disclaim the said peerages for my life under the above-mentioned Act;

And Whereas I attained the age of twenty-one years before the said date;

Now Therefore, I, the said Sir Alexander Frederick Douglas-Home, in accordance with the provisions of the said Act, hereby disclaim the said peerages for my life;

In Witness whereof I have hereunto set my hand and seal this twenty-third day of October One thousand nine hundred and sixty-three.

Signed and Sealed by the said Sir Alexander Frederick Douglas-Home in the presence of:

T. J. Bligh, 10 Downing Street, S.W.1., Civil Servant.

[The Earl of Home's instrument of disclaimer.]

*Lord Home disclaimed six peerages thereby becoming Sir Alec Douglas-Home and was able to be elected to the House of Commons, having been appointed Prime Minister in succession to Harold Macmillan.*

### (2) ALIENAGE

And whereas it is requisite and necessary that some further provision be made for securing our religion laws and liberties from and after the death of his Majesty and the Princess Ann of Denmark and in default of issue of the body of the said princess and of his Majesty respectively Be it enacted by the Kings most excellent Majesty by and with the advice and consent of the lords spirituall and temporall and commons in Parliament assembled and by the authority of the same.

That whosoever shall hereafter come to the possession of this crown shall joyn in communion with the Church of England as by law established.

That in case the crown and imperiall dignity of this realm shall hereafter come to any person not being a native of this kingdom of England this nation be not obliged to ingage in any warr for the defence of any dominions or territories which do not belong to the crown of England without the consent of Parliament . . .

That after the said limitation shall take effect as aforesaid no person born out of the kingdoms of England Scotland or Ireland or the dominions thereunto belonging (although he be . . . made a denizen (except such as are born of English parents) shall be capable to be of the privy councill or a member of either House of Parliament or to enjoy any office or place of trust either civill or military or to have any grant of lands tenements or hereditaments from the Crown to himself or to any other or others in trust for him . . .

[Act of Settlement 1701, s. 3.]

In this Act, unless the context otherwise requires—

. . .

'alien' means a person who is neither a Commonwealth citizen nor a British protected person nor a citizen of the Republic of Ireland; . . .

[British Nationality Act 1981, s. 50(1).]

## (3) BANKRUPTCY

(1) Where a court in England and Wales or Northern Ireland adjudges an individual bankrupt or a court in Scotland awards sequestration of an individual's estate, the individual is disqualified—

(*a*) for sitting or voting in the House of Lords,

(*b*) for being elected to, or sitting or voting in, the House of Commons, and

(*c*) for sitting or voting in a committee of either House.

(2) Where an individual is disqualified under this section, the disqualification ceases—

(*a*) except where the adjudication is annulled or the award recalled or reduced without the individual having been first discharged, on the discharge of the individual, and

(*b*) in the excepted case, on the annulment, recall or reduction, as the case may be.

(3) No writ of summons shall be issued to any lord of Parliament who is for the time being disqualified under this section for sitting and voting in the House of Lords.

(4) Where a member of the House of Commons who is disqualified under this section continues to be so disqualified until the end of the period of 6 months beginning with the day of the adjudication or award, his seat shall be vacated at the end of that period.

(5) A court which makes an adjudication or award such as is mentioned in subsection (1) in relation to any lord of Parliament or member of the House of Commons shall forthwith certify the adjudication or award to the Speaker of the House of Lords or, as the case may be, to the Speaker of the House of Commons.

(6) Where a court has certified an adjudication or award to the Speaker of the House of Commons under subsection (5), then immediately after it becomes apparent which of the following certificates is applicable, the court shall certify to the Speaker of the House of Commons—

(*a*) that the period of 6 months beginning with the day of the adjudication or award has expired without the adjudication or award having been annulled, recalled or reduced, or

(*b*) that the adjudication or award has been annulled, recalled or reduced before the end of that period.

(7) Subject to the preceding provisions of this section, so much of this Act and any other enactment (whenever passed) and of any subordinate legislation (whenever made) as—

(*a*) makes provision for or in connection with bankruptcy in one or more parts of the United Kingdom, or

(*b*) makes provision conferring a power of arrest in connection with the winding up or insolvency of companies in one or more parts of the United Kingdom,

applies in relation to persons having privilege of Parliament or peerage as it applies in relation to persons not having such privilege.

[Insolvency Act 1986, s. 427.]

## (4) TREASON

Provided nevertheless, that if any person hereafter convicted of treason . . . shall at the time of such conviction hold any military or naval office, or any civil office under the Crown or other public employment . . . or any place, office, or emolument in any university, college, or other corporation, or be entitled to any pension or superannuation allowance payable by the public, or out of any public fund, such office . . . employment, or place shall forthwith become vacant, and such pension or superannuation allowance or emolument shall forthwith determine and cease to be payable, unless such person shall receive a free pardon from Her Majesty, within two months after such conviction, or before the filling up of such office . . . employment, or place if given at a later period; and such person shall become, and (until he shall have suffered the punishment to which he had been sentenced, or such other punishment as by competent authority may be substituted for the same, or shall receive a free pardon from Her Majesty), shall continue thenceforth incapable of holding any military or naval office, or any civil office under the Crown or other public employment . . . or of being elected, or sitting, or voting as a member of either House of Parliament, or of exercising any right of suffrage or other parliamentary or municipal franchise whatever within England, Wales, or Ireland.

[Forfeiture Act 1870, s. 2.]

### (5) MINORITY

The following, if not under the age of twenty one, are members of the House of Lords . . .

[House of Lords Standing Order No. 2: see above, p. 494.]

*The House of Lords has no power to expel any member. None of the other types of disqualification which may affect M.P.s (on which see above p. 449) can affect peers.*

## 4. LEAVE OF ABSENCE

Lords are to attend the sittings of the House or, if they cannot do so, obtain leave of absence, which the House may grant at pleasure. But a Lord who is unable to attend regularly is not required to apply for leave of absence, if he proposes to attend as often as he reasonably can.

A Lord may apply for leave of absence at any time during a Parliament for the remainder of the Parliament. Applications for leave of absence should be addressed to the Clerk of the Parliaments.

Before the beginning of every Parliament the Lord Chancellor in writing asks each Lord (with such exceptions as the Leave of Absence and Lords' Expenses Committee may direct), to answer within eight weeks whether or not he wishes to apply for leave of absence. In the case of those Lords who have not by the date specified in the letter either (a) indicated their wishes or (b) attended the House (other than for the purpose of taking the Oath of Allegiance) reminder letters are sent stating that if they do not indicate their wishes within a further period of two weeks they will be considered to have applied for leave of absence. At the expiry of that period, the Leave of Absence and Lords' Expenses Committee meet to consider lists of those Lords who have (a) applied for leave of absence and (b) failed to reply to the reminder letter. Subject to any deletions which the Committee may decide to make, the Lords on the lists are granted leave of absence by the House.

(1) A Lord who has been granted leave of absence is expected not to attend sittings of the house until his leave has expired or been terminated, except to take the Oath of Allegiance.

(2) If a Lord on leave of absence wishes to attend during the period for which leave was granted, he is expected to give notice in writing to the Clerk of the Parliaments at least one month before the day on which he wishes to attend; and his leave is terminated one month from the date of this notice, or sooner if the House so direct.

(3) A Lord who has leave of absence may not act as a supporter of a Lord who is being introduced.

(4) Lords who have leave of absence may apply for places for their wives at the State Opening of Parliament, and the usual number of places at such functions as The Queen's Birthday Parade (Trooping the Colour). They may not apply for places on such occasions as visits to naval or military establishments which are organised to assist the active members of the House in their Parliamentary duties.

(5) Lords who have leave of absence may use the Library, Dining Room, Guest Room, etc, and may obtain tickets for the Strangers' Gallery. Their wives and sons enjoy the same facilities as those of other Lords.

(6) Lords who have leave of absence may sit on the steps of the Throne during a sitting of the House.

(7) Lords who have leave of absence may, on application, receive copies of Hansard and Parliamentary Papers.

*The Standing Order has since been amended as shown below.*

[House of Lords Standing Order No. 20.]

The Leave of Absence Committee have considered the operation of the leave of absence scheme, following experience of administering the scheme at the beginning of this Parliament. They noted that, when the scheme was initiated some 30 years ago, the proportion of Lords who took advantage of the scheme was higher than it is today, when the activity of the House and numbers who attend regularly have risen sharply. An elaborate administrative machinery exists for the purpose of identifying those Lords who should be granted leave of absence. For the majority of Lords, the inquiry whether they do or do not wish to be granted leave establishes what is already self-evident.

The Leave of Absence Committee have concluded that in modern circumstances the scheme is of marginal relevance and does not require a general trawl of Lords, which takes months to complete and which, in the current Session, produced the result that of the 162 Lords who applied for leave, 124 were already on leave at the end of the last Parliament.

However, the Committee recognise that the scheme does give to those Lords who take seriously the demands of their Writ of Summons, but who, for whatever reason, cannot attend, the opportunity to have their position regularised. For this reason, the Committee do not recommend that the scheme be abolished but, instead, propose that it be reformed to operate on the principle that leave of absence should be granted only to those Peers who ask for leave and that it should not be granted by default.

The Committee accordingly recommend that in future:

(*a*) At the beginning of each Parliament the Clerk of the Parliaments should write to those Lords who were on leave at the end of the previous Parliament asking them if they wish to apply for leave for the new Parliament. Leave will be granted only to those Lords who so apply;

(*b*) To ensure that all Lords are made aware of the leave of absence scheme, the Dissolution Notice, which is sent to all Lords giving details of the opening of a new Parliament and the procedure for taking the Oath, will include the following notice:

'Leave of Absence

Letters asking all Lords whether they wish to apply for leave of absence are being sent only to those Lords who were on leave at the end of the last Parliament. Other Lords who wish so to apply are asked to communicate with the Clerk of the Parliaments.'

(*c*) Details of the scheme will be included in the 'new Peers' Kit' of general information which is given to Lords on their introduction and to hereditary Lords when first taking their seat.

[1st Report from the Procedure Committee, H.L. 46 (1987–88), accepted by the House at 494 H.L. Deb. 430 (7 March 1988).]

*Between 130 and 150 peers have leave of absence at any one time; in the 1988–89 session the number was 156.*

## Organization in the House

### 1. SOME STATISTICS

#### (1) DAILY ATTENDANCE 1987–88 SESSION

Average daily attendance: 333

[Source: Sessional Statistics 1987–88.]

#### (2) PARTY ALLEGIANCES IN MAY 1989

| Party | Number |
|---|---|
| Conservative | 426 |
| Labour | 113 |
| Social and Liberal Democrat | 57 |
| SDP | 23 |
| Cross-bench | 288 |

[Source: Journal and Information Office, House of Lords.]

LORD BESWICK: My Lords, I beg leave to ask the Question standing in my name on the Order Paper.

The Question was as follows:

To ask Her Majesty's Government whether they will provide the figures on which they base the statement made in the House on 26th April that, 'In almost every case and almost every way of looking at it, the Government do not have an overall majority in this House' (col. 149).

LORD DENHAM: Yes, my Lords, the figures are these. On 26th April of this year, the day on which I made the claim quoted by the noble Lord, 1,097 Peers were in receipt of a Writ of Summons of whom 462 were Government Peers, or 42.1 per cent of this total. If you exclude those Lords who were on leave of absence the figure becomes 936, of whom 424 were Government Peers or 45.3 per cent. If you exclude again those Lords who had not taken the Oath during the current Session the figure becomes 865, of whom 398 were Government Peers, or 46 per cent.

Alternatively, during 1982–83, the last full Session for which figures are available, 281 Peers attended half or more of the sittings and of these 122 were Government Peers or 43.4 per cent; 343 Peers attended a third or more of the sittings of whom 147 were Conservative, or 42.6 per cent; whereas 754 Peers attended on at least one occasion, of whom 344 were Government Peers, or 45.6 per cent. The total number of Peer attendances recorded during that Session was 27,226 and, of these, 11,816 were by Government Peers—which makes 43.4 per cent. If the noble Lord, Lord Beswick, can think up any set of criteria that does give the Government an overall majority in your Lordships' House, I, as Chief Whip, would be very grateful to him.

LORD BESWICK: My Lords, I am grateful to the noble Lord for that Answer, and particularly grateful to him that he handed me the figures separately beforehand. But is he aware that to an extent he supports the case that I have made? Is it not a fact that in the general run of the revisionary business of this House, there may not be a preponderance of Conservative Peers but that when it comes to the crunch and a decisive issue in the Division Lobby, then the noble Lord certainly does have, as on April 9th, an overall majority? May I refer him to more simple figures published by the Journal and Information Office of this House which states the position as follows: 136 Labour, 41 Liberal, 41 SDP—an Opposition total of 218 against a total figure of Conservative Peers of 418. If one takes the Cross-Bench peers, that total is 219, which certainly gives a minority to the Government of 20. But does it not require an undignified degree of gullibility to accept that all but 20 of Cross-Bench Peers are potential Opposition supporters?

LORD DENHAM: My Lords, the words that I was defending, the words that I used in answer to the noble Lord, Lord Beswick, some days ago, were that the Conservative Government did not have an overall majority in this House. I think that I have substantiated that by the figures that I have quoted; and that is what I was asked to do by the noble Lord. I wonder how noble Lords on the Cross-benches will react to the suggestion of the noble Lord, Lord Beswick, that they are Conservatives in sheep's clothing. Many years ago when he was Opposition Chief Whip and I was acting Government Chief Whip, this may have been true. Noble Lords sat on the Cross-Benches because they held office of profit under the Crown or for some other identifiable reason and their voting was usually predictable. But nowadays they are genuinely independent and examine each proposition on its merits. Only last week they divided 28 to 1 against the Government. Not even my noble friends behind me do that!

[451 H.L. Deb. 1506–7 (17 May 1984).]

### (3) DAILY SITTING

*The House sits each year on about 150 days (compared with the Commons' average of some 175 days). The 1985–6 session was a heavy one, peers sitting on 165 days; the lowest annual total of sitting days in recent years was 143 in 1980–1.)*

## 2. ARRANGEMENT OF BUSINESS; ORDER IN THE HOUSE

*The Leader of the House of Lords and the Government Chief Whip, in consultation with the other parties represented in the House, arrange the order of daily business. The House as a whole regulates its proceedings and maintains order, advised by the Leader of the House.*

14. The overwhelming majority of the House opposed the introduction of a Speaker with controlling powers. A small number

based their opposition on practical arguments concerning the position of the Lord Chancellor as Speaker, and the self evident problems which would have to be faced if a change were made, including those relating to the other ministerial and judicial duties of the Lord Chancellor. The nomination or election of another person to fill the role would be no solution, giving rise to procedural and practical difficulty.

15. For most, the reasons against such a change are positive; Peers have pride in our system of self-regulation and the 'liberal spirit' it embodies. The introduction of a Speakership with powers would encourage time-wasting points of order, worsen conduct, and curtail the ancient liberties of the House.

[Report of the Group on the Working of the House, H.L. 9 (1987–8), paras. 14–15.]

If in a speech a Lord is thought to be seriously transgressing the accepted practice of the House, it is open to another Lord to move That the noble Lord be no longer heard. This Motion however is very rare; it is debatable and seldom needs to be decided on Question since Lords generally conform to the sense of the House as soon as this sense becomes clear.

The effect of agreeing to this Motion is to prohibit the Lord in question from speaking further on the substantive Motion, but not on any subsequent Motion.

[Sainty, *House of Lords Standing Orders*, 41.]

BARONESS SEEAR: I am sorry to interrupt the noble Lord but this is the third Second Reading speech [delivered during the committee stage] that we have had this afternoon. We have a great number of amendments to get through. Many of us have our names down to amendments to be taken later. Perhaps I may move that the noble Lord be no longer heard.

Moved, That the noble Lord, Lord Sefton of Garston, be no longer heard.

On Question, Motion agreed to.

[496 H.L. Deb. 428 (3 May 1988).]

## 3. ALLOWANCES AND PAY

*Peers are entitled to the following allowances:*

| | |
|---|---|
| Attendance allowance | £21 a day |
| Overnight allowance | £57 a day |
| Office, secretarial and research allowance | £22 a day |

[Resolution of the House, 478 H.L. Deb. 906 (16 July 1986), as amended by Resolution of the House, 488 H.L. Deb. 1531–46 (23 July 1987).]

*Travel expenses within the United Kingdom on parliamentary business are reimbursed.*

Salaries

| Office | Annual Amount (£) |
|---|---|
| Lord Chancellor | 91,500 |
| Leader of the Opposition | 33,241 |
| Government Chief Whip | 39,641 |
| Deputy Government Chief Whip | 33,241 |
| Government Whip | 29,971 |
| Opposition Chief Whip | 29,971 |
| Lord Chairman of Committees | 39,641 |
| Principal Deputy Chairman of Committees | 36,131 |
| Lord of Appeal in Ordinary | 82,750 |
| Cabinet Minister in Lords | 44,591 |
| Minister of State in Lords | 39,641 |
| Parliamentary Secretary in Lords | 33,241 |

## 4. FINANCIAL INTERESTS

*There is no register of peers' interests, but peers are honour-bound to declare any personal financial interest during debate. The rules governing the contributions to debates by peers who are members of public boards are governed by the Addison Rules.*

A Lord who is a member of a public Board, whether commercial or non-commercial in character, is not by reason of such membership debarred from exercising his right to speak in the House of Lords, even on matters affecting the Board of which he is a member; and it is recognised that, in the last resort, only the Lord concerned can himself decide whether he can properly speak on a particular occasion. By custom, the Lord should inform the House of his interest if he does decide to speak.

The following guidance (based upon that given in 1951 by the then Leader of the House, Viscount Addison, after consultation and agreement between the Parties) may be helpful to Lords who are considering whether or not to take part in a particular debate:

(i) When questions affecting public Boards arise in Parliament, the Government (in general) and the responsible Minister (in particular) are alone responsible to Parliament. The duty of reply rests with Ministers only, and cannot devolve upon members of public Boards who may also be members of the House of Lords. There can be no question of Board members replacing, or usurping the functions of, Ministers.

(ii) It is important that, except where otherwise provided, public Boards should be free to conduct their day-to-day administration without the intervention of Parliament or Ministers. If Board members who happen also to be Lords were to give the House information about the day-to-day operations of the Board or to answer criticisms respecting it, the House would in fact be exercising a measure of Parliamentary supervision over matters of management. It would also be difficult for the responsible Minister not to give similar information to the House of Commons.

(iii) There is no duty upon the Board member to answer questions put to him in debate, and no criticism should attach to any member of a Board who refrains from speaking in a debate. Nor should the fact that a member spoke in a particular debate be regarded in any way as a precedent for him or any other member to speak in any other debate.

(iv) The foregoing applies only to debates relating to public Boards. Experience acquired as a member of a public Board will often be relevant to general debates in which the same considerations do not arise, and the contributions of Board members who are Lords may be all the more valuable because of that experience.

[Sainty, *House of Lords Standing Orders*, 42–3.]

## Work of the Lords

### 1. ALLOCATION OF TIME

| Topic | Time spent (%) |
| --- | --- |
| Public Bills from Commons | 60 |
| General debates | 14 |
| Unstarred questions (debated) | 5 |
| Other questions | 5 |
| Ministerial statements | 2 |
| Subordinate legislation | 4 |
| European Community Committee reports | 1.5 |
| Private Bills | 1 |
| Other | 8.5 |

[Source: Sessional Statistics 1987–8.]

### 2. PUBLIC BILLS FROM THE COMMONS

*Some 1,500 amendments are made to such Bills by the House of Lords in an average session—although most of them are proposed by Ministers. Most Commons' public Bills are passed entirely unamended in any session.*

After receiving a Second Reading, a Bill is, unless the House otherwise orders, committed to a Committee of the Whole House without question put.

[Sainty, *House of Lords Standing Orders*, 86.]

### 3. BACK-BENCH PEERS' BILLS

*Any back-bench peer may introduce a Bill without giving notice, without going through any ballot, and without needing the leave of the House. About a dozen such Bills are introduced each year; less than half of them will be enacted.*

## 4. GENERAL DEBATES

*One day a week is devoted to a debate on a neutral motion calling for papers or on a motion to take note; an additional day a month is given over to a short general debate. The topics are chosen by back-bench peers through a ballot.*

## 5. QUESTIONS

Questions are addressed to Her Majesty's Government and not to a particular Minister.

Questions may also be addressed to certain Lords as holders of official positions but not as members of the Government. Thus, for instance, the Leader of the House has been questioned on matters concerning procedure, and the Chairman of Committees concerning any matters within the duties of his office and matters relating to the House of Lords' Offices Committee and its Sub-committees.

Starred Questions (marked * on the Order Paper) are asked for information only, and not with a view to making a speech or to raising a debate. They may be put on the Order Paper for any day on which the House is sitting, and are entered before other business. No Starred Question may be tabled less than twenty-four hours before it is due to be asked. The number of Starred Questions for any one day is limited to four, and to two for any individual Lord. No Lord may have more than three Starred Questions on the Order Paper at any one time. Starred Questions are asked by leave of the House, and may be disallowed by the House. The proper form of words to be used is: 'My Lords, I beg leave to ask the Question standing in my name on the Order Paper.' If a Lord is not present to ask a Question standing in his name, the Question may be asked by another Lord on his behalf but only with his authority.

Supplementary questions may be asked provided they are short and confined to the subject of the original Question, but debate may not take place. The essential purpose of Starred Questions and supplementaries is to elicit information from the Government, and so they should not incorporate statements of opinion.

Where the Minister's answer contains material which is too

lengthy or too complicated to be given orally in the House this may be published in Hansard.

The rule against the reading of speeches applies also to the reading of supplementary questions.

Question time should normally be concluded in 20 minutes.

A Lord who wishes to give Her Majesty's Government private notice of his intention to ask a Question on a matter of urgency should submit his Question in writing to the Leader of the House by Twelve noon on the day on which he proposes to ask the Question (by 10 am on days when the House sits before 1 pm). The decision whether the Question is of sufficient urgency to justify an immediate reply rests in the first place with the Leader of the House and ultimately with the general sense of the House.

If a Lord challenges the preliminary decision of the Leader of the House on the question of urgency he should, as a matter of courtesy:

(*a*) give as much notice as possible to the Leader that he proposes to challenge his preliminary decision in the House; and

(*b*) make clear to the House, when he rises to ask his Question, that he is appealing to the House to support him against the preliminary decision of the Leader.

A Lord should not seek to raise the issue of his Private Notice Question on any motion on the day of that question, unless it is relevant to it.

Private Notice Questions are taken immediately after Starred Questions. Where there is a similar Private Notice Question in the Commons the answer is usually given so as to synchronise with the answer in the Commons.

A Lord who wishes to ask a Question but does not desire an oral reply may enter it on the Order Paper under the heading 'Questions for Written Answer'. The answer to such a question is printed in Hansard and a copy is sent to the Lord. Answers are issued to the Press Gallery at 4.30 pm without an embargo on use and publication. There is no limit to the number of Questions which may be put down; they should be answered within a fortnight; and, where appropriate, they may be answered on the day on which they are tabled.

The simultaneous tabling of large numbers of Questions for

Written Answer is considered undesirable as is the tabling of what is, in effect, a series of different requests for information under the guise of a single Question for Written Answer.

When a Minister undertakes in the House to write to a Lord on a matter of general interest to the House, it is open to that Lord or any other Lord to ensure that the Minister's reply is available in the House by putting down a Question for Written Answer.

A Question which may give rise to debate, known as an Unstarred Question, may be put down upon the Order Paper for any day on which the House is sitting. It is usual to consult the Government Whip's Office to agree upon a suitable date. An Unstarred Question is entered last.

Speeches may be made upon an Unstarred Question, but no Lord may speak more than once except, with the leave of the House, for the purpose of explaining himself in some material point (no new matter being introduced). The Lord who asks the Question has no right of reply since he moves no Motion. It is the practice for the Minister who is to reply on behalf of the Government to wait until he is satisfied that no other Lord wishes to speak before he rises. It is considered undesirable for Lords to continue the debate after the Government's reply has been given, save for questions to the Minister before he sits down.

It is considered undesirable, as a general rule, for a second Unstarred Question to be taken after 8 o'clock. A second Unstarred Question should be put down only on a day when business appears to be light; and if subsequently the pressure of business increases, the Lord concerned should be prepared to postpone his Question to a later date, subject to the convenience of the House and of other Lords who may wish to speak.

[Sainty, *House of Lords Standing Orders*, 75–7.]

## 6. COMMITTEES

*Most Lords' committees are select committees, but there is no understanding as exists in the Commons that the government will have a majority of members on each committee. Reports critical of government policy have been published by such committees and have been approved by the House: see, e.g., the Report of the Select Committee on Unemployment, H.L. 142 (1981–2), debated at 436 H.L. Deb.*

*425–513 (16 November 1982); 1st Report from the Science and Technology Committee, H.L. 20 (1986—7), agreed to at 484 H.L. Deb. 1251–332 (19 February 1987). The European Communities Committee and the Science and Technology Committee are particularly important.*

## Lords and Government in Conflict

### 1. THE STATUTORY RULES

Whereas it is expedient that provision should be made for regulating the relations between the two Houses of Parliament:

And whereas it is intended to substitute for the House of Lords as it at present exists a Second Chamber constituted on a popular instead of hereditary basis, but such substitution cannot be immediately brought into operation:

And whereas provision will require hereafter to be made by Parliament in a measure effecting such substitution for limiting and defining the powers of the new Second Chamber, but it is expedient to make such provision as in this Act appears for restricting the existing powers of the House of Lords:

1.—(1) If a Money Bill, having been passed by the House of Commons, and sent up to the House of Lords at least one month before the end of the session, is not passed by the House of Lords without amendment within one month after it is so sent up to that House, the Bill shall, unless the House of Commons direct to the contrary, be presented to His Majesty and become an Act of Parliament on the Royal Assent being signified, notwithstanding that the House of Lords have not consented to the Bill.

(2) A Money Bill means a Public Bill which in the opinion of the Speaker of the House of Commons contains only provisions dealing with all or any of the following subjects, namely, the imposition, repeal, remission, alteration, or regulation of taxation; the imposition for the payment of debt or other financial purposes of charges on the Consolidated Fund, the National Loans Fund or on money provided by Parliament, or the variation or repeal of any such charges; supply; the appropriation, receipt, custody, issue or audit of accounts of public money; the raising or guarantee of any loan or the repayment thereof; or subordinate matters incidental to those

subjects or any of them. In this subsection the expressions 'taxation', 'public money', and 'loan' respectively do not include any taxation, money, or loan raised by local authorities or bodies for local purposes.

(3) There shall be endorsed on every Money Bill when it is sent up to the House of Lords and when it is presented to His Majesty for assent the certificate of the Speaker of the House of Commons signed by him that it is a Money Bill. Before giving his certificate, the Speaker shall consult, if practicable, two members to be appointed from the Chairmen's Panel at the beginning of each Session by the Committee of Selection.

2.—(1) If any Public Bill (other than a Money Bill or a Bill containing any provision to extend the maximum duration of Parliament beyond five years) is passed by the House of Commons in two successive sessions (whether of the same Parliament or not), and, having been sent up to the House of Lords at least one month before the end of the session, is rejected by the House of Lords in each of those sessions, that Bill shall, on its rejection for the second time by the House of Lords, unless the House of Commons direct to the contrary, be presented to His Majesty and become an Act of Parliament on the Royal Assent being signified thereto, notwithstanding that the House of Lords have not consented to the Bill: Provided that this provision shall not take effect unless one year has elapsed between the date of the second reading in the first of those sessions of the Bill in the House of Commons and the date on which it passes the House of Commons in the second of those sessions.

(2) When a Bill is presented to His Majesty for assent in pursuance of the provisions of this section, there shall be endorsed on the Bill the certificate of the Speaker of the House of Commons signed by him that the provisions of this section have been duly complied with.

(3) A Bill shall be deemed to be rejected by the House of Lords if it is not passed by the House of Lords either without amendment or with such amendments only as may be agreed to by both Houses.

(4) A Bill shall be deemed to be the same Bill as a former Bill sent up to the House of Lords in the preceding session if, when it is sent up to the House of Lords, it is identical with the former Bill or contains only such alterations as are certified by the Speaker of the House of Commons to be necessary owing to the time which has elapsed since the date of the former Bill, or to represent any

amendments which have been made by the House of Lords in the former Bill in the preceding session, and any amendments which are certified by the Speaker to have been made by the House of Lords in the second session and agreed to by the House of Commons shall be inserted in the Bill as presented for Royal Assent in pursuance of this section:

Provided that the House of Commons may, if they think fit, on the passage of such a Bill through the House in the second session, suggest any further amendments without inserting the amendments in the Bill, and any such suggested amendments shall be considered by the House of Lords, and, if agreed to by that House, shall be treated as amendments made by the House of Lords and agreed to by the House of Commons; but the exercise of this power by the House of Commons shall not affect the operation of this section in the event of the Bill being rejected by the House of Lords.

3. Any certificate of the Speaker of the House of Commons given under this Act shall be conclusive for all purposes, and shall not be questioned in any court of law.

4.—(1) In every Bill presented to His Majesty under the preceding provisions of this Act, the words of enactment shall be as follows, that is to say:—

> 'Be it enacted by the King's most Excellent Majesty, by and with the advice and consent of the Commons in this present Parliament assembled, in accordance with the provisions of the Parliament Acts, 1911 and 1949, and by authority of the same, as follows.'

(2) Any alteration of a Bill necessary to give effect to this section shall not be deemed to be an amendment of the Bill.

5. In this Act the expression 'Public Bill' does not include any Bill for confirming a Provisional Order.

6. Nothing in this Act shall diminish or qualify the existing rights and privileges of the House of Commons.

7. Five years shall be substituted for seven years as the time fixed for the maximum duration of Parliament under the Septennial Act, 1715.

8. This Act may be cited as the Parliament Act, 1911.

[Parliament Act 1911, ss. 1 to 8, as amended by the Parliament Act 1949, s. 1 and the National Loans Act 1968, s. 1(5).]

## 2. GOVERNMENT LEGISLATIVE DEFEATS

| Government | Number of Lords' legislative defeats |
|---|---|
| Labour 1964–70 | 116 |
| Conservative 1970–74 | 26 |
| Labour 1974–79 | 355 |
| Conservative 1979–86 | 100 |

[Sources: Brigid Hadfield, 'Whether or Whither the House of Lords?' (1984) 35 *Northern Ireland Legal Quarterly* 313; Journal and Information Office, House of Lords.]

## 3. 'THE SALISBURY RULES'

Cranborne [Leader of the House of Lords] reckoned that it was not the duty of the House of Lords to make our system of government inoperable. Nor, he considered, was it justified that the Opposition peers should use their voting strength to wreck any measure which the Government had made plain at a General Election that they proposed to introduce. He thus evolved guidelines, now unofficially known as the Salisbury Rules, which meant that the Lords should, if they saw fit, amend, but should not destroy or alter beyond recognition, any Bill on which the country had, by implication, given its verdict. The Lords, in other words, should not frustrate the declared will of the people.

I doubt if this amounted to a formal constitutional doctrine but as a way of behaving it seemed to be very sensible, and Cranborne's conduct of Opposition was exemplary. He had the confidence of the entire party, he dominated the House however distinguished its membership, he was wise, encouraging, clever and kind: he taught me most of whatever I've learned in politics. His parliamentary problem, of course, was that he had to give his followers a taste of blood from time to time. Many of us might feel deeply about some particular measure, which it was within our constitutional power to amend beyond repair or delay to a degree we knew could make a nonsense of Government administration. Cranborne had to allow some robust words and tactics, but still retain sufficient control to prevent the passing by the Opposition of 'wrecking' amendments—as opposed to those which could perhaps draw a good deal of the poison from a Bill without seeming to destroy it utterly. There was, of course, argument about what constituted a wrecking amendment and what did not: but, by and large, the Salisbury strategy worked and the Salisbury convention—of no wrecking amendments—was observed. To this day the convention continues that the House of Lords may amend but does not reject Bills on matters of formal and declared Government policy which have received a second reading in the Commons. Later in life I applied the same convention myself. I owed it to Cranborne. And in leading us in those days Bobbety Cranborne was brilliantly supported by his second-in-command, Philip Swinton, one of the ablest men I have ever known . . .

But my principal responsibility during these years of Shadow Cabinet and Opposition in the 1960s was to lead the Tory peers, and from the first I remembered and appreciated the example set me during my parliamentary novitiate by Bobbety Salisbury, and tried to follow the same broad principles. To lead the Tories in the Lords when there was a Conservative Government was a comparatively simple matter at that time, although there would always be some dissidents, or some who thought our policy inadequately robust. To lead them in Opposition, when they had a majority in the House and strongly objected to many of the Labour Government's measures, needed more delicate handling. Of course there was plenty of straight politics with little difficulty in producing a united party. The Prime Minister, Wilson, began by taking an attitude towards the Polaris project—that our nuclear armoury should not and would not be truly independent because of the American provenance of some of it—which I knew to be nonsense in logic and reckoned (and said) was a viewpoint advanced to placate the left wing of his own party, like much else. If we chose, our deterrent force would be entirely independent, because we would command and control it. But many issues were more controversial on our side.

I tried to apply the Salisbury Convention: and, like Salisbury, I found the greatest difficulty lay in striking a proper balance between, on the one hand, giving my troops a taste of battle, allowing enough uninhibited passion to find voice; and, on the other hand, keeping them sufficiently minded that it was not our job to provoke a constitutional crisis, that the House of Commons had been elected by the people, that the Government had a majority in that House and that Government must go on. Both sides of the balance were necessary. We had to behave responsibly; but I couldn't expect our supporters to lie down and be silent when something to which they took strong and principled objection was being proposed. Plenty of them felt that their right and their duty was to protest; and they could protest both with their voices and with their votes. The former need not be discouraged, but the latter needed handling. On the whole, matters went tolerably well.

[Lord Carrington, *Reflect on Things Past* (London, 1988), 77–8, 203–4.]

## The Parliament (No. 2) Bill

*The last government attempt to reform the House of Lords was contained in the Parliament (No. 2) Bill 1968–9. It was, however, withdrawn because of hostility to it from government and Opposition M.P.s. It is reproduced in full here as one coherent model of possible reform of the House of Lords.*

A

# BILL

TO

Amend the law relating to the composition and powers of the House of Lords; to make related provision as to the parliamentary franchise and qualification; and for purposes connected therewith.

Whereas it is expedient to make further provision with respect to the composition and powers of the House of Lords, and in particular to exclude from membership of that House persons not already members thereof who are peers by virtue only of succession to a hereditary peerage; to establish within the House a body of voting members exclusively entitled to participate in decisions relating to legislation and other matters, being qualified in that behalf by virtue of their attendance to the business of Parliament or by their official position; to reduce the number of the Lords Spiritual in the House; to substitute for section 2 of the Parliament Act 1911 as amended new provisions limiting the power of the House to prevent or delay the enactment of Bills passed by the House of Commons; and to secure the predominance of the House of Commons in case of disagreement between the two Houses in respect of subordinate legislation:

And whereas proposals for the purposes aforesaid were presented to Parliament by Command of Her Majesty on 1st November 1968, together with proposals (to which effect would properly be given by means of the exercise of Her Majesty's Prerogative in respect of the creation of new peers) designed to secure—

(*a*) the preservation within the said body of voting members of the reformed House of Lords of a proper balance between members adhering to the party of Her Majesty's Government, members adhering to other parties and members adhering to no party; and

(*b*) the inclusion in that House, and in the said body of voting members, of suitable numbers of peers with knowledge of and experience in matters of special concern to the various countries, nations and regions of the United Kingdom:

Be it therefore enacted by the Queen's most Excellent Majesty, by and with the advice and consent of the Lords Spiritual and Temporal, and Commons, in this present Parliament assembled, and by the authority of the same, as follows:—

*Composition of the House of Lords*

1.—(1) Except as provided by subsection (2) below, the holder by succession of a hereditary peerage, whether in the peerage of England, Scotland, Great Britain or the United Kingdom, shall not in right of that peerage receive a writ of summons to attend the House of Lords in any Parliament summoned after the commencement of this Act.

(2) Subsection (1) of this section shall not affect the right to receive writs of summons to attend the House of Lords of any holder by succession of a hereditary peerage who

(*a*) had received such a writ in right of that peerage at any time before the date of the commencement of this Act; or

(*b*) being qualified at that date to receive such a writ, had applied for it before that date or applies for it within six months thereafter.

(3) For the purposes of this section a notice in writing given by a peer to the Lord Chancellor that he intends to apply for a writ shall be treated as an application for the writ.

(4) Any holder of a hereditary peerage to whom subsection (2) of this section applies may, by notice in writing given to the Lord Chancellor within one year after the commencement of this Act, disclaim his membership of the House of Lords; and thereupon the said subsection (2) shall cease to apply to him and any writ of summons to attend that House previously issued to him shall cease to have effect.

2.—(1) In any Parliament summoned after the commencement of this Act, the House of Lords shall be composed of members possessing full voting rights (in this Act referred to as voting peers) and other members; and the voting peers shall consist only of those peers of first creation who are qualified as such under the following provisions of this Act.

(2) A peer who is not a voting peer shall not be qualified to vote—

(*a*) on any question to be determined by the House (including any Committee of the whole House); or

(*b*) as a member of any Committee for the consideration of any Bill or Measure or of any instrument or draft instrument to which section 14 or section 15 of this Act applies.

(3) In this section 'vote' means to give voice upon question put or take part in a division.

(4) Nothing in this section affects the right of any peer to move any motion or to take part, otherwise than by vote, in any proceedings of the House or any Committee of the House.

3.—(1) A peer of first creation shall be qualified as a voting peer in any Parliament summoned after the commencement of this Act if he has deposited with the Lord Chancellor in respect of that Parliament a voting declaration (that is, a declaration in writing that he wishes to be so qualified), and that declaration is for the time being in force.

(2) A voting declaration duly deposited in accordance with this section shall, unless previously withdrawn, continue in force until the dissolution of the Parliament to which it relates.

(3) A voting declaration in respect of any Parliament summoned after such date as Her Majesty may prescribe by Order in Council (being an Order of which a draft has been laid before Parliament and approved by resolution of each House) shall not be deposited by a peer who had attained the age of seventy-two years before the dissolution of the last previous Parliament.

(4) A voting declaration in respect of a Parliament shall not be deposited by any peer after the end of the period of one month from the issue of the writ summoning him to attend the House in that Parliament, or such extended period as the House may for special reasons allow.

(5) A voting declaration deposited by a peer in respect of any Parliament may at any time be withdrawn by notice in writing given by him to the Lord Chancellor.

4.—(1) Subject to the provisions of this section, if a peer who has deposited a voting declaration in respect of any Parliament fails to comply with the minimum attendance requirement in any Session of that Parliament, he shall be treated as having withdrawn that declaration at the end of that Session.

(2) The minimum attendance requirement in any Session is attendance at the sittings of the House (or sittings of Committees of the House) on a number of days equal to not less than one-third of the total number of days on which the House meets during the Session (other than days on which it meets for judicial business only): but in calculating that total number there shall be disregarded—

(*a*) in the case of a peer created after the commencement of the Session, any days before the issue of the writ summoning him to attend the House;

(*b*) in the case of a peer who, at any time during the Session, is absent with the leave of the House on account of ill-health or of Parliamentary or other public business, or is disqualified to sit in the House, any days when he is so absent or disqualified.

(3) Leave of absence for the purposes of paragraph (*b*) of subsection (2) of this section may be given either before, during or after the period for which it is given, and either before or after the end of the Session to which it relates.

(4) Subsection (1) of this section shall not apply in relation to any

Session of Parliament in which the number of days on which the House of Lords meets as aforesaid is less than thirty.

(5) For the purposes of this section attendance on a day on which the House sits until after midnight shall be treated as attendance on one day only.

5.—(1) A peer of first creation who is for the time being the holder of an office to which this section applies, that is—

(*a*) any office in respect of which salary is payable under the Ministerial Salaries Consolidation Act 1965;

(*b*) any high judicial office within the meaning of the Appellate Jurisdiction Act 1876 as amended by section 5 of the Appellate Jurisdiction Act 1887

shall be qualified as a voting peer whether or not he is or could be so qualified by virtue of a voting declaration under the foregoing provisions of this Act.

(2) If any such peer ceases during a Parliament to be the holder of an office to which this section applies—

(*a*) he shall continue to be qualified as a voting peer until the end of the Session then current; and

(*b*) he may (subject to subsection (3) of section 3 of this Act) deposit a voting declaration or further voting declaration in respect of that Parliament within one month after the opening of the next Session or within such extended period as the House may for special reasons allow.

(3) Without prejudice to subsection (1) of this section, any peer of first creation who is one of the Lords of Appeal within the meaning of the Appellate Jurisdiction Act 1876 shall be qualified as a voting peer for the purposes of any judicial business.

6.—(1) The number of Lords Spiritual who are Lords of Parliament shall be progressively reduced, as provided by subsection (2) of this section, from twenty-six to sixteen.

(2) Of the next twenty vacancies among the Lords Spiritual who are Lords of Parliament which arise after the commencement of this Act on the avoidance of sees other than those of Canterbury, York, London, Durham and Winchester, only ten shall be supplied pursuant to section 5 of the Bishoprics Act 1878; and the vacancies to be so supplied shall be the second of each two which so arise.

(3) The bishop of any see other than those of Canterbury, York, London, Durham and Winchester may, by notice in writing given to

the Lord Chancellor, disclaim for himself the right to sit as a Lord of Parliament as such; and where such notice is given—

(*a*) if at the time of the notice the bishop is one of the Lords of Parliament, section 5 of the Bishoprics Act 1878 as amended by this section shall apply as if the see were avoided by his retirement;

(*b*) whether or not he is then one of the Lords of Parliament, he shall be left out of account for the purpose of supplying pursuant to that section any vacancy among the Lords Spiritual which arises during his tenure of the see on the avoidance of any such see.

(4) Sections 2 to 4 and subsection (1) of section 5 of this Act shall apply to the Lords Spiritual who are Lords of Parliament as they apply to peers of first creation, and as if the sees of Canterbury, York, London, Durham and Winchester were offices to which the said section 5 applies.

7. A person who, by virtue of any process under the Mental Health Act 1959, the Mental Health (Scotland) Act 1960 or any other enactment, is liable to be detained on the ground (however formulated) that he is a person suffering from mental illness shall not be qualified, so long as he remains so liable, to sit or vote in or to receive writs of summons to attend the House of Lords.

*Legislative powers*

8.—(1) The next four sections of this Act shall apply to any public Bill which is passed by the House of Commons and sent up to the House of Lords, not being a Money Bill within the meaning of section 1 of the Parliament Act 1911 or a Bill containing any provision to extend the maximum duration of Parliament.

(2) In this section 'Public Bill' does not include a Bill to confirm a provisional order, but includes a Bill presented under section 6 of the Statutory Orders (Special Procedure) Act 1945.

(3) Section 2 of the Parliament Act 1911 shall cease to have effect.

9.—(1) If a Bill to which this section applies is disagreed to by the House of Lords, the House of Commons may, subject to the provisions of this section, resolve that the Bill be presented to Her Majesty for Her Royal Assent under this Act; and on the Royal Assent being signified the Bill shall become an Act of Parliament accordingly notwithstanding that the House of Lords have not consented to it.

(2) A resolution under this section for the presentation of a Bill for Royal Assent shall not be moved in the House of Commons until after the following period of delay, namely six calendar months from the day on which the Bill was disagreed to by the House of Lords or, if it was so disagreed to more than sixty parliamentary days after being sent to that House, from the last of those days.

(3) A resolution for the presentation of a Bill for Royal Assent under this section may be passed, and the Royal Assent may be signified accordingly, notwithstanding any prorogation or dissolution of Parliament during the period of delay: but in any such case the resolution shall not take effect unless passed within thirty parliamentary days after the end of the period of delay.

10.—(1) For the purposes of this Act a Bill shall be treated as disagreed to by the House of Lords in the following circumstances (and not otherwise) namely—

(*a*) if a motion for the rejection of the Bill is carried, or the motion that the Bill be read at any stage or passed is rejected or amended, by that House;

(*b*) if that House insist on any amendment of the Bill not agreed to by the House of Commons, or, having disagreed to an amendment made by the House of Commons on consideration of Lords' amendments, insist on their disagreement;

(*c*) if, at any time after the end of the period of sixty parliamentary days from the day on which the Bill was sent up to the House of Lords and within the Session in which it was so sent—

(i) any motion relevant to the progress of the Bill, made in that House by the peer in charge of the Bill and expressed to be made pursuant to this section, is rejected by that House; or

(ii) the House of Commons resolve, on a motion of which at least ten parliamentary days' notice has been given, that the Bill be treated for the purposes of this Act as disagreed to by the House of Lords.

(2) The date on which a Bill is disagreed to by the House of Lords within the meaning of this section shall be endorsed on the Bill by

the Clerk of the Parliaments or, if the Bill is then in the possession of the House of Commons, by the Clerk of that House; and on the expiration of the period of delay, the Bill shall, unless it is then in the possession of the House of Commons, be returned to that House.

11.—(1) Nothing in this Act shall prevent the taking, in the case of a Bill which is disagreed to within the meaning of the last foregoing section, of any proceeding which could otherwise lawfully be taken in either House, or the enactment otherwise than under section 9 of this Act of a Bill as agreed to by both Houses.

(2) Without prejudice to subsection (1) of this section, either House may, at any time during the period of delay and notwithstanding any intervening prorogation or dissolution of Parliament, propose to the other House amendments with which they would agree to the Bill; and if agreement is reached between both Houses in respect of those proposals—

(*a*) the period of delay shall thereupon expire and a resolution under the said section 9 for the presentation of the Bill for Royal Assent may be passed accordingly; and

(*b*) for the purposes of the Royal Assent pursuant to such a resolution the amendments shall be treated as amendments of the Bill made by the House of Lords and agreed to by the House of Commons.

12.—(1) The Bill to be presented to Her Majesty for Her Royal Assent pursuant to a resolution of the House of Commons under section 9 of this Act shall be the Bill as sent up to the House of Lords with the following amendments and no others, namely—

(*a*) any amendments made by the House of Lords and agreed to by the House of Commons (including any amendment treated as so made and agreed to under the last foregoing section);

(*b*) any amendments made by the House of Commons on consideration of Lords' amendments and agreed to by the House of Lords;

(*c*) such other amendments (if any) made by either House as may be specified in the resolution under the said section 9.

(2) When a Bill is presented to Her Majesty for Her Royal Assent pursuant to such a resolution, there shall be endorsed on the Bill the certificate of the Speaker of the House of Commons, signed

by him, that the provisions of this Act have been duly complied with; and any such certificate shall be conclusive for all purposes and shall not be called in question in any court of law.

(3) In every Bill so presented to Her Majesty, the words of enactment shall be as follows:

> 'Be it enacted by the Queen's Most Excellent Majesty in Parliament, pursuant to section 9 of the Parliament Act 1968, as follows'

and the alteration of the words of enactment to give effect to this subsection shall not be deemed to be an amendment of the Bill.

*Subordinate legislation*

13.—(1) The provisions of the next two sections of this Act shall have effect for securing that in cases where each House of Parliament has power, by passing or rejecting the appropriate resolution or motion, to control the making, coming into operation or continuance in force of an instrument laid or laid in draft before it, a decision of the House of Lords may be overruled by the House of Commons.

(2) References in the said provisions to the annulment or approval of an instrument or draft include references to the presentation to Her Majesty of an address to the like effect in relation to an instrument or draft, and references to resolutions or motions for annulment or approval shall be construed accordingly.

14.—(1) A resolution passed by the House of Lords pursuant to subsection (1) of section 5 of the Statutory Instruments Act 1946 (instruments subject to annulment by resolution of either House) or subsection (1) of section 6 of that Act (draft instruments subject to disapproval by resolution of either House) shall be of no effect until the end of whichever of the following periods expires later, namely—

(*a*) the period of forty days prescribed in subsection (1) of the said section 5 or section 6, as the case may be;

(*b*) the period of twenty parliamentary days from the date of the resolution.

(2) If during the period for which a resolution of the House of Lords is suspended as aforesaid a corresponding motion in respect of the instrument or draft is rejected by the House of Commons or

the instrument or draft is approved by resolution of that House, the resolution of the House of Lords shall be of no effect thereafter.

15.—(1) This section applies to any enactment, including any future enactment, which provides (by whatever form of words) that an Order in Council, order or other instrument of any description—

(*a*) may be made only after approval in draft by resolutions of each House of Parliament;

(*b*) shall not come into force unless or until approved by such resolutions; or

(*c*) shall cease to have effect at the end of a specified period unless so approved within that period.

(2) For the purposes of any enactment to which this section applies, an instrument or draft shall be treated as approved by resolution of each House of Parliament, notwithstanding that a motion for such approval is rejected by the House of Lords, if the instrument or draft had previously been approved by resolution of the House of Commons and that resolution is subsequently confirmed by that House.

(3) If in the case of an instrument falling within paragraph (*c*) of subsection (1) of this section a motion for approval is rejected by the House of Lords less than ten parliamentary days before the end of the period specified in the relevant enactment, that period shall be extended by virtue of this section until ten parliamentary days after the rejection.

(4) For the purposes of this section a motion for the approval of an instrument or draft shall be treated as rejected by the House of Lords if it is not passed within ten parliamentary days after the day on which it is moved and, in the case of an instrument falling within paragraph (*c*) of subsection (1) of this section, within the period referred to in that paragraph.

*Parliamentary franchise and qualification*

16. A person shall not be disqualified for voting at elections to the House of Commons—

(*a*) as being the holder of a peerage, whether or not he is entitled to receive writs of summons to attend the House of Lords as such; or

(*b*) as being one of the Lords Spiritual.

17. The holder of a peerage who is not entitled to receive writs of summons to attend the House of Lords shall not be disqualified as such for being, or being elected as, a member of the House of Commons.

*Supplemental*

18.—(1) In this Act the following expressions have the meanings hereby assigned to them, that is to say—

'Committee', in relation to the House of Lords, includes a committee composed of Members of that House and of the House of Commons;

'Enactment' includes an enactment of the Parliament of Northern Ireland;

'Judicial business' means proceedings falling within section 5 of the Appellate Jurisdiction Act 1876 as extended by any subsequent enactment;

'Parliamentary days' means—

(*a*) days on which either House meets (but disregarding any meeting of the House of Lords for judicial business only), and

(*b*) days comprised in any period when both Houses are adjourned if the number of days so comprised does not exceed four, and periods of parliamentary days shall be calculated accordingly;

'Peer' includes peeress, and 'peer of first creation' means the holder of a life peerage or the first holder of a hereditary peerage.

(2) In calculating for the purposes of this Act any period from or after a specified day or event, that day, or the day on which that event occurs, shall be excluded.

19.—(1) This Act shall come into force at the end of the Session of Parliament in which it is passed.

(2) For the purposes of this Act, the remaining Sessions of the present Parliament shall be treated as a separate Parliament summoned after the commencement of this Act; and in relation to that Parliament the reference in section 3(4) of this Act to the issue of the writ summoning a peer to attend the House of Lords shall be construed as a reference to the commencement of this Act.

(3) In relation to a peer who, immediately after the commencement of this Act, is disqualified to receive a writ of summons to attend the House of Lords—

(*a*) by virtue only of his adjudication in bankruptcy or the sequestration of his estate; or

(*b*) by virtue only of section 7 of this Act,

subsection (2) of section 1 of this Act shall apply as if for references in paragraph (*b*) to the date of the commencement of this Act there were substituted references to the date on which he ceases to be so disqualified.

20.—(1) This Act may be cited as the Parliament Act 1968.

(2) The enactments described in the Schedule to this Act (which include certain obsolete or unnecessary enactments relating to the House of Lords) are hereby repealed to the extent specified in column 3 of that Schedule.

[Schedule not reproduced.]

# [11]

# THE CONSTITUTIONAL POSITION OF THE JUDGES

## Appointment, Pay, and Promotion

### 1. APPOINTMENT

#### (1) LAY MAGISTRATES

6.—(1) Subject to the following provisions of this Act, justices of the peace for any commission area shall be appointed by the Lord Chancellor by instrument on behalf and in the name of Her Majesty, and a justice so appointed may be removed from office in like manner.

[Justices of the Peace Act 1979, s. 6(1), as replaced by the Administration of Justice Act 1982, s. 65.]

68.—(1) Sections 6 (1), 7 and 11 of this Act shall have effect in relation to the counties of Greater Manchester, Merseyside and Lancashire with the substitution, for any reference to the Lord Chancellor, of a reference to the Chancellor of the Duchy of Lancaster.

(2) In relation to the entry in or removal from the supplemental list of the name of a person who is a justice of the peace only for any of the counties of Greater Manchester, Merseyside and Lancashire, subsections (4) to (6) of section 8 and section 9 of this Act shall have effect respectively with the substitution, for any reference to the Lord Chancellor, of a reference to the Chancellor of the Duchy of Lancaster.

[Justices of the Peace Act 1979, s. 68.]

The Commission of the Peace is a document issued by the Crown setting out in very general terms the functions of the justices. There is one Commission for each county, each of five London commission areas and the City of London. Justices of the peace for any commission area are appointed in the name of the Queen by the Lord Chancellor, or, in Greater Manchester, Merseyside and Lancashire, by the Chancellor of the Duchy of Lancaster.

The only qualification for appointment laid down by statute is that the person resides in or within 15 miles of the commission area for which he is appointed. However, the booklet on 'The appointment and duties of Justices of the Peace in England and Wales' published on behalf of the Lord Chancellor, makes it clear that the following will not be appointed:

(a) a person over 60 years of age;
(b) a person convicted of certain offences, or subject to certain court orders;
(c) an undischarged bankrupt;
(d) a person whose sight or hearing is impaired, or who by reason of infirmity cannot carry out all the duties of a Justice;
(e) a serving member of Her Majesty's Forces; a member of the Police;
(f) a close relative of a person who is already a Justice on the same Bench.

The notes on the application/recommendation form state that certain other classes of person will not be appointed:

(g) a traffic warden;
(h) a close relative of a member of the local police force;
(i) an officer or servant of a magistrates' court in his own Petty Sessional Division;
(j) an M.P., adopted candidate or full-time political agent for the local constituency;
(k) 'a person, the nature of whose work is such that it would conflict, or clearly be incompatible with, the duties of a magistrate.'

The person must also be a British subject. There is no property qualification and women became eligible in 1919.

The Lord Chancellor's booklet states that justices: 'should be personally suitable in character, integrity and understanding . . . and . . . should be generally recognised as such by those among whom they live and work.'

They are appointed on the advice of Advisory Committees. These were first established following recommendations of the

Royal Commission on the Selection of Justices of the Peace of 1910 in response to complaints that the Benches were dominated by Conservatives.

There are about 100 committees, generally one for each non-metropolitan county and metropolitan district, the City of London, some of the larger urban areas and each London commission area. Most of the county committees have sub-committees or area panels. County committees are normally chaired by the Lord Lieutenant, the London Committees by Circuit judges. Most committees have eight to ten members, and sub-committees about six to eight. The term of office is normally six years. Appointments to a committee are made by the Lord Chancellor, usually after consulting the chairman. Members are almost invariably existing magistrates. Each committee has at least one Conservative and one Labour member; most have a Liberal, and some in Wales a member of Plaid Cymru. It is the practice to check with the party headquarters that they are known supporters. The names of the committee members are normally kept secret in order to keep them free from pressure and lobbying, although the name and address of the secretary is published. A candidate can be recommended to a committee by any person or organisation, or can put himself or herself forward. In turn, the recommendations of the committee can be rejected by the Lord Chancellor.

The main areas of difficulty have been those of politics and social background. The problems here are linked. The official position as to politics is stated in the Lord Chancellor's booklet: 'Political views are neither a qualification nor a disqualification for appointment as a Justice of the Peace. The Lord Chancellor, when making appointments, has regard to political affiliations only in order that he may ensure that no Bench becomes unduly overweighted in favour of any one political party.'

As regards politics, there have been a number of separate strands of thought. First, some people have been recommended for appointment as a reward for political services rather than because of their fitness for the office. This was condemned by the Royal Commissions of both 1910 and 1946–8. The latter noted that there were still 'political appointments' in this sense, although their extent could not be stated with precision.

Secondly, the 1910 Royal Commission stated unequivocally that 'it is not in the public interest that there should be an undue preponderance of Justices drawn from one political party.' It is not clear whether this was intended to refer to the position nationally or the composition of particular benches, but the latter view seems to be emphasised today. It was certainly the contemporary preponderance of Conservatives on the bench that led to the appointment of both the Royal Commissions of 1910 and 1946–8, by, respectively, a Liberal and a Labour government. However, overall statistics kept of political affiliation are largely based on the declared position of each justice at the time of appointment and are thus of limited reliability. There is no policy to maintain 'proportional representation' on the benches. Conversely, it is not at all unusual for the Lord Chancellor to refuse to accept recommendations because a certain party is under-represented.

Thirdly, the attention may be focused on the political affiliation of *new appointees*. This was emphasised by the 1946–8 Royal Commission, which stated that if after preliminary selection on merit:

> it is found that a considerable majority of the proposed new justices are of one political faith, the list should be revised with a view to seeing whether equally good, or better, nominations can be made from among members of political parties. If the answer is that they cannot, then the original list should stand.

Fourthly, some have argued that political opinions should be ignored entirely. This has, however, been regarded as impractical by successive Lord Chancellors.

[P. F. Smith and S. H. Bailey, *The Modern English Legal System* (London, 1984), 134–6.]

THE LORD CHANCELLOR: My Lords, as your Lordships know, the advisory committees are local organisations, and we have asked them to take steps to make themselves known. About half of the advisory committees for which I have responsibility—95 altogether—will have made their identity public by the end of this year. We have said that all should do so by 1992 for reasons unconnected with another important matter in 1992. On the Chancellor of the Duchy's committees, I understand that it is likely that they will start making themselves more public from the beginning of next year.

LORD CLEDWYN OF PENRHOS: My Lords, on the question of time, can the noble and learned Lord explain why such a long time is needed to publish? Why wait another three years?

THE LORD CHANCELLOR: My Lords, we consulted widely on this matter. We have encouraged local advisory committees to go public immediately. Many of them have done that. However, there are some people who took membership on local advisory committees under a regime when their identity was not public. We felt it right to go to 1992 in order to enable those people, if they wish, to retire from the committees, all of which will be constituted by 1992. I felt that it was reasonable to bring this in gradually. It is a voluntary matter. People have so far done it voluntarily. It will become compulsory by 1992. Those who have taken office on the committees on the understanding that their identity would not be revealed would have the option of retiring from their committee before it happens to their committee. That is, if there are people in that position.

All the indications I have are that this move has been generally welcomed, and I believe that the advisory committees themselves generally welcome it. I do not believe that many people will wish to take advantage of that option. However, in making the change, we thought that we should give people that opportunity; but we expressed the hope that they may be willing to have their names made public as soon as possible.

[Lord Mackay of Clashfern LC, 499 H.L. Deb. 1312 (20 July 1988).]

## (2) ACTING STIPENDIARY MAGISTRATES

13.—(1) It shall be lawful for Her Majesty to appoint a barrister or solicitor of not less than seven years' standing to be, during Her Majesty's pleasure, a whole-time stipendiary magistrate in any commission area or areas outside the inner London area and the City of London, and to appoint more than one such magistrate in the same area or areas.

(2) A person so appointed to be a magistrate in any commission area shall by virtue of his office be a justice of the peace for that area.

(3) Any appointment of a stipendiary magistrate under this section shall be of a person recommended to Her Majesty by the Lord Chancellor, and a stipendiary magistrate appointed under this

section shall not be removed from office except on the Lord Chancellor's recommendation.

(4) The number of stipendiary magistrates appointed under this section shall not at any time exceed forty or such larger number as Her Majesty may from time to time by Order in Council specify.

(5) Her Majesty shall not be recommended to make an Order in Council under subsection (4) above unless a draft of the Order has been laid before Parliament and approved by resolution of each House.

15.—(1) Where it appears to the Lord Chancellor that it is expedient to do so in order to avoid delays in the administration of justice in any commission area in which a stipendiary magistrate can be appointed under section 13 of this Act, the Lord Chancellor—

(*a*) may authorise any person qualified to be so appointed to act as a stipendiary magistrate in the area during such period (not exceeding three months at one time) as the Lord Chancellor thinks fit, or

(*b*) may require so to act any stipendiary magistrate appointed under that section in another commission area.

(2) While acting as a stipendiary magistrate in any commission area under subsection (1) above, a person shall have the same jurisdiction, powers and duties as if he had been appointed stipendiary magistrate in that area and were a justice of the peace for that area.

(3) The Lord Chancellor may, out of moneys provided by Parliament, pay to any person authorised to act under this section, not being a stipendiary magistrate, such remuneration as he may, with the approval of the Minister for the Civil Service, determine.

34.—(1) If it appears to the Lord Chancellor that it is expedient to do so in order to avoid delays in the administration of justice in the inner London area, he may authorise any person, who is a barrister or solicitor of not less than seven years' standing, to act as a metropolitan stipendiary magistrate during such period (not exceeding three months at any one time) as the Lord Chancellor thinks fit.

(2) All things required or authorised by law to be done by, to or before a metropolitan stipendiary magistrate may be done by, to or before any person acting as such in pursuance of this section.

[Justices of the Peace Act 1979, ss. 13, 15, 34.]

## (3) STIPENDIARY MAGISTRATES

31.—(1) Metropolitan stipendiary magistrates shall be appointed by Her Majesty, and Her Majesty shall from time to time appoint such number of persons as is necessary; but the number of metropolitan stipendiary magistrates shall not at any time exceed sixty or such larger number as Her Majesty may from time to time by Order in Council specify.

(2) A person shall not be qualified to be appointed a metropolitan stipendiary magistrate unless he is a barrister or solicitor of not less than seven years' standing.

(3) The Lord Chancellor shall designate one of the metropolitan stipendiary magistrates to be the chief metropolitan stipendiary magistrate.

(4) The following provisions shall apply to each metropolitan stipendiary magistrate, that is to say—

(*a*) he shall by virtue of his office be a justice of the peace for each of the London commission areas and for the counties of Essex, Hertfordshire, Kent and Surrey;

(*b*) he shall not during his continuance in office practise as a barrister or solicitor;

(*c*) he may be removed from office by the Lord Chancellor for inability or misbehaviour.

(5) A metropolitan stipendiary magistrate who is by virtue of his office a justice of the peace for any area mentioned in subsection (4) above shall not, by reason only of his being a justice of the peace for that area by virtue of that office, be qualified to be chosen under section 17 (1) of this Act as chairman or deputy chairman of the justices for a petty sessional division of that area or to vote under that subsection at the election of any such chairman or deputy chairman.

(6) Section 14 of this Act shall apply to metropolitan stipendiary magistrates as well as to other stipendiary magistrates in England or Wales.

(7) Her Majesty shall not be recommended to make an Order in Council under subsection (1) above unless a draft of the Order has been laid before Parliament and approved by resolution of each House.

[Justices of the Peace Act 1979, s. 31.]

*Qualifications*

Metropolitan Stipendiary Magistrates are appointed by The Queen on the recommendation of the Lord Chancellor to serve in the Inner London magistrates' courts. The statutory qualification is to be a barrister or solicitor of seven years' standing. In practice, the Lord Chancellor recommends candidates who have proved themselves as acting Stipendiaries in London over a period of not less than two or three years and who are over the age of 40. It is unusual for a candidate to be appointed much after the age of 55, the retirement age for the Metropolitan Bench being, at 70, two years lower than that of the Circuit Bench and most other judicial offices.

*Appointment*

Barristers and solicitors interested in being appointed to the Metropolitan Bench should apply to the Lord Chancellor. When vacancies occur, normally about two or three times a year, a short-list of applicants is prepared by the Lord Chancellor's Department in consultation with the Chief Magistrate from among those acting Stipendiaries who are considered to have the best prospect of appointment. The candidates are invited to an interview board, which includes the Chief Magistrate, and which then advises the Lord Chancellor.

*Provincial Stipendiary Magistrates*

There are relatively few Provincial Stipendiary Magistrates (14 at present) and vacancies occur only intermittently. When a full-time vacancy occurs, those acting Stipendiaries who have expressed an interest in an appointment in that part of the country, or in the provinces generally, will be asked if they wish to be considered and a short-list of candidates will be prepared for interview. The Lord Chancellor is unlikely in practice to recommend any candidate who has not had experience as an acting Stipendiary.

The procedure for the appointment of acting Stipendiaries and the selection of full-time Stipendiaries is similar to that for appointments in London.

[*Judicial Appointments* (Lord Chancellor's Department, 1986), 15–16.]

## (4) ASSISTANT RECORDERS

146. For section 24 of the Courts Act 1971 (deputy High Court and Circuit judges) there shall be substituted—

*Deputy Circuit judges and assistant Recorders*

24.—(1) If it appears to the Lord Chancellor that it is expedient as a temporary measure to make an appointment under this section in order to facilitate the disposal of business in the Crown Court or a county court or official referees' business in the High Court, he may—

(*a*) appoint to be a deputy Circuit judge, during such period or on such occasions as he thinks fit, any person who has held office as a judge of the Court of Appeal or of the High Court or as a Circuit judge; or

(*b*) appoint to be an assistant Recorder, during such period or on such occasions as he thinks fit, any barrister or solicitor of at least ten years' standing.

(2) Except as provided by subsection (3) below, during the period or on the occasions for which a deputy Circuit judge or assistant Recorder is appointed under this section he shall be treated for all purposes as, and accordingly may perform any of the functions of, a Circuit judge or a Recorder, as the case may be.

(3) A deputy Circuit judge appointed under this section shall not be treated as a Circuit judge for the purpose of any provision made by or under any enactment and relating to the appointment, retirement, removal or disqualification of Circuit judges, the tenure of office and oaths to be taken by such judges, or the remuneration, allowances or pensions of such judges; and section 21 of this Act shall not apply to an assistant Recorder appointed under this section.

Notwithstanding the expiry of any period for which a person is appointed under this section a deputy Circuit judge or an assistant Recorder, he may attend at the Crown Court or a county court or, as regards any official referees' business, at the High Court for the purpose of continuing to deal with, giving judgment in, or dealing with any ancillary matter relating to, any case which may have been begun before him when sitting as a deputy Circuit judge or an assistant Recorder, and for that purpose and for the purpose of any proceedings subsequent thereon he shall be treated as a Circuit judge or a Recorder, as the case may be.

(5) There shall be paid out of money provided by Parliament to deputy Circuit judges and assistant Recorders appointed under this section such remuneration and allowances as the Lord Chancellor may, with the approval of the Minister for the Civil Service, determine.

[Courts Act 1971, s. 24 as replaced by the Supreme Court Act 1981, s. 146.]

*Qualifications*

Assistant Recorders are appointed by the Lord Chancellor to sit part-time in the Crown Court and County Courts. The appointment can be made and terminated as the needs of the courts require. Assistant Recorders are therefore approved to sit generally, and are then usually appointed for short periodic terms to sit as needed by arrangement with the Circuit Administrator. The qualification for appointment is to be a barrister or solicitor of ten years' standing. In practice, the Lord Chancellor is looking for practitioners of at least 35 and below 50 years of age, who are of above-average ability and judged to be so by the professional community, are professionally and personally suitable to sit judicially, and who seem likely to qualify in due course for promotion to Recorderships.

*Applications*

As mentioned above, solicitors are required to apply for Assistant Recorderships; but it is not strictly necessary for barristers to do so since the annual review process covers every barrister of ten years' standing under the age of 50. However, it is helpful, and therefore sensible, for barristers to apply as well. Applicants are invited to complete a form giving factual information about themselves. Applications may be made by those who have reached the necessary age and standing to the Lord Chancellor's Department.

Once made, there is no particular time within which such applications can be decided upon. It may not be, and indeed typically is not, possible to give an immediate positive answer. It takes time, often several years, to build up enough information about a candidate to enable a decision to be made about whether he or she is not up to the required standard. But an applicant who asks how he stands will always be told as plainly as possible.

Candidates for Assistant Recorderships are not now normally approved to sit until they have been interviewed by a senior member of the Judicial Appointments Group.

First appointment as an Assistant Recorder happens when the Lord Chancellor is satisfied that the person in question is suitable, and the decision is not normally taken with reference to the candidate's age or seniority in relation to that of other candidates. This means that appointment does not always follow the order of age or strict professional seniority. This does not necessarily have any long-term career significance.

### *Training*

Those approved to sit as Assistant Recorders receive notification of the fact by a letter from the Circuit Administrator of their Circuit, which sets out the preliminary requirements regarding training which they must fulfil before they can begin sitting. These requirements are laid down by the Lord Chancellor, on the advice of the Judicial Studies Board. They differ according to whether the Assistant Recorder has been authorized to sit in both the Crown Court and the County Courts or, as the Lord Chancellor now allows in a minority of cases, to sit in the County Courts only. In the case of those authorized to sit in the Crown Court, the new Assistant Recorder is required, before undertaking any judicial sitting on his own, to attend an induction seminar organized by the Judicial Studies Board, and to sit on the Bench with a Circuit Judge in the Crown Court for at least a week, or more if necessary.

[*Judicial Appointments*, 10–12.]

## (5) RECORDERS

21.—(1) Her Majesty may from time to time appoint qualified persons, to be known as Recorders, to act as part-time judges of the Crown Court and to carry out such other judicial functions as may be conferred on them under this or any other enactment.

(2) Every appointment of a person to be a Recorder shall be of a person recommended to Her Majesty by the Lord Chancellor, and no person shall be qualified to be appointed a Recorder unless he is a barrister or solicitor of at least ten years' standing.

(3) The appointment of a person as a Recorder shall specify the term for which he is appointed and the frequency and duration of

the occasions during that term on which he will be required to be available to undertake the duties of a Recorder.

(4) Subject to subsection (5) below the Lord Chancellor may, with the agreement of the Recorder concerned, from time to time extend for such period as he thinks appropriate the term for which a Recorder is appointed.

(5) Neither the initial term for which a Recorder is appointed nor any extension of that term under subsection (4) above shall be such as to continue his appointment as a Recorder after the end of the completed year of service in which he attains the age of seventy-two.

(6) The Lord Chancellor may if he thinks fit terminate the appointment of a Recorder on the ground of incapacity or misbehaviour or of a failure to comply with any requirement specified under subsection (3) above in the terms of his appointment.

(7) There shall be paid to Recorders out of money provided by Parliament such remuneration and allowances as the Lord Chancellor may, with the approval of the Minister for the Civil Service, determine.

[Courts Act 1971, s. 21.]

### *Qualifications and terms of service*

Recorders are appointed by The Queen on the recommendation of the Lord Chancellor. The statutory qualification is to be a barrister or solicitor of ten years' standing. In addition, the Lord Chancellor will not now recommend the appointment of a Recorder unless he is at least 38 years of age and, as mentioned above, he has first proved himself as an Assistant Recorder. Recorders are normally appointed for a period of three years (sometimes rather more or less in their first term, in order to make their appointment terminate at the end of a calendar year). Their appointments are thereafter renewable by the Lord Chancellor, until the end of the completed year of appointment in which the Recorder attains the age of 72. Until then, though no Recorder has any right or guarantee of renewal, the Lord Chancellor will normally renew a Recorder's appointment for further terms of three years at a time, unless the Recorder's judicial performance is unsatisfactory or he has broken the terms of his appointment. The most important of these terms is the commitment given by every Recorder (save in a few exceptional cases) to make himself available to sit judicially for at least 20 days a year, of which at least ten days must be in one continual period. Recorders, like Assistant Recorders, are not normally allowed to sit for more than 50 days a year.

*Renewal of appointment*

Where the terms of the appointment have been kept, the Lord Chancellor decides not to renew a Recorder's appointment only when he is personally satisfied that the Recorder has failed to measure up to the standard required. Where possible, the Recorder is warned in advance of any cause for concern, so as to give him a chance to improve. However, this cannot always be done. And, if he considers it necessary in the public interest, the Lord Chancellor will direct that a serving Recorder is not to be asked to sit further.

[*Judicial Appointments*, 13.]

16.—(3) Subject to subsection (5) below, a stipendiary magistrate so appointed, sitting at a place appointed for the purpose, shall have power to do any act, and to exercise alone any jurisdiction, which can be done or exercised by two justices under any law, other than any law made, after the 2nd August 1858 which contains an express provision to the contrary; and all the provisions of any Act which are auxiliary to the jurisdiction exercisable by two justices of the peace shall apply also to the jurisdiction of such a stipendiary magistrate.

(4) Subsection (3) above shall apply to cases where the act or jurisdiction in question is expressly required to be done or exercised by justices sitting or acting in petty sessions as it applies to other cases; and any enactment authorising or requiring persons to be summoned or to appear at petty sessions shall in the like cases authorise or require persons to be summoned or to appear before such a stipendiary magistrate at the place appointed for his sitting.

33.—(1) In the inner London area the jurisdiction conferred on justices of the peace by any enactment, by their commission or by the common law shall be exercisable both by metropolitan stipendiary magistrates and by justices of the peace for that area who are not metropolitan stipendiary magistrates (hereafter in this Part of this Act referred to as 'lay justices').

(2) Metropolitan stipendiary magistrates shall continue to exercise the jurisdiction conferred on them as such by any enactment; and the inner London area (having taken the place of the metropolitan stipendiary courts area) shall continue to be the area for which magistrates' courts are to be held by metropolitan stipendiary magistrates.

(3) Lay justices for the inner London area may, in addition to exercising the jurisdiction mentioned in subsection (1) above, exercise the jurisdiction conferred on metropolitan stipendiary magistrates as such by any enactment except the following, that is to say—

(*a*) the Extradition Acts 1870 to 1935;

(*b*) section 28 of the Pilotage Act 1913 (which relates to appeals by pilots against certain actions of pilotage authorities);

(*c*) section 25 of the Children and Young Persons Act 1933 (restrictions on persons under 18 going abroad for the purpose of performing for profit); and

(*d*) the Fugitive Offenders Act 1967;

but a magistrates' court consisting of lay justices for the inner London area shall not by virtue of this subsection try an information summarily or hear a complaint except when composed of at least two justices.

(4) Without prejudice to subsection (1) above, subsections (3) to (5) of section 16 of this Act shall have effect in relation to a metropolitan stipendiary magistrate as they have effect in relation to a stipendiary magistrate appointed under section 13 of this Act.

[Justices of the Peace Act 1979, ss. 16(3), (4), 33.]

## (6) CIRCUIT JUDGES

16.—(1) Her Majesty may from time to time appoint as Circuit judges, to serve in the Crown Court and county courts and to carry out such other judicial functions as may be conferred on them under this or any other enactment, such qualified persons as may be recommended to Her by the Lord Chancellor.

(2) The maximum number of Circuit judges shall be such as may be determined from time to time by the Lord Chancellor with the concurrence of the Minister for the Civil Service.

(3) No person shall be qualified to be appointed a Circuit judge

unless he is a barrister of at least ten years' standing or a Recorder who has held that office for at least three years.

(4) Before recommending any person to Her Majesty for appointment as a Circuit judge, the Lord Chancellor shall take steps to satisfy himself that that person's health is satisfactory.

(5) The provisions of Part I of Schedule 2 to this Act shall have effect with respect to the appointment as Circuit judges of the holders of certain judicial offices, and the supplementary provisions in Part II of that Schedule shall have effect.

[Courts Act 1971, s. 16 as amended by the Administration of Justice Act 1977, s. 12.]

*Qualifications*

Circuit Judges are appointed by The Queen on the recommendation of the Lord Chancellor. The statutory qualification is to be a barrister of ten years' standing or to have been a Recorder for at least three years. (This second limb enables solicitors to qualify.) Candidates for appointment as Circuit Judges are normally expected to have proved themselves first by sitting as Assistant Recorders and Recorders. The Lord Chancellor will not normally recommend the appointment of a candidate who is under 45 or over about 62. Candidates are expected to apply for appointment, and it is helpful if they do so; but potential candidates are often approached first.

*Ability and experience*

The Lord Chancellor will not recommend an applicant for appointment as a Circuit Judge unless satisfied that he or she has not only attained a high standard of professional ability and experience, but is also suited by personal character and temperament. These alone are the criteria in choosing between applicants, and appointment is not affected by rank or branch of the profession. Queen's Counsel, members of the junior Bar and solicitors are all given equal consideration on their merits.

*Appointment*

Before considering a candidate for appointment, the Lord Chancellor requires him to have been interviewed at least once by a senior member of his staff. Among the matters on which he seeks information are the precise history, nature and size of the candidate's practice, his judicial experience, and his domestic and personal position so far as relevant. A serious candidate, actual or potential, will also be asked to have a separate meeting with the Circuit Administrator of the Circuit on which he would like to sit to discuss his likely initial places and pattern of sittings if he becomes a judge. In this connection, the Lord Chancellor needs to be satisfied that a candidate will, if appointed, live near enough to the main court centres at which he will sit. (This is normally interpreted as within one hour's travelling by car.) If the Lord Chancellor decides that the candidate is suitable for appointment to the Circuit Bench, he will authorize him to be sent a formal offer of appointment. This will include a brief description of the terms and conditions of service and of the requirements for medical examination. The Lord Chancellor's offer must be kept confidential until the appointment has been approved by The Queen and announced. Once it is announced the prospective judge can no longer, by the etiquette of the profession, appear as an advocate in court, though he may advise and do paperwork. There is normally only a short interval between the announcement and the new judge's swearing-in by the Lord Chancellor at the House of Lords.

[*Judicial Appointments*, 16–17.]

## (7) QUEEN'S COUNSEL

### *Timetable for applications*

Queen's Counsel are appointed by The Queen on the recommendation of the Lord Chancellor. There is a fixed annual timetable. An announcement is made in the newspapers and the professional journals about the beginning of October inviting applications from the Bar. A fresh application is required on each occasion, and application forms are not available until after the announcement has been made. The closing date for applications is specified in the announcement, and is about the middle of November. Every applicant is informed of the success or otherwise of his application, but not until just before Maundy Thursday in the following year, which is the date when, by tradition, the names of the new Silks are announced. They are sworn in by the Lord Chancellor on the first day of the Easter Term, which is normally the Tuesday week after Maundy Thursday.

### *Qualifications*

The Lord Chancellor will recommend the grant of Silk only to barristers of sufficient standing (normally at least ten years or more) whom he is satisfied have reached an appropriate level of professional eminence and distinction. Applicants must be British subjects, Commonwealth citizens or citizens of member states of the European Community. For the most part, Silk is granted only to practising members of the English Bar. The Lord Chancellor will also accept applications from employed barristers who have attained sufficient professional eminence and distinction, and have also made a significant and appropriate contribution to the public life of the profession, such as service to the Senate or the Inns of Court. In addition, the Lord Chancellor recommends the occasional grant of honorary Silk to barristers who have given distinguished service to the law in the public service or the academic world. Honorary Silk is granted by invitation and not on application.

### *Consultations*

After the closing date for applications, the Lord Chancellor arranges for extensive consultations to take place, first with the Leaders of the various sections of the Bar concerned, and then with the Presiding and equivalent judges with special knowledge and authority, all of whose opinions and views are studied by the Lord Chancellor. Before reaching final decisions about whom to recommend for Silk, the Lord Chancellor consults the Law Officers and the four heads of Divisions.

### *Numbers*

In considering the numbers of Silks to be appointed, the Lord Chancellor has regard, in the light of the public interest, to the needs of the various fields of practice into which the Bar is functionally divided. Depending on current demand, it may be desirable to recommend sometimes rather more, and sometimes rather fewer, Silks in each particular field. The Lord Chancellor is concerned to ensure that the ablest and most suitable candidates in a particular Circuit or specialisation are appointed to Silk. For this reason the number of existing or potential Silks in an applicant's set of Chambers is not normally a factor which the Lord Chancellor takes into consideration.

*Effect on judicial appointment*

The Lord Chancellor considers that Silk should be a working rank at the Bar, and not an immediate stepping-stone to judicial appointment. He therefore expects Queen's Counsel appointed from the practising Bar to practise as such for a reasonable period thereafter. His normal policy is not to consider them for full-time judicial appointments until they have been in Silk for at least two years.

[*Judicial Appointments*, 7–8.]

## (8) HIGH COURT JUDGES

10.—(2) Subject to the limits on numbers for the time being imposed by sections 2 (1) and 4 (1), Her Majesty may from time to time by letters patent appoint qualified persons as Lords Justices of Appeal or as puisne judges of the High Court.

(3) No person shall be qualified for appointment—

(*a*) as Lord Chief Justice, Master of the Rolls, President of the Family Division or Vice-Chancellor, unless he is qualified for appointment as a Lord Justice of Appeal or is a judge of the Court of Appeal;

(*b*) as a Lord Justice of Appeal, unless he is a barrister of at least fifteen years' standing or a judge of the High Court; or

(*c*) as a puisne judge of the High Court, unless he is a barrister of at least ten years' standing.

[Supreme Court Act 1981, s. 10(2), (3).]

4.—(1) The High Court shall consist of—

(*a*) the Lord Chancellor;

(*b*) the Lord Chief Justice;

(*c*) the President of the Family Division;

(*d*) the Vice-Chancellor; and

(*e*) not more than eighty puisne judges of that court.

(2) The puisne judges of the High Court shall be styled 'Justices of the High Court'.

(3) All the judges of the High Court shall, except where this Act expressly provides otherwise, have in all respects equal power, authority and jurisdiction.

(4) Her Majesty may by Order in Council from time to time amend subsection (1) so as to increase or further increase the maximum number of puisne judges of the High Court.

(5) No recommendation shall be made to Her Majesty in Council to make an Order under subsection (4) unless a draft of the Order has been laid before Parliament and approved by resolution of each House of Parliament.

(6) The High Court shall be taken to be duly constituted notwithstanding any vacancy in the office of Lord Chancellor, Lord Chief Justice, President of the Family Division or Vice-Chancellor.

[Supreme Court Act 1981, s. 4(1).]

*Qualifications*

High Court Judges are appointed by The Queen on the recommendation of the Lord Chancellor. The statutory qualification is to be a barrister of ten years' standing. In practice, High Court Judges are selected from the most eminent and able members of the Bar. They are, for the most part, leading Silks, except in the special case of Treasury Counsel. From time to time, appointments are also made by the promotion of Circuit Judges. Each appointment is made to fill a particular vacancy and is by invitation, so that it is not appropriate to apply. In every case, the Lord Chancellor personally reviews the field of choice in detail, in close consultation with the heads of Division and other senior members of the Judiciary.

[*Judicial Appointments*, 17.]

## (9) LORDS JUSTICES OF APPEAL

2.—(1) The Court of Appeal shall consist of ex-officio judges and not more than eighteen ordinary judges.

(2) The following shall be ex-officio judges of the Court of Appeal—

- (*a*) the Lord Chancellor;
- (*b*) any person who has been Lord Chancellor;
- (*c*) any Lord of Appeal in Ordinary who at the date of his appointment was, or was qualified for appointment as, an ordinary judge of the Court of Appeal or held an office within paragraphs (*d*) to (*g*);

(*d*) the Lord Chief Justice;
(*e*) the Master of the Rolls;
(*f*) the President of the Family Division; and
(*g*) the Vice-Chancellor;

but a person within paragraph (*b*) or (*c*) shall not be required to sit and act as a judge of the Court of Appeal unless at the Lord Chancellor's request he consents to do so.

(3) The ordinary judges of the Court of Appeal (including the vice-president, if any, of either division) shall be styled 'Lords Justices of Appeal'.

(4) Her Majesty may by Order in Council from time to time amend subsection (1) so as to increase or further increase the maximum number of ordinary judges of the Court of Appeal.

(5) No recommendation shall be made to Her Majesty in Council to make an Order under subsection (4) unless a draft of the Order has been laid before Parliament and approved by resolution of each House of Parliament.

10.—(2) Subject to the limits on numbers for the time being imposed by sections 2 (1) and 4 (1), Her Majesty may from time to time by letters patent appoint qualified persons as Lords Justices of Appeal or as puisne judges of the High Court.

(3) No person shall be qualified for appointment—

(*a*) as Lord Chief Justice, Master of the Rolls, President of the Family Division or Vice-Chancellor, unless he is qualified for appointment as a Lord Justice of Appeal or is a judge of the Court of Appeal;
(*b*) as a Lord Justice of Appeal, unless he is a barrister of at least fifteen years' standing or a judge of the High Court; or
(*c*) as a puisne judge of the High Court, unless he is a barrister of at least ten years' standing.

[Supreme Court Act 1981, ss. 2, 10(2), (3).]

## (10) LORDS OF APPEAL IN ORDINARY

For the purpose of aiding the House of Lords in the hearing and determination of appeals, Her Majesty may . . . by letters patent appoint . . . qualified persons to be Lords of Appeal in Ordinary . . .

A person shall not be qualified to be appointed by Her Majesty a Lord of Appeal in Ordinary unless he has been at or before the time of his appointment the holder for a period of not less than two years of some one or more of the offices in this Act described as high judicial offices, or has been at or before such time as aforesaid, for not less than fifteen years, a practising barrister in England or Ireland, or a practising advocate in Scotland.

Every Lord of Appeal in Ordinary shall hold his office during good behaviour, and shall continue to hold the same notwithstanding the demise of the Crown, but he may be removed from such office on the address of both Houses of Parliament.

. . .

Every Lord of Appeal in Ordinary, unless he is otherwise entitled to sit as a member of the House of Lords, shall by virtue and according to the date of his appointment be entitled during his life to rank as a Baron by such style as Her Majesty may be pleased to appoint, and shall . . . be entitled to a writ of summons to attend, and to sit and vote in the House of Lords; his dignity as a Lord of Parliament shall not descend to his heirs.

On any Lord of Appeal in Ordinary vacating his office, by death resignation or otherwise, Her Majesty may fill up the vacancy by the appointment of another qualified person.

A Lord of Appeal in Ordinary shall, if a Privy Councillor, be a member of the Judicial Committee of the Privy Council, and, subject to the due performance by a Lord of Appeal in Ordinary of his duties as to the hearing and determining of appeals in the House of Lords, it shall be his duty, being a Privy Councillor, to sit and act as a member of the Judicial Committee of the Privy Council.

25.—In this Act, if not inconsistent with the context, the following expressions have the meaning herein-after respectively assigned to them; that is to say,

'High judicial office' means any of the following offices; that is to say, The office of Lord Chancellor of Great Britain . . . or of Judge of one of Her Majesty's superior courts of Great Britain and Ireland:

'Superior courts of Great Britain and Ireland' means and includes—

As to England, Her Majesty's High Court of Justice and Her Majesty's Court of Appeal . . . and

As to Ireland, the superior courts of law and equity at Dublin; and

As to Scotland, the Court of Session . . .

[Appellate Jurisdiction Act 1876, ss. 6, 25.]

1.—(1) The maximum number—

(*a*) of Lords of Appeal in Ordinary shall be eleven . . .

[Administration of Justice Act 1968, s. 1.]

## 2. THE LORD CHANCELLOR'S POLICY ON APPOINTMENTS

This pamphlet outlines the Lord Chancellor's main policies and procedures in selecting candidates for professional judicial appointments in England and Wales and in recommending the appointment of Queen's Counsel. (It does not deal with lay Justices of the Peace.) It is not comprehensive and aims only to be an informal guide to the main points likely to be of interest to lawyers. The Lord Chancellor's Department will always be willing to give whatever further information it can in reply to individual inquiries.

The Lord Chancellor's policy is to appoint to every judicial post the candidate who appears to him to be the best qualified to fill it and to perform its duties, regardless of party, sex, religion or ethnic origin. Professional ability, experience, standing and integrity alone are the criteria, with the requirements that the candidate must be physically capable of carrying out the duties of the post, and not disqualified by any personal unsuitability.

The overriding consideration in the Lord Chancellor's approach is always the public interest in maintaining the quality of the Bench and confidence in its competence and independence. In any conflict, this consideration has to take precedence over all else. Subject however to that overriding consideration, the Lord Chancellor does his utmost to deal fairly and openly with individual candidates.

### *The Lord Chancellor's staff and their functions*

The Lord Chancellor's staff for this branch of his work consists, under his Permanent Secretary, of the Judicial Appointments Group of the Lord Chancellor's Department; and when this pamphlet refers to the Lord Chancellor's Department, it means the Judicial Appointments Group.

The Judicial Appointments Group is headed by a Deputy Secretary, and consists at present of two Assistant Solicitors and one Senior Legal Assistant, all of whom are legally-qualified, together with four Higher Executive Officers. The Group is divided into two Divisions. Judicial Appointments Division 1 deals with staff work on the appointment of Assistant Recorders, Recorders, Circuit and High Court Judges. Judicial Appointments Division 2 deals with Masters, Registrars, Stipendiary Magistrates and tribunal appointments. They have a small supporting staff, most of which comprises the Records Section. The address of all these officers is: Lord Chancellor's Department, House of Lords, London SW1A 0PW. Judicial Appointments Division 1 is also associated with the Secretariat of the Judicial Studies Board, which is headed by a Principal and is located at Thames House North, Millbank, London SW1P 4QE. (The appointment of lay Justices of the Peace, with which this pamphlet is not concerned, is dealt with by the Secretary of Commissions, whose address is also Thames House North, Millbank, London SW1P 4QE.)

Within the Department, the main function of the Judicial Appointments Group is to ensure that the Lord Chancellor has all the information and advice he needs in order to fulfil his responsibilities in this field. Their duties include corresponding with and interviewing barristers and solicitors who are, or may become, candidates for appointment, consulting judges and senior members of the profession, filing and recording the results, and taking and carrying out the Lord Chancellor's instructions and guidance, through the Permanent Secretary where necessary, both on individual appointments and candidates, and on his general policy. Broadly speaking, the Permanent Secretary and Deputy Secretary deal with appointments to the High Court and above; the Deputy Secretary with Queen's Counsel, the Circuit Bench (and equivalent tribunal appointments) and Recorderships; and the Assistant Solicitors and the Senior Legal Assistant with other appointments.

The Lord Chancellor also increasingly regards it as one of the functions of his Department to help members of the legal profession with 'career advice' in relation to appointments. Any barrister or solicitor of ten years' standing or more who would like to discuss his or her chances of an appointment, or what an appointment would involve, is welcome to write personally to the Deputy Secretary at the House of Lords. The address appears at the front of the booklet. He or one of his team will be glad to arrange to see the person concerned and to give him, in confidence, whatever advice they can about his position.

The Department aims to provide the Lord Chancellor with the material he needs for a fair and informed judgment about every appointment. To this end, its senior members obtain factual data from the candidate personally, and sometimes opinions from referees named by him. In the case of all permanent, and an increasing proportion of part-time, judicial appointments, they also interview him at least once and sometimes more often. They also seek to ascertain, by wider consultations, the views of the judicial and professional community about the candidate or candidates concerned.

*Guiding principles*

A guiding principle of the Lord Chancellor's approach is that, as far as possible, no one person's view about a candidate, whether positive or negative, should be regarded as decisive in itself, however authoritative or eminent the person giving it. By contrast, the independent view of a spread of observers and colleagues in a position to assess the candidate's work and personality over a sufficiently long time is treated as having great weight, especially if it reveals a consensus or a clear predominance of view. This approach is applied extensively in relation to the appointments of High Court and Circuit Judges and their associated part-time appointments, and to the appointment of Queen's Counsel. It is being progressively applied, as circumstances allow, to other appointments in the courts and tribunals.

Another guiding principle is that, as far as possible, candidates should be appointed to permanent judicial posts only when they have successfully prepared and proved themselves by experience in an associated part-time capacity. This is already fully applied to the Circuit Bench and to most of the lower judicial and tribunal appointments. The Lord Chancellor's intention is that it should be progressively applied to all other judicial appointments, including the High Court.

To enable the Lord Chancellor to apply these principles, the

Permanent and Deputy Secretaries undertake continuous consultations with judges and senior members of the profession. In particular, the Deputy Secretary follows an annual programme of reviews of appointments on each of the six Circuits, undertaken in consultation with the Presiding Judges, as well as co-ordinating the separate annual round of consultations about applications for Silk. The purpose of this is to enable the Lord Chancellor to gain a wide spread of advice from those who are well fitted to express views on the candidates' suitability for judicial office. The Lord Chancellor attaches particular importance to ensuring that the advice he receives is broadly based and is not derived from only a limited number of advisers.

[*Judicial Appointments*, pp. (iv), 2–3.]

It must be remembered that Lord Chancellors in making their appointments to the High Court have a relatively small group to select from. Effectively, the group consists of experienced barristers between the ages of forty-five and sixty and the number of genuine possibilities—the short list—may be as small as half a dozen.

[J. A. G. Griffith, *The Politics of the Judiciary* (London, 3rd edn., 1985), 24.]

However, much controversy surrounded the appointment of Sir Gordon Hewart as Lord Chief Justice. In 1921 it was arranged that Lord Reading C.J. was to become Viceroy of India. Hewart, as Attorney-General, pressed his claim to the position of Lord Chief Justice but could not be spared from the Commons. Lloyd George appointed a 77 year-old Queen's Bench judge, A. T. Lawrence J., on the understanding that he would retire when called upon, although neither Lord Birkenhead L.C. nor Hewart approved of the plan. Nevertheless, in 1922 Lord Trevethin (as Lawrence became) read of his own resignation in *The Times*, and Hewart duly succeeded him. To add injury to insult, Hewart proved to be 'perhaps the worst Lord Chief Justice of England since the seventeenth century. Although no imputation of corruption or dishonesty could be brought against him, as against Scroggs and Jeffreys, on the bench he rivalled them in arbitrary and unjudicial behaviour.' Since 1945 the position seems to have changed significantly. In 1946, Viscount Caldecote C.J. was succeeded by a Lord of Appeal, Lord Goddard, after the post had been declined by Sir Hartley

Shawcross, the Attorney-General. Lord Goddard and his successors have not had political careers. Lord Goddard was followed by Lord Parker, who subsequently commented that the non-political nature of the appointment, made clear by the appointments of Lord Goddard, himself and Lord Widgery, was of 'vital importance for the administration of justice in this country.' The only Law Officers subsequently appointed to the bench have been Lynn Ungoed-Thomas and Sir Jocelyn Simon, and only two of the others have become Lord Chancellor. The appointment of Lord Chief Justices from amongst the ranks of the judiciary has been generally welcomed.

It has become progressively more difficult to combine membership of the Commons with a successful practice at the Bar. Lord Hailsham has regretted that he was unable to appoint a single High Court judge from among MPs. There is something of a vicious circle in that the lack of a reasonable prospect of elevation to the Bench may discourage the ablest lawyers from seeking a political career. Political experience has been regarded by some as an asset for an appointee. Lord Simon has argued that:

> although no one would wish to see a predominantly political Bench, a seasoning of judges with experience of politics and administration is far from disadvantageous; constituency duties, for example, are calculated to develop a social awareness which ordinary forensic work is not apt to inculcate.

[Smith and Bailey, *Modern English Legal System*, 162–3.]

## 3. PAY

| Office | Current annual salary (£) |
|---|---|
| Lord of Appeal in Ordinary | 82,750 |
| Lord Justice of Appeal | 79,750 |
| Lord Chief Justice | 82,750 |
| Master of the Rolls | 82,750 |
| President, Family Division | 79,500 |
| Vice-Chancellor | 79,500 |
| High Court judge | 72,000 |
| Circuit judge | 48,100 |
| Stipendiary magistrate | 39,400 |

9.—(1) Subject to the following subsections, there shall be paid to—

(*a*) Lords of Appeal in Ordinary;
(*b*) judges of the Supreme Court in England and Wales other than the Lord Chancellor;
(*c*) judges of the Court of Session;
(*d*) judges of the Supreme Court in Northern Ireland;
(*e*) metropolitan stipendiary magistrates;
(*f*) stipendiary magistrates appointed under this Act;

such salaries as may be determined, with the consent of the Minister for the Civil Service, by the Lord Chancellor or, in the case of judges of the Court of Session, by the Secretary of State.

(2) Until otherwise determined under this section, there shall be paid to the holders of judicial office mentioned in paragraphs (*a*) to (*e*) of subsection (1) above the same salaries as at the coming into force of this section.

(3) Any salary payable under this section may be increased, but not reduced, by a determination or further determination under this section.

(4) The salary payable to any holder of judicial office under this section shall in each case be abated by the amount of any pension payable to him in respect of any public office in the United Kingdom or elsewhere to which he had previously been appointed or elected; but any abatement under this subsection shall be disregarded for the purposes of computing the pension payable to him in respect of that judicial office and any derivative benefit within the meaning of the Administration of Justice (Pensions) Act 1950 which depends upon eligibility for such a pension.

(5) Salaries payable under this section shall be charged on and paid out of the Consolidated Fund of the United Kingdom.

[Administration of Justice Act 1973, s. 9.]

12.—(1) Subject to subsections (2) and (3), there shall be paid to judges of the Supreme Court, other than the Lord Chancellor, such salaries as may be determined by the Lord Chancellor with the concurrence of the Minister for the Civil Service.

(2) Until otherwise determined under this section, there shall be paid to the judges mentioned in subsection (1) the same salaries as at the commencement of this Act.

(3) Any salary payable under this section may be increased, but not reduced, by a determination or further determination under this section.

(4) The salary payable to any holder of judicial office under this section shall in each case be abated by the amount of any pension payable to him in respect of any public office in the United Kingdom or elsewhere to which he had previously been appointed or elected; but any abatement under this subsection shall be disregarded for the purposes of computing the pension payable to him in respect of that judicial office and any derivative benefit within the meaning of Part II of the Judicial Pensions Act 1981 which depends upon eligibility for such a pension.

(5) Salaries payable under this section shall be charged on and paid out of the Consolidated Fund.

[Supreme Court Act 1981, s. 12.]

21.—(7) There shall be paid to Recorders out of money provided by Parliament such remuneration and allowances as the Lord Chancellor may, with the approval of the Minister for the Civil Service, determine.

[Courts Act 1971, ss. 21(7), 24 as replaced by the Supreme Court Act 1981, s. 146.]

## 4. PROMOTION

*As is clear from* Judicial Appointments *(see above, p. 564), there has been a judicial promotion system in place for some years. This proceeds from Assistant Recorder to Recorder to Circuit judge, and from Recorder to Circuit judge (and sometimes deputy High Court judge) to High Court judge, and from High Court judge to Lord Justice of Appeal to Lord of Appeal in Ordinary. Promotion carries with it a knighthood for a High Court judge, a Privy Councillorship for Lords Justices, and a life peerage for Lords of Appeal.*

## Judges and Parliament

### 1. JUDICIAL CRITICISM OF PARLIAMENT

*In the course of conducting cases judges may criticize both the technical form of legislation and the policy behind it—provided that this is done in a measured and responsible way. Judges may also be forthright in criticizing ministerial conduct, but they must obviously avoid taking sides in politically controversial issues in any way which would show them as favouring one political party. In the main judges stay well within these precepts.*

### 2. PARLIAMENTARY CRITICISM OF THE JUDICIARY

*Matters to be dealt with by a substantive motion*

Certain matters cannot be debated, except upon a substantive motion which admits of a distinct vote of the House. Amongst these . . . are the conduct of the sovereign, the heir to the throne or other members of the Royal Family, a Governor-General of an independent territory, the Lord Chancellor, the Speaker, the Chairman of Ways and Means, Members of either House of Parliament and judges of the superior courts of the United Kingdom, including persons holding the position of a judge, such as a judge in a court of bankruptcy and a county court, or a recorder. These matters cannot, therefore, be raised by way of amendment, or upon any motion for adjournment. For the same reason, no charge of a personal character can be raised, save upon a direct and substantive motion to that effect. No statement of that kind can, therefore be embodied in a notice to call the attention of the House to a stated matter.

Subject to the discretion of the Chair and to the right of the House to legislate on any matter or to discuss any matters of delegated legislation, matters awaiting the adjudication of a court of law should not be brought forward in debate.

Following the First Report of the Select Committee on Procedure, 1962–3, the House passed a resolution (23 July 1963) which set out the rule in detail. This resolution bars references in debate (as well as in motions, including motions for leave to bring in bills, and questions, including supplementary questions) to matters awaiting or under adjudication in all courts exercising a criminal jurisdiction from the moment the law is set in motion by a charge being made to the time when verdict and sentence have been announced, and again when notice of appeal is given until the appeal is decided; and in courts martial from when the charge is made until the sentence of the court has been confirmed and promulgated, and again when the convicted man petitions the Army Council, the Air Council, or the Board of Admiralty).

The resolution of 23 July 1963 also applies to the civil courts, and in general bars reference to matters awaiting or under adjudication in a civil court from the time that the case has been set down for trial or otherwise brought before the court, as for example by notice of motion for injunction; such matters may be referred to before such date unless it appears to the Chair that there is a real and substantial danger of prejudice to the trial of the case. The ban again applies from when notice of appeal is given until judgment is given.

On 28 June 1972 the House came to a further resolution, that notwithstanding the Resolution of 23 July 1963 and subject to the discretion of the Chair, reference may be made in questions, motions or debate to matters awaiting or under adjudication in all civil courts, in so far as such matters relate to a ministerial decision which cannot be challenged in court except on grounds of misdirection or bad faith, or concern issues of national importance such as the national economy, public order or the essentials of life; and that in exercising its discretion the Chair should not allow reference to such matters if it appears that there is a real and substantial danger of prejudice to the proceedings; and should have regard to the considerations set out in paragraphs 25 to 28 of the Fourth Report from the Select Committee on Procedure of session 1971–2. The restriction on reference in debate also applies in the case of any judicial body to which the House has expressly referred a specific matter for decision and report, from the time when the resolution of the House is passed, but ceases to have effect as soon as the report is laid before the House.

The Speaker has exercised his discretion to allow questions asking for a statement on or an inquiry into the circumstances surrounding a case which was the subject of a coroner's inquest. The Speaker has also exercised his discretion to allow a debate under SO

No. 20 to proceed when it seemed possible that civil proceedings in relation to the subject might be instituted. Deliberations of non-domestic courts, such as the courts of the European community, are not subject to the sub-judice rule.

[Erskine May, *Parliamentary Practice* (London, 21st edn., 1989), 377–9.]

## (1) MINISTERS' COMMENTS ON JUDGES

*Ministers and particularly Prime Ministers are usually only drawn into commenting on individual judges during Parliamentary Questions.*

LIEUT.-COLONEL SIR ARNOLD WILSON asked the Prime Minister whether his attention has been drawn to an article under the signature of Lord Hewart of Bury, as Lord Chief Justice of England and a signatory of the treaty of December, 1921, between Great Britain and Ireland, commenting upon and explaining the purport and possible effects of recent decisions of the Judicial Committee of the Privy Council announced on 6th June; and whether he will invite His Majesty's Judges voluntarily to apply to themselves the restrictions in respect of communications to the Press adopted by His Majesty's advisers and announced to this House on 3rd March, 1927, and which bind all civil servants?

THE PRIME MINISTER: My attention has been called to this article. I do not propose to communicate to His Majesty's Judges in the sense suggested by my hon. and gallant Friend. It is obviously undesirable that His Majesty's Judges should write for publication on matters of political controversy or on questions upon which they may have to decide judicially, but the limit of action in this respect must be left to the good sense of each individual Judge.

[303 H.C. Deb. 799 (24 June 1935).]

The Chief [Lord Hewart L.C.J.] believed it was his duty to help to unite a disunited nation in order to meet Hitler's threats, and had started to write newspaper articles again. But this time his themes were general and patriotic, and his brother-judges were not critical.

A few years before, at the request of Sir Emsley Carr, the editor, Hewart agreed to write a series for the *News of the World* on such controversial topics as 'Should a Man be Hanged?', 'Reform of the Law Courts,' 'Licensing Law Reform,' and 'The Meaning of Democracy.' The articles were to be paid for at the rate of £100 each, and Carr wrote, as one old newspaperman to another, that they would 'appear on the leader-page, in primer, and should extend to some 2000 words. If they are illustrated they will be by photographs in a very dignified and imposing manner.'

When the articles began to appear Hewart's colleagues adopted a censorious attitude, and argued that the Lord Chief Justice of England should not contribute to the Press, except on rare occasions, when a non-controversial article might be permitted. 'Ah, yes,' replied Hewart, when the subject was mentioned, 'but I write, not as Lord Chief Justice of England, but as a peer of the realm.' (On a previous occasion Hewart had made an after-dinner joke on his dual position, remarking that he could be as sober as a judge and at the same time as drunk as a lord.) 'Besides,' said the Chief, as an afterthought, 'I need the money.'

Hewart was a regular reader of the *News of the World*, and always asserted that his brother-judges took the newspaper to find out what sort of sentences they each imposed up and down the country. One Sunday morning, after attending a service at the Temple Church, Hewart approached a street newsagent's stand and asked for a copy of the newspaper. 'Not when you are out with me,' said Lady Hewart firmly. 'If you insist on reading the *News of the World* on the way home I shall get into another carriage.' The Chief agreed to read the newspaper at home, and later told the story to Sir Emsley, who reproached Lady Hewart. 'I thought you were a friend of mine, Jean.'

'Well,' said Lady Hewart, 'I am. But you must agree that a top-hat and the *News of the World* do not really go well together.'

Hewart was not serious when he said he needed the money for his articles. He was a wealthy man—his estate was proved at £150,947—who lived modestly and reacted violently to ostentation of any kind. During a discussion one evening on a new motor-car Lady Hewart remarked that they ought to be able to afford a Rolls-Royce. 'Yes,' said the Chief, 'we can afford a Rolls. If you really want one I will buy a Rolls. But remember this. Lots of the other judges not only cannot afford a Rolls, but cannot afford a car of any sort.

The last thing I want,' added Hewart, 'is to appear to be ostentatious.' The new car was not a Rolls.

[Robert Jackson, *The Chief: A Biography of Gordon Hewart* (1959), 327–8.]

Q1. MR PAGET asked the Prime Minister whether he is aware that there is concern that the holder of a high judicial office upon resignation or retirement may be offered paid employment in industry; and if he will consider introducing legislation prohibiting such transfers.

Q3. MR MASON asked the Prime Minister if he is aware that there is concern that highly placed civil servants upon retirement, and Ministers of the Crown following resignation, are quickly offered executive positions in industry and commerce; and if he will consider introducing legislation prohibiting these immediate transfers during a specified period.

Q5. MR LIPTON asked the Prime Minister if he will seek power to apply to ex-Ministers, who become directors of commercial undertakings with which their former Departments had business dealings, regulations similar to those governing senior civil servants taking comparable directorships on their retirement.

THE PRIME MINISTER (MR HAROLD MACMILLAN): I do not think that such legislation would be wise or necessary.

MR PAGET: Is the right hon. Gentleman aware that judicial pensions proportionate to Service men's pay are vastly higher than those of any other branch of the public service, and, in particular, that the Lord Chancellor, unlike any other Cabinet Minister, receives a pension of £5,000 a year precisely so that judges need not hang around their necks a 'For Hire' label? Does he consider it desirable for industry to be in a position to run its eye down the High Court Bench and decide whom it will buy? Does he think that justice appears to be done when judges might have appearing before them a potential employer who is in a position to quadruple their screw? Is not this a serious matter?

THE PRIME MINISTER: There are two points. First, I think that it is desirable and beneficial to the country that men of considerable experience should be available, when they leave the Government, to the service of industry and commerce. Secondly, I understood that Lord Kilmuir, like other Lord Chancellors, does not draw his pension while he is not fulfilling a judicial function.

MR MASON: Is the Prime Minister not aware that there has been widespread concern over a long period about this quick switch from Minister of the Crown to executive member, director or adviser of big business?

MR ROSS: Jobs for the boys.

MR MASON: This is especially so if the Ministers happen to have been in negotiations previously with the firm which they are joining. Is the Prime Minister not aware that Cabinet Ministers, with their intimate knowledge of forward Government thinking and their personal contacts in high places in the Civil Service and in the Government, are in big demand? Would he not therefore consider, even if he avoids legislation, whether there should be some introduction of either a higher code of conduct or a period of restraint so that this quick switch from Minister of the Crown to big business does not seem so unseemly and so connected with the previous office?

THE PRIME MINISTER: No, Sir. Dealing with the specific point, I know of no case in which the ex-Ministers concerned have been concerned with contracts or negotiations with the firms in question. As for the wider issue, I think that the hon. Member, like so many of his hon. Friends, is living rather in the past. He seems to expect that in future nobody will be able to enter public life unless he has a large private income.

MR LIPTON: Does not the Prime Minister appreciate that there has been some marked falling off recently in standards of conduct? Does he recall that when this House was considering in 1959 the Lord Chancellor's pension, Sir Jocelyn Simon, then Solicitor-General, said that it was not altogether in accordance with custom for an ex-Lord Chancellor to take an outside post?

MR SPEAKER: I do not know from what the hon. Member is quoting, but verbatim quotation in Questions is not allowed unless it is an exceptional case.

MR LIPTON: It was not a verbatim quotation, Mr Speaker, but the sense of what the Solicitor-General told the House on that occasion. In the light of these circumstances, is it not more and more crudely obvious that the Tory Party and big business are just one and the same thing?

THE PRIME MINISTER: No, Sir. I do not think that considerations relevant to what should be the pension of a Minister apply when the Minister in question does not draw the pension.

SIR R. NUGENT: Is my right hon. Friend aware that there have been many men from industry and commerce who have given valuable service in the House, on both sides of it and on both Front Benches and back benches, and that to place any restrictions on movement from industry and commerce or back again would be against the best interests of the country?

THE PRIME MINISTER: Yes, Sir. I find myself in complete agreement with my right hon. Friend.

MR GAITSKELL: Does the Prime Minister recall exactly what Sir Jocelyn Simon, when Solicitor-General, said on this subject when he was introducing the Judicial Pensions Bill? Is the right hon. Gentleman aware that Sir Jocelyn Simon said that there was a moral obligation upon an ex-Lord Chancellor to continue to preside over the Judicial Committee of the Privy Council and the House of Lords Law Lords? How can an ex-Lord Chancellor do this if he occupies a full-time post in industry? Can the Prime Minister give us any example of a former Lord Chancellor taking a post in industry, except that of Lord Birkenhead, and would he not agree that this was bitterly criticised at the time? The Prime Minister has accused us of being in the past, but is he aware that, with the exception of Lord Birkenhead, the conduct of ex-Ministers in the past was very much better than it is today?

THE PRIME MINISTER: Ex-Lord Chancellors in the eighteenth and nineteenth centuries no doubt accumulated in those periods of small taxation and high fees during their period of service very large capital resources. All that has changed. I think that it is not only fair but generally beneficial that there should be this interchange between industry and commerce in this way.

MR GAITSKELL: How can the Prime Minister defend the Judicial Pensions Bill, which specifically increased the pension of the Lord Chancellor in order to prevent this kind of thing happening? Is the right hon. Gentleman now saying to us that all that is nonsense, that all that is in the past, and that in future Lord Chancellors can take any job they like?

THE PRIME MINISTER: No, Sir. I am saying that the justification for the pension was that, if the Lord Chancellor was sitting as a judge—as a Law Lord or in other ways—although he was not obliged to do so, but so long as he had his health and strength, if he drew the pension and did nothing else, he was expected to sit as a Law Lord. In this case my noble Friend Lord Kilmuir, who is being attacked now—though why I do not understand—does not draw the pension.

[667 H.C. Deb. 999–1003 (20 November 1962).]

MR NELSON: Has my right hon. Friend seen reports today of the 12-month sentence, eight months of which have been suspended, which was passed at the Leeds crown court on a man who pleaded guilty to two charges of raping a girl who was only six years old? Does my right hon. Friend understand that most people will regard such a lenient sentence as wholly incomprehensible?

THE PRIME MINISTER: Yes, I do. Indeed, I am one such person. I have been in touch with the Lord Chancellor, as has my hon. Friend the Member for Sowerby (Mr Thompson), and he has called for all the papers on this case to ascertain the facts. As an interim measure the Lord Chancellor has given instructions to all circuit administrators that in no circumstances is a charge of rape to be listed for hearing except before one of the judges authorised to try murders or before a judge expressly approved by the presiding judge of the circuit. The Lord Chancellor fully supports the guidance given by the Lord Chief Justice to the effect that, except in wholly exceptional circumstances, rape always calls for an immediate custodial sentence and that the sentence must reflect the seriousness of the crime.

MR CHRISTOPHER PRICE: On a point of order, Mr Speaker—

MR SPEAKER: Order. I always stop questions at 3.30 pm, except when I have said that I shall allow extra time for a given reason.

MR PRICE: On a point of order, Mr Speaker. On several occasions in this House, I have been told by you that it is out of order to criticize a judge who has made a certain decision.

MR CANAVAN: So have I.

MR PRICE: Is that ruling simply to be applied in one case and not in another? If it is the ruling, it should be applied to everyone, including the Prime Minister.

MR SPEAKER: The hon. Gentleman is correct. I have from time to time ruled that a judge can be criticized only if there is a motion on the Order Paper.

MR CANAVAN: Throw her out then.

MR SPEAKER: I took the view that I did today because no judge was named. I do not know who it was. [Interruption.] The hon. Gentleman may be satisfied that he has outlined what is normally the correct position. [Interruption.] There is no point in pursuing the matter now. The question has been asked and answered.

MR CRYER: On a point of order, Mr Speaker. Over several weeks the Prime Minister appears to have deliberately misled the House in quoting the number of nuclear warheads on both sides. In fact, the figures are—

MR SPEAKER: Order. Points of order are not for that sort of thing.

MR FOOT: Further to that point of order raised by—

MR SPEAKER: Order. I just ruled that that was not a point of order. Perhaps I have misunderstood the right hon. Gentleman. Is the right hon. Gentleman referring to the criticism of the judge?

MR FOOT: In view of your reply, Mr Speaker, to my hon. Friend the Member for Lewisham West, (Mr Price) would it not be helpful to the House, both in this and in future instances—the name of the judge and knowledge of the case is in the possession of the House—for you to make a statement on this matter tomorrow so that we can see whether there has been a breach of our rules in this instance? That would guide the House in dealing with such questions in future.

MR SPEAKER: Order. There is no need to wait until tomorrow. The hon. Member for Lewisham West (Mr Price) drew my attention to a breach of our rules, which I said had taken place—[Interruption.] Order. The responsibility is mine. I allowed the question and therefore—[Interruption.] Order. I do not intend to speak against competition. I allowed the question. I believe I made a mistake, but I did allow it. Therefore, I can only say to the House that in future the rule will stand and be observed. I hope that that satisfies the House.

THE PRIME MINISTER: It may regularise the matter if, as the Leader of the Opposition and the hon. Member for Lewisham West (Mr

Price) appear to wish, I withdraw the use of the word 'incomprehensible' in connection with that prison sentence. That I do. With all due respect, I stand by the arrangements that the Lord Chancellor has made . . .

[34 H.C. Deb. 124–6 (14 December 1982).]

MR KINNOCK: On another type of inner city question, the 1985 insider dealing legislation made provision for two-year prison sentences. Does the Prime Minister think that a £25,000 fine and a suspended sentence is a punishment that adequately fits the crime?

THE PRIME MINISTER: The right hon. Gentleman is aware, as he indicated, that we were the first to make insider dealing a crime. The maximum penalty is two years' imprisonment, but there is a measure before the House that puts up the penalty to seven years. The right hon. Gentleman is also aware that it is Parliament's duty to ensure that the maximum penalty is available, but he knows full well that one is not able to comment on any particular sentence.

[118 H.C. Deb. 622 (2 July 1987).]

MR NORMAN TEBBIT (Chingford): On a point of order, Mr Speaker, arising from Prime Minister's questions. During Prime Minister's questions you very rightly prevented one of my hon. Friends from raising a question concerning the problems in another political party, saying—quite correctly—that they were not of course within the responsibility of the Prime Minister. May I therefore take your advice on exactly how you see the Prime Minister's responsibility for a particular sentence passed by a particular judge in a particular court, because you did, after all, allow a question to be put on that matter?

MR SPEAKER: It is not unusual for questions of that kind to be put to the Front Bench. I listened carefully to the Prime Minister's reply, as I listened carefully to the reply of the Leader of the House on exactly the same matter.

MR TEBBIT: Further to that point of order, Mr Speaker. I did not ask for your advice on whether such questions were or were not usual. I asked for your advice on what was the responsibility of the Prime Minister, which was being questioned.

MR SPEAKER: The right hon. Gentleman has been here for a long time. It is perfectly in order to criticize or to question a sentence; but it is not in order to criticize a judge. That has to be done by motion.

MR TEBBIT *rose*—

MR SPEAKER: Order. I do not think that I can help the right hon. Gentleman further.

MR TEBBIT: But I hope, Mr Speaker, that you will be able to help me because, as a Back Bencher, I would want to address questions to Ministers and I would want to be sure that, as I understand it, those questions might be addressed to a Minister, despite the fact that the Minister has no departmental responsibility and that there is no Government responsibility for the matter. Is that what you are telling me, Sir?

MR SPEAKER: I am telling the right hon. Gentleman what he knows very well: that in this Chamber, and in his presence when he was on the Front Bench, questions of this kind have been asked and have been answered.

MR D. N. CAMPBELL-SAVOURS (Workington): On a point of order, Mr Speaker. Will you confirm that in the past 12 months the Prime Minister has replied to and commented upon penalties that have been imposed?

MR SPEAKER: I have no more to say on the matter. The whole House knows the rules. It is not in order to criticize a judge. That must be done by motion. However, it has always been in order to comment upon sentences.

[118 H.C. Deb. 641 (2 July 1987).]

### (2) BACK-BENCHERS' COMMENTS ON JUDGES

Questions which reflect on the decision of a court of law are not in order. The Speaker has ruled privately that questions relating to a sentence passed by a judge, and to the circumstances under which rules of court were made and issued by the Lord Chancellor, were inadmissible.

[May, *Parliamentary Practice,* 344.]

MR SPEAKER: Before I call the right hon. Member for East Ham, North (Mr Prentice) to move the motion, I want to say this to the House. Certain inquiries and representations have been made to me about the scope of this debate. I do not in general believe in ruling upon hypothetical situations, but on this occasion however it might be helpful if I try to give some guidance.

Any Act of Parliament which the courts have to operate can be criticised as strongly as hon. or right hon. Members desire. It can be argued that a judge has made a mistake, that he was wrong, and the reasons for those contentions can be given, within certain limits.

I wonder whether I might read to the House what Lord Atkin, one of the great judges of this century, said some years ago on this subject. He said:

> But whether the authority and position of an individual judge, or the due administration of justice is concerned, no wrong is committed by any member of the public who exercises the ordinary right of criticising, in good faith, in private or public, the public act done in the seat of justice. The path of criticism is a public way, the wrong headed are permitted to err therein: provided that members of the public abstain from imputing improper motives to those taking part in the administration of justice, and are genuinely exercising a right of criticism, and not acting in malice or attempting to impair the administration of justice, they are immune. Justice is not a cloistered virtue: she must be allowed to suffer the scrutiny and respectful, even though outspoken, comments of ordinary men.

That is very much the attitude of mind with which the Chair will approach this debate. Reflections on the judge's character or motives cannot be made except on a motion. No charge of a personal nature can be raised except on a motion. Any suggestion that a judge should be dismissed can be made only on a motion. As for today's debate, the only motion that can be debated is that in the name of the Leader of the Opposition and his hon. and right hon. Friends.

[865 H.C. Deb. 1092 (4 December 1973).]

*In order to make their comments on judicial behaviour within the rules of debate, back-bench M.P.s put down early-day motions (see above p. 477). Although these are rarely debated, reference can be made to them during, for example, business questions each Thursday. M.P.s may also try to slip in their comments during a supplementary question.*

MR ROBERT PARRY: (Liverpool, Riverside): The Leader of the House will have seen early-day motion 112 concerning the imprisonment against strong medical advice of a young pregnant woman for a first-time minor offence. The baby is due to be born next week.

[*That this House deplores the decision of Judge John Edward Jones in rejecting an appeal against the three month prison sentence imposed on Paula Otemah, a 20-year-old pregnant woman; notes that Ms Otemah is 35 weeks pregnant and that according to the Senior Registrar in obstetrics and gynaecology at Liverpool Maternity Hospital is in danger of having an induced birth due to intrauterine growth retardation of the foetus; condemns the possibility of an innocent baby being born in prison; and calls upon the Home Secretary to order the release of this young woman, a first offender, on compassionate and humanitarian grounds and for the Lord Chancellor to put Judge John Edward Jones on the retired list forthwith.*]

Will the Leader of the House and his right hon. Friend the Home Secretary order the release of this young lady on compassionate grounds? Will he also ask the Lord Chancellor permanently to retire geriatric judges who are in their middle 70s?

MR WAKEHAM: I shall certainly refer the matter to my right hon. Friend the Home Secretary.

[120 H.C. Deb. 492 (23 July 1987).]

MR JEFFREY THOMAS: Does the Solicitor-General agree that many people fear that Lord Denning's judgment, which was made at the weekend, has hardly helped the matter? Many people also fear that that judgment will provide more explosive material in an already dangerous minefield. Lord Denning has made the law even more uncertain, and he is therefore bringing the law, and the rule of law, into disrepute. Will the Solicitor-General advise his noble Friend that, although hon. Members may have respected Lord Denning in the past, the time has now come for him to retire?

MR SPEAKER: Order. Such remarks should be made only when there is a motion on the Order Paper. Judges are not to be criticised unless there is a substantive motion before the House.

[977 H.C. Deb. 930 (28 January 1980).]

## (3) THE SUB JUDICE RULE

MR SPEAKER: Yesterday I was asked to give a ruling. The hon. Member for Lewisham West (Mr Price) made a considered submission to me on how the Chair should exercise its discretion in permitting reference to be made to matters that are *sub judice* before the civil courts, in the light of the resolution of the House on the Question of 28th June 1972. I now want to reply to the important issues that he raised.

In the first place, I draw attention to the fact that the resolution of 1972 is prefaced by the phrase 'subject to the discretion of the Chain'. This governs all that follows, and places upon me the responsibility of exercising my judgment in each particular case. The remainder of the resolution constitutes guidance by the House as to how it wishes me to exercise my discretion in certain classes of case. Of course I pay very close attention to that guidance.

I assure the hon. Gentleman that in the case with which he is particularly concerned I have considered whether the ministerial decision was one that could be challenged only on grounds of misdirection or of bad faith, and also whether the issues of national importance set out in the resolution of 1972 applied. I do not think that it would be helpful for me to seek to define those issues more closely than the resolution itself does, although the hon. Member invited me to do so.

I should like to say a word about the *sub judice* rule in general. It is, as the hon. Member quoted from the 1972 report, 'the fundamental responsibility of Parliament to be the supreme inquest of the nation with the overall responsibility to discuss anything it likes.'

It is to enable them to perform that function that hon. Members enjoy absolute privilege to speak in this Chamber without any court being able to question them.

It is also an important principle that Parliament shall not influence, or seem to be seeking to influence, the administration of justice. The *sub judice* rule is therefore a self-denying ordinance instituted by the House in order to protect that principle. The fact that newspapers sometimes feel free to comment on issues that are still *sub judice*, as the hon. Member remarked, is another matter, since the courts may deal with them for contempt, and their views do not carry with them the weight of having been delivered in Parliament.

Having made those general remarks, I assure the hon. Gentleman that I recognise that the resolution of 1972 constituted a deliberate relaxation by the House of the *sub judice* rule in the area of public policy; that it does go wider than the Industrial Relations Act; and that I shall exercise my discretion in favour of freer debate in every case in which I consider that I may properly do so.

The hon. Member and the hon. Member for Penistone (Mr Mendelson) made a final point about the freedom of Back Benchers to make submissions to me about the exercise of my discretion in particular cases. I assure them that I am always prepared to consider submissions—provided that they do not anticipate my decision by commenting on the matter that is awaiting judicial decision or contain comments that are out of order on other grounds.

In this particular case the hon. Member's object on Tuesday was to submit to me arguments that this particular issue did not fall within our rule on *sub judice* matters. Had he put forward his argument purely on the basis of the resolutions of the House and past precedents, as indeed he did yesterday, I would certainly have been prepared to hear him out. It was solely because, in my view, he began by reflecting on the courts that I intervened.

MR CHRISTOPHER PRICE: On a point of order, Mr Speaker. Thank you very much for that ruling, which has clarified the matter. The 1972 resolution mentioned, among other things, that you should take into account 'the essentials of life'. I asked you to rule on that, but I understand that you have not felt able to say what it means, just as previous Leaders of the House have not felt able to say what it means. I submit that it can cover social issues, such as the row we had earlier this week, which is continuing, as well as economic and national defence issues.

I very much hope that you would be willing to see the 1972 resolution in that wider context, which includes social issues, when using your proper discretion on this matter in future.

MR SPEAKER: I thank the hon. Member very much.

[916 H.C. Deb. 882–4 (29 July 1976).]

Resolved, that—

(1) notwithstanding the Resolution of 23rd July, 1963, and subject to the discretion of the Chair reference may be made in Questions, Motions or debate to matters awaiting or under adjudication in all civil courts, including the National Industrial Relations Court, insofar as such matters relate to a Ministerial decision which cannot be challenged in court except on grounds of misdirection or bad faith, or concern issues of national importance such as the national economy, public order or the essentials of life;

(2) in exercising its discretion the Chair should not allow reference to such matters if it appears that there is a real and substantial danger of prejudice to the proceedings; and should have regard to the considerations set out in Paragraphs 25 to 28 of the Fourth Report from the Select Committee on Procedure.

[839 H.C. Deb. 1627 (28 June 1972).]

MR SPEAKER: Order. I am bound by the resolutions of the House. Let me repeat the rule that matters are sub judice if they are awaiting trial, or under adjudication by any court exercising a criminal jurisdiction, and should not be referred to in any motion—including a motion for leave to bring in a Bill—in debate, or in questions to Ministers. I am bound by that resolution passed on 23 July 1963. If the House wants to change the resolutions, it is a matter for the House. I have already said that I am not prepared to exercise my discretion in this case.

[119 H.C. Deb. 708 (13 July 1987).]

## 3. LAW LORDS AS LEGISLATORS

*The Lord Chancellor, the Lords of Appeal in Ordinary, and other judges who are peers are both judges and legislators. This calls for tact and sensitivity by them, but has not prevented some trenchant interventions in the legislative House of Lords.*

But more dramatic and more political was Lord Salmon's contribution in 1975 to the debates on the government's controversial Trade Union and Labour Relations (Amendment) Bill. He said:

We cannot shut our eyes to the fact that there are groups, very small numerically but extremely cohesive and tenacious, who have infiltrated the unions with the intention of seizing power if they can. Their objects and ideas are entirely different from those of the trade unions, which we all know and respect. Their avowed purpose is to wreck the Social Contract and the democratic system under which we live. Their ethos derives from foreign lands where individual liberty is dead, and where the courts and trade unions are mere tools of the Executive, to do its will.

The argument is familiar—Lord Gordon-Walker said he had heard it for forty years—but, even more, it is a political argument. Lord Salmon clearly felt strongly and spoke in the name of freedom and democracy. He posed the question whether the disadvantage of a judge speaking on matters which in one form or another—such as unfair dismissal from employment or from a trade union—might well come before him when he was on the bench was outweighed by the advantage of hearing his views or by the argument that he should not be prevented, by convention or otherwise, from speaking in Parliament on such a matter.

[Griffith, *Politics of the Judiciary*, 47.]

LORD LANE (Lord Chief Justice): No doubt if the Lord Chancellor's Department had been left to its own devices it would have appreciated the position in which the judges find themselves; but the language of Chapter 1 of the Green paper [The Work and Organisation of the Legal Profession] betrays clearly the influences which have been at work. Such expressions as:

'a market providing legal services',
'the widest possible choice of cost-effective services',
'the discipline of the market',
and
'the discipline of competition',

are classic Department of Trade and Industry jargon. The expressions show that the draftsman has failed to realise that he is, or at least should be, dealing with complex human relationships, with standards of integrity, and with concepts of freedom which go far beyond the ideas of the market place, and its limitations, where the prime consideration is what is the best buy . . .

However, throughout the Green Paper and in the various situations with which it deals, the so-called Lord Chancellor's Advisory Committee on Legal Education and Conduct makes its appearance.

It is an ill-sorted conglomerate, comprising, *inter alia*, a majority of lay persons. It is expressly to be staffed by civil servants from the Lord Chancellor's own department. It will advise the Lord Chancellor. He will on some matters consult the judges; but one wonders how much or how little in practice that would in fact mean. This in short is an elaborate mechanism which threatens, whether intentionally or unintentionally, to give the civil servants control of who is to be the advocate, how he shall be educated, how he shall behave in court and indeed in what courts he shall appear. These are matters which up to now have been the province of the judges, acting in some instances through the intermediary of the Inns of Court. With all those powers in the hands of the executive, if these proposals become law, the one thing which at all costs must be avoided is likely to come about: and that is control by the executive of the principal means available to the ordinary citizen of controlling that same executive.

No doubt the fears which I have expressed will be pooh-poohed in some quarters: of course they will. But loss of freedom seldom happens overnight, as the experiences of the noble and learned Lord, Lord Elwyn-Jones, in Europe immediately after the war taught him. Oppression does not stand on the doorstep with a toothbrush moustache and a swastika armband. It creeps up insidiously; it creeps up step by step; and all of a sudden the unfortunate citizen realises that it has gone.

In some common law jurisdictions in other parts of the world with British-style systems of government, the administration of justice has indeed come under the heel of government. Judges there are no longer independent. The principle of the rule of law is observed so long as it suits the government and no longer. The private legal profession is bullied. We are told, and people say, 'Of course it couldn't happen here'. Could it not? The growth in the powers of the executive, and therefore of the Government, over the administration of justice has steadily increased in recent years. The signs are that it will extend still further, and one asks whether we are now seeing tools being fashioned which by some future, perhaps less scrupulous government may be used to weaken the independent administration of justice and so undermine the rule of law.

One may ask: to what purpose are all these proposals directed? They are populist proposals which inevitably will be applauded by the tabloid press, and have been. They do nothing to alleviate the popular complaints, and those popular complaints are two-fold: first of all, the expense of justice; and, secondly, the delays in justice. Indeed, the proposals which are made are likely in their effect to increase both.

If there are to be changes is it too much to ask that they should be made cautiously, leaving room to retreat if they prove unworkable or counter productive? Is it asking too much that the judges—that is to say, those people who have the task of operating any changes—should receive a little more courtesy and a little more consideration than has so far been extended to them? Much in this sphere can be done gradually by co-operation: nothing in this sphere can be done by confrontation.

[505 H.L. Deb. 1329–32 (7 April 1989).]

LORD DONALDSON OF LYMINGTON (Master of the Rolls): . . . As I am a serving judge and with so many noble Lords wishing to speak, I shall limit my contribution strictly to the effects which the Green Paper proposals would have upon the administration of justice in the courts. For centuries it has been axiomatic that judges must be wholly independent of the government of the day. That is something we all know and that Government accept. However, it is worth remembering why that situation is essential. All governments enjoy great power; all governments know that they know best; all governments, in seeking to further what they regard as the public interest, are tempted, through no doubt the most impeccable of motives, to ride roughshod over the rights of minorities who disagree with them. The record of the present Government is no better, even if it is no worse, than that of previous governments.

Those who find that their rights are threatened can appeal to the media and to public opinion. But, by definition, minorities—in particular, unpopular minorities—are not likely to have public opinion on their side. Alternatively they can appeal to Parliament either through a Member of this House or of the other place. However, the parliamentary timetable and the fact that a majority of Members support the Government limits the effectiveness of this remedy. In the end, their only real hope lies in the enforcement of their rights through the courts . . .

I say nothing about the dispute between the two branches of the profession with regard to rights of audience. Both branches of the legal profession and the Government seem to be agreed on the need for specialist advocates. The issue is simply whether the Government's proposals would produce this result more economically and without any sacrifice of quality. I do not know the answer and I am pretty sure that the Government do not either. It seems to me that we would do very much better to indulge in a little more research and a little less rhetoric. For my part I am loath to follow the Government in an irreversible plunge into the unknown. To follow them in an irreversible plunge into the known would be something different on which we could form a judgment—but not into the unknown, which I fear is the present position. However, despite all the thunder, that is not the real issue. The real issue is who shall prescribe the standards of education and training and the standards of professional conduct of those engaged at the heart of the administration of justice. Who shall decide who does what, and who shall supervise complaints procedures? The Government's answer is simply to say that the Government will do that and that they will do so by statutory instrument.

That approach was condemned by Lord Chief Justice Hewart in his book *The New Despotism* published exactly 60 years ago. He rightly described it as using the sovereignty of Parliament to frustrate the rule of law. In the present context it is, in my judgment, an affront to the constitutional doctrine of the separation of power. It spells dependence, not independence, for the legal profession as administrators of justice. That the effects may not be, and probably will not be, felt in the immediate future is absolutely no comfort. As that very great Scottish judge the late Lord Reid remarked in a case in this House, we have too often seen freedom disappear in other countries not only by *coup d'état* but by gradual erosion.

There is a better way and one which preserves the constitutional propriety. It is to have a legal profession which is bound by primary legislation to seek to achieve specific objects determined by Parliament; it is to give the judiciary statutory powers which will enable it to exercise greater supervision of both branches of the legal profession in so far as they are involved in the administration of justice; it is to establish a truly independent advisory body containing elements and representatives of all those concerned—consumers, lawyers, administrators, government—in fact, the lot; and it is to establish a truly independent advisory body which will point out to the profession and to the judiciary the respects in which the parliamentary objectives are not being achieved and to suggest remedies for any such failures.

In my judgment that is the way forward to better and cheaper justice and also constitutional justice. We are told that this is a listening government. I hope so. I hope that the Government will not misinterpret the moderate language used by many of your Lordships as indicating mild anxiety. My anxiety for the future of the rule of law, if the Government are given the powers they seek, is quite profound. It should not be necessary for me to spell out my message in the terms reportedly employed by a distinguished former Prime Minister to a distinguished former president of the AUEW. The former Prime Minister said: 'Get your tanks off my lawn'. But, if necessary, I shall say just that.

[505 H.L. Deb. 1365–69 (7 April 1989).]

## Extra-Judicial Activities

### 1. DISQUALIFICATION FROM THE HOUSE OF COMMONS

1.—(1) Subject to the provisions of this Act, a person is disqualified for membership of the House of Commons who for the time being—

(*a*) holds any of the judicial offices specified in Part I of Schedule 1 to this Act;

(*b*) is employed in the civil service of the Crown, whether in an established capacity or not, and whether for the whole or part of his time;

(*c*) is a member of any of the regular armed forces of the Crown;

(*d*) is a member of any police force maintained by a police authority;

(*e*) is a member of the legislature of any country or territory outside the Commonwealth; or

(*f*) holds any office described in Part II or Part III of Schedule 1.

(2) A person who for the time being holds any office described in Part IV of Schedule 1 is disqualified for membership of the House of

Commons for any constituency specified in relation to that office in the second column of Part IV.

(3) In this section—

'civil service of the Crown' includes the civil service of Northern Ireland, Her Majesty's Diplomatic Service and Her Majesty's Overseas Civil Service;

'police authority' means any police authority within the meaning of the Police Act 1964 or the Police (Scotland) Act 1967, or the Police Authority for Northern Ireland; and 'member' in relation to a police force means a person employed as a full-time constable;

'regular armed forces of the Crown' means the Royal Navy, the regular forces as defined by section 225 of the Army Act 1955, the regular air force as defined by section 223 of the Air Force Act 1955, the Women's Royal Naval Service, Queen Alexandra's Royal Naval Nursing Service and Voluntary Aid Detachments serving with the Royal Navy.

(4) Except as provided by this Act, a person shall not be disqualified for membership of the House of Commons by reason of his holding an office or place of profit under the Crown or any other office or place; and a person shall not be disqualified for appointment to or for holding any office or place by reason of his being a member of that House . . .

## SCHEDULE I

### OFFICES DISQUALIFYING FOR MEMBERSHIP

### Part I

*Judicial offices*

Judge of the High Court of Justice or Court of Appeal.
Judge of the Court of Session.
Judge of the High Court of Justice or Court of Appeal in Northern Ireland.
Judge of the Courts-Martial Appeal Court.
Chairman of the Scottish Land Court.
Circuit Judge.
Sheriff Principal or Sheriff (other than Honorary Sheriff appointed under the Sheriff Courts (Scotland) Act 1907, or Temporary Sheriff Principal or Temporary Sheriff appointed under the Sheriff Courts (Scotland) Act 1971.
County Court Judge or Temporary County Court Judge in Northern Ireland within the meaning of the Government of Ireland Act 1920, or the deputy of such a Judge.

Stipendiary Magistrate within the meaning of the Justices of the Peace Act 1949.
Stipendiary Magistrate in Scotland.
Resident Magistrate appointed under the Summary Jurisdiction and Criminal Justice Act (Northern Ireland) 1935 or the Magistrates' Courts Act (Northern Ireland) 1964.
Chief or other National Insurance Commissioner.
Chief or other National Insurance Commissioner for Northern Ireland.
Umpire or Deputy Umpire appointed for the purposes of section 43 of the National Service Act 1948.

[House of Commons Disqualification Act 1975, s. 1(1) and Schedule 1, Part I.]

*Assistant Recorders, Recorders and lay magistrates are not barred from being M.P.s.*

## 2. AVOIDANCE OF PARTY POLITICAL CONTROVERSY

Lord Hewart's name stirred political controversy again before the year was out, when a Liberal panel put forward his name as a member of the Ullswater Committee on Electoral Law Reform. It was a subject in which Hewart, in common with other Liberals, had taken an interest for years. Hewart had agreed to serve on the Committee five months before, and no one had raised objection. But when the members were announced publicly Baldwin, in the Commons, said he was surprised to see the name of a High Court judge on the Committee, and objected to Hewart's membership.

Baldwin was clearly uneasy when he spoke, and stressed the fact that, in voicing the Conservative Party's objection, he had no personal feelings against Hewart. 'No one has a greater admiration for Lord Hewart's character and attainments, and I have had the honour to enjoy his personal friendship for many years. It is not because Lord Hewart is Lord Hewart that I have any objection, but because I object to any member of the judicial bench being included on any committee where his selection depends on his office,' said Baldwin.

Lloyd George at once took personal responsibility for the Chief's nomination. He and his colleagues believed the Committee was to be entirely non-party, he said. Hewart was a constitutional authority who had a knowledge of the law and experience in the House of Commons, and it was felt that he would be a valuable member of the Committee. But Lloyd George had no desire to press Hewart's name, and produced a letter the Chief had written to him, expressing Hewart's great surprise at the Conservative attitude. It had never occurred to him, Hewart had written, that the Committee was a party one, or that the matter would be approached in a party spirit. However, the fact that this was the view of a responsible leader of one of the political parties satisfied him that the better course was to take no part in the work of the Committee. He proposed, therefore, to ask Lord Ullswater to release him.

In *The Times* next morning Hewart repeated his 'astonishment' at the objection to his name, and added a few tart words on his position as Lord Chief Justice in relation to public affairs:

> It would be quite wrong [he said] if anyone were . . . to imagine that I regard myself as being prevented by my judicial office from holding or expressing an opinion upon such a topic as Electoral Law Reform.
>
> Nothing, indeed, could be farther from the truth. More than one speaker in the discussion [in the Commons] appeared to think that where political questions arise my position is analogous to that of a High Court judge who has previously happened to be a member of the House of Commons.
>
> But the analogy entirely fails. These speakers apparently forget that, in addition to being Lord Chief Justice of England, I am also a peer of the United Kingdom, and in that capacity am summoned by writ, issued from the Crown Office, to be present in the House of Lords 'to treat and give Council' upon the affairs of the State. 'And this,' the writ from the Crown concludes, 'as you regard Us and our Honour and the safety and defence of the said United Kingdom and Church and dispatch of the said affairs in no wise do you omit!'

Hewart added pungent words which gave his critics points for reflection:

> These are not privileges to be enjoyed. They are responsibilities to be discharged. And I have not the smallest intention of handing on my office shorn of any of its duties or obligations, or of submitting whether by actual conduct or by passive acquiescence to any diminution of the rights exercised by my illustrious predecessors.

The occasion was soon forgotten, but Hewart was admired for his stand and the respect he showed for his office.

[Jackson, *The Chief: Gordon Hewart*, 216–17.]

Judges are frequently called on by the government to preside over royal commissions, departmental committees and inquiries conducted under the Tribunals of Inquiry (Evidence) Act 1921. From 1953 to 1973, not including judges who served on permanent committees for law reform, 79 such appointments were made. Many judges are well suited for this work but there are potential dangers to judicial independence in the practice, particularly when matters of acute political controversy are referred to a judge for an impartial opinion. Examples may be found in the inquiries by Lord Wilberforce in 1970 and 1972 into industrial disputes and in the regular use of judges (including Lords Radcliffe, Diplock and Bridge) to chair the Security Commission which investigates shortcomings in the work of British intelligence services. Particularly controversial references were the investigations conducted by Lord Denning on the request of the Prime Minister into the security aspects arising out of the resignation of a minister (J. Profumo) in 1963 and by the Lord Chief Justice, Lord Widgery, in 1972 into the Londonderry riot deaths. Such references may give rise to allegations that the government of the day is using the judiciary for its own ends; and they may expose the judge in question, particularly if he is the sole member of the inquiry, to political criticism by those who disagree with his report. It needs to be stressed that such work is not the primary task of the judges and that the government may not assume that the services of a judge will be available whenever an awkward political situation might be eased by an impartial inquiry.

While the government may invite judges to take part in inquiries into current problems, the political parties are not entitled to ask judges to assist them in the preparation of their policies.

In 1968, the leader of the Opposition, Mr Heath, appointed a committee to consider possible changes in the constitutional position of Scotland. Included in the committee, which was chaired by a former Conservative Prime Minister, Sir Alec Douglas-Home, was a judge of the Court of Session, Lord Avonside, nominated at the request of Mr Heath by the Lord President of the Court of Session. In the ensuing controversy, the Lord Advocate maintained that the nomination of a judge to this committee was in breach of 'a long-standing constitutional convention' by which the judiciary did not participate in the activities of a political party. When the Scottish National Party asked the Lord President to nominate a judge to serve on that party's constitutional committee, the Lord President declined. Lord Avonside thereupon resigned from the Douglas-Home committee, while denying that a judge in Scotland could be bound against his will to eschew party politics.

Despite the judge's assertions to the contrary, these unusual events reinforced the strong constitutional convention that a judge should not become involved in party political activities. All salaried judges are disqualified from membership of the Commons. While the Lords of Appeal in Ordinary and other senior judges are members of the House of Lords, they sit on the cross-benches and do not take part in the legislative work of the House as party supporters.

[Wade and Bradley, *Constitutional and Administrative Law* (London, 10th edn., 1985, by A. W. Bradley), 336–7.]

## 3. RULES ABOUT PRACTISING LAW

17.—(6) So long as he holds office as such, no Circuit judge shall practise as a barrister, or act for any remuneration to himself as arbitrator or referee, or be directly or indirectly concerned as a conveyancer, notary public or solicitor.

[Courts Act 1971, s. 17(6).]

31.—(4) . . .

(*b*) he [a metropolitan stipendiary magistrate] shall not during his continuance in office practise as a barrister or solicitor; . . .

[Justices of the Peace Act 1979, s. 31(4)(*b*).]

*Solicitors and barristers who are Recorders must comply with the Lord Chancellor's requirement that they do not appear as advocates in courts in which they sit judicially.*

38.—(1) Subject to the provisions of this section, it shall not be lawful for any solicitor who is one of the justices of the peace for any area, or for any partner of his, to act in connection with proceedings before any of those justices as solicitor or agent for the solicitor of any person concerned in those proceedings.

(2) Where the area for which a solicitor is a justice of the peace is divided into petty sessional divisions, his being a justice for the area shall not subject him or any partner of his to any disqualification

under this section in relation to proceedings before justices acting for a petty sessional division for which he does not ordinarily act.

(3) Where a solicitor is a justice of the peace for any area, that shall not subject him or any partner of his to any disqualification under this section if his name is entered in the supplemental list kept under section 1 of the Administration of Justice Act 1973.

(4) Where a solicitor is, as being Lord Mayor or alderman, a justice of the peace for the City of London, that shall not subject him or any partner of his to any disqualification under this section, if he is in accordance with section 1 (6) of the Administration of Justice Act 1973 excluded from the exercise of his functions as a justice for the City.

[Solicitors Act 1974, s. 38.]

## 4. THE KILMUIR RULES

Lord Chancellor's Office
House of Lords
London S.W.1

12th December, 1955

Dear Jacob,

On July 14 last you wrote to me about a project you had in mind for broadcasting a series of lectures in The Third Programme about great Judges of the past. I sent you an interim reply saying that while I was far from unsympathetic to the proposal I was obliged as Head of the Judiciary to give it critical examination, and that I should want to consult with some of my senior colleagues.

Since I wrote to you I have in fact given a great deal of thought to this matter. The Lord Chief Justice, the Master of the Rolls, and the President of the Probate, Divorce and Admiralty Division have been good enough to give me the benefit of their considered views, and what I write hereafter has their united approval.

It is, I think, agreed that there are positive advantages to the public when serious and important topics are dealt with through the medium of broadcasting by the highest authorities. We are likely, for example, to get a better assessment of the qualities of some eminent Judge of the past through an existing member of the Judiciary than from anyone else.

But the overriding consideration, in the opinion of myself and of my colleagues, is the importance of keeping the Judiciary in this country isolated from the controversies of the day. So long as a Judge keeps silent his reputation for wisdom and impartiality remains unassailable: but every utterance which he makes in public, except in the course of the actual performance of his judicial duties, must necessarily bring him within the focus of criticism. It would, moreover, be inappropriate for the Judiciary to be associated with any series of talks or anything which could be fairly interpreted as entertainment: and in no circumstances, of course, should a Judge take a fee in connection with a broadcast.

My colleagues and I, therefore, are agreed that as a general rule it is undesirable for members of the Judiciary to broadcast on the wireless or to appear on television. We recognise, however, that there may be occasions, for example charitable appeals, when no exception could be taken to a broadcast by a Judge. We consider that if Judges are approached by the broadcasting authorities with a request to take part in a broadcast on some special occasion, the Judge concerned ought to consult the Lord Chancellor, who would always be ready to express his opinion on the particular request.

The expression of views contained in the foregoing paragraph is subject to the important qualification that, as you are already aware, the Lord Chancellor has no sort of disciplinary jurisdiction over Her Majesty's Judges, each of whom, if asked to broadcast, would have to decide for himself whether he considered it compatible with his office to accept.

I am sorry to think that the foregoing expression of my views and those of my senior colleagues will be a disappointment to you. As I said before, I am by no means unsympathetic to the proposal you have made to me which, as I think I have made plain, raises issues of principle of the first importance.

Yours sincerely,
Kilmuir

Lieutenant-General
Sir Ian Jacob, K.B.E., C.B.

[A. W. Bradley, 'Judges and the Media—The Kilmuir Rules' [1986] *Public Law* 383 at 384–6.]

*Within days of becoming Lord Chancellor in 1987 Lord Mackay of Clashfern stated that while judges should obey the spirit of the Rules they would be trusted to decide for themselves whether to talk to the media; they should in any case be careful not to say anything which might damage their authority or prejudice the performance of their work.*

## 5. JUDGES AS CHAIRMEN

All governments ask senior judges to preside over some Royal Commissions, departmental committees, and committees of inquiry. This is done for fairly obvious reasons. Judges are trained to ascertain facts in complex issues, to preside over inquiries, and are seen as impartial; setting up an inquiry may also delay the need for the government to take an awkward decision, and the judge as chairman may helpfully take the responsibility for an inconvenient result. The remits entrusted to the judiciary, and which they take to be part of their public duty to accept, have been extremely varied, from matters of social concern (such as the working of the Abortion Act 1967), to issues involving entirely political choices (like the proper levels of police pay), and to highly controversial matters (including the legal procedures to deal with terrorists and the events of 'Bloody Sunday' in Northern Ireland). There are two clear drawbacks in using judges in these ways. First, in a controversial inquiry the judge may be criticized by the losing side for producing a whitewash or a wrongheaded report, the result of which is to drag him into further disputes. In any inquiry with political, and to an extent social, implications that result is likely—and even the government which commissioned the report may reject it. The second danger arises in the use of judges in those standing bodies in which political considerations must necessarily be present. The National Industrial Relations Court was fatally flawed from the start because trade unionists saw it as an enforcement arm of the government's industrial relations policy. The Security Commission, of which a Lord of Appeal is Chairman, has to carry out investigations and to supervise matters which arguably could more appropriately and effectively be discharged through parliamentary machinery. On the other hand, the deployment of judges on standing official law reform bodies like the Law Commissions, the Criminal Law Revision Committee, and the Law Reform Committee is unexceptionable, because although they have to grapple with social issues their work will only infrequently be controversial in the eyes of politicians and the public.

[Rodney Brazier, *Constitutional Practice* (Oxford, 1988), 244–5.]

## Tenure, Discipline, and Removal

### 1. TENURE

11.—(2) A person appointed to an office to which this section applies shall vacate it on the day on which he attains the age of seventy-five years unless by virtue of this section he has ceased to hold it before then.

(3) A person appointed to an office to which this section applies shall hold that office during good behaviour, subject to a power of removal by Her Majesty on an address presented to Her by both Houses of Parliament.

[Supreme Court Act 1981, s. 11(2), (3).]

*See also Appellate Jurisdiction Act 1876, s. 6, above p. 499.*

2.—(1) A person who holds an office listed in the First Schedule to this Act shall vacate that office on the day on which he attains the age of seventy-five years.

[Judicial Pensions Act 1959, s. 2(1).]

8.–(2) Subject to the following provisions of this section, there shall be entered in the supplemental list—

(*a*) the name of any justice of the peace who is of the age of 70 years or over and neither holds nor has held high judicial office within the meaning of the Appellate Jurisdiction Act 1876, and

(*b*) the name of any justice of the peace who holds or has held such office and is of the age of 75 years or over.

[Justices of the Peace Act 1979, s. 8(2).]

21.—(5) Neither the initial term for which a Recorder is appointed nor any extension of that term under subsection (4) above shall be such as to continue his appointment as a Recorder after the end of the completed year of service in which he attains the age of seventy-two.

[Courts Act 1971, s. 21(5).]

31.—(4)

. . .

(*c*) he [a metropolitan stipendiary magistrate] may be removed from office by the Lord Chancellor for inability or misbehaviour.

[Justices of the Peace Act 1979, s. 31(4)(c).]

17.—(4) The Lord Chancellor may, if he thinks fit, remove a Circuit judge from office on the ground of incapacity or misbehaviour.

[Courts Act 1971, s. 17(4).]

21.—(6) The Lord Chancellor may if he thinks fit terminate the appointment of a Recorder on the ground of incapacity or misbehaviour or of a failure to comply with any requirement specified under subsection (3) above in the terms of his appointment.

[Courts Act 1971, s. 21(6).]

## 2. DISCIPLINE

### (1) CRITICISM AND REVERSAL ON APPEAL

*A judge may be criticized, and a decision of his court may be reversed, by his senior brethren on appeal: this is a form of discipline.*

The mechanisms for disciplining judges who misbehave are more significant in practice than the procedures for removal. Judges may be criticised in Parliament. An extreme case is that of Lord Westbury L.C., who resigned in 1865 following votes of censure passed in both Houses concerning certain appointments he had made.

Judges are often criticized in the press. 'Scurrilous abuse' of a judge may, however, be punished as contempt for 'scandalising the court.' This head of contempt must be distinguished from that concerned with publications likely to interfere with the administration of justice in particular proceedings, by, for example, influencing juries. The former head was thought to be obsolete in 1899. However, proceedings were taken against the editor of the *Birmingham Daily Argus* for a spirited attack on Darling J. (an 'impudent little man in horsehair, a microcosm of conceit and empty headedness'). He apologised, and was fined £100, with £25 costs. According to Abel-Smith and Stevens 'within a decade the criticism of judicial behaviour which had been so outspoken was replaced in the press by almost unbroken sycophantic praise for the judges.' Similar proceedings were taken on a number of occasions in the 1920s and 1930s. Since then, press criticism of the judiciary has become more commonplace, without matching the personal insults expressed by Mr Gray. Proceedings against Quintin Hogg (as he then was), arising out of criticisms of the Court of Appeal published in *Punch*, were dismissed. Salmon L.J. said:

> The authority and reputation of our courts are not so frail that their judgments need to be shielded from criticism, even from the criticism of Mr Quintin Hogg . . .[N]o criticism of a judgment, however vigorous, can amount to contempt of court, provided it keeps within the limits of reasonable courtesy and good faith.

Judges are from time to time rebuked in appellate courts. Censure may be coupled with the setting aside of a conviction or the reversal of a judgment. Thus, judges have been censured for excessive interruptions, threatening a jury, improper behaviour on the Bench, falling asleep, incompetence, and disloyalty to the decisions of superior courts. Lord Hailsham has written that there are judges who become subject to 'judge's disease, that is to say a condition of which the symptoms may be pomposity, irritability, talkativeness, proneness to *obiter dicta*, a tendency to take short cuts'.

There may be complaints from barristers, solicitors or litigants either expressed in court or in private to the judge personally, or made in some other quarter. Complaints may be made to the Lord Chief Justice or the Lord Chancellor. They may be channelled through a head of chambers, the Chairman of the Senate of the Inns of Court, the Attorney-General, The Law Society, an M.P., or some other intermediary. There is generally a preference for taking action privately. Confrontations in court between counsel and judge may be to the client's disadvantage; it is impossible to assess the extent to which they may also be, or be feared to be, to the barrister's future disadvantage. The upshot may be an interview between the Lord Chancellor and the judge, or even, on occasion, a public rebuke.

It has been doubted whether the informal pressures on judges are sufficient. Over the years there have been a few judges whose conduct has often been criticised, but who have nevertheless remained on the Bench. On the other hand, this small minority seems to have dwindled. The JUSTICE Sub-Committee argued that some form of complaints machinery should be established, probably in the form of a complaints tribunal or judicial commission. Such a reform is unlikely to occur in the foreseeable future, and, on the present evidence, the case for it is not made out. Finally, it must be remembered that criticisms of judges in the popular press are commonly marred by such weaknesses as a failure to report accurately the full facts, a failure to understand basic principles of the conduct of trials and a failure to distinguish defects of the law from the defects of the judge.

[Smith and Bailey, *Modern English Legal System*, 167–8.]

## (2) CRITICISM BY THE LORD CHANCELLOR OR THE LORD CHIEF JUSTICE

*The Lord Chancellor or the Lord Chief Justice have on occasions interviewed judges privately. This has been followed by administrative action and sometimes by a public rebuke.*

LORD CAMPBELL OF ALLOWAY asked Her Majesty's Government what action has the Lord Chancellor taken in respect of a speech made by His Honour Judge Argyll QC at Trent Polytechnic, Nottingham, on 13th March 1987.

THE LORD CHANCELLOR (LORD HAVERS): I have written to the judge severely reprimanding him for a number of unfortunate remarks made in the course of the speech referred to by my noble friend.

[488 H.L. Deb. *1376* (written answers 21 July 1987).]

## 3. REMOVAL

11.—(8) The Lord Chancellor, if satisfied by means of a medical certificate that a person holding an office to which this section applies—

(*a*) is disabled by permanent infirmity from the performance of the duties of his office; and

(*b*) is for the time being incapacitated from resigning his office,

may, subject to subsection (9), by instrument under his hand declare that person's office to have been vacated; and the instrument shall have the like effect for all purposes as if that person had on the date of the instrument resigned his office.

(9) A declaration under subsection (8) with respect to a person shall be of no effect unless it is made—

(*a*) in the case of any of the Lord Chief Justice, the Master of the Rolls, the President of the Family Division and the Vice-Chancellor, with the concurrence of two others of them;

(*b*) in the case of a Lord Justice of Appeal, with the concurrence of the Master of the Rolls;

(*c*) in the case of a puisne judge of any Division of the High Court, with the concurrence of the senior judge of that Division.

[Supreme Court Act 1981, s. 11(8), (9).]

*For the Lord Chancellor's statutory powers to remove junior judges from office, see above p. 598.*

MR MEADOWCROFT asked the Attorney-General what criteria are applied by the Lord Chancellor when he decides not to renew recorderships.

THE ATTORNEY-GENERAL: Under section 21 of the Courts Act 1971 recordership is a part-time judicial office which is held for a specified term (usually about three years) and is renewable by the Lord Chancellor until the age of 72. Until then, the Lord Chancellor will normally renew the appointment provided that he is satisfied as to the recorder's continuing fitness for it, particularly with reference to his judicial performance and behaviour, and whether or not he has complied with the terms of his appointment. In making these decisions, the Lord Chancellor always acts after receiving advice in writing from officials and relevant presiding judges. This advice is based on consultations with the judiciary and the profession. The Lord Chancellor has in fact never decided not to renew a recordership except in accordance with such advice from officials and presiding judges. His overriding consideration, as with all judicial appointments, is always the maintenance of public confidence in the competence and independence of the judiciary, and in the integrity and impartiality of the administration of justice.

[101 H.C. Deb. *167* (written answers 9 July 1986).]

MR D. E. THOMAS asked the Attorney-General in how many cases since May 1979 the Lord Chancellor has not renewed the appointments of recorders at the Crown court, willing to continue to serve as such, on the grounds of alleged incompetence.

THE ATTORNEY-GENERAL: The figures from 1979 are not immediately available. Since 1 January 1981 the appointments of 27 recorders have expired and not been extended. In some of the cases, the recorders had reached the age limit of 72. In some others, the Lord Chancellor was not satisfied of their continuing fitness or suitability to be recorders.

[107 H.C. Deb. *429* (written answers 16 December 1986).]

MR D. E. THOMAS asked the Attorney-General whether the figures given by him in his reply to the hon. Member for Meirionnydd Nant Conwy on 16 December 1986, *Official Report*, column 431, refer to both recorders and assistant recorders or only to recorders.

THE ATTORNEY-GENERAL: To recorders only. The statutory provisions have no application to assistant recorders.

[108 H.C. Deb. *574* (written answers 21 January 1987).]

The safeguard usually quoted as protecting the public from corrupt or spiteful judges is the power to remove a judge from office. This of itself offers little comfort to the man who suffers imprisonment as a result of an improper refusal of bail, or leave to appeal, or who is convicted by virtue of a deliberate misdirection. Nor will the removal of the judge compensate the party who suffers financially from a malicious refusal of costs or whose case is improperly put back on the list. However as far as the power to remove a judge goes, it is a power which becomes progressively less likely to be effective the higher the rank of the judge. A magistrate may be removed from the commission of the peace as the Lord Chancellor sees fit. There is no requirement for a formal hearing but it does not seem to be a power widely abused. A person dissatisfied by the behaviour of a magistrate should address a formal complaint to the Lord Chancellor. Further up the scale, a circuit judge may be dismissed by the Lord Chancellor for incapacity or misbehaviour. So a citizen believing that such a judge has behaved improperly or with gross incompetence should address a memorial to the Lord Chancellor. He must then exercise his powers fairly and judicially for it would seem that he is in this matter subject to the control of the court. The judge must be notified of the charges made, given an opportunity to be heard and the complaints must relate to his incapacity or some act of misbehaviour. Subject to these restrictions the Lord Chancellor's decision is final, there is no power to examine whether his assessment of the evidence before him is correct.

This leaves the judges of the High Court, whose immunity from suit appears impregnable and who in practice are virtually irremovable. They hold office under the terms of the Supreme Court of Judicature (Consolidation) Act 1925, s. 12 (1), derived with slight changes of wording from the Act of Settlement 1701, during good behaviour, subject to a power of removal by Her Majesty on an Address presented to Her Majesty by both Houses of Parliament. Theoretically then a High Court judge could be removed *either* on grounds of proven misbehaviour *or* for any reason satisfactory to Parliament. This is the view now supported by most writers on constitutional law. The latter procedure at first sight confers on Parliament vast and arbitrary powers. A glance at British constitutional history should reassure those whose fears are still for the independence of the judiciary. Only once since the Act of Settlement of 1701 has a judge been removed from office. In the nineteenth century a cumbersome procedure evolved, usually requiring the investigation of charges against judges by committees of both Houses. The judge was entitled to be heard at all stages in person and by counsel. The process dragged on for many months.

Nevertheless an individual who believed that a judge of the High

Court had maliciously made an order against him, knowing it to be unjustified, could still complain to his M.P. Unfortunately the M.P. will probably not be able to do much in the way of eliciting further information relating to the judge's behaviour. While he may ask questions and seek further evidence, he will find his way blocked by the convention of the House that a judge may only be criticised on a motion. The House was reminded of this convention in 1973 during a debate on Industrial Relations when the Speaker ruled to M.P.s that:

> Reflections on a judge's character cannot be made except on a motion. No charge of a political nature can be raised except on a motion. Any suggestion that a judge should be dismissed can be made only on a motion.

Whether the motion before the House must be the commencement of an attempt to move an Address to Her Majesty to dismiss the judge, or whether it may simply be one of censure or criticism, is not clear. In the nineteenth-century cases a motion to criticise a judge seems nearly always to have been treated as a first step towards investigating whether the judge should be removed. In view of the serious nature of such a step this preliminary motion was required to be supported by prima facie evidence before it would be considered by the House. Furthermore distinct and substantial allegations had to be made. The unsupported evidence provided by an injured constituent would be unlikely to be sufficient. In this century again the cumbersome nature of this Parliamentary process has been illustrated, as well as Parliament's unwillingness to proceed against a judge. In 1906 certain allegations were made as to the conduct of the Great Yarmouth election petition by Grantham J. The allegations were debated on a motion to criticise the judge. Yet the motion was later withdrawn by leave because of the Prime Minister's view that such a motion could be regarded only as instituting process to remove the judge. The judge's comments on Parliament's treatment of himself were again the subject of discussion in the House in 1911 when the Prime Minister expressed the strong disapproval of Parliament, the judiciary, and the public of the judge's behaviour but still refused to move an Address for his dismissal. The tenor of these debates seems to be that only where real *moral* delinquency can be shown will a judge be dismissed. It might be observed that the safeguards inserted at every stage to protect the judge and the awesome nature of the proceedings are such that no opportunity to prove real moral delinquency is afforded to the complainant M.P. He is required to have acted as judge and jury before he commences the prosecution. Perhaps the aggrieved party might seek help from the press in formulating the charges and substantiating them by investigation. The newspapers will be wary of such intervention, for while they are at liberty to criticise decisions of the courts as contrary to law or ill-judged as a matter of policy the editors risk committal to gaol for contempt should they attack the fairness or impartiality of the judge. This will be the case even if they use reasonable and temperate language, although the Attorney-General may choose not to prosecute. Finally it was suggested earlier that a judge could be removed for misbehaviour otherwise than by Parliament. The means that exist at common law are the writ of *scire facias* and the laying of a criminal information by the Attorney-General. Both remedies survive the Crown Proceedings Act 1947 which dealt exclusively with civil matters. Unfortunately by its nature the latter remedy is available only to the Attorney-General and the former requires his fiat to proceed. Therefore, as there is no ordinary judicial remedy for the citizen against the action of a corrupt judge, any power to prevent injustice appears to lie with the Government of the day. With due respect to the independence of the Attorney-General he is unlikely to consent to or initiate the common law proceedings outlined above in circumstances where his colleagues are unwilling to support attempts to move an Address in Parliament. So the individual should address his complaints to his M.P. but his problems in gathering evidence which will persuade the government to act are formidable.

Pressure of parliamentary time and a laudable desire not to seem to interfere with the independence of the judiciary are further deterrents to government action. Rather than await a crisis and be obliged to create an *ad hoc* procedure, consideration should be given now to the question of alternative means of removing High Court judges introduced in the Canadian Parliament. A procedure in some number of constitutions provide for removal of a judge by the Head of State, after investigation of allegations made, by and on the recommendation of a judicial tribunal not necessarily composed of national judges. In order to avoid any major change in procedure the most acceptable model may be found in Burma. Judges can be removed only for infirmity or misbehaviour. A motion to dismiss a judge has to be introduced in one of the Chambers of Parliament supported by at least a quarter of the number of members. The charges are then referred to a Special Tribunal of judges. The report and recommendation of the tribunal is referred to Parliament and the judge will be dismissed if both Chambers vote to that effect. In 1965, when allegations of a serious nature were made against a Canadian judge, and a motion to remove the judge introduced in the Canadian Parliament, a procedure in some ways similar to that required in Burma was resolved on by the Canadian Parliament. A retired judge was invited to report on the allegations in an inquiry instituted under the Inquiries Act R.S.C. 1952 c. 154. When the report was delivered a motion for an Address to remove the judge was introduced and the judge resigned. Certainly the latter example illustrates that the present procedure can be adapted and worked today, but why not provide for such a contingency in advance? Parliament could certainly not afford the time to proceed as it did in the last century. The existence of a body established to deal with allegations should assist public confidence and alleviate Parliament's timidity in allowing allegations to be made. The actual decision to remove the judge would still be taken by Parliament, but Parliament's power should be formally restricted to removal for misbehaviour or incapacity. The criticism that this kind of revision might attract would be that, although it may simplify matters for Parliament if it is presented with a report from experienced judges, effectively it places the power to dismiss a judge with judges. Will they protect their own? First, if they must report as well as recommend, Members of Parliament will be able to make their own assessment as to whether the facts found do prove misbehaviour despite the judicial recommendation. The ultimate sanction remains with Parliament. Secondly at present most lawyers would finally agree that the real protection against judicial malice or folly is that the 'bad' judge will be persuaded to go by his virtuous brethren. Little evidence to support or refute this can be advanced. However this power, such as it is, is exercised behind closed doors in the drawing rooms and studies of legal London. The procedure suggested would at least be open to the light of public examination and criticism.

[Margaret Brazier, 'Judicial Immunity and the Independence of the Judiciary' [1976] *Public Law* 397 at 400–4.]

## Reform

*The government is currently proposing changes to the ways in which lawyers would qualify to address the courts, and also in the qualifications needed for appointment to judicial office.*

3.8. . . . the Government proposes that the existing complex arrangements for rights of audience under statute and common law should be replaced by statutory rights of audience in all courts, and by statutory rights of audience before appropriate tribunals.

3.9. The Government considers that it is for the professional bodies and other organisations whose members provide legal services to satisfy the courts and the public that their members can meet the high standards of competence and conduct required for rights of audience. The Government therefore proposes that it should be for the professional bodies and other organisations to determine that particular persons are qualified in accordance with the appropriate rules to appear in the courts. The standards they apply, and the mechanisms by which they monitor those standards, should, however, be subject to independent scrutiny and public comment.

*The Bar*

3.10. Primary legislation should recognise that any person called to the Bar by one of the Inns of Court (under their new arrangements to apply from October) in accordance with the regulations on education and training will have rights of audience which can be exercised in all courts and appropriate tribunals when pupillage is complete. That will depend only on their complying with the rules of conduct made by the Bar. After the legislation comes into force, any change in either set of rules will be subject to the concurrence of the Lord Chancellor and of the Lord Chief Justice, the Master of the Rolls, the President of the Family Division and the Vice-Chancellor. Both the Lord Chancellor and those judges will act having regard to advice from the Lord Chancellor's Advisory Committee on Legal Education and Conduct. Further details of the procedure for making the rules are set out in Chapters 7 and 8.

*The Law Society*

3.11. Primary legislation should provide that the Law Society should be able to recognise a solicitor as qualified according to the rules for education and training to be an advocate, in a particular court or courts, and in particular tribunals. Any person so qualified will be recognised as having a right of audience in that court or those courts or tribunals, provided that he or she complies with the relevant rules of conduct made by the Law Society. To be effective, both sets of rules will require the concurrence of the Lord Chancellor and the same senior judges as those for the Bar.

3.12. The rules will determine the training and experience necessary for a solicitor to have rights of audience in a particular court. But it is envisaged that such qualifications will be obtained in stages. On qualification, all solicitors should receive rights of audience which will be equivalent to their existing rights. It is likely that many solicitors will find these rights adequate for the work they wish to do.

3.13. Those who wish to proceed to further rights of audience will then be expected to undertake a subsequent period of practical experience in advocacy under supervision. The Government does not expect the progress to further rights to be automatic in any way but to be conditional on the attainment of a standard of competence to be determined by the rules appropriate for the court or courts concerned. Conclusion of the period of training will need to be tested by considering the individual standard of competence achieved.

3.14. In order to provide for possible developments in the future, it is proposed that a power be provided to add to the list of bodies which can grant rights of audience, should that become appropriate. Such a power would be exercised only in the light of advice to that effect from the Advisory Committee, and with the concurrence of the senior judges referred to above. The addition would be made by an Order in Council made on the recommendation of the Lord Chancellor. The Order would be subject to approval in draft by affirmative resolution of both Houses of Parliament.

3.15. As with the current statutory arrangements in the county courts, these proposals will not be a restriction on the judges' discretion to control proceedings in the courts over which they preside. It should remain open for a judge to hear any advocate, professional or lay, who does not possess the appropriate, or even any, right of audience. Similarly, subject to giving reasons the judge may refuse to hear any individual advocate, whatever his right of audience, if his conduct towards the court falls short of what is required.

3.16. It will be a principle of the proposed legislation that no individual or class of advocates will lose any existing rights. In particular:

—all barristers and solicitors will retain all their existing rights of audience;

—all categories of lay and professional advocates who currently have specific rights of audience before any court or tribunal will be given corresponding rights. For example, those rights before magistrates' courts conferred upon local authority members and officers by section 223 of the Local Government Act 1972 will be preserved in full.

3.17. The exercise of rights of audience by a person who holds them may be limited by professional rules of conduct. Current examples include the limited rights accorded to employed barristers or solicitors. The extent of those limitations under the rules will be a matter for early consideration by the Advisory Committee, and should be kept under review by the professional body concerned.

15.1. The Government regards it as a matter of great importance that the highest standards of intellect and character should be maintained in appointments to the judiciary. The prospect of appointment to the Bench should also be an encouragement for the men and women who have made the law their career to reach the highest standards of service to the public. But that encouragement should be open to all if it is to operate as an effective stimulus to excellence in all parts of our legal system, and if the Lord Chancellor is to be free to consider the best practitioners of all kinds for appointment.

15.2. For these reasons the Green Papers proposed that all those who had held the appropriate advocacy qualifications for suitable lengths of time should be eligible for judicial appointments; and that the judges in a lower court should be eligible for promotion to a higher one on the basis of their judicial experience in the lower court.

15.3. The suggestion that the highest judicial offices should be open to all with suitable experience was widely welcomed in the consultation. It was agreed that a practitioner's early decisions on form of training should not limit his or her chances of proceeding through merit and character to hold some of the most important offices under the Crown.

15.4. The Government accordingly proposes to revise and extend the conditions for appointment to judicial office. The simplification of the proposals for granting rights of audience will, however, make it possible to simplify significantly the system of eligibility requirements proposed in the Green Paper.

15.5. Under the adversarial system in this country, experience as an advocate in work of an appropriate range and complexity is required in order to preside effectively as a judge. Experience of past appointments demonstrates, however, that it is not necessary for a new judge to have practised in all of the areas in which he or she may be called to sit. The Government accordingly proposes that the minimum qualifications for a practitioner for appointment to the Bench should be rights of audience as set out below:

(i) *Lord of Appeal In Ordinary*
General rights of audience in the Supreme Court for 15 years.

(ii) *Lord Justice of Appeal, Judge of the High Court, Deputy High Court Judge*
General rights of audience in the High Court and the Court of Appeal for 10 years.

(iii) *Circuit Judge, Recorder, Assistant Recorder*
General rights of audience in the Crown Court or the county courts for 10 years.

(iv) *Master or Registrar of the Supreme Court, County Court Registrar, Stipendiary Magistrate*
Rights of audience in the Supreme Court or a general right of audience in the county courts for 7 years.

15.6. The present qualification for appointment as a Lord of Appeal in Ordinary of at least two years of service as Lord Chancellor or as a judge of one of the Superior Courts in Great Britain and Northern Ireland will remain unchanged. Any person who has been a Circuit Judge for at least two years should be eligible for appointment as a judge of the Supreme Court. Any person who has been a Registrar, or an equivalent judicial officer, for at least 3 years should be eligible for appointment as a Circuit Judge. The provision requiring a solicitor to serve for at least 3 years as a Recorder before becoming eligible for appointment to the Circuit Bench will be removed.